UNIVERSITY DICTIONARY OF
BUSINESS AND FINANCE

UNIVERSITY DICTIONARY OF BUSINESS AND FINANCE

DONALD T. CLARK

AND

BERT A. GOTTFRIED

Thomas Y. Crowell, Publishers
Established 1834
New York

First published under the title
Dictionary of Business and Finance

Copyright © 1957 by Harper & Row, Publishers, Inc.

Manufactured in the United States of America

Library of Congress Catalog Card No. 57-14560

ISBN 0-8152-0143-5

APOLLO EDITION, 1967

78   79   80   81   82   10   9   8   7   6   5   4

Preface

Two authorities compiled this *University Dictionary of Business and Finance*. Donald T. Clark, Librarian, University of California at Vera Cruz, formerly at the Harvard University Graduate School of Business Administration, has taught at the University of Western Ontario, the University of Hawaii, Simmons College, and Harvard University. He has served with the Oregon State Library, the Berkeley Public Library, California, and The New York Public Library. Bert A. Gottfried, Chief Economist with The Research Institute of America, Inc., began his business career as a research assistant at the National Bureau of Economic Research in New York City. Then followed service with the War Production Board in Washington, D. C., and the Research and Statistics Division of the Office of Chief Quartermaster, European Theater of Operations. He has been a research expert in economics and marketing for Dun and Bradstreet, Inc., and for Amos Parrish and Company, Inc. Messrs. Clark and Gottfried thus bring to the *Dictionary of Business and Finance* extensive knowledge of the operation and history of contemporary business practice.

The authors organized the *Dictionary of Business and Finance* to give information quickly and easily. They particularly kept in mind the two general kinds of users of this *Dictionary*: first, the experienced businessman who wants precise knowledge about a particular subject and, secondly, the newcomer, student, or professional man who wants general information. To meet these needs the editors supplied both master entries and specific entries. To take an example: an experienced businessman will probably have general knowledge about *bonds*. If he wants particular information about *negotiable bonds,* he simply looks for that entry in its usual place under the *N*'s. But the less experienced man may be more interested in learning the distinctions between all the bonds. He should then turn to the master entry *bond,* listed in its proper place under the *B*'s. Here, in quick sequence, he will find all the types of bonds. With this arrangement he can compare the definitions in order to fix their distinctions in his mind. The *Dictionary of Business and Finance,* with its "umbrella" entries on the one hand and its multiplicity of individual entries on the other, is indeed an exceptionally versatile reference tool.

The *Dictionary*'s scope is broad. It includes accounting, advertising, banking, commodities, credit, export, finance, government, imports, insurance, investments, labor, law, merchandising, personnel, purchasing, retailing, real estate, selling, shipping, statistics, the stock market, traffic, warehousing, work measurement. The entries supply the most recent information, and the examples and illustrations are taken from contemporary business practice. The text closes with an Appendix of exceptionally useful information presented in tabular form for quick reference. There is a complete alphabetical "Table of Equivalents," an "Income Table," "Compound Interest Tables," "Bond Interest Tables," and others which day in and day out have proved useful to businessmen.

A

abandonment. 1. In law, the voluntary relinquishment or surrender of property, rights, or interest, without regard to future ownership or possession, and with the intent or appearance of never again resuming the rights or interest abandoned. Mere non-use, however, is not necessarily evidence of *abandonment*. *Abandonment* has been held to differ from SURRENDER in that surrender involves another party, and from FORFEITURE in that forfeiture may be against one's wish or intent.

2. With regard to a patent, trademark, or copyright, the cession of rights by the owner, by intent or by negligence as defined in the patent laws, in which event the invention, design, or name falls into the public domain. Examples of negligent acts which may lead to *abandonment* include the failure to prosecute infringers, the failure to manufacture or license the manufacture of an invention, etc.

3. In insurance, the act, by an insured owner of damaged property, of relinquishing his property to the insurer, for the purpose of claiming a total loss. In this event, any remaining value in the property is surrendered to the insurer.

~ **clause.** In the standard fire insurance policy, a clause stating that the insured may not abandon the property, but must take all reasonable steps to prevent further damage or loss. In marine insurance, on the other hand, it is a clause providing that the insured may abandon his ship, cargo, or other damaged property to the insurer, and call on the insurer to take possession and make full payment for a total loss.

4. In shipping practice, the refusal of a consignee to accept delivery of freight which has been so badly damaged in transit as to render it worthless. The carrier is thus held responsible for the value of the goods.

abatement. The extinguishment or reduction of a claim or debt. In connection with taxes, the cancellation, in whole or in part, of taxes assessed but not actually paid, as distinguished from a REFUND or REBATE. For example, municipalities will often offer *abate-ment* of real estate taxes as an inducement to builders to clear slum property and rebuild.

A bond, B bond, *etc*. See under BOND (1).

above par. See PAR (1).

abrasion. The loss in weight sustained by coinage due to ordinary wear and tear while in circulation.

abrogate. To repeal, cancel, or annul a right or agreement by higher authority. A higher court, for example, may *abrogate* an order, sentence, or agreement of a lower court; or a state law may *abrogate* a local ordinance.

absentee. In general, one who is absent or missing from his regular place. In personnel usage, one who is absent from work, especially, but not necessarily, one who is absent without good cause.

absenteeism. In general, the practice of being absent from work. More particularly, the personnel management problem created by such frequent absences.

absentee owner. An owner of land, particularly farm land, who does not himself live on the land and work it. By expansion, an owner or part owner of an industrial plant who does not take an active part in its management or operation. A non-profit institution, insurance company, investment company, etc., may be an *absentee owner* of a business through stock holdings.

absentee rate. A measure of the amount of absenteeism in an industrial establishment, usually obtained by dividing the total number of employee days or hours lost by absence by the total number of employee days or hours assigned for work during the period. The *absentee rate* may be used to compare one time period with another, or different departments or plants with each other.

absolute. In general, with no reservations or conditions; full, not limited or qualified; not subject to cancellation. See each of the following under the principal listing: ~ ACCEPTANCE (3); ~ CONTRACT (1); ~ ENDORSEMENT; ~ ESTATE; ~ SALE; ~ TITLE.

absorbed. With respect to an issue of stock, bonds, or other securities, one which has passed completely into the hands of the public. When an issue has been *absorbed,* it is out of the hands of the original issuers or UNDERWRITERS, and is being traded normally.

absorption. In freight practice, the partial or complete payment of freight charges by a seller. To the extent that such payment gives an advantage to one or more buyers over others, *absorption* is an illegal practice under the anti-trust laws. Also, the payment by a freight carrier of some of the costs of a shipment, instead of passing them along to a shipper. Examples of charges which might be absorbed include lighterage, switching, and terminal charges.

abstract. A document in which another document, or documents, is summarized; a legal record summarizing the key points of a more detailed record or transcript.

  ~ **of title.** A legal document summarizing all the pertinent facts, proceedings, claims, and instruments by which TITLE to land or other property is evidenced.

abutting foot. See FRONT FOOT.

acceleration. A provision sometimes included in a mortgage or other obligation, granting the debtor the right to make advance payment of part or all of the remaining principal under certain specified conditions. Also, a provision giving the creditor the right to demand advance payment of the principal, under conditions such as the failure of the debtor to pay an installment when due.

accept. 1. In shipping, to take or receive, with the intent to retain. A consignee may *accept* a shipment by taking and using the delivered goods, or simply by failing to refuse delivery, or failing to return the goods.

  2. In general, to agree to the terms of an offer, or to agree to perform some obligation; to acknowledge as correct and binding. A person may *accept* a BILL OF EXCHANGE, for example, by writing his name across the face, with the date and the word *accepted,* thereby agreeing to pay the bill when it matures or falls due. See also ACCEPTANCE (3).

acceptance. 1. Under the law of contracts, an indication by the second party to a contract of his willingness to be bound by the terms of the offer of the first party. In a sales contract, for example, it is the physical receipt of the goods with the intention of retaining them. See also CONTRACT.

  conditional ~. A tentative acceptance which depends on the fulfillment of some special condition. It is in effect a counteroffer,

which must then be accepted by both parties.

  express ~. A direct oral or written agreement to be bound by terms, made by a principal or his agent.

  implied ~. One which may be deduced from the circumstances, in the absence of an EXPRESS ACCEPTANCE, which see above. For example, the retention and use of defective or damaged goods delivered may be held to be *implied acceptance* of the terms of the sales offer.

  2. Acknowledgment by a consignee of the receipt of a shipment, thereby relieving the shipper and carrier of further responsibility.

  3. In banking and finance, the agreement to pay a BILL OF EXCHANGE or DRAFT when due, by the one on whom it is drawn, by his writing on the face of it his name, the date, place of payment, etc. Also, in common usage, the instrument offered for *acceptance* itself.

  absolute ~. An express and positive agreement to pay; an EXPRESS or GENERAL ACCEPTANCE, which see below.

  bank ~. As defined by the Federal Reserve Board, a draft or bill of exchange of which the acceptor is a bank or trust company. *Bank acceptances* are used to finance trade, to effect currency exchange, and for business borrowing. When accepted for payment by the bank, the *acceptance* is known as a *banker's acceptance* and may be used by the drawer or payee as collateral, or may be sold or discounted.

  conditional ~. An *acceptance* under which payment depends on the fulfillment of some special or future condition.

  general ~. One which contains no qualifications or conditions. The usual form contains simply the date, place of payment, the word "accepted," and the signature of the acceptor. It is sometimes called a *clean acceptance.*

  partial ~. An *acceptance* which varies from the terms of the bill itself; for example, one calling for payment of only part of the amount, or at a different time.

  qualified ~. An *acceptance* which places some qualification or special limitation on payment, such as a PARTIAL or CONDITIONAL ACCEPTANCE, which see above.

  special ~. See QUALIFIED ACCEPTANCE above.

  trade ~. A draft which accompanies a shipment of goods, calling on the buyer to pay the amount involved at a specified future date. Under the Uniform Negotiable Instruments Act, and the requirements of the Federal Reserve Board, there are certain forms which must be included in a valid and legal *trade acceptance.* The *acceptance* must state that it is for a specific amount and transaction; there must be a specific date of maturity; and the payer must indicate in his *acceptance* the name and location of the bank or other place at which payment will be made when due. The National Association of Credit Men has designed a standard *trade acceptance* form which meets all legal requirements.

acceptance bill. See under BILL OF EXCHANGE.

acceptance credit. See under CREDIT (3).

acceptance for honor. The act of one who AC-CEPTS (2) a bill of exchange or other instrument, of which he himself is not the drawee, to protect or save the credit of another person, or for the other person's HONOR. The other person, who has failed to accept the bill when due, is obligated to reimburse the one who has accepted the bill for his honor.

acceptance supra protest. See SUPRA PROTEST.

acceptor. The drawee of a draft for acceptance, who, upon signing his name on the face of a draft or bill agrees to pay it when due. See also ACCEPTANCE (3).

accessory. Anything joined to or used with another as an ornament, or to make it more perfect or useful. For example, a frame for a picture or a bridle for a horse is an *accessory* but a storage battery was held to be an intrinsic part of an automobile, and not an *accessory* for tax purposes. Strictly, an *accessory* relates only to personal property, and an APPURTENANCE to real property. See also EQUIPMENT.

access right. The right of an owner of property to free access to the property, without obstruction. If the property abuts on a public way, this is known as a direct *access right,* and if there is other property intervening between the owned property and the public way, the right is known as an EASEMENT right.

accident. In contract law and insurance practice, any unforeseen event occurring without will or design; something unexpected, unusual, or of unknown cause. The term excludes occurrences which are the result of negligence, or the failure to exercise reasonable caution or care.

accidental death benefit clause. In insurance, a supplementary provision frequently added to life insurance policies, providing that an additional amount (usually equal to the face value of the policy) will be paid in the event that death occurs as the result of certain accidental causes. There is normally a small additional premium charge for the inclusion of this clause. The common phrase "double indemnity" refers to this clause.

accident insurance. See under INSURANCE, LIFE, ACCIDENT, AND HEALTH.

accident rate. The measure of the frequency of industrial accidents. The standard ratio is the number of reported disabling injuries per million employee-hours worked.

accommodation. Originally, the lending of money by one who has it to one who needs it, without any consideration or collateral. In this sense, the lender accommodates the borrower. Today, in a narrower sense, it indicates the lending of one's credit or honor to another, without any consideration, for the purpose of enabling the other to obtain borrowed funds.

~ **endorsement.** The ENDORSEMENT of a note, bill, draft, or other form of loan instrument by one person for a second, when the purpose of the endorsement is to enable the second to obtain the loan, which he would not be able to do on the strength of his own credit. In this case, the endorser signs the note as an *accommodation* to the borrower, and not because of any direct interest in or benefit from the loan. See also ENDORSER, ACCOMMODATION.

~ **note.** See ACCOMMODATION PAPER below.

~ **paper.** A note, bill, draft, or other form of loan instrument which is made, accepted, or endorsed by one person for the benefit of another, without consideration or collateral. The accommodator, by making or endorsing the loan, in effect assumes the risk, and guarantees the credit of the other person. See also BILL OF EXCHANGE, ACCOMMODATION.

~ **party.** Under the Uniform Negotiable Instrument Law, one who has signed an instrument as maker, drawer, acceptor, or endorser, without receiving value therefore, and for the purpose of lending his name to some other person. Under the law, such a person is liable on the instrument to a holder for value, notwithstanding the fact that such holder at the time of taking the instrument knew him to be an *accommodation party*. In other words, one who has signed a note as an *accommodation party* may have an agreement with the first holder of the note that he is not to be held liable for payment, but if the note is negotiable, any second or subsequent holder of the note is not bound by such an agreement.

accommodation line. In the insurance trade, a term for a policy written on a risk that would not ordinarily be accepted, as an accommodation to the customer in anticipation of additional business, or as an accommodation to the agent or broker in return for his continued business.

accord and satisfaction. The settlement of a claim, demand, or debt by the arranging of a new agreement, under which the creditor agrees to accept a lesser amount, or payment over a longer period of time. Technically, the new agreement itself is the *accord,* and its performance is the *satisfaction.* Also, any new agreement which both parties accept and perform as a substitute for an original agreement. See also COMPOSITION.

account. 1. A statement of goods sold or services rendered, together with a record of the amounts due therefore, such as might be submitted by a seller to a customer; an INVOICE, or a STATEMENT OF ACCOUNT.

2. In accounting, any of various records of business transactions, entered in a book of record, usually in the form of DEBITS and CREDITS. *Accounts* may be classified in many different ways, the principal ones of which are listed and defined below.

balance sheet ∼. Any of the records of assets, liabilities, capital, surplus, etc., which are summarized to make up the periodic BALANCE SHEET or FINANCIAL STATEMENT of a business. These are sometimes called REAL ACCOUNTS, which see below.

income statement ∼. See NOMINAL ACCOUNT, below.

liquidation ∼. See REALIZATION ACCOUNT, below.

nominal ∼. Any of the records of income and expenditures kept by a business, so called because they are kept in the names of particular customers, suppliers, etc., rather than because they are in any way immaterial. These are the *accounts* which are summarized to make up the INCOME STATEMENT of the business.

real ∼. Any of the various *accounts* of assets and liabilities, which are summarized to make up the company balance sheet. See also BALANCE SHEET ACCOUNT, above.

realization ∼. One which is set up specifically for summarizing and adjusting the *accounts* of a business which is being wound up or dissolved. It is sometimes known as a *liquidation account.*

summary ∼. One in which several other *accounts,* covering particular classes of items or particular time periods, are merged or summarized. Examples include controlling *accounts,* in which various LEDGER *accounts* are merged, and clearing and closing *accounts,* which are used to summarize, balance, and transfer various income and expense *accounts* to a final statement.

3. In banking and finance, the term for a credit established in a particular name, by deposit or otherwise, against which the depositor or other authorized person may make withdrawals under specified conditions. The major types of financial *accounts* are listed and defined below.

active ∼. A banking term for one in which there are frequent deposits and withdrawals. Sometimes, an *account* in which there has been a deposit or withdrawal within a specified period of time, such as a day.

bank ∼. In general, a credit established in a BANK OF DEPOSIT, for purposes of making withdrawals or earning interest.

checking ∼. A form of BANK ACCOUNT, which see above, set up primarily for the purpose of enabling the depositor to draw CHECKS against the balance maintained.

compound-interest ∼. See THRIFT ACCOUNT, below.

demand ∼. The name for one from which withdrawals may be made on demand, without prior notice, as distinguished from a TIME ACCOUNT, which see below. The common example is a CHECKING ACCOUNT, which see above.

inactive ∼. A banking term for one in which there are infrequent deposits and withdrawals. Also, sometimes, one in which there was no deposit or withdrawal on the previous day.

insured ∼. A term for one which is insured under the program of the Federal Deposit Insurance Corporation, under which bank *accounts* are insured up to a limit of $10,000.

joint ∼. One opened in the names of two or more persons jointly. Depending on the exact terms of the deposit agreement, withdrawals from such an *account* may be made by either of the joint depositors alone, or only by the signatures of all of them together. In some cases, it may be specified that withdrawals can be made, for example, by any two of the three joint depositors.

savings ∼. One in which interest is paid periodically on the balance on deposit, and which is intended primarily for the accumulation of savings. Such *accounts* are TIME ACCOUNTS, which see below.

special checking ∼. A form of CHECKING ACCOUNT, which see above, in which a charge, called an ACTIVITY CHARGE, is made for each check drawn, and sometimes for each deposit made. There is also sometimes a periodic service charge. No minimum balance is required, and the charges are made to offset the costs of handling the *account.*

survivorship ∼. A form of JOINT ACCOUNT, which see above, in which withdrawals may be made by either depositor, or by the survivor. It is sometimes known as a *joint account with right of survivorship.*

thrift ∼. A term for a SAVINGS ACCOUNT, which see above, which is used in some states for such *accounts* in commercial banks. In these states, the law prescribes that only banks chartered as savings banks may offer savings *accounts,* so that the interest-bearing *accounts* in commercial banks are known as *thrift accounts,* compound-interest *accounts,* etc.

time ∼. One on which withdrawals may only be made after due notice has been given a specified period of time in advance, or on which the bank reserves the right to require such advance notice. See, for example, SAVINGS ACCOUNT, above.

two-name ∼. See JOINT ACCOUNT, above.

4. In business generally, a name for the relationship established when one business grants another the privilege of purchasing on credit. The term has also come to be used to refer to any regular customer of a business, whether on a cash or credit basis. The principal types of business accounts are listed and defined below.

book ∼. See OPEN ACCOUNT, below.

cash ∼. The term for a basis of trading under which the customer is required to make immediate payment in cash, either at the time of ordering or on delivery, for all goods purchased. Also, a term for a CHARGE ACCOUNT, which see below, on which no interest or service charges are made, so that the customer is given the same privileges as if he bought for cash. See also TERMS OF SALE.

charge ∼. A system of purchasing and selling on credit, under which the customer agrees to settle his outstanding balance periodically, in return for which he is given credit privileges. Normally, *charge accounts* at retail provide for monthly settlement, but the exact terms vary. Under a budget or revolving *charge account,* a store may set a limit on the total amount of credit outstanding, and may make an interest or service charge on outstanding balances.

current ∼. See OPEN ACCOUNT, below.

open ∼. A basis of trading on credit, under which the customer is not required to give a note for each purchase, or to pay interest, but is required to settle his outstanding balance in full periodically, or within a specified period after each purchase. Since the only record of the credit outstanding is that on the account books of the seller, this form of *account* is sometimes called a *book account.* An *open account* which must be settled periodically is sometimes known as a *current* or *running account.*

accountability. In general, the liability to keep and to render an account, or to be answerable for carrying out a given task, assignment, or responsibility.

accountancy. In general, the profession of ACCOUNTING; the work done by an ACCOUNTANT.

account and risk. A term describing the usual method of trading in commodities and securities. The blank forms provided by brokers for the use of customers usually bear the inscription, "Buy (or sell) for my *account and risk,"* meaning that the customer is the principal in the transaction, and that he holds himself responsible for paying for or delivering the commodities or securities traded. The broker is thus acting merely as his agent and is relieved of all risk unless due to his own negligence.

accountant. One who is professionally trained and skilled in the practice of ACCOUNTING, or of one of its branches. See also AUDITOR; CONTROLLER.

certified public ∼. A PUBLIC ACCOUNTANT, which see below, who has been certified by a state examining body after meeting certain requirements of training, experience, and ability. In many states, certain accounting records, analyses, etc. must be prepared or examined by a *certified public accountant.*

chartered ∼. In England, and in some of the Dominions, an *accountant* who has been chartered by the Institute of Chartered Accountants, as one fully competent to undertake professional accounting work.

public ∼. An *accountant* who is skilled in the establishment and examination of business accounting records, and who makes his services available to business organizations on a fee or contract basis. In some states, the calling of *public accountant* is recognized as separate from, and on a lower level than that of CERTIFIED PUBLIC ACCOUNTANT, which see above.

account executive. In an advertising agency, research organization, securities trading house, or similar business firm, the individual who maintains direct personal contact with one or more clients. His usual duties include transmitting the client's wishes to the operating units of his company, and presenting the results of the company's work to the client.

accounting. 1. According to the Committee on Terminology of the American Institute of Accounting, the art of recording, classifying, and summarizing in a significant manner and in terms of money, transactions and events which are in part, at least, of a financial character, and interpreting the results thereof. Generally, *accounting* is considered to be concerned with the design, installation, and analysis of record-keeping systems, as distinguished from BOOKKEEPING, which is concerned with the direct work of making entries in the books and records of account. See also COST ACCOUNTING.

2. The rendering or furnishing of a statement of accounts, by one who is held accountable, legally or otherwise, for property, money, or other things of value. Typically, *accountings* are required of executors under a will, guardians, trustees in bankruptcy, and so on.

accounting period. A period of time or portion of a business year, at the close of which summary operating and balance statements are prepared, and new records begun for the next period. Most incorporated businesses today operate with quarterly (three month) *accounting periods,* but such periods may be of longer or shorter duration. See also FISCAL YEAR.

account opener. 1. An advertising or sales promotion campaign by mail or newspaper, designed primarily to obtain new charge account business for a retail store. More generally, any special item or special price, promoted for the purpose of getting such new charge account business.

2. A person or firm engaged in the business of organizing and running *account opener* promotional campaigns for retail stores, for a fee.

account sales. A statement sent by a broker, agent, auctioneer, or other to a principal, client, or customer, giving the details of sales made on behalf of the principal. The statement usually indicates the goods sold, the prices, and the net amount due the principal after all charges, expenses, and commissions are deducted.

accounts payable. On a BALANCE SHEET, the liabilities account reflecting the amounts owed by the business for goods and services purchased other than for cash. It does not include indebtedness due on long-term installment purchases, or to direct borrowing of any kind. See also LIABILITY, CURRENT.

accounts receivable. On a BALANCE SHEET, the assets account reflecting the amounts currently owed to the business by its customers, usually for goods and services sold or rented. It does not include amounts due on notes, or on long-term installment purchasing contracts. See also ASSET, CURRENT.

accounts receivable financing. The use of ACCOUNTS RECEIVABLE on the books of a business as a basis for obtaining working capital, either by borrowing with the accounts used as collateral, or by the outright sale of the

rights in the accounts, called factoring. Both commercial banks and sales finance companies grant accounts receivable loans, while factoring is usually engaged in by finance companies specializing in this activity. See also FACTOR; SALES FINANCE COMPANY.

accounts receivable insurance. See under INSURANCE, CASUALTY.

accounts receivable ledger. See LEDGER, SALES.

account stated. See STATEMENT OF ACCOUNT.

accretion. In real estate law, any increase in size of a piece of land due to deposits by a stream or river, the falling of the water level, etc. See also ALLUVION.

accrual basis accounting. A method of accounting, usually for income tax purposes, under which income and expenses are charged to the period to which they are applicable, regardless of when the money is actually received or spent. It is the opposite of CASH BASIS ACCOUNTING.

accrual clause. A clause inserted in a deed or will, bequeathing property of value to two or more persons as TENANTS IN COMMON, providing that on the death of one his share shall go equally and jointly to the survivors. His share thus ACCRUES to the others.

accrue. 1. To accumulate, grow, or increase, usually in an orderly manner, in the sense that interest *accrues* on money invested. To come into being or develop, as an enforceable claim or right. A claim or right which *accrues* ordinarily does so to the benefit of a particular person.

2. To record sales, expenses, and similar items of business income and outgo as they are incurred or earned, rather than as they are paid or received. To keep records on an ACCRUAL BASIS.

accrued. Earned but not yet received, or incurred but not yet paid. See each of the following under the principal listing: ~ DIVIDEND; ~ EXPENSE (2); ~ INCOME; ~ INTEREST (2); ~ LIABILITY (2).

accumulated. Added on to what was previously in existence, or due. In addition, or the result of previous additions. See each of the following under the principal listing: ~ DIVIDEND; ~ INTEREST (2); ~ SURPLUS.

accumulation. 1. Earnings or profits which are not distributed to stockholders as dividends, but instead are transferred to a capital account. See also SURPLUS, EARNED.

2. In law, the process of adding income from dividends, rent, interest, or other continuing source to the principal amount of a fund, and the subsequent treatment of such additions as capital.

3. In securities trade usage, the purchase

or *accumulation* of shares of stock at a time when prices are low, to be held for sale after a future expected increase in prices.

accumulation trust. See under TRUST (1).

accumulative stock. See STOCK (1), CUMULATIVE.

acetate. A form of man-made textile fiber or yarn, manufactured essentially from cellulose chemical materials. Under present federal regulations, only products made by the so-called *acetate* process are known as *acetate,* and those made by the viscose process are called RAYON. Frequently, the two types of fiber or yarn are blended to obtain a resulting mixture with the best characteristics of each.

acid test ratio. One of the ratios used in analyzing the financial condition of a business, or in considering the granting of credit. It is the ratio of quick or liquid current assets, not including inventories, deferred items, and other assets not readily convertible into cash, to current liabilities. In general practice, a one-to-one ratio is considered satisfactory, though actually the proper ratio varies considerably from one type of business to another. See also OPERATING RATIO.

acknowledgement. In law, the appearance before an authorized official, such as a notary, commissioner, or judge, for the purpose of making and signing a declaration or admission to be attached to a bond, mortgage, deed, etc. The purpose of making an *acknowledgement* is to furnish satisfactory evidence that the instrument was actually signed by the person whose name it bears and that he is the person described in the instrument.

acquittance. A written agreement discharging a person from the obligation to pay a sum of money; an acknowledgement of the payment in full of a debt.

acquisition cost. In insurance, the cost of inducing an insurer to place his insurance with a broker, agent, or underwriter; the selling costs of the insurance business. Generally, the cost of acquiring any asset, new business, etc.

acre. Originally, any field or piece of open ground, but now specifically a measure of land area. The English and American statute *acre* contains 160 square rods, 4,840 square yards, or 43,560 square feet. There are 640 *acres* in a square mile. One square *acre* measures 208.71 feet on a side. The English and American *acre* is smaller than that used in Ireland and Scotland. An *acre* is equal to about two-fifths, .40467 to be exact, of a metric hectare, the land measure used in

Europe and in most countries outside of the British Empire.

across the board. General and uniform, or applying to all classes, such as, for example, an *across the board* reduction in taxes, or an *across the board* increase in wages. Also, in radio and television usage, programming which schedules the same program for the same hour each weekday.

actio in personam. A Latin term, meaning a legal ACTION in which the proceeding is against a person, as distinguished from an action against property. See also ACTIO IN REM.

actio in rem. A Latin term, meaning a legal ACTION in which the proceeding is against property, as distinguished from an action against a person. See also ACTIO IN PERSONAM.

action. 1. In law, the legal and formal demand for rights, made in a court. Any proceeding in a court in which one party prosecutes another for the enforcement or protection of a right, the redress or prevention of a wrong, or the punishment of an offense; a SUIT.

cause of ∼. The basis or grounds on which an *action* is brought; the facts or state of affairs to which the particular law under which the *action* is brought applies.

civil ∼. An *action* brought on behalf of a person, to enforce his rights against other individuals or parties.

criminal ∼. An *action* instituted by a government, to punish or prevent an offense against public law or order.

real ∼. An *action* brought at common law, including especially those concerning land or inheritances.

2. In finance, a term used in France, and sometimes in other countries, meaning a share of stock in a business enterprise. Thus, an actionnaire or actionary is a shareholder.

actionable negligence. See under NEGLIGENCE.

active. In general, being used, or in use. Frequently used, as distinguished from that which is infrequently used, or inactive. See each of the following under the principal listing: ∼ ACCOUNT (3); ∼ ASSET (2); ∼ CAPITAL (3); ∼ PARTNER; ∼ STOCK (1).

active market. In securities trade usage, a market marked by frequent transactions, as distinguished from a dull, flat, narrow, or stagnant market. See also BROAD MARKET; INACTIVE MARKET; NARROW MARKET.

active trust. See TRUST (1), SPECIAL.

activity charge. A charge made by a bank against a checking account for deposits and checks, where the balance maintained in the account is not large enough to offset the costs of handling the activity. See ACCOUNT (3), SPECIAL CHECKING.

activity depreciation. See under DEPRECIATION, PRODUCTION.

act of God. Any unusual, extraordinary, or overwhelming natural phenomenon, such as an earthquake, storm, lightning, flood, or drought, which produces loss of property or life. Any natural cause of loss or damage, which is not attributable to human agency, and which it is not within the power of man to foresee, prevent, control, or avoid by reasonable precautions.

~ **clause.** In contracts, a clause providing that damages are not recoverable where the loss or damage can be shown to be due to an *act of God.* Such clauses are normally included in maritime BILLS OF LADING, and in common carrier contracts for freight haulage. Some insurance contracts also carry this type of clause with reference to certain risks.

act of honor. A term used for the instrument that is drawn up when a person desires to accept a bill for HONOR. See also ACCEPTANCE FOR HONOR.

actual. That which exists in fact or in act; real; in action or being at a given time. See each of the following under the principal listing: ~ ASSET (2); ~ COST; ~ LOSS (2); ~ PARTNER; ~ PRICE; ~ TARE.

actual cash value. See under VALUE (2).

actual damages. See DAMAGES, SUBSTANTIAL.

actual delivery. See DELIVERY (1).

actually issued. A term applied to securities which have been ISSUED (2) and sold to a bona fide purchaser for valuable consideration, and under such conditions that the purchaser holds the securities free from control by the issuing corporation. See also NOMINALLY ISSUED.

actuary. In general, one skilled in the mathematical sciences of probability, compound interest, and vital statistics. Specifically, the officer in an insurance company who is a trained specialist in actuarial science, and who calculates, mathematically and statistically, the rates or premiums to be charged for different types of insurance, based on the probable duration of the lives to be insured, and on the probability of occurrence of the hazards insured against.

addition. 1. In insurance, a part added or joined to a main building. It may be an added story, or a wing, or even in some cases a subsidiary building not physically attached to the main one.

2. In law, as a term used in a mechanic's lien, it is specifically a lateral *addition,* one

covering ground adjacent to the main building. In this terminology, an added story or an excavated cellar are alterations, not *additions.*

additional insured. In insurance, a person, other than the one named as the insured in an insurance policy, who is also protected against loss, either by being specifically listed as an *additional insured,* or by definition, according to the terms of the policy. See also INSURANCE; NAMED INSURED.

additions and betterments. A term sometimes used, especially in common carrier accounting, for those IMPROVEMENTS that increase the value of property, as distinguished from MAINTENANCE or REPAIR expenditures, which merely keep up the present value of the property.

ademption. In law, the revocation or extinction of a legacy, according to the implied intention of the testator from acts done by him in life, though there may have been no express revocation. For example, a testator may have paid to a legatee, as a gift during his life, that which by his will he proposes to give him at his death. In this event, it will be held that the legacy has been extinguished by the gift.

ad hoc. A Latin term meaning, literally, for this. Hence, for this special purpose; as, for example, an *ad hoc* committee, which is appointed to hold hearings on a particular matter, or an *ad hoc* attorney, who represents a client in a particular case.

adjourned sale. See under SALE (1).

adjudication. In law, the final order disposing of any legal action or special proceeding, such as a bankruptcy proceeding. More broadly, any recognized method of settling controversies.

adjudication order. An order by a court of bankruptcy, declaring or adjudging a debtor to be BANKRUPT, so that his estate may be vested in a trustee and wound up for the benefit of his creditors. The order may be granted either on the petition of a creditor, or on the voluntary application of the debtor.

adjustable currency. See CURRENCY, ELASTIC.

adjuster. 1. In a retail store, one who determines the validity of customer complaints concerning merchandise, service, or errors in price, and who is authorized to make refunds or other adjustments.

2. In insurance, one who determines the amount of a claim against an insurance company or one of its insureds, and who may recommend settlement for the amount determined. In many states, public *adjusters* are

licensed to make such determinations as independent parties.

adjustment. 1. In insurance, the determination of the amount of a loss, and the proper distribution of it among those liable to pay it; the settling of the indemnity which the insured is entitled to receive, and the proportion which each underwriter of the risk is liable to pay.

2. In accounting, an entry made to correct or compensate for a discovered error or difference in an account.

adjustment bond. See under BOND (1).

adjustment mortgage. See MORTGAGE, IMPROVEMENT.

administrative expense. See under EXPENSE (2).

administrator. 1. In general, one who directs, coordinates, integrates, and controls the affairs of an organization; an executive manager.

2. In law, a person appointed by a court for the purpose of winding up the estate of one who has died intestate, or who has left a will but has not named an EXECUTOR.

administrator's bond. See under BOND (2).

admiralty court. A court exercising jurisdiction over all actions arising out of maritime contracts or operations. The term derives from traditional British usage.

admiralty law. The term for the laws governing occurrences at sea, and the settling of disputes involving maritime commerce. It is partly the national law of the several countries, and partly a branch of international law.

admiralty mile. See MILE, NAUTICAL.

adult. In law, any person who is no longer an INFANT. The age at which a person becomes an *adult,* and therefore able to undertake obligations, enter into contracts, stand criminal trial, and so forth, varies from state to state, and often from purpose to purpose within a state. A person may be an *adult* at 16 under criminal law, for example, but at 18 for other purposes. In some states, a person who has reached the age of discretion, but who is not yet legally an *adult,* is called a MINOR.

adulteration. In general, the act of corrupting or debasing anything by the addition of inferior materials. As usually and specifically used, the term refers to the intentional deception of buyers as to the quality or purity of a product by the mixing in of inferior or impure elements, the removal of needed elements, or similar practices. Under various federal laws, such as the Pure Food and Drug Act, the Filled Meat Act, etc., the

adulteration of products entering interstate commerce is forbidden. Many states have similar laws governing the sale of products made within the state.

ad valorem. A Latin term meaning, literally, at value. According to the value, rather than according to the weight or number. Thus, any charge or tax which is levied as a percentage of the value of the item taxed. See, for example, TARIFF (2), AD VALOREM; TAX (2), AD VALOREM.

advance. In general, any payment made before it is due, or before the completion of an obligation for which it is to be paid. Examples include money paid to a contractor at the beginning of a contract, to aid him in undertaking the work, or money paid to the consignee of a shipment, to enable him to meet expenses, and to be repaid upon sale of the shipment.

advance bill. See under BILL (4).

advancement. 1. In law, a gift, made by an intestate person during life, to a child, of a portion of what will be the child's share of the intestate's estate, and to be taken into account in the distribution of the estate. See also ADEMPTION.

2. A promotion, such as to a better position, or to a higher rate of pay.

adventure. 1. In general, any hazardous or speculative enterprise or business venture. The term was formerly commonly used to describe a shipment of goods sent to a new or untried market, to be sold at the best price obtainable, as a test of the acceptance of the product in the market.

joint ∼. A commercial or maritime undertaking by two or more persons, which is ordinarily, but not necessarily, limited to a single venture. As generally used, a *joint adventure* is similar to a limited PARTNERSHIP, and is governed by the same rules of law, except that it is limited in purpose and duration, rather than in other ways.

2. In marine insurance, a term frequently used to mean PERIL.

adverse possession. See under POSSESSION. See also TITLE (2) BY ADVERSE POSSESSION.

adverse title. See TITLE (2) BY ADVERSE POSSESSION.

advertise. To announce publicly; to offer for public sale; to place an ADVERTISEMENT in any form of advertising medium.

advertisement. In general, any public announcement or notice, or offer to sell, placed in any public medium, either by printing or by the use of sight or sound.

advertising. In general, any form of paid public announcement or presentation, which is aimed at the promotion of the sale of goods or services, or at gaining acceptance for an idea or point of view. In modern usage, *advertising* may involve the use of many media and techniques, the major ones of which are listed and defined below.

classified ∼. *Advertising* appearing in specified sections of newspapers, magazines, and similar publications, consisting usually of brief announcements or notices classified under certain headings. These headings may include help wanted, situations wanted, homes for rent, house for sale, lost and found, etc. Charges for such *advertising* are usually made by the word, by the line of print, or by the COLUMN INCH.

consumer ∼. *Advertising* directed at the general consuming public, as distinguished from INDUSTRIAL ADVERTISING, or TRADE ADVERTISING, which see below, and placed in media which reach the consuming public.

cooperative ∼. *Advertising* which is paid for jointly by a manufacturer and the dealers or distributors of his products. The usual practice is for the manufacturer to make funds available for such *advertising* in proportion to the purchases of his products by those who cooperate in the *advertising*. See also ADVERTISING ALLOWANCE.

direct ∼. *Advertising* by the original producer of goods or services, and aimed at the final consumer, as distinguished from *advertising* to the trade, or by the trade to the consumer.

direct mail ∼. *Advertising* by means of letters, cards, literature, and other promotional material sent through the mail to potential customers. Such *advertising* may solicit direct orders by return mail, or may urge the recipient to visit a retail store, or to take some other action. See also MAIL-ORDER ADVERTISING, below.

display ∼. *Advertising* which consists primarily of illustration, headline, brief phrases in distinctive type, and blank space, as distinguished from *advertising* which consists largely or entirely of text or COPY (2). Also, loosely but incorrectly, the term sometimes refers to *advertising* which consists of display posters, working models, and similar setup material, such as would be used in POINT-OF-PURCHASE ADVERTISING, which see below.

industrial ∼. Advertising directed at industrial consumers of the products advertised, rather than at the general public. Such *advertising* may be placed in publications which are read in the industries covered, or it may be direct mail or some other form of *advertising*.

institutional ∼. *Advertising* which is aimed at keeping the name of a company or group before the public, rather than at promoting the merits of a particular product. It may be undertaken for general public relations purposes, or, as in wartime, to keep the company's name before the public when its regular products or services are unavailable.

keyed ∼. See directly.

local ∼. *Advertising* which is directed at a particular limited area, such as a city or even a neighborhood, and which consists of material placed in local newspapers and other local publications, announcements on local radio and television stations, billboards, posters, localized direct mail *advertising*, etc. The campaign may be undertaken by a local distributor or dealer, or by a manufacturer on behalf of his local distributors.

mail-order ∼. *Advertising* which is designed to encourage the consumer to order merchandise or services by mail, directly from the advertiser, who may be a retail store, a specialized mail-order distributor, or a manufacturer. The *advertising* itself may be placed in a newspaper, or it may consist of catalogs, brochures, and other material sent to the customer by direct mail.

media ∼. In general, any of the various types of *advertising* which appears in an *advertising* medium, such as a newspaper or magazine. Though radio, television, billboards, etc. are *advertising media,* the term as used usually refers to printed media only.

national ∼. That which is designed to reach the entire consuming public, or an entire trade or industry, and is therefore placed in publications with nationwide circulation and readership, or in radio or television network programs, etc. Such *advertising* is frequently combined with LOCAL ADVERTISING, which see above, aimed at directing the buying impulses created by the national campaign to the particular local sources for the advertised products.

outdoor ∼. *Advertising* placed on billboards, posters, illuminated signs, etc., which are located in prominent or heavily travelled locations, such as atop buildings, along highways, and so forth.

point-of-purchase ∼. The various forms of *advertising* and promotion material used in retail stores, at the point of purchase or sale. These include counter cards, displays, working models of products, literature for distribution to customers, etc. It is also known as *point-of-sale advertising*.

trade ∼. That *advertising* which is directed at the wholesale and retail distributors of a product or service, rather than at the industrial consumers or the general consuming public. Such *advertising* is usually placed in the trade magazines and newspapers which are read in the wholesale and retail fields, and includes also *advertising* material sent by direct mail or other means to the members of the trade.

transit ∿. *Advertising* placed in buses, rapid transit cars, rapid transit stations, and other locations in the transportation field. It usually consists of posters, cards placed in special brackets in the vehicles, and similar material.

advertising agency. A business organization which specializes in the creation and placing of ADVERTISING for other businesses. The services offered by a large modern *advertising agency* may include the planning of national advertising campaigns and their local counterparts, marketing research, the creation of advertising art and copy, the checking of various advertising media, the selection of media and the placement of the advertising. Some agencies now have facilities for preparing complete radio or television broadcasts as well. Except for special services, the standard method of payment for the services of an *advertising agency* is a fee of 15 percent of the cost of the space or time purchased in advertising media. For smaller accounts, which do not place enough advertising to justify this method of payment, fixed fees are sometimes negotiated.

advertising allowance. A payment, either in money or as an allowance against the cost of goods purchased, which a manufacturer or wholesale distributor makes to a distributor or retailer to defray all or part of the costs of advertising a product. Such allowances may be based on total dollar purchases, or on the number of units purchased, or on some other basis. When the allowance is conditioned on a matching expenditure by the retailer in some fixed proportion to the amount granted by the manufacturer, such as an exactly equal expenditure, the allowance is known as cooperative advertising. Under the terms of the Robinson-Patman Act, any *advertising allowances* granted must be available on proportionately equal terms to all other customers competing in the distribution of the advertiser's products or commodities.

advertising campaign. The coordinated employment of various media and methods of advertising to gain acceptance for a certain idea or product, or to increase the sales of a particular product or service. The placement of isolated and uncoordinated advertisements does not comprise a campaign.

advertising medium. Any means or instrument through which an advertising message is brought to the attention of the public. Some of the principal *advertising media* include newspapers, magazines, both general and trade, radio and television, outdoor displays, transit cards, direct mail material, dealer selling aids such as counter displays, novelties and specialties, directories, and registers, programs, menus, etc.

advice. A term for commercial or other information conveyed by letter or note, wherein one party advises another of something which has been done, or is about to be done, on his account. For example, an *advice* may be the statement that certain goods or securities have been bought or sold, or that they have been offered for sale at a particular price. See also LETTER OF ADVICE.

affidavit. In law, a written declaration or statement of facts, made voluntarily and under oath or affirmation before a proper authority. An *affidavit* is sometimes distinguished from a DEPOSITION, which is elicited by questioning, and which may afford an opportunity for cross-examination.

affiliated company. See under COMPANY.

afloat. A term used in commerce and in commercial statistics to distinguish commodities or goods which are en route on board ship from those which are actually on land. Statistics on the supply of a given commodity, for example, may contain a figure for the amount on hand and *afloat*. See also VISIBLE SUPPLY.

after date. A term used in drawing up a bill of exchange, draft, or note, meaning any date after the date on which the bill or note is originally drawn or executed. For example, a note made payable 30 days *after date* is payable on the 30th day after the day on which the note is originally made out and dated.

after sight. A term used in a bill or draft, determining the date on which payment is due, and meaning after the bill is presented to the drawee for ACCEPTANCE. For example, a bill which is due 30 days *after sight* is payable within 30 days after it is presented for acceptance, rather than 30 days after the date on which the bill is drawn. On bills so drawn, the acceptance date must, of course, be specifically stated.

agate. A measure of TYPE SIZE, approximately one-fourteenth of an inch high, or 5 POINTS. It is the basic unit used in measuring advertising space in newspapers. See also AGATE LINE.

agate line. A standard measurement used in measuring advertising space for billing purposes. It is a line one column wide and one *agate* high. Thus, there are 14 *agate lines* to the COLUMN INCH, but the total area involved may vary from publication to publication, depending on the width of column used.

agency. In law, the relationship existing between one person, the PRINCIPAL, who authorizes or empowers a second person to act for him, and the second person, or AGENT. Also, the corporation, group, or person that acts as an agent for another, such as an ADVERTISING AGENCY.

agenda. The order of business at a meeting; the list of matters to be considered or acted upon.

agent. In general, one who is authorized or empowered to act for another, in particular matters or in general. Under law, any contracts or arrangements made by an *agent* in the ordinary course of business are binding upon his PRINCIPAL. The chief types of *agent* are listed and defined below.

advertising ∼. See ADVERTISING AGENCY.

buying ∼. One authorized to buy goods for another, such as, for example, an importer's representative who buys for the importer's account in a foreign country, or a food processor's representative who buys agricultural products at the farm.

commission ∼. One who sells goods for a principal, under an arrangement or commission. A SALES AGENT, which see below, or COMMISSION MERCHANT.

fiscal ∼. See under FISCAL.

forwarding ∼. See FORWARDER.

general ∼. An *agent* who is authorized to act for a principal in all matters, or with broad powers. One who represents a principal in all matters in a given class of functions, in a given territory, etc.

insurance ∼. A person who represents an INSURANCE COMPANY in its dealings with buyers or with brokers. In life insurance, the *agent* is often essentially a salesman for the company, except that he operates under a specific agreement or contract, and is frequently not considered an employee of the company. Under recent rulings, however, such *agents* are considered employees for such purposes as social security taxes, etc. In property and liability insurance, the *agent* is typically an independent business man, who represents the insurance company locally, and is empowered to accept business, pending a review by the company. He differs from an insurance BROKER, who represents the insurance buyer, and places insurance through an *agent* or directly with the insurance company. In practice, however, there is often little difference between the activities or services of an *agent* and those of a broker.

manufacturer's ∼. A person or organization engaged in selling the goods of one or more manufacturers to retailers or users. An *agent* frequently performs many of the services of a wholesaler, and sells in a fixed territory or to specified trades, as a wholesaler would. He does not, however, take title to the goods he sells. He differs from a BROKER in that he acts under a continuing contractual arrangement with the manufacturer, while the broker makes a new arrangement for each sale.

purchasing ∼. See directly.

sales ∼. One authorized specifically to sell the goods of another. Frequently, a manufacturer, such as a textile mill, will authorize a selling organization, or perhaps another manufacturer of non-competitive but related products, to act as *sales agent* for all or certain classes of the manufacturer's products.

special ∼. One authorized to act for a principal in only certain specified or limited matters, or in a particular transaction.

transfer ∼. An *agent,* usually a bank, trust company, or similar organization, which acts for a corporation in the transfer of stock from one owner to another.

universal ∼. One who has virtually unlimited powers to act for a principal.

aggregate-of-intermediates clause. In rail transport, a clause in the Interstate Commerce Act, prohibiting the setting of a through freight or passenger rate between two points which is higher than the sum of the rates between intermediate points. The Interstate Commerce Commission may specifically authorize such a rate after investigation, however.

aging. The act or practice of classifying and analyzing something by its age. In a department store, for example, it is the usual practice to *age* inventory, by classifying it according to the number of months it has been held. The *aging* of accounts receivable is a classification according to the number of months the amount has been due.

agio. The difference between the real and nominal value of a currency, as shown by the rates of exchange. Sometimes, it is the difference between the value of paper and metal currency in a country. See also DISAGIO.

agreement. In law and business usage, a mutual understanding between two or more persons, involving a CONSIDERATION. An agreement exists when one party has made an OFFER, and the offer has been accepted by the other party. An agreement enforceable by law is a CONTRACT.

agreement in restraint of trade. As defined by the federal anti-trust laws, any agreement that lessens the competition in a particular field, restricts the free entry of new competitors into the field, or otherwise serves to restrain free trade. Such an agreement may be horizontal, or between companies at the same level of production or distribution; or vertical, between companies at different levels of an industry or distribution process. See also RESTRAINT OF TRADE.

agricultural paper. See under COMMERCIAL PAPER.

air cargo. Any items transported by aircraft, including AIR FREIGHT, AIR EXPRESS, AIR MAIL, etc.

air express. A transport service provided by the RAILWAY EXPRESS AGENCY in conjunction with the airlines, by which parcels and small freight shipments are carried, on a door-to-door basis, by either passenger aircraft or cargo flights, when available. The service is thus roughly comparable to the regular railway express service offered by the Railway Express Agency in conjunction with the railroads.

air freight. Commercial freight transported by aircraft, either on passenger flights or on regular freight flights.

airline. A company offering passenger and/or cargo transportation between points by aircraft. Also, the route covered by such a company.

  scheduled ∼. One licensed by the Civil Aeronautics Administration to carry passengers or freight over regular routes on regularly scheduled flights.

  non-scheduled ∼. One licensed by the Civil Aeronautics Administration to carry passengers or freight between authorized points only, as frequently as the demand requires, rather than on a regular schedule. In fact, a *non-scheduled airline* which advertises or gives notice of specified departure times in advance risks the withdrawal of its license. In many particulars, the regulations governing the operation of *non-scheduled airlines* differ from those for the *scheduled lines*.

air mail. See under POSTAL SERVICE.

air mile. See MILE, NAUTICAL.

air parcel post. See POSTAL SERVICE, AIRMAIL.

aleatory contract. See under CONTRACT (1).

alias. Literally, in the Latin, otherwise. Hence, otherwise known as. For example, "John Doe, *alias* Richard Roe" means "John Doe, otherwise known as Richard Roe." The term is especially used for a false name used for illegal purposes.

alien. Belonging to another country. An *alien* corporation, for example, is one incorporated in a foreign country, while under the laws of many states a FOREIGN corporation is one incorporated outside the state, though perhaps in the same country.

alienate. With reference to property, to transfer title or specified rights to another.

alimony. In law, a maintenance or living allowance, paid under a court order by a husband to a wife who is legally separated or divorced from him, or is about to be. Temporary *alimony* may be ordered paid while the separation or divorce action is pending, and permanent *alimony* ordered paid after the arrangement is set.

aliquot part. Strictly, a share or part which is contained in a larger amount an exactly even number of times. Seven, for example, is an *aliquot part* of 42. As generally used, however, any fractional part, or definite share of the whole is known as an *aliquot part*.

all-around price. See under PRICE.

allegation. In law, a declaration or statement of charges which a party to a legal proceding expects to prove. Hence, in general usage, any unproved charge.

all faults. See WITH ALL FAULTS.

Allison Act. See BLAND-ALLISON ACT.

allocate. To allot or assign shares, especially of an item in short supply. To distribute, as to *allocate* items under the proper accounts in bookkeeping.

all-loss insurance. See INSURANCE, ALL-RISK.

allonge. In banking and finance, the name for a slip attached to a BILL OF EXCHANGE, note, or other negotiable instrument, on which an endorser may sign his name when there is no further room on the original bill for additional endorsements.

all or any part. In the securities trade, a phrase used in a contract for UNDERWRITING a securities issue, indicating that the bidder agrees to be prepared to accept *all or any part* of the issue that is allotted to him. In the event of several similar bids, for example, the issuing company may wish to divide the issue among several underwriters. See also ALL OR NONE.

all or none. In the securities trade, a phrase used in a bid or agreement for UNDERWRITING a securities issue, indicating that the bidder has submitted his price for underwriting the issue on the assumption that he will receive the entire issue. In some cases, a prospective underwriter may want to quote one price if he is given an entire issue, but a higher price if he is to have only part. On the other hand, the issuer of the securities may ask for bids on both an *all or none* basis and on an ALL OR ANY PART basis, or on only one or the other basis.

allotment. A share, portion, or allowance. Also, the act of sharing out or apportioning, such as for example, the distribution of a securities issue among underwriters. Originally, it was a distribution by lot, but in current usage it is any sharing or apportionment.

allowance. 1. A reduction, especially a reduction in price. For example, an *allowance* for imperfections or damage, or an *allowance* for a trade-in. In sales accounting, such *allowances* are frequently grouped under the heading *sales allowance*.

2. In commercial practice, a reduction from invoice weights or measurements, based on custom in the trade or on an agreement between buyer or seller. Such *allowances* may be made for package weight, shrinkage, breakage, waste, etc.

3. A RESERVE, or an amount set aside, such as an *allowance* for bad debts, or for depreciation.

alloy. Any combination or mixture of two or more metals, to obtain a resulting metallic substance with properties different from those of any of the individual components. For example, the addition of nickel and chromium to steel to make it stainless steel, or the mixture of copper and tin to create bronze. An *alloy* may also contain non-metallic substances, such as, for example, carbon steel, which contains pure carbon.

all-risk insurance. See under INSURANCE.

alluvion. In law, an addition or accretion to land, due to the deposit of soil by the water which washes on it. The *alluvion* belongs to the owner of the land on which it is deposited. See also ACCRETION.

alongside. In commercial usage, at the side of the ship. Goods to be delivered *alongside* are to be delivered to the dock or lighter from which they can be loaded aboard ship. See also FREE ALONGSIDE.

alternative will. See under WILL.

amalgamated union. See under UNION.

amalgamation. In business, a joining together of two or more companies into one surviving company. It may be either a MERGER, in which one company absorbs another, or a CONSOLIDATION, in which both are joined into a new company.

American Stock Exchange. One of the two major SECURITIES EXCHANGES in New York City. It was formerly known as the curb exchange, due to the fact that its members originally conducted their trading activities on the curb, or street, outside the stock exchange, before becoming organized as a regular exchange.

American value. See UNITED STATES VALUE.

amicus curiae. Literally, in Latin, a friend of the court. The name for a brief entered in a case by a party who is not directly involved, but who has an interest in the outcome of the case, or in the principle involved. For example, when one company brings suit against another on charges of unfair competition, the government might submit a brief for the guidance of the court, as a friend of the court, or *amicus curiae*.

amnesty. In law, a decree or order by a government granting a mass PARDON to a large number of prisoners convicted of specified crimes, especially political crimes. It is common, in some states, for the governor to grant an *amnesty* at Christmas to large numbers of prisoners convicted of minor crimes. Also, an order by a government promising freedom from prosecution to those who have committed certain crimes, on the acceptance of specified conditions.

amortization fund. See SINKING FUND.

amortize. 1. In accounting and finance, to extinguish or wipe out the value of an asset, or the value at which it is carried on the books of a company, gradually and evenly over a period of time. This is done especially in the case of such assets as leases, patents, copyrights, and so forth, which do not undergo DEPRECIATION in the ordinary sense, but which are nevertheless of decreasing value to the company as they near the end of their existence. Such assets may be *amortized* by reducing their value by an equal amount each period, or by following one of the various depreciation formulas.

2. In finance, to reduce or pay off a debt or obligation by making payments on the principal each period, along with a payment of interest. In some cases, as in real estate mortgages, the payments may be of equal size, becoming more principal and less interest as the debt is reduced.

amortized loan. See under LOAN.

amortized mortgage. See under MORTGAGE.

ampere. The basic unit of measurement of the rate of flow of an electric current. It is defined as the rate of flow of a current under a pressure of one VOLT across a conductor with a resistance of one OHM. In the basic relationship of WATTS, VOLTS and *amperes, amperes* equal watts divided by volts. In other words, a 500 watt appliance, operating on a 110 volt house circuit, causes current to flow at a rate of about 5 *amperes*. Most ordinary home lighting circuits are designed to carry current at a maximum of 15 *amperes,* and have a fuse in the circuit which will blow or burn out if a heavier flow is drawn.

and interest. A term used in quoting the selling price of a bond, meaning that any interest which has accrued or accumulated on the bond since the last payment date up to the date of the transaction is to be added to the market price of the bond and paid to the seller. Under this method of quoting bond prices, the market price itself does not regularly rise from interest date to interest date. See also EX-INTEREST.

angstrom unit. In physics, the unit used to measure the length of light waves. One *angstrom* is one hundred millionth part of a centimeter. The unit is named after A. J. Ångström, a Swedish physicist.

annual. Occurring or recurring once each year, or over a period of a year; yearly. For example, *annual* income or earnings is the amount of money received over the period of a year, but an *annual* payment of interest is an amount paid once each year, rather than more often. Similarly, an *annual* PREMIUM, in insurance, is one paid yearly, rather than more or less frequently.

annual wage plan. Any of several plans under which an employer guarantees to his employees a stated amount of work during a year, or pay for a stated amount of work or number of weeks of work, whether worked or not. Under one plan, for example, employees are paid a fixed amount each week, regardless of the amount of overtime worked during the peak season, or the amount of time not worked during the slack season. Any net balance of overtime is paid at the end of the year, but any net pay for time not worked is absorbed by the employer. Wages paid under such a plan are sometimes called a guaranteed annual wage.

annuitant. A person who is receiving, or who is to receive, payments under an ANNUITY.

annuity. A series of sums of money to be paid to a specified person or persons for a period of years, for life, or in perpetuity. Strictly speaking, the sum is to be paid annually, as the term implies, but in practice it may be paid in any regular amount in any specified frequency of payment. It differs from an INCOME, which is paid out of earnings and interest only, in that it is paid out of a combination of both the principal amount and the interest of the fund that establishes it. In insurance, an *annuity* may be purchased by the payment of a single lump sum amount, or by a number of payments over a period of time, or by the conversion of the face amount of a matured or payable insurance policy. The principal types and classes of *annuity* are listed and defined below. See also BOND (1), ANNUITY.

~ certain. One which is to be paid to the annuitant for life, but under which a fixed number of payments are guaranteed in any event, to be made either to the annuitant or to a named beneficiary. The terms of the agreement, for example, may provide for payments for ten years *certain,* meaning that if the annuitant should live for less than ten years, the remaining payments of the ten will be paid to whoever he names.

~ due. The term for an *annuity* in which the regular payments are made at the beginning of each period, instead of at the close of the period, starting with the beginning of the first period. One established to make rental payments, for example, might be of this type.

contingent ~. One for which the necessary funds have been set up, but which is to become payable only in the event of some uncertain event happening, such as the death of a named person while the intended annuitant is still alive.

deferred ~. One providing for payments for a fixed number of years, or for life, the payments to start at the end of some agreed period. A person who comes into a large sum of money, for example, might use it to buy a single payment *deferred annuity,* to provide for his retirement. See also SINGLE PAYMENT ANNUITY, below.

equity ~. See VARIABLE ANNUITY, below.

immediate ~. One which is to start immediately upon purchase, as distinguished from a DEFERRED ANNUITY, which see above. It may be either a SINGLE PAYMENT or a PREMIUM ANNUITY, which see below.

joint-and-survivor ~. One which is specified to be payable jointly to two or more annuitants as long as they are all alive, and to the surviving annuitant as long as he lives.

joint life ~. One which is specified to be payable jointly to two or more persons as long as they all remain alive. As soon as one dies, the annuity ceases, and any remaining principal is paid in a single sum to the others.

last survivor ~. One which is payable jointly to two or more annuitants as long as they all live, and to the last survivor as long as he lives. It differs from the usual JOINT-AND-SURVIVOR ANNUITY, which see above, in that any remaining principal is paid to the estate of the last survivor.

life ~. One which is specified to be payable to a named person as long as he lives, and to cease when he dies, as distinguished from a TEMPORARY ANNUITY, which see below, which is for a specified number of years.

ordinary ~. One under which payments are made at the end of each period, beginning one full period after the completion of purchase, as distinguished from an ANNUITY DUE, which see above.

perpetual ~. One which is specified to be payable for an indefinite period of time, not limited to a number of years or to the life of a person. It continues without limit, as long as the need exists, and funds are available, but not literally in perpetuity. The annuitant in such a case may be a religious or charitable organization.

premium ~. One which is purchased over a period of time by a series of premium payments, rather than by means of a single large payment, as in the case of a SINGLE PAYMENT ANNUITY, which see below. The *annuity* purchased may be either an IMMEDIATE or DEFERRED ANNUITY, which see above.

single payment ~. One which is purchased by means of a single large payment, rather than through the payment of a series of small amounts over a period of time, as in the case of a PREMIUM ANNUITY, which see above. The annuity purchased may be either an IMMEDIATE or DEFERRED ANNUITY, which see above.

survivorship ~. One which is payable to the beneficiary named in a life insurance policy, upon the death of the insured. It is purchased, in effect, with the proceeds of the policy, and is an ANNUITY CERTAIN, LIFE ANNUITY, which see above, or other form, depending on the choice of the insured or the beneficiary.

temporary ~. One which is specified to be payable for a fixed number of years, rather than for life. See also LIFE ANNUITY, above.

variable ~. A form of PREMIUM ANNUITY, which see above, in which the regular payments are invested in common stocks, rather than in more conservative securities, with the thought that the increase in value of the fund built up will offset the effects of future inflation. It is sometimes known as an *equity annuity,* since the funds are invested in equity securities. The sale of such *annuities* is so far permitted in only a few states.

annuity bond. See under BOND (1).

annul. In law, to make void; to rescind or abolish. As used, to *annul* is different from to CANCEL, in that it implies a wiping out of what has happened, and a return to the situation existing at a previous time, while cancellation affects only those things which have not yet happened. When a marriage is *annulled,* for example, the legal effect is as if neither party had been married at all.

antedate. To affix an earlier date than the actual one; to give an effective starting date to an instrument earlier than that at which

it was actually written. A life insurance policy may be *antedated* by a full year in some states, for example, by paying an extra year's premium, so that the annual premium, maturity value, cash reserve value, etc. will be calculated as of an age one year younger than that at which the policy actually started. On the other hand, to *antedate* a negotiable instrument is unlawful. The term predate is sometimes used, but this is not recommended, since it may be confused with POSTDATE.

anticipated profit. See under PROFIT.

anticipation. 1. In business, the payment of an account before the actual due date, to take advantage of a cash discount allowed. Also, sometimes, the amount deducted from the full price, when payment is *anticipated.* See also DISCOUNT (1), CASH.

2. In accounting, the act of assigning, making charges against, or otherwise dealing with income or profit before it is actually realized.

3. In patent law, the condition in which a claimed invention is shown to be known already in the country in which it is submitted for patenting, whether the *anticipating* invention has itself been patented or not.

anticipation rate. A term for the rate of the cash discount allowed. See DISCOUNT (1), CASH.

anti-dumping tariff. See under TARIFF (2).

anti-trust laws. Any of a number of federal laws intended to prevent or eliminate MONOPOLIES, TRUSTS, RESTRAINT OF TRADE, etc. The principal federal anti-trust laws are the Sherman Act, passed in 1890; the Clayton Act, passed in 1914; the Federal Trade Commission Act, passed in 1914; the Robinson-Patman Act, passed in 1936; the Miller-Tydings Act, passed in 1937; and the McGuire Act, which replaced the Miller-Tydings Act after the former was declared unconstitutional. Several of the states have similar laws, to cover the few cases of monopolistic practices which do not involve interstate commerce.

A-one. First class; of the highest quality; in perfect condition. Now used generally, the term originated in the practice of marine insurance underwriters, who classified vessels as A, B, or C risks for rating purposes, with A-1 as the highest possible rating.

apothecaries' measure. A system of measurement of liquid volume, used in the fields of medicine and pharmacy. The principal units are fractions of the standard fluid OUNCE, with 60 MINIMS equal to one fluid DRAM, and 8 drams equal to one ounce.

apothecaries' weight. A system of measurement of weight, used in the fields of medicine and pharmacy. It is similar to TROY WEIGHT, in that it is based on a POUND of 12 OUNCES or 5,760 GRAINS, but the intermediate units are the SCRUPLE of 20 grains and the DRAM of 60 grains or 3 scruples. There are 8 drams in an ounce. See also AVOIRDUPOIS.

apparent. In general, obvious, manifest, or evident to view; having the superficial or immediate appearance of reality. For example, an *apparent* danger connected with any work or employment is one of which the employee can be assumed to be aware. See also DEFECT, PATENT.

apparent heir. See HEIR APPARENT.

appeal. In law, a move by one of the parties to a legal action or suit to have the correctness of the decision of a lower court reviewed by a higher court, and reversed or modified. In civil law, or in equity, either the plaintiff or defendant may *appeal* an adverse decision or ruling, but in criminal law, while the defendant may always *appeal,* the state is restricted to *appeals* based only on certain grounds, as specified in the particular state or federal laws.

appeal bond. See under BOND (2).

appearance. In law, the formal coming into court of a party to a suit or action, which is necessary to give the court jurisdiction over the person who is required to *appear.* Actually, in civil cases, this is frequently accomplished by the filing of specified papers effecting *appearance,* rather than by an actual physical *appearance* in the court.

apportion. To divide into proportionate parts; to distribute in proportion to some uniform basis of comparison, such as value, legal status, etc. For example, total taxes on real estate in a community may be *apportioned* in proportion to the ASSESSED VALUATION of the taxable property in the community, and an estate may be *apportioned* among the heirs according to the terms of a will or according to the laws of the state if there is no will.

appraisal. In general, an evaluation of the worth of anything, whether of real property or of an intangible, such as a program or plan of action, or method of operation. More particularly, in real estate and insurance, a formal and detailed evaluation of property, usually undertaken by an expert in such work, known as an APPRAISER. *Appraisals* may be prepared to determine the necessary amount of insurance, the taxable value of property, its fair price for sale, etc. See also RETROSPECTIVE APPRAISAL.

appraisal surplus. See under SURPLUS.

appraise. To set a value upon something; to estimate a fair price or value for purposes of sale, purchase, taxation, insurance, etc. To make an APPRAISAL.

appraiser. A specially trained and skilled person employed or appointed to ascertain or determine the true value of some item of property. In some states, such persons are licensed and must be qualified to perform their duties. The services of an *appraiser* may be used to determine the insurable value of property before or after a loss, to determine the value for tariff purposes of an imported item, to set the value of real or personal property in an estate for purposes of distributing it among the heirs, etc.

appraiser's store. In the United States Customs Service, the government warehouse or storeroom in which imported goods are held under security while awaiting and during inspection, examination, or appraisal by the customs officials. One or more such *appraiser's stores* is maintained at every customs port of entry into the country.

appreciate. In business, to increase in value, especially in market value, due to changes in circumstances, rather than as the result of any deliberate action taken. For example, real estate may *appreciate* in value due to changes in the character of the neighborhood in which it is located, or goods in inventory may *appreciate* in value due to changes in their market price while held. However, property which increases in value due only to improvements made by the owner is not considered to have *appreciated.* See also DEPRECIATE.

appreciation surplus. See SURPLUS, APPRAISAL.

apprentice. Originally, under the guild system of skilled trades, one who was bound to a MASTER for a period of years to learn a trade or skill before becoming a JOURNEYMAN. As used today, anyone who learns a specified trade by working at it under supervision by a skilled worker, or by a combination of this training with more formal school or individual instruction. The *apprentice* system of training is used especially in the printing and building trades, and in skilled machine tool work.

appropriate. 1. In business generally, to make funds available for a specific purpose. To authorize or set aside money to be spent for some particular project, or to meet some particular payment when due. In a corporation, for example, the by-laws may require that all expenditures of over some amount be specifically *appropriated* by the board of directors.

2. In law, to make something one's own, or to take over possession of something. The

term is used especially to refer to the taking over of something to which one has no right, such as property belonging to an employer, or public property. The CONVERSION of property.

appropriated surplus. See under SURPLUS.

appropriation. A formal and official authorization or setting aside of money to be spent for a specific purpose, and usually, to be spent during a specified period of time. For example, a legislature may make an *appropriation* to meet the costs of a regular government department or program during a year, or it may make an *appropriation* of the funds called for to carry out a specific item of legislation.

approval sale. See SALE (1) ON APPROVAL.

appurtenance. With respect to real property, anything which is appended or annexed to it, or which is closely related to it, though not necessarily physically attached. The right and title to an *appurtenance* is ordinarily transferred with the property itself, unless otherwise specified. For example, a garden is an *appurtenance* to its house, and a right of way is an *appurtenance* to the property which it benefits. In the case of personal property, such as tools or equipment, the things in similar relationship are called ACCESSORIES.

arbiter. See ARBITRATOR.

arbitrage. Literally, the act of looking into. The buying of securities, negotiable instruments, or currency in one market for immediate resale in another, when a small price difference exists between the two markets. The profit on such transactions is relatively very small, but they are usually carried on in large volume. In practice, the fact that professional *arbitragers* or *arbitragists* will take advantage of such price differences promptly serves to keep the prices for freely traded securities or currencies from differing by very much in the various markets of the world. Also, the trading in two securities, one of which is convertible into the other, to take advantage of any small price differential which may exist, is known as *arbitrage* in the securities trade.

arbitrary. Originally, according to the decision or discretion of an ARBITRATOR, rather than according to a preset rule. As used, based on opinion or will, with no cause or reason given or apparent; capricious, rather than based on reasonable judgment.

arbitration. Literally the act of looking into something, or of deciding its merits. The process by which a dispute between two contending parties is turned over to one or more disinterested parties for investigation and a final decision. The disinterested party, or ARBITRATOR, may be chosen by the parties themselves, or may be appointed by some superior body whose authority is accepted by the parties. Under an *arbitration* procedure, both contending parties agree in advance to accept the decision of the arbitrator, and there is no appeal. In most states, a uniform statute provides for the acceptance of such arbitrated decisions by the courts. *Arbitration* may be VOLUNTARY, in that it is agreed to by the parties on their own initiative, or it may be COMPULSORY, in that it is provided for under a previous agreement, such as a union contract, sales contract, etc. See also CONCILIATION; MEDIATION.

arbitration of exchange. In a free currency or foreign exchange market, a calculation by means of which the value of three or more currencies in terms of each other is determined. The calculations are based on the relative value of each of the currencies in terms of the others at three or more different places. When only three places or markets are involved, the process is known as *simple arbitration,* and when four or more places are involved it is known as *compound arbitration.*

arbitrator. A private, disinterested person, who is chosen or agreed to by the parties to a dispute to examine the circumstances of the dispute and reach a final and binding decision. Sometimes the term arbiter is used for an *arbitrator* who operates informally, outside of any regular system or agreement for ARBITRATION proceedings. Strictly, an *arbitrator* is distinguished from a REFEREE, in that the latter is employed to interpret or clarify the terms of a judicial decision or award, while the former deals with private contracts, agreements, or disputes.

are. In the METRIC SYSTEM, the basic unit of square land measure. It is an area equivalent to a square ten METERS on each side, or 100 square meters. A more widely used measure is the hectare, or 100 *ares,* including 10,000 square meters, and the equivalent of 2.471 ACRES in the American system of land measure.

area sample. See under SAMPLE (3).

arise. In law, to come into existence or action; to follow from a given set of causes or circumstances. For example, in WORKMEN'S COMPENSATION laws, those injuries *arising* out of employment are those which have some causal connection with the work done or the place of work, rather than merely those which coincidentally occur during the time of employment.

arithmetic mean. See under AVERAGE (1).

armed forces leave bond. The name for an issue of registered, non-negotiable, five-year bonds which were issued by the federal government to discharged servicemen at the end of World War II, in payment for unused leave time. Virtually all of the bonds were redeemed within a short time, since they could be used to pay premiums on National Service Life Insurance or for other purposes.

arms length. An expression used in reference to business dealings, meaning without any personal influence or close relations. An agreement between a parent company and a subsidiary, for example, is said to be negotiated at *arms length* when it is done according to established business practices, with no implication of influence or collusion, and is executed at fair market prices.

arrangement. In general, a settlement, especially one between parties involved in a legal action. As defined in the federal BANKRUPTCY laws, an *arrangement* is any plan of a debtor, offered to his creditors, intended to provide a settlement, satisfaction, or extension of the payment of his unsecured debts. A debtor who can conclude such an *arrangement* with his creditors may be able to avoid formal bankruptcy procedures.

array. In statistics, an arrangement of individual observations or items in ranked order, from the greatest to the least or the reverse. Data may be put in an *array* to determine the median, or to calculate the rank correlation. See also AVERAGE (1), MEDIAN; CORRELATION, RANK.

arrears. In accounting and finance, the term for amounts which are due and not yet paid at the date fixed for payment, or after the period of time allowed for payment has expired. A person or debtor who has not paid a debt or obligation by the time it is due is said to be *in arrears* on the payment. Similarly, a bond or preferred stock on which interest or dividends due have not been paid is said to be *in arrears*.

arson. In law, the malicious and intentional burning of the house or other property of another. Also, the burning of one's own property, when done to defraud an insurance company. Originally, the term referred specifically to the burning of a dwelling place, but it now covers any building or structure, a ship, standing timber, etc.

art. In patent law, any useful principle, device, or machine which is put into manufacture. Any beneficial feature which is included in an invention and is exactly described in the patent. More broadly, the body of knowledge and skill which is connected with the accomplishment of a result.

   prior ∼. As used in the patent laws, those things which any person skilled in the existing principles and practices of a field could be expected to know, or to discover by reasonable diligence. Features which are included in the *prior art* in any field are not patentable.

articles of agreement. A term for any contract or agreement between two or more persons which is reduced to a written memorandum. It sets forth the intent and purposes of the agreement, any promises made, the details of the things to be given or performed, and provides for a termination date, if appropriate. A memorandum of this form may be drawn up, for example, before the preparation of a more formal document, such as a DEED.

articles of association. A written memorandum of agreement drawn up and signed by the members of a joint stock company, or an association, setting forth the purposes of the organization, the form, amount of capital, and any other appropriate details. However, it is not the CHARTER of the organization, which is issued by the state or other authority.

articles of incorporation. The authorization issued to a corporation by the Secretary of State or other officer of a state, to operate and do business within the state. Strictly, the *articles of incorporation* of a corporation are distinguished from its CERTIFICATE OF INCORPORATION, in that the latter is the form filed by the incorporators, and the former is the form issued by the state. Both documents contain essentially the same information, and either may be known, loosely, as the corporation's charter.

articles of partnership. See PARTNERSHIP AGREEMENT.

articles of war. The set of rules established by Congress for the government of members of the armed forces, and persons under their direct jurisdiction outside of the United States; the military law. This is distinguished from MARTIAL LAW, which is the emergency government of civilians by the military in time of emergency.

artificial person. See under PERSON.

artisan. Originally, one who practices any of the arts, but more specifically, one of the industrial arts. Hence, a skilled craftsman, or a mechanic, as distinguished from an ordinary laborer, on the one hand, and from a professional technician on the other. Under state laws, *artisans* are frequently listed as being entitled to a mechanic's lien for any unpaid work done. See also LIEN, MECHANIC'S.

as is. A term meaning that a thing is to be taken in its present condition, with no repair or improvement work done. A sale of merchandise *as is*, for example, is a sale of something in its actual condition as shown, with whatever defects, faults, marks of wear, etc. it may have. Such a sale is usually made at a reduction from the original price. See also SALE WITH ALL FAULTS.

asked price. See under PRICE.

as per advice. A phrase frequently used in a BILL OF EXCHANGE. It means that the person against whom the bill has been drawn, the drawee, has been properly notified or advised that the bill has been drawn. It does not mean, however, that the drawee has guaranteed payment of the bill when presented.

assay. To test or analyze a metal or mineral, or an ore, chemically, to determine its metallic content, and its degree of purity. The term is used particularly to refer to the analysis of precious metals, such as gold and silver.

  ~ **office.** One of several establishments maintained by the federal government to analyze the content of gold and silver delivered to the government. It will also analyze metal which is not being delivered or sold to the government, for a small charge.

  ~ **office bar.** The term for a bar of fine or pure gold or silver which has been analyzed, or perhaps made, by a United States government *assay* office, and bearing a mark to this effect. A bar which has been privately *assayed* or analyzed is known as a commercial bar.

assembling. In marketing and distribution, the function of bringing together or concentrating goods to facilitate their further distribution or final sale. For example, a WHOLESALER brings together the products of many manufacturers to distribute them together to retail dealers, a FORWARDER assembles small shipments to forward them more economically, and an assembler of components makes finished products out of the manufactured parts produced by others. Such assemblers as this last type are classified as MANUFACTURERS by the Bureau of the Census.

assent. In general, compliance; the approval of something already done; acquiescence to an existing state of affairs. Strictly speaking, *assent* is distinguished from CONSENT, which is an agreement or willingness that something be done which has not yet occurred. It is sometimes said that consent is active, while *assent* is passive.

assented stock. See under STOCK (1).

assess. To ascertain the value of something, or to fix its value for tax purposes. This is usually done according to certain established rules or practices in the particular state or community. In some communities, for example, residential property is *assessed* at a lower percentage of its true market value than is commercial property. The tax to be paid by each property is determined by multiplying the TAX RATE in the community by the ASSESSED VALUATION of the property.

assessable policy. See under POLICY (2).

assessable security. See under SECURITY (1).

assessable stock. See under STOCK (1).

assessed valuation. The value which is assigned to property for tax purposes, by the city, town, or other taxing authority. It is established according to the rules, practices, and customs of the state or community. See also ASSESS.

assessment. 1. In taxation, a charge made against property to pay the costs of public improvements which will benefit the property. The costs of new sewers, street paving, etc. are frequently charged against the property in the area by *assessment*. Thus, an *assessment* differs from a TAX in that it is imposed against specified property to pay for a specific improvement, while a tax is imposed against all property in a given class, for the general revenue, or to pay for a general class of costs, such as all highway costs. It is sometimes called a *local assessment*.

  2. In corporate finance, a demand for funds from a company upon its shareholders to pay into the company treasury a specified amount per share to meet the obligations of the company. An *assessment* differs from a CALL (2) in that it is a demand for funds over and above the par value of the stock, while the latter is a demand for funds to bring each shareholder's paid in amount up to the par value. Presently, most stocks are non-assessable.

  3. In insurance, a charge made by an insurance company, especially a mutual company, against all of its policy holders, to cover the amounts paid out to meet excessive losses. Presently, most insurance policies are of the non-assessable type. See also POLICY, ASSESSABLE; POLICY, NON-ASSESSABLE.

assessment insurance company. See under INSURANCE COMPANY.

asset. 1. In law, a part of the goods or property, both real and personal, belonging to a deceased person, and which is available to his estate.

  2. In business, anything of value which is

owned by a business organization, whether tangible or intangible, and which can be applied, directly or indirectly, to cover the liabilities of the business. In accounting and in general practice, the following types and classifications of *assets* are recognized.

active ∼. The term for one which is being used in the conduct of the business, or in production, including materials, equipment, machinery, etc.

actual ∼. One which is carried at its true or known value, such as money or securities, as distinguished from a NOMINAL ASSET, which see below.

available ∼. In one sense, one which is free to be converted into cash; a LIQUID ASSET, which see below. In another sense, one which is not pledged against a loan, or covered by a lien.

capital ∼. One which is held as a long term investment, or for the production of income, rather than for consumption or for resale. Thus, the term includes such items as plant and equipment, patents owned, etc.

cash ∼. One consisting either of cash in hand or in a bank, or of things of value which can immediately be converted into cash, such as checks, drafts, etc.

current ∼. In general, all of the TANGIBLE ASSETS of a company, which see below, except the FIXED ASSETS, which see below. Thus, the term includes cash, securities, goods and materials in inventory, accounts and notes receivable, etc.

deferred ∼. An accounting term for an item which has been paid in advance, for a future expense not yet incurred. For accounting purposes, such amounts are carried as *assets* until they are liquidated by the occurring of the event or time period for which they were paid out. Examples include rent, insurance premiums, taxes, and other costs paid in advance.

doubtful ∼. A term used in the analysis of a financial statement for an *asset* which is believed to be of lower actual value than that at which it is carried on the company books. Also, one which may not be capable of being converted into cash.

fixed ∼. Any one of those TANGIBLE ASSETS, which see below, which is used more or less permanently in the conduct of the business, rather than held for consumption or resale, and which cannot readily be converted into cash. *Fixed assets* are essentially identical with CAPITAL ASSETS, which see above, though they may not necessarily be held directly for investment or the production of income.

frozen ∼. A term for one which is not convertible into cash within a reasonable period of time, such as an inventory of

obsolete goods, or an investment in real estate which cannot be readily marketed. Also, sometimes, an *asset* which cannot be disposed of because of some governmental restriction or regulation.

hidden ∼. A term sometimes used for the difference between the value at which an *asset* is carried on the books, and its true higher value. A company may sometimes deliberately reduce the value at which it carries some *assets,* to mislead competitors, or the government, or for other reasons.

intangible ∼. One which is of value to the company, and which may produce income, but which does not have a readily determinable value. Examples include good will, subscription lists, secret processes, trade names, etc. In conservative accounting practice, such *intangible assets* are carried at a nominal value on the books of the company, though they may bring a large sum of money on the sale of the business.

liquid ∼. A term for those *assets* of a person or a business which are in cash, or a form readily convertible into cash, such as securities, current accounts receivable, etc. In general, *liquid assets* consist of CURRENT ASSETS, which see above, less goods in inventory. The term *quick assets* is sometimes used.

net ∼. The total *assets* of a business less its total LIABILITIES. In other words, the NET WORTH of the business.

nominal ∼. A term for the face or book value of an *asset,* as distinguished from its actual value. See also ACTUAL ASSET, above.

quick ∼. See LIQUID ASSET, above.

slow ∼. See FIXED ASSET, above.

tangible ∼. Literally, one which is capable of being touched, and hence, one which has a physical existence, such as goods, equipment, land, etc. More broadly, one on which a definite value can be placed, as distinguished from an INTANGIBLE ASSET, which see above. Thus, a patent has been held to be a *tangible asset* for tax purposes, since it produces a measurable income and can therefore be capitalized.

wasting ∼. A term for a FIXED ASSET, which see above, which decreases gradually in amount and value during use, such as a quarry, mine, timber land, etc. See also DEPLETION.

watered ∼. One which is carried at a book value higher than its fair, or reasonable market value. See also STOCK (1), WATERED.

asset currency. See under CURRENCY.

asset value. See NET ASSET VALUE.

assign. To make over, or to transfer to another; to convey property to another; to endorse a right or goods to another. Also, a person to whom property or goods are thus transferred; as, for example, in the phrase "heirs and *assigns.*"

assigned account. In the commercial credit field, the term for an ACCOUNT RECEIVABLE which has been pledged to a FACTOR (1), SALES FINANCE COMPANY, or bank as security for a loan. The customer whose account has been thus pledged or assigned may be informed of the fact or not, depending on whether NOTIFICATION is included in the agreement. See also ACCOUNTS RECEIVABLE FINANCING.

assigned stock. See under STOCK (1).

assignee. Any person to whom some right or property has been ASSIGNED or transferred; one who receives an ASSIGNMENT.

assignment. A TRANSFER (1) of real or personal property, or of some right or interest. Specifically, it is a transfer of a total interest, or of an undivided share of an interest, as distinguished from a LICENSE, which is restricted. In PATENT law, for example, an *assignment* of a patent right transfers the monopoly granted under the patent to the assignee, while a license leaves the monopoly itself in the control of the inventor. Also, the document by which the transfer is accomplished. An assignment may be either revocable or irrevocable by the one who makes it, and may be either voluntary, as in the case of a patent assignment, or involuntary, as in the case of an involuntary ASSIGNMENT FOR BENEFIT OF CREDITORS.

assignment for benefit of creditors. The transfer by a debtor of all or some part of his property to another person in trust, the proceeds of the property to be devoted to paying off the debts of the person making the assignment. Such an assignment may be either voluntary, when it is initiated by the debtor himself, or involuntary, when it is initiated by the creditors. The federal BANKRUPTCY laws provide that the TRUSTEE IN BANKRUPTCY may require such an assignment.

assignment in blank. The term for the formal assignment of a stock, bond, or other transferrable property or right, which has been left with a broker or dealer to be sold or transferred. The owner or holder signs his name to the assignment form on the reverse of the stock or bond certificate, leaving the name of the new owner and the date of transfer blank, to be filled in after the sale is made. See also STOCK (1), ASSIGNED.

assignor. The person who makes an ASSIGNMENT, or who transfers some right or property which he holds to another.

associated bank. See under BANK.

associated buying office. See BUYING OFFICE.

associated company. See COMPANY, AFFILIATED.

association. In general any grouping of persons for mutually beneficial purposes or for the furtherance of some object. More particularly, in law, an unincorporated society, not formed for profit. The laws of the various states differ considerably as to the status of an *association,* and the rights and responsibilities of *association* members.

assume. In business, to take on, to undertake; to engage to do or perform. For example, one person may, for various reasons, *assume* the debts of another, and a corporation which acquires another by merger *assumes* all of the liabilities and responsibilities of the merged corporation.

assumed bond. See under BOND (1).

assumed name. In business, one made up or devised by a person or persons under which to conduct a business. In many states, the law prohibits any person or persons, except corporations, from transacting business under an *assumed name* unless the full and true names of all persons with an interest in the business, together with the post office address of each, are filed in the designated public office. See also TRADE NAME.

assumed risk. The term for a RISK which is taken on voluntarily by contract; one which is accepted knowingly under any formal or informal agreement.

assurance. In general, a pledge, or guaranty; anything making a person secure. As frequently used, the word is a synonym for INSURANCE.

assured. In insurance, the term for the person to whom an insurance policy is payable on maturity, and to whom any dividends are payable, whether or not the person is the owner of the insured property, or is the person whose life is insured. For example, if a husband takes out an insurance policy on the life of his wife, pays the premiums, and controls the policy, he is the *assured,* and she the INSURED.

A stock, B stock, etc. See under STOCK (1).

at par. See PAR (1).

attachment. In law, a writ authorizing or ordering the seizure by the sheriff of property, rights, etc., belonging to the defendant in a legal action, and the holding of it to satisfy any judgment that may be awarded against the defendant. Thus, it is a temporary measure, intended to protect the interest of a creditor or plaintiff, not a permanent seizure. Sometimes, the creditor who requests an *attachment* is required to post a bond to cover any possible loss or damage suffered by the defendant as a result of the *attachment*. An *attachment* is distinguished from a GARNISHMENT, which is an order issued to others who hold property of the debtor, not to dispose of it until the action is settled. See also BOND (2), ATTACHMENT; LIEN.

attainder. Originally, in English law, the loss of rights which followed after conviction and sentencing for certain crimes, or after the flight of a person to escape prosecution. Later, any loss of rights by a particular person, ordered by a court or prescribed by a special law. See also BILL OF ATTAINDER.

attest. In general, to testify, or to bear witness. As used in the laws of many states, to witness a signature and affirm the fact in writing, or to examine any written instrument and verify that it is an exact and correct copy of an original. A person who so verifies an instrument in writing is called an *attesting* witness.

attested copy. The name for a copy made directly from an original document, rather than from another copy, and which has been examined, compared, and declared to be a true and exact copy by a declaration to this effect, signed by the person or persons making the examination. It is also known as a certified COPY.

at the market. A phrase used in an order given to a securities broker, authorizing him to buy or sell a particular stock at the current market price, rather than at some particular price. See also ORDER (4), MARKET.

attitude audit. See AUDIT (2).

attorney. Originally, any person to whom one turns over a right or duty; hence, an agent, or substitute. Now, as most frequently used, a legal agent, or representative at law. In British usage, a legal representative who prepares and conducts cases in the COMMON LAW, but who does not normally appear in open court, as distinguished from a SOLICITOR, who handles cases in EQUITY, and from a BARRISTER, who pleads the case in open court. In the United States no distinction in terms is made, but in practice before the Supreme Court an *attorney* has been recognized as the regular representative of a party, while a COUNSEL is a special representative engaged for the particular case.

attorney at law. Technically, any person engaged by another to represent him in court, or to manage a legal matter for him. More generally, a professional lawyer; a person duly trained, qualified, and admitted to the practice of law.

Attorney-General. In the federal government, the chief officer of the Department of Justice, and a member of the cabinet. He, or one of his representatives, appears in the Supreme Court in all cases in which the government is involved. He also supervises all of the legal and law-enforcing activities of the Department of Justice. In an individual state, he is the chief legal officer of the state, who represents the state in the courts, conducts investigations related to the state constitution, etc.

attorney in fact. Any person who is authorized by another to act in his place, either in a particular matter or generally. The authorization is embodied in a document known as a LETTER OF ATTORNEY, while the authority itself is a POWER OF ATTORNEY.

attorney of record. In law, the particular lawyer whose name is entered in the court records as the representative of a party in a legal action or suit. He may actually be only one of several lawyers involved, and need not be the principal one.

attractive nuisance. See under NUISANCE.

au besoin. See IN CASE OF NEED.

auction. A form of public sale, in which property or a right passes to the highest bidder, through successively increased offers. In more restricted form, any sale or purchase by bidding, such as a sale in which each prospective buyer is entitled to submit only one bid, or a purchase of goods or services in which each seller or performer submits a single bid. In the latter case, the lowest, rather than the highest bid is accepted.

    Chinese, Dutch, etc. ∼. One of a number of names for a form of *auction* in which the bidding is started at a high price, and the seller progressively lowers his asking price until someone offers to buy the goods. The prospective buyer must decide whether to wait for a lower price or to secure the goods at a particular price level.

    public ∼. Actually a redundancy, the term for an *auction* which is held after advertising or other public notice.

auctioneer. A person who is authorized or licensed to sell property at AUCTION. He is legally the agent of the seller until the property is awarded to a bidder, and as such he is responsible for trying to obtain the maximum price for the property. Once the award has been made, he becomes the agent of both the buyer and seller in completing the sale.

audit. 1. Originally, a hearing. An examination of records, accounts, or procedures, conducted by a person trained in such examinations. The purpose usually is to determine whether expenditures have been properly made, receipts properly accounted for, assets properly evaluated, and so forth. It may be conducted either by an employee of the company or by a person specifically engaged for the purpose, or by a government agency. In ordinary business, the principal reason for conducting an *audit* is to determine whether the accounts and statements of the company are kept in conformity with accepted accounting principles, and whether they represent a fair statement of the condition of the company.

continuous ~. One which is conducted more or less on a continuing basis throughout the fiscal year, sometimes involving the *audit* of one department or activity at a time, in rotation.

independent ~. One conducted by a person not connected with the company in any way, who is engaged expressly for the purpose. Some statutes, and many organization by-laws, require such *independent audits* at periodic intervals.

internal ~. One conducted within an organization by its own employees, or by persons engaged to conduct it under the supervision of an employee, rather than by an independent outside agency.

2. In marketing and opinion research work, a term for any examination or survey made on a quantitative basis. A *store audit,* for example, is a study of the merchandise held and sold by retail stores, and an *attitude audit* is a survey of the opinions and attitudes held by a group on any particular subject.

Audit Bureau of Circulation. A non-profit, co-operative organization established for the purpose of measuring, auditing and certifying the net paid circulation of various publications, such as newspapers and magazines. It operates by checking the subscription and individual copy sale of each publication for stated periods, and analyzing the geographic, occupational, and other classifications of the purchasers of the publication. See also CIRCULATION (3).

auditor. In general, any person who is qualified to conduct an AUDIT, and who is engaged to do so. He may be a *public auditor,* who is in the business of examining the accounting records of private companies for a fee, or a *state auditor,* who examines the records of state departments and agencies, and various public bodies.

authenticate. To give authority, to establish the legal validity of something; to verify, or to establish the genuineness of a statement.

Also, to sign a statement to the effect that one has verified the validity or genuineness of a document, signature, etc.

authority. The name used for any of various autonomous municipal, state, or interstate boards, corporations, commissions, etc., which perform some public or semi-governmental function. Common examples of functions performed by *authorities* include the operation of bridges, tunnels, highways, rapid transit systems, etc. The members of the *authority* are usually appointed for long terms by the governor of the state in which the *authority* operates.

authority to purchase. A term for a document used in foreign trade, similar to a commercial LETTER OF CREDIT. In its usual form it is a letter from a foreign bank, especially a Far Eastern bank, to an American correspondent, directing him to negotiate drafts covering an export transaction. It is sometimes known as an Oriental letter of credit.

authorized capital. See under CAPITAL (2).

authorized stock. See under STOCK (1).

automatic. Self-acting, or self-regulating; not initiated or controlled by human means. Occurring as a result of previous firm commitments or contractual agreements. The *automatic* CHECKOFF of union dues, for example, is a deduction of union dues from wages according to an agreement between an employer and a union.

automatic premium loan. A provision inserted in some life insurance policies, providing that in the event the insured person fails to pay a premium when due, the amount of the premium will be automatically borrowed from the cash reserve fund of the policy, and used to pay the premium. This will be done as long as the amount of the lendable cash surrender value of the policy will permit.

automatic selling. A term for the selling of merchandise of any sort through the medium of automatic vending machines, rather than through retail stores. In the Census of Business, *automatic selling* companies are classified as non-store retailers.

automatic wage adjustment. The name of a clause sometimes occurring in union labor agreements, providing that wage rates will rise or fall automatically, according to an established formula. The formula is usually based on the cost of living, prevailing wage rates, company sales volume or profits, etc.

automobile insurance. See under INSURANCE, CASUALTY AND LIABILITY.

available asset. See under ASSET (2).

avails. A term for the amount received by a borrower after the DISCOUNT has been deducted in advance from a note; the PROCEEDS of the note.

average. 1. In general, any value which is representative of the central tendency of a group of values or observations; a middle or mean value. The most commonly used *average* is the ARITHMETIC MEAN, which see below, but there are several other measures of central tendency which have special significance and particular applications. The principal ones of these are listed and defined below.

arithmetic mean. That *average* which is typical of all of the values in a group in the sense that the *average* value, multiplied by the total number of values, results in the total of all of the original values. It is computed by dividing the sum of the individual values by the number of items. Thus, if the five items to be *averaged* are 2, 4, 6, 8, and 10, their *arithmetic mean* is 30 divided by 5, or 6.

geometric mean. A form of *average* designed to give equal weight to equal percentage differences among the values included, rather than to simple arithmetic differences. It is computed by multiplying together all of the values, and extracting the nth root of the product, where n is the number of values *averaged*. The *geometric mean* of the five values given above is the 5th root of 3,840, or approximately 5.21.

harmonic mean. A form of *average* designed to minimize the effect of isolated large values on the *average* value. It is computed as the reciprocal of the ARITHMETIC MEAN of the reciprocals of the individual items. The *harmonic mean* of the five values given above is approximately 4.38.

median. The middle value in an ARRAY or FREQUENCY DISTRIBUTION. It is the *average* value in the sense that as many values are greater than it as are smaller. The *median* of the five values given above is the middle number in rank, or 6.

mode. The value in an ARRAY or FREQUENCY DISTRIBUTION which is *average* or typical in the sense that it occurs most frequently, or is the one about which most individual values tend to cluster. It is not possible to speak of the *mode* of a simple series of numbers such as the five values given above.

simple ~. One in which each of the values to be *averaged* is given the same importance, or weight; one in which each item is counted only once, as distinguished from a WEIGHTED AVERAGE, which see below.

weighted ~. One in which each of the values to be *averaged* is counted in proportion to the importance, or weight assigned to it. To compute a weighted ARITHMETIC MEAN, for example, each value is first multiplied by a weight, or assigned number, and the total of the products is then divided by the sum of the weights. Many price indexes are *weighted averages* of the prices included, with each price weighted according to the relative importance of the product or service it represents.

2. In a broad sense, normal, typical, or ordinary; not special, superior, inferior, or otherwise out of the ordinary.

3. In marine insurance, a term meaning loss or damage, or the expense caused by a loss or damage to a ship or its cargo. Originally, the term referred to the adjustment of the loss among the owners and shippers, but has come to mean the loss itself as well. The principal terms used in connection with *average* in this sense are listed and defined below.

free of all ~. A term sometimes used in marine insurance policies, meaning that the policy does not cover any claims for GENERAL AVERAGE or PARTICULAR AVERAGE, which see below. In other words, the policy insures against total loss of the goods or ship insured only.

free of particular ~. A term sometimes used in a marine insurance policy, meaning that the policy does not cover any PARTICULAR AVERAGE, which see below, unless it results from a catastrophe to the entire ship, such as the stranding, sinking, burning, or collision of the ship. In other words, the policy does not cover any partial loss to the shipment insured which is due to a cause other than a catastrophe.

general ~. Any loss or damage, or expense from loss or damage, which results from actions taken by the captain or other ship's officer to protect or preserve the ship itself, or the passengers and crew, or the cargo in general. An example would be the throwing overboard of a part of the cargo in order to lighten and balance the ship. Such losses are adjusted by means of a *general average contribution,* under which the expense is proportioned among the shipowners and shippers in proportion to their interests, since all benefit from the loss suffered by the owner of the cargo thrown over.

particular ~. Any partial loss or damage, or expense from loss or damage, resulting from an accident or from the normal perils of the sea, which occurs to a ship or to part of its cargo. A common example is the damage to cargo from the action of sea water. The expense of such a loss is not apportioned among the shipowners and other shippers, but is borne entirely by the owner of the particular thing damaged, or by his insurance company.

with ∼. A term used in marine insurance policies in two ways. In the so-called narrow form, it means that the policy will cover PARTICULAR AVERAGE losses in excess of some specified percentage of the value of the item, such as 3 percent. In the broad form, it means that the policy covers all PARTICULAR AVERAGE losses without restriction.

with particular ∼. A term meaning that the marine insurance policy covers PARTICULAR AVERAGE losses, and that the insurance company will pay for any partial damage to cargo resulting from damage, deterioration, etc. It is the opposite of FREE OF PARTICULAR AVERAGE, which see above.

average adjustor. A person skilled in the rules and usages of marine insurance, who is employed to help determine the relative burdens to be borne by the shipowners and the various shippers in the event of AVERAGE (3) losses to an insured cargo or ship.

average clause. In fire insurance, a name sometimes given to the COINSURANCE CLAUSE. In connection with marine insurance, see AVERAGE (3).

average collection period. See COLLECTION PERIOD.

average deviation. See DEVIATION (3).

average hourly earnings. In labor statistics, a measure of the average amount of wages per hour worked which is paid to all workers in a particular group. It is computed by totalling the gross amount of compensation paid to all in the group, and dividing this by the total number of hours worked or paid for. The resulting figure is usually higher than the going average wage rate, since it includes overtime periods, premiums, bonuses, etc.

average loss. See AVERAGE (3).

average tare. See under TARE.

average unit cost. See under UNIT COST.

averaging. In the securities trade, the term for any of several methods of attempting to improve the average price paid or received for securities by buying or selling at a variable rate as prices rise or fall. See also DOLLAR AVERAGING.

∼ **down.** The practice of buying additional shares of a particular stock as prices fall, to lower the average price paid for the total. The theory behind such a plan is that the price need only recover part of the way to the original purchase price in order to show an average profit on the entire investment.

∼ **up.** The practice of selling SHORT additional shares of a particular stock as prices continue to rise. The theory is that prices need only fall part of the way back to the level of the original short sale to wipe out any loss and result in an average profit on the entire operation.

averment. In law, a positive statement of the facts involved in a legal action or suit, as distinguished from the CLAIMS or arguments of the contending parties. Also, the proofs offered to support a claim or argument as distinguished from the argument itself.

avoirdupois. Literally, from the French, to have weight. The name given to the system of weights used in commerce in English-speaking countries. It is the system generally used for measuring the weight of all things except precious stones, metals, and medicine. The system is based on a POUND of 7,000 grains, or 16 OUNCES of 437.5 grains each. See also APOTHECARIES' WEIGHT; TROY WEIGHT.

award. 1. In law, the written decision of an arbitrator, referee, commissioner, or other extra-judicial person to whom a dispute is brought for settlement. Also, the amount of money or other things involved in such a decision.

2. The acceptance of a bid, or the assigning of work on the basis of an offer made. For example, a contract may be *awarded* to the lowest bidder.

B

babbitt metal. A soft alloy of lead, containing tin, antimony, and copper, used as an anti-friction bearing metal.

baby bank. See CREDIT UNION.

baby bond. See under BOND (1).

back. To sponsor, finance, or ENDORSE. For example, to *back* a scheme financially means to invest in or lend to the plan. To *back* a promissory note, on the other hand, implies that the BACKER endorses the note, and stands ready to be financially responsible.

back bill. See under BILL (4).

backed bond. See BOND (1), SECURED.

backer. Any person who gives financial support to a scheme or enterprise; a PROMOTER.

back-haul. In rail and motor freight, to carry goods back over a portion of a route already covered. A shipment from St. Louis to Harrisburg, Pa., for example, might be routed by fast freight to Philadelphia, then *back-hauled* to Harrisburg. See also CROSS-HAULING.

back label. The label or part of the label on the back of a container or package. Particularly, the label containing the detailed specifications and ingredients of the product, such as a blended whiskey, vitamin preparation, etc.

backlog. An accumulation, especially of unfilled orders. In some lines, such as the manufacture of machine tools, the existence of a *backlog* is normal, while in other lines it would represent an unusually prosperous condition. To *backlog* an order is to add it to a list of orders waiting to be filled or processed.

back-order. Part of an original order which could not be filled along with the original shipment, and is automatically entered as a new order and shipped when ready, without the necessity of a re-order from the customer. Also, to arrange for shipping a subsequent partial order in this manner. In usual practice, the invoice sent with the original shipment will carry the items *back-ordered,* but bearing a notation next to each such item to this effect, so that the customer will know

that it is not necessary to place a second order.

back pay. Wages or salary due an employee for past services, such as might arise due to a retroactive promotion, or a retroactive wage rate settlement in a union dispute.

back spread. A term used in ARBITRAGE operations in commodities, stocks, etc., to describe the situation in which the difference between the prices in two markets is less than the normal difference, as distinguished from a SPREAD situation in which the difference is greater than normal. Prices for the same commodity will normally differ in separate markets due to the costs of transportation, insurance, interest, etc., which would occur in an actual transfer between markets.

back-to-work movement. A tactic used to defeat a strike, wherein an employer or a group of employees attempts to obtain pledges from a majority of the striking employees that they are ready and desirous of returning to work. In the past, violence has often resulted from attempts to put such pledges into operation.

backtracking. See BUMPING.

Bacon-Davis Act. The federal law, also known as the PREVAILING WAGE LAW, which empowers the Secretary of Labor to set wage rates on public construction and improvement projects. The general aim of the act is to insure that the wage rates paid on such projects will be the same as those currently paid for similar private work in the same area.

bad check. See under CHECK.

bad debt. In general, a debt which is unpaid and uncollectible; an accounts receivable item on which the customer has not paid after repeated notices. As defined by the National Bank Act, a *bad debt* is one on which interest or payment is past due and unpaid for six months, except for debts which are secured or are in the process of collection.

　　reserve for ~. A reserve set aside on the books of a business to provide for the normal or expected proportion of *bad debt* losses

27

over a period of time. Such a reserve offsets the possible strain which might result if a few large *bad debt* losses should occur at the same time. The size of the reserve is usually determined on the basis of the past experience of the business or of similar businesses. It is sometimes known as a provision for doubtful accounts.

bad delivery. In the securities trade, a term for a security or other certificate not properly signed or transferred, or one in poor condition. Less frequently, any delivery of merchandise which does not conform to the terms of the agreement. See also GOOD DELIVERY.

bad faith. As generally used, involving actual or constructive FRAUD, or the intention to deceive or mislead; a neglect or deliberate refusal to fulfill a duty or obligation. An act in *bad faith* is one not prompted by an honest mistake or by ignorance, but by some sinister or self-interested motive. See also GOOD FAITH.

badger. Originally, in England, one who bought grain or other foodstuffs in one market, and carried them to another market to sell at a profit. Thus, a licensed huckster, or one who wore a badge. Hence, in current usage, a *badger game* is a scheme to obtain a profit, usually involving sharp or fraudulent dealings.

baggage. The parcels of clothing and other useful or necessary items a traveler takes with him on a trip. Household furnishings transported with a family, however, are not considered *baggage*. LUGGAGE is *hand-baggage,* or the *baggage* actually carried with the person.

bail. From the Latin, meaning to carry, or to care for. Thus, to deliver a person or thing into the custody of someone, usually on the condition of a BOND (2) or security deposited to assure the future appearance at the specified time. Also, the bond or security itself which is deposited. See also BOND (2), BAIL.

bailee. Any person who has the custody of the property of another; one who has received the property of another under a BAILMENT contract, and is liable under the contract to care for the property, and to return it in good condition when the contract is performed.

bailment. A transfer of property, but not of title, from one person to another under an agreement or contract providing that the property will be returned when the object or purpose of the contract has been fulfilled. The one who delivers the property is the BAILOR, and the one who receives the property is the BAILEE. Examples of *bailment* contracts are the deposit of goods for storage or repair, or the lease of equipment for hire. When a contract provides for the alternative of paying for the property and keeping it, instead of returning it, it is actually a CONDITIONAL SALE, though it may be called a *bailment* sale to avoid the terms of the conditional sale law. See also SALE (1), BAILMENT.

bailor. One who entrusts property to the custody of another; one who delivers property to another under the terms of a BAILMENT contract.

bait. Merchandise offered or advertised at a very low price, to induce customers to come into a store, or to make further inquiry which can then be followed up by a salesman. A LOSS-LEADER.

  ∼ **advertising.** The use in advertisements of very low prices or exceptional values, for the purpose of inducing customers to contact the seller, who then attempts to sell the customer higher priced and more profitable goods. Often, the *bait* offered in the advertisement is entirely fictitious and nonexistent, in which case the advertisement is illegal under federal law and under various statutes.

baker's dozen. See LONG DOZEN.

balance. Generally, the amount needed to make two quantities equal; a remainder. Thus, the net remainder or difference between the debit and credit entries in an account, or the net amount open or unpaid in an account receivable. Also, to make two amounts or accounts equal by making a *balancing* entry in one or the other.

balanced fund. See INVESTMENT COMPANY, MUTUAL FUND.

balance due. An item appearing on a STATEMENT or INVOICE, indicating the amount still owed on an account, after deducting payments made to date and including any charges added since the last statement or invoice was prepared. A statement may be made a request for payment by the addition of a phrase such as "please pay *balance due.*"

balance of payments. As defined by the U. S. Department of Commerce, an itemized account of the commercial and financial transactions conducted within a stated period of time, by all the people of one nation with the people of all other nations. The transactions included in determining the *balance of payments* include current transactions, such as imports, exports, and tourist spending; capital transactions, such as investments in another country; and so-called gold transactions, which represent the transfer of gold or other valuables to offset deficits in trade balances. See also BALANCE OF TRADE.

balance of trade. The net difference between the value of the exports and imports of a country. This may be the balance with respect to a particular country, or with respect to the rest of the world in general. A country is said to have a favorable *balance of trade* when exports exceed imports, and an unfavorable balance when imports exceed exports. Since imports and exports make up only a part of the total of payments between countries, the *balance of trade* should not be confused with the BALANCE OF PAYMENTS.

balance sheet. A statement of the assets and liabilities of a business at a given time, as distinguished from an INCOME STATEMENT, which reports what has happened over a period of time. As defined specifically by the American Institute of Accountants, it is a tabular statement or summary of debit and credit balances carried forward after an actual or constructive closing of the books of account kept by double-entry methods. See also FINANCIAL STATEMENT.

comparative ∼. One containing data for more than one accounting period, and thus providing a basis for comparing the financial condition at the present time with that at the end of the previous period, or at various times in the past.

condensed ∼. A term for one in which several of the detailed accounts have been combined and condensed, to show a quick picture of the status of the business in summary form.

consolidated ∼. One covering the combined operations of several affiliated companies, subsidiaries, or divisions. In such a *balance sheet,* any interlocking assets or liabilities are deducted, and only the net aggregates are shown. An item which is an asset to a parent company and a liability to its subsidiary, for example, would not appear at all. See also PRO FORMA.

balance sheet account. See under ACCOUNT (2).

balance sheet item. In accounting, a term for an account balance or total which represents an asset or liability, and would therefore appear on a company's BALANCE SHEET, as distinguished from an income item, which would appear on its INCOME STATEMENT.

balancing. In accounting, the periodic closing and adjusting of all accounts by banks or businesses, for the purpose of ascertaining the profits or losses accumulated over a period of time.

balbriggan. A knit cotton fabric, often with a napped back, sometimes, incorrectly, known as cotton flannel. Also, garments, such as pyjamas, made of *balbriggan* fabric.

bale. In general, any large package or bundle of goods, usually wrapped in cloth or paper, and bound by cords, metal strapping, or wire. Specifically, a measure of weight, used to measure cotton. The official U. S. *bale,* as set by the Department of Agriculture, is 500 pounds gross weight, and 480 pounds net. Some foreign *bale* weights differ from the American.

ballast. Any heavy material, such as stone, water, etc., placed in the hold of a ship to make it ride steady when not fully loaded. Also, crushed stone or gravel laid under and between railway ties to provide a bed and to anchor them solidly.

balloon freight. In railroading, a term for light, bulky cargo, such as will fill a freight car without reaching the minimum carload weight.

ballooning. The manipulating of prices to push them above safe or real values.

bank. Any one of many different types of financial institutions, which performs one or more of a variety of services such as lending, borrowing, issuing notes, caring for money, acting as a depository for valuables, financing business operations, etc. *Banks* may be chartered under the laws of the state in which they are located, or under the National Bank Act. In the latter case, the *bank* is permitted to use the term *national bank* in its title, and only such *banks* may use this name. The principal types of *banks,* and terms used in describing *banks* are listed and defined below:

acceptance ∼. A banking company which assists in financing foreign and domestic trade by buying and selling ACCEPTANCES. See also DISCOUNT BANK, below.

associated ∼. One of a group of *banks* associated for the purpose of making daily clearances at the same CLEARING HOUSE. The member *banks* of the New York Clearing House, for example, are known as the Associated Banks of New York.

∼ of circulation. See BANK OF ISSUE, below.

∼ of deposit. A *bank* which receives deposits of money, and holds such deposits subject to payment on checks drawn against them.

∼ of discount. A *bank* which DISCOUNTS negotiable instruments, such as promissory notes, bills of exchange, commercial paper, etc. All COMMERCIAL BANKS, which see below, including national banks, Federal Reserve Banks and state banks, are *banks of dis-*

count, while no SAVINGS BANKS, which also see below, are.

~ **of issue.** A *bank* which is authorized to issue its own BANK NOTES for circulation as money. Each of the twelve Federal Reserve District Banks, and many national banks are banks of issue.

branch ~. A *bank* which is a subsidiary branch of another *bank.* National banks may not have domestic branches, but are permitted to set up additional offices in the same city which are not strictly branches. State laws vary greatly on the subject of branch banks, with some states permitting branches liberally and other restricting them severely. See also BANKING, BRANCH.

central ~. One which occupies a central position in the monetary and financial system of the country in which it operates. Usually it is one controlled or owned by the government, with power to issue currency, act as fiscal agent for the government, and supervise other *banks,* as well as to carry on the usual activities of banking. Examples include the Bank of England, Bank of France, etc. The nearest thing to a central bank in this country is the FEDERAL RESERVE SYSTEM.

central reserve ~. Any NATIONAL BANK, which see below, located in either of the central reserve cities of New York or Chicago. See also FEDERAL RESERVE SYSTEM.

commercial ~. Any *bank* which is primarily in the business of accepting demand deposits, and making loans of various sorts to individuals, businesses, and governmental units. *Commercial banks* may also accept time deposits in interest-bearing accounts, provide safe-deposit facilities, and perform other services, but the acceptance of demand deposits is the distinguishing feature.

cooperative ~. A general term for the class of financial institutions including SAVINGS AND LOAN ASSOCIATIONS, BUILDING AND LOAN ASSOCIATIONS, CREDIT UNIONS, and similar organizations.

country ~. A *bank* which, for purposes of establishing reserve ratios, etc., is designated as a *bank* not located in a reserve city or a central reserve city. See also RESERVE CITY.

discount ~. A *bank* which is organized primarily to trade in foreign and domestic bills of exchange, to facilitate the business of importing and exporting. These *discount banks,* or discount companies exist primarily in London, and there are very few of them in the United States.

industrial ~. Originally, one organized to extend loans and other financial assistance to industrial wage earners. The source of funds for such loans were deposits and long

term notes sold by the *bank.* The so-called Morris Plan Banks were among the first *industrial banks,* but these and the institution in general have now been merged into the commercial banking system.

interior ~. In banking circles, a term used to refer to all *banks* outside of New York City.

intermediate credit ~. See FEDERAL INTERMEDIATE CREDIT BANK.

labor ~. A COMMERCIAL BANK, which see above, organized and sponsored by one or more labor unions. While the stock is usually owned by the union or its members, the facilities of the *bank* are available to the entire community.

member ~. Any national bank, and any state bank that is a member of the FEDERAL RESERVE SYSTEM. Also, sometimes, a *bank* that is a member of a local CLEARING HOUSE ASSOCIATION.

mutual savings ~. A SAVINGS BANK, which see below, conducted wholly for the benefit of its depositors, who receive in the form of interest or dividends all profits over and above necessary expenses and reserves. The affairs of the *bank* are usually directed by a board of directors or trustees made up of prominent members of the local community.

national ~. A private *bank* organized to do business under the National Bank Act, and under the Federal Reserve Act and amendments. *National banks* are organized as stock companies.

non-member ~. A *bank* that is not a member of the Federal Reserve System. Also, one that is not a member of a local CLEARING HOUSE ASSOCIATION, but clears through another *bank* that is a member.

private ~. Any unincorporated individual or group of individuals engaging in one or more phases of the banking business, such as making loans, trading in foreign exchange, etc. See also BANKER.

savings ~. A BANK OF DEPOSIT, which see above, organized for the purpose of receiving and investing savings, which pays interest on the savings at a rate depending on the *bank's* profits from its investments. In most cases, the *bank* is a mutual one; that is, it is run solely for the benefit of the depositors. Under the laws of the various states, *savings banks* are usually restricted in the nature of the investments they may make, and the collateral they may accept on loans.

state ~. One chartered under the laws of the particular state in which it is located. Though it is not a NATIONAL BANK, which see above, it may be a member of the Federal Reserve System.

stock savings ~. A SAVINGS BANK, which

see above, organized as a stock company, in which the stockholders receive dividends over and above the interest paid to depositors. See also MUTUAL SAVINGS BANK, above.

wildcat ∿. The term used for a *bank,* especially one existing prior to the passage of the National Bank Act of 1863, which issued banknotes, known as *wildcat* notes, far in excess of its reserve capacity to redeem them. The term was first applied to *banks* in the *wildcat,* or backwoods part of Wisconsin, a state with particularly loose banking laws at the time.

bankable bill. See under BILL OF EXCHANGE.

bankable paper. See COMMERCIAL PAPER, BANK.

bank acceptance. See under ACCEPTANCE (3).

bank accommodation. A term used to describe a short term loan made by a bank to a customer, either on his own note or on his endorsement of another's note owed to him. It is not an ACCOMMODATION in the usual sense, since there is usually a consideration and security involved.

bank account. See under ACCOUNT (3).

bank balance. The amount standing to the credit of an individual, firm, corporation, or other depositor in a BANK. The balance in favor of or against a bank at the local CLEARING HOUSE.

bank bill. See BANK NOTE.

bankbook. See PASSBOOK.

bank call. The demand which a state superintendent of banks may send to all banks and trust companies in the state at any time during each quarter of the year, calling for a sworn statement of their condition as of a given date. The CONTROLLER OF THE CURRENCY issues a similar call to national banks three or more times a year.

bank check. See under CHECK (1).

bank clearings. 1. The term for the items, such as checks, drafts, etc., presented by member banks at a local CLEARING HOUSE for collection. The banks exchange, or clear, items representing claims against each other, and settle their net outstanding balances.

2. In financial statistics, the total dollar volume of all items presented and exchanged among the members of a local clearing house, or of all clearing houses. The published figures are usually divided into New York *clearings* and all others, but the reports of other clearing house associations are usually available locally.

bank collection code. A uniform statute covering the procedures for items offered for collection at or by banks, which has been adopted by several states.

bank commissioner. A state official who is charged with the duty of making examinations into the affairs of banks and trust companies operating within the state.

bank credit. See under CREDIT (3).

bank currency. See BANK NOTE.

bank debits. In financial statistics, the total of cash withdrawals and transfers by check from the deposit accounts of all banks in a specified area within a given time. This total is used as a measure of the volume of general trade activity in the area during the time covered.

bank deposit. See under DEPOSIT (2).

bank deposit insurance. See FEDERAL DEPOSIT INSURANCE CORPORATION.

bank discount. See DISCOUNT (2).

bank draft. See under DRAFT (2).

bank-eligible bond. See BOND (1), ELIGIBLE.

banker. In general, any person or firm engaging in the business of banking. In common usage, the term often refers specifically to a private *banker,* an unincorporated individual who engages in one or more phases of the banking business, such as making loans, trading in foreign exchange, etc. See also BANK, PRIVATE.

banker's acceptance. See ACCEPTANCE (3), BANK.

bankers' bank. A term generally applied to a central bank, which deals primarily with other banks, rather than with the public. In the United States, for example, the Federal Reserve Banks are *bankers' banks.*

banker's bill. See under BILL OF EXCHANGE.

banker's check. See DRAFT (2).

banker's credit. See under CREDIT (3).

bank examiner. A representative named by a state or federal banking official, and empowered to examine into the affairs and records of any bank or banking institution in his jurisdiction. Agencies appointing such examiners include state banking commissions, the Controller of the Currency, the Federal Reserve System, and the Federal Deposit Insurance Corporation. The examiners appointed by the Controller of the Currency are known as national bank examiners.

bank exchanges. See BANK CLEARINGS; EXCHANGE (4), BANK.

Bank for Cooperatives. One of twelve district banks, originally established in 1933, to provide credit for farmers' cooperatives, to finance their purchases of commodities, to provide working capital, to finance the construction of processing facilities, etc. The funds of the banks come mainly from the FEDERAL INTERMEDIATE CREDIT BANK.

bank holiday. 1. Specifically, the period from Monday, March 6, through Thursday, March 9, 1933, when all banks in the United States were closed by a proclamation issued on Saturday, March 4, by President F. D. Roosevelt. The *bank holiday* followed a period during which many banks were forced to close due to the panicky depositor withdrawal of funds after a number of sensational bank failures. During the four-day holiday, steps were taken to restore confidence, and to create monetary and exchange controls.

2. In general, any day, such as a legal holiday, on which all banks are ordered to remain closed.

banking. In general, the business of dealing in money, securities, and negotiable instruments. The accepting of deposits, for convenience or for interest, and the making of loans, with or without collateral, using the money placed on deposit. The buying, selling, exchanging, or holding of currency, negotiable instruments, or other items of direct monetary value as a regular business.

branch ∼. The operation of a *banking* company through the establishment of branches. National banks, by law, may have domestic branches only in the city or county in which they are established, though a state bank with branches which becomes a national bank may keep such branches as it has. Some states permit state chartered banks to have branches, some permit them only in the same city or county, and some do not permit them at all.

chain ∼. A system in which a person or group owns a controlling interest in a number of separately organized banks, and coordinates their operations.

deposit ∼. The term for that portion of the *banking* field which involves the receipt and handling of deposits, the paying out of withdrawals, and the lending of money or the extension of credit on the basis of the deposits received. See also BANK, COMMERCIAL.

group ∼. Actually, a form of CHAIN BANKING, which see above, in which control is held by a holding company established to own the stock of a number of banks. Such systems are now limited in their operations by the Bank Holding Company Act.

investment ∼. As defined by the Investment Bankers' Association, the business of UNDERWRITING or distributing issues of bonds, stocks, or other securities, of purchasing such securities and offering them for sale as a dealer, or of purchasing and selling such securities on the order and for the account of others.

unit ∼. A *banking* system based on separate, independent, local banks, rather than on branch or chain banks.

bank money order. See under MONEY ORDER.

bank note. A promissory note in the form of paper currency, issued by an authorized bank, and payable to the bearer on demand, which circulates as money. Notes issued by banks under present federal laws are redeemable in money and are full legal tender. They are sometimes known as bank bills or bank currency.

Federal Reserve ∼. Currency issued by the several Federal Reserve Banks, backed by the security of government bonds and notes held by the banks. In addition, FEDERAL RESERVE NOTES are issued by the Federal Reserve Banks upon application of member banks, on deposit of the proper collateral. Federal Reserve notes are issued in greater volume than are *Federal Reserve bank notes,* and, in fact, make up a large proportion of the total currency in circulation in the $5, $10, $20, $50, and $100 denominations in which they are issued.

national ∼. A *bank note* issued by a national bank, secured by government bonds deposited with the U. S. Treasury. They are full legal tender, and are redeemable in lawful money.

bank paper. See under COMMERCIAL PAPER.

bank rate. A term referring to the prevailing central bank discount rate in a financial market. In London, for example, it means specifically the discount rate established by the Bank of England; in Paris, the rate of the Bank of France, etc. In New York and other American cities, it is the uniform rate set by the leading banks. It is distinguished from the OPEN MARKET RATE, set by secondary banks and other dealers in commercial paper. See also DISCOUNT RATE; RATE OF INTEREST.

bank reserve. See RESERVE (2).

bankrupt. One who is unable to meet his obligations; a debtor who is unable to pay his creditors in full; an insolvent person. More strictly, one who has been declared by a court to be *bankrupt,* and whose assets or estate have been assigned for the payment of his debts. The word derives from the practice of the early Venetian moneylenders and bankers, under which the *banco,* or bench, of an insolvent or failed banker was literally broken.

bankruptcy. I. The state or condition of being BANKRUPT, or unable to meet one's obligations; the state of insolvency. Strictly, the state or condition of a debtor who has been adjudged or declared a bankrupt by a court.

2. The legal procedure under which the affairs of an insolvent person or business are turned over to a receiver or trustee for administration and the payment of debts. The procedure is initiated by the filing of a petition of *bankruptcy,* either by the debtor himself or by his creditors, under the National Bankruptcy Act.

involuntary ∼. A proceeding in which one or more creditors of an insolvent debtor file a petition to have the debtor declared a bankrupt. Within a fixed period of time after filing the petition, the creditors must show that the debtor has committed an act of *bankruptcy;* that is, that he has transferred, concealed, or removed any property to defraud his creditors, has made payments to one creditor in favor over others, or has made an assignment of his property, permitted a receiver to be named, admitted his insolvency in writing, or taken similar steps indicating a willingness to be declared a bankrupt. If the debtor opposes the petition, a referee is named by the court to conduct an investigation, arrive at a settlement, if possible, and preside over the arrangements made. When, to the satisfaction of the referee, receiver, trustee, or court, the bankrupt has paid his debts to the best of his abilities and resources, he may be discharged from *bankruptcy,* and relieved of all further liability for the remaining balance of debts involved.

voluntary ∼. A proceeding under which a debtor files a petition stating his inability to meet his debts, and his willingness to be declared a bankrupt. A receiver or trustee is then named either by a committee of his creditors or by the court. Any individual, firm, or corporation may file a petition of *voluntary bankruptcy* except a banking, insurance, municipal, or railroad corporation.

bank statement. I. A balance sheet or financial statement reporting the financial condition of a bank. National banks are required to publish such statements at least three times a year, and under various state laws, banks may be required to publish statements as often as four times yearly.

2. A statement provided by a bank to a depositing customer, showing a listing of all transactions in his account during a period, including deposits, checks drawn, etc. Customarily, banks send statements to regular depositors monthly, including the cancelled checks for the period with the statement.

bare boat charter. See under CHARTER.

bargain. I. A compact or agreement, written or oral, for the sale or purchase of anything; a SALE (I) contract, sometimes called in legal terminology a *bargain* and sale. Also, loosely, the terms of such an agreement.

2. Something for sale or purchased at a low or advantageous price; a good buy.

3. To come to terms, to reach agreement over the terms of a sale or purchase; to haggle or dicker over terms.

bargain and sale. See BARGAIN (I).

bargain basement. A basement or downstairs selling area, particularly in a department store, in which lower-priced goods are sold, and in which goods from the upstairs or main store are sold at reduced prices to clear them out. Hence, as an adjective, low-priced, inexpensive, cheap, of poor workmanship.

bargain counter. A counter or area in a retail store at which goods are sold at reduced prices, to clear out discontinued or outdated stocks. Hence, any item being offered for sale at a reduced price, or below its worth, is said to be on the *bargain counter.*

bargaining agent. A local union, chosen by employees and recognized by the employer, to represent the employees in COLLECTIVE BARGAINING.

bargaining rights. The legally recognized rights of employees to bargain collectively with their employers. The right of a designated union to represent the employees in COLLECTIVE BARGAINING.

bargaining unit. A group of employees who join together voluntarily, or are designated by an agency such as the National Labor Relations Board, to act as an appropriate unit in COLLECTIVE BARGAINING. It may be the employees of a single department, a plant, all the plants of a company, or even all the workers in a given area.

bargain money. Money paid by one party to a BARGAIN to the other party, to bind the bargain. See also EARNEST.

barleycorn. As a unit of linear measure, ⅓ of an INCH. It is now practically unused, except to define other units of measure.

barratry. I. In maritime law, any action by the master or crew of a ship, for their own benefit or for any unlawful or fraudulent purpose, which results in a loss or injury to the owners of the ship. Acts of gross negligence are included within the definition. For example, the sale of part of the ship's cargo to unauthorized purchasers would obviously be *barratry,* but so would the wanton failure to protect the cargo against the weather.

2. In criminal law, literally, the act of throwing up barriers. The offense of stirring up or exciting frequent quarrels or groundless legal suits, especially for the purpose of obstructing the normal conduct of business by a competitor.

barrel. A measure of volume of liquid or dry commodities, the capacity, volume or weight of which varies with the commodity and with custom. Under U. S. law, various standard *barrels* have been established, including that for fruits, vegetables, and other dry commodities, of 105 dry QUARTS. The standard *barrel* for liquid measure in the U. S. is set by usage at 31½ GALLONS.

barrister. In English usage, a lawyer or counsel who pleads cases in open court, as distinguished from an ATTORNEY, who prepares cases and handles out-of-court legal matters.

barter. The direct exchange of commodities for commodities, or of commodities for services, without the use of money. It differs from a SALE, in which a money consideration is always all or part of the price. A *barter* contract is completed by the delivery of the bartered goods on each side, rather than by the delivery of goods and a money payment in exchange.

base. Originally, low; hence, inferior, servile, or impure. Specifically, adulterated, or alloyed with inferior metals. The opposite of FINE (3).

~ **bullion.** Silver or gold, in bars, but including various proportions of alloying metals.

~ **coin.** One that is adulterated, or that contains inferior metals other than gold or silver; a coin that has been DEBASED, or is part of a debased coinage, in that all coins have had alloying metals added to replace some of the gold or silver.

~ **metal.** Any metal less valuable than gold or silver, such as copper, nickel, lead, etc., especially when used in coinage or jewelry. See also MONEY, BASE METAL.

base period. The time interval used as the point of reference for any business and economic statistics. In the construction of an INDEX NUMBER, for example, the average value for the *base period* (usually a year or several years) is set at 100, and all later values related to it. The *base period* is often chosen as a period of normal or average activity, but not necessarily.

base price. See under PRICE.

base rate. Under an INCENTIVE SYSTEM, the regular or established rate at which a task or job is to be done, in terms of pieces per hour or per shift, for example, and upon which the incentive payment is based. Also,

the rate of pay for the standard or regular amount of work, to which the incentives are added.

basic stock. See INVENTORY CONTROL.

basing point. An arbitrary location, chosen as the theoretical originating point in a BASING POINT PRICING system, from which freight charges are calculated in setting delivered prices.

basing point pricing. A system of setting delivered prices for a manufacturer's products, or for similar products of several manufacturers. The price in a given market is set as the factory price plus the cost of freight from the nearest of one or more BASING POINTS, which may or may not be the actual place of manufacture of the product. The price for steel, for example, may be quoted including freight from Pittsburgh, Birmingham, or some other center, though actually shipped from another city, nearer or more distant. Common or joint *basing point pricing* systems established by competing manufacturers have been held to be illegal as in restraint of trade. See also ZONE PRICING; PRICE, BASE.

basis. 1. The effective rate of return on a bond or other investment. A bond with a nominal 3 percent interest rate, for example, may be priced to sell at a 5 percent *basis*. The YIELD.

2. In computing capital gains or losses for tax purposes, the value used as the original cost of the property, which may or may not be the actual cost, depending on circumstances and the particular tax regulations applicable. It is sometimes referred to as the cost basis.

batch process. In manufacturing, any operation, such as in the manufacture of chemicals, or in the making of glassware, pottery, etc., in which a single load or *batch* of product is processed to completion as a unit, before another load of materials is placed into processing. It is distinguished from a CONTINUOUS PROCESS, in which materials are continuously fed in and finished product drawn off, while the process is in operation.

bazaar. Originally, from the Persian, a market place or exchange. Hence, any special fair or sale, such as one to raise funds for charitable purposes.

bear. In the securities market, a trader or speculator who makes his profit on falling prices. Typically, this is done by selling SHORT, and buying back at a lower price. The *bear* is the opposite of a BULL, who makes his profit by buying and selling on rising prices. The same trader may be a *bear* at one time and a bull at another. In general, one who expects or counts on lower prices; a pessimist.

bearer. 1. As defined by the Negotiable Instruments Act, the person who holds or possesses any negotiable instrument, such as a bill, note, check, or draft, which is made payable to the *bearer* on demand. It is important to note that the term is not limited to the lawful or proper possession of the instrument.

2. As an adjective, in reference to a negotiable instrument, one that is payable to the *bearer* on demand. An indication that title passes by mere delivery, with no endorsement required.

bearer bond. See under BOND (1).

bearer certificate. The term for a certificate, such as one for shares of corporate stock, which is not made out in the name of a specific individual. Such certificates are negotiable without endorsement. See also STOCK CERTIFICATE.

bearer note. See NOTE (1), NEGOTIABLE.

bear market. In the securities trade, a declining market. One characterized by falling prices, and thus favorable to BEARS.

beat down. In business slang, to bargain; to secure a lower price by haggling.

Bedeaux system. An incentive wage system developed and introduced by Bedeaux, a French industrialist. Under it, the worker is paid an incentive for production above a standard amount, based on a unit called the "B," which is the computed normal amount of output per minute, so that normal hourly production is 60 Bs. See also INCENTIVE.

beginning inventory. See under INVENTORY.

Belo plan. The name for a formula adopted to meet the requirements of businesses with long, irregular work weeks, within the wage-hour law. The plan, named for the company which first devised it and obtained approval in the courts, provides that where employees frequently work as much as 60 hours a week, they may be paid for the 60 hours whether worked or not, with any hours over 60 being paid for at overtime rates figured on the basis of a 40 hour week. For example, employees may be paid regularly on the basis of $105 for a 60 hour week, calculated as 40 hours at $1.50 an hour plus 20 hours at $2.25 per hour. Any overtime beyond 60 hours, therefore, is paid at $2.25 per hour.

below par. See PAR (1).

belt-line railroad. A railroad which operates in and around a rail terminal center, especially and originally one which encircles the center.

bench warrant. See under WARRANT.

beneficial interest. See CERTIFICATE OF BENEFICIAL INTEREST.

beneficial society. See FRATERNAL SOCIETY.

beneficial trust. See under TRUST (1).

beneficiary. 1. In general, the person who will receive the benefits or advantages of some action. For example, the person for whose benefit a TRUST has been created is called the *beneficiary.* Also, loosely, one who inherits under a will is sometimes called the *beneficiary.*

2. Specifically, in life insurance, a person named in a policy as the one to whom all or part of the proceeds of the policy are to be payable. A *primary beneficiary* is the one directly named to receive the payments, and a *contingent beneficiary* is one named to receive the payments in the event that the *primary beneficiary* is no longer living, or is otherwise ineligible to receive the payments.

benefit. 1. In general, any gain, advantage, or privilege that accrues or is paid to a person or to property. For example, the advantage accruing to real property as the result of some local improvement, such as the re-paving of a road, is known as a *special benefit.*

2. In insurance, especially health, hospital, workmen's compensation, or similar types of insurance, the amount of indemnity to be paid periodically or otherwise under the terms of the policy. For example, a hospitalization insurance policy usually specifies a weekly *benefit* to be paid to hospitalized policy holders, and a specific dollar *benefit* to be paid for certain types of hospital or surgical services.

benefit association. See FRATERNAL SOCIETY.

bequeath. In law, to give personal property by the terms of a will. Strictly speaking, to give real property by a will is to DEVISE, and only personal property is *bequeathed.* For this reason, the usual wording used in wills is "I do hereby *bequeath* and devise."

bequest. A gift or transfer of personal property by the terms of a will; a LEGACY. Loosely, any gift made by the terms of a document, such as a GRANT, or the establishment of a TRUST, is known as a *bequest,* but this usage is incorrect.

best bid. See under BID (2).

best efforts. In the securities trade, a basis on which one or more investment bankers may agree to act as agent for the sale of a new issue of securities. Unlike a firm agreement to UNDERWRITE an issue, a *best efforts* agreement does not bind the investment bankers to absorb any securities not sold to the public, but merely to sell as much of the issue as they can by their *best efforts*. Public sale of securities of small or unknown companies is frequently made on this basis, since investment bankers may be unwilling to underwrite the sale of the securities of an unknown company.

best paper. See under COMMERCIAL PAPER.

best seller. Any article of merchandise, but more particularly a book, the sales of which are of much greater volume than those of other articles with which it competes. A particular style of dress, or model of furniture, for example, may become a *best seller* in its class. Popularly, books whose current sales are among the ten or so largest are known as *best sellers*. See also RUNNER.

better business bureau. One of a great many local voluntary organizations of business men, set up in cities and towns to improve business practices, and to establish fair standards under which business is to be conducted. The activities of a *better business bureau* include the policing of newspaper and other advertisements by retail stores, the checking of manufacturer and distributor claims of product performance, the investigation of credit sales practices, and similar efforts to improve the ethical level of business. The local *better business bureaus* are associated through a national organization, the Association of Better Business Bureaus, Inc.

betterment. An improvement made to real property which increases its value more than would ordinary MAINTENANCE (1) or REPAIR work. For example, repair work on the roof of a building would be considered maintenance, but a completely new roof would be a *betterment*. Other examples include such things as partitions, lighting fixtures, flooring, etc. In most states, *betterments* to rented property become the property of the landlord at the termination of the lease, and in some states title to the *betterment* passes to the landlord proportionately over the life of the lease. In insurance contracts, the phrase "improvements and *betterments*" is used, to make certain that all possibilities are included in the policy terms. See also IMPROVEMENT.

bias. 1. Originally and literally, oblique, or on a slant. Hence, in law, a leaning or predisposition; a failure to maintain an open mind. Strictly speaking, *bias* is less than PREJUDICE, which implies a prejudging of a question, or a completely closed mind.

2. With reference to textiles, an obliquely cut fabric. Fabric with the cross-threads running diagonally across the fabric, rather than directly across the width or along the length, is said to be *on the bias*.

bicameral. Having two chambers; said of a legislature which is composed of two chambers, or houses. The Congress of the United States, for example, includes a Senate and House of Representatives. Most of the state legislatures are also *bicameral*, with one house elected on the basis of population, and the other on a territorial basis.

bid. 1. In general business usage, an offer to perform work, provide a service, or supply materials, under the terms of a contract, for a specified price or rate of pay; a TENDER.

2. In a public sale, especially at an auction, an offer to pay a specified price for goods, property, securities, etc., being sold. See also OFFER.

    best ~. One which is not necessarily the lowest or the highest, but which is best for the interests of the person or company inviting the *bid*, taking into account the price named, the solvency of the bidder, the quality of the work to be done, future relations, etc. In many cases, public bodies buying or selling by means of *bids* are not required to accept the lowest or highest *bid*, but may accept one of the lowest or highest as a *best bid*.

    competitive ~. One which is submitted as the result of public notice and advertising of an intended purchase or sale, regardless of the fact that it may be the only *bid* submitted. Frequently, however, public bodies are permitted to refuse to accept any *bid* if fewer than a specified number are submitted.

    sealed ~. One which is submitted under seal, as requested, and which is not to be opened until an appointed time, at which all such *bids* are to be opened and compared. Such *bids* are usually requested in the letting of construction contracts, to assure that all *bids* are independently made.

bid and asked. In the securities trade, a form of price quotation for securities which are not actively traded, so that frequent actual sale quotations are not available. The *bid* part of the quotation represents the highest price prospective purchasers are willing to pay for the security, and the *asked* part represents the lowest price at which present holders are willing to sell. Sales take place when a buyer is willing to raise his *bid*, or a seller is willing to lower his *asked* price. Usually, *bid and asked* quotations are maintained and reported by the broker who specializes in the particular security issue. See also PRICE, BID; PRICE, ASKED.

bid bond. See under BOND (2).

bid in. The practice followed by an owner of property being auctioned, or by another with an interest in or encumbrance on the property, in bidding for and buying the property, particularly if a high enough price has not been offered by an outside bidder. When industrial or railroad property is being sold on liquidation of a company, for example, it is common for the property to be *bid in* by the bond holders or other principal creditors. See also BUYING IN.

bid price. See under PRICE.

bid up. To raise the price which is bid for something being sold at auction by a series of bids, each one higher than the other. This practice, when followed collusively by one or more persons with an interest in raising the final bid price, is unlawful.

big board. In securities trade usage, the New York Stock Exchange. Also, a price quotation board maintained in a stock broker's office, reporting prices of securities on the New York Stock Exchange.

big business. 1. In general, and collectively, those industrial and commercial organizations which account for a large share of the total assets and sales volume of all business. There is no precise or generally accepted definition of this group, but it is usually agreed to include the major manufacturers of steel, other metals, automobiles, electrical appliances, etc., and the major department stores, banks, insurance companies, and other large non-manufacturing organizations.

2. As distinguished from SMALL BUSINESS in some state and federal laws, any business with more than a prescribed number of employees, usually set at 500, or with more than a prescribed sales volume, which usually varies with the type of business concerned.

big steel. In the securities trade, and now in general usage, the United States Steel Company. Also, as sometimes used, the several major steel producing companies as a group, as distinguished from the rest of the steel industry, including the smaller companies and the specialized producers and processors, which are referred to collectively as LITTLE STEEL.

big three. In the American automobile industry, the Ford Motor Company, General Motors, and the Chrysler Corporation, as distinguished from the smaller manufacturers in the field. Also, in other industries or retail fields, a term used within the trade to refer to the three leading organizations, whichever they may be.

bilateral. Two-sided, or applying to both or all of two or more persons or things. A

bilateral contract or agreement, for example, is one under which both parties are bound to perform or fulfill reciprocal obligations, such as to sell and to buy specified property. See also UNILATERAL.

bill. 1. In law, a formal statement of a complaint, presented to a court. It normally contains the names of the parties involved in a controversy, an alleged statement of facts, and the proposed or claimed relief. A *bill* may be presented by a plaintiff in a suit, by either party to an action, or by the prosecution in a criminal case. It is sometimes referred to as a *bill of particulars*.

2. In law, a formal statement or declaration of a court, or of a grand jury, reporting its findings. When a grand jury reports a TRUE BILL, for example, it indicates that it accepts as true the facts alleged by the prosecution in its presentation.

3. In legislation, a proposed law; one that has been presented to the legislature, or to one of its committees, but has not yet been either enacted into law or rejected.

4. In business in general, a list of charges or costs presented by a person who has sold goods, performed work, provided a service, etc., to the person who has contracted to pay the costs. Such a *bill* usually contains a list of the individual items being charged, their unit cost and total cost, and a statement of the terms of sale. An INVOICE.

advance ∿. One which has been prepared and submitted in advance of the shipment or delivery of the goods or services covered. A purchaser may request an *advance bill* in order to include a payment in a particular budget period or tax year.

back ∿. An unpaid *bill* or invoice, or one submitted covering charges previously submitted and not yet paid.

∿ rendered. A statement submitted by a creditor to a debtor, covering an account of money due, and including the particulars of the transactions for which the debt is due. See also ACCOUNT (1).

memorandum ∿. One which is intended to be for information only, and is not a request for payment. For example, a shipment of samples for examination and return may include a *memorandum bill* stating prices, terms of sale, delivery times, and other particulars.

5. In law, a petition or list of claims or exceptions filed in connection with a suit. A CREDITORS' BILL, for example, is a petition filed by all of the creditors of a bankrupt, calling for an accounting of the assets of the bankrupt business.

6. A promissory NOTE. In current usage,

the term is seldom used, except in particular cases such as those defined below.

due ∼. A written acknowledgement of indebtedness that is not a promise to pay at any particular time; an I.O.U. It is usually non-interest-bearing, and may be made non-negotiable. In some lines of trade, *due bills* may be given to creditors with the limitation that they will not be paid in cash but may only be exchanged for the products or services of the debtor. A restaurant which is short of working capital, for example, may obtain needed supplies by giving *due bills* exchangeable for meals to local suppliers.

treasury ∼. A form of promissory note sold by the United States Treasury to obtain short-term funds. The most popular form are those sold publicly with a term of 91 days. These *bills* or notes do not bear interest, but are sold, by bidding, at a discount from the face value, so that when they are redeemed the holder receives an effective interest, at the current market rate.

7. A written statement of evidence of a contract or transaction. See, for example, BILL OF LADING; BILL OF SALE.

8. A BANK NOTE, FEDERAL RESERVE NOTE, or other piece of paper money, popularly referred to as a one-dollar *bill,* five-dollar *bill,* etc.

9. A BILL OF EXCHANGE, which see directly.

billboard. A large, flat-surfaced display board, placed in a conspicuous location, or on the outside of a business establishment, and carrying an advertising or public information message. See also ADVERTISING, OUTDOOR.

bill broker. See BROKER (1), NOTE.

billed cost. See under COST.

billing. In general, the process of submitting invoices or bills. In particular, in advertising, the term used for the total value of all of the advertising placed by an advertising agency for its clients during a specific time period. The amount of such *billings* can be measured independently, since the rates of the various advertising media, and the total amount of space and time arranged for by each agency are known, and it is used as a measure of the relative importance of the various agencies.

bill of adventure. In transportation, a written statement or declaration by a shipper or carrier to the effect that a shipment is the venture or property of another person, and that the shipper or carrier is responsible only for its delivery as consigned.

bill of attainder. Any law directed against a particular person, declaring him to be guilty of some crime without regular court procedures, and prescribing sentencing, loss of rights, or other punishment. Such laws are forbidden by Article I of the United States Constitution, and the Supreme Court has held that any law claimed to be general, but so worded that it affects only a small part of the population is such a *bill of attainder.* An example might be a law confiscating the property of members of any religious sect or other group.

bill of credit. 1. A promissory note or bill, issued by a state government, secured only by the faith and credit of the state, and intended to circulate as money. Section 10 of Article I of the United States Constitution specifically forbids any state to emit or issue such *bills of credit.*

2. In commercial law, a written request by a person to a bank or merchant, calling for the delivery of money to the bearer on the credit or account of the writer. Hence, a CHECK, or DRAFT.

bill of entry. A printed form for the use of the customs officers, which is filled out by an importer. It includes a description of the goods, their value, etc., and when accepted by the collector's office it authorizes the inspector or searcher to permit the goods to be unloaded and moved from the pier. When the importer does not have enough information to prepare such a bill, he prepares a BILL OF SIGHT, which permits the goods to be unloaded for inspection.

bill of exchange. As defined by the Uniform Negotiable Instruments Law, an unconditional written order, addressed by one person to another, calling on the person to whom it is addressed to pay, on demand or at a fixed or determinable future time, a sum of money to the order of a specified person or to bearer. ACCEPTANCES, CHECKS, and DRAFTS are forms of *bills of exchange.* For the many particular types of such bills, and their uses, see below.

acceptance ∼. One which is to be presented for ACCEPTANCE, as distinguished from one which is to be presented directly for payment. There are three parties to such a *bill;* the drawer, the payee, and the acceptor. See also PAYMENT BILL OF EXCHANGE, below.

accommodation ∼. One which is drawn and accepted with no consideration passing or value given or received. If accepted, it is essentially a promissory note, for the benefit of the drawer, with payment guaranteed by the acceptor. See also ACCOMMODATION.

bankable ∼. One that is of such good quality that a bank will readily discount or buy it. Any bill already endorsed by a bank is thus in this category.

banker's ~. One that is drawn by one bank or banker and is payable by another bank or banker. Such bills are considered to be of excellent quality, and usually sell at a lower rate of discount than ordinary commercial *bills of exchange*.

~ at sight. See SIGHT BILL OF EXCHANGE, below.

~ payable. A term used in accounting for a *bill of exchange* or other instrument which is a current liability of the person who must pay it. The term NOTE PAYABLE is more common.

~ receivable. A term used in accounting for a *bill of exchange* or other instrument which is currently payable to the holder. The term NOTE RECEIVABLE is more common.

blank ~. A bill or draft which is drawn without the name of a specific payee being inserted. It is thus, in effect, payable to bearer until a bearer writes in his or another's name.

clean ~. A term for a FOREIGN BILL OF EXCHANGE, which see below, which has no documents attached. See also DOCUMENTARY BILL OF EXCHANGE, below.

commercial ~. One drawn in connection with payment for a shipment of goods; ordinarily a draft drawn upon and payable by the one to whom the shipment is consigned. See also COMMERCIAL PAPER.

continental ~. One which is payable on the continent of Europe. Dealers in negotiable paper, when quoting prices, may name different rates for bills payable in London in sterling, for example, and those payable on the continent.

demand ~. One which is payable on presentation or on demand; a SIGHT BILL OF EXCHANGE, which see below.

documentary ~. A commercial bill, usually a FOREIGN BILL OF EXCHANGE, which see below, to which are attached the documents of the transaction in connection with which it is drawn. The documents usually include the bill of lading, the insurance papers, etc. Such a bill may be either an ACCEPTANCE BILL OF EXCHANGE, which see above, in which case the documents are surrendered to the consignee and he may take possession of the goods as soon as he accepts the bill, or it may be a PAYMENT BILL OF EXCHANGE, which see below, so that it must be paid before the consignee may receive the documents and get possession of the goods.

domestic ~. One drawn and made payable in the same country; one arising out of a purely domestic commercial transaction. Sometimes known as an inland bill.

domiciled ~. One on which the place of payment is not noted until the time of acceptance. When it is accepted, the acceptor notes the place or domicile at which the bill will be honored for payment.

finance ~. A long-term bill drawn by a bank in one country on a bank in another. It is usually drawn against security held, but the term also is used to apply to unsecured bills.

foreign ~. One drawn in one country and payable in another; one arising out of foreign trade operations. Such bills are usually made up in sets, with different copies sent by different routes, so that if one is lost the others will arrive; see also FIRST OF EXCHANGE. In the United States, a bill drawn in one state and payable in another is strictly speaking a *foreign bill of exchange*.

inland ~. See DOMESTIC BILL OF EXCHANGE, above.

investment ~. A bill of high quality, bought at a discount and held as an investment for the profit that will be taken when it is later paid at its face value.

long ~. A term used in financial circles for a bill or other instrument with a term of 60 days or more, or sometimes for one with a term of more than 30 days. See also SHORT BILL OF EXCHANGE, below.

negotiable ~. One which may be endorsed by the named payee, so that it becomes payable to another person. Thus, the holder may sell his interest in it to another, usually at a discount. A *negotiable bill of exchange* is usually made payable "to the order of John Doe," and is therefore sometimes called an order bill. See also NON-NEGOTIABLE BILL OF EXCHANGE, below.

non-negotiable ~. One which may not be paid to anyone but the named payee, and thus may not be sold or discounted. A bill is usually made non-negotiable by making it payable "only to the account of John Doe." The use of the word "only" prevents the named payee from endorsing the bill to another. See also NEGOTIABLE BILL OF EXCHANGE, above.

non-value ~. An ACCOMMODATION BILL OF EXCHANGE, which see above. See also VALUE BILL OF EXCHANGE, below.

original ~. In financial circles, a term for a bill which has been sold for the first time, without having been previously endorsed.

payment ~. One which is to be presented directly for payment, as distinguished from one which is to be presented for acceptance. There are only two parties to such a bill, the drawer and the payee. See also ACCEPTANCE BILL OF EXCHANGE, above.

prime ~. One which is of excellent financial quality; one of which there is no question at all as to whether it will be paid. See also COMMERCIAL PAPER, FIRST CLASS.

sales ∼. One drawn on the purchaser of goods in a commercial sale; a COMMERCIAL BILL OF EXCHANGE, which see above.

short ∼. A term used in financial circles for a bill or other instrument with a term of less than 60 days, or sometimes for one with a term of 30 days or less. It includes SIGHT BILLS OF EXCHANGE, which see below.

sight ∼. One which is payable on presentation, or at the end of a grace period after presentation, where statutes provide for such a period; one which is payable at sight. A *sight bill of exchange* which is payable absolutely on presentation, with no grace period, is called a demand bill of exchange. Under some statutes, however, a grace period is compulsory for both demand and *sight bills of exchange*.

sold ∼. In financial circles, a term for a bill which has, in effect, been sold short. A person may draw a bill which is payable by another person, and sell it for cash. He must then return cash to the person who will pay the bill, before the bill becomes due. Thus, by trading on the credit of the payer, the drawer has had the use of the proceeds of the bill for its term.

sterling ∼. One which is payable in pounds sterling. See also CONTINENTAL BILL, above.

time ∼. One which is payable at a specified future date, as distinguished from a SIGHT BILL OF EXCHANGE, which see above. The term includes bills with both short and long terms of maturity.

trade ∼. One drawn in the usual course of trade; a COMMERCIAL BILL OF EXCHANGE, which see above.

value ∼. One which is drawn against value received, as distinguished from an ACCOMMODATION BILL OF EXCHANGE, which see above. A typical *value bill of exchange* is one drawn to cover payment on a shipment of goods in commerce.

bill of health. A certificate given by the port or customs authorities to the captain of a departing ship at the time of his leaving port, attesting to the state of health of the ship's crew at the time. A *clean bill of health* signifies that no contagious disease was known to exist at the time. Thus, in general usage, to give anything a *clean bill of health* is to imply that it has been investigated and found to be in good order. A ship may also be given a *suspected bill*, indicating that while no contagion was found, there was reason to believe it might appear; or a *foul*

bill, indicating that one or more cases of contagious disease were found at the time.

bill of indictment. In law, the list of charges drawn up by the state and presented to a grand jury, in an attempt to obtain an INDICTMENT. If the jury finds the charges to be true, or sufficiently sustained by the evidence to warrant a trial, it returns a TRUE BILL report.

bill of lading. In general, a receipt given by a carrier to a shipper for goods received, stating that the goods have been accepted for shipment and detailing the terms and conditions under which they will be transported. It is thus, in effect, a contract between the shipper and carrier for the transport and delivery of the goods shipped. The original copy of the *bill of lading* carries with it title to the goods shipped, and is negotiable. This is the copy which is therefore attached to the BILL OF EXCHANGE or DRAFT which is used to effect payment for the shipment. The various types of *bills of lading* are defined below.

clean ∼. One on which the carrier, such as the ship owner or captain, has made no marginal or other notes indicating qualifications due to deviations or defects in the goods, and is therefore said to be clean of qualifications or limitations.

foul ∼. One carrying notations by the carrier indicating that shortages or damages existed in the shipment at the time it was picked up, so that it no longer matches the description as carried in the *bill of lading.* The opposite of a CLEAN BILL OF LADING, which see above.

maritime ∼. One covering a shipment by sea. *Maritime bills of lading* are usually made up in several copies; one each for the shipper, consignee, and carrier, and one or more for the various export and import control authorities, consulates, and customs offices which may be involved.

negotiable ∼. One which may be transferred by endorsement, thus transferring title to the goods shipped. See ORDER BILL OF LADING, below.

ocean ∼. See MARITIME BILL OF LADING, above.

order ∼. One in which the goods are consigned to the order of a person named in the bill, so that the named consignee may endorse the bill to another, transferring title to the goods in the shipment by so doing.

original ∼. The original copy of the *bill of lading,* which carries with it the title to the goods shipped, and is used in connection with a BILL OF EXCHANGE or DRAFT.

rail ∽. One covering a shipment by railroad. Such a *bill of lading* is supported by the WAYBILL covering the shipment, which contains the detailed description of the goods shipped.

straight ∽. One in which the goods are consigned specifically to a named consignee, so that the bill may not be negotiated or endorsed to another.

through ∽. The form of bill given when a shipment is to be transported on the route of one carrier, then on the route of one or more others, using a single set of covering documents. Also, a *bill of lading* covering a shipment which is sent first by rail to a port and then exported, using a single set of documents.

bill of materials. In manufacturing, a listing of the materials, parts, and components required to manufacture each unit of a product. It is prepared from the specifications and engineering drawings, and may be used as the basis for requisitioning or ordering materials and parts to produce a given number of units. During periods of government allocation of materials, such as in wartime, *bills of materials* may be used as the basis of a program of allocation of critical materials for the production of needed items.

bill of particulars. See BILL (1).

bill of sale. A formal written agreement by which one person transfers to another his rights, interest, and title in specified personal property. Since a *bill of sale* is considered to be sufficient warranty of the seller's title to the property and his right to sell, it need not be recorded as is a DEED for real property. It may be given as security for a debt, in which case the creditor may take full title to the property on non-payment of the debt.

conditional ∽. The form given the buyer in a conditional or installment sale. It usually provides that title passes only after the price and service charges have been paid in full, and that the seller may reclaim the property on non-payment of the balance due. In this case, the buyer is not entitled to any refund, all payments to date counting as rent or liquidated damages. State laws vary as to the exact rights of buyers and sellers under such sales. See also SALE, CONDITIONAL; SALE, INSTALLMENT.

bill of sight. A temporary form of entry permit for imported goods, which permits goods to be unloaded from the ship so that they may be examined in the presence of a customs inspector to determine their exact nature. This form is used when the BILL OF LADING does not give sufficient information about the goods to allow the preparation of a BILL OF ENTRY, which would permit the goods to be unloaded and removed.

bills in a set. See FIRST OF EXCHANGE.

bimetallic standard. A MONETARY STANDARD based on both gold and silver, in which the two metals are valued at a legally established ratio to each other. For many years, the creation of a *bimetallic standard* in the United States, with gold and silver fixed at a ratio of sixteen to one in value, was an election issue in national politics.

bimetallism. The name for a system of coinage in which two metals, usually gold and silver, are both freely coined, at an established ratio of value to each other, and are both part of the MONETARY STANDARD of the country. It is distinguished from MONOMETALLISM, which is the term for a system based on the coinage of only one metal, either gold or silver, but not both. See also BIMETALLIC STANDARD.

binder. In insurance, a term for a temporary contract of protection issued pending the preparation and execution of the permanent POLICY itself. A *binder* need not be a written agreement, and in fact may be created by a telephone conversation between an insurance agent and the insured person. It is regular practice to place a *binder* when preparing fire insurance or similar protection for property.

bit. Originally, in the western states, the popular name for the Mexican *real,* a small silver coin worth approximately 12½ cents. Hence, a QUARTER-DOLLAR is sometimes called *two bits,* and this is the only usage in which the term remains. Sometimes, a HALF-DOLLAR is referred to as *four bits,* but not in common usage.

black Friday. The designation for one of several Fridays on which various financial panics are understood to have begun. By coincidence, the panics of 1869 and 1873, and the great stock market crash of 1929, all first became serious on Fridays, and hence the term, indicating a day of evil.

black ink. The ink used for positive, or profitable, entries in books of record or account. The use of *black ink* indicates that the figure is to be added to the other figures, rather than deducted, which would be the case if RED INK were used. Hence, in an income statement, a balance in *black ink* indicates that the business has been profitable during the period covered, and a business which is making money is said to be "in the black."

blacklist. Originally, a list of persons, such as members of a club, who had behaved poorly, or who had incurred censure in some other way. Hence, in current usage, a list of persons to be avoided, or to whom credit is not to be advanced, or who are not to be given employment in a given field, etc. Also, to place a person's name on such a list.

blackmail. Originally, a form of extortion practiced by marauding bands along the English-Scotch border, in which payments were demanded from local landholders for protection from harm. The term mail, in this usage, is an old Scotch word for rent, or tribute. Hence, today, any extortion based on threats of harm or exposure, especially when based on the threatened release of damaging documents, photographs, or other information.

black market. A place or system for buying and selling scarce or allocated goods in violation of government regulations, or at a higher price than that on the regular market. During time of war or emergency, for example, scarce goods which are rationed and sold at fixed prices may be traded on the *black market* at prices far above the fixed price. Similarly, when any product, such as a new drug, is in short supply and informally allocated by the manufacturers, a *black market* in the drug may develop in which buyers with low priority are able to procure the drug by paying very high prices. See also GRAY MARKET.

Bland-Allison Act. The federal act, originally passed in 1878, providing for the purchase of a stated amount of silver bullion by the federal government each month, and its coinage into silver dollars. The silver purchase clauses of the act were repealed in 1890.

blank assignment. See ASSIGNMENT IN BLANK.

blank bill. See under BILL OF EXCHANGE.

blank check. See under CHECK.

blank credit. See under CREDIT (3).

blank endorsement. See ENDORSEMENT IN BLANK.

blanket. A term generally meaning all-inclusive, or broad; covering more than one specific subject, or more than one article of property. See each of the following under the principal listing: $\sim$ BOND (1); $\sim$ BOND (2); $\sim$ INJUNCTION; $\sim$ POLICY (2); $\sim$ PRICE.

blanket mortgage. See MORTGAGE, GENERAL.

blank transfer. See ASSIGNMENT IN BLANK.

blind selling. In business slang, an expression for the practice of selling goods or services to a customer without the customer having the opportunity to examine what he buys. In the motion picture distribution field, for example, the term is applied to the leasing of a film to a distributor before the latter has had an opportunity to examine or view it.

block. 1. In general, a large amount of something in a single unit or transaction. In the securities trade, for example, a large *block* of shares offered for sale at one time may include 5,000 or 10,000 shares. Similarly, at a stockholders' meeting of a corporation, a group of stockholders may vote their shares as a *block,* or as a single unit, for or against a proposition.

2. In finance and foreign exchange, to place restrictions on the free exchange of currency, or on its free movement out of and into a country. See, for example, CURRENCY, BLOCKED.

blockade. The act or process of preventing trade with a particular port or country, such as in time of war, by physically preventing ships or other cargo carriers from entering the affected port or area. Strictly, it is distinguished from an EMBARGO, which prohibits the departure of ships from specified ports, or the departure of shipments for specified countries.

block booking. In the motion picture distribution field, the practice of requiring a distributor or exhibitor to accept a full series of films at one time, rather than permitting him to chose the particular films he wishes. The purpose is to obtain distribution for the less favored films along with those which are in strong demand. In its extreme forms, this practice is the equivalent of a TIE-IN SALE, and is illegal under the anti-trust laws.

blocked currency. See under CURRENCY.

block policy. See POLICY (2), FLOATER.

blotter. The popular name for a book of accounts or journal used for making the first or temporary entries of transactions or happenings. The name is derived from the fact that such books are frequently made with alternate pages of blotting paper, so that the book may be closed immediately after each entry is made, if desired. Similar books, with the same name, are used at police precinct stations to record all of the events that occur during each tour of duty, the names of criminals and suspects brought in, etc.

B.L.S. See BUREAU OF LABOR STATISTICS.

blue-chip stock. See under STOCK (1).

Blue Cross Plan. The name of a large, voluntary, non-profit organization providing hospitalization insurance, or a prepaid hospital expense plan, to groups and individuals. In the typical group, all or most of the employees of a company pay a regular premium, in return for which they are assured of the payment of any hospital costs for room, board, special services, etc., which they may incur. In many companies the employer pays

part or all of the premium. The exact benefits offered by the plan may vary from time
to time, and sometimes from state to state.
See also INSURANCE, LIFE, ACCIDENT, AND
HEALTH.

blue law. Originally, the popular name for the
extremely severe religious and moral conduct
code of laws drawn up for the Connecticut
Colony. Today, the name for any state or
local laws regulating or restricting Sunday
commerce or activity. In many cities and
states, for example, the law prohibits any
manufacturing or trade on Sunday, with the
exception of certain retail services during
certain restricted hours. In other localities,
the laws affect sports and entertainment activities as well.

blue note. See under NOTE (1).

Blue Shield Plan. The name of a large, voluntary, non-profit organization providing medical expense insurance, or prepaid medical
care, to groups and individuals. In the typical group, all or most of the employees of a
company pay a regular premium, in return
for which they are assured of the payment of
any medical expenses they may incur in connection with hospitalization. These include
doctors' visits, surgical fees, post-operative
care, etc., in the hospital, and in some cases
in private clinics or offices. In many companies the employer pays part or all of the
premium. The exact benefits offered by the
plan may vary from time to time, and sometimes from state to state. See also INSURANCE,
LIFE, ACCIDENT, AND HEALTH.

blue-sky law. The popular name for any of the
various state laws designed to protect the investing public from unscrupulous or highly
speculative investment schemes. The typical
law requires any securities offered for sale
in the state to meet certain standards, and
regulates the methods of selling or promoting
the sale of securities. The term is derived
from the fact that the promoters of such
schemes are accused of offering prospective
investors the *blue sky,* or unlimited profits.

blurb. In advertising slang, any brief but
highly commendatory promotional statement,
such as a quotation from a book review on
the jacket of a newly published book. More
broadly, any extravagant praise or claim,
when repeated in promotional or advertising
matter.

board. 1. Any group or committee duly authorized to control, administer, or supervise
activities of some form. Examples include
the *board* of DIRECTORS of a corporation, the
board of governors of the FEDERAL RESERVE
SYSTEM, etc.

2. Strictly, as used in rental agreements,
food supplied by the host, or landlord. The
term is often understood to include also
room rent, when used alone, but it ordinarily appears only in the expression "room
and *board."* Thus, a contract for employment which provides that *board* shall be included in the benefits provided for the employee may or may not mean that living quarters shall also be provided, and the exact
conditions should be specified.

board foot. A unit of measure of the volume of
lumber or, in some cases, of standing timber. It is the equivalent of a piece of lumber
one foot square and one inch thick, or 144
cubic inches of wood.

board measure. The standard system of measuring the size of pieces of cut and dressed
lumber. In this system, the actual thickness
and width of the lumber is usually ¼ to ⅜
of an inch less than the nominal or marked
size. Thus, a one-inch board may actually be
¾ of an inch thick, and a two-by-four inch
beam may be 1¾ by 3⅝ inches. The exact
measures are set by the lumber trade associations, and may be revised from time to time.
They may also differ in detail according to
the building codes of the various states.

board of directors. See DIRECTOR.

Board of Governors. The name for the governing body of the FEDERAL RESERVE SYSTEM. It
consists of seven members, appointed by the
President. It sets the policy for the system,
establishes reserve requirements, determines
the DISCOUNT RATE, and generally regulates
the amount of credit available. Through its
staff, it supervises the twelve FEDERAL RESERVE
BANKS and the member banks of the system.
It replaced the original Federal Reserve
Board, and is still frequently known by this
name.

board of trade. In some cities, the organized
group of business men which operates the
local commodities exchange. In Chicago, for
example, the commodities exchange is known
as the *board of trade.* In other cities, merely
a CHAMBER OF COMMERCE. In England, the
government department equivalent to the
Department of Commerce in the United
States.

board of trustees. See TRUSTEE.

board room. In the securities trade, the large
room in a securities brokerage office, open
to the public, in which the current prices of
active securities are posted on a quotation
board, either by chalk or mechanically. The
customer representatives of the brokerage
firm have their desks in this room, and
orders to buy or sell securities are taken. The

term is also used for the trading room, or trading floor, of a securities exchange itself. In a corporate headquarters office, the *board room* is frequently the room reserved for meetings of the board of directors and other important conferences.

boat. Originally, a small open-decked vessel, propelled by oars, pole, or sail, rather than by mechanical means. In some statutes, a *boat* is distinguished from a SHIP in that it is not decked over, but in other cases the two terms are used interchangeably. In common usage, a *boat* is a vessel small enough to be carried aboard another vessel, whether decked or not, and whether power driven or not.

body. 1. The main part or substance of any document, text, or written matter of any sort. The *body* of a letter, for example, excludes the salutation and the closing. The *body* of an advertisement is that part set in normal type, rather than the headline, display matter, or illustration.

2. In law, any artificial person or group, constituted for any proper purpose. A *body corporate,* for example, is another term for a CORPORATION. See also PERSON, ARTIFICIAL.

bogey. A goal, standard, or quota. The term was originally used in golf, and referred to the imaginary Colonel Bogey, or the imaginary partner against whom a player going alone considers himself to be playing. Hence, in golf, it means PAR, or in some usages one over par. In selling, a *bogey* is the standard of performance, and may be the volume of sales above which a bonus or extra commission is paid. Similarly, in production, a *bogey* may be the standard or expected volume of output, above which production bonuses are paid.

bogus. False, spurious, or sham; counterfeit or fraudulent; non-existent. *Bogus* money, for example, is counterfeit money, and a *bogus* check is one drawn on a non-existent account, or on a non-existent bank. Similarly, a *bogus* transaction is a sham or imaginary one, such as a WASH SALE.

boiler and machinery insurance. See EXPLOSION INSURANCE, under INSURANCE, CASUALTY AND LIABILITY.

boiler room. In securities trade slang, a room or office from which stock promoters or their representatives conduct a telephone campaign to sell speculative and unreliable securities to the general public. Often, the activities of such establishments are in violation of the state BLUE-SKY LAWS, or of Securities and Exchange Commission regulations. The term probably derives from the fact that such places are located in out of the way or hard

to find locations, though not literally in basements or *boiler rooms.*

bona fide. Literally, from the Latin, in good faith; with honest intent. A *bona fide* action is one undertaken with no intention to deceive, and with no knowledge of any wrong or defect in connection with the action. A *bona fide* holder of a negotiable instrument, for example, is one who has accepted it in good faith, or a HOLDER IN DUE COURSE. A *bona fide* purchaser is one who has purchased and paid for goods with no knowledge of the fact that the seller may be insolvent, or that some other person has a claim against the goods. See also MALA FIDE.

bonanza. Originally a Spanish or Mexican term meaning prosperity, or exceptional riches. A very rich discovery of ore, especially of gold or silver; a highly profitable mine. More generally, any undertaking which produces exceptionally high profits, or which becomes highly profitable at a very rapid rate.

bond. 1. A written promissory agreement, under seal, by which one party, which may be a corporation, governmental unit, or other body, promises to pay a stated sum of money at some specified future time, known as the maturity date, and to pay interest at a stated rate at specified dates until the maturity date. An obligation or debt, evidenced by a written certificate, for a stated amount and for a stated term. The term is usually for a period of one year or longer. *Bonds* may be classified according to the nature of the security for the obligation, according to the method of paying interest, according to the terms under which the principal amount will be paid, according to the purpose for which they are issued, according to the currency in which they will be paid, according to the type of organization issuing them, etc. The chief classifications are listed and defined below. See also MORTGAGE.

A∼, B∼, etc. Terms used to distinguish one series of *bonds* from another when they are issued by the same corporation or government. Consecutive series of *bonds* may or may not have different maturity periods, rates of interest, etc.

adjustment ∼. One issued by a corporation which is in the process of a reorganization of its finances. Interest is payable only to the extent it is earned after payment of all prior obligations. Hence, it is a form of INCOME BOND, which see below.

annuity ∼. One which has no maturity date, but on which interest is to be paid in perpetuity. It is not actually a true bond, but is a mixture of a *bond* and an ANNUITY.

assumed ∼. One originally issued by a

corporation the identity of which has been lost by merger, and which has been assumed as an obligation by the successor corporation.

baby ～. In popular usage, a *bond* having a face value of $100 or less, or sometimes, of less than $1,000.

backed ～. See SECURED BOND, below.

bearer ～. In British usage, a COUPON BOND, which see below.

blanket ～. One which is secured by a general lien on all of the property of the issuer, but subject to any possible number of prior or underlying liens.

bottomry ～. One secured by a mortgage on a ship, or more specifically on her hull or bottom, and issued by a shipowner to obtain funds for outfitting, repairing, etc. Should the ship be lost, the *bond* is cancelled, since it is issued specifically on the ship itself, with no alternate security.

callable ～. One in which the issuer has reserved the right to retire, or call for payment, all or any part of the issue at any date or dates before the maturity date.

called ～. A CALLABLE BOND, which see above, which has been called in for payment, but not yet surrendered. Interest on such a *bond* is no longer paid after the date of call.

car trust ～. See EQUIPMENT TRUST BOND, below.

chattel mortgage ～. One issued on the security of a CHATTEL MORTGAGE, which see under MORTGAGE.

classified ～. One of a series of *bonds* in different classes, or series, which may bear different maturity dates, rates of interest, etc. They are usually noted as Class or Series A, B, etc.

clean ～. A COUPON BOND, which see below, on the back of which no endorsements or other writings have yet been placed. See also ENDORSED BOND, below.

collateral trust ～. One secured by a deposit of securities with a trustee. The securities deposited may be those of a subsidiary company, held by the parent company which is issuing the *bond* against them.

consolidated ～. One issued to refund, that is, to provide for the retirement and replacement of two or more previous issues. The step may be taken to simplify the debt structure of the corporation, or to take advantage of more favorable interest rates. Sometimes called a unified *bond*. See also CONSOL.

consolidated mortgage ～. One issued to replace two or more previous issues of MORTGAGE BONDS, which see below. Also, sometimes, a *bond* secured by a consolidated mortgage.

construction ～. One issued to secure funds for carrying on construction. It is usually secured by a mortgage against the work under construction.

continued ～. One which need not be presented for redemption at the maturity date, but which may be held for an indefinite period at the same or a different rate of interest. See also EXTENDED BOND, below.

convertible ～. One issued by a corporation, which may be converted by the holder into stock of the corporation within a specified time period, and at a specified price. *Bonds* of this type are usually DEBENTURE BONDS, which see below.

corporate ～. In general, any bond issued by a corporation, as distinguished from one issued by a governmental or other body.

corporate mortgage ～. One issued on the security of a mortgage on the property of the corporation. The mortgage is usually made to a trustee, who holds it for the benefit of the bondholders.

coupon ～. One not registered in the name of the owner on the books of the corporation or government issuing it, but negotiable, and payable to the bearer. The interest on such a *bond* is paid on the basis of coupons or certificates attached to it, the appropriate one being detached and forwarded to the corporation or paying agent, as each interest payment becomes due. Sometimes such *bonds* are marked "registered as to principal only," in which case they are negotiable only by endorsement, but the interest is payable by coupon in the same manner.

currency ～. One payable in the legal tender of a particular country, rather than in gold, or in a currency of the holder's choice.

debenture ～. One with a stated maturity date and rate of interest, but with no security. Such *bonds* frequently sell at a discount, since the interest and redemption is less certain, but when they are issued as CONVERTIBLE BONDS, which see above, they are popular with investors.

deferred ～. One on which the first interest payment is deferred for some specified period.

definitive ～. A complete and final *bond* which is eventually issued to a holder when the issue was not ready for delivery at the time of sale, so that the purchasers were given temporary certificates, later exchanged for the *definitive bond*.

development ～. One issued to raise funds for the development of property. See also IMPROVEMENT MORTGAGE BOND, below.

dollar ～. One on which the interest and principal are payable in United States dollars, whether or not issued by the United States government. Some foreign governments have issued such *bonds* from time to time, to make them more acceptable to American investors.

drawn ∼. A CALLABLE BOND, which see above, which has been drawn by lot for redemption, on one of a series of such redemption dates.

eligible ∼. One which, either through legislation or administrative ruling, has been declared eligible for purchase as an investment by savings banks, insurance companies, trustees, etc. Sometimes known as legal *bonds*.

endorsed ∼. A *bond* issued to bearer but which has been endorsed for some special purpose. For example, it may have been deposited as security, and must bear a releasing endorsement before it is deliverable to a new holder.

equipment trust ∼. One issued by a railroad or similar carrier, to raise funds for the purchase of new equipment. For a more detailed discussion see TRUST CERTIFICATE.

extended ∼. One which has reached maturity but has been extended for an additional fixed period, at the same or a different rate of interest. When the United States Savings Bonds, Series E, reached maturity, for example, they were extended for an additional ten years at the same rate of interest.

first and refunding mortgage ∼. One issued to refund or replace one or more previous issues, and secured by a first mortgage on at least part of the same property. As the original issues mature and are paid off, the refunding mortgage becomes a first mortgage on the entire property.

first lien collateral trust ∼. Strictly speaking, a form of COLLATERAL TRUST BOND, which see above, under which practically all of the *bonds* of subsidiary companies are deposited as collateral, so that the trust has in effect a first mortgage lien on the subsidiary property. The term is sometimes loosely used, however, to mean only that the holders of the trust *bond* have a first lien on the collateral itself.

first mortgage ∼. In general, one that represents a first claim on the property of the issuer. In some cases, the first mortgage is on only part of the property, some being subject to prior bonds.

first mortgage and collateral trust ∼. One that is, in effect, a combination of a FIRST MORTGAGE BOND and a COLLATERAL TRUST BOND, which see above. It is secured in part by a mortgage on the property of the company and in part by the deposit of securities.

first refunding ∼. A term used primarily to confuse investors. It does not mean that the *bond* is secured by a first mortgage, but merely that it is secured by the first refunding mortgage, or in other words, that this is the first of the REFUNDING BONDS, which see below.

general mortgage ∼. One secured by a general mortgage on the property of the issuer. That is, it is secured by a mortgage on all of the property of the company.

gold ∼. One which is specified as payable, both principal and interest, in gold. Such *bonds* were sometimes offered by foreign governments as inflation-proof investments.

government ∼. Specifically, one issued by a national government. Such *bonds* are secured by the good faith and ability to pay of the government issuing them, rather than by any particular property or income.

guaranteed ∼. One for which some party other than the issuer guarantees the payment of interest and principal. For example, when one railroad leases the property of another, it may guarantee the *bonds* and other securities of the leased railroad as part of the transaction.

improvement mortgage ∼. One issued to finance improvements or developments on already existing construction. It is usually secured by a first mortgage on the property and the improvement.

income ∼. One that is, in effect, a lien on the net income or earnings of a corporation. Interest is paid only when it is earned in sufficient amount to cover prior claims, such as taxes, mortgage *bonds,* etc. Such a *bond* is entitled to interest before payments are made on corporate stock, however, either preferred or common. This form of *bond* is frequently used as a part of the financial reorganization of a corporation, and in such cases is called an ADJUSTMENT BOND, which see above. Infrequently, this type of *bond* is known as a *preference bond*.

installment ∼. One on which the principal is to be paid in specified installments at specified times over a period of years. It differs from a SERIAL BOND, which see below, in that periodic payments are made on each certificate, rather than specified certificates being paid in full at different times.

interchangeable ∼. One on which the holder may request a change from a COUPON to a REGISTERED BOND, which see below. Sometimes, the change in the opposite direction may also be made on request.

interest ∼. One issued instead of monetary interest on another *bond,* when cash to make the interest payment is not available. It is essentially an interest-bearing promissory note for the interest.

interest-bearing ∼. In general, one on which interest at a fixed rate is payable until maturity. More specifically, a type of short-term *bond* on which interest is payable at maturity.

interim ~. A short-term bond issued by a corporation to raise money needed only temporarily, such as during a period of financial difficulty. It is sometimes called a temporary bond.

investment ~. A general term used for the entire type of promissory obligation covered by this definition.

irredeemable ~. See ANNUITY BOND, above.

joint ~. One which is issued jointly by two or more companies, and on which the issuers are jointly liable for the interest and principal. Such *bonds* may be issued, for example, by two railroads to finance the purchase or operation of a third road, in which both have an interest.

junior lien ~. A term used to describe any *bond* which is junior or inferior in its claim on the property by which it is secured to some other *bond* or mortgage.

legal ~. See ELIGIBLE BOND, above.

legal tender ~. One which is specified to be payable in any legal tender.

Liberty ~. One of a series of *bonds* issued by the United States government in 1917–1918 to finance the costs of World War I.

matured ~. One on which the principal has become due on its maturity date. Unless it is specified as a CONTINUED BOND, which see above, interest ceases to be earned after the maturity date.

mortgage ~. One of a variety of *bonds* the payment of which is secured by a MORTGAGE on the property of the issuer. Thus, the *bond* represents an actual claim against property, rather than merely against income or against the good name of the issuer. It may be a claim against specific property, or against all of the property of the issuer in general. Usually, the mortgage itself is held by a trustee, for the benefit of the bondholders. See, for example, FIRST MORTGAGE, CONSOLIDATED MORTGAGE, and GENERAL MORTGAGE BONDS, above.

municipal ~. Any of a variety of general or special purpose *bonds* issued by towns, counties, water or school districts, or other subdivisions of a state. Like GOVERNMENT BONDS, which see above, they are secured by good faith, rather than by specific property. Income from particular sources, such as bridge tolls, however, may be specifically pledged to meet the interest payments.

negotiable ~. One on which the interest and principal are payable either to the named holder or to his order, that is, to a new holder to whom he transfers his title by endorsement. REGISTERED BONDS, which see be-

low, may be either *negotiable* or *non-negotiable*.

non-callable ~. One which may not be called or redeemed for payment of the principal until the stated maturity date. It is sometimes known as a non-redeemable *bond*, but in this case should not be confused with an IRREDEEMABLE BOND, which see above. See also CALLABLE BOND, above.

non-interest-bearing ~. One which does not provide for the payment of interest to the holder. Usually, only SURETY BONDS are of this type. See BOND (2).

non-negotiable ~. One which is payable, both in interest and principal, only to the person named as payee on the *bond*, and on which title may not be transferred to another person.

non-redeemable ~. See NON-CALLABLE BOND, above.

optional ~. One which has a stated maturity date, but which may be redeemed by the issuer on or after a stated earlier date. For example, a *bond* maturing in 50 years may be specified to be redeemable after 10 years. It differs from a CALLABLE BOND, which see above, in that it is redeemable only on or after the specified date.

overlying ~. One secured by a mortgage which is inferior or subsequent to another, underlying, mortgage in its claim.

participating ~. One which, in addition to the stated interest, may be entitled to share in the distribution of the corporate profits. Under some circumstances, such *bonds* may also have voting rights in the operation of the corporation. Sometimes known as a profit-sharing *bond*.

passive ~. One which pays no present interest, but which carries some stated future benefit to the holder. An example is an ADJUSTMENT BOND, which see above.

perpetual ~. See ANNUITY BOND, above.

plain ~. See DEBENTURE BOND, above.

preference ~. See INCOME BOND, above.

prior lien ~. One which represents a lien or claim on property which is ahead of, or must be satisfied before, all others.

profit-sharing ~. See PARTICIPATING BOND, above.

rail ~. A general term for the *bonds* of railroad operating or holding companies.

real estate ~. One which is secured in whole or in part by a mortgage on real estate.

redeemable ~. See CALLABLE BOND, above.

refunding ~. One issued for the purpose of refunding or refinancing an existing mortgage. For example, a company with an already existing mortgage on its property, represented by a *bond* issue, may issue another series of *bonds* secured by a second mortgage on the property. Part of the issue may be sold to raise immediate funds, and the rest reserved to pay for the first mortgage bonds as they mature. Thus, the refunding issue eventually becomes a first mortgage *bond* on the property.

registered ∼. One registered in the name of the holder on the books of the company and on the *bond* certificate itself. The interest on a *registered bond* is payable by check to the registered owner. When such a bond is negotiable, a form for assignment and transfer on the reverse is filled out, and the certificate is surrendered to the company. Then, a new certificate, registered in the name of the new owner is issued.

registered coupon ∼. A COUPON BOND, which see above, which is registered as to principal, but on which the interest is still payable to the bearer of the coupons.

renewal ∼. One issued in renewal or redemption of an older issue which has become due.

respondentia ∼. One which is similar to a BOTTOMRY BOND, which see above, but which is secured by both the hull and cargo of the ship on which it is issued. Its payment is similarly contingent on the safe arrival of the ship and its cargo.

revenue ∼. One issued by a national, state or local government for the purpose of raising funds in anticipation of tax receipts. The understanding is that the *bond* will be redeemed out of the revenue or income of the governmental unit which issues it.

secured ∼. One which is secured by a mortgage or by a pledge of collateral, as distinguished from a DEBENTURE BOND, which see above. The term is not frequently used.

serial ∼. One of a series of bonds issued with maturity dates spread over a period of time. For example, a total issue of $10,000,000 may be issued in ten series, of $1,000,000 each, redeemable at periods of from eleven to twenty years after the original issue date. It differs from an INSTALLMENT BOND, which see above, on which periodic repayments are made on each certificate.

sinking fund ∼. One containing a provision that stated amounts or proportions of income will be paid each year into a SINKING FUND, to provide for the redemption of the *bond* issue. There are a wide variety of particular arrangements, under which the issuer may be required to retire part of the issue as funds become available, or may reinvest the sinking fund, to be used for payment on maturity, etc. The fund may be set up as a trust, which buys in the *bonds* and holds them itself, collecting the interest and applying it against the redemption of the remaining outstanding certificates. Corporations engaged in mining or other extractive industries, in which the corporate capital is continuously depleted, frequently issue such *bonds,* providing for payments into the sinking fund of so many cents per ton of coal mined, gallon of oil pumped, etc.

temporary ∼. See INTERIM BOND, above.

sterling ∼. One which is specified to be payable, both principal and interest, in pounds sterling.

tax ∼. One issued by a governmental unit in anticipation of tax receipts, and acceptable by it as tax payment. Such a *bond* is bought by those who must pay taxes as a means of investing the money put aside or reserved for tax payment.

temporary ∼ See INTERIM BOND, above.

treasury ∼. In general, any of the many series of *bonds* issued by the United States Treasury; a GOVERNMENT BOND. Also, a corporate *bond* which has been repurchased by the corporation and held in its treasury, either for resale at another time or to avoid paying interest when the borrowed funds are no longer needed but the *bond* has not yet matured.

underlying ∼. One secured by a mortgage which is prior or ahead of other claims on the corporate property.

unified ∼. See CONSOLIDATED BOND, above.

unsecured ∼. See DEBENTURE BOND, above.

2. Any of various forms of agreements or covenants between two or more parties, under which one party agrees to bind himself as a SURETY for one or more others, or agrees to INDEMNIFY one or more others against specified loss or damages. Also, the instrument containing such an agreement. *Bonds* of this type are classified according to their purpose, the person who binds himself, or the person who benefits. The principal types and classifications are listed and defined below.

administrator's ∼. A form of OFFICIAL BOND, which see below, required of an ADMINISTRATOR of an estate, to protect the interests of all those benefiting from the estate from loss due to any possible malfeasance or errors on the part of the administrator.

appeal ∼. One which may be required of a person who appeals from a court decision, to assure that any costs, damages awarded, etc., will be paid if the appeal is lost.

attachment ∼. One which a court may require of a person who has obtained an ATTACHMENT, or seizure of property, pending a final judgment, to cover any possible loss or damage that might be suffered by the defendant as a result.

bail ∼. One given by a defendant, or by a person who has agreed to give BAIL for a defendant, to guarantee the appearance of the defendant for trial or sentencing.

bid ⁓. One sometimes required to be posted by a person who submits a bid on a contract, such as one for public works, to guarantee that the person will enter into a contract if his bid is accepted, or forfeit the *bond*.

blanket ⁓. A term for a FIDELITY or SURETY BOND, which see below, covering all of the employees of a company, rather than specified employees or specified positions.

contract ⁓. One which may be required of a person who has undertaken a contract, such as one for public works, to protect the government or others from loss due to his inability to complete the contract as agreed. It is also frequently known as a performance *bond*.

customs ⁓. One required of importers, warehousemen, truckers, and others who may import or handle goods subject to customs tariff, to protect the government's interest while such goods are stored, processed, etc., before payment of the tariff.

executor's ⁓. A form of OFFICIAL BOND, which see below, required to be posted by the EXECUTOR of an estate under a will, to protect the interests of all those benefiting from the estate from any loss due to possible malfeasance or errors on the part of the executor.

export ⁓. A special form of CUSTOMS BOND, which see above, which may be required of a person who removes goods from a bonded warehouse for export, to cover the payment of any tariffs or excises if the goods are later reimported.

fidelity ⁓. A form of agreement or contract under which a person or organization agrees to indemnify an employer against any losses due to the dishonesty or infidelity of one or more of his employees. Strictly, it is distinguished from a SURETY BOND, which see below, which protects against failure to fulfill an obligation, rather than against dishonesty, but the two are frequently combined. *Fidelity bonds* are usually of one of three major types; BLANKET BONDS, which see above, NAME, or POSITION BONDS, which see below.

guaranty ⁓. A term for a form of combined FIDELITY BOND, which see above, and SURETY BOND, which see below, required of persons holding positions of public or private trust, such as FIDUCIARIES or TRUSTEES, to assure faithful performance of their duties.

guardian's ⁓. One which may be required of an appointed GUARDIAN, to protect his wards and others against possible loss due to malfeasance or errors on his part.

indemnity ⁓. A term for any of a wide variety of *bonds* given by one person to protect and indemnify others against loss due to the actions of the bonded person, or due to the performance of his duties in any position he may hold.

injunction ⁓. One which may be required by a court of a person who seeks and obtains an INJUNCTION against another, to protect the latter against any loss or damage he may wrongfully suffer as a result of the interference with his rights or property.

judgment ⁓. One required to be posted by a person who has appealed from a JUDGMENT awarded against him, to assure the payment of the judgment if the appeal is denied. The posting of the *bond* makes it unnecessary to pay the judgment itself unless and until the appeal is lost. See also APPEAL BOND, above.

judicial ⁓. A general term for any of the *bonds* required of persons who act under the orders or control of a court. Examples include ADMINISTRATOR'S and GUARDIAN'S BONDS, which see above, and RECEIVER'S BONDS, which see below. See also OFFICIAL BOND, below.

name ⁓. A term for a FIDELITY BOND, which see above, or SURETY BOND, which see below, covering only one or more specifically named persons, regardless of the positions they hold.

official ⁓. A general term for any of the class of *bonds* required of persons who hold public office, or positions of public trust, or who have responsibilities to the public as a result of a position or office held. Such *bonds* are frequently required of a wide variety of elected or appointed officials, government employees, administrators, trustees, executors, etc.

penalty ⁓. A term for a form of *bond* under which a person agrees to pay a specified sum or penalty at a future time, under condition that if some named event happens or does not happen meanwhile, the penalty need not be paid. Thus, it differs from the typical INDEMNITY BOND, which see above, in that the person binding himself conditionally agrees to make a specific payment at a specific time, rather than to cover uncertain losses which may or may not occur.

performance ⁓. See CONTRACT BOND, above.

position ⁓. A term for a FIDELITY BOND, which see above, or a SURETY BOND, which see below, covering one or more specifically listed positions of employment, such as treasurer, paymaster, accountant, etc., regardless of which employee currently holds the position.

receiver's ⁓. One required to be posted

by a person who has been named by a court as RECEIVER of the property or assets of another, such as a RECEIVER IN BANKRUPTCY, to protect the interests of the owner of the property, his creditors, and others, from any loss due to possible malfeasance or errors on the part of the receiver.

redelivery ～. One which may be posted by a person whose property has been placed under ATTACHMENT, pending a final court judgment, when the person wishes to obtain possession and use of the property, on condition that it will be redelivered to the custody of the court if and when the judgment becomes final. It should not be confused with an ATTACHMENT BOND, which see above, which is posted by the person obtaining the attachment.

removal ～. A form of CUSTOMS BOND, which see above, required to be posted by a person who removes imported goods from a bonded warehouse, such as for processing before export, to cover the tariff or excise which would have to be paid if the goods were sold domestically.

replevin ～. One required to be posted by a person who has recovered his property under a REPLEVIN action, to indemnify the public officer or private person from whom the property is recovered, in the event that it is later shown that the property was not wrongfully detained in the first instance.

security ～. See SURETY BOND, below.

surety ～. One required to be posted by a person who agrees to be a SURETY for another. More generally, a form of agreement or contract under which a person or organization agrees to indemnify an employer or other person against any losses due to the failure of an employee or other person to fulfill an obligation undertaken, such as to perform the duties of an office. Strictly, it is distinguished from a FIDELITY BOND, which see above, which protects against dishonesty, but the two are frequently combined. *Surety bonds* are usually of one of three major types; BLANKET, NAME, or POSITION BONDS, which see above.

warehouse ～. One required under customs regulations of the operator of a bonded warehouse, to assure payment of any tariffs or excises due on property stored and wrongfully removed from the warehouse. See also WAREHOUSE, BONDED.

bond broker. See under BROKER (2).

bond dividend. See under DIVIDEND.

bonded. 1. In general, secured or protected by a pledge of property, or by a BOND (2). A messenger who carries valuables, for example, is usually *bonded,* or protected by a fidelity or surety *bond.* See also BOND (2), SURETY.

2. Held or produced IN BOND. Having had a *bond* posted as security that the necessary tax or tariff will be paid at the proper time. See also WAREHOUSE, BONDED.

bonded debt. See under DEBT.

bonded warehouse. See under WAREHOUSE.

bonding company. A financial institution engaged primarily in the business of entering into contracts of SURETY, and of providing BONDS (2) for those persons or organizations needing them in the course of their business or other activities.

bond rating. A method or system of appraising and rating the worth of individual *bond* issues as investments. Such ratings are based on the character of the issuing company or governmental unit, on its income possibilities, its previous record of interest payments, etc. There are several systems in use, but they are generally similar, and represent the relative rating of each issue in alphabetic code, with a triple-A, or AAA bond as the most secure, and others rated below, through AA, A, B, etc.

bond redemption. The process of making payment for a *bond* issue, or of repaying the loan represented by the *bond.* This may be done in various ways, including a total repayment at maturity in cash accumulated through a SINKING FUND; the calling or redeeming of some of the bonds each year, using funds available out of income to make the payment; converting the bond into company stock; REFUNDING, or replacing the bond with a newly issued one for another period, etc.

bondsman. A person who provides BONDS (2), especially bail bonds or surety bonds; a BONDING COMPANY.

bond value table. A table or schedule used to determine the present value of a bond, or the actual YIELD, when the purchase price, redemption price, interest rate, and number of years until maturity or redemption are known. Thus, by the use of one of these tables, the price which should be paid for a bond in order to produce a particular yield, or the yield which will be produced by a purchase at any particular price, may be determined.

bonification. Literally, the giving of a benefit. In taxation, the remission or returning of a tax paid, such as an excise tax paid on goods intended for export, or for sale to the government. Manufacturers, for example, are not required to pay excise taxes on electrical appliances intended for export. If the tax is paid before it is known that the goods are to be exported, it is returned upon the filing of the necessary report, and this process is known as *bonification*.

bonus. Literally, something good. A premium or extra payment over and above what is due or expected. Workers in a factory, for example, may be paid a *bonus* at year end, if the company is prosperous. Since such payments are a result of the extra efforts of the employees, or are made in order to stimulate future production, they have been held to be wages, for tax purposes, not gifts.

bonus stock. See under STOCK (1).

boodle. In slang, a fund set aside or collected to pay bribes or for other corrupt purposes. Also, in some usages, the proceeds from illegal activities. The term is believed to derive from a Pennsylvania Dutch word for property, or wealth.

book. 1. Pertaining to a BOOK OF ACCOUNTS, or to entries in an account *book*. A *book* DEBT, for example, is one standing on the *books* of a business, or one resulting from its regular trading activities. The *book* VALUE of an asset is the value at which the asset is carried on the account *books* of the company. See each of the following under the principal listing: ~ CREDIT (3); ~ INVENTORY; ~ PROFIT; ~ VALUE (2).

2. To enter or record in a *book* or register; to engage. A theater seat or hotel room, for example, may be *booked* for a particular date. Similarly, a company may *book* sales, or may *book* its productive capacity to fill orders received.

book account. See ACCOUNT (4), OPEN.

bookkeeping. The art or trade of keeping BOOKS OF ACCOUNT. The work of entering or recording the transactions of a business enterprise in the accounts and other records kept for this purpose. *Bookkeeping* is distinguished from ACCOUNTING, which is primarily the interpreting and analysis of such entries, and the design of systems for keeping records.

book of account. In business, one of the books or forms in which are recorded the information relating to all of the transactions of a business enterprise. The two basic *books of account* in the typical business are the JOURNAL (1), which is the BOOK OF ORIGINAL ENTRY, and the LEDGER, which is the final register of accounts in which entries are posted from the journal. In some businesses, the VOUCHER REGISTER is the book of original entry. In actual use, a *book of account* may not be a book at all, but a collection of forms, cards, or other means of recording data.

book of original entry. The BOOK OF ACCOUNT in which are entered the first records of each business transaction made by a company. Examples of such transactions include sales, purchases, payments made and received, etc. In the typical business, the JOURNAL, or one of its subdivisions, is the *book of original entry*. In a company operating on the VOUCHER SYSTEM, the *book of original entry* is one of the VOUCHER REGISTERS. See also ORIGINAL ENTRY.

book right. In publishing, the right to publish a literary product in book form, either before or after it has appeared in a periodical in serial form, or on the stage in play form. This right, and the compensation connected with it, should always be specifically disposed of in any contract between author and publisher. See also SERIAL RIGHT.

book sizes. The various common page sizes in which books are printed. Originally, all book paper came in only one sheet size, approximately 19 by 25 inches, so that page sizes were limited to folds of this standard sheet. Thus, a sheet folded once made a *folio* page of about 12½ by 19 inches; a sheet folded into fourths made a *quarto* page of approximately 9½ by 12½ inches, and so forth. Today, book paper comes in many sheet sizes, and pages may be folded and trimmed to practically any desired size. Pages of approximately the original dimensions, however, are still known by the traditional names. The more common *book sizes* now in use are the following; in order of decreasing size:

quarto (4to). Approximately 9½ by 12½ inches.
imperial octavo. About 7½ by 11½ inches.
royal octavo. About 7 by 10½ inches.
octavo (8vo). About 6¼ by 9½ inches.
crown octavo. About 5½ by 8½ inches.
duodecimo (12mo). About 4¾ by 8¼ inches.
sixteenmo (16mo). About 4½ by 6¼ inches.
twenty-fourmo (24mo). About 3¼ by 6¼ inches.
thirty-twomo (32mo). About 3⅛ by 4½ inches.

boom. In economics, a rapid expansion in the volume of business activity, usually accompanied by price inflation and increased speculation in securities, commodities, etc. Some writers differentiate between a *boom* and PROSPERITY, to the extent that the former is largely psychological, and represents an expansion in activity, rather than in the actual amounts of production and consumption, while the latter is based on a real increase in the national product and income.

boot. Originally, something which makes another thing better; something given into the bargain, as extra compensation. More broadly, anything added, as when one party to a bargain throws in an additional benefit or thing of value *to boot*.

bootleg. Originally, to sell illegal liquor. The term originated, supposedly, from the practice of transporting flasks of such liquor in the leg of a boot. As used, the term includes both the sale of illegally produced liquor, and the sale of liquor which was legally produced in one place, but which may not be sold in another place. More broadly, to transport, distribute, or sell any product illegally, or contrary to established trade practices; to smuggle. See also MOONSHINE.

boot money. Money given as added or extra compensation by one of the parties to a bargain. When a BARTER transaction takes place, for example, the things exchanged may not be of equal value, so that one of the parties gives the other a sum of money in addition, or *to boot*.

borax. In retail merchandising, the name for a class of inexpensive but generally poorly designed furniture. It is used primarily as a promotional device, being featured in advertisements and then used to encourage the buyer to raise his intentions to higher priced and better designed goods. The origin of the term is obscure, and there are several conflicting explanations of its derivation, such as that the units resembled the large ungainly box in which borax was shipped.

bordereau. In insurance, and in some other fields, a statement or digest of the transactions between an insurer and a reinsurer, or between an agent and an insurance company, or between any agent or broker and his principal.

borough. Originally, a walled or fortified town. Now, in the United States, a part of a township, or of a city, established for administrative purposes, but not politically independent.

borrow. To solicit and receive something of value from another, temporarily, on the promise to return it or its equivalent. One who *borrows* machinery, for example, may be expected to return the exact thing *borrowed*, but one who *borrows* money may return any money of the same total amount. Originally, *borrow* was distinguished from RENT (1), in that it involved no payment or interest, but this distinction has disappeared. Today, the distinction tends to be in

terms of the thing received or used; one *borrows* money or personal property, but one RENTS real property or capital equipment. See also LEND.

Boston interest. See INTEREST (2), ORDINARY.

bottleneck. Anything which restricts the free flow of goods, information, money, etc. Particularly, any obstruction or limit to capacity which slows the normal rate of operation of a business or production operation. In an assembly line, for example, one machine operating at a slower rate than others is a *bottleneck*, while in an administrative office, a person who delays papers in their normal routing is also a *bottleneck*.

bottomry. In maritime usage, a form of mortgage in which a loan is made with a ship, or its cargo, as security. The borrower keeps the use of the vessel, however, and the terms of the loan provide that if the ship is lost the lender loses his money also, since repayment of the loan is contingent on the safe arrival of the ship in port. See also BOND (1), BOTTOMRY; HYPOTHECATION.

bought note. See under NOTE (2).

bouncing check. See CHECK, BAD.

bounty. Any unusual or additional benefit paid; a premium, or reward, especially one paid by a government. A *bounty* may be paid to those who join the armed forces, for example, or it may be paid to a particular branch of industry to encourage its expansion. Sometimes, a *bounty* is distinguished from a BONUS in that it is paid to encourage future action, while a bonus is a reward for past action, but the two terms are interchangeable in many usages.

bourgeois. Literally, in French, a city-dweller. In economics, a term for the class of self-employed persons, such as shopkeepers, craftsmen, etc., who are neither PROLETARIAT, since they do not work for others, nor CAPITALISTS, since they do not employ others. More broadly, the middle classes in general, sometimes referred to as the *petit-bourgeois*.

bourse. In French, an EXCHANGE (2); especially a securities exchange, or a money exchange. A market.

boycott. In general, any conspiracy, or concerted action by a group of persons, directly or indirectly, to prevent the carrying on of a lawful business, by preventing would-be customers from trading with the affected business. The action may take the form of appeals, coercive notices, threats, etc. In labor relations particularly, it is the action of a combination of employees in refusing to continue dealing with a company, and in attempting to persuade or coerce others to refuse to have business dealings with the affected company. The term derives from a Capt. Boycott, a land agent for absentee English owners in Ireland, whose methods of collecting rents were so harsh that the farmers eventually organized against him, refusing to provide him with supplies, or to have any relations with him whatever.

primary ∼. In labor, one in which a union and its members refuse to deal with a company whose policies they oppose, but without involving the general public or other parties. In the case of a large and powerful union, or one which is important in the company's own market area, such a *boycott* can be very effective.

secondary ∼. In labor, one in which a union attempts to persuade or coerce others into not dealing with the affected firm. This may be done, for example, by approaching customers and suppliers of the company being *boycotted,* and threatening that they will be *boycotted* themselves if they continue to deal with the company. Such *secondary boycotts* are illegal under the Labor-Management Relations Act.

branch. A subordinate unit or division of a business, located at a different place from the principal operation. Also, as used, a division of an industry or trade. For example, one may speak of the retail *branch* of the apparel trade. See also each of the following under the principal listing: ∼ BANK; ∼ BANKING.

branch line. In railroading, a line or route which diverges from a MAIN LINE or TRUNK LINE, to serve subsidiary cities or areas which are not along the principal route. A short *branch line* to serve a particular city or industrial plant is sometimes known as a SPUR LINE. See also FEEDER LINE.

brand. Originally, a mark made by burning, with a firebrand or hot iron. More generally, any identifying mark, used by an owner or producer of goods or services to identify his product. Any name, term, symbol, or design, or a combination of these, which serves to identify the goods or services of a seller or group of sellers, and to distinguish them from those of competitors; a TRADEMARK. A *brand* may be used by a manufacturer, wholesaler, or retailer, depending on the product and the nature of the distribution pattern in the trade.

fighting ∼. One used by a manufacturer or distributor for the purpose of combatting competitive *brands,* to drive them out of the market. For example, a manufacturer may introduce a new *brand* of canned food in a local market at a very low price, and

continue to sell it until a local competitive *brand* has been eliminated. At this point the *fighting brand* is withdrawn and replaced by one of the manufacturer's regular *brands,* at the regular price. Such tactics are now illegal under the Robinson-Patman Act and other anti-trust laws.

manufacturer's ∼. One used by the original manufacturer of an item, rather than by a wholesale or retail distributor. In many fields, such as foods, drugs, appliances, etc., some of the existing *brands* are *manufacturer's brands,* but many are not. See also PACKER'S BRAND, below.

national ∼. One which is widely, though not necessarily literally nationally distributed and advertised. A *national brand* is often a MANUFACTURER'S BRAND, which see above, but it may be the *brand* of a large wholesale distributing organization or retail chain.

packer's ∼. One used by the original packer of a product, rather than by a distributor. In the meat packing industry, for example, some packers distribute all or some of their production under their own *packer's brands,* while others pack for distribution under *brands* owned by distributors. The term is also used in the vegetable packing industry.

private ∼. One which is used exclusively by a distributor of products made by a manufacturer. A manufacturer of *branded* products, for example, may reserve part of his production to be marked with the *private brand* of a large retailer, and sold only through the retailer's stores. One reason for such distribution is to permit the retailer to charge a lower price for products which are regularly sold on a RESALE PRICE MAINTENANCE basis.

wildcat ∼. One which is generally unknown, and usually of inferior quality. The term is used especially to describe unknown and substandard *brands* of food products, such as canned goods.

brass. 1. One of a class of copper-base alloys, containing copper, tin, and sometimes zinc and other metals in small proportions. It is typically a very hard and corrosion resistant metal, used for plating and protecting other metal surfaces. See also WHITE BRASS; YELLOW BRASS.

2. In business slang, derived from military slang, the top-ranking persons in the management of a company or organization; the officers of a corporation. The term is based originally on the shiny *brass* buttons, gold braid, and other distinctive ornamentation of the uniforms of high military officers.

breach. Literally, a breaking, or violation. A

failure to carry out the terms of an agreement, or to follow the requirements of a law or regulation, either by doing something which it has been promised would not be done, or by failing to do something which should have been done. A *breach* of contract, for example, is a failure to perform according to the terms of the agreement in any manner. A *breach* of the peace is a violation of public peace and order, especially in an illegal manner. In fire insurance, a *breach* of WARRANTY may be a failure to perform as promised, or a false statement made in the policy declaration.

breakage. 1. An allowance made for losses due to the breaking of products, either in transit, in storage, or in use. A manufacturer of china, for example, may give a *breakage* allowance to retail stores, under which they may receive replacements or credit for pieces which break while in storage or on display, up to a given percentage of the total amount purchased. In some cases, the allowance may be in the form of extra units included without charge in each order, to cover expected or average *breakage*.

2. In monetary transactions, the fractional pennies due either party as a result of percentage calculations, etc. In computing interest, for example, it is the practice of some banks to credit amounts of one half cent or more to the depositor, while others drop all fractional amounts, taking the *breakage* for themselves. Similarly, in computing taxes, it is the practice of many governmental units to take all *breakage* for themselves.

break-bulk service. See under FORWARDER.

break-even chart. Any graphic portrayal or analysis of the BREAK-EVEN POINT of a business.

break-even point. The level of production or sales volume in a business at which operations are neither profitable nor unprofitable. The point at which total net income just covers total costs. Since at least some costs are fixed, and do not vary with sales volume, any increase in volume above the *break-even point* will begin to produce a profit, while any drop in volume below this point will result in an operating loss. A company which can operate profitably at a very low level of operation is said to have a low *break-even point,* while one which must operate at a high level to be profitable is said to have a high *break-even point.* Typically, however, a company with a low *break-even point* has a rate of profit which is relatively stable, while one with a high *break-even point* has rapidly increasing profits once the point is passed, and is said to have high LEVERAGE.

breakup value. See VALUE, BOOK; SALVAGE VALUE.

bribe. Something of value, especially money, given to a person in a position of trust or authority, to persuade him to violate or permit the violation of some law or regulation, or to give preferred treatment, or otherwise to permit his conduct to be influenced in favor of the giver. In current usage, the term refers especially to amounts given to persons in public office, or employed by government.

brief. In general, any short or condensed document. In law, a summary of the basis of the case to be presented by one side in a legal action, which is prepared for the information of the court, as requested, and is submitted before the case is to be tried or heard. In some cases, the court may rule on the admission of certain evidence, or on other aspects of the conduct of the case, on the basis of the *briefs* submitted by the attorneys.

Brinell hardness. A standard method and scale for measuring the hardness or impenetrability of a metal. It is measured in terms of the depth of penetration of a hard steel ball, driven into the surface of the metal being tested. See also ROCKWELL HARDNESS.

British Thermal Unit. The standard unit of measure for the heat content of fuels, and of the energy content of some foodstuffs. It is the amount of heat required to raise the temperature of one pound of water, at 39.1 degrees Fahrenheit, by one degree Fahrenheit. The *British Thermal Unit* is the equivalent of approximately $\frac{1}{4}$ kilogram-calories, or 252 gram-calories, in the metric system. It is abbreviated as B.T.U. See also CALORIE.

broad gauge. See GAUGE (1).

broad market. In the securities trade, a term for a situation in which a wide range of securities is traded, and in which trading in general is active and spirited, as distinguished from a NARROW MARKET, in which trading is dull and listless. See also ACTIVE MARKET; INACTIVE MARKET.

broadside. In advertising, a large size, single sheet advertisement, intended to be displayed as a poster, or distributed as a handbill. In the latter case, it may be folded, although the advertising material printed on it is still usually a single large unit, rather than broken into several pages.

broken lot. See ODD LOT.

broker. 1. Originally, one who broached, or tapped, casks of wine or beer, to resell the contents by the glass. Hence, by extension, any merchant or middleman who bought in gross to resell in smaller quantities. In modern usage, however, the meaning of the term has completely changed, to the extent that the original definition is excluded from the present one. A *broker* is now an independent agent who is engaged in negotiating bargains or agreements between two or more parties. He does not take title to the goods for the exchange of which he negotiates, and usually does not take possession of them. He does not act in his own name, but in the names of his customers on both sides. A *broker* is sometimes distinguished from an AGENT in that the latter has a continuing relation with his principal, while a broker, though he may serve the same principal in many transactions, handles each separately. Some of the more important types of commercial *brokers* are listed and defined below.

bill ∼. See NOTE BROKER below.

customs ∼. A service company engaged in handling the work involved in bringing imported goods through the customs procedure, and in preparing export shipments for the customs and other requirements of foreign countries. This service is usually provided by foreign freight FORWARDERS.

exchange ∼. One who negotiates the purchase and sale of foreign currencies, acceptances, bills of exchange, and other instruments of foreign commerce.

export ∼. One who acts to sell goods to the export trade for manufacturers and others. He does not export goods for his own account, and is therefore not an EXPORTER himself.

import ∼. One who negotiates to buy foreign goods, either in the country of origin or at a domestic port, for the account of customers, rather than for his own account.

insurance ∼. A person who acts to obtain insurance for individuals and companies, from insurance companies or their agents. He differs from an insurance AGENT in that he does not represent any particular companies, but is free to place the insurance with any insurer. His compensation is technically obtained from the insurance buyer, whereas the agent is paid by the insurance company directly. In practice, however, there is often little difference between the activities or services of the *broker* and those of an independent agent.

money ∼. One who deals in foreign currencies and foreign negotiable instruments. He is not strictly a *broker*, since he sometimes buys and sells currencies for his own account. Also, sometimes, a money lender, or PAWNBROKER.

note ∼. One who negotiates the sale and purchase of promissory notes, bills of exchange, and other commercial paper, especially such paper which is not of first quality. See also COMMERCIAL PAPER, STREET.

real estate ∼. One whose activities are confined to bringing together buyers and sellers of real estate, or in some cases, leasers and renters of real estate. Under the laws of many states, the *real estate broker* may take a commission from either the buyer or seller, but not from both on the same transaction.

ship ∼. An independent agent who is engaged by ship owners to obtain cargo and passengers for their vessels. He may also arrange for the insurance of the cargo, prepare the bill of lading, arrange for the loading and unloading, and provide other services of a FORWARDER. The *ship broker* may also arrange for the charter of an entire ship, for a voyage or for a period of time.

2. A dealer in securities; a member of a securities exchange who acts in the purchase and sale of securities for the investing public. Many such *brokers* are also traders or dealers, in that they sometimes buy or sell securities for their own account, in the course of their regular activities. The principal types of securities *brokers* are listed and defined below. See also TRADER.

bond ∼. One who specializes in the purchase and sale of bonds, debentures, and other similar securities.

curb ∼. Originally, one who transacted his business on the street, or curb, since he was not a member of an organized exchange. Eventually, however, the *curb brokers* in New York City formed the New York Curb Exchange, now the American Stock Exchange. See also OUTSIDE BROKER, below.

investment ∼. Strictly, one who handles only cash transactions, rather than MARGIN transactions. Presumably, securities bought for cash are more likely to be held as investments, while those bought on margin are more likely to be bought for speculative purposes. The term is falling into disuse, however, since margin requirements have been raised.

odd-lot ∼. One who specializes in handling ODD-LOT transactions, or those involving less than 100 shares of stock. He serves other *brokers*, and is strictly speaking a dealer, since he typically buys ROUND LOTS on his own account and holds them to fill odd-lot orders, and accumulates odd-lot amounts on his own account to make later round-lot sales. His compensation is the TRADING DIFFERENCE, or fraction of a point per share, which he charges for his services.

outside ∼. One who is not a member of an organized exchange, but who operates through others who are. Also, one who deals in securities not registered on an exchange. He is sometimes called an OVER THE COUNTER broker, or STREET broker.

two-dollar ~. See directly.

brokerage. In general, the business of serving as a BROKER. A firm organized for the purpose of negotiating purchases and sales, such as of securities, commodities, textiles, foodstuffs, etc., for the accounts of others, on a commission basis; a *brokerage* house. Also, the fee or commission charged by a broker, usually a percentage of the value of the thing bought or sold.

brokers' broker. See TRADER, FLOOR.

broker's contract. See under CONTRACT (1).

broker's loan. See under LOAN.

brokers' market. In the securities trade, a term describing the condition in which the investing public is generally inactive in securities trading, while the members of the exchange themselves are trading relatively heavily for their own accounts.

broker's ticket. In the securities trade, the name for the written memorandum or note prepared by a securities broker on each sale or purchase he executes. It records the date, name and amount of the security traded, the price, customer's name, name of broker from or to whom the security is traded, etc. These are balanced and cleared at the end of the trading day through the stock CLEARING HOUSE serving the exchange. See also STOCK CLEARING CORPORATION.

bronze. A metal alloy of copper and tin, and sometimes containing small amounts of lead or zinc.

brotherhood. In trade-union usage, the title used in the name of some unions, especially those in the railroad, construction, and similar fields. The term is carried over from the fact that many of these unions were originally established as fraternal or beneficial societies.

bubble. A highly speculative scheme or undertaking, especially one based on false representation. Also, the inflationary and false expansion which may result from such a scheme, before it is exposed and the *bubble* breaks. One of the most notorious such schemes was the famous South Seas *bubble,* in which thousands of persons lost their savings, which had been invested in the supposed highly profitable development of the South Seas trade.

bucketing. In the securities trade, a term for the practice of a broker in executing a customer's order for his own account, rather than on the market, in the hope of profiting from a balancing transaction later. For ex-

ample, if an investor places an order to buy stock A, which the broker feels sure will soon drop in price, the *bucketing* broker will sell the stock to the investor directly, either from his own holdings or in a SHORT sale, planning to buy the stock later, at a lower price, to balance out the transaction. Similarly, if the investor places an order to sell stock B, which the broker is sure will rise, he may buy the stock for his own account, holding it until the expected rise occurs. The term derives from the fact that the broker holds, or *buckets* the transaction, until he completes it later. Such operations are forbidden in regular exchange trading.

bucket shop. In the securities trade, an unauthorized or irregularly operated business for dealing in securities off the regular exchanges. Specifically, a *bucket shop* is an unlicensed business in which customers, in effect, place bets on the rise or fall of stock prices on the regular exchange. No actual orders are filled, but the customers are paid a profit or charged a loss on the basis of the action of their chosen stocks on the regular exchange, with a commission charged on each transaction or bet. More broadly, the term is applied to any unscrupulous or disreputable brokerage operation, such as one which regularly engages in BUCKETING, or betting against the judgment of its customers.

budget. In general, a plan or estimate of future activities, especially of income and expenses during a particular future time period. A government prepares an annual *budget* on the basis of anticipated tax revenues and expenditures, and a business may prepare a *budget* on the basis of expected sales, output, and expenses. The term itself derives from the leather bag, or *bougette,* in which the funds to meet expected expenses were originally set aside. The principal types of *budgets* which might be prepared by a business are listed and defined below.

capital ~. One covering the planned capital expenditures of the company over the coming period, such as those for the purchase of new machinery or equipment, or for new construction. It also provides for the source of the needed capital funds to cover these expenditures.

cash ~. One covering the planned needs of the company for cash, or liquid assets, during the coming period, based on expected cash receipts and expenditures during the period, and the desired level of cash reserves. It may also provide for the necessary amount of short term borrowing to produce the desired amount of working cash.

fixed ~. One set up for a definite period of time, and which is intended not to be adjusted or modified during the period covered. A government *budget* is relatively fixed, in that it establishes a definite tax rate and definite expenditures for each department, which will not be changed except in emergency situations. It is distinguished from a VARIABLE BUDGET, which see below.

flexible ~. See VARIABLE BUDGET, below.

operating ~. Broadly, one covering all of the regular operations of the business. More particularly, one covering the production and distribution operations, as distinguished from the selling and financial operations of the business.

sales ~. One planning for the selling activities of the business, covering the expected realistic level of sales for the *budget* period, and the levels of sales staff, advertising, promotion, etc. needed to support this level of sales. A detailed *sales budget* may provide separately for each product, price line, territory, and industrial market covered by the company.

variable ~. One including two or more alternative plans, depending on a higher or lower developing level of activity or business volume. Also, one which is subject to adjustment or revision during the *budget* period, as distinguished from a FIXED BUDGET, which see above.

budgetary control. In general, the plan or system of directing and operating a business enterprise according to a prepared plan of operations. The control of income and expenditures to adhere to a previously established BUDGET.

budget plan. See INSTALLMENT PLAN.

builder's risk insurance. See under INSURANCE, PROPERTY.

building. As defined in various statutes and regulations, any STRUCTURE designed or suitable to be occupied by man, as distinguished from a dam, bridge, oil well, or other structure not intended to be so occupied. Also, the activity of constructing such structures, as differentiated from other construction activity, such as in construction statistics.

building and loan association. Strictly, a co-operative banking society, formed to accumulate money from its members in the form of savings and subscriptions, and to lend this money, in the form of mortgages and modernization loans. The society's activities may be limited to its own members, but in current usage, loans are made to the general public as well. Under modern statutes, a *building and loan association* is simply a special variety of SAVINGS AND LOAN ASSOCIATION.

building permit. An authorization by a local government to undertake and complete construction. It may be for a new building, or for a major alteration or addition to an existing building. The value of *building permits* issued, or the value of the construction planned under such permits, is a widely used statistical indicator of the volume of construction activity. It is not an exact indicator, however, since many buildings for which plans are filed and permits issued are never built, and many finally involve expenditures much more or less than the amount stated in the original permit.

bulk. In general, large amounts or units of any goods or commodity, or large amounts in a single package. In another sense, large amounts not exactly measured, counted, or weighed, but sold or bought by quantity or approximate volume. Also, unpacked, loose, or without a special container. Thus, a *bulk* shipment may be one of an unpackaged commodity, such as grain, or it may be simply a large shipment of any goods.

bulk sale. In one sense, a sale of an entire shipment, cargo, or lot of goods at a single price and in a single transaction. More particularly, a sale of the entire stock of goods or assets of a BANKRUPT business to a single buyer, under a BULK SALES LAW.

bulk sales law. The name for a statute, adopted in more or less the same form by all of the states, governing the conditions under which the entire stock of goods or assets of a BANKRUPT business may be sold to a single buyer. The purpose of the law is to prevent the defrauding of creditors through such a sale of a business.

bull. In the securities trade, a speculative trader who makes his profits on rising prices. Hence, one who favors or believes in rising prices or improving business activity; an optimist. Typically, a *bull* operates by buying securities at low prices and reselling after the expected rise. The same trader, however, may be a *bull* during rising prices, and a BEAR during a period of falling prices.

bulling the market. In the securities trade, an expression for the activities of speculators aimed at forcing upward the level of prices. These may include the spreading of optimistic rumors, the entering of purchase orders at levels slightly above the prevailing price levels, etc.

bullion. Strictly, gold or silver metal intended for coinage. In other words, gold or silver of the required degree of purity or fineness, in bars, ingots, or some other suitable form. More loosely, any gold or silver in bar or ingot form. In some cases, foreign coins suitable for melting and coinage are included in the definition.

bull market. In the securities trade, a market characterized by a long-term trend of rising prices. Hence, a market favorable to the speculative activities of BULLS.

bumping. In labor, the practice of a senior employee in claiming the job of a junior employee at a time of reduction of staff. Most union contracts, for example, provide that in the event of a LAYOFF, workers must be let go in order of SENIORITY. Thus, if the layoff involves the elimination of the job of an employee with high seniority, he has the right to take an equally or lower rated job, so that the employee filling that job must be laid off instead. It is sometimes called backtracking.

bunco game. A name for a CONFIDENCE GAME.

burden. In general, a load or obligation, or anything which is added on as an additional loading or obligation. See OVERHEAD.

Bureau of Customs. The bureau in the Treasury Department, established in its present form in 1927, which is responsible for the collection of customs tariffs, the regulation and licensing of vessels, etc. It operates offices of the Collector of Customs in all PORTS OF ENTRY.

Bureau of Labor Statistics. The federal bureau, in the Department of Labor, which is responsible for the collection, analysis, and publishing of statistics in connection with employment, the labor force, construction, wages, etc. The bureau also maintains the CONSUMER PRICE INDEX, which measures the prices paid by working-class families.

Bureau of the Budget. The federal agency, originally in the Treasury Department and now under the Executive Office of the President, which is responsible for the presentation of the federal budget. It also supervises the statistical activities of the various federal agencies, and attempts to coordinate and standardize these activities.

Bureau of the Census. The federal agency, in the Department of Commerce, which is responsible for conducting the various censuses of population, housing, agriculture, manufactures, and business. It also collects and publishes many other statistical series, and conducts special surveys at the request of the Congress, or of other federal agencies.

burglary. In law, strictly, the breaking and entering of a home or place of business with the intention of committing LARCENY. Thus,

it is a form of THEFT, and differs from ROBBERY, which is theft from one's person, and from EMBEZZLEMENT, which is the larceny of that which is left in a person's care.

burglary insurance. See INSURANCE, CASUALTY AND LIABILITY.

bushel. A unit of capacity used in the dry measure of various commodities. The standard United States *bushel* contains 2150.42 cubic inches, and is the equivalent of 4 PECKS, 8 dry GALLONS, or 32 dry QUARTS. The weight of a *bushel* obviously varies from commodity to commodity, but for a wide variety of products it ranges from about 48 to 60 pounds. In some cases, the *heaped bushel* is a permitted measure, consisting of a *bushel* container piled or heaped to a cone, and containing one and one fourth *bushels*.

business. In general, any commercial, industrial, or financial activity. Any and all of those activities connected with the production and exchange of goods or services, and the financial affairs connected with these activities. Hence, any undertaking or enterprise in one of these lines of activity, or any transaction or affair connected with *business* activity. As commonly used, a COMPANY or CORPORATION. See each of the following under the principal listing: ∼ COMMERCIAL PAPER; ∼ CORPORATION; ∼ MONTH; ∼ TRUST (3).

business agent. An employee or officer of a local UNION, whose duties include the initiating of negotiations for agreements with the employers, the supervision of the agreements and the settlement of disputes arising under them. Not all unions operate on the *business agent* basis, but in those that do he is usually the most important single officer in the local union.

business cycle. In economics, the name for the periodic major swings in the level of business activity. In most modern economic theory, the typical *business cycle* is considered as including a period of EXPANSION leading to a PEAK, or period of PROSPERITY, followed by a downturn through a period of CONTRACTION to a TROUGH or period of DEPRESSION. This in turn is followed by a new upturn and a new period of expansion in the next cycle. In duration, the definition is usually limited to those cycles which are longer than one year, but not longer than about seven years.

business establishment. As defined by the Bureau of the Census, any separate place or establishment at which some business is conducted, as distinguished from a COMPANY. Thus, a company may operate several *busi-*

ness establishments, and, conceivably, several companies may jointly operate one *business establishment.* Examples include factories, warehouses, shops, stores, offices, etc.

business hours. As used in contracts, insurance, and various statutes, the hours of each day during which a business establishment is normally and regularly open for the conduct of business. With regard to a factory, they are the hours during which employees normally work, for example, and with regard to a retail store they are the hours during which customers are normally served.

business interruption insurance. See under IN-SURANCE, PROPERTY.

business life insurance. See under INSURANCE, LIFE, ACCIDENT, AND HEALTH.

business machine. The general name for a wide class of machines and equipment which are designed to perform the operations required in business. They include adding machines, calculating machines, accounting and billing machines, punch card tabulating and sorting equipment, etc. The newest business machines are electronically operated, and are able to handle tremendous masses of data at extremely rapid speeds.

business paper. See under COMMERCIAL PAPER.

business publication. The term for a newspaper, magazine, or other periodical which is addressed to the needs and interests of business executives in general, rather than to the interests of one particular business, industry, or trade. Publications of the latter type are known, usually, as TRADE PUBLICATIONS.

business savings. See under SAVINGS.

business year. See COMMERCIAL YEAR.

butt. A measure of liquid volume, equivalent to one half a TUN, or two HOGSHEADS, and thus containing 126 liquid GALLONS; a PIPE. It is seldom now used, and the volume actually contained may vary according to usage in particular trades.

buy. To acquire ownership of something from another in return for the payment of a monetary consideration. To obtain title to property by PURCHASE. See also SELL.

buyer. In general, any person who BUYS. In retail merchandising in particular, the person who is responsible for buying the merchandise to be resold by a retail store. In a department store, especially, the *buyer* for a department is the person in charge of all of the operations of the department. He not only decides what merchandise to buy, but arranges for its display, plans for sales, advertising promotion, training of sales personnel, etc. See also PURCHASING AGENT.

buyers' market. A descriptive term for the situation in which supply is greater than demand, so that the buyers in a particular market tend to set the prices and terms of sale. Hence, a market characterized by low or falling prices. It is the opposite of a SELLERS' MARKET.

buyer's option. See OPTION (1, 2).

buyers' strike. A term describing the situation in which relatively large numbers of potential buyers for a class of products, or for goods in general, refrain from buying in normal quantities as a protest, conscious or unconscious, against the high level of prices.

buying. In general, the process of obtaining title to goods by PURCHASE. More particularly, the activity of obtaining the needed materials, goods, services, and supplies for a business operation. The normal activities of a BUYER or PURCHASING AGENT.

buying agent. See under AGENT.

buying in. The buying of property at an auction or foreclosure sale by the original owner, or by a party with an interest in the property or the proceeds of the sale. For example, if bidding at an auction does not produce a high enough price to make selling worth the owner's while, he may *buy in* the property by placing a bid himself. Similarly, if the assets of an industrial company or railroad are being auctioned in a foreclosure sale, it is common for the property to be *bought in* by the bond holders or other creditors of the business. See also BID IN.

buying office. The name for an agency or office maintained by a number of retail stores, to do joint buying of merchandise for all of the stores. A *buying office* may be an independent business, serving a number of stores as separate customers, but passing on to all any benefits of its volume buying operations, or it may be one serving the member stores of a CHAIN. The latter type is usually known as an *associated buying office.*

buying power. See PURCHASING POWER.

buy on a scale. See ON A SCALE.

buy out. To purchase all of the assets, stock, etc. of a going business; to purchase the interest in a business which someone else owns. For example, an outsider may *buy out* the owners of a going business, and take over its operation, or one partner in a business may *buy out* the interest of another partner and take over a larger share, or all, of the business.

by-bidder. A term for a person who is engaged to make fictitious bids at an auction, on behalf of the owner or seller of the goods, for the purpose of obtaining a higher price or to stimulate additional bidding. See also PUFFER.

by-law. One of a set of rules enacted or adopted by a private organization for its own government or control. A *by-law* is never a public law or regulation, but always a private rule. Examples include the *by-laws* of FRATERNAL SOCIETIES, CORPORATIONS, etc.

by-product. A product which is produced more or less incidentally to the manufacture of another principal product. An example is the glycerine produced in soap-making operations, or the coke produced in the manufacture of illuminating gas. It is distinguished from a JOINT PRODUCT, which is the result of a manufacturing process specifically designed to result in more than one finished product.

C

C.A.A. See CIVIL AERONAUTICS ADMINISTRATION.

C.A.B. See CIVIL AERONAUTICS BOARD.

cable. 1. A unit of length in marine measure, originally 100 fathoms, 200 yards, or roughly one tenth of a nautical mile. Now, however, the U.S. Navy standard *cable* length of 120 FATHOMS or 240 yards is more widely used.

2. A cablegram; a message sent by telegraph *cable,* especially across the Atlantic between the United States and Europe.

3. In business usage, a CABLE TRANSFER, or similar credit instrument arranged through a cablegram.

cable address. A coded address, used for indicating the delivery address of CABLE messages in abbreviated form. For example, the *cable address* for Thomas Y. Crowell Company is TYCROWELL, NEW YORK.

cable credit. A commercial LETTER OF CREDIT authorized by cablegram.

cable transfer. A method for putting funds in the immediate possession of a person in a foreign country, using a cablegram. The funds are, deposited with a local bank in the name of the person to receive the funds, and the bank cables instructions to a correspondent bank in the foreign country, to make the funds available to the person in question. A similar cable is sent to the person receiving the funds, instructing him to call for them at the bank.

cabotage. Originally, from the French, coastwise navigation and shipping, as distinguished from ocean trade. Today, in air transport, domestic operations as opposed to international operations.

C.A.F. See COST AND FREIGHT.

calendar day. See under DAY.

calendar month. Any of the twelve months into which the year is divided, with the number of days assigned to the month by the calendar, rather than 30 days, as in the usual business month. The elapsed time from any date of one month to the corresponding date in the next month, regardless of the exact number of intervening days. See also MONTH.

calendar year. The period of 365 days (366 in leap year) from January 1 through December 31 in any year, as distinguished from a FISCAL YEAR, which runs from the first day of any month to the last day of the preceding month in the next year.

calends. In the Roman calendar, the first day of any month, as distinguished from the IDES, or middle day of the month. See also NONES.

call. 1. In the securities trade, a written agreement representing an option to buy a named security on or before a specified date at a given price. In effect, the buyer of a *call* is betting its price that the stock will go up in value. See also PUT; STRADDLE.

2. An assessment of shareholders in a corporation to pay in additional capital, usually up to the subscribed value of the capital stock.

3. To redeem; to *call* in for redemption, as a bond or loan.

callable. A term denoting that a security or obligation is subject to being redeemed, or paid in full, by the issuer at any time on due notice, before the date of maturity (if it carries a maturity date). The security itself usually carries the notice, subject to call, or subject to redemption. See also REDEEM; BOND (1), CALLABLE.

callable stock. See STOCK (1), REDEEMABLE.

call-back pay. Extra pay due to an employee who is required to return to work after leaving at the end of his regular shift, such as for emergency maintenance work. It is usually set at some minimum amount, such as an hour's pay, and paid at a premium above the regular rate of pay.

called bond. See under BOND (1).

calling. Literally, a vocation; hence any business, occupation, or profession.

call-in pay. The pay due an employee who reports for work at his regular time, or who is called in for work, and then finds that there is no work to do. The amount is usually set at a certain number of hours' pay, such as four hours or half a regular shift.

call loan. See under LOAN.

call, margin. See under MARGIN (2).

call money. Borrowed money which is returnable on the *call* or demand of the lender. Also, money or credit which is available for lending on this basis.

call note. See NOTE (1), DEMAND.

calorie. In the metric system, the unit of measurement for heat. The *calorie* used in measuring the heat energy equivalent of various foods is the *great calorie* or *kilogram-calorie*, defined as the amount of heat required to raise the temperature of one kilogram (or liter) of water one degree centigrade. The *small* or *gram-calorie*, used in chemical and physical research, is the amount of heat required to raise one gram of water one degree centigrade. The comparable unit in the English system of measurement is the BRITISH THERMAL UNIT (B.T.U.), which is the amount of heat required to raise the temperature of one pound of water one degree Fahrenheit. One *kilogram-calorie* equals 3.968 B.T.U.

cambist. One who deals in foreign notes and bills of exchange, and exchanges foreign money. Also, a handbook in which the currencies of various countries are converted into the currency of the country for which the handbook is issued.

cancel. To obliterate, or to cross out, as a record or report. To revoke or recall, as an order or directive. Also, to wipe out by paying, as a debt or obligation. See also ANNUL.

canceled check. See under CHECK (1).

canvass. To count or examine, as, for example, to count the vote of the shareholders of a corporation in an election of directors. Also, to examine, or to go through a particular area. For example, an area may be *canvassed* by a salesman soliciting orders for merchandise.

capacity. 1. In accounting and industrial usage, the ability of a plant to produce at a given level. The output possible with the available amounts of plant, equipment, machinery, and personnel committed to production.

2. In transport, the amount of freight or cargo which can be carried by a freight car, truck, vessel, etc., usually measured either in cubic *capacity* or TONNAGE.

3. In law, competency or legal authority; as, the *capacity* to enter into an agreement.

capital. 1. In general, wealth, especially in the form of property or equipment which can be used in the production or creation of value. In the broadest sense, it is the stock of funds or valuable assets possessed by any person or business. In classical economics, it is one of the three factors of production, the other two being labor and land.

2. In corporate finance, the money or assets contributed to a business by the owners or stockholders, to be used in the conduct of the business. Together with SURPLUS, it constitutes the owners' NET WORTH in the business. The principal classifications of business *capital* are listed and defined below.

authorized $\sim$. With respect to a corporation or limited liability company, the total value of the shares of *capital* stock which the business authorizes itself to issue. See also STOCK (1), AUTHORIZED.

equity $\sim$. A term for that portion of the funds to be used in a business which have been invested by the owners, rather than loaned by creditors. Loosely, any security, such as common stock, representing ownership in a business.

invested $\sim$. A term sometimes used to represent the total of cash and assets paid into a business plus all earned surplus turned back into the business. Thus, it is a synonym for the NET WORTH of the business.

nominal $\sim$. In a corporation with par value stock, the total par value of the authorized stock of the corporation, as distinguished from the actual value of the SUBSCRIBED CAPITAL, which see below. See also STOCK (1), PAR VALUE.

paid-in $\sim$. See SUBSCRIBED CAPITAL, below.

paid-up $\sim$. A term for the total amount which has been paid on shares of *capital* stock, when the total par value or NOMINAL CAPITAL, which see above, has not been paid in full.

risk $\sim$. See VENTURE CAPITAL, below.

subscribed $\sim$. The total amount of money which is promised, or guaranteed, by the shareholders of a business. When the total *subscribed capital* has been contributed, it is usually known as the *paid-in capital*.

venture $\sim$. A term for the funds invested by shareholders or owners in a business enterprise in which there is a relatively large element of risk. More broadly, any investment in a business enterprise. It is sometimes known as *risk capital*.

3. That part of the assets of a business which are invested in the conduct of the business, and which are therefore the source of the profits of the business. The principal types of such *capital* are listed and defined below. See also ASSET, CAPITAL.

active $\sim$. That *capital* being actively used in the conduct of the business, including both the WORKING CAPITAL, which see below, and that FIXED CAPITAL, which see below, which is invested in profit-contributing assets.

circulating ∽. A term for the *capital* invested in current assets, such as inventories, accounts receivable, and cash funds. It is sometimes known as the *current capital,* or gross WORKING CAPITAL, which see below.

current ∽. See CIRCULATING CAPITAL, above.

fixed ∽. The *capital* invested in fixed assets, or assets of a permanent nature, such as land, building, machinery, equipment, etc., as distinguished from CIRCULATING CAPITAL, which see above, or WORKING CAPITAL, which see below. See also GOODS, CAPITAL.

floating ∽. A term for that portion of *capital* which is temporarily invested, such as in work in process, materials, finished goods, etc., and which will become available for other investment.

gross working ∽. See CIRCULATING CAPITAL, above.

working ∽. In general, that *capital* being used in the conduct of the business, to buy materials, pay wages, etc., as distinguished from the *capital* invested in fixed assets, or FIXED CAPITAL, which see above. Specifically, as used in accounting, it is the excess of total current assets over total current liabilities, or the *net working capital*. See also CIRCULATING CAPITAL, above.

capital amount. With respect to an amount invested at interest, the original amount, or the PRINCIPAL.

capital asset. See under ASSET (2).

capital budget. See under BUDGET.

capital equipment. See under EQUIPMENT.

capital expenditure. An expenditure for plant, or for equipment, rather than for operating expenses. Broadly, any expenditure which adds to the value of the property of a business.

capital gain (or loss). The gain or loss realized from the sale or exchange of a capital asset at a price which is higher or lower than the price originally paid for the asset, or higher or lower than its BASIS. In federal tax regulations, a profit realized from the sale of an asset held less than six months, or a *short-term capital gain,* is not recognized as a *capital gain,* but is treated as regular income for tax purposes. The profits from *long-term capital gains,* or those resulting from the sale of an asset held for six months or longer, are taxed at half the regular rate.

capital goods. See under GOODS (3).

capitalist. A person who invests funds in a productive business enterprise. More broadly, a person who supplies CAPITAL (1), and who employs others to work with the capital to produce a profit. In economics, he is distinguished from the PROLETARIAT, or working class, and from the BOURGEOIS, or self-employed class.

capitalization. 1. The total value of all of the securities, both stocks and bonds, outstanding in a business enterprise. The total amount which would have to be paid off to investors and long term creditors on liquidation of the enterprise.

2. The act or process of converting something into CAPITAL (2), or the act of placing a value on something which produces income or profit. See also CAPITALIZE.

capitalize. In general, to convert into CAPITAL (2). To place a value on something, and to treat it as if it is part of the capital of a business. For example, if a new machine is designed which produces at a rate far in excess of that expected, the increased earning power created by the machine may be *capitalized,* or added to the capital of the business. When such conversions have been made at an excessive rate, or the values assigned have been unreasonably high, a business is said to be *overcapitalized,* and this is usually evidenced by its inability to earn a fair rate of return on its stated capital.

capital liability. See under LIABILITY (2).

capital loss. See CAPITAL GAIN.

capital market. In general, any place or system in which the capital fund requirements of business enterprises can be met. The market in which newly issued securities are bought and sold. Thus, in general, it includes the INVESTMENT BANKING system, the SECURITIES EXCHANGES, etc.

capital outlay. See CAPITAL EXPENDITURE.

capital stock. See STOCK (1).

capital sum. In general, the CAPITAL AMOUNT, or PRINCIPAL. Specifically, in insurance, a term used for the maximum amount which is payable for each type of loss specified in the policy.

capital surplus. See under SURPLUS.

capitation tax. See under TAX (2).

captive mine. A coal mine owned by a railroad or steel company, the output of which is used almost exclusively by the owning company.

carat. 1. A unit of weight, originally Arabian, for the measure of diamonds and other precious stones. Traditionally, one *carat* was 4 grains, but today the international *carat* is 200 milligrams, or about 3.1 grains troy.

2. As a measure of the fineness of gold, one

twenty-fourth part of pure gold. Thus, 24 *carat* gold is pure gold, eighteen *carat* gold is three-fourths pure gold, etc.

car card. An advertisement or poster designed to be displayed in street cars, buses, subways, rapid transit cars, etc. See also ADVERTISING, TRANSIT.

cargo. Literally, from the Italian, a load or charge. Thus, the merchandise or freight carried by a vessel, other than supplies for the passengers or crew. In general, it may be classified as *special cargo,* consisting of one specialized commodity, such as oil, lumber, etc., or as *general cargo,* consisting of mixed and varied commodities, such as might normally be carried in foreign trade.

cargo tonnage. See under TONNAGE.

carload. In railroad freight, the amount of a commodity or product that will fill a freight car, or the amount that is sufficient to be treated as if it filled a car. If a standard car will carry 30,000 lbs. of an item, for example, 20,000 lbs. or more may qualify as a *carload.*

~ **lot.** A shipment which is of sufficient quantity to be treated as a *carload,* and to be carried at the *carload* rate; as distinguished from a LESS-THAN-CARLOAD lot.

~ **rate.** The FREIGHT RATE charged for *carload* lots. This is usually considerably lower than the rate per pound for less-than-carload lots.

carloading company. See under FORWARDER.

carloadings. A statistic used to measure rail freight activity, and as an indicator of general business activity. It is the number of freight cars loaded during a specified period of time on one railroad or on a number of railroads. The Association of American Railroads collects and issues data on the number of *carloadings* of revenue freight weekly on all Class I (and some Class II) railroads. These are classified into eight freight categories and according to eight geographic regions.

car-mile. A statistic used in measuring transportation activity. It represents the movement of one car, passenger or freight, a distance of one mile. Thus, the movement of a ten car train for ten miles creates one hundred *car-miles.*

carriage. The charge made, such as by a railroad, for carrying goods from one place to another.

carrier. 1. A person or company who undertakes to transport passengers or goods from one place to another.

common ~. A *carrier,* usually operating under public franchise or regulation, who offers to carry any person or goods for payment. A *common carrier* may restrict the classes of passengers or goods carried, but must accept all business offered in these classes. Railroads, barge lines, motor truck freight haulers, bus lines, pipelines, etc. are *common carriers.*

contract ~. As *carrier* who offers his services under contract, either on a one-trip basis, or for a period of time. Many motor truck freight *carriers* operate as *contract carriers.*

2. In insurance, the company which bears or carries the risk; an UNDERWRITER; an INSURANCE COMPANY.

carry. 1. To transport or convey; to haul.

2. In accounting, to transfer a sum or balance; to CARRY FORWARD.

3. To maintain a stock of merchandise for sale. To offer for sale the goods of a particular manufacturer, as, to *carry* a brand.

4. To extend credit, or to hold off demand for payment on a debt; to accommodate.

carry-back. A provision of the Internal Revenue Code, which allows individuals or corporations, under specified circumstances, to use operating or capital losses incurred in one year to offset operating or capital profits in a subsequent or preceding year, and thus reduce taxes. Actually, therefore, the losses may be either *carried back* or forward, but the same general term is applied in both cases.

carry forward. In accounting, to transfer a sum or balance from one page, ledger, or accounting period to the next, or to any later one.

carrying charge. 1. The continuing cost of owning or holding property or goods, such as rental, taxes, insurance, interest, maintenance, etc.

2. In retail credit, the charge paid by the buyer for the privilege of paying in installments, aside from any interest charge on the unpaid balance. A service charge.

3. In the securities trade, the interest charged by a broker on the difference between the amount of MARGIN deposited and the purchase price of the security, when securities are purchased on margin.

carry-over. See CARRY-BACK.

cartage. The charge made by railroads or other common carriers for the local hauling of goods, such as for pick-up and delivery service, or for hauling to shipside.

carte blanche. From the French, literally, a blank check. Instructions or orders conferring unlimited authority or discretion of action. In securities and commodities trading, for example, a *carte blanche* ORDER (4) is one giving the broker or agent unlimited authority in buying or selling.

cartel. Literally, a small card, and later one with writing; thus any written agreement, such as one for the exchange of prisoners, or one made between political parties. In business, primarily in European usage, an agreement between business organizations to control the prices, production, or marketing of a product or an industry. Also, the group of organizations itself, as the steel *cartel.* A TRUST (2).

car trust bond. See BOND (1), EQUIPMENT TRUST.

cart wheel. In popular usage, a United States silver dollar, so called because of its large, unwieldy size.

cash. 1. In general, any ready money or legal tender, including coins and paper money. Sometimes, in a narrow sense, coins only, as in the phrase, *cash* and bills.

2. In accounting, money and negotiable instruments which are readily convertible into money, including bank deposits, drafts, money orders, travelers' checks, cashier's checks, certified checks, etc.

3. As a term of sales, any of a variety of conditions calling for payment before, at the time of, or immediately after the delivery of goods. In many lines of trade, *cash* terms has come to mean that payment is to be made after a certain number of days, with or without a discount allowed for earlier payment. Thus, such terms as NET *cash* and SPOT *cash* have been introduced to specify the original meaning of immediate *cash* payment required. See also TERMS OF SALE.

4. To convert an instrument into money, as, to *cash* a check, to *cash* a coupon or warrant, etc. See also each of the following under the principal listing: ∼ ACCOUNT (4); ∼ ASSET (2); ∼ BUDGET; ∼ CREDIT (3); ∼ DISCOUNT (1); ∼ DIVIDEND.

cash against documents. In the export trade, a term meaning that the buyer must make payment for the goods before the shipping documents which will give him control of the goods are surrendered to him.

cash and carry. In retail selling, a method of operation under which the customer pays cash for his purchases, which he must take with him or pay to have delivered. More generally, a *cash and carry* operation is one in which none of the many store services, such as credit, free delivery, extended return privileges, etc. are offered.

cash basis accounting. A method of accounting under which income and expenses are charged to the period in which the actual payment is made or received, rather than to the period in which they are earned or incurred. The opposite of ACCRUAL BASIS ACCOUNTING.

cash before delivery (C.B.D.). A sales term indicating that payment is required before the goods are delivered. See also TERMS OF SALE.

cash book. In accounting practice, a JOURNAL (1) or book of original entry in which are recorded all cash transactions. In practice, the *cash book* is usually divided into two books, the cash receipts journal and the cash disbursements journal. Each is usually set up in columns, to classify the various types of transactions. The receipts journal, for example, may contain columns for gross sales, allowances, net sales, miscellaneous receipts, etc., while the disbursements journal may provide for merchandise purchases, supplies, payroll, etc.

cash collection. See CASH ITEM.

cash disbursement basis. A method of recording and dating expenditures under which the expenditure is considered to be made when the actual disbursement of cash is made to pay the check presented, rather than when the check is originally written. See also CHECKS-ISSUED BASIS; DAILY TREASURY STATEMENT BASIS.

cash disbursements journal. See CASH BOOK.

cashier. The person in a business organization who is charged with the duties and responsibilities of taking in and paying out cash, and for the care of all cash on hand. In a bank, the officer who is charged with the direct responsibility for the bank's assets, and sometimes, especially in small banks, for the administration of the bank.

cashier's check. See under CHECK (1).

cash in. To turn in for cash; to convert rights or property into money; to realize a cash profit on an investment.

cash in advance. A sales term indicating that the buyer must make payment in full before the goods will be shipped, although not necessarily before they are manufactured to his order. If shipping costs are to be borne by the buyer, these are usually included in the advance payment required. See also TERMS OF SALE.

cash in bank. A balance sheet term, indicating money which has been deposited in banks and which can be freely withdrawn to meet current needs. See also CASH ON HAND.

cash item. In banking, a deposit item, such as cash, certified checks, or certain other checks which will be immediately credited to the depositor's balance, as distinguished from those deposit items, such as personal checks, which will be credited to his balance only when they have been presented for payment and the funds collected by the bank. These latter are known as COLLECTION ITEMS. Those items for which a bank is willing to give immediate credit, though they must actually be collected, such as some drafts, acceptances, etc., are known as cash collections.

cash journal. See CASH BOOK.

cash on delivery (C.O.D.). A term commonly used in selling, indicating that payment is to be made when the merchandise is delivered. In retail trade, such terms are used to cover purchases made by customers who do not wish to pay at the time of buying, or who order by mail or telephone, but who do not maintain a charge account or other credit arrangement. In industrial selling, these terms are usually used when selling to a customer whose credit rating is poor, or has not yet been established. See also TERMS OF SALE.

cash on hand. A balance sheet term, indicating the cash that is immediately available. In this sense, cash includes currency, bank notes, money orders, and similar negotiable instruments that are readily accepted as money. As often stated, the term is, *cash on hand and in banks,* recognizing the fact that the modern business does not keep its cash assets literally on hand.

cash on receipt of merchandise. In export trade, a sales term indicating that while the shipping documents are sent directly to the buyer, he does not pay until the merchandise itself is received.

cash position. The state or degree of liquidity of a business; the relative amount of quick assets. A balance sheet is spoken of as showing a strong or weak *cash position,* depending on the relative amount of current assets which are in cash or are readily convertible into cash. See also OPERATING RATIO.

cash receipts journal. See CASH BOOK.

cash register. A business machine used primarily in retailing, to total and record the amount of each sale, and to store the cash taken in from customers. Modern *cash registers* provide an itemized receipt for the customer, and may contain several internal tapes or dials for recording separate totals of sales made in various categories or by various salesmen.

cash reserve value. See RESERVE VALUE.

cash sale. 1. In retail selling, a SALE (1) in which immediate cash payment is made at the time of purchase, as distinguished from a credit, charge account, or c.o.d. sale.

2. In industrial or wholesale selling, a sale for which payment is to be made within a stated period of time, such as within 10 or 30 days, or by the end of the month, or by the tenth day of the following month. See also TERMS OF SALE.

3. In the law of contracts, a sale which is completed, and in which title passes, upon payment of the price asked; as distinguished from a conditional sale.

cash statement. An accounting statement drawn up periodically, showing the cash balances in a business, and summarizing cash receipts and disbursement.

cash surrender value. In insurance, the amount due to an insured under a life insurance contract, should he at a given time decide to surrender or cancel his contract. The *cash surrender value* after any number of years is usually stated in the policy. The amount is determined by the RESERVE VALUE built up by the payment of premiums over and above the amount needed to buy pure term insurance, less any SURRENDER CHARGE made by the insurance company.

cash value. See VALUE (2), MARKET.

cash with order. A term used in sales contracts, directing that the buyer must make payment when he places his order with the vendor. Such terms are used in mail-order selling, and sometimes when selling for the first time to a customer whose credit rating cannot be established. See also TERMS OF SALE.

cask. In general, any large barrel. As a measure of quantity, the amount contained in a *cask.* It is a measure of variable amount, depending on the commodity.

cast up. To compute, or to add up to a total; as, to *cast up* an account.

casual employment. Occasional, irregular, or temporary employment, as distinguished from regular employment. See also EMPLOYMENT.

casualty. An unforeseen event, one not to be guarded against. An ACCIDENT.

casualty insurance. See under INSURANCE, CASUALTY AND LIABILITY.

casual worker. A worker who has no regular or steady employment. Such workers frequently move from one part of the country to another to meet seasonal or fluctuating demands for employment. Typically, *casual workers* have no seniority or other status rights with either employers or unions.

catalog. In business, a listing of the products or services available for sale. In industrial selling, *catalogs* are widely used, but in retail trade they are used primarily by firms specializing in this type of selling.

~ **house.** A type of wholesale distributor, which operates by placing sales *catalogs* in the hands of retailers, from which the retailer's customers make their selections. The retailer carries no stock, but places orders for the selected items with the wholesaler, which orders are delivered either to the retailer or directly to the customer.

mail-order ~. A *catalog* from which customers may order merchandise by mail, for delivery direct from the distributor of the *catalog.* See also RETAILER, NON-STORE.

catching a bargain. The making of an agreement whereby one who is expecting a legacy or inheritance transfers his rights to another for cash, usually in a smaller amount than the value of the expected legacy. Such agreements may be voided on grounds of the gross inadequacy of the cash consideration offered, or on grounds of fraud, deceit, or concealment on the part of the one who offers the consideration. It is sometimes called a catch-bargain, or a catching bargain.

cats and dogs. In securities trade usage, shares which are highly speculative and of low investment quality. In commerce generally, merchandise items which do not have satisfactory sales turnover, and which accumulate in inventory; DEAD STOCK.

cattle paper. See under COMMERCIAL PAPER.

causa mortis. In Latin, in contemplation of death. Under tax law, for example, certain actions taken in contemplation of death, such as the transfer of property, are considered to be void for purposes of computing estate taxes.

cause. In law, that which produces an observed result or effect. The law recognizes several classifications of *causes,* which are listed and defined below.

immediate ~. That *cause,* or causal factor, which is nearest in time, though not necessarily in effect, to the produced result. For example, if a cable breaks and a piece of equipment falls, striking an employee, the *immediate cause* of the employee's injury is being struck by the equipment. In effect, the *immediate cause* is the last INTERVENING CAUSE, which see below.

intervening ~. Any independent act or condition coming between an original wrongful act, or ORIGINAL CAUSE, which see below, and a resulting damage or injury, in such a way that the injury is due to the *intervening cause,* among others, even though the original *cause* might have produced an injury alone. In this case, for example, if the original *cause* was the overloading of the cable,

intervening causes might include the breaking of the cable, the presence of the employee in an unauthorized place, his being struck by the equipment, etc.

original ~. The first or basic factor in a series of *causes,* which might not have produced the damage or injury itself, but without which the loss would not have occurred. In this case, the *original cause* might be said to be the overloading of the cable.

proximate ~. The *cause* which, in a natural and unbroken sequence of events, is responsible for an injury or damage. It is the last negligent act committed, and therefore the *cause* closest to the result in order of effect, though not necessarily in time. There may be more than one *proximate cause* for the same loss. In this case, it might be held that the employee's presence in an unauthorized place was the last negligent act, and therefore the *proximate cause* of the loss.

cause of action. See under ACTION (1).

caveat. 1. In Latin, let him beware. Any written notice, warning, or caution, the main purpose of which is to provide an opportunity for the giver of the notice to be heard before a matter is decided or an action is completed. In a financial transaction, it is usually a notice to stop payment.

2. In law, a written warning issued by a court, sometimes at the request of a party to an action. Usually, it is a notice to some judicial or adminstrative officer to stop, refrain from, or delay some action in which the court or other CAVEATOR is interested, until further order. In probate cases, for example, it is used to defer the appointment of an administrator until the caveator can be heard.

caveat emptor. In Latin, let the buyer beware. A rule in English and American common law that the purchaser buys at his own risk in the absence of any express WARRANTY, or unless the law implies a seller's warranty. For example, a buyer has the right to expect that merchandise will be as described, and will be in good condition.

caveator. One who sends or files a CAVEAT.

caveat venditor. In Latin, let the seller beware, a phrase which gained currency at the time of the enactment of the Securities Act of 1933. In his message of March 29, 1933, President Roosevelt wrote of this act, "It adds to the ancient rule of CAVEAT EMPTOR the further doctrine let the seller also beware. It puts the burden of telling the whole truth on the seller."

cease and desist. An order issued by a court or governmental agency, calling on a person or company to stop some activity. For example, the Federal Trade Commission may issue an order to a company to stop some unfair competitive practice, or the National Labor Relations Board may issue an order to *cease and desist* from some unfair labor practice.

cede. 1. In general, to yield, to grant, or give up; to assign, as rights or income.

2. In insurance, to reduce the risk of loss by transferring all or part of the liability assumed as an insurer to another insurance company. See also REINSURANCE.

ceiling. A maximum, especially one fixed or allowed by law or regulation, as in time of war. Examples include *ceiling* prices, wages, rents, etc. See also PRICE, CEILING.

cellarage. A charge for storage or warehousing, especially of wines or liquors.

cent. In United States coinage, the minor coin valued at one hundredth part of a DOLLAR. The coin itself is made of a copper-base alloy. Previously, the cent was not, strictly speaking, LEGAL TENDER, but since 1934 all coins have been full legal tender.

cental. See HUNDREDWEIGHT.

center spread. An advertisement or editorial matter occupying the two central facing pages of a magazine or newspaper.

centi-. In the METRIC SYSTEM, the prefix used for any unit of measure which is one-hundredth of a basic unit. It is now also frequently used for any unit which is one-hundredth of another, whether or not in the metric system. Examples include the centigram, centimeter, etc.

centigrade. In general, divided into 100 divisions or degrees. The scale of temperature used in the metric system and in scientific research, in which 0° is set at the freezing point of water, and 100° at its boiling point. See also FAHRENHEIT SCALE.

centner. See HUNDREDWEIGHT.

central bank. See under BANK.

centralization. Concentration. The bringing into a central point, or under one system or control. For example, the *centralization* of industry refers to the concentration of industry in one or a few areas, and the *centralization* of authority refers to the concentration of managerial or other power in one person or a small group.

central reserve bank. See under BANK.

central reserve city. See FEDERAL RESERVE SYSTEM.

central trades and labor council. An organization of all of the local UNIONS in a city, or in a metropolitan area. Formerly, it was made up of those unions belonging to the American Federation of Labor, but since the merger

with the Congress of Industrial Organizations, local unions of both groups are eligible to join.

certificate. 1. A formal, written statement, giving assurance that some act or event has or has not occurred, that some requirement has been met or will be met, etc. A statement made by a person having either public or private authority to do so, concerning the truth or existence of some matter.

2. A form of United States paper money, issued against gold or silver deposited in the Treasury. *Gold certificates* are now issued only for use within the Federal Reserve System, to transfer balances, and not for circulation. *Silver certificates* are widely circulated in small denominations, making up a large proportion of all one-dollar bills in use, and are full legal tender. Each bears the statement; "This certifies that there is on deposit in the Treasury of the United States of America one dollar (for example) in silver payable to the bearer on demand." Thus they are, in effect, negotiable warehouse receipts for the metal on deposit in the Treasury.

certificate of beneficial interest. One representing a share of the ownership of a business, when such ownership has been deposited with a trustee. The holder of the certificate receives the income from, and retains an interest in the assets of the business, but gives up management power. It is used when a business is operated as a TRUST (3).

certificate of deposit. A transferable or negotiable receipt from a bank, stating that a certain sum of money has been placed in a special deposit, against which checks or withdrawals cannot be made. The certificate is payable by the bank, and may be either a demand certificate, payable on demand, or a time certificate, payable on or after a stated future date. In the latter case, the certificate usually bears interest.

certificate of incorporation. A statement filed, under the laws of the particular state, by persons wishing to form a CORPORATION. Ordinarily it includes, among other things, the name of the proposed corporation, its purpose, the amount and kind of capital stock, the number and names of the officers and directors, the location of the corporate offices, etc. When it has been properly filed with and approved by the Secretary of State or other appropriate officer of the state, it is commonly known as the corporation charter, or its ARTICLES OF INCORPORATION.

certificate of indebtedness. In general, any formal written acknowledgement of a debt. Specifically, the short-term, interest-bearing negotiable obligations of the United States Treasury which are known by this term.

certificate of insurance. A written statement to the effect that an insurance POLICY has been written covering a particular risk, and containing a summary of the terms of the policy. Such a *certificate of insurance* may be filed as proof of insurance, when required by law.

certificate of manufacture. A non-negotiable document, used in foreign trade. It is a statement, signed by an exporter or by the beneficiary of a LETTER OF CREDIT, declaring that the particular goods ordered by the importer have been manufactured and are ready for shipment in accordance with the terms of the credit, and have been set apart for the account of the importer.

certificate of necessity. A certificate issued by a federal agency, for example during time of war, stating that the construction or purchase of a given building, plant, or item of equipment is considered necessary to the national defense. Such a certificate may grant a priority in the acquisition of materials, and permit accelerated depreciation of the property.

certificate of origin. A statement which must be submitted by an importer, certifying the country of origin of imported goods. Unless the goods themselves are clearly marked, this certificate must accompany the goods in domestic trade after they are imported.

certificate of participation. One sometimes issued by an INVESTMENT COMPANY, in place of shares of stock, as evidence of a proportionate interest owned by the certificate holder in the various securities owned by the company. Also, a certificate issued to a person who participates in a mortgage or bond loan. Each purchaser of a portion of the mortgage or bond is issued a *certificate of participation*, stating the extent of his fractional interest.

certificate of registry. One issued by the proper registration authority of a port or country, indicating the name, tonnage, owner, etc., of a vessel, and serving to certify the nationality of the vessel.

certification. 1. In banking, an assurance by a bank that the drawer of a check has sufficient funds on deposit to meet payment on the check, and that the funds have been set aside to meet the check when presented. The *certification* is usually written or stamped across the face of the check in the terms, good when endorsed, certified, or a similar phrase, with the date and the signature of a proper official. See also CHECK, CERTIFIED.
  2. The assurance by some public or private

officer that a condition exists, a requirement has been met, an act performed, etc. The granting of a license or franchise to do business, engage in trade, or undertake some other activity.
  3. In COLLECTIVE BARGAINING, the statement by the National Labor Relations Board or an equivalent state agency that a particular union is designated as the representative of the employees in a bargaining unit.

certification mark. See under TRADEMARK.

certified check. See under CHECK (1).

certified copy. See ATTESTED COPY.

certified mail. See under POSTAL SERVICE.

certified public accountant. See under ACCOUNTANT.

certiorari. Literally, in Latin, certified. A writ issued by a higher or superior court, directing a lower or inferior court to certify and pass up to the higher court some pending proceeding, or all the records of a case, for review of the propriety or legality of the procedure or decision of the lower court.

cestui que trust. In law, a French adaptation of a Latin phrase, now meaning the person for whose benefit a TRUST has been created; a BENEFICIARY.

chain. 1. In surveying, a measure of length, equal to 66 feet, 22 yards, or 4 rods. It is divided into 100 LINKS, each 7.92 inches long.
  2. In engineering, a measure of distance equal to 100 feet, divided into 100 links of one foot each.
  3. In business, a group of stores, newspapers, radio, or television stations, etc. which are associated under a common management or common ownership, and follow a common policy. The member units may be owned by a single organization, or they may be independently owned, as in a VOLUNTARY CHAIN, which see.

chain banking. See under BANKING.

chain discount. See under DISCOUNT (1).

chain store. See under RETAIL STORE.

chairman of the board. The highest executive officer of a corporation which is governed by a board of directors and chairman. In a corporation in which the directors, acting as a board, elect a chairman, he is the top policy-making officer of the corporation, ranking higher than the president. In some corporations, the president may also hold the title of *chairman of the board.*

chamber of commerce. A local, state, national, or international association of business and professional men and organizations, formed for the purpose of protecting and promoting the interests of the business community, and of the areas, regions, or trades in which they are organized. In various localities, the *chamber of commerce* may be known as a board of trade, commerce and industry association, or similar name. Over 3,000 such local organizations are affiliated with the United States Chamber of Commerce.

chancery. A corruption of chancellery; presided over by a chancellor; hence a court of EQUITY. The usage is primarily English, and is used in the United States only in a few special terms. See, for example, MASTER IN CHANCERY.

change. 1. The amount of money returned to a payer who offers a larger sum of money in payment than is required. For example, a buyer may offer a one-dollar bill in payment for a 79-cent item, and receive 21 cents in *change*. Hence, any small coins less than one dollar are popularly known as *change,* or *small change*.

2. In general, any alteration, modification, or substitution, such as might be made in the text of a regulation, in the terms of an agreement, etc.

3. In its several uses, a contraction for EXCHANGE.

change of venue. See under VENUE.

channel of distribution. The route or method by which goods are distributed from the original grower, manufacturer, or importer to the final consumer. Also, the various businesses which are part of the distribution operation, such as wholesale distributors, retail dealers, etc. For example, the typical *channel of distribution* for packaged food products is from manufacturer or processor to food wholesaler or jobber, to retail grocer, and finally to the individual consumer. The usual *channel of distribution* for automobiles, on the other hand, is from manufacturer to franchised retail agency, to final purchaser.

chapel. In some unions, such as those in the printing trades, a membership unit consisting of the union members in a single shop or plant. It is a smaller unit than a UNION LOCAL, and is usually subordinate to a local, which may include all of the shops in a given branch of the industry in a city or region.

Charga-plate. See CHARGE PLATE.

charge. 1. A money demand made by one party upon another, in return for goods sold, work done, or services rendered, in accordance with an agreement; the price demanded.

2. In accounting, a cost or expense allocated or assigned to a specific account; a DEBIT to an account.

3. In law, the instructions given to a jury by a presiding judge, specifying the limitations under which they may deliberate, the various verdicts which they may reach, and the weight they are to give to various items of testimony or evidence.

4. To buy for credit, or without making immediate payment. One who instructs a retailer to *charge* a purchase usually means that he wishes the cost of the purchase to be added to his monthly or periodic account. See also ACCOUNT (4), CHARGE.

charge off. To reduce the value at which an asset is carried; to treat as an expense. To treat an uncollected or uncollectable debt as a loss; to write off. For example, a business may periodically *charge off* as operating losses accounts which are unpaid for a long period of time.

charge plate. In retail selling, a metal or plastic plate, bearing a stencil of a charge customer's name, address, and charge account number, used as a means of identification in making charge purchases. In many stores, a special device is maintained at each cash register in which the plate is inserted to stamp the customer's name and other information on the sales check at the time of purchase. The plates are often known by the trade name of a particular style of plate, the *Charga-plate*.

charges forward. A term used in price quotations, meaning that the buyer is to pay the shipping charges, insurance, etc., upon receipt of the goods. Essentially it is the same as quoting a price F.O.B. FACTORY. The comparable term used in the shipping documents is FREIGHT FORWARD, or FREIGHT COLLECT.

charitable trust. See under TRUST (1).

charter. 1. In business, an authority conferred upon a company or organization by special act of Congress or of a state legislature, defining the special purposes and prescribing the privileges conferred on the company. It is typical, for example, for non-profit corporations such as veterans' organizations, trade associations, charitable corporations, and others to apply for and receive *charters*.

2. In common but incorrect usage, the CERTIFICATE OF INCORPORATION of a business corporation.

3. In maritime law, the lease of a vessel for one or more voyages, or a contract for the use of all or part of the cargo space on a vessel for a single voyage or for a period of time. See also CHARTER PARTY.

   bare boat ∼. One under which the ship owner provides only the ship itself, and the charterer provides the personnel, equipment, insurance, and other materials and expenses needed for the operation of the ship during the period of the *charter* or lease. When one steamship line *charters* a ship from another, it is usually on a *bare boat* basis. The opposite of a GROSS CHARTER, which see below.

gross ~. One under which the ship owner is required to pay all expenses and provide all needed personnel and equipment. Under such a *charter* the owner pays all port charges, unloading and loading costs, as well as operating costs, and the charterer pays only a single specified amount for the use of the ship. A ship *chartered* for an excursion, for example, would usually be taken on a *gross charter* basis.

time ~. One under which a ship is leased for a specified period of time, rather than for a particular voyage. Such *charters* are usually, but not necessarily, BARE BOAT CHARTERS, which see above.

trip ~. One under which a ship, or part of a ship, is leased for a single trip or voyage between two specified ports. Such charters are made either as BARE BOAT CHARTERS or GROSS CHARTERS, depending on the particular circumstances.

chartered accountant. See under ACCOUNTANT.

charter party. The contract between a ship owner and one who wishes to use a ship or part of it for a period of time or for a particular voyage. The *charter party* states the rate, terms, and conditions under which the ship is to be chartered, including the route to be followed, the demurrage arrangements, etc. Also, as sometimes used, one of the parties to a *charter party* agreement.

chart of accounts. In accounting, a list or table of the particular accounts used in a business, and to which all costs and expenses are charged. Usually, the various accounts are grouped under logical headings, with detailed accounts listed under the more general accounts in each category. A stationery account, for example, may be listed under the office expense account, and an overtime wages account listed under the direct labor account. Usually, each account in the *chart of accounts* is given a number, indicating the general group to which it belongs.

chasing eighths and quarters. In the securities trade, a colloquial expression for the practice of taking quick, small profits from the day to day fluctuations in the market; taking profits in eighths or quarters of a dollar per share. This practice is typical of the activities of a SCALPER, who trades on his own account, paying no commissions, and thus can afford to take very small profits.

chattel. In law, any PROPERTY except real property. It is a broader term than GOODS, in that it includes such things as livestock, intangible property such as rights, leases, etc., and similar personal property. In documents, the phrase GOODS AND CHATTELS is usually used to make certain that nothing is excepted.

chattel mortgage. A mortgage on personal property. See under MORTGAGE.

chattel mortgage bond. See under BOND (1).

cheap money. See MONEY, EASY.

check. 1. As defined by the Uniform Commercial Code and the Negotiable Instruments Act, a DRAFT or BILL OF EXCHANGE drawn upon a bank, and payable on demand. A *check* is distinguished from other drafts or bills in that it is always payable on demand; always purports to be drawn against funds already on deposit; cannot be withdrawn once signed, except by the act of stopping payment; and needs no act of acceptance to make it valid and payable. The principal types of *check* are listed and defined below.

bad ~. One which has been drawn with the knowledge that there are insufficient funds on deposit to pay it, or that no account exists in the name of the drawer; one which will be refused on presentation, or will bounce.

bank ~. A normal *check*, drawn upon a bank by a depositor. It should not be confused with a bank draft, which is a *check* drawn by one bank upon another. See DRAFT, BANK.

blank ~. One which has been signed but on which the amount payable, and perhaps the name of the payee, has been left blank. It is not unusual, for example, for a trusted agent to be sent to negotiate a bargain with a *blank check* in his possession, to be filled in after the terms of the bargain are set. Hence, any complete and unconditional power to negotiate given to an agent is known as a *blank check*. See also CARTE BLANCHE.

cancelled ~. One which has been paid by a bank, charged against the drawer's account, and then perforated so that it cannot be presented again. The perforations, which are distinctive for each bank, are called the cancellation.

cashier's ~. One drawn by a bank upon itself. It is signed by an authorized officer of the bank, such as the cashier, hence its name. It is distinguished from a CERTIFIED CHECK, which see below, in that it is drawn against the funds of the bank itself, not against the funds in a particular depositor's account, though both imply that the funds are on deposit to meet the *check*. This form of *check* may be issued, for example, to a bank customer who wishes to make a payment by check but who does not have a checking account. He gives the necessary cash to the bank, which gives him the *check* in exchange.

certified ∽. One which has written across its face the name of the proper officer of the bank on which it is drawn, certifying to the signature of the drawer as a depositor of the bank, and to the fact that the funds to meet the *check* are on deposit and have been reserved to make payment. Once a *check* has been *certified,* all holders and endorsers are freed of liability for its payment, and the bank alone is responsible. The certifying bank is absolutely liable for payment of the *check* unless it is later fraudulently raised. Thus, such a *check* is practically the equivalent of money, and is considered as such for many purposes.

counter ∽. One which is kept on hand by a bank for the convenience of depositors, to be used in making withdrawals from the bank, but not for ordinary commercial purposes. It is so named because a supply is usually kept available at the bank counter, and usually has the words *counter check* printed across it.

initialed ∽. One on which the bank cashier or a teller has placed his initials, signifying that the signature of the drawer is valid. This in no way certifies the *check,* however, since it does not attest that funds to meet it are on deposit.

marked ∽. One on which a confidential mark has been made by the company against whose account it is drawn. Many business organizations place a private mark on *checks* when they are written, so that the bank of deposit will challenge any *check* presented without the mark. This is done to prevent the forgery of *checks,* but it is no protection against a RAISED CHECK, which see below.

memorandum ∽. One drawn by a borrower and made payable to his creditor, with the understanding that it will be redeemed by the borrower by the repayment of the loan, and will not be deposited or cashed by the creditor. In some cases, the *memorandum check* may be dated ahead to the due date of the loan, so that the creditor cannot act on it unless and until the loan is not repaid when due.

out-of-town ∽. With respect to any particular bank at which a *check* is presented for deposit or collection, a check drawn on a bank which is located outside the territory of the clearing house with which the collecting bank is identified. Hence, a *check* on which collection must be made by a special transfer. Many banks reserve the right to claim a collection charge for *out-of-town checks.*

postdated ∽. One which is written with a date later than the actual date on which it is made and signed. Such a check is illegal, since it is not a demand instrument but a time promissory note. In many cases, however, *postdated checks* are written, as a form of delayed payment for work not yet accepted or not yet completed.

raised ∽. One on which the amount as originally written has been fraudulently increased. The bank which pays such a *check* is ordinarily responsible for restoring to the depositor the difference between the original amount and the raised amount. Most banks carry insurance to protect them against loss from this occurrence.

register ∽. One prepared by a teller, using funds recorded and set aside in a special register, for the convenience of members of the general public who may desire to make a payment by *check,* but who do not maintain checking accounts. Thus, it is actually a form of MONEY ORDER, prepared in the form of a *check.* It differs from a CASHIER'S CHECK, which see above, which is used primarily for the convenience of regular customers of the bank. The bank charges a small fee for each *register check* sold.

stale ∽. A term used for a *check* which has remained outstanding and unpaid for a considerable period of time, whatever the cause.

travelers' ∽. One which is actually a form of LETTER OF CREDIT. They are sold by most banks, in amounts which are even multiples of ten dollars, for use by persons who do not wish to carry cash or negotiable instruments with them when they travel. The *check* is signed once by the purchaser when bought, and again when it is used to make a payment. Thus, only the original purchaser can use the *check.*

voucher ∽. One which is used in connection with a VOUCHER SYSTEM of accounting. The *check* or an attached stub contains a statement of the particular item for which the *check* is payment, including invoice number, date, and other pertinent information. A copy of this statement is retained for accounting purposes, and serves as the basis for entries in the VOUCHER REGISTER.

2. A brief indication of ownership; an identification ticket or token, such as a *hat check, baggage check,* etc.

3. A summary inspection or test, such as might be made of product quality, worker performance, etc.

checkbook. A book or pad of blank checks supplied by a bank to a depositor, for use by him in drawing checks against his account. Companies using specially designed checks, such as voucher checks, may arrange to supply their own *checkbooks.*

check collection charge. See COLLECTION CHARGE.

checking account. See under ACCOUNT (3).

checkoff. An amount of money deducted in advance by an employer from an employee's pay or wages, to be turned over to a union as dues or to meet a special assessment. Such a deduction may be compulsory or automatic, under an agreement between the employer and the union, or it may be voluntary, at the request of the individual employee. Also, the system under which such a deduction is made. See also UNION SECURITY.

checks-issued basis. A method of recording and dating expenditures in which the expenditure is considered as made when the check is written in payment, rather than at the time the actual disbursement is made to pay the check. In the United States Treasury, government expenditures are recorded on a *checks-issued basis,* but the DAILY TREASURY STATEMENT is issued on a CASH DISBURSEMENT BASIS.

Chicago Board of Trade. The primary commodity market for wheat and other grain products in the United States. It is the trading floor of the Board of Trade that is widely known as the PIT in commodities trading.

Chinese auction. See under AUCTION.

chose. In French, a thing. A term used in some legal phrases, such as a *chose* in action, meaning a RIGHT.

churning. In the securities trade, a term for the practice of creating a large number of transactions in a stock, by such tactics as WASH SALES, as well as by legitimate trading back and forth, with the purpose of giving an impression of a very active market in a particular stock. Speculators may engage in *churning* a stock in order to dispose of large amounts of it to unsuspecting investors who are convinced that the activity foretells a price increase. See also RIGGING.

C.I.F. See COST, INSURANCE, AND FREIGHT.

cipher. 1. A symbol, and hence any symbolic or secret writing; a code. Also, the key to translating or *deciphering* a code.

2. In arabic numerals, the symbol for zero. Hence, a number which is said to be followed by three *ciphers,* for example, is a number counted in thousands.

3. To compute or calculate; to figure arithmetically.

circuit. In the theatrical field, a group of associated theaters; a chain of theaters; a series of theaters in which plays, films, or other productions are shown in turn.

Circuit Court of Appeals. One of a number of three-judge federal courts, established to hear appeals from decisions and rulings of the various federal district courts. The name derives from the fact that the court originally travelled a regular route from district to district hearing appeals. See also FEDERAL COURT SYSTEM.

circular. A letter or notice prepared for wide distribution in quantity; a *circular* letter. A notice or advertisement prepared for wide distribution by mail or by house-to-house circulation; a HANDBILL.

circular letter of credit. See LETTER OF CREDIT, TRAVELER'S.

circular measure. The system of measurement used for measuring relative distances along the circumference of a circle, or of a circular segment. It is also used for measuring angles. In this system, a circle is divided into 360 equal parts called degrees, or four quadrants of 90 degrees each; each degree is divided into 60 minutes, and each minute into 60 seconds.

circular note. See under NOTE (1).

circulating capital. See under CAPITAL (3).

circulating medium. The *circulating medium* of exchange; the recognized means of making payments in ordinary commerce, including coins, currency, bank notes, checks, bills of exchange, notes, etc.; the measures of value by which trade is carried on in any country. See also MEDIUM OF EXCHANGE.

circulation. 1. A term used for the total amount of CURRENCY IN CIRCULATION; the total of the coins, bills, notes, and other instruments accepted as money which are in use at any given time.

2. In banking, the total value of the issued bank notes of a bank which are in use, rather than in reserve in the bank.

3. In publishing, the total number of copies of a given issue of a periodical publication, such as a newspaper or magazine, which are issued, distributed, or sold; the average number of several successive issues which are distributed or sold.

controlled ~. Distribution of a periodical to a list of customers, especially to those who are presumed to be good prospects for the goods and services advertised therein. This form of *circulation* is frequently used for trade and technical magazines, sometimes in addition to PAID CIRCULATION, which see below. Also, the number of copies, or average number of copies of a periodical distributed by this method.

paid ~. The distribution of a periodical publication to customers who pay for it, either by subscription or by purchasing individual copies at newsstands or other places. Also, the number of copies, or average number of copies of a periodical distributed by this method. When the average *paid circulation* for a period of time has been checked or audited by an independent agency, such as the AUDIT BUREAU OF CIRCULATION, it is known as the *net paid circulation.*

circumstantial evidence. See under EVIDENCE.

city item. In banking, a term for a check, draft, or other instrument which is collectible in the territory covered by the local clearing house with which the bank at which it has been presented is associated. It is distinguished from an OUT-OF-TOWN ITEM, which is collectible elsewhere, and on which there may be a collection charge. See also COLLECTION ITEM.

civil action. See under ACTION (1).

Civil Aeronautics Administration. The federal agency, within the Department of Commerce, which is responsible for the supervision of airports, the regulation of air navigation, and the enforcement of the air safety regulations and other regulations of the CIVIL AERONAUTICS BOARD.

Civil Aeronautics Board. The independent federal agency, originally established in 1940, which regulates air carriers. It operates primarily through the staff of the CIVIL AERONAUTICS ADMINISTRATION. The Board assigns certificates to carriers, licensing them to provide public service either as scheduled or non-scheduled carriers, depending on whether they are licensed to cover regularly scheduled routes. It also sets air safety standards, investigates air accidents, etc.

civil court. See under COURT.

civil law. That branch of the written law which deals with the rights of private individuals, and with the settlement of disputes between individuals. Thus, it is distinguished from the CRIMINAL LAW, which deals with offenses against the state, or against public interest.

claim. 1. A RIGHT (1) or INTEREST (1) which is asserted, but not yet determined or verified; a demand by one person on another, under asserted legal or judicial rights. For example, a demand by an insured person for payment or recovery under an insurance policy is known as a *claim.*

2. In land law, a tract or parcel of land taken up or appropriated by a settler or miner, under the federal land laws. Also, the assertion of rightful occupancy or ownership to such land which is filed with the LAND OFFICE.

mining ~. One which is based on the presence of valuable mineral deposits in the subsoil or rock under a parcel of land, and which is filed with the purpose of mining these deposits, under the special regulations for such *claims* in the land laws.

3. In patent law, that part of the patent application in which the inventor states the detailed specifications and description of the invention, showing the reasons why the device is novel and patentable. The *claim* is thus the heart of the patent application.

claim-jumping. The act of taking over and filing for a land or mining CLAIM (2) already filed by another. This is sometimes done in the hope that the original claim may be proved defective, but is often an outright matter of fraudulent seizure.

classification of accounts. 1. The systematic, logical listing of the internal accounts of a business. See also CHART OF ACCOUNTS; ACCOUNT (2).

2. An arrangement of the outstanding current liabilities of a business, according to their age, size, likelihood of prompt payment, etc.; an arrangement of business customers according to volume of activity, reliability, credit rating, etc. See also ACCOUNT (4).

classification of motor carriers. A division of all common and contract motor CARRIERS into three classes, for rate-making and statistical purposes, by the Interstate Commerce Commission. Class I includes all those motor carriers with an annual gross operating revenue of over $200,000; Class II those with revenue of from $50,000 to $200,000; and Class III those with revenue of less than $50,000.

classification of railroads. A division of all passenger and freight railroads, or steam railways, into three classes, for rate-making and statistical purposes, by the Interstate Commerce Commission. Class I includes all those railroads with an annual gross operating revenue of $1,000,000 or more; Class II those with revenue of from $100,000 to $1,000,000; and Class III those with revenue of less than $100,000.

classification of risks. In insurance, the term for the listing of the location, nature, and value of the properties and articles specifically insured under a particular policy. Also, sometimes, a listing of all of the risks insured by a particular company, grouped according to their type, vulnerability to loss, etc.

classified advertising. See under ADVERTISING.

classified bond. See under BOND (1).

classified stock. See under STOCK (1).

class interval. In statistics, the difference between the higher and lower values which define a particular class or group in a

FREQUENCY DISTRIBUTION. For example, the income class of all incomes from $3,000 to $5,000 has a *class interval* of $2,000. In accepted statistical practice, it is desirable for all of the *class intervals* in a distribution, with the possible exception of the highest and lowest, to have the same size. It is also important that the intervals be consistent; that is, for example, if one interval is given as, from $3,000 up to but not including $5,000, the interval next above should not begin at over $5,000.

Class one, two, or three motor carrier. See CLASSIFICATION OF MOTOR CARRIERS.

Class one, two, or three railroad (or steam railway). See CLASSIFICATION OF RAILROADS.

class rate. See under FREIGHT RATE.

clean. Free of defects or fraud; free of encumbrances or reservations; with no attachments or endorsements. See each of the following under the principal listing: ∼ BILL OF EXCHANGE; ∼ BILL OF HEALTH; ∼ BILL OF LADING; ∼ BOND (1); ∼ DRAFT (2).

clean acceptance. See ACCEPTANCE (3), GENERAL.

clean bill. See BILL OF HEALTH.

clean bill of exchange. See under BILL OF EXCHANGE.

clean hands. In law, the doctrine that the plaintiff in a case at EQUITY must come to court with *clean hands;* that is, with no record of misconduct on his own part in the same area as that in which he is complaining against the defendant. For example, in a case in which one party charges another with unfair competition, the suit may be dismissed if it can be shown that the complaining party has followed similar practices.

clean up. To make a large and quick profit; to take all available profits in a market. For example, a person who introduces a new and popular product in a market may *clean up,* or make a large profit, due to the demand for his product and the lack of competition.

clear. 1. To make a net profit or gain. For example, it may be said that a business *clears* $1,000 per month, meaning that this is the amount of profit remaining after expenses.
2. To arrange for or give permission; to investigate and approve. For example, a ship is given permission to *clear* port; imported goods are *cleared* through customs; a deposited check is *cleared* through a bank; or a prospective employee is *cleared* after an investigation.
3. To sell at reduced prices in order to eliminate or *clear* out obsolete or slow-moving merchandise; to hold a CLEARANCE (3).

4. Free of ENCUMBRANCES or conditions; as, for example, a *clear* TITLE (2).

clearance. 1. In general, the act or process of CLEARING; the investigation, approval, adjustment or settlement of persons or documents.
2. A certificate of authority issued by the customs officials or other proper authority, giving a ship permission to leave or enter a port, and stating that all legal requirements have been met. It is known as the ship's *clearance paper.*
3. In retailing, a special sale, at reduced prices, intended to sell large amounts of obsolete or slow-moving stock. See also SALE (2).

clear day. See under DAY.

clearing. 1. In banking, the process of presenting at a local CLEARING HOUSE of various items for collection, including checks, drafts, etc., which are held by one bank, and the receipt in exchange by the bank of similar items which are payable by it. In practice, the collectible and payable amounts for each bank are balanced, and only the net amount or balance paid between the various banks. Only exchanges and settlements between banks of the same local clearing house are referred to as *clearings;* the nationwide exchange of items for clearance is known as TRANSIT OPERATIONS.
2. Any process of exchange and settlement of reciprocal obligations, as between brokers, merchants, railroad ticket offices, airlines, etc.

clearing account. See ACCOUNT (2), SUMMARY.

clearing agreement. An agreement between two banks or other agencies for the periodic exchange of obligations and balances, and the settlement of net balances outstanding. In international finance, for example, several nations or national banks may have *clearing agreements* through which outstanding foreign exchange accounts are periodically settled, and the net balances paid in gold or acceptable currencies.

clearing house. An association, and the place in which it meets, organized to permit banks in a local area to exchange daily the checks, drafts, and other instruments drawn on each other, and to settle outstanding balances. Also, any similar organization set up to handle settlements between members of a securities exchange, commodities exchange, etc. See also STOCK CLEARING CORPORATION.
∼ **association.** The voluntary association of local banks which operates the local *clearing house.* In addition, many such associations serve as a medium for discussing and solving various local banking problems.
∼ **balance.** The statement provided to

each bank of the payments required to the other member banks of the local *clearing house* in settlement, or the amounts due from other banks for similar settlement.

~ **statement.** A statement, issued periodically, of the total resources and liabilities of the member banks of a local *clearing house*.

clearing-house stock. See under STOCK (1).

clearing the market. In the securities and commodities trade, a term used to describe the condition existing when the volume of supply of a particular security or commodity is exactly matched by the volume of demand at the supply price, so that the resulting transactions are said to *clear the market;* that is, to leave no unsatisfied supply or demand at the price.

clear profit. See PROFIT, NET.

clear tare. See TARE, ACTUAL.

clerk. 1. In business, any employee who handles more or less routine office, warehouse, or factory record-keeping duties. A payroll *clerk,* for example, keeps payroll records and makes out payrolls, while a stock *clerk* makes physical inventories of goods on hand and keeps records of stock receipts and deliveries.

2. In municipal and state governments, a public official whose duty it is to keep certain public records or accounts, to issue various licenses and permits and record their issuance, etc.

client. A customer; one who engages the services of an accountant, lawyer, consultant, advertising agency, or other professional man or service.

clientele. The clients or customers of a professional man or of a business in general, as a group. Also, the general class of customers who patronize a particular professional service or business establishment, not necessarily limited to the specific individual customers.

clip joint. In slang, a dishonest business establishment; one which charges excessive prices, gives inferior service, or is otherwise dishonest in its dealings with customers.

clipping coupons. The practice of detaching dividend or interest COUPONS from bonds and presenting them for payment. A retired or wealthy person whose income is largely from such interest payments is sometimes said to be employed at *clipping coupons.* See also BOND (1), COUPON.

close. 1. To finish, to wind up. To *close* an account, for example, is to determine the final balance, and make the appropriate *closing* entry. Similarly, to *close* the books of a business is to summarize its operations at the end of an accounting period.

2. To conclude a sale or an agreement; to obtain the necessary signatures of the parties concerned to a contract, deed, or other agreement.

3. In selling, that part of a sales presentation which is intended to lead the prospective customer to conclude the sale. It is not necessarily the last part of the presentation, and may be repeated in various forms during the presentation in an attempt to *close* the sale.

4. In the securities trade, the price paid for a given security in the last or *closing* transaction of a period; as, for example, the daily *close,* weekly *close,* etc. See also HIGH; LOW.

close (or closed) corporation. See under CORPORATION.

closed-end investment company. See under INVESTMENT COMPANY.

closed mortgage. See under MORTGAGE.

closed shop. The term for a shop, plant, or other establishment in which, by agreement with the union, only union members may be hired, and in which employees must remain union members in order to retain their jobs. It differs from a UNION SHOP, in which nonunion workers may be hired, provided they join the union within a period of time. See also OPEN SHOP.

closed stock. A term sometimes used for merchandise, such as china or silverware, which is sold only in sets, with no assurance that it will be available for any long period of time for replacement or additions, as distinguished from OPEN STOCK.

closed trade. In the securities and commodities trade, a term for a completed transaction, especially a speculative one. When a speculator who has sold short has bought the necessary securities to cover the sale, for example, the transaction is said to be a *closed trade.* Similarly, when a dealer who has bought a commodity contract with the intention of reselling it before delivery has done so, the trade is *closed.* See also OPEN TRADE.

closed union. See under UNION.

close out. 1. To liquidate; to make a final disposition. For example, when a retail or wholesale distributor stops carrying a particular line or brand of goods, he *closes out,* or disposes of, his existing stocks. Also, when an investor fails to provide sufficient MARGIN when it is called for, the broker may *close out* his account by selling the securities he holds on margin.

2. Goods or merchandise which are to be or have been disposed of in a *close out* operation. Since such merchandise represents discontinued lines, it is usually in incomplete assortments by size, style, color, etc.,

and is disposed of at reduced prices. In some fields, manufacturers' discontinued lines are known as drops, rather than as *close outs.*

closing account. See ACCOUNT (2), SUMMARY.

closing date. In the publishing and advertising fields, the last day on which advertisements can be accepted for publication in a particular issue of a magazine or other periodical. In the larger magazines, there may be two *closing dates;* the *first closing,* on which date the printing forms for one section of the magazine are closed, and the *final closing,* on which date the last of the printing forms are closed.

closing entry. See under ENTRY (1).

closing inventory. See INVENTORY, ENDING.

closing of transfer book. See TRANSFER BOOK.

closing price. See CLOSE (4); PRICE, CLOSING.

co-. A prefix indicating that two or more persons are associated or bound together in a relationship. The use of the prefix usually implies either a JOINT or COMMON relationship, depending on the usage of the term and on local statutes. Examples include *co*-tenant, *co*-defendant, *co*-trustee, *co*-owner, *co*-executor, etc.

code. 1. In law, a compilation or collection of existing laws into a systematic whole. A body of laws representing a comprehensive coverage of a particular field. For example, the INTERNAL REVENUE CODE of 1954 is a collection and simplification of the previously existing tax laws of the United States, with modifications and amendments.

2. In general, a special arrangement of letters, numbers, or symbols to represent other letters, words, or phrases. It may be used to assure secrecy, or to conserve message space. Telegraphic *codes,* for example, are designed more to condense long messages into a few *code* words than to provide secrecy.

codicil. A subsequent addition made to a WILL, which changes, amplifies, explains, adds to, or substracts from the provisions of the original. It is subject to the same requirements concerning witnesses, etc., as the will itself, and must be admitted to probate along with the original will.

cognovit note. See NOTE (1), JUDGMENT.

coin. 1. A piece of metal, especially gold, silver, or other valuable metal, of prescribed size, shape, weight, and fineness, stamped with special designs and marks by governmental authority, and used as MONEY. The presently used *coins* of the United States Government are the DOLLAR, HALF-DOLLAR, QUARTER-DOLLAR, DIME, NICKEL, and PENNY or CENT.

   minor ~. In the United States, the nickel and cent; those *coins* which are not made of precious metal.

   subsidiary ~. In the United States, one of less than one dollar in value; hence, any of the currently used *coins* except the silver dollar.

2. To fashion metal into *coins.* Also, to stamp out metal pieces for any use, using similar equipment and processes as those used in the making of *coins.* A *coining* machine is one that stamps *coins* or other pieces out of strip or coils of metal.

coinage. 1. The process of making coins. Also, the pieces coined, collectively.

2. The system of metallic money used in a country. Together with CURRENCY, it makes up the monetary system of the country.

coin of the realm. A figurative expression for anything which passes as money in a country. It does not mean strictly the metal coinage only, but includes all forms of money.

coinsurance. 1. In property insurance, a requirement that the insured person carry an amount of insurance equal to a specified percentage of the value of the insured property, usually 80 percent. In the event of a partial loss to the property, the insurance company determines whether the insurance maintained is equal to the required percentage of total value. If it is less, the amount the insurance company will pay on the claim is reduced proportionately, and the insured becomes a *coinsurer* to the extent to which he shares in the loss. For example, under a policy with an 80 percent *coinsurance* requirement, a home valued at $10,000 should be insured for at least $8,000. If it is insured for only $6,000, or 75 percent of the required amount, a loss of $1,000 would be settled for only $750 by the insurance company. A total loss, of course, would be settled for the full $6,000 of the policy. *Coinsurance* is required in most marine insurance, and in fire insurance on commercial property in many states. It is required on residential property only in certain areas. See also COINSURANCE CLAUSE; INSURANCE, PROPERTY.

2. In some forms of casualty insurance, a requirement that the insured share, or participate, in each loss for a given percentage of the loss, large or small. It is more commonly known as PARTICIPATION.

coinsurance clause. A clause inserted in fire insurance policies when the insurance is written under a COINSURANCE requirement. In return for such a clause, there is usually a reduction in the premium. The typical *coinsurance clause* reads as follows: "In consideration of the reduced rate under which this policy is written, this company shall be liable for no greater proportion of any loss than the amount hereby insured bears to the percentage specified of the actual cash value of the property described herein at the time when such loss shall happen." It is sometimes called the reduced rate contribution clause, or average clause.

collapse. In business usage, a sudden decline or fall, as in business activity or prices. With respect to an individual company, failure or ruin.

collapsible corporation. See under CORPORATION.

collateral. Literally, at the side. Hence, in business, a SECURITY (2) which is in addition to the borrower's good name; pertaining to an obligation which is secured by something of value, especially something which is readily convertible into money. See each of the following under the principal listing: ∼ LOAN; ∼ NOTE (1); ∼ SECURITY. See also BOND (1), COLLATERAL TRUST.

collect. In general, to demand and receive payment for something; to recover value for something sold. Thus, pertaining to a service or product for which payment is to be made after use or completion, such as a *collect* telegram, a *collect* telephone call, or a *collect* freight shipment.

collection. 1. In general, the presentation for payment of any obligation, bill, or instrument, and the obtaining of such payment. Also, any money so obtained in payment.

2. In banking, the presentation for payment, at the bank on which it was drawn, of a check or draft, or the presentation of any item presented for deposit at the place at which it is payable. In modern banking, all local *collection* is effected through CLEARING (1), or the exchange of checks and drafts among the banks in a local area. *Collection* of items which are payable outside of the local clearing area is effected through the FEDERAL RESERVE SYSTEM.

collection charge. The charge made by a bank, under some circumstances, for the collection of a check, draft, note, or other instrument which is collectible or payable in some other city, or which is not collectible through the local CLEARING HOUSE. See also CLEARING (1).

collection item. In banking, the term for an ITEM (2) offered for deposit which is not credited immediately to the depositor's account, but is first presented for payment or collection, as distinguished from a CASH ITEM, which is immediately credited and may be drawn against as soon as deposited. Examples include personal checks, business checks on out of town banks, and similar items.

collection period. In general, the number of

days between the time an invoice is presented, and the time it is paid. As usually used, it is the average number of days between presentation and payment of all of the accounts receivable of a business. The standard method used to compute the average *collection period* is as follows: for the period concerned, the average value of ACCOUNTS RECEIVABLE is divided by the average daily sales, and the resulting figure is the average number of days' sales which are outstanding for collection, or the average *collection period*.

collections basis. The term for the method of reporting tax receipts used by the Internal Revenue Service, under which receipts are counted at the time they are received at the local offices of the service from taxpayers and from collecting officers in the field. This differs from the method used by the U. S. Treasury, under which receipts are counted when they are turned over to the Treasury by the Internal Revenue offices, on the DAILY TREASURY STATEMENT BASIS.

collective agreement. A contract signed between an employer and a union setting the wages, working conditions, and other specifications under which the employees represented by the union will work; a UNION CONTRACT.

collective bargaining. The process of negotiation through which an agreement on wages, working conditions, and other subjects for discussion is reached between an employer and his employees, as represented by a union. When the employers of a given industry or segment of an industry negotiate jointly with the union or unions representing the employees in the industry, the form of *collective bargaining* that occurs is usually known as industry-wide bargaining. See also UNION CONTRACT; BARGAINING AGENT; BARGAINING RIGHTS.

collective mark. See under TRADEMARK.

collect on delivery. A term used in the orders given by a seller to the delivering carrier or to the post office, instructing that the payment for the goods is to be obtained from the buyer at the time of delivery. Sometimes the term may be used to refer only to the shipping charges on the goods, or to a balance payment due on delivery. See also CASH ON DELIVERY.

collision clause. In marine insurance, a clause under which the insurance company agrees to cover a stated proportion of the damage inflicted by the insured ship on other ships. It is sometimes referred to as a running down clause.

collusion. In general, any secret agreement between two or more persons, to take cooperative action to deceive or defraud other persons. Particularly, it is a secret agreement between persons who are supposedly contending at law, to use the legal action for some fraudulent purpose. For example, a person carrying liability insurance and another person may enter into *collusion,* by testifying as to a non-existent accident, to defraud an insurance company.

color. In law, the appearance or resemblance of a thing, but not the thing itself. In one sense, the word implies an imitation of the real thing, but in another sense it means to support, or to make apparent. For example, one party in a legal suit may give *color* to the arguments of the other by failing to deny them.

   ~ of title. Those conditions and facts which tend to support a claim to title to property, but which are technically not strong enough to establish the title legally. See also TITLE (2), COLORABLE.

colorable. In law, tending to give support or COLOR, or contributing to the appearance of facts as claimed. As usually used, the term refers to attempts to give an appearance which is not warranted by the true facts, and which tends to deceive.

   ~ alteration. A change made in a design or in an artistic composition which is really not a substantial change at all, but which is made deliberately to give the appearance of difference, and thus to evade the patent and copyright laws. See also INFRINGEMENT (2).

   ~ imitation. In the language of the trademark laws, a deliberate attempt to give the appearance of another thing, such as a label or trademark, for the purpose of deceiving prospective customers. A *colorable imitation* is one which is likely to deceive, whether an exact replica of the real thing or not.

   ~ title. See under TITLE (2).

column inch. In printing and advertising, a standard measure of space, one column wide and one inch deep. Thus there are fourteen standard AGATE LINES to one *column inch,* but the total page area involved depends on the width of the column used in the particular publication.

comaker. A person who agrees to share the responsibility for payment of a note or loan by signing his name to it along with that of the MAKER (1) or borrower. The exact responsibility of the *comaker* depends on the laws of the particular state.

combination. In business, an agreement or association between two or more companies to achieve some joint purpose, but without an outright MERGER or CONSOLIDATION. Examples include TRUSTS, POOLS, etc. Such *combina-*

tions are usually for the purpose of promoting the interests of the members at the expense of others, and in such cases are illegal under the anti-trust laws.

   ~ in restraint of trade. As defined under the anti-trust laws, any conspiracy, association, or *combination* which is intended to obstruct the free flow of interstate or foreign commerce, or which is an attempt to monopolize or control the production, traffic, or sale of any commodity, or which is an attempt to stifle free competition. See also RESTRAINT OF TRADE; AGREEMENT IN RESTRAINT OF TRADE.

combination advertising rate. In advertising, a rate charged by a publisher when advertising space is bought in two or more of his publication at the same time. It is usually lower than the total of the two separate rates would be.

combination freight rate. See under FREIGHT RATE.

combine. As a noun, a business slang term for a COMBINATION, or TRUST. Also, a SYNDICATE, or CHAIN.

combustible. As used in fire insurance, anything which will burn with an open flame, or which is inflammable, as distinguished from things which will merely be destroyed by fire. As sometimes used, the word applies to things which will easily or readily burst into flame, but this is not the proper meaning.

commerce. In general, the interchange of goods, property, or services, including the use of all of the facilities and services normally associated with this interchange. Thus it includes not only buying and selling, but storage, transportation, financing, and so forth. Sometimes, *commerce* is distinguished from TRADE (2) in that it takes place between different areas, while trade is among persons in one area, and the phrase *commerce and trade* is used in some legislation and documents for this reason. See also DOMESTIC COMMERCE; FOREIGN COMMERCE; INTERSTATE COMMERCE; INTRASTATE COMMERCE.

commerce and industry association. See CHAMBER OF COMMERCE.

commerce clause. A term for the clause in Article I, Section 8, of the United States Constitution, which provides that Congress shall have power "to regulate commerce with foreign nations, and among the several states . . ."

commercial. 1. In general, pertaining to COMMERCE, or to business. As usually used, it refers to the buying and selling of goods and services, rather than to their production or use. See also MERCANTILE.

2. In advertising, a paid advertising announcement on a radio or television program. More loosely, any announcement, program, or publication which is paid for by a sponsor for advertising purposes.

3. Of the kind, quality, or grade generally used or traded in business or commerce, as distinguished, for example, from that used in research. See also COMMERCIAL GRADE.

commercial agency. A MERCANTILE AGENCY.

commercial agreement. An agreement or treaty between countries or states concerning their business relationships, or the commerce between the countries or between their citizens; a COMMERCIAL TREATY. See also TRADE AGREEMENT, RECIPROCAL.

commercial bill. See under BILL OF EXCHANGE.

commercial code. See UNIFORM COMMERCIAL CODE.

commercial credit. See under CREDIT (3).

commercial credit company. See SALES FINANCE COMPANY.

commercial discount. See DISCOUNT (1), TRADE.

commercial exhibit. A regular or periodic display of goods for sale by various sellers in the same or related fields, under one roof or in adjoining places. The purpose of such a display is usually both to promote the sale of the goods and to make direct sales to the potential customers who visit the exhibit. See also FAIR.

commercial finance company. See SALES FINANCE COMPANY.

commercial grade. In general, that grade or quality which is used, or is suitable for use, in business or commerce. Depending on the particular field, it may refer to a specific degree of purity or fineness of a chemical or metal, to a quality of meat, to a weight or grade of paper, etc. In most usages, *commercial* is a lower grade than others for the same commodity, but this depends on the customs of the individual trades.

commercial law. In general, the whole body of law, including federal, state, and local laws and regulations, dealing with business, commerce, and trade. That part of *commercial law* which is embodied in the common law is known as the LEX MERCATORIA.

commercial letter of credit. See under LETTER OF CREDIT.

commercial loan. See under LOAN.

commercial month. See MONTH.

commercial paper. Any of the various forms of short-term, negotiable, credit instruments which arise out of business transactions, including BILLS OF EXCHANGE, DRAFTS, ACCEPT-

ANCES, NOTES, etc. There are no exact limits to the application of the term, but in financial circles it is generally used to refer to credit which has a term of six months or less, and which is for an amount of $50,000 or less. The various types of *commercial paper* in use are listed and defined below. In business usage, these are usually referred to as agricultural paper, bank paper, best paper, etc., without the use of the word commercial itself.

agricultural ～. As defined in the regulations of the Federal Reserve Board, any negotiable instrument drawn or issued for agricultural purposes, or based on livestock as security. The various Federal Reserve Banks may buy and sell such paper under specified conditions.

bank (or bankable) ～. A commercial negotiable instrument which is of sufficiently high quality that a bank will buy or discount it. Also, any instrument which has already been discounted by a bank, and which therefore bears the bank's endorsement.

best ～. A term for those instruments which are of the highest quality, such as BANK PAPER, which see above.

business ～. Those instruments which are given in exchange for merchandise or commodities in normal business sales.

cattle ～. The term for a note which is secured by a chattel mortgage on cattle or other livestock.

commodity ～. As defined by the Federal Reserve Act, a negotiable instrument which is secured by a warehouse receipt or shipping documents covering approved, insured, and readily marketable staple commodities.

corporation ～. An instrument drawn by a corporation, as distinguished from that of individual proprietors, partnerships, etc.

double-name ～. See TWO-NAME PAPER, below.

eligible ～. Those negotiable instruments which, under the rules established by the Federal Reserve Board, may be accepted for purchase, discount, or rediscount by a Federal Reserve Bank, as distinguished from NON-ELIGIBLE PAPER, which see below.

first-class ～. Any which has been drawn or endorsed by a person with the highest financial standing, and which will therefore be most readily bought or discounted in the market, as distinguished from SECOND-CLASS or THIRD-CLASS PAPER, which see below.

ineligible ～. See NON-ELIGIBLE PAPER, below.

mercantile ～. A term for those instruments which arise out of normal buying and selling transactions, rather than out of transportation, finance, storage, or other business services.

non-eligible ~. Those negotiable instruments which, under the rules established by the Federal Reserve Board, do not meet the requirements which would make them acceptable for purchase, discount, or rediscount by a Federal Reserve Bank, as distinguished from ELIGIBLE PAPER, which see above.

one-name ~. See SINGLE-NAME PAPER, below.

prime ~. See FIRST-CLASS PAPER, above.

purchased ~. A negotiable instrument which has been bought from a broker or dealer in such instruments, rather than directly from the person to whom it was originally given. See also STREET PAPER, below.

second class ~. In general, instruments which have been drawn or endorsed by persons of average financial standing and business reputation. Such instruments are not as readily accepted in the market as FIRST-CLASS PAPER, which see above, but are more readily accepted than THIRD-CLASS PAPER, which see below.

single-name ~. A negotiable instrument which is drawn or issued by only one person, and which is not endorsed, so that only one person is responsible for its payment.

street ~. A term for those instruments which have been sold through a broker or dealer, rather than to a bank. Thus, it is usually *paper* which is of a lower quality than BANK PAPER, which see above.

third-class ~. The term for those negotiable instruments drawn or issued by persons of the lowest financial standing, and which are therefore not readily accepted in the market, except at a considerably higher than average discount.

time ~. An instrument which is payable at some future definite time, such as 30 or 60 days from the date it is drawn.

two-name ~. Any negotiable instrument for whose payment two or more persons are responsible. It may have more than one maker or drawer, or it may be endorsed by one or more persons.

commercial paper rate. In the financial market, the prevailing rate at which COMMERCIAL PAPER is DISCOUNTED (2). Actually, there are several rates, for 30, 60, and 90 day paper, for first-class and other paper, etc. See also DISCOUNT RATE.

commercial set. A term for the set of the four principal documents covering a shipment in trade, including the INVOICE, BILL OF LADING, CERTIFICATE OF INSURANCE, and BILL OF EXCHANGE or DRAFT.

commercial standard. See under STANDARD.

commercial traveler. A TRAVELING SALESMAN. More specifically, a sales representative who travels about, taking orders for goods, but not making delivery or collecting payment. Thus, he is different from a local ROUTE MAN, who performs these services for his employer.

commercial treaty. A treaty or agreement between nations, dealing with such matters as tariffs, regulations governing export and import, monetary exchange, the treatment of citizens engaged in business, and so forth. In some cases, such treaties may also provide for the exchange of specified amounts of goods between the two countries involved, and set the conditions under which these will be exchanged. See also TRADE AGREEMENT, RECIPROCAL.

commercial year. The business year, as opposed to the CALENDAR YEAR. For purposes of computing interest, and for similar operations, the year is assumed to consist of 12 months of 30 days each, so that the *commercial year* has 360 days. See also INTEREST (2), ORDINARY.

commingled trust fund. See TRUST FUND, COMMON.

commissary store. See INDUSTRIAL STORE.

commission. 1. A warrant or authorization, from a government or court, conferring on some person or group the right to do certain things or perform certain services. Also, loosely, a similar authorization in private business, from a company to its agent or other person, authorizing such person to act for the company.

2. A group or committee, duly named to perform some public act or service, and to whom a *commission* or authorization is given. Examples include the Interstate Commerce Commission, the Federal Communications Commission, and the many *commissions* appointed from time to time to investigate conditions in some field, regulate sports, and other activities, etc.

3. The compensation paid to an agent or representative, especially a sales representative, which is based on the amount or value of sales. It is usually computed as a percentage of the sales volume or the profit, but may also be a stated amount of money per unit of sales. Strictly speaking, only an employee or agent receives a *commission*. A similar percentage of sales paid to a distributor or wholesaler is his MARGIN or DISCOUNT. See also FEE (1); SALARY; WAGES.

commission agent. See under AGENT.

commissioner. 1. A member of a commission, whether a permanent or special commission. Also, a person commissioned by a court to inquire into some matter and prepare a report, to take testimony, or perform some other service in connection with an action before the court.

2. A person authorized to administer certain laws, to administer oaths, take acknowledgements, register documents, etc. In some states, for example, the *commissioner of deeds* performs these services.

commission house. In the securities and commodities trades, a term for a securities or commodities dealer or broker who buys and sells only for customers, and does not speculate or trade on its own account.

commission merchant. A form of distributor, who accepts goods from manufacturers for sale, and receives his compensation out of the proceeds of the sale. His powers and services are broader than those of a BROKER, since he usually takes possession of the goods, does business in his own name, and exercises some discretion over the prices and terms of sale. He is not a true WHOLESALER, however, since he does not take title to the goods he sells. Depending on the line of business, a *commission merchant* may arrange for shipment or delivery, extend credit, collect payment, and provide other services. See also FACTORS (2).

commitment. An engagement or obligation to perform some act, or engage in some transaction. More particularly, an engagement to buy or sell something, or the written acknowledgement of such an engagement.

committee. In general, a group of persons duly selected or appointed to perform some specific acts or services, to consider some particular matter, or to administer some operation. In business, examples include an EXECUTIVE COMMITTEE, a PROTECTIVE COMMITTEE of stockholders, etc.

commodities clause. The popular name given to Article 8, of Section 1, Part I, of the federal Interstate Commerce Act, which forbids railroads to transport in interstate commerce for commercial sale any commodities which the railroads themselves manufacture, mine, or produce, or in which they have an interest. Timber and timber products are excepted. A railroad owning a coal mine, for example, may transport coal from the mine for its own use, but if the coal is to be sold commercially it must be transported across state lines by a railroad or other carrier other than the railroad owning the mine. The purpose of the clause is to discourage railroads from competing with their own customers, and to eliminate the possibility that they might give unfair advantages to their own commodities over those of regular shippers.

commodity. Originally, anything providing a convenience or accommodation. More generally, any movable and tangible article in commerce and trade, including GOODS, MERCHANDISE, PRODUCE, etc. In various court decisions, the term as used in federal laws has been held to be of broader application than the usual definition, including such intangible services as telephone communication, advertising, etc. See each of the following under the principal listing: ∼ COMMERCIAL PAPER; ∼ CONTRACT (3); ∼ EXCHANGE (2); ∼ FREIGHT RATE; ∼ LOAN; ∼ MONEY.

Commodity Credit Corporation. The federal agency, originally established in 1933, and transferred to the Department of Agriculture in 1939, which operates the federal crop price support programs, makes crop loans to farmers, provides facilities for the storage of surplus crops, etc.

commodity dollar. In economics, the popular name for a plan or proposal under which the gold content of the dollar was to be increased or decreased to compensate for changes in commodity prices. The object of the plan was to assure that the dollar would buy a fixed quantity of goods, or have a stable purchasing power. Though widely discussed at the time the country was on a true gold standard, the plan was never tested in use, so that its practicality remains in doubt. It was also known as the compensated dollar plan.

Commodity Exchange Authority. The federal agency, within the Department of Agriculture, established in 1936 to supervise trading activities on the several CONTRACT MARKETS established under the Commodities Exchange Act. It carries out the policies and decisions of the COMMODITY EXCHANGE COMMISSION. It was formerly known as the Grain Futures Administration.

Commodity Exchange Commission. The independent federal agency, established under the Commodities Exchange Act of 1922, to administer the provisions of the act. It supervises the activities of the several CONTRACT MARKETS established under the act, investigates violations of the act, etc. It operates primarily through the staff of the COMMODITY EXCHANGE AUTHORITY.

commodity gold. The term for the gold, in the form of bars, ingots, or sometimes foreign coins, which formerly was bought and sold on the open market. Under present laws, however, all highly refined gold can be sold only to the federal government, so that there is no trade in *commodity gold* in this country.

commodity market. Broadly speaking, the regular trade in commodities, as carried on through the several organized commodity exchanges. More specifically, one of the commodity exchanges itself. See also EXCHANGE (2), COMMODITY.

commodity price index. Any one of the various PRICE INDEXES designed to measure changes in the wholesale prices of selected basic commodities. Such indexes are prepared by the U. S. Department of Commerce, and by various trade publications, financial organizations, etc.

commodity reserve currency. In economics, a proposed system under which currency was to be based on a fixed combination of selected basic commodities, and would only be redeemable in units of these commodities. Stocks of the selected commodities would be held in reserve to provide a partial backing for the currency, hence the name of the system. As the plan was intended to operate, any increase in the price level of the commodities included would result in an increase in the value of the currency, so that the net result would be a general stability of prices. The plan was never tested in use.

common. 1. Originally, shared or owned by the community in general; public. Hence, equal, joint, or combined, as distinguished from private or separate.

2. Standard or ordinary; of a class or quality enjoyed or owned by the public at large; not special or superior.

common average. See AVERAGE (3), PARTICULAR.

common carrier. See under CARRIER.

common injunction. See INJUNCTION, TEMPORARY.

common labor. See under LABOR.

common law. That body of law which has developed out of customs, usage, precedent, rulings, court decisions, etc., rather than through specific legislation. More specifically, the term refers to the English *common law,* which included all of English *common law* as well as those English statutes which were in existence at the time of formation of the United States. Most state constitutions recognize the validity of *common law,* and many such constitutions provide specifically that the English *common law* shall apply, except where it is in conflict with the United States Constitution or with the particular statutes of the state. In Louisiana, however, the Napoleonic Code has been adopted, instead of the English *common law.* The *common law* in general is distinguished both from CIVIL LAW, which is in written statutes, and from EQUITY, which is modified to meet the needs of each case.

common law trust. See under TRUST (3).

common stock. See under STOCK (1).

common stock fund. See INVESTMENT COMPANY, MUTUAL FUND.

common trust fund. See under TRUST FUND.

community. In general, any group of persons with the same or closely associated interests, as for example, the business *community.* In a geographic sense, a group of people living together in a village, town, or city. Also, the place or locality itself, in which the members of a *community* live.

community of interest. In general, the existence of common or joint interests among several persons or companies. More specifically, an organization of the interests and activities of several businesses under a common policy or management, and for a common end. This may be achieved through the ownership of a controlling stock interest in the several companies by a single person or group, or by a pooling of interests by the several companies. To the extent that such an arrangement leads to monopolistic control or lessens competition it is illegal under the anti-trust laws.

community property. Property which is owned jointly or in common by a husband and wife by the mere fact of their marriage, according to the laws of several states. The various state laws vary widely, but in those states known as *community property* states a husband and wife are generally considered to share equally in all of each other's property which is acquired during the marriage, and in any income or increase in value during the marriage. This should not be confused with the joint ownership of particular property by a husband and wife under a specific contract or deed.

commutation. The substitution of a single or lesser thing for a greater amount or a series of amounts. The payment in a lump sum of the present value of a series of agreed future payments.

~ **of interest.** The substitution and payment of a single sum, representing the present value of a series of interest payments which are due to be paid over a period of time. This may take place at any time over the life of a debt, and when it takes place at the time of the loan it is, in effect, DISCOUNTING (2) the loan.

~ **of sentence.** The substitution of a shorter term of imprisonment for the longer term originally called for. Depending on the particular state laws, this may be done by the sentencing judge, by the state pardon or parole authority, or by action of the governor.

~ **of taxes.** The payment, in advance, of a

single lump sum tax in place of a series of payments which are to be due over a period of time under the law. Many tax regulations provide for such advance payment, usually at a small discount, at the option of the taxpayer.

~ **ticket.** One under which, for a lump sum payment, a traveler receives the right to make a large number of trips, or to use the facilities of a carrier without limit over a specified period of time. Thus, a reduced rate ticket of the type issued to a regular traveler, especially to a person who makes daily use of a railroad or bus line for traveling to and from a place of work or business.

commutative contract. See under CONTRACT (1).

commute. 1. To change or exchange one thing for another, especially to substitute a simpler or combined thing for a series, such as to substitute a single lump sum payment for a series of interest payments. See also COMMUTATION.

2. To travel regularly, as on a COMMUTATION TICKET; especially to travel on such a ticket to and from a regular place of work or business.

compact. Any agreement, bargain, or contract mutually arrived at among two or more persons, under which all of those concerned have both obligations and rights.

company. In general, any association of persons for the purpose of carrying out some joint venture or of achieving some common goal. In business, an association of individual persons, usually based on a contribution of capital funds, skills, and time, to carry out some commercial or industrial undertaking. Some prefer to limit the use of the term to CORPORATIONS and similar limited liability *companies,* and to use the term FIRM for other business organizations. In general use, however, no such distinction is made, and many organizations with *company* as part of their name are not incorporated. The principal types and classifications of *companies* are listed and defined below.

affiliated ~. As defined by the Securities and Exchange Commission, one which directly or through intermediaries is either controlled by or controls another *company,* or is controlled by the same group of interests with another *affiliated company.* See also SUBSIDIARY COMPANY, below.

controlled ~. In some states, the term for a SUBSIDIARY COMPANY, which see below.

controlling ~. In some states, the term for a HOLDING COMPANY, or PARENT COMPANY, which see below.

holding ~. Strictly, one formed for the purpose of investing in the securities of other *companies,* and for exercising control of such *companies* through these holdings. The Public Utility Act, for example, defines a *holding company* as any which directly or indirectly owns, controls, or has the power to vote 10 percent or more of the outstanding voting securities of any public utility *company.* More generally, any *company* which has a controlling interest in another, though it may also be an OPERATING COMPANY, which see below, is a *holding company* with respect to the one it controls. See also PERSONAL HOLDING COMPANY, below.

joint stock ~. A form of business organization in which the members hold shares of stock, but in which the members are usually individually liable for all of its debts. See also directly.

limited liability ~. One in which the shareholders are limited in their liability for the *company's* debts to the amount they have paid for their stock; for example, a CORPORATION.

operating ~. One which is actively and directly engaged in business, as distinguished from one which is purely a HOLDING COMPANY, which see above, though a company may be both at the same time. Sometimes, a SUBSIDIARY COMPANY, which see below, which owns and operates facilities under the control of another *company.*

parent ~. One holding a controlling interest in one or more SUBSIDIARY COMPANIES, which see below. It may be an OPERATING COMPANY, which see above, but with respect to its subsidiary it is a HOLDING COMPANY, which see above.

personal holding ~. Under the federal tax laws, one formed by an individual or a small group of individuals specifically for the purpose of holding securities and receiving the income therefrom. The purpose of such a *company* is usually to avoid or reduce the taxes which the individual would ordinarily pay on the income from the securities held.

proprietary ~. A term for a PARENT or HOLDING COMPANY, which see above.

stock ~. Any business organization whose capital stock is divided into shares which are held by its members, whether or not it is actually a CORPORATION.

subsidiary ~. One which is controlled by another company, usually through ownership of all or a majority of its outstanding stock. When all of the outstanding stock is owned by the PARENT COMPANY, which see above, the *subsidiary* is known as a *wholly-owned subsidiary.*

company magazine. See HOUSE ORGAN.

company store. See INDUSTRIAL STORE.

company town. A community established by a company primarily or exclusively for its own employees, in which all or most of the homes and other property are owned by the company or a subsidiary formed for the purpose. Such communities were frequently established by mining companies, steel mills, etc. which were originally located in isolated places, but are much less common today.

company union. See under UNION.

comparative balance sheet. See under BALANCE SHEET.

comparative negligence. See under NEGLIGENCE.

comparison. In the securities trade, a term for the process of verification, by brokers, of the accuracy of the written notes or tickets which they have made during the day covering sales of securities. This takes place after the close of the market by an exchange of tickets among brokers through the STOCK CLEARING CORPORATION.

comparison shopper. A person employed to shop or investigate the prices, goods, and services of competing stores. Usually such a person is employed by one retail store to shop others, but he may be employed by a manufacturer to investigate the way in which his product is being sold in retail stores.

compensated dollar. See COMMODITY DOLLAR.

compensating balance. In banking, the proportion of a loan which a bank may require a borrower to keep on deposit, or the average balance which must be maintained in a deposit account set up by a borrower. In effect, the requirement for such a balance reduces the amount of the loan, and thus raises the interest which the borrower actually pays for the money he is able to use.

compensating error. In accounting, or in statistics, an error which matches, counteracts, or equalizes an error of similar magnitude but in the opposite direction, thus giving a false appearance of accuracy to a balance or to comparative totals.

compensation. In general, an equal amount of money given for value received. Thus, payment or remuneration for services rendered. Also, any payment as an indemnity for damage or loss, as, for example, under the WORKMEN'S COMPENSATION laws.

compensatory damages. See under DAMAGES.

compensatory tariff. See under TARIFF (2).

competent. In law, qualified; capable or skilled; legally suitable or acceptable. For example, a *competent* witness in a legal proceeding is one who has special knowledge or training in the field about which he is testifying.

competition. In economics, the continuing struggle among different business organizations for a share of a given market, or for business advantages of one sort or another. It is usually evidenced by such activities as price adjustments, the offering of special services and inducements, improvements in quality, advertising and sales promotion, and so forth. *Competition* is said to be free when all buyers and sellers have equal access to the market, and is limited to the extent that any do not have such access. This may result, for example, when some sellers have more opportunity to advertise their products, or when some buyers are offered more advantageous prices. See also UNFAIR COMPETITION.

competitive bid. See under BID (2).

compilation. A collection of extracts or selections from various authors and sources in one literary work; especially one arranged in a particular logical or methodical manner. Though the particular selections included in a *compilation* may not be copyrighted by the compiler, the *compilation* itself, as an original arrangement and analysis of material may receive a copyright.

complainant. In law, one who applies for legal redress of a wrong; the one who brings a suit. In a case in EQUITY, the equivalent of a PLAINTIFF. Also, in a criminal case, any person who makes an accusation against another.

complaint. In law, the initial statement or pleading of a COMPLAINANT or PLAINTIFF in a civil case. Though the exact requirements vary from state to state, it usually includes a statement of the alleged facts, the names of all of the parties concerned, and the particular relief demanded. In criminal law, it is the charge filed by the COMPLAINANT before a magistrate. See also PLEA; REPLICATION.

composition. An agreement between an insolvent debtor and his creditors, under which the latter agree to accept as full payment an amount less than the amount due them. The debtor is permitted to retain his other assets, if any, and to continue in business without being forced into BANKRUPTCY. Also the particular amount or proportion of the debt accepted as a settlement is sometimes referred to as the *composition*. It is distinguished from an ACCORD, which is an agreement between a debtor and one particular creditor.

compound arbitration. See under ARBITRATION OF EXCHANGE.

compounding. A term sometimes used for COMMUTATION.

compound interest. See under INTEREST (2).

compound-interest account. See ACCOUNT (3), THRIFT.

compound tariff. See under TARIFF (2).

comprehensive insurance. See under INSURANCE.

compromise. Literally, a mutual promise or agreement. A settlement of a dispute between two parties by an adjustment of differences, and by concessions made on both sides, rather than by a resort to legal proceedings. Also, in a derogatory sense, a concession that results in a weakening of one's position or in a lowering of moral standards.

comptroller. See CONTROLLER.

compulsory. Involuntary or obligatory; forced or by coercion. See, for example, ARBITRATION, COMPULSORY.

concern. Originally, an interest or matter of responsibility. Hence, any business activity or business organization, such as a company, corporation, firm, etc. Sometimes, the term is limited to mercantile or commercial organizations, rather than to those in manufacturing, finance, communications, etc., but this distinction is not generally followed.

concession. 1. A grant of a special privilege, or of permission to operate an enterprise, especially one given by a government but also one given by a private company. For example, a state may grant a *concession* to operate a refreshment stand in a state park, or the owners of a department store may grant another company a *concession* to operate a cafeteria in the store. Hence, also, any business operated under such a grant of privilege.

2. A reduction or rebate; an allowance or yielding from the established price or rate. For example, one country may give a tariff *concession* to certain goods from another country, or a landlord may give a *concession*, such as one month's free occupancy, to encourage the renewal of a lease.

concessionaire. A person or company operating a business under the terms of a CONCESSION. Since the various attractions and refreshment stands at fairs, circuses, sports events, and similar enterprises usually operate under concession arrangements, any proprietor of such a business is frequently known as a *concessionaire*, whether or not he is one in fact.

conciliation. The process of bringing together the two or more parties involved in a dispute, and encouraging them to settle or compromise their differences. It is essentially the same as MEDIATION, but it is sometimes distinguished by the fact that a conciliator takes an active part in the proceedings, and may suggest particular solutions to the dispute, while a mediator merely attempts to keep the parties together until they reach their own solution. See also ARBITRATION.

concurrent. Literally, running together. Con-temporary, at the same time, or overlapping in period of effect. Also, for the same or similar purposes. For example, two leases with the same periods are said to be *concurrent,* and similar resolutions passed by the two houses of a legislature are *concurrent* resolutions. See also WILL, CONCURRENT.

concurring opinion. See under OPINION.

condemnation. 1. The process by which land or other property is taken over for public use or benefit. Under a *condemnation* proceeding, the property is taken with or without the consent of the owner, but upon the payment of just compensation, under the right of EMINENT DOMAIN. See also CONFISCATION.

2. In general, the process of declaring any commodity unfit for use or consumption, or below the minimum or stated standard or grade. The federal Food and Drug Administration, for example, has the power of *condemnation* over any foods or drugs shipped in interstate commerce which it finds unfit for use or consumption. The condemned goods are usually destroyed after seizure.

condition. Any restriction, qualification, limitation, requirement, or stipulation, relating to the performance of some agreement or contract. Anything which makes the performance of an agreement or operation of a contract tentative, uncertain, or dependent on future events.

conditional. Subject to, or dependent on, some uncertain CONDITION, which may or may not be fulfilled. Not to come into full effect until some condition or restriction is removed. See each of the following under the principal listing: ~ ACCEPTANCE (1,3); ~ BILL OF SALE; ~ CONTRACT; ~ FEE (2); ~ ESTATE (1); ~ ENDORSEMENT (2); ~ SALE (1).

conditional sales contract. The form of contract used for conditional or installment sales, under which the seller retains full title until payment is completed. Under the Uniform Conditional Sales Act, which has been adopted in many states, such a contract must be recorded, in a similar manner to a chattel mortgage or deed of trust. See also SALE, CONDITIONAL.

conditions of sale. A statement, such as on an order form, invoice, shipping document, or sales contract, of the terms and conditions under which a sale will be made. See also TERMS OF SALE.

confession of judgment. In some states, a formal and verified statement given by a debtor to a creditor, acknowledging the existence of a debt. The statement may be filed in the proper court as a means of permitting the creditor to obtain a JUDGMENT against the debtor without going through a more complicated procedure. The exact status of the *confession,* and the procedures to be followed, vary from state to state.

confidence game. A colloquial term for any scheme for obtaining money or property from an unsuspecting victim by trickery, fraud, etc. The name derives from the fact that the success of the scheme depends on taking advantage of the misplaced confidence of the victim in the operator of the scheme.

confidence man. An operator of a CONFIDENCE GAME; a professional swindler.

confirm. To authenticate or corroborate; to make certain or final; to make firm. For example, a person who has placed an order by telephone may *confirm* it in writing, or a person who has made an oral offer of any sort may *confirm* it later in more formal terms.

confirmation. A written memorandum or letter making a tentative, informal, or oral offer certain and final. In the law of contracts, many forms of oral contract must be converted into a written contract by a *confirmation* in order to be considered valid.

confirmed credit. See under CREDIT (3).

confirmed letter of credit. See under LETTER OF CREDIT.

confiscation. The appropriation or seizure of property by the government or a public agency for the use of protection of the state, with or without just compensation. For example, the *confiscation* of property for public use is accomplished by CONDEMNATION, which involves compensation, but the *confiscation* of illegal weapons, smuggled merchandise, gambling devices, etc., is by FORFEITURE, with no compensation involved.

consent. In law, agreement or approval that something be done or not done. Strictly, *consent* is distinguished from ASSENT in that it refers to that which has not yet occurred, while assent is approval of what has already happened. It is sometimes said that *consent* is active, and assent is passive.

consequential. In general, following from a preceding event, as a result follows from a cause. The term implies a causal relationship, rather than a mere sequence in time. See each of the following under the principal listing: ~ DAMAGE; ~ DAMAGES; ~ LOSS (2).

consent decree. See under DECREE.

consideration. In commercial law, the thing of value given by one party to a contract which induces the other party to enter into the contract. It may be a physical thing, or an act or performance. Ordinarily, the exchange of *considerations* is mutual, each party giving something up to the other. Strictly speaking, a contract is not valid without a *consideration,* which should be of substantial value in proportion to the benefit to be derived from the contract. The principal forms and classifications of *considerations* are listed and defined below. See also CONTRACT; VALUE RECEIVED.

good ~. Strictly, one founded on motives other than gain, such as natural affection, duty, moral obligation, etc. Generally, it consists of a promise to do some lawful thing, or to forbear from doing some lawful thing which one has a right to do. It is also known as a valid *consideration.*

illegal ~. One which contravenes some statute, or is against public policy, or is otherwise one which the courts will neither sanction nor enforce. A *consideration* may be illegal whether it is the result of a deliberate attempt to accomplish some unlawful purpose, or is based on fraud or deceit, or is merely the result of a misunderstanding or mistake.

impossible ~. One which for any reason cannot be carried out, or which has subsequently been nullified by some act or happening; hence, one which will not be recognized by the courts.

legal ~. One which the authority of the state, through the courts, will sanction and enforce; one which does not contravene any statute or violate public policy, as distinguished from an ILLEGAL CONSIDERATION, which see above.

mutual ~. One of the *considerations* exchanged by both parties to a contract.

onerous ~. One which puts a real or substantial burden or demand on the giver, rather than a nominal or token burden. An *onerous consideration* may be required by the laws of some states for some types of contracts. See also SUFFICIENT CONSIDERATION, below.

partial ~. One which is merely a portion of the total *consideration* to be given, as when both money and the performance of some act are to make up the *consideration.* In another sense, one which is legal and valid, and is separable from another part of the *consideration* which is held to be illegal or invalid.

sufficient ~. Any one which a court, upon examination, will hold to be enough to make a contract binding, and to support a claim for non-performance brought by the party giving the *consideration.*

valid ~. See GOOD CONSIDERATION, above.

valuable ~. In general, money, or something with monetary value. In a contract of sale, for example, it is the price paid. More broadly, it is one by which the person giving suffers some immediate, substantial, and material loss.

consign. To forward goods from one person or place to another; to deliver goods into the custody of another, such as a carrier, storage company, or sales agent. To deposit goods with an agent or distributor for sale, with title kept by the deliverer.

consignee. In general, the one to whom goods or property is CONSIGNED. In transportation, the person to whom a shipment of goods is to be delivered; the one who is authorized to accept delivery from a carrier. The *consignee* need not be the purchaser of the goods, nor the one to whom title is to pass, but merely the acceptor.

consignment. In general, a shipment for delivery. More particularly, a delivery of goods from a seller or consignor to a distributor or dealer, who is to act as selling agent for the goods, without taking title to them at the time of delivery. In the simplest case, the distributor merely acts as a commission agent, selling the goods in the name of the owner, and receiving a commission. In some trades, however, the goods are considered to change hands from the original consignor to the distributor and then to the final customer at the time of sale, so that the customer has made his purchase from the distributor, rather than from the consignor of the goods. This method of distribution is commonly known as *consignment* selling. See also SALE (1) ON CONSIGNMENT.

consignor. In general, the person who makes delivery of a shipment, or who turns it over to a carrier for transportation and delivery. More particularly, one who makes delivery of goods on CONSIGNMENT to a distributor or agent to be sold, without giving up title to the goods.

consistency. In general, an internal agreement or harmony; a congruity. In accounting, for example, it is the use of a uniform system of accounts and a uniform practice of posting to accounts over a long period of time, so that the accounting results obtained over the period are in agreement, and may be compared with each other.

consol. In the securities trade, a term for a bond issue that is a consolidation of previous issues. Specifically, the term is used to refer to the consolidated bonds of England, which were first consolidated from nine separate loans in 1751. The market price of *consols* was long regarded as a barometer of the British credit position, and British government bonds are still frequently referred to as *consols,* whether or not they are related to the original consolidation. See also BOND (1), CONSOLIDATED.

consolidated. Joined or combined into a single body or issue. Merged into a common corporation, security, document, etc. See each of the following under the principal listing: ~ BALANCE SHEET; ~ BOND (1); ~ BOND (1), MORTGAGE.

consolidation. In business, the joining together of two or more corporations into a new one, which is the surviving corporation. Strictly, a *consolidation* differs from a MERGER, in that in the latter case one corporation absorbs one or more others, while in the case of a *consolidation* a new corporation is formed to take over the assets and business of all of the existing corporations involved. Both are forms of AMALGAMATION.

consortium. The term for an agreement under which several nations, or the financial institutions of several nations, join together for some common purpose, usually to help one of the nations involved. It is also the name for the international body or organization formed under such an aid agreement. More broadly, any association formed for a common end; a temporary partnership.

constant dollars. A method of expressing statistical series in a form that eliminates the effect of the changing purchasing power of the dollar. A series of statistics on sales volume, consumer expenditures, or production, for example, expressed in *constant dollars,* is the physical amount of goods or services sold, bought, or produced over a period of time, valued at the prices existing at one particular time. In NATIONAL INCOME statistics, various measures are frequently given both in current or actual dollars and in *constant 1947 dollars.* See also CURRENT DOLLARS.

construction bond. See under BOND (1).

constructive. That which may be inferred, construed, or implied, from the surrounding circumstances, or from the actions or absence of actions of the person concerned. For example, the receipt of a shipment of goods may be *constructive,* rather than actual, when it has been accepted by an agent for delivery to a warehouse, though the goods themselves have not yet been delivered to the warehouse. In such a case, the warehouse becomes liable for the goods at the time of their *constructive* receipt, rather than their actual receipt. See also LOSS, CONSTRUCTIVE; TRUST (1), CONSTRUCTIVE.

constructive delivery. See DELIVERY (1).

consul. The commercial representative of a government in a foreign state. In general, the duties of a *consul* are to promote the commercial interests of his country and its citizens in the foreign country, to observe the operation of commercial treaties, to provide services and facilities for citizens of his country doing business in the foreign country, and for citizens of the foreign country doing business with his country, etc. *Consuls* are not considered diplomatic representatives of their countries, and are not granted many of the usual diplomatic immunities. Major countries may establish consulates in several cities of other countries, rather than only in the capital city.

consular invoice. In foreign trade, the name for a special copy of an INVOICE accompanying or relating to a shipment of goods into a country which has been reviewed and signed by the CONSUL of the receiving country who resides in the country of origin of the shipment. Many countries require such invoices on all imports, and charge a fee for the signature of the consul. The *consular invoice* then becomes the document on which the import tariffs and other charges and regulations are based.

consumer. In general, one who uses or consumes goods or services, rather than one who distributes or produces them. In economic statistics, *consumers* are those private individuals or families who buy goods and services for their own personal use or consumption, rather than for resale or for further processing or manufacture. However, a manufacturing company may also be a *consumer* of those supplies, maintenance goods, communications services, etc., which it uses but which it does not resell or incorporate into its products for resale. The term *ultimate consumer* is sometimes used to specify one who finally consumes a product, as distinguished from one who is a *consumer* with respect to his supplier, but who may not be a true *consumer* in the strict sense.

consumer advertising. See under ADVERTISING.

consumer credit. In general, the entire system of the extension of credit to CONSUMERS, both in connection with the purchase of particular products and services, and the making of loans to private individuals for unspecified purposes. In economic statistics, the figures on *consumer credit* include credit extended in connection with installment sales, consumer loans, both installment and single payment, retail charge accounts outstanding, repair and modernization loans for housing, etc. Real estate mortgage credit outstanding, however, is not included.

consumer jury. See CONSUMER PANEL.

consumer loan. See LOAN, PERSONAL.

consumer panel. In marketing research, the term for a selected group of representative private consumers which is used by a manufacturer, advertising agency, or marketing research company to help determine consumer reactions to new products, services, or advertising campaigns. The product, service, or advertising material being tested is submitted to the panel, or to some of the members of it, and they are then asked for their opinions, or are required to fill out a report or questionnaire form. They are also sometimes known as consumer juries.

Consumer Price Index. The index of prices paid by urban wage earning families, maintained by the Bureau of Labor Statistics. It is based on the actual retail prices of a wide variety of consumer goods and services, collected in a number of cities across the country each month. The present index is calculated with reference to average prices during a base period of 1947 to 1949. Thus, when the index stands at 118, for example, it indicates that consumer prices, on the average, have risen 18 percent since the base period.

consumers' cooperative. See under COOPERATIVE.

consumers' goods. See under GOODS (3).

consumption. In economics, the use of goods or services, as distinguished from their PRODUCTION or DISTRIBUTION. The purchase or obtaining of goods or services by final consumers, rather than for further processing or for resale.

consumption tax. See under TAX (2).

contact man. A term for an ACCOUNT EXECUTIVE.

container. In general, any outside or confining medium; a box, crate, can, bag, or other object that contains, or is designed to contain any product or material. In some usages, a *container* is distinguished from a PACKAGE in that it is the object which directly contains the product or material, while a package may be either a *container* or an outer packaging for shipment. This distinction is not consistently made in common business usage, however, and a *container* may be spoken of as an inner or outer *container*.

continental bill of exchange. See under BILL OF EXCHANGE.

contingency. In general, any event that may or may not happen. An event that depends on some future uncertain event or condition for its own happening. A *contingency* RESERVE, for example, is one set aside against the possible occurrence of some uncertain or indefinite future event which may involve cost to the company.

contingent. Conditional or dependent on the happening of some future event; doubtful or uncertain; not definite. See each of the following under the principal listing: ∼ ANNUITY; ∼ BENEFICIARY (2); ∼ FEE (1); ∼ LIABILITY (3).

contingent business interruption insurance. See under INSURANCE, PROPERTY.

continued bond. See under BOND (1).

continuing agreement. A term for the form of agreement entered into between a borrower and a bank or other lender from which he is a regular borrower. It sets forth the terms and conditions under which loans will be made and repaid, and obviates the necessity of making a separate note or instrument each time a loan is made. Such an agreement usually is set up to cover unsecured call loans only, and may specify the total amount of such loans which may be outstanding at any one time. See also LINE OF CREDIT.

continuing partner. See under PARTNER.

continuous audit. See under AUDIT (1).

continuous process. In manufacturing, any operation, such as in the manufacture of chemicals, petroleum products, etc. which must run continuously, with raw materials being fed in and the finished product being drawn off while the process is in operation. The distillation of alcohol is an example of such a process. It is distinguished from a BATCH PROCESS, in which a single loading or batch of materials is processed to completion before another load of materials is fed into the process.

contra. A Latin word meaning against. In law, accounting, and other fields, it is used to mean against, opposite, or offsetting, in combination with a large variety of standard terms. In accounting, for example, a *contra account* is one which offsets or is offset by another; one which is entered on the opposite side of a statement from another particular account.

contraband. Strictly speaking, under international law, any goods which a neutral may not furnish to or transport for a belligerent without violating its neutrality. Examples include weapons, munitions, fuel, or any other materials or products declared vital to carrying on a war. In more general usage, any goods which may not legally be transported, imported, or exported, especially such goods which have been seized by the authorities.

contract. 1. In law, a promissory agreement between two or more persons or parties that creates, modifies, or cancels some legal relationship. An agreement to do or not to do a specified thing, in exchange for a proper CONSIDERATION. Also, the written evidence of such an agreement. To be enforceable under law, a *contract* must have the following elements: an expression of mutual agreement, or an OFFER and an ACCEPTANCE; evidence of the capacity of both parties to enter into the agreement; a legal object and legal means of accomplishing it; and a sufficient consideration. The principal types and classes of *contract* are listed and defined below.

  absolute ∼. One in which a simple, unconditional, and unlimited promise or agreement is made. One which will not be limited or affected by the happening of some future event. See also CONDITIONAL CONTRACT, below.

  aleatory ∼. One which is contingent for its fulfillment upon some future event. Examples include insurance *contracts* and all forms of wager agreements.

  broker's ∼. The name for the oral agreement under which a security broker buys, sells, delivers, or receives a certain number of shares of stock, or a certain amount of bonds, for the account of a customer.

  commutative ∼. One under which each of the parties gives and receives an equivalent benefit. See also RECIPROCAL CONTRACT, below.

  conditional ∼. One, the performance of which is conditioned upon the prior performance by one or the other party of something at some future time, or upon the removal of some restriction which is specified.

  conditional sales ∼. See directly.

  delivery ∼. A term sometimes used for the type of *contract* under which each party is specifically bound, one to deliver and one to accept delivery, at a particular time and place.

  entire ∼. A form of *contract* in which all of the commitments made by one party must be carried out before the other party is bound to perform or pay that which he has promised in return. If the first party abandons his promises after only partial fulfillment, he is not entitled to any payment at all from the other for the partial performance.

  executed ∼. One in which nothing more now remains to be done by either party to discharge his obligations under the agreement. One which has been put into effect by all of the parties. Such a *contract* actually exists in name only, since it is fulfilled, but its existence prohibits any future impairment or questioning of the settled obligations.

executory ⁓. One which has not been fully carried out or put into effect, or which cannot be put into effect at the time of the agreement. For example, a *contract* to lend money at some future date, or one to build a house after the purchase of land at a future date, is *executory* at the time it is made.

express ⁓. One representing an open and actual agreement between the parties, with terms which are directly stated, and which have been agreed to by all the parties, as distinguished from an IMPLIED CONTRACT, which see below.

formal ⁓. One prepared according to the specified forms established by law for the particular type of *contract,* and which observes the formalities specified by the law, such as the use of a seal. Examples include DEEDS, MORTGAGES, etc. It is also known as a special *contract.*

gratuitous ⁓. One in which all of the benefits are to one party, with no offsetting requirements, and with no profits or advantages to the other party. Such a *contract* will not be enforced by a court, since there is no sufficient consideration. See also NAKED CONTRACT, below.

illegal ⁓. One which is entered into for an unlawful purpose, or which will have an unlawful result, regardless of the intent. Examples include any *contracts* to defraud a third person, *contracts* to violate a law, etc. All *illegal contracts* are VOID CONTRACTS, which see below, and are not enforceable.

implied ⁓. One which may not exist directly in writing, but which is inferred from the acts of one or both parties, or from circumstances which make the assumption that an agreement exists a reasonable one. For example, an order submitted implies an agreement to pay for the goods if the order is accepted.

impossible ⁓. One which cannot be carried out because its terms are physically impossible, or because circumstances have changed since the agreement was made, or because the object of the *contract* no longer exists. For example, a *contract* to buy a house becomes impossible and void if the house burns down before the *contract* is executed. All such *contracts* are void and unenforceable.

informal ⁓. One which does not depend for its validity on the form in which it is made, or on a recording under seal, but on an enforceable agreement between competent parties, and a sufficient consideration. It is sometimes known as a simple *contract,* and is distinguished from a special or FORMAL CONTRACT, which see above.

joint and several ⁓. One in which the obligation to perform rests on two or more parties, who are liable both together and separately for its performance. In the event of a failure to perform, they may be sued both jointly and separately by the person to whom they are obligated.

labor ⁓. See directly.

land ⁓. The term sometimes used for the preliminary agreement prepared in the sale and purchase of land, which is binding upon the buyer and seller until the formal DEED can be prepared and executed.

legal ⁓. One with lawful object and means; one which the state, through the courts, will enforce, as distinguished from an ILLEGAL CONTRACT, which see above.

marine ⁓. One relating exclusively to business transacted on the high seas, or in ports, or on navigable inland waters, and dealing with maritime commerce; one within the jurisdiction of the ADMIRALTY COURTS.

naked ⁓. One which is incomplete in some particular, especially one in which there is no consideration present. Such a *contract* is a VOID CONTRACT, which see below.

open end ⁓. One, especially a sales *contract,* in which all of the terms are not fixed, but are deliberately left indefinite or open. An example is a *contract* for goods in which the total amount is not specified, so that additional amounts may be ordered under the same terms for the life of the *contract.*

option ⁓. One which, for a consideration, gives a privilege or OPTION, such as the right to have an offer held open for a specified period of time.

oral ⁓. See PAROL CONTRACT, below.

parol ⁓. One which is not reduced to writing, but is by word of mouth only; an oral or verbal *contract.* More broadly, one which is in the form of a memorandum or other informal note, rather than a FORMAL CONTRACT, which see above.

quasi ⁓. A form of agreement which arises out of the actions or transactions of the parties, without an express agreement. A *contract* which is imposed or assumed by law. See also IMPLIED CONTRACT, above.

reciprocal ⁓. One in which the parties each agree to perform some service or give some benefit to the other, in return for considerations exchanged. The benefits need not be of equal value, as long as those on each side are substantial. See also COMMUTATIVE CONTRACT, above.

requirement ⁓. The name for one requiring a buyer or a lessee of equipment to obtain all of his supplies or other requirements from the same source. Such *contracts* have been held to be in restraint of trade and illegal under the anti-trust laws. See also TIE-IN SALE.

sale ∿. See SALE (1).

several ∿. See JOINT AND SEVERAL CONTRACT, above.

simple ∿. See INFORMAL CONTRACT, above.

special ∿. See FORMAL CONTRACT, above.

sub- ∿. One which is made under or within the terms of another *contract,* which is the master *contract* with respect to the *sub-contract.* For example, a person who has received a *contract* to perform certain work on a building being constructed may sign a *sub-contract* with another person to perform the actual work, or a part of it.

void ∿. Any one which is not enforceable under law, either because it is illegal, or is incomplete, or lacks a sufficient consideration, or for some other reason. A *contract* may be legal but VOID, however.

voidable ∿. One which is presently in force and effective, but which may be made void by either of the parties, or by circumstances. For example, it may be discovered that one of the parties was not competent to sign, or that there is some fraud in the terms, etc. State laws differ as to the conditions under which a *contract* is VOIDABLE.

written ∿. Any one which is reduced to writing, as distinguished from a PAROL CONTRACT, which see above.

2. To agree, or to enter into a contractual arrangement. To bind one's self to perform some act, or deliver some goods, in a formal agreement with one or more other persons. For example, a person who offers to sell goods at a price *contracts* to make the goods available, and to deliver them, at that price.

3. In the commodities trade, a term for the established or customary unit of trading. For example, the standard recognized cotton *contract* is an agreement to deliver 50,000 pounds, or 100 bales, of cotton in the month named. In the FUTURES market, different prices are set for *contracts* to be delivered in different months in the future.

contract bond. See under BOND (2).

contract carrier. See under CARRIER.

contract clause. The popular name for the provision in Section 10, Article I, of the United States Constitution, that "No state shall . . . pass any . . . law impairing the obligation of contracts." See also IMPAIR.

contract grade. In the commodities trade, any one of the various established and standardized qualities or grades set for the different commodities which are traded on the open market in terms of which contracts are made. The establishment of such uniformly defined grades facilitates the buying and selling of commodities.

contraction. In economics, the phase of a BUSINESS CYCLE leading from PROSPERITY to DEPRESSION. The period during which business volume is becoming smaller, unemployment is increasing, etc. It is the opposite phase from an EXPANSION, which is the period of generally rising activity, leading from depression back to prosperity.

contract market. Under the Commodity Exchange Act, one of the eighteen commodity exchanges which are authorized to deal in FUTURES contracts in the various commodities. The *contract markets* are administered by the Commodities Exchange Commission, through the Commodities Exchange Authority. See also EXCHANGE (2), COMMODITY.

contract month. In the commodities trade, the month during which a FUTURES contract matures. The month during which the commodity involved is to be delivered, if the contract is held.

contractor. In general, any person who enters into a contract, or is a party to a bargain or agreement. As used, any person or company doing work or performing services for others, or supplying materials to others, for compensation, but not as an EMPLOYEE or AGENT. In some trades, such as construction, apparel manufacturing, etc., one who does work with or on materials belonging to the person for whom the work is being done. A *contractor,* for example, may perform the sewing operations on men's clothing, with the work in process remaining the property of another manufacturer. See also INDEPENDENT CONTRACTOR.

contractual liability insurance. See under INSURANCE, CASUALTY AND LIABILITY.

contributed surplus. See SURPLUS, PAID IN.

contribution. In general, any amount given, or provided, to supply aid, or for some other special purpose. Any share, or sharing, of a loss, obligation, or payment among several persons or companies. The heirs of a person with debts, for example, may be called on to make a *contribution* to pay the debts out of their respective shares of the estate.

contribution clause. In insurance, a clause now inserted in many fire insurance and similar policies providing that in the event of a loss covered by more than one policy, the particular policy will pay only that proportion of the total loss that the amount of the insurance bears to all of the insurance covering the loss. If a home is insured for $10,000 under one policy with a *contribution clause,* for example, and insured for another $20,000 under other policies, the first policy will contribute only one third of the amount of any loss, up to the value of the policy. This form of clause has largely replaced the former EXCESS COVERAGE CLAUSE, under which each policy claimed to cover only the excess of loss over that covered by all other policies. Such clauses obviously led to impossible situations.

contributory infringement. See under INFRINGEMENT (2).

contributory pension plan. See PENSION PLAN.

contributory negligence. See under NEGLIGENCE.

control. 1. Originally, to check, or verify, by comparison with a counter-roll, or independent duplicate register of accounts. Thus, in accounting, to check and regulate the accounts of a business, and to compare actual performance against plans, standards, or budgets. More broadly, to analyze and interpret all of the accounting and statistical records of a business, for the purpose of reaching management decisions.

2. In statistics and quality control, the condition in which all of the variation in the measured characteristic of a product can be explained by chance, or random variations, rather than by errors or biases in the production operation. A manufacturing process is said to be in *control* when the individual variations in the measured characteristics are distributed above and below the desired level in a pattern that can be explained by chance variation.

controlled circulation. See under CIRCULATION (3).

controlled company. See under COMPANY.

controller. In a business organization, the key executive whose duty it is to CONTROL, or to analyze and interpret the financial results of the organization. The typical *controller* is also the chief accounting executive of the company, and is responsible for the design of accounting systems, the preparation of budgets and financial forecasts, the internal auditing of the company's operations and records, etc. In many companies, the duties of the *controller* are performed by the company treasurer, and in others they are largely performed by the chief accounting officer, whatever his title. The term is sometimes spelled *comptroller,* though this is becoming less common in American usage.

Controller (or Comptroller) of the Currency. The federal officer, in the Treasury Department, who is charged with the supervision of the national banks, and with enforcement and administration of the National Bank Act. The BANK EXAMINERS who examine national

banks are agents of the *Controller of the Currency.*

controlling account. See ACCOUNT (2), SUMMARY.

controlling company. See under COMPANY.

convenience goods. See under GOODS (3).

convention. 1. A pact or agreement among a number of states, or a number of countries, providing for uniform action or treatment on some matter of mutual interest. There are international *conventions,* for example, on the treatment of prisoners of war, on air travel rates and services, on postage service, and so forth. Generally, a *convention* is regarded as less formal than a treaty, but is just as binding.

2. A meeting, especially a large, periodic meeting, called to take action. The *convention* of a political party, for example, is called to prepare the platform of the party, and to nominate candidates for office. A company sales *convention* is called to prepare the sales campaign for the coming period, and to formulate sales policy with the help of the selling representatives who attend.

conventional interest. See under INTEREST (2).

conversion. 1. In general, the exchange or transformation of one thing into another. Examples include the *conversion* of preferred stock into common stock under specified conditions, the *conversion* of bonds into stock, the *conversion* of one currency into another, or the *conversion* of raw materials into finished products in a manufacturing process. See also CONVERTIBLE.

2. In law, any unauthorized taking over of the rights and privileges of ownership over goods or property belonging to another. The application to one's own uses and enjoyment of property belonging to another. As usually used, it is assumed to be without the permission of the owner, and therefore unlawful.

3. In tax law, the changing of wealth from real property to personal property, or the reverse. In general, any profit arising from such a *conversion* must be reported as income. The sale of a house for money, for example, is a *conversion* of property that may produce taxable income. If a *conversion* is involuntary, however, such as the collection of insurance on a house destroyed by fire, there will be no taxable income under certain conditions.

convertible. In general, capable of being changed from one form of property into another. As usually used, with reference to securities, currency, etc., authorized for exchange into other securities or currency of different form or class, but of similar value. See each of the following under the principal listing: ~ BOND (1); ~ CURRENCY; ~ MONEY; ~ STOCK (1).

convey. In law, to transfer property, or the title to property, from one person to another by means of the appropriate legal instruments, such as a DEED or other document. As used, the term usually refers to the transfer of real property.

conveyance. In law, the act of transfering property, or the title to it, from one owner to another. Also, an instrument by the terms of which such title is transferred, including a DEED, MORTGAGE, etc. However, in modern usage a WILL is not considered a *conveyance,* though it actually does convey title to property.

cooling-off period. In financial trade slang, the term for the period of time, usually 20 days, which must elapse between the filing of a registration for new securities and their public sale, under the regulations of the Securities and Exchange Commission. Also, in labor practice, the period prescribed by legislation or contract between the filing of a notice to strike and the actual strike. See also WAITING PERIOD (2, 3).

cooperative. In general, any enterprise, activity, or association which is created and owned jointly by its members, and is operated for their mutual benefit, with a sharing of any profits among the total membership. Frequently, the *cooperative* is formed by an association of persons who have a common need for some service or product, such as a marketing facility, milk delivery, etc., and is operated exclusively to serve its members. Often, however, the *cooperative* is formed by the operators of the facility itself, and its products or services are offered to the general public, with the operators sharing in the profits. In different states, the required form of organization for a *cooperative* differs, so that it may be an unincorporated ASSOCIATION, a non-profit CORPORATION, or a special form of *cooperative* corporation. The principal types of *cooperatives* in business are listed and defined below.

consumers' ~. One formed by private consumers of products or services, such as milk, gasoline, foodstuffs, laundry service, etc., to buy such products and services jointly at favorable prices, for distribution to members. Some *consumers' cooperatives* sell their products through their own stores at competitive market prices, to the general public as well as to their members. In this case, the accumu-

lated profits are usually returned to the members of the *cooperative* in the form of patronage refunds, based on the total amount of purchases made by each member. Some of the larger *consumers' cooperatives* now own their own sources of supply for products, such as canning plants, gasoline refining and storage facilities, dairy plants, etc.

housing ~. One formed for the purpose of supplying housing accommodations to its members. Usually, each member's stock ownership in the *cooperative* entitles him to occupy one dwelling unit, and the operating and carrying costs of the project are shared by the members in the form of monthly payments similar to rent. In some *housing cooperatives,* the title to all dwelling units is kept by the organization, and the member has only the right of occupancy. In others, however, the individual dwelling units are sold outright to the members, with the organization supplying operating and maintenance services.

marketing ~. One formed by farmers to market their produce jointly, usually under a single brand name. The *cooperative* may supply storage, processing, transportation, and other services, as well as the actual marketing and promotion of the products. Such *cooperatives* have been formed, for example, by the nut growers, orange growers, and other farm groups.

producers' ~. One formed by the original producers of a product, usually an agricultural product but not necessarily so, to obtain the benefits of the joint use of various equipment, services, facilities, etc. The *cooperative* may sell its products to the regular distributing trade, or it may operate also as a MARKETING COOPERATIVE, which see above.

purchasing ~. One formed by a group of independent retail stores, to buy products for resale and obtain the benefits of mass purchasing practices and volume discounts. The *cooperative* may serve strictly as a BUYING OFFICE for the stores, or it may also engage in the promotion of a common store name, brand name, etc., in which case the stores operate as a VOLUNTARY CHAIN.

service ~. One formed for the purpose of supplying any of a number of services to its members. Examples include medical care associations, electric utility companies, insurance societies, CREDIT UNIONS, etc. The *cooperative* may buy its services from commercial sources for resale to its members, or, as in the case of an insurance society, credit union, etc., it may organize its own facilities to perform the services.

cooperative advertising. See under ADVERTISING.

cooperative bank. See SAVINGS AND LOAN ASSOCIATION.

co-ownership. An indistinct term which may refer to JOINT ownership by two or more persons, or to ownership IN COMMON, or sometimes to SEVERAL ownership, under which each retains title to a distinct portion of the whole. The term is also frequently used in reference to a PARTNERSHIP arrangement. Since the meaning is inexact and confused, the term should be avoided in contracts and other documents.

copartner. See PARTNER.

copy. 1. In general, a reproduction, imitation, or transcript of writing, or of any work. A copy of a document, for example, may be made by reproducing it with writing or typing materials, or by the use of duplicating equipment. A copy of a literary work, or work of art, is a violation of the laws of COPYRIGHT, unless authorized. See also ATTESTED COPY.

2. In advertising, the term for the text, or reading matter in an advertisement, as distinguished from the illustrative or display material.

3. In printing and publishing, the term for any text material which is ready to be printed or to be set in type. More particularly, *rough copy* still needs editorial work, while *final copy* is ready for the printer.

copyright. The exclusive right or privilege, secured by law, granting to authors, artists, designers, or other creators of literary or artistic works the benefits of the publication of their work for a limited period. Under the present *copyright* laws, an original *copyright* is granted for 28 years, with the right of renewal by the creator or his estate for another 28 years. The actual right granted is the sole right to make copies of the material, for use or for sale, and the right to take action against others who make unauthorized copies, or who infringe the *copyright*. In practice, *copyright* is obtained by the publication of the work with a *copyright* notice in the proper form, and the filing of the proper application, with a copy of the work bearing the notice and the required fee, with the Copyright Office of the Library of Congress. Provision is also made for the *copyright* of unpublished works, such as lectures, plays, etc. Under recent rulings, a *copyright* may be obtained on a work of art intended to be incorporated in a manufactured product, provided the work is submitted as purely a work of art, and provided that each item of the final product carries the proper *copyright* notice. Ordinarily, however, a *copyright* may not be obtained for the design of a utilitarian product, which must be protected under the design section of the PATENT laws.

cord. A unit of measurement of wood, especially of logs or firewood. It is the amount of wood in a load or pile 8 feet long, 4 feet high, and 4 feet wide. It is thus the equivalent of 128 cubic feet of wood. The actual amount of wood contained, however, may vary according to the size of the pieces, the amount of air space between them, etc.

∼ **foot.** A unit of volume of wood, equivalent to one foot of the length of a standard *cord* which is piled 4 feet wide and 4 feet high. Thus, it contains 16 cubic feet, or ⅛ of a *cord*.

corner. To attempt to purchase all of the available supply of a commodity, with the intention of controlling the market and advancing the price at will, obtaining a large profit by so doing. In the securities trade, it is an attempt to purchase all of the stock of a company which is available in the market, so that those wishing to buy the stock, especially speculators who have sold it SHORT and must make purchases to cover their sales, will have to pay a high price. Such activities are now prohibited under the Commodities Exchange Act and the Securities Exchange Act. The practice is sometimes known as ENGROSSING.

corporate. Pertaining to or affecting CORPORATIONS, or their activities. Having the form, or performing some of the functions, of a corporation. See, for example, BOND (1), CORPORATE; TRUST (2), CORPORATE.

corporate agent. See FISCAL AGENT.

corporate charter. See CERTIFICATE OF INCORPORATION.

corporate income tax. See under TAX (2).

corporate mortgage bond. See under BOND (1).

corporate tax. Any one of various taxes levied by states or the federal government against corporations or their income or profit. See TAX, CORPORATE INCOME; TAX, EXCESS PROFITS; TAX, UNDISTRIBUTED PROFITS.

corporation. A legal entity or artificial person, created under the laws of a state to carry on some business or other authorized activity. It may be formed for a perpetual or limited period of time, has a name and identity under which it may be sued, and is authorized to enter into contractual agreements and perform all other functions which a person may perform under the laws of the state. The model *corporation* law, adopted in more or less the same form by many states, provides for the basic form of organization, officers, directors, meetings, etc. of *corpora-*

tions within each state. In general, a *corporation* may be a public, quasi-public, or private organization. The principal types and classifications of *corporations* are listed and defined below:

business ∿. One formed for the purpose of carrying on some legitimate business or commercial activity, as distinguished from one formed for non-business purposes. The principal distinction between a *business corporation* and other forms of business organization is the fact that the liability of the owners is limited to the capital of the *corporation,* so that the personal estates of the owners may not be held liable for the debts or losses of the business. This is not the case, for example, with a PROPRIETORSHIP or PARTNERSHIP.

close (or closed) ∿. One in which all of the shares of ownership, or stock, are held by a relatively few persons, and are not for sale to the public. In some cases, the owners may sign an agreement that they will not dispose of their shares without first offering them to the other owners. When a small part of the total stock of a *corporation* is held by the public, it is called a *closely held corporation,* though not strictly a *close corporation.* See also OPEN CORPORATION, below.

collapsible ∿. Under the federal income tax laws, the term for one formed for the purpose of avoiding the payment of corporate income taxes by means of a particular device. According to the federal Internal Revenue Code, it is a *corporation* formed to make, construct, or purchase property, to be held in inventory for sale but not sold, with the intention of making a distribution of the corporate assets to the shareholders before any substantial profit is realized on their normal sale. The shareholders may then realize the gain on the sale as individuals, avoiding the payment of a double tax, once on the corporate income and once on the dividend received. The code provides penalty taxes for the formation of such a *corporation.*

domestic ∿. According to the laws of most states, one organized under the laws of the particular state, and domiciled within the state. In some cases, the definition includes a *corporation* formed under a federal law as well. It is distinguished from a FOREIGN CORPORATION, which see below.

eleemosynary ∿. Under the laws of most states, one organized strictly for the carrying on of charitable activities. It may be severely limited regarding the ownership of property, the accumulation of income or assets, and so forth.

foreign ∿. According to the laws of most states, one organized under the laws of a foreign country, or of another state, or, in some cases, under federal laws, and domiciled elsewhere than in the particular state. It is distinguished from a DOMESTIC CORPORATION, which see above.

government ∿. A stock *corporation* formed and wholly owned by a government, particularly the federal government. Examples include the Federal Deposit Insurance Corporation, the Commodity Credit Corporation, etc.

lay ∿. One formed for any secular purpose, whether for commercial profit or not, as distinguished from a RELIGIOUS CORPORATION, which see below.

municipal ∿. A term for a town, borough, village, city, county, or other governmental unit smaller than a state, which is chartered as a *corporation* under the state law covering such *corporations.* Also, sometimes, a *corporation* wholly owned by such a political subdivision; a PUBLIC CORPORATION, which see below.

non-profit ∿. One not organized for commercial profit, but to carry on other activities, such as those of a FRATERNAL SOCIETY, political, religious, or charitable organization. A COOPERATIVE, etc.

non-stock ∿. One organized under the *corporation law,* or under a special law, but in which ownership is not represented by shares of stock. Examples include MUNICIPAL CORPORATIONS, which see above, and some PUBLIC CORPORATIONS, which see below. See also STOCK CORPORATION, below.

open ∿. One whose stock is available for sale to the general public, as distinguished from a CLOSE CORPORATION, which see above. It is possible for a majority, or a controlling share, of the stock of an *open corporation* to be held by a few persons, as long as a substantial share is held by the general public.

personal service ∿. The term for one whose income is derived primarily from the personal activities or services of the owners, rather than from the employment of invested capital. In states where architects, lawyers, doctors, etc., are permitted to incorporate, they form such *personal service corporations.*

public ∿. One formed for the purpose of carrying on some function of government, or of providing a government or public service. Examples might include a bank, library, water company, etc.

quasi ∿. The legal term for any public or private organization possessing some of the attributes of a *corporation,* and entitled to some of its privileges, but not yet strictly a *corporation*. An example is a JOINT STOCK COMPANY.

religious ∼. One organized specifically for the purpose of transacting matters connected with religion, or with a religious institution. Such a *corporation,* for example, may be formed to hold the property of a church, to conduct a religious school, etc. Under the laws of many states, they are entitled to special privileges and exemptions.

stock ∼. A term for the common form of *corporation,* in which ownership is represented by shares of stock, which are subscribed to and paid for by the individuals who form the *corporation.* It may be a regular BUSINESS CORPORATION or a PUBLIC CORPORATION, which see above. See also NONSTOCK CORPORATION, above.

corporation calendar. An agenda or list of the required and prescribed duties which a corporation or its officers must discharge over the course of a year, to comply with state law, its articles of incorporation, and its by-laws, arranged chronologically for the convenience of the corporate officers. Such a calendar assures that the corporation will prepare and submit the required reports, notices, etc., will hold the necessary elections, and so forth.

corporation charter. See ARTICLES OF INCORPORATION; CERTIFICATE OF INCORPORATION.

corporation paper. See under COMMERCIAL PAPER.

corpus. Literally, the body. With reference to a trust fund, annuity, estate, etc., it is the PRINCIPAL amount, or the capital, as distinguished from any interest or income. Thus, a person may establish a trust fund, providing that the income is to go to one person, and the *corpus* eventually to go to another. See also TRUST.

correlation. In statistics, the relationship existing between two or more characteristics or factors, which is such that when the value or behavior of one or more of the factors are known, the value or behavior of another can be predicted with a known degree of certainty. For a simple business example, there is a high degree of relationship, or *correlation,* between advertising expenditures and sales volume, especially in certain fields. Given the amount spent on advertising a product in one of these fields, and a measure of the *correlation* between advertising and sales, it is possible to predict sales volume with a known range of error. The various formulas and methods of calculating the coefficient of *correlation* may be found in texts on statistics. The more important classifications of *correlation,* or of regression, as

it is sometimes called, are listed and defined below.

multiple ∼. The measured relationship between one factor, on the one hand, and two or more factors on the other, taking into account the joint effects of the two or more factors and the interactions between them. An example would be the *correlation* between sales volume, on the one hand, and advertising expenditures, the number of salesmen, and the volume of sales promotion activities on the other.

partial ∼. The measured relationship between one factor, on the one hand, and one or more factors on the other, taking into account but artificially holding constant the effects of one or more additional known factors. An example would be the *correlation* between sales volume, on the one hand, and advertising expenditures on the other, with the number of salesmen known and held constant.

rank ∼. A method of measuring the relationship between two factors, by making paired observations on the two together, arranging the observations on one factor in order of size, and measuring the degree to which the other factor is also in order of size on this basis. For example, if the advertising expenditures of a number of companies are listed in order of size, and the corresponding sales volume of each company listed in an adjoining column, the *rank correlation* may be calculated from the degree to which the sales volume listing is in order of size.

simple ∼. The measured relationship between two factors, ignoring any possible or known effects on either of other factors. An example is the *correlation* between advertising and sales volume, ignoring the number of salesmen, promotional expenditures and any other factors.

correspondent. In business usage, any person or organization which maintains regular business relations with another, particularly with one in another city or another country. Typically, a *correspondent* acts as AGENT for the other company in any business which it must transact locally. For example, a *correspondent* bank accepts the BILLS OF EXCHANGE of another bank in another country, according to an agreement between the two banks.

cost. In general, the amount paid or expended for a particular product or service. The amount of money which is actually laid out or charged up for the purchase of goods or services, or the amount expended internally on the production of goods or services. In accounting, *cost* is distinguished from EX-

PENSE in that the former is the actual expenditure or charge, and the latter is the amount of the *cost* which is applicable to a particular accounting period. The amount expended on an item of capital equipment, for example, is a *cost*, but the DEPRECIATION charges on the equipment are expenses to the appropriate accounting period. The principal classifications of *costs* in business are listed and defined below.

actual ∼. In one sense, the *cost* of manufacture or production, not including storage or selling *costs*. In another sense, the ORIGINAL COST, which see below.

billed ∼. The purchase *cost* of an item as listed on the invoice, after deduction of the usual trade and quantity DISCOUNTS. Any cash discount allowed may or may not be deducted before figuring the *billed cost,* depending on the practice in the particular trade, or the accounting practices of the particular company.

direct ∼. The *cost* of materials and labor directly expended on the production of a product or service, as distinguished from the INDIRECT COSTS, which see below. See also VARIABLE COST, below.

factory ∼. The *cost* of a manufactured product as it leaves the factory, including materials, labor, and OVERHEAD, but excluding any non-manufacturing *costs*. Depending on the practice of the company, packaging and storage *costs* may or may not be included.

first ∼. See INITIAL COST, below.

fixed ∼. One which is not affected, or affected only slightly, by changes in the volume of business activity. One which does not vary with the amount of activity or output, as distinguished from a VARIABLE COST, which see below. Examples include rent, heat and light, maintenance, etc. See also INDIRECT COST, below.

imputed ∼. See directly.

indirect ∼. One expended on activities not directly associated with the production of a product or service, as distinguished from a DIRECT COST, which see above. *Indirect costs* are essentially the same as FIXED COSTS, which see above.

initial ∼. The first *cost* of acquiring an asset, not including the *costs* of maintaining or operating it. See also ORIGINAL COST, below.

joint ∼. A *cost* of producing two or more goods or services which are produced in a common or simultaneous manufacturing operation. See also JOINT PRODUCT.

marginal ∼. The *cost* of producing one additional unit of a product. Hence, the DIRECT COST, which see above, of the last unit produced at the actual operating rate of a plant or factory. See also directly.

net ∼. The BILLED COST, which see above, after all allowances and discounts have been deducted.

original ∼. The actual *cost* of an asset to a company when first purchased or constructed, as distinguished from the REPLACEMENT or REPRODUCTION COST, which see below. The term is especially used in the public utilities field. Loosely, the INITIAL COST, which see above.

replacement ∼. The *cost* of replacing an existing asset with the same materials at current *costs* of materials and labor. The term is frequently specified as *replacement cost new,* to make it clear that the asset is not to be replaced in its used or depreciated condition.

reproduction ∼. In the public utilities field, a special term for the calculated REPLACEMENT COST, which see above, of the assets of a public utility. The exact meaning of the term has varied in different court decisions, and is important in the setting of utility rates, which depend on the return on investment of the company.

unit ∼. See directly.

variable ∼. One which changes, or varies, in proportion to the volume of production, as distinguished from a FIXED COST, which see above. Examples include materials, labor, power, selling commissions, etc.

cost accounting. The branch of ACCOUNTING which is concerned with designing methods and systems for recording, allocating, and analyzing the costs of production and distribution in a company. The costs involved are the actual or projected outlays or expenditures for materials, labor, services, etc. involved in the regular operations of manufacturing or distributing a product or service. The particular functions of a *cost accounting* system include the proper recording of costs, their distribution or allocation to the appropriate accounts, and the analysis of total, average, or summary costs with those of other products, other periods of time, other methods of operation, etc.

cost and freight (C.A.F.). A term used in sales price quotations, for both domestic and export sales, meaning, in general, that the quoted price includes the cost of the goods and freight charges to a named destination, but not insurance fees and any other special charges. Under such terms, the seller is responsible for arranging for the transportation of the goods to the named point, and for paying the freight charges, but the buyer is responsible for any loss or damage during shipment, for arranging for local delivery of the goods, and for the payment of any import duties on the goods. See also COST, INSURANCE, AND FREIGHT; FREE ON BOARD; FREIGHT ALLOWED.

cost basis. See BASIS (2).

cost center. In COST ACCOUNTING, any machine, operating unit, department, etc., for which cost records are maintained, and to which OVERHEAD costs are allocated. Examples include a packaging operation, a single department in a department store, a connected series of metalworking operations in a factory, etc. It is sometimes known as a load center, due to the fact that overhead costs are loaded on the operating costs of the particular unit.

cost, insurance, and freight (C.I.F.). A term used in sales price quotations, for both domestic and export sales, meaning, in general, that the quoted price includes the cost of the goods, the freight charges to a named destination, and the insurance charges on the shipment of the goods. Under such terms, the seller is responsible for arranging for the transportation of the goods to the named point, for paying the freight charges, and for either insuring the shipment or assuming responsibility for any loss or damage during shipment. The buyer is responsible only for local delivery of the goods, and for paying any import duties on the goods. See also COST AND FREIGHT; FREE ON BOARD; FREIGHT ALLOWED.

cost markup. See MARKUP.

cost method. See under INVENTORY VALUATION.

cost of goods sold. In retail and wholesale accounting, a term used in an INCOME STATEMENT or other record, including the invoice cost of all goods sold during a period, plus the costs of transportation, handling, storage, alteration, etc. In standard retailing practice the term also includes costs of articles lost, destroyed, or stolen, depreciation on the goods in stock, and other costs of holding goods for sale. The term *cost of sales* is sometimes used.

cost of living. In economics, the average cost of providing the so-called necessities of life; the average of the retail prices of all of the goods and services needed to maintain a reasonable STANDARD OF LIVING by the average family. Various PRICE INDEXES have been constructed from time to time to measure changes in the *cost of living,* but in fact it is virtually impossible to include in such an index a combination of goods and services which will measure the *cost of living* for all families. The present CONSUMER PRICE INDEX of the Bureau of Labor Statistics is designed to measure changes in the prices of the goods and services bought by the typical urban wage-earning family, and to this extent measures changes in the *cost of living* of these families.

cost of living adjustment. In a union contract, a provision for an increase or decrease in wages in some fixed proportion to any increase or decrease in the COST OF LIVING, usually as measured by the Consumer Price Index of the Bureau of Labor Statistics. See also ESCALATOR CLAUSE (2).

cost of sales. See COST OF GOODS SOLD.

cost or market, whichever is lower. A popular basis for the valuation of inventory, under which each item in inventory is valued at either its original cost or the present market or replacement cost, whichever is lower. In some systems, depreciation is taken into account by figuring the market price as the price for similar goods in similar condition, or the price at which the item could be sold in a free market in its present condition. See also INVENTORY VALUATION.

cost-plus. A term pertaining to a method of setting a price for goods or services, under which the price charged is the cost of the goods, or the cost of producing them, plus a stated percentage of the cost or plus a stated amount. The latter form of arrangement is known as *cost-plus fixed fee.* Such arrangements are frequently included in contracts for the manufacture of war materials, or the construction of military bases, when the need to get the work done is more urgent than the desire for economy, so that the contractor is guaranteed that any costs he incurs will be reimbursed plus an assured profit. See also PRICE, COST-PLUS.

cost price. See under PRICE.

costs in law. See COURT COSTS.

cotton contract. See CONTRACT (3).

cotton linters. The name for the coarse, short-staple cotton fiber removed from the seed and husk by a second ginning, or by a linter machine. It is an inferior grade of cotton and is seldom used for textiles, but is used for mattress padding and similar packing.

coulomb. The basic unit used as a measure of the amount of electricity that flows in a given period of time. It is the amount of electricity that flows in a circuit at a rate of one AMPERE in one second. In a circuit of constant voltage, the number of *coulombs* that flow in a period of time are directly proportional to the number of WATTS of electric energy being consumed in the circuit.

counsel. In general, an advisor. As used, a lawyer, especially one who prepares and pleads a case in court; one who represents a client in a legal suit or action. In the records of a court proceeding, the term *of counsel* is used to identify the names of the lawyer or lawyers who represent the various parties before the court. See also ATTORNEY OF RECORD.

counter. A bench, table, or shelf on which goods may be displayed, and on which transactions are completed, especially in retail trade. The term is apparently derived from the counting table, on which money was counted out in the original banks, or counting houses. It appears now in such business phrases as OVER THE COUNTER; UNDER THE COUNTER; BARGAIN COUNTER, etc.

counter check. See under CHECK (1).

counterclaim. In law, an opposing action brought by a defendant against whom a claim is pending. It is usually an independent action against his opponent, as distinguished from a SET-OFF, which is a suit brought to reduce or eliminate the original claim, and based on the same circumstances.

counterfeit. Anything made in imitation of something else, with the intent to defraud; an illegal copy; false, such as a coin or currency. The term is derived from the old French, and originally meant to press a soft mold against something, such as a coin, for the purpose of making copies. Thus, it is distinguished from FORGERY in that it refers to things which are engraved, such as coins or printing plates, while forgery generally refers to written instruments.

counterfoil. A stub or part of a check, money order, or other instrument, which is retained by the person who issues or draws it, and which contains a record of the details of the transaction. It is not a receipt unless it is signed or acknowledged by both parties to the transaction.

countersign. To authenticate a document by adding another signature. For example, it may be required that a person receiving a salary check or other instrument sign it once as an acknowledgment of receipt, and to *countersign* it as an ENDORSEMENT when cashing or depositing it.

countervailing tariff. See under TARIFF (2).

county. Originally, in England, the district or territory governed by a count or earl. Now, in the United States, the basic political subdivision of a state, for political and administrative purposes. Forty-seven of the states are divided into *counties*, but Louisiana is divided into parishes, after the French custom, which are essentially the same as *coun-*

ties. Altogether, there are over 3,000 *counties* in the United States.

coupon. Originally, something to be cut off. Hence, in business and finance, a small piece of paper attached to a bond, note, or other interest-bearing instrument, as evidence of an interest payment to be made. The *coupon* is cut from the bond or note on or after the date on which the particular interest payment is due, and presented for payment. Each *coupon* is numbered to identify the specific interest payment for which it is to be presented. More generally, it is any certificate which is to be cut from an advertisement and presented as an order for goods, a request for information, etc. See also BOND (1), COUPON; NOTE (1), COUPON.

court. Any judicial organ of government, established to administer justice, interpret the law, or reach decisions in equity. Also, the judges, collectively, who make up a *court,* and the building or place in which it meets. The major classifications of *courts* in general are listed and defined below.

civil ∼. One which hears and decides on suits involving private rights, and disputes between individuals, rather than cases involving the breaking of laws or the breach of public order.

∼ of equity. One in which decisions are based on EQUITY (1), or on the principles of right and fair dealing, rather than on the written law.

∼ of law. One in which justice is administered according to the written and common law, rather than according to the principles of equity.

∼ of record. One whose acts, proceedings, and decisions are recorded. Generally, it is a *court* which has the power to fine or imprison, as distinguished from a *court* which is not of record, and can only settle disputes, without meting out punishment to one side or the other.

criminal ∼. One which administers the criminal law, and is empowered to deal out punishment to offenders against the law who are found guilty.

inferior ∼. Generally, one of limited jurisdiction, whose decisions or sentences are subject to appeal to, or review by, a higher or SUPERIOR COURT, which see below.

superior ∼. Generally, one of broad jurisdiction, with the power of review and supervision over lower or INFERIOR COURTS, which see above.

court costs. In law, those expenses or costs which are incurred in the prosecution or defense of a legal suit or action. Reimbursement for such costs may be granted by the court to the party which is successful in a suit. The costs which may be thus reimbursed are defined by statute in each state, and may or may not include attorney's fees, printing costs, etc.

Court of Appeals. See FEDERAL COURT SYSTEM.

Court of Claims. The federal court, established in 1855 to handle claims against the federal government. Before the establishment of this court, every claim against the government had to be handled by an act of Congress. Several of the states have similar courts.

Court of Customs and Patent Appeals. The federal court, created in 1910, and given broader powers in 1929, which hears appeals from decisions and rulings of the Customs Court, the Board of Patent Appeals, and the Tariff Commission.

covenant. Originally, in law, a written document, under seal, in which one person promises another that something will be done or not done. In current usage, the requirement of a seal has been abolished in most states, so that a *covenant* is any formal document promising performance or non-performance, such as a DEED.

cover. In business usage, to protect, or to provide payment. An investor, for example, may leave a *cover,* or deposit, with a securities broker, to protect the broker in the event of speculative losses by the investor. In this sense, *cover* is not the same as MARGIN, since it is not applied against a specific stock purchase. Similarly, a businessman may draw a check to *cover* his expenses on a forthcoming trip. An insurance company issues a contract of insurance to *cover* possible loss from specified causes.

coverage. In insurance, a term loosely used either as the amount of monetary protection or indemnity provided by an insurance contract, or as the hazards against which protection is given. A property insurance contract, for example, may be said to provide *coverage* of $50,000 against losses, or it may be said to provide broad *coverage* against a variety of hazards. In credit insurance, in particular, it is a term for the proportion of the loss from any one debtor that the insurance company agrees to repay.

cover-all clause. A term for a clause sometimes inserted in a real estate MORTGAGE, providing that the mortgaged property shall stand as security not only for the present loan given, but for all other present and future indebtedness of the borrower to the lender. See also MORTGAGE, OPEN END.

covering. In general, the act of meeting an obligation. As used, the term frequently refers specifically to the process of meeting one obligation by undertaking another. In foreign exchange dealings, for example, *covering* is the act of paying one bill of exchange, which is due, with another which has been purchased or drawn for the purpose. In the securities trade, *covering* is used with reference to SHORT selling, as the process of buying a stock to make the transfer of stock already promised by the short sale.

covert. In general, hidden, not open, not easily observable. A *covert* act is one carried out in secret, or one carried out under the disguise of some other act. It is the opposite of OVERT.

craft. 1. Originally, knowledge, skill, or cunning. Hence, an occupation or calling requiring special skill or art, especially the skills of manual dexterity. As used in modern industry, any of the various skilled trades, such as carpentry, bricklaying, printing, plumbing, etc., which may be used in several different industries.

2. In maritime usage, and in marine insurance contracts, any boat, ship, or vessel, whether for use on the open seas, on inland waters, or in harbors. Thus, it includes lighters, barges, tugs, etc., as well as regular passenger or cargo carrying vessels.

craft union. See under UNION.

crash. In economics, a sudden, precipitous, and disastrous decline in business activity, security values, prices, etc. The term is sometimes applied to a single business enterprise, meaning a sudden bankruptcy or failure of the business. In business cycle terms, the distinction between a *crash* and an ordinary CONTRACTION is not in the amount of the decline, but in the length of the time period over which it occurs.

credentials. In general, any documents intended to create belief. Any documents or papers used to verify a person's identity, or as evidence of his authority to act. A bill collector, for example, will usually carry *credentials,* identifying him as an agent or employee of the company for which he is collecting, and stating his authority to accept payment and to give a receipt in the company's name.

credit. 1. Broadly speaking, the ability to borrow money, or the ability to transact business or obtain delivery of goods or services, on the promise of future payment. The term itself is derived from the Latin word for belief, and implies trust, faith, and a reliance on the borrower's integrity. A person is said to have good *credit* when he can borrow easily, and poor *credit* when he can borrow only by pledging a high security. In business, a company's *credit* is based on its solvency, and on its past reputation for reliability in the payment of debts.

2. In accounting, an entry made on the liability side of a ledger or account. A *credit* entry represents a liability to the company, bank, or other organization keeping the ledger, and an asset or potential asset to the person, company, or depositor in whose ledger account it is entered. See also DEBIT (1).

3. In finance, an amount loaned, or the amount due to a CREDITOR; the counterpart of a DEBT. In business and finance, there are a wide variety of methods and forms of the extension of *credit,* the principal ones of which are listed and defined below.

acceptance ~. The *credit* established by the ACCEPTANCE (3) by a bank of a BILL OF EXCHANGE or other instrument made out to the order of the person in whose name the *credit* is now established.

bank ~. *Credit* established by a bank, usually in the form of a deposit against which a person may draw checks up to an agreed amount. *Bank credit* may be either SECURED or UNSECURED CREDIT, which see below.

banker's ~. A general term for any of the forms of commercial *credit* extended or arranged by banks, including BILLS OF EXCHANGE, LETTERS OF CREDIT, ACCEPTANCES (3), etc.

blank ~. In general, unlimited *credit;* any *credit* instrument which is signed without a specific amount or limit being filled in. See also CHECK, BLANK.

book ~. A term for the *credit* established on the account books of a company by allowing a customer to make a purchase without paying cash and without submitting a specific credit instrument, such as a NOTE. See also ACCOUNT (4).

cash ~. A term for a BANK CREDIT, which see above, set up to enable a business to borrow amounts from time to time to meet its everyday cash needs. Interest is charged only on the amounts outstanding and only for the period of time they are actually outstanding.

commercial ~. In general, any of the forms of *credit,* or *credit* instruments, issued in connection with business activities. See, for example, BILL OF EXCHANGE; COMMERCIAL PAPER. See also CONSUMER CREDIT.

confirmed ~. One extended by a bank to a customer on the basis of a commercial transaction, and confirmed, or stated to exist, by the bank in a letter. Such a *credit* becomes an IRREVOCABLE CREDIT, which see below. See also LETTER OF CREDIT, CONFIRMED.

consumer ~. See directly.

export ~. The credit established in favor of an exporter on the basis of the shipping documents and other required instruments, against which he is able to draw before his foreign customer makes payment.

import ~. The counterpart of an EXPORT CREDIT, which see above. It is the *credit* issued to an importer to permit him to make payment for imported goods, or to forward foreign currency to the foreign exporter if necessary.

irrevocable ~. One which cannot be withdrawn, revoked, or canceled before its expiration date, without the consent of all of the parties concerned; a CONFIRMED CREDIT, which see above.

marginal ~. A term for an EXPORT or IMPORT CREDIT, which see above, which may be drawn against, for any amount up to the margin or limit specified in the *credit* instrument.

open ~. One established by a bank, against which a customer may draw, without depositing security, up to a specified limit, or one established by a supplier, against which a customer may order goods, up to a limit, without making immediate payment. See also ACCOUNT (4), OPEN.

paper ~. A term for *credit* granted on the basis of a written obligation representing property, rather than on the basis of the property itself. Examples are *credit* extended on the basis of a mortgage, pawn ticket, or other paper put up as security.

revocable ~. One which has not been confirmed by the bank issuing it, and is therefore subject to being revoked or cancelled at any time by either of the parties involved. It is the opposite of a CONFIRMED or IRREVOCABLE CREDIT, which see above.

revolving ~. One established by a bank or supplier, permitting a customer to make withdrawals or order goods up to a limit, with the amount of *credit* available being automatically renewed as payments are made.

secured ~. One granted on the basis of a SECURITY (2) or COLLATERAL pledged or deposited to assure repayment, as distinguished from an UNSECURED CREDIT, which see below.

service ~. In general, a term for *credit* granted in connection with service, or with work in one of the professions, or the performance of professional work, such as by a lawyer, doctor, accountant, etc., without demand for immediate payment. It is not, strictly speaking, COMMERCIAL CREDIT, which see above.

store ~. See BOOK CREDIT, above.

trade ~. A term for the usual *credit* terms granted to buyers in any line of trade. In many trades, for example, it is thirty days from the date of the invoice, after which payment becomes due. See also TERMS OF SALE.

unconfirmed ∼. See REVOCABLE CREDIT, above.

unsecured ∼. One granted without requiring a pledge or deposit of COLLATERAL. Strictly speaking, such *credit* is secured by the SECURITY (2) of the borrower's good name and integrity.

credit agency. See MERCANTILE AGENCY.

credit balance. With respect to the account of a customer or depositor, the condition of having a net excess of *credit* over DEBIT entries. Hence, showing a net asset balance, or showing a net profit.

credit bureau. A term for a credit agency, or MERCANTILE AGENCY, especially one which limits its coverage to one or more particular lines of trade, or to a particular geographic area. *Credit bureaus* are frequently operated by trade associations for the benefit of their members, or by local chambers of commerce for the benefit of local manufacturers and distributors.

credit control. In general, the control of the use of credit facilities, or of the total amount of credit available or outstanding, either by governmental agencies or by the banking system itself. Since the RATE OF INTEREST is determined by the demand and supply of credit, and helps determine the demand for credit, the control of credit is in large part the control of the rate of interest.

credit cooperative. See CREDIT UNION.

credit currency. See under CURRENCY.

credit instrument. In finance and commerce, any written promise or order to pay, other than actual currency or bank notes, which serves the purposes of money in completing commercial transactions. There are many forms of such credit instruments, some of which are used for special types of commercial transactions, including ACCEPTANCES (3), BILLS OF EXCHANGE, CHECKS, DRAFTS, NOTES, MONEY ORDERS, LETTERS OF CREDIT, etc. Credit instruments may be either NEGOTIABLE or NON-NEGOTIABLE. See also NEGOTIABLE INSTRUMENT.

credit insurance See under INSURANCE, CASUALTY AND LIABILITY.

credit line. See LINE OF CREDIT.

credit manager. The title of the person in a business concern whose responsibility it is to make decisions in the field of the extension of credit. He must decide whether or not credit is to be extended to a particular customer, the amount of credit to be extended, and the terms under which it is to be extended. Together with the officers of the company, he also determines the general policy of the company with regard to credit selling, the extension of credit, and the terms of credit.

credit memorandum. The name for a document given by a supplier to a customer, stating that a credit for a stated amount has been set up in the customer's account. Such a *credit memorandum* may be sent, for example, when a customer has returned goods for credit, or when the price has been reduced and the agreement provides that the customer shall be given the benefit of any such reductions. It is common, for example, for suppliers to give their dealers the benefit of any price reduction on goods held in the dealer's inventory, and to carry this out by means of a *credit memorandum*. Ordinarily, the *credit memorandum* may not be converted into cash, but must be used in the purchase of additional goods. See also INVENTORY PROTECTION.

creditor. In general, any person who, in confidence of future payment, has transferred or rendered something of value to another. One who has made a LOAN, or to whom a DEBT is due. More broadly, any person who has an enforceable right to demand and recover a sum of money from another, whether arising originally out of a loan or not. Especially in connection with BANKRUPTCY proceedings, there are several recognized classes of *creditors*, which are listed and defined below.

general ∼. One whose demand for payment is secured only by the general credit or personal security of the borrower; hence, an UNSECURED CREDITOR, which see below.

judgment ∼. One whose claim against a delinquent debtor has been reduced to a JUDGMENT, or to an order for payment by a court.

petitioning ∼. In bankruptcy practice, the term for a *creditor* who has joined in a petition requesting a court to declare a debtor to be a bankrupt.

preferred ∼. One who is entitled under law to have his claim against a bankrupt, or against the estate of a deceased, satisfied before other claims. The holder of a first mortgage or other prior lien is a *preferred creditor*.

secondary ∼. One whose claim is second in priority to that of a PREFERRED CREDITOR, which see above. Thus, all *creditors* except preferred *creditors* are *secondary creditors* if there are any preferred *creditors* at all.

secured ∼. One whose claim is secured or evidenced by a pledge or deposit or property, or by some form of COLLATERAL, such as a mortgage.

unsecured ~. One who holds no COL-LATERAL to secure the payment of his debt, but who depends on the personal security of the borrower.

creditor nation. Any nation whose total obligations to foreign nations and individuals are less than the sum of all obligations owed to it. Hence, a nation with a net credit balance in its international transactions, and the opposite of a DEBTOR NATION. See also BALANCE OF PAYMENTS.

creditors' bill. In BANKRUPTCY proceedings, the name for the bill or petition filed in court on behalf of all of the creditors of a bankrupt business, and calling for an accounting of the assets of the business.

credit rating. An estimate, particularly one made by a MERCANTILE AGENCY or CREDIT BUREAU, of the CREDIT (1) of a person or company. Typically, a *credit rating* includes an estimate of the financial strength of the company, its ability to repay advances, and its record in paying commercial debts. See also RATING.

credit sale. See SALE (1) ON CREDIT.

credit union. A form of cooperative society, organized for the purpose of creating a source of credit for its members at reasonable rates of interest. The credit is usually granted in the form of small, short-term, personal loans, with or without security. The source of the funds to be loaned is usually the members themselves, who deposit savings with the *credit union* at interest, to be loaned out to other members. Typically, *credit unions* are organized among members of a common group, such as employees of a company, residents of a community, etc. A federal *credit union* is one organized under a charter from the Federal Deposit Insurance Corporation. Other names for *credit union* include baby bank, people's bank, etc.

crime. In law, a wrong or offense committed against the state, or against the public interest. More specifically, any act which is defined as a *crime* under the laws of a city, state, or government. In legal practice, a *crime* is distinguished from a TORT, which is a wrong committed against another person, such as LIBEL.

criminal action. See under ACTION (1).

criminal court. See under COURT.

criminal law. The branch of the written law which deals with offenses against the state, or against the public interest, and with the punishment for such offenses. Thus, it is distinguished from the CIVIL LAW, which deals with the rights of private individuals, and with disputes between individuals.

criminal libel. See under LIBEL.

criminal negligence. See under NEGLIGENCE.

crisis. In economics, a term previously used for the culmination of forces which bring about a downturn in a business cycle. The turning point at which the prosperity breaks and the depression begins. The term is seldom used in modern economic thinking.

crop insurance. The name for a special form of insurance provided to farmers, protecting them against financial loss due to hail, drought, insects, floods, etc., which may destroy their crops. Such *crop insurance* is made available to farmers by the Department of Agriculture at reasonable rates, and is also available commercially for certain areas and crops.

cross exchange. See under EXCHANGE (4).

cross hauling. In freight practice, the shipment of goods from one factory or source of supply to a distant market at the same time that goods from a source at or near that market are being shipped to the area of the first source. Thus, it is possible that the shipments might actually pass in being *cross hauled* from their respective sources to markets. In time of war, such *cross hauling* may be prohibited, in the interests of conservation.

cross licensing. In the field of PATENT licensing, the mutual exchange of LICENSES (2) by two or more patent holders, so that each may manufacture or use the products or processes patented by the other. Such *cross licensing* may be limited to particular named patents, or it may be general, applying to all of the patents of each participant.

cross order. See under ORDER (4).

cross trade. See MATCHED ORDER; WASH SALE.

crown octavo. See under BOOK SIZES.

cumulative. In general, additive; adding up from one to the other or from period to period, rather than starting anew each time. See each of the following under the principal listing: ~ DIVIDEND; ~ STOCK (1).

cumulative voting. A method of voting used for electing DIRECTORS of corporations, in those states in which the method is permitted. Under this method, each stockholder is entitled to vote for as many directors as are to be elected, or to cast the same number of votes for a single director, or for two or more directors, as long as the total number of votes cast by each stockholder is the same as it would be if he voted once for each vacancy. Under this method of voting, it is possible for minority stockholder groups, by concentrating their votes, to elect one or more representatives to a board of directors.

curb. In the securities trade, a term used originally in reference to trading activities other than those on the regular stock exchange. The term derives from the fact that stocks not listed on the exchange were usually traded on the sidewalk or *curb*. The term is now used primarily with reference to activities on the American Stock Exchange, formerly the New York Curb Exchange, which was organized by the brokers who trade on the *curb*. See also BROKER (2), CURB; STOCK (1), CURB.

curb exchange. In general, any secondary market for securities not listed on the primary or regular stock exchange. The name derives from the fact that trading in such securities was conducted on the sidewalk or curb near the regular exchange. Today, it refers specifically to the American Stock Exchange, formerly the New York Curb Exchange.

curfew. A term derived from the French expression *couvre-feu,* to cover the fire. Originally, it was a bell rung at a given time each evening as a signal to cover or bank fires, to conserve fuel. Hence, any regulation putting a restriction on activities after a certain hour of the evening, such as a *curfew* law requiring retail establishments or places of entertainment to be closed by a certain hour.

currency. Generally, anything which circulates freely and is widely accepted as a MEDIUM OF EXCHANGE. More particularly, the official MONEY of any country, including both metal and paper money, and such media as BANK NOTES which circulate as money. As usually used, the term is restricted to those forms of money which are actually issued and circulated, as distinguished from those which are only MONEY OF ACCOUNT. In popular usage, *currency* is sometimes used loosely to refer only to paper money, so that the term *coins and currency* is sometimes found even in legislation. The principal types and classifications of *currency* are listed and defined below.

   adjustable ~. See ELASTIC CURRENCY, below.

   asset ~. *Currency,* such as bank notes, secured by the assets of the issuing bank, rather than by deposits of government bonds, as is the usual practice.

   blocked ~. One which is restricted by the issuing government, so that it cannot be exported, or exchanged for foreign currency, except at fixed rates and in limited amounts under strict regulations. Usually, a currency is blocked by a government that has an unfavorable balance of trade, to prevent foreign traders from taking currency out of the country, and to force them to accept the goods and services of the country instead.

   convertible ~. A term for paper *currency* which is convertible, or redeemable, in metal coinage on demand at the Treasury or at the bank of issue. See also IRREDEEMABLE CURRENCY, below.

   credit ~. One which is based on the credit of the issuing government, rather than on deposits of gold or silver. See also MONEY, FIAT.

   elastic ~. A system of *currency* which permits the expansion of the amount of *currency* as the demand increases, and its contraction when there is less demand. The FEDERAL RESERVE SYSTEM provides an *elastic currency* for the United States.

   fractional ~. In general, those units of *currency* which are less than one dollar, such as the half-dollar, quarter, dime, nickel, and cent. See also SHINPLASTER.

   irredeemable ~. A term for paper *currency* which is not redeemable in precious metal or in gold or silver, but is only exchangeable for other legal tender. See also CREDIT CURRENCY, above; MONEY, FIAT.

   managed ~. One over which various governmental agencies exert control, altering the amount in circulation in order to regulate the price level, control the supply of credit, and otherwise attempt to affect the course of business fluctuations. See also ELASTIC CURRENCY, above.

   mixed ~. One consisting partly of precious metal coins, partly of paper *currency* convertible in precious metals, and partly of paper which is legal tender but is not convertible or redeemable. See also CONVERTIBLE CURRENCY and IRREDEEMABLE CURRENCY, above.

currency bond. See under BOND (1).

currency exchange. A financial organization, other than a bank, credit union, or similar institution, which is engaged primarily in providing facilities for the cashing of checks, money orders, etc., and which charges a fee for its services. Such *currency exchanges* usually are established near large industrial plants, where employees are paid by check but are not able to cash their checks immediately at a nearby, open bank.

currency in circulation. The total amount of all currency, including both paper money and coins, which are in use at any given time. As defined in economic statistics, it is the total of existing currency not held by the Federal Reserve Banks or the U. S. Treasury, and thus includes both that held by individuals and that held by banks as cash reserves. The phrase MONEY IN CIRCULATION is sometimes used with the same meaning.

current. As used in business, presently in force or effect; presently running, or not expired. Due and payable or receivable, but not yet overdue, especially due to be paid or received within the present fiscal period. Also, up to date, or existing at the present date. See each of the following under the principal listing: ~ ASSET (2); ~ DEBT; ~ EXPENSE (2); ~ LIABILITY (2); ~ YIELD.

current account. See ACCOUNT (4), OPEN.

current capital. See CAPITAL (3), CIRCULATING.

current dollars. A term used in economic statistics, meaning that a particular figure is expressed in the dollars actually existing at the time to which it refers, rather than in CONSTANT DOLLARS, or dollars which have been adjusted to eliminate the effect of price changes.

current money. Any money which is acceptable as lawful money. See also LEGAL TENDER.

current price. See PRICE, GOING.

current ratio. See under OPERATING RATIO.

curtailing. A term used with respect to a NOTE or other instrument, meaning a reduction in the principal of an outstanding note. This may be done by making a partial payment on the note while it is outstanding, or by renewing or extending it for a lesser amount at the time it falls due, either by making a partial payment or by agreement with the holder of the note.

custody. In law and business, the care and keeping of anything, or the responsibility for such care and keeping; guardianship. A person may have *custody* of the property of another without having actual possession at all times. In insurance, such property is normally excluded from the coverage of a property insurance contract, and the one who has such CUSTODY, or the BAILEE, should carry special liability insurance to cover his responsibility for the property.

custom. The usual or common practice or usage of a place or trade. Many statutes recognize the *custom of the trade* as an established procedure to be followed in the absence of specific laws or regulations to the contrary. Also, as sometimes used, the persons who usually or regularly trade with a particular business, or its CUSTOMERS.

customary tare. See under TARE.

customer. A person who makes a purchase; a client. The term is used especially for a regular *customer,* or one who usually or regularly buys or does business with a particular establishment.

customer's man. In the securities trade, a term for an ACCOUNT EXECUTIVE. A person who deals directly with the customers or clients of a securities broker, taking their orders and transmitting them to the traders, advising them on securities, and generally servicing their accounts.

customhouse broker. See BROKER (1), CUSTOMS.

custom-made. Made to the individual order of a customer. Made to the particular specifications and measurements of the customer, as distinguished from READY-MADE, or made to standard or average measurements. In the apparel field, *custom-made* clothes are cut directly from the cloth to the measurements of the customer, as distinguished from CUSTOM-TAILORED clothes, which are tailored or adjusted from the standard garments to fit the customer's individual measurements.

customs. Originally, the rents, duties, or taxes customarily paid to a feudal lord, especially those paid for the privilege of moving goods to a market. Now, the taxes imposed by a government on the import or export of goods; TARIFFS, or DUTIES. Also, in common usage, the process or procedure involved in bringing goods into the country from abroad, having them evaluated, and the *customs,* or tariff, paid. Goods are said to go through *customs* when they follow this procedure.

customs bond. See under BOND (2).

customs broker. See under BROKER (1).

Customs Court. The federal court, created in 1926 to replace the Board of General Appraisers, which reviews customs appraisals, settles disputed classifications, reviews cases in which the exclusion of imported goods is protested, etc. Its decisions may be appealed to the Court of Customs and Patent Appeals.

customs house. In general, the place at a port where imported goods are examined, evaluated, the tariff decided and paid, and otherwise processed for admission, and where incoming and outgoing ships are cleared. In particular, there is a United States Customs House in each of the major PORTS OF ENTRY. The term *custom house* is also used, with the same meaning.

customs tare. See under TARE.

custom-tailored. In the apparel field, a term for garments which are cut to standard sizes and partly manufactured, then finished or tailored to meet the individual measurements of the purchaser. Thus, it is distinguished both from CUSTOM-MADE, which is completely made to individual measurements, and from READY-MADE, which is completely manufactured to standard sizes.

cut a melon. In business slang, to make a large extra distribution of money or stock to stockholders, especially when this is done as the result of a particularly profitable transaction, such as the profitable sale of a subsidiary, or the disposal of some of the corporate assets at more than their stated or depreciated value.

cut back. To reduce, especially to reduce to a former level. Production may be *cut back*, for example, in a time of slack demand, or prices may be *cut back* to a previous level under a price control regulation. More generally, to reduce in amount, or to eliminate certain provisions or features, regardless of previous levels or terms.

cut price. See under PRICE.

cut-throat competition. A term for COMPETITION which is so severe and violent as to be destructive, especially when it is destructive of both companies that engage in it, so that they may be said to be cutting their own throats. For example, two competing companies may successively reduce prices, in an attempt to capture each other's share of a market, until each is selling below costs and losing money.

cwt. See HUNDREDWEIGHT.

cycle. See BUSINESS CYCLE.

D

daily. Occurring every day, or during the course of a day, or lasting for the period of a day. The term appears in such business phrases as *daily* allowance, *daily* balance, *daily* circulation, *daily* sales, *daily* wages, etc.

daily Treasury Statement basis. The most commonly used method of reporting receipts and expenditures of the federal government. On this basis, receipts are recorded when actually received by the Treasury, and expenditures are recorded when the checks are paid by the Treasury. See also CHECKS-ISSUED BASIS; COLLECTIONS BASIS.

damage. Any loss suffered by a person or property, whether resulting from unavoidable accident or from carelessness, premeditation, or negligence of another.

   consequential ～. *Damage* which flows from the necessary and connected effects of an act or cause, or from its consequences, rather than directly from the act itself.

   direct ～. *Damage* which follows directly from the act done, or from the cause.

damages. In law, the sum of money allowed or awarded by a court or other body as an INDEMNITY or recompense for some damage, injury, or loss sustained at the hands of another. Under some statutes, double or treble *damages,* twice or three times the value of the loss actually suffered, are provided for. The major classifications of *damages* which may be awarded are listed and defined below.

   actual ～. See SUBSTANTIAL DAMAGES, below.

   compensatory ～. Those awarded in an amount, and for the purpose, of recompensing a person for the loss actually suffered, as distinguished from PUNITIVE DAMAGES, which see below.

   consequential ～. Those awarded for any loss which is directly attributable to an act committed by another, and which is complained of before a court or other body with the power to award *damages.*

   exemplary ～. See PUNITIVE DAMAGES, below.

   nominal ～. A trifling sum awarded to the plaintiff in an action, when an infraction of his rights is recognized, but he has been unable to demonstrate any substantial loss or injury. See also SUBSTANTIAL DAMAGES, below.

   punitive ～. Those awarded, not in proportion to the loss suffered, but as punishment for a malicious act. In awarding *damages* for LIBEL, for example, the court may decide that the actual damage done is small, but may still award heavy *damages* because the libel was committed maliciously, and with intent to injure. These are sometimes known as *exemplary damages,* since they are intended to make an example of the one who is required to pay.

   substantial ～. Those awarded in relation to a real loss suffered, or in any event in an amount which recognizes that a substantial loss has been suffered, as distinguished from NOMINAL DAMAGES, which see above.

damask. Silk, linen, or cotton material with a pattern woven into it. *Damask* is frequently used for table linen, and sometimes as material for formal gowns.

dangerous machine. See under MACHINE.

data. Literally, from the Latin, given. Thus, those facts, figures, or other information used as a basis for discussion or calculation, or from which inferences may be drawn. It is the plural of *datum,* but the singular is rarely used.

date. 1. The particular point in time at which an occurrence takes place, as fixed by the year, month, and day of the month. In some instances, as in certain types of insurance contracts, the hour of the day must also be specified.

   2. To specify a particular day on which an action has occurred, or is to occur. To place a *date* on a document or instrument.

dated billing. See DATING.

dating. A commonly used method of extending credit beyond the period for which it is ostensibly or nominally granted. For example, if a buyer of goods is normally to receive

108

30 days in which to make payment, his invoice may be dated 30, 60, or some other number of days after the actual purchase, so that in effect he has 60, 90, or more days in which to make the payment. Such *dating* is often granted as an inducement to dealers to place orders for seasonal goods in advance of the season. It's sometimes called dated billing. See also TERMS OF SALE.

day. Strictly, a consecutive period of 24 hours, during one complete revolution of the earth. Unless otherwise specified, the *day* is understood to begin at 12:01 A.M., or one minute after midnight. In special usages, however, it may be any 24 hour period, such as from noon to noon, which is specified. More loosely, it is the period of time between sunrise and sunset, as distinguished from NIGHT. Some of the particular types of *day* used in business are listed and defined below.

    calendar ～. One counted or reckoned strictly according to the calendar. For example, a note dated January 1, and payable in 30 *calendar days,* is due on January 31, while one payable simply in 30 *days* is usually understood to be payable on the same *day* of the following month, or in this case, February 1.

    clear ～. One full intervening *day.* One of the number of *days* in a time period not including the first and last *days* of the period.

    entire ～. A term meaning one full *day,* running from midnight to midnight, rather than a 24 hour period including parts of two successive *days.*

    running ～. One of a number of consecutive days, including Sundays and holidays. Thus, a charter or contract covering five *running days* beginning with a Friday would include only three business or working *days.*

day book. A BOOK OF ORIGINAL ENTRY, in which all of the daily transactions of a business related to goods and money are recorded. It is in the nature of a memorandum or diary, normally suited for small businesses only. A JOURNAL. See also BLOTTER.

daylight saving time. A method of adjusting the time during the longer summer days to give an extra hour of daylight at the close of the day, to conserve fuel and power, and to provide additional usable time for outdoor activities. *Daylight saving time* is one hour later than the STANDARD TIME for the locality. In some local areas, *double-daylight saving time* is used for part of the summer, so that during this period the time is two hours later than standard time.

day loan. See under LOAN.

day order. See under ORDER (4).

days' date. A term used in bills of exchange, meaning a number of days after the date on which the bill is drawn. A bill payable in 30 *days' date,* for example, is payable within 30 days after the date of the bill. See also AFTER DATE.

days of grace. 1. The number of days, usually three, allowed for the on-time payment of a negotiable instrument after it has become due. The practice has been abolished under the Negotiable Instruments Law, but is still permitted in some states. In general, any additional days allowed after the due date for the fulfillment of an obligation. In computing *days of grace,* Sundays and business holidays are excluded.

    2. The days allowed, usually 30, for the payment of a life insurance policy premium without penalty, after it is due. On monthly premiums, there may be an interest charge during the grace period.

days' sight. A term used in bills of exchange, meaning a number of days after the bill is presented for acceptance. A bill payable in 30 *days' sight,* for example, is payable within 30 days after the bill is presented for ACCEPTANCE. On bills so drawn, the acceptance date must, of course, be specified. See also DAYS' DATE.

daywork. Work done and paid for by the hour or day. Thus, a *daywork* rate is an hourly or daily rate of pay. Work not paid for on a PIECE WORK or INCENTIVE basis, and therefore understood to be unskilled work. Also, the group of employees who perform unskilled jobs, as distinguished from the skilled or piece rate workers. See also TIME WORK.

dead beat. In business slang, one who is unable to meet his debts; or, more specifically, one who buys on credit with no intention of meeting the payments.

dead freight. See under FREIGHT.

deadhead. 1. In railroad usage, an empty freight or passenger car, usually one being returned to its point of origin, or to a terminal or yards. To *deadhead* a car is to attach it, empty, to a train going in the direction in which the empty is to be returned. The term has now generally been extended to use in connection with buses, trucks, and other motor vehicles, with the same meaning.

    2. A passenger who rides a train, bus, or other public conveyance without charge, such as on a pass. In general, anyone who obtains services or privileges without charge, or on pass.

    3. To move a train crew or individual workers, as passengers, from one terminal to another for the convenience of the railroad, whether with or without pay.

dead stock. Goods on hand or in inventory, for which there is no demand. See also CATS AND DOGS.

dead storage. See under STORAGE.

dead time. In work measurement, time which through no fault of the worker is lost from working time; idle time. It may include time during machine breakdowns, time waiting for materials, etc.

deadweight capacity. A basis for measuring the capacity of a vessel, consisting of the difference between its DISPLACEMENT loaded and its displacement empty. It is measured in gross tons of 2,240 pounds. The tonnage so measured is sometimes called the vessel's deadweight TONNAGE.

deadweight tonnage. See under TONNAGE.

deal. In business slang, a bargain, agreement, or transaction of some kind. To *deal* in a commodity or product is to engage in buying, selling, or transferring it.

dealer. 1. One who deals in merchandise or goods; one who buys for resale to final consumers; a TRADER. A *dealer* may buy directly from a manufacturer, or from a wholesale distributor, but as a *dealer* he is not himself a wholesale distributor, since he sells only for consumption.
   2. Specifically, in the securities trade, one who buys and sells for his own account, as distinguished from a BROKER (2), who acts as a buying and selling agent for others. The two functions now frequently overlap.

dealer acceptance. In marketing and advertising, a term for the condition under which retail dealers are willing to buy and promote a product, because they have been convinced that consumers know of the product and will be willing to buy it.

dealer aids. Promotional material supplied by a manufacturer to his dealers to assist them in selling the manufacturer's products. It may include point-of-purchase displays, counter cards, literature for distribution to customers, window displays, mats for newspaper advertising, etc. These are also called dealer helps.

dear. Costly, expensive, high-priced. In financial circles, for example, money is said to be *dear* when loans can only be obtained at a high rate of interest, due to the supply and demand situation for commercial credit.

death sentence clause. The popular name given to a section of the Public Utility Holding Company Act of 1935, which required corporate simplification of public utility holding companies, and in effect passed a *death sentence* on the major utility holding combinations. Hence, any clause or act giving to an official the power to force the dissolution of a corporation, or to revoke a corporate charter. See also COMPANY, HOLDING.

death tax. See TAX (2), ESTATE; TAX (2), INHERITANCE.

debase. To reduce from a higher to a lower grade or quality; to reduce the intrinsic value of a thing. The coinage of a country may be *debased,* for example, by a reduction in the official gold or silver content of the coins themselves.

debenture. Originally, from the Latin, anything which is owed. Currently, in the term United States, the term usually refers to an unsecured debt, such as a *debenture* BOND (1). Corporations frequently issue *debentures* which are convertible into the common STOCK (1) of the corporation at a given price. The investor who buys the *debenture,* therefore, has the opportunity to profit if the stock rises above the conversion price.

debenture bond. See under BOND (1).

debenture stock. See under STOCK (1).

debit. 1. In accounting, an entry made on the ASSET side of a ledger or account. A *debit* entry represents an asset or potential asset to the company, bank, or other organization keeping the ledger, and a liability or debt to the person, company, or depositor in whose ledger account the entry is made. Also, to make a *debit* entry, or to charge a person or his account with the cost of something. See also CREDIT (2).
   2. In insurance, a specified territory in which an agent or salesman solicits business, services customers, and collects the premiums, or *debit* amounts, due the company from policy-holders.

debit balance. With respect to the account of a customer or depositor, the condition of having an excess of DEBIT over CREDIT entries. Hence, showing a net debt owed, or a net loss.

debt. From the Latin, that which is owed by one person to another, including money, goods, or services. Of the many ways in which *debts* may be classified, the most important are listed and defined below.
   bad ∼. As defined by the National Bank Act, an UNSECURED DEBT, which see below, on which interest or payment is past due and unpaid for at least six months. See also directly.
   bonded ∼. Those *debts* of a corporation or governmental unit which are represented by BONDS (1), as distinguished from the CURRENT, or FLOATING DEBT, which see below.
   current ∼. A *debt* of a business which is

due to be paid within the current fiscal year; the short-term *debt.* See also LIABILITY, CURRENT.

∼ **of record.** One which is stated or recorded to be due according to a judgment of a court, or according to a deed, or other recorded document. See also JUDGMENT DEBT, below.

fixed ∼. One which is fixed over a long period of time, or which will continue to exist for a long time; a long-term *debt,* or FUNDED DEBT, which see below.

floating ∼. The indebtedness of a business which is not represented by securities, usually the short-term or CURRENT DEBT, which see above. In general, the opposite of FUNDED DEBT, which see below.

funded ∼. Those *debts* which are represented by, or which have been converted into, bonds or other securities which are payable at a fixed future date. A business may fund its outstanding *debts,* for example, by floating a bond issue and using the proceeds to repay the other obligations.

government ∼. See NATIONAL DEBT, below.

installment ∼. One which is specified to be repaid in installments, rather than in a single sum. Also, sometimes, one resulting from an INSTALLMENT PLAN purchase. See also LOAN, INSTALLMENT.

judgment ∼. One found by a court to be legally due and owing, and awarded under a JUDGMENT; a DEBT OF RECORD, which see above.

legal ∼. One that is recoverable by legal action in a court of law, if necessary. Examples include the *debts* created under bonds, contracts, bills of exchange, etc.

national ∼. A term for the total indebtedness of the federal government, represented by all outstanding bonds, notes, certificates, bills, and other securities. In general, the amounts owed by any government to individuals and institutions, as well as to foreign governments.

outstanding ∼. A term for all of the undischarged obligations of an individual or company.

privileged ∼. Any of the obligations which must be paid before others out of the estate of a person who has died. Statutes vary as to the particular *debts* included, and as to their order of priority, but the term generally includes funeral expenses, medical expenses, wages due employees, administrative expenses, etc.

public ∼. See NATIONAL DEBT, above.

secured ∼. One, the payment of which has been secured by the deposit of some COLLATERAL, such as a deed, mortgage, securities, etc.

unfunded ∼. See FLOATING DEBT, above.

unsecured ∼. One which is not formally secured by the deposit or pledge of COLLATERAL. Strictly, an *unsecured debt* is secured by the word and good faith of the borrower.

debt limit. The amount of total indebtedness and obligation beyond which a governmental unit is prohibited by law from assuming or creating additional indebtedness. The amount may be fixed by law, or by a state constitution. In the case of municipalities and similar governmental units, the *debt limit* is usually set at a given percentage of the assessed valuation of all taxable real property within the limits of the municipality.

debtor. A person or party who owes money to another, called the CREDITOR; one who is in DEBT.

judgment ∼. One who owes money as the result of a judgment obtained in court by a creditor.

debtor nation. A nation whose total obligations to foreign powers and individuals are greater than the sum of all obligations owed to it. It is the opposite of a CREDITOR NATION. See also BALANCE OF PAYMENTS.

debt reduction reserve. See under RESERVE (1).

debt service. The payment of interest and capital reduction or retirement charges on corporate or governmental bonds or other long-term debts. In a corporate or governmental budget, the amount set for *debt service* is the total of such payments to be made during the fiscal year.

deca-. In the metric system, the prefix used for any measure which is ten times a basic measure. It is now also frequently used to indicate ten of any unit, whether in the true metric system or not. Examples include decagram, decaliter, decameter, decastere, decasyllabic, decaton, etc.

decasualization. The elimination of casual labor, or of irregular hiring and work practices, and the substitution of regular work groups and working periods. With respect to longshore labor, for example, *decasualization* involves the elimination of the SHAPEUP, and the formation of regular work groups, which are then employed through organized hiring halls, providing steadier work for a smaller number of workers.

decedent. In law, one who is deceased, especially one who has recently died. Frequently, as used, a person who has left an estate; one from whom others inherit.

deceit. An attempt to deceive by trickery, FRAUD, or by underhanded dealing. At law, the four elements that constitute *deceit* include fraudulent representations, the inability of the person defrauded to detect the trickery or deception, reliance upon this condition by the deceiver, and resultant damage to the person defrauded.

decentralization. The breaking up of that which is concentrated or centralized, and the distribution of its elements elsewhere. For example, the *decentralization* of industry includes the removal of factories from a concentrated area and their relocation in less industrial areas. The *decentralization* of authority involves the removal of some authority from the few and its distribution among several persons or offices.

deci-. In the metric system, the prefix used to indicate a unit of measure which is one tenth the value of a basic unit. It is now also frequently used to indicate any value which is one tenth of another. Examples include decibel, decigram, decimeter, decivolt, etc.

decibel. The commonly used measure of the relative loudness of a sound or noise. It is one tenth of a bel, which in turn is a measure of the number of times more powerful one sound is than another. For example, if one sound is 3 bels louder than another, it is 10^3 times as loud, or 1,000 times as loud. A *decibel* of change is $10^{0.1}$, or 1.259 times as strong as the base level. In the measurement of sound levels, the first *decibel* of change is measured in relation to the sound level that is at the threshold of hearing for the average individual. The first *decibel* is the amount of change required to make the sound barely discernible. Thus, the sound volume level of 60 *decibels,* which is typical of many locations, is a level $10^{6.0}$ times more powerful than that at the threshold of hearing. A level of 120 *decibels* is considered to be the loudest that the human ear can bear.

decile. In statistics, any one of the nine values in a ranked distribution of values or scores which divide the whole into ten parts of equal numbers of elements. The *deciles* are usually numbered from the lower to the higher values, so that, for example, the ninth *decile* of a distribution of scores is the value that divides the top 10 percent of the scores from the rest of the distribution. The fifth *decile,* counting in either direction, is the MEDIAN of the distribution. Sometimes, loosely but incorrectly, *decile* is used to refer to the groups of values themselves, which each include 10 percent of the distribution. See also QUARTILE.

decimal system. Any system of computation, notation, and measurement based upon the number ten and the powers of ten. For example, in the METRIC SYSTEM, which is a *decimal system,* all units of weight, volume or linear measure are developed by raising to a power of ten the basic measures of *gram, liter* and *meter,* respectively. Fractional units are obtained by using the negative powers of ten. The monetary system of the United States is also basically a *decimal system,* with CENTS, DIMES, DOLLARS and EAGLES (ten dollars) related to each other as consecutive powers of ten.

decision. The JUDGMENT or DECREE pronounced by a court of law or equity, or by any judicial or quasi-judicial body, in settlement of a controversy before it. Usually, it includes both the FINDING of the facts in the case, and the OPINION on the judicial questions involved. It roughly corresponds to the jury's VERDICT and the SENTENCE of the court in a criminal case.

deck cargo. Ship's CARGO which is customarily carried on deck, rather than in the hold, such as lumber, cattle, large vehicles, etc.

declaration. 1. In law, the first pleading in an action; a methodical and consecutive statement of the facts of a matter, made by a party thereto or one having an interest therein.

2. The listing or full disclosure of goods, property, or income subject to taxation, such as a customs *declaration* of goods subject to import duties, or an income *declaration* for income tax purposes.

3. In insurance, one of the several statements made or attested to by the insured, regarding the nature of the risk, on the basis of which the premium rate is set and the policy contract is issued. The *declarations* include statements of the nature, location, condition, and value of the property to be insured.

declaration of trust. A formal acknowledgement or statement that property to which one person holds title actually belongs to another, for whose benefit the title is held. For example, an adult may open a savings account in his own name, but make a *declaration of trust* to the effect that the account is being held in TRUST, or for the benefit of, a minor child.

declaratory. That which defines, explains, or merely makes statements. A *declaratory* statute, for example, is one enacted for the purpose of clarifying or resolving doubts about the prevailing policy or attitude of a state.

declared value. The claimed or stated value of an item of goods, property, or income as listed in a declaration made for import duty or taxation purposes. It is not necessarily the TAXABLE VALUE.

decline. 1. A lessening, falling off, or deterioration in value or amount. Hence, a *decline* in prices, a *decline* in stock values, a business *decline,* etc.

2. To refuse to accept, to turn aside, to reject politely; as to *decline* an offer of purchase or sale.

decontrol. To remove from control, or to end control, particularly governmental control. For example, at the end of a period of war or national emergency, the federal government may act to *decontrol* prices, wages, industry, and trade.

decree. The DECISION or JUDGMENT of a court in a case in equity, or of a quasi-judicial body with decision-making powers. In strict usage, a *decree* is more flexible than a judgment, in that it may be relative, while a judgment is in favor of one party or the other.

consent ~. One entered by agreement or consent between the contending parties. Strictly speaking, such an agreement is not binding on the court, but in practice the court will accept the *decree* as its own decision.

~ nisi. One which is provisional, but which will become final unless some intervening event occurs first, or unless good reasons are presented to advise against it. Such a *decree* is usually subject to review by the court before it becomes final.

final ~. One which completely and finally disposes of a case, leaving no questions to be decided.

interlocutory ~. One which leaves some questions unsettled, pending further information or action; one which is handed down while the proceedings are still pending, such as a temporary injunction.

dedication. 1. In law, an appropriation or grant of property, such as land, by its owner to the public, or for public use.

2. In copyright law, the term for the first publication of an original work not bearing a copyright notice. Such publication is a *dedication* of the work to the public, and it may afterwards be published by anyone without permission or the payment of a fee or royalty.

deductible clause. A clause used in various types of insurance, providing that the insured will absorb the first part (such as $50 or $100 or some other amount) of each loss, and that the insurance company will pay the excess, if any. Where there is a possibility of many small losses, as in automobile damage insurance, such a clause can materially reduce the insurance company's exposure, and hence the premium charge. It differs from a FRAN-

CHISE CLAUSE, which provides that the insured will absorb all losses below a certain amount, but that the insurer will pay the total loss on all larger claims.

deed. A formal, written instrument of transfer, by which title to an estate in real property is conveyed from one person to another.

~ of release. A written release in the form of a *deed,* whereby a person gives up, abandons, surrenders and transfers claim or interest in something to another. See also QUITCLAIM DEED, below.

~ of trust. A conveyance of property to a party who is to hold it in trust for another. Not to be confused with TRUST DEED, which see below.

~ poll. One made by a single party, transferring property to a single party. It is made in one undivided part, with no duplicate copies. The term derives from an old English expression, meaning that it has clean, sharp edges, as opposed to an INDENTURE DEED, which see below.

escrow ~. One made and then delivered to a third person, or put in ESCROW, until the happening of some specified event. If the event fails to occur, or to occur within the specified time, the *deed* becomes null and void. If and when the event occurs, the *deed* is delivered.

indenture ~. One which transfers property to several persons, jointly, each of whom undertakes an obligation toward the others. It is so called because such *deeds* were originally prepared in several attached parts, one for each party, with a crease or *indent* between the parts. The *deed* was then torn or cut along the creases, and each party given his part or copy. The exact contour of the tear or cut could then be used to establish the genuineness of the copy. Thus, it is distinguished from a DEED POLL, which see above, which has smooth-trimmed edges.

quitclaim ~. A *deed* in the form of a release. It passes any title, interest, or claim the grantor may have in the property, without professing that there is any valid title. Under such a *deed,* the grantor thus quits all claim, *if any.* It differs from a DEED OF RELEASE, which see above, which gives up a valid claim or interest.

trust ~. A *deed* conveying property of a corporation to a trustee, to be held as collateral for a bond issue by the corporation. Hence, it is essentially a mortgage on the property, given to the trustee, and the bonds issued are mortgage bonds.

warranty ~. A *deed* or conveyance in which the seller warrants the title to the property to be a perfect one, in contrast to a QUITCLAIM DEED, which see above.

de facto. Literally, in fact. A phrase used to refer to a state of affairs which actually exists, and must be accepted for practical purposes, though illegal or illegitimate. It is the opposite of DE JURE, which means by law, or rightfully.

defalcation. In general, the act of defaulting. As used, the act of defaulting in some duty or trust which one has assumed. Hence, the wrongful disposition or appropriation of money or property by one who holds it in trust; EMBEZZLEMENT by a trustee or fiduciary.

defamation. In law, the injury of another's reputation or good name by the making of false and malicious statements. It includes both LIBEL and SLANDER.

default. In general, the omission or failure to perform or fulfill some obligation or duty; the failure to fulfill an obligation when due, especially under contract. Particularly, as used, the failure to make a payment, such as an installment on a promissory note, bond, or mortgage, or a dividend or interest payment on a bond or other security, when due. A bond on which the issuer has failed to make one or more interest payments, or a preferred stock on which the company has failed to pay one or more dividends is said to be *in default*.

defeasance. Any act or instrument which defeats or annuls the force or effect of another. For example, a simple releasing or annulling contract may serve as a *defeasance* to a previous contract to do or provide something.

defect. In general, a lack of some required feature or component; an imperfection or blemish. In law, a weakness, or absence of some substantial part, which may destroy or nullify an agreement.

  fatal ∼. One of such seriousness that it will nullify or defeat a contract or agreement, or cancel a sale.

  latent ∼. One, such as in a title to property, or in delivered goods, which is not apparent to the buyer, and is not discoverable by reasonable observation, though it may be known to the seller.

  patent ∼. One which is clear or apparent, or which can be discovered by simple inspection, in contrast to a LATENT DEFECT, which see above.

defective title. See under TITLE (2).

deferred. Delayed or put off; postponed until a future time; to begin at some future date; chargeable against some future period. See each of the following under the principal listing: ∼ ANNUITY; ∼ ASSET (2); ∼ BOND (1); ∼ DIVIDEND; ∼ INCOME; ∼ LIABILITY (2); ∼ PREMIUM (2); ∼ STOCK (1).

deferred charge. In accounting, a payment made for a long-term service or benefit, all or part of which will be received in future accounting periods. Examples include payments for insurance, long-term product development costs, discounts on bond issues, etc. A *deferred charge* differs from a prepaid expense, in that the latter is simply a payment for a short term or current expense item which will be received or consumed in the near future, usually in the next accounting period, while the former is a prepayment for something continuing over a long period of time.

deferred payment plan. See INSTALLMENT PLAN.

deficiency. In general, a shortage, or an amount lacking from a desired or prescribed total. In law, that part of a total debt which is not covered by the proceeds of a forced sale of the property mortgaged as security for the debt. A *deficiency* JUDGMENT, for example, is one obtained from a court by a creditor for the balance of the debt remaining after the sale of the security.

  ∼ account. A term for the statement sometimes prepared in the course of a bankruptcy proceeding, showing the detailed amounts involved in the deficit of the bankrupt's assets in comparison with his debts.

deficit. In general, something which is wanting or lacking. Particularly, as used in business, an amount of money which is needed to make up the difference between receipts and expenditures, between assets and liabilities, etc.

  ∼ financing. In federal fiscal policy, the practice of deliberately budgeting larger expenditures than the actual receipts of the government will cover, with the intent thereby of expanding business activity and bringing about an improvement in general economic conditions. The resulting *deficit* is covered by the issuance of government bonds.

definitive bond. See under BOND (1).

deflation. A relatively sharp decline in prices, or an increase in the value of money, such as might be brought about by a decrease in the amount of money in circulation relative to the amount of goods and services available. The condition may be deliberately brought about by a government by withdrawing money from circulation, by raising the interest rate so that credit outstanding contracts, or by other means. It may also come about during a recession or depression due to an abundance of goods available in the face of reduced consumer demand. See also INFLATION.

defraud. To cheat by deception or fraud; to wrongfully deprive someone of a right or interest by deceitful means or practices. For example, to obtain goods or materials by presenting a false or fraudulent check is to *defraud* the merchant involved.

defray. To pay, or to provide for payment; to bear an expense. A settlement in favor of one party or another in a legal controversy, for example, will often include an amount to *defray* the legal costs of the favored party.

defunct. Literally, dead; finished. A *defunct* business concern is one which is no longer in existence, for whatever reason. As frequently used, however, the term implies that the concern has failed, or gone bankrupt.

degree. In circular measure, one 360th part of a full circle, or one 90th part of a QUADRANT, containing 60 MINUTES and 3600 SECONDS.

de jure. Literally, by right; rightful, legitimate, just; according to law or equity. A term used to describe a state of affairs or a condition which exists according to right and just title, or according to law, as distinguished from one which exists purely as fact, or DE FACTO, with no basis in right.

del credere. From the Italian, the name for a form of agreement entered into by an AGENT and his PRINCIPAL, under which the agent, in return for an additional premium or consideration, guarantees the payment for all goods he sells for the principal, whether or not he himself receives payment. The extra payment made is often called a *del credere* commission, and an agent who operates under such an agreement is a *del credere* agent.

delectus personae. Literally, in Latin, choice of persons; the right which a partner has as to which, if any, new members shall be admitted to the partnership. This right of choice or selection is one of the features which distinguishes a PARTNERSHIP from a CORPORATION.

delegate. 1. A representative, or deputy. One who is sent to a meeting of representatives in the name of a group or organization. For example, members of legislatures are frequently known as *delegates.*

2. To assign or entrust responsibility, authority, power, etc., to an individual who is authorized to act as an agent, deputy, or representative. To pass authority or responsibility down to a lower level of operations. See also LETTER OF DELEGATION.

delinquent. Failing in some duty or obligation.

For example, a *delinquent* debtor is one who has failed to pay his debt, or the next installment on his debt, when due. Similarly, *delinquent* taxes are tax payments which are overdue and unpaid.

delist. In the securities market, to remove a security from the list of those which have trading privileges on an exchange. To change a security from a listed to an unlisted security, which see under SECURITY. A security may be *delisted* because it no longer meets the requirements as to number of shares outstanding, or because of undesirable speculative activity in its shares.

delivered price. See under PRICE.

delivery. 1. In law, the final transfer of something, such as property or an instrument, in such a manner as to deprive the transferer of any future control over the thing *delivered*. In the law of sales, for example, an *actual delivery* is the physical transfer of the thing sold from the possession of the seller to that of the purchaser. A *constructive delivery,* on the other hand, may include such steps as marking and setting the item aside in a warehouse, with notice to and consent of the purchaser, changing the listed title to the goods on record, charging rent for continuing to hold them, etc.

2. In general, the transporting of property, such as commercial goods or merchandise, to any place designated by the purchaser.

delivery contract. See under CONTRACT.

delivery day. In the commodities trade, formally the first day of the month during which delivery is to be made under a FUTURES contract. Since all sales are made at the seller's option, however, the seller may, in practice, make delivery on any day of the DELIVERY MONTH, after due notice to the purchaser.

delivery month. In the commodities trade, the specified month during which delivery is to be made under the terms of a FUTURES contract. In organized futures markets, various futures contracts which are actively traded are often known by the *delivery month* specified therein; as, for example, an October contract, January contract, etc. See also CONTRACT MONTH.

demand. 1. In economics, the total potential purchase or consumption of an item or service at given price levels. The relative amount of a given commodity which will be exchanged for money or other commodities at various price relationships. The *demand* for a commodity is said to be relatively elastic if it increases or decreases rapidly with small changes in price, and inelastic if it changes relatively little with large changes in price. In general, luxury goods, such as jewelry, have elastic *demands,* while staples, such as bread, have relatively inelastic *demands.* See also SUPPLY; ELASTICITY OF DEMAND.

2. In law, a claim, or the forceful assertion of a legal right.

3. In finance, a request or call for payment, or for the discharge of an obligation. See each of the following under the principal listing: ~ ACCOUNT (3); ~ BILL OF EXCHANGE; ~ DEPOSIT; ~ LOAN; ~ NOTE (1). See also CALL; SIGHT.

demand draft. See DRAFT (2), SIGHT.

de minimus. Literally, in Latin, of the least, or smallest. In law, a term used for something, such as an error or infraction, which is too small or minor for the law to be concerned with. Examples include minor errors in calculation on a tax return, insignificant damage to property, etc.

demise. 1. Originally, from the Latin phrase, "I have sent away", which was used in leases; hence, to create an estate by LEASE; to let out for a term. In modern leases, the phrase "granted, *demised* and let" is frequently used.

2. In current usage, to transfer an estate by a document, whether by lease, by will, or otherwise; hence, to transmit property by succession or bequest. Also, incorrectly, death or decease.

demonetize. To remove or withdraw from use as money; to reduce coins from the rank of legal tender to that of token money. Also, to withdraw a particular metal from use as coinage. In the United States, for example, gold has been *demonetized,* and all gold coins withdrawn from circulation.

demonstrative legacy. See under LEGACY.

demonstrator. In retail selling, a trained person who exhibits, explains, and demonstrates the use of a product in retail stores, to stimulate demand and create sales. The salary of the *demonstrator* is usually paid by the manufacturer or distributor of the product, but all sales made are credited to the retailer in whose establishment the *demonstrator* is working. Also, sometimes, the particular product unit so used, which may later be sold at a reduced price.

demurrage. In transportation, a charge made for the use of equipment during unloading or loading beyond the specified amount of free time allowed. The term is derived from the Latin, meaning to hesitate, or delay. In railroad practice, *demurrage* is charged for the use of freight cars, after arrival at their destination, beyond the number of free days allowed to unload the cars, usually two days.

A similar charge may be made for the holding of highway trailers, freight barges, shipping containers, and other equipment. In marine practice, *demurrage* is charged for the use of a ship while loading or unloading beyond the number of LYING DAYS specified in the charter agreement.

demurrer. In law, a plea or allegation by the defendant in a case, admitting to the facts in a charge but denying that they are sufficient cause for action, or stating that the charge contains defects or omissions, or holding that the court lacks jurisdiction, and, in any event, that therefore there is no reason to continue with the trial. The laws of the several states differ as to when a *demurrer* may be entered.

denomination. Literally, a name; a category or classification. In the case of currency, for example, the *denomination* is the face value of the various values of bills or notes.

density of traffic. See TRAFFIC DENSITY.

department. In business, usually a separate or distinct branch, section, or division of a company. The concept differs widely from company to company. In retailing, a section of a store handling a distinct classification of goods, such as clothing, furniture, housewares, etc.

department store. See under RETAIL STORE.

dependent. In law, a person who derives his main support from another; one who depends on another for his normal needs. Under the 1954 Revenue Code, one person may claim another as a *dependent* if he contributes the major part of that person's support.

depletion. Literally, a using up, a reduction, or emptying. A DEPRECIATION or reduction in the value of an asset, due to its gradual consumption in use. Assets in the form of mineral deposits, oil, standing timber, etc., are normally depreciated by *depletion.* Such assets are often known as wasting assets. See also RESERVE, DEPLETION; ASSET, WASTING.

~ **allowance.** Under the tax laws, a special allowance or deduction from income allowed to companies engaged in extractive industry, such as mining, oil production, timber cutting, etc., which reduces their income tax. The allowance is given on the grounds that part of the income of the company is actually a reduction in its assets, rather than the result of production operations.

deponent. In law, the name for the person who makes a DEPOSITION; a person who testifies, under oath, in writing, as part of some legal action, proceeding or investigation; one who makes an AFFIDAVIT. More generally, any one who gives evidence, whether in writing or not.

deposit. 1. In selling, an amount of money given in partial payment for goods, to reserve them until the remainder of the payment is made; an EARNEST.

2. In general, property or money put into the custody of another, for safekeeping, for investment, or as a pledge. The various classes of *deposit* are listed and defined below.

bank ∼. Funds, in the form of coins, currency, checks, drafts, etc., placed by a customer in the care of a bank, to be kept to the customer's account, and returned to the customer under stated circumstances. A *bank deposit* may be a DEMAND DEPOSIT or a TIME DEPOSIT, which see below.

demand ∼. A BANK DEPOSIT, which see above, which may be withdrawn at any time at the option of the depositor, without prior notice to the bank. The usual means for making a withdrawal from a *demand deposit* is a CHECK. Since the *deposit* is held at the convenience of the depositor, no interest is usually paid, except on very large balances maintained. In fact, the current practice is for banks to make a service charge on the basis of the number of checks handled, unless a sizable balance is maintained.

derivative ∼. A form of BANK DEPOSIT, which see above, which results from the making of a loan or discount, rather than from an actual *deposit* of money. See also LOAN, DEPOSIT.

general ∼. A BANK DEPOSIT, which see above, which is placed in the general funds of the bank, though placed to the credit of the depositor. Title to the funds technically passes to the bank, which then becomes a debtor to the depositor. This is the usual form of demand or time *deposit*. See also SPECIAL DEPOSIT, below.

gratuitous ∼. A *deposit* of property or other thing of value from which the holder, or depositary, receives no benefit, or for which no consideration is paid. In essence, it is a form of BAILMENT without hire.

involuntary ∼. One resulting from an accidental or unintentional *deposit* of money, goods, or other valuables, or one arising out of a fire, flood, or other calamity in which a person is compelled to leave valuables with another. Under law, the person with whom such an *involuntary deposit* is left is required to care for and protect the things deposited to the best of his ability, but is not responsible for losses beyond his ability to control.

special ∼. A *deposit* of anything of value with a bank or other place of trust and safekeeping, with the understanding that the thing deposited will be kept separate from the other assets of the bank, and not loaned out or used as security. Title to such *deposits*

remains with the depositor. An example is property placed in a SAFE DEPOSIT VAULT.

time ∼. A BANK DEPOSIT, which see above, which is to remain for a specified period of time, or on which notice must be given to the bank before withdrawal. Savings deposits are *time deposits,* and the bank reserves the right to require 30 days' notice before withdrawal, though this right is seldom exercised under normal circumstances.

deposit account. See ACCOUNT (3).

depositary. A person or institution named as one to be intrusted with something of value for safekeeping; a FIDUCIARY. A bank or trust company, for example, may be named as *depositary* for shares of foreign stock, when the stock is to be traded on an American stock exchange. It is not to be confused with a DEPOSITORY, which is a physical place in which valuables are stored for safekeeping. See also DEPOSITARY RECEIPT.

depositary receipt. A device used to permit trading in foreign stocks on American stock exchanges, when the foreign government involved will not permit foreign ownership of the stock of domestic corporations. The shares of stock are deposited with a bank or trust company in the country in which the corporation is located, and an affiliated or correspondent bank in this country issues *depositary receipts* for the shares. These receipts are then sold to American investors, and are traded on the stock exchange in the same way as regular stocks. Dividends paid on the original stock are transmitted to the receipt holders. The receipts, however, do not represent ownership of the stock, which remains technically in the country of the foreign corporation.

deposit banking. See under BANKING.

deposit book. See PASSBOOK.

deposition. In law, testimony taken by written or oral questioning, but not in open court. The questions and answers are reduced to writing and signed and witnessed, and may then be submitted as testimony in the trial of a case or in the conduct of a suit. *Depositions* are usually taken when a person is unable to appear in person, due to illness or other strong reason, or when it is desired to take testimony in advance of a trial to save time. See also AFFIDAVIT.

deposit loan. See under LOAN.

depositor. In general, a person who deposits money or the equivalent of money in a bank or similar institution, to be held to his credit. As defined by the banking laws of several states, a *depositor* is any person who deposits money or commercial paper in any bank, either on open account, subject to check, or to be withdrawn otherwise than by check, whether interest is allowed or not.

depositors' guaranty fund. Under the banking laws of some states, a fund required to be set apart by banks chartered in the state, to be used in reimbursing the depositors in any banks which become insolvent. See also FEDERAL DEPOSIT INSURANCE CORPORATION.

depository. A place for the deposit of valuables. A bank or trust company in which funds or securities are deposited; a storage warehouse, safe deposit company, or other company in which valuable papers or property may be deposited for safekeeping. Thus, it is distinguished from a DEPOSITARY, which is the person or institution taking the responsibility for the safekeeping of valuables, rather than the place itself.

government ~. A national bank which has been designated by the federal government to receive deposits of taxes and other money collected in the name of the government. A bank in which the federal government maintains an account.

public ~. One which is designated by the state in which it is located to receive deposits of state funds, or of funds of local governments. The *depository* may be required to post a bond for the safekeeping of the deposits, and may be required to pay a rate of interest on them which is fixed by the state law.

special ~. One designated by law to receive deposits of special public or private funds, such as trusts, pension funds, etc. It may be required to post a bond, to pay interest on the funds, etc.

United States ~. See GOVERNMENT DEPOSITORY, above.

deposit rate. A term for the RATE OF INTEREST paid by a bank on deposits left with it.

deposit slip. The name for the printed form provided by a bank on which the depositor enters the amount of his deposit, segregated according to checks, bills, coins, etc. It is not a formal document of record unless and until it is receipted by an officer or authorized employee of the bank.

depot. Originally, a place for the deposit or storage of goods. The term is still used in this sense by the armed forces, but not generally in business. In the United States, a railroad or other station, for passengers or freight.

depreciate. To decrease in value or price, especially due to age, or to normal wear and tear. Also, to WRITE DOWN the value of an asset or of property which has *depreciated* in value.

depreciation. The decline in value of a tangible asset, such as a building, tool, machine, furniture, etc., due to age, and to the normal wear and tear of use. It is distinguished from OBSOLESCENCE, which is the loss in value due to changes in style, new improvements, etc., and from DEPLETION, which is a loss in value due to an actual using up of part of the asset, such as a mineral deposit. In accounting, various methods of calculating the *depreciation* of an asset are used, the principal ones being listed and defined below.

diminishing balance ~. The calculation in which the value of the asset in each succeeding year is taken as a fixed percentage of its value in the preceding year. For example, an automobile valued new at $5,000 may be depreciated at a fixed percentage rate of 20 percent per year. At the end of the first year, its value will be $4,000, at the end of the second year $3,200, and so on, until eventually the remaining calculated value is less than the scrap value of the equipment. This method has the advantage of charging the largest amounts in the early years, and the further attraction of being a close approximation of the way in which the relative value of some equipment actually declines.

production ~. The *depreciation* calculated by assuming that the machine has an expected life of a certain number of hours of use, or of a certain number of units of production. A record is kept of the use of the machine, and a proportionate amount of value deducted for each hour of use or each unit of production. In the case of the $5,000 automobile, for example, it might be assumed to have a useful life of 50,000 miles of travel, and be depreciated at a rate of ten cents per mile of travel.

sinking fund ~. Under this method, the asset is considered to be an investment to be AMORTIZED, and a fund is put aside at interest to accomplish this result. For example, if the $5,000 automobile is considered to have a useful life of five years, with no scrap value at the end of the period, an annual payment of $956.10, at 3 percent interest, will produce a total fund of $5,000 in five years. Thus, at the end of the first year, the asset will be valued at $4,043.90. At the end of the second year, the first payment will have earned interest of $28.68, so that the total in the *depreciation* fund is now $1,940.88, and the asset is valued at $3,059.12.

straight line ~. In this method, the asset is considered to lose an equal share of its total value each year of its life. Thus, the $5,000 automobile, with a 5 year useful life, is valued at $4,000 after one year, $3,000 after two years, etc. This is the simplest method of *depreciation* calculation, though not necessarily the most realistic, and is widely used.

sum-of-digits ∼. This method of calculation, approved under the 1954 Internal Revenue Code, produces high deductions in the early years of the life of the asset, and has the advantage over the DIMINISHING BALANCE method, which see above, of reducing the value of the asset to zero over its life. The amount of *depreciation* each year is calculated by assigning a numerical value to each year of expected life of the asset, in descending order, so that if the asset has a life of 5 years, for example, the number or digit for the first year is 5, for the second year 4, etc. The digit for each year is then divided by the sum of all of the digits for all of the years to determine the proportion of the total value of the asset which will be *depreciated* in that year. In this case, for example, the *depreciation* in the first year is 5/15ths of the total, in the second year 4/15ths, etc. For the $5,000 automobile, the value at the end of the first year will thus be $3,333.33, at the end of the second year $2,000.00, etc.

depreciation reserve. See under RESERVE (1).

depression. In economics, a period of low activity in business, characterized by high unemployment, low production, little consumer buying, a contraction of credit, etc. In current usage, a *depression* is a relatively severe contraction of business, as compared with a RECESSION, which is relatively milder and shorter in duration. See also PROSPERITY.

derelict. In maritime law, a vessel found deserted or abandoned at sea, with no indication of any intent of reboarding or recovery. It is the property of any finder who claims it. More broadly, any property forsaken, abandoned, or thrown away in a manner indicating the owner has no further use or need of it. See also FLOTSAM; JETSAM; WRECK.

derivative deposit. See under DEPOSIT (2).

derogation. A term for the partial repeal of a statute or regulation, such as by a limiting act or amendment. It is distinguished from ABROGATION, which is total repeal or abolition. In another sense, tending to decrease or lower authority or respect.

descent. In law, the passing of property, or of the TITLE (2) to property, from generation to generation by inheritance, rather than by bequest or purchase. The particular regulations governing the passage of property by *descent* may vary from state to state.

descriptive label. See under LABEL.

descriptive standard. See under STANDARD.

design patent. See PATENT.

desk jobber. See DROP SHIPPER.

destitute. Originally, deprived or forsaken; neglected or abandoned. Today, without the minimum necessities of life; without any means of support. Abjectly poor.

detachable warrant. See WARRANT (4).

detainer. In law, a writ or order authorizing the keeper or warden of a prison to keep in custody a named person, especially one who is already in custody and would otherwise have to be released. Also, the act of withholding from any person the lawful possession of his property or goods.

deterioration. With respect to property or an asset, any diminishing of value due to breakage, lack of maintenance, exposure, fire, flood, etc. It is distinguished from DEPRECIATION, which is the decrease in value due to normal wear and tear, and from OBSOLESCENCE, which is a decrease due to changing styles, new improvements, etc.

determinable. In law, subject to being decided, settled, or terminated. For example, the end of a time period is *determinable* if it can be computed or decided from the available information, or from the course of events. See FEE (2), DETERMINABLE.

devaluation. A deliberate reduction in value, especially in the value of a currency or of a standard monetary unit. It may be accomplished, for example, by reducing the weight or fineness of the metallic content of the monetary unit, or by changing the equivalent value of the currency in terms of other currencies.

development. In general, an expansion or growth; an improvement in property or in conditions. In real estate usage, a project for the improvement of a large tract of land, such as by the construction of a large number of dwelling units, the building of stores, office buildings, etc. See also BOND (1), DEVELOPMENT; MORTGAGE, DEVELOPMENT.

deviation. 1. In insurance, any change or variation in the condition or state of the property insured from that which existed at the time it was insured, without necessity or a just reason. Examples include a change in the announced course of a ship, a change in regular operating practices in a factory, an introduction of business use into a residence, etc. Such a *deviation* may void the responsibility of the insurance company in the event of a loss associated with the change made.

2. In general, any change in the performance of a contract, whether agreed upon or not, such as a change in the design of a product, in the materials used, etc. A *deviation* not agreed on, but made secretly, is

cause for a claim for damages if it results in loss or injury.

3. In statistics, a measure of the DISPERSION of the items or observations in a FREQUENCY DISTRIBUTION. In general, it is the average amount by which the items deviate from the arithmetic mean of the distribution. The *standard deviation,* sometimes called the root-mean-square *deviation,* is the geometric mean of the *deviations,* and the average, or *mean deviation* is the arithmetic mean of the *deviations,* both calculated without regard to the direction of the difference above or below the mean.

devise. In law, the technical term for a disposition of real property according to the terms of a WILL. Strictly, it is distinguished from a BEQUEST or LEGACY, which is a gift of personal property by a will. The various classifications of legacy are applied with the same meanings to *devise.*

dictum. In law, a statement or remark made by a presiding judge; a judicial opinion which is not based on the full argument or consideration of the case in question, but on general principles. See also OBITER DICTUM.

differential. In general, a difference existing between two rates, such as freight rates, tax rates, wage rates, tariffs, etc. A rate or price which is different for different classes of customers or service. See, for example, TARIFF (2), DIFFERENTIAL.

dime. Originally, from the Latin term *decima,* a tenth part. A fractional silver coin of the United States, valued at ten cents, or the tenth part of the dollar.

dime store. See under RETAIL STORE.

diminishing balance depreciation. See under DEPRECIATION.

direct. 1. To guide, control, manage, or regulate the affairs of a business, association or government; to instruct, order, or command.

2. Without any intermediate steps; without any conditions; certain or definite. See each of the following under the principal listing:
~ ADVERTISING; ~ COST; ~ DAMAGE; ~ EVIDENCE; ~ EXCHANGE (4); ~ EXPORTER; ~ LABOR (1); ~ LIABILITY (3); ~ LOSS (2); ~ TAX (2).

direct endorsement. See ENDORSEMENT (2) IN FULL.

direct investments. In statistics on foreign trade and the BALANCE OF PAYMENTS, those investments in foreign corporations or other enterprises which are held in such a form that the investors have a direct controlling interest in the foreign business. Common stocks of the foreign corporations, for example, are *direct investments* in this sense.

direct mail advertising. See under ADVERTISING.

director. In general, one who DIRECTS; one who manages the affairs of an enterprise, a government bureau, a department or division of a company, etc. In business, specifically, a person elected by the stockholders of a corporation to manage the affairs and set the general policies of the corporation. The several *directors* together constitute the board of *directors,* which is the policy making body of the corporation. The laws of the various states differ in their requirements concerning the number of *directors,* voting, term of office, etc. In some cases, *directors* may be elected for terms of more than one year, with a proportion of the board replaced each year, and in other cases the entire board may be elected each year. Customarily, the principal officers of the company, including the president, vice-president, and secretary, are *directors,* but this is not generally required by state law. See also CUMULATIVE VOTING.

  inside ~. The term for a *director* who is also an employee, officer, or principal stockholder of a corporation, as distinguished from an OUTSIDE DIRECTOR, which see below, who has no direct connection with the corporation other than his directorship.

  interlocking ~. A person who is a *director* of more than one corporation, especially in corporations having allied business interests, or which are supposedly in competition with each other. The existence of *interlocking directors* in competitive corporations is generally illegal under the various anti-trust laws.

  outside ~. The term for a *director* of a corporation who has no direct connection with the corporation except his directorship, and except for the minimum stock ownership which may be required of *directors* in the particular state, as distinguished from an INSIDE DIRECTOR, which see above.

directory. A listing, usually in book form, of the names and addresses of persons, companies, associations, or other classifications, usually grouped according to some logical arrangement or other to facilitate locating. Examples in business include city *directories,* classified telephone *directories,* trade *directories,* etc.

direct placement. See PLACEMENT (2).

direct reduction mortgage. See MORTGAGE, AMORTIZED.

direct selling. In general, the practice of selling directly to final customers or consumers, rather than to distributors or dealers. The term is also applied to any pattern of selling which skips one or more of the normal steps in the particular field. For example, a manufacturer who sells directly to retail stores instead of to wholesalers, or a wholesale distributor who sells directly to private consumers, instead of to retailers, is said to be a *direct seller*. Companies specializing in selling directly to consumers, either by HOUSE-TO-HOUSE SELLING or by MAIL-ORDER, are known as *direct selling* companies.

direct trust. See TRUST (1), EXPRESS.

direct-writing insurance company. See under INSURANCE COMPANY.

disability. In general, the lack of ability or capacity to perform. In insurance, a temporary or permanent state of bodily injury or illness that wholly or partially prevents a person from performing useful work. As interpreted in insurance policies, it is usually an incapacity with respect to one's normal or usual work. The *disability* resulting from an injury or illness which is so severe that a person is not able to engage in any form of work is known as *total disability,* while that which permits the performance of some form of useful work is known as *partial disability*.

disability clause. In a life or health insurance contract, a clause which may be of either of the following types. It may provide for the payment of an indemnity or regular benefits in the event of total and permanent disability, or it may provide for the suspension of premium payments and the continuation of the insurance in the event of total disability lasting more than a specified period of time. The latter type is also known as a waiver of premium clause.

disability insurance. See under INSURANCE, LIFE, ACCIDENT, AND HEALTH.

disagio. In foreign exchange operations, a term for the discount charged for exchanging a depreciated foreign currency. Also, the charge or discount deducted for exchanging abraded or worn coins. See also AGIO.

disbursement. In accounting and finance, an actual paying out of cash. It is distinguished from an APPROPRIATION, which is an authorization for payment, and from an EXPENDITURE, which is the creation of a liability, such as by a purchase, rather than the extinguishment of the liability by payment. Sometimes, the term is restricted to payments for expenses, rather than for capital assets.

discharge. 1. In law, to cancel or to release from an obligation, by completing or performing what is to be done. A debt is *discharged,* for example, by payment. In another sense, a person is *discharged* from bankruptcy

by settling his debts to the best of his ability, though not necessarily in full.

2. In personnel management, to dismiss an employee at the initiative of the employer, usually for cause. It is distinguished from a LAYOFF, which is always for reasons beyond the control of the employee, such as a necessary reduction of the workforce. Ordinarily, a *discharged* employee loses his seniority rights, while a laid off employee keeps his. Similarly, under most state unemployment insurance laws, an employee *discharged* for cause is not entitled to insurance payments.

disclaimer. In law, any repudiation or renouncing of a claim, right, or interest. Usually, it is a signed, written statement, but it may be an oral statement as well, if made in the presence of witnesses. A RELEASE.

disclosure. In patent law, the term for the section of a patent application which covers the specification of the subject matter and the method of operation of the invention. Thus, it is one of the two basic parts of the application, the other being the CLAIM (3), which describes what the invention will accomplish, and the extent to which it is new, rather than how it accomplishes the intent. More broadly, a *disclosure* of an invention is a public revelation of the operation of the invention, whether in a patent application or otherwise.

discount. 1. Literally, a counting down, or a reduction; an amount deducted in advance, such as from a payment due. Thus it is distinguished from a REBATE, which is an amount given back after payment, rather than an amount deducted in advance. A *discount* may be allowed for any of a number of reasons, and take various forms, the principal ones of which are listed and defined below:

cash ∼. An amount allowed from the full total of an account due in return for prompt payment. Typically, a *cash discount* may be allowed for payment within ten days of the date of an invoice, and may be, for example, 2 percent of the total amount. The notation for such a discount in stated TERMS OF SALE is 2/10. See also ANTICIPATION.

chain ∼. A *discount* allowed on a price which has already been reduced by a *discount;* a series of such *discounts*. For example, a distributor may be allowed a basic TRADE DISCOUNT, which see below, of 15 percent, and additional *discounts* of 10 percent and 5 percent. Thus, if the list price is $100, the first *discount* would make it $85, the second would reduce it by $8.50 to $76.50, and the last would reduce the price by $3.82 to $72.68. Thus, a *chain discount* of 15, 10, and 5 is essentially the same as a single *discount* of about 27.5 percent.

commercial ∼. See TRADE DISCOUNT below.

quantity ∼. One allowed for purchases made in large amounts. The justification for such a *discount* is supposedly the savings in costs of handling, billing, packing, etc., but in practice the *discounts* allowed are often simply inducements to customers to make larger purchases. Under the Robinson-Patman Act, however, *quantity discounts* must be justified by savings.

time ∼. In advertising, a *discount* allowed to an advertiser by a publisher for a stated number of insertions of an advertisement within a period of time, or for a continued regularity of insertion over a period of time. Also, a name for a CASH DISCOUNT, which see above.

trade ∼. A reduction from the list or suggested retail price of a product which is allowed to a retail, wholesale, or other distributor who qualifies for the reduction as a member of a class of trade. Thus, a system of *trade discounts* established by a manufacturer is actually a schedule of prices to be charged to different classes of customers. See also NET PRICING.

2. In banking and finance, a deduction made in advance from an amount loaned, as a form of interest. For example, a bank making a loan of $100 to a borrower may deduct a *discount* of $5 in advance, so that the borrower actually receives only $95. If the loan is for a full year, such a *discount* of 5 percent is the equivalent of an interest charge of 10 percent per year on the unpaid balance of a loan repaid in equal installments over the year. The *discount* figured on the amount actually made available to the borrower, rather than on the face amount of the loan is called the *true discount,* and in this case would be approximately 5.26 percent. Similarly, a bank may purchase a BILL OF EXCHANGE, deducting a *discount* from the face value in determining the amount it pays for the bill, as an interest charge until the bill becomes due, and as payment for the risk involved in purchasing the bill. See also COMMUTATION OF INTEREST.

discount company. A name for a FACTOR, or SALES FINANCE COMPANY.

discount rate. In general, the percentage rate of DISCOUNT (2) which a bank or other lender deducts in advance from loans made, or from the face value of commercial paper bought. In particular, in financial statistics, the rate charged by the various Federal Reserve Banks to their member banks in the

purchase of COMMERCIAL PAPER. It is also known as the *rediscount rate,* since the paper sold by the member banks has already been once purchased by them at a discount.

discretionary order. See under ORDER (4).

discretionary trust. See under TRUST (1).

discrimination. In general, the failure to treat all alike. In business, particularly, the failure to treat all customers alike, by charging different prices, giving unequal service, etc. The most common form of *discrimination* is PRICE DISCRIMINATION, which is specifically declared to be illegal under the anti-trust laws.

dishonor. In general, to refuse to meet a claim or obligation when due. Specifically, to refuse or neglect to pay a bill of exchange, note or other instrument when due, or to refuse to accept a negotiable instrument when presented for acceptance. A note or other instrument is said to have been *dishonored* when the holder is unable to have it either paid or accepted for payment. See also HONOR.

dismiss. 1. In law, to dispose of a case without a trial of the issues. This may be done because the court has decided that the basis for a case doesn't exist, or at the request of one or both of the parties, who decide not to contest the issues. If the case is *dismissed* with PREJUDICE, the plaintiff may not again bring suit on the same grounds, but if it is *dismissed* without prejudice, the plaintiff retains the right to bring suit of the same issues again.

2. In personnel management, to sever an employee at the initiative of the management. The term includes both DISCHARGE, which is usually for cause, and LAYOFF, which is for necessary reasons beyond control of the employee. However, it excludes any form of voluntary resignation, and any form of temporary LEAVE or FURLOUGH in which the employee technically remains on the payroll.

dismissal pay. See SEVERANCE PAY.

dispatch money. In connection with ship chartering contracts, an allowance or bonus sometimes paid by the owner of a vessel to the charterer or shipper for loading or unloading cargo with dispatch, or less time than the number of LYING DAYS allowed.

dispersion. In statistics, the spread of values in a FREQUENCY DISTRIBUTION, as distinguished from the clustering or central tendency in the distribution. The *dispersion* is measured by such statistics as the RANGE and the STANDARD DEVIATION.

displacement. In shipping, the volume or weight of water which is pushed aside, or displaced, by a floating ship. Since any floating body displaces its own weight in water, the *displacement* of a ship is the equivalent of its floating weight. See also TON, DISPLACEMENT; TONNAGE, DISPLACEMENT.

display advertising. See under ADVERTISING.

disposable personal income. In economic statistics, the total income remaining to individuals after payment of state and federal income taxes, and other payments to government. In another sense, it is the total of all personal consumption expenditures and personal savings.

dispossess. In law, to eject, especially from land occupancy, by legal steps. An action taken by a landlord to remove from occupancy a tenant who has violated the terms of a lease, or who has failed to make rental payments, by obtaining a special order from a local court or from the county sheriff.

dissenting opinion. See under OPINION.

dissolution. In law, the cancellation of a contract or agreement, by the mutual consent and action of the parties involved. The *dissolution* of a PARTNERSHIP agreement is an example. More broadly, the termination or liquidation of any business enterprise, whether by voluntary action of its owners, or by the expiration of its charter, or by legal or legislative action, such as through BANKRUPTCY procedures.

distant. With respect to commodities, and to FUTURES contracts for commodities, a term meaning a month in the distant future, or one for which contract trading has only recently begun. See also NEARBY; CONTRACT MONTH.

distressed goods. In retail and wholesale distribution, a term for goods or inventories which have been seized for failure to pay, and which have subsequently been resold at low prices to raise cash. More broadly, any inventory which has been disposed of to a dealer or distributor at a low price to raise cash, whether or not a seizure or forced sale is actually involved. Such *distressed goods* are usually resold to the public at sale prices, often through OUTLET stores.

distribution. 1. In business, the area of activity including the selling, shipping, storing, and promotion of goods; the movement of merchandise or commodities from the producer to the final consumer. It is a broader term than MARKETING, since it includes not only the advertising, selling, packaging, and similar activities, but the physical movement and preparation of the goods as well.
2. In law, any division of funds, such as the *distribution* of a residual ESTATE, or of the estate of one who has died intestate, among the heirs, or a *distribution* of the funds of a BANKRUPT among his creditors.
3. In accounting, the process of allocating income and expenses to the proper subsidiary accounts. The costs of maintaining equipment, for example, must be distributed on some basis among the various products made on the equipment, and the income from a combination sale must be distributed among the various products and departments involved. See also COST ACCOUNTING.

distribution clause. See PRO RATA DISTRIBUTION CLAUSE.

distributive share. In law, the portion or share of each particular heir in the DISTRIBUTION (2) of an estate, especially the share provided for by law as the portion of each class of heir in the estate of an intestate. More broadly, the proportionate share of any person in a distribution of funds, as, for example, the share of a particular creditor in the distribution of the funds of a bankrupt. See also STATUTE OF DISTRIBUTION.

distributor. In general, any person or organization performing the function of distributing the products of a manufacturer to customers or to DEALERS. As used, the term is generally understood to exclude RETAIL STORES, but to include both regular WHOLESALERS and dealers who sell to industrial consumers of the product. The latter are known as *industrial distributors*.

diversification. In general, any spreading out, or turning in several directions. Thus, the *diversification* of a company's product line involves the adding of new products with different uses, different markets, etc. Similarly the *diversification* of risk in insurance is obtained by spreading the liabilities assumed by the insurance company over a great many individual risks. In investment practice, *diversification* is obtained by investing funds in the securities of a number of different companies, engaged in different kinds of activities.

diversified investment company. See INVESTMENT COMPANY, MUTUAL FUND.

dividend. Literally, that which is to be divided. Any funds, out of earnings, or out of the proceeds of sale of property, to be divided or distributed among shareholders or creditors. Generally, it is a distribution of a share of profits, but it may also be a distribution of property or assets, or of funds obtained from the sale of assets. Ordinarily, a *dividend* is paid in proportion to the share of ownership of each shareholder, or in proportion to the amount owed to each creditor. The principal types and classifications of *dividends* are listed and defined below.

accrued ∿. That portion of a regular *dividend* which has been earned during a partial time period since the last regular payment. Ordinarily, in the sale of stocks, such *accrued dividends* are not taken into account directly, but tend to gradually raise the price at which the stock sells, from one *dividend* date to the next.

accumulated ∿. A CUMULATIVE DIVIDEND, which see below, which has not been paid when due, and which therefore has *accumulated,* or been added to the amount to be paid in the future.

bond ∿. One paid in the form of bonds of the company. Such a *dividend* may be paid, for example, when a large proportion of the assets of the company are in the form of real estate investments, and the company wishes to conserve its cash for additional investments in the future. A *dividend* in the form of bonds of another company held by the paying company is a form of PROPERTY DIVIDEND, which see below.

cash ∿. One paid in cash, or more frequently, by check immediately convertible into cash. This is the most common form of *dividend* payment.

cumulative ∿. One which, if it is not paid at the regular time it is due to be paid, will be automatically accumulated, to be paid in the future. Some preferred stocks pay *cumulative dividends,* but common stocks practically never do so. See also STOCK, CUMULATIVE.

deferred ∿. One declared at present, but due to be paid at some future time. Such a *dividend* may be declared, for example, on an insurance policy, to be paid at maturity.

extra ∿. One paid in addition to the REGULAR DIVIDEND, which see below, at the regular date for *dividend* payment. Such a *dividend* may be paid, for example, if the profits of the company during the period covered by the *dividend* are exceptionally high.

insurance ∿. One paid to the policy holders of an insurance company, especially those of a mutual life insurance company. Such a *dividend* may be paid out of the income of the company from its investments, or out of surpluses which accumulate due to better actuarial experience than expected. Such *dividends* are also sometimes paid by fire, liability, and other insurance companies, usually in the form of reductions on future premium payments.

interim ∿. One paid before the final determination of the regular rate of *dividend,* or before the preparation of the final financial statement for the accounting period. Such a *dividend* may be paid, for example, by a new corporation which has not yet begun to make regular payments, or by one which has previously discontinued payments and has again begun to earn a profit.

Irish ∿. In financial slang, a facetious term for an ASSESSMENT (2) levied against stockholders of a corporation.

irregular ∿. One paid from time to time, at irregular time intervals, rather than at regular periodic dates. Also, sometimes, one paid in between regular *dividend* payment dates. See also REGULAR DIVIDEND, below.

liquidation ∿. One paid out of assets, to the owners of a corporation being dissolved, or to the creditors of a company being liquidated, or in bankruptcy, or to the heirs of an estate being settled. It may be paid in cash or in property. See also DISTRIBUTION (2).

optional ∿. A term for one which will be paid in cash or in stock, or perhaps in some other form, at the option or election of the shareholder.

passed ∿. One which, in a company ordinarily paying REGULAR DIVIDENDS, has not been paid when due. Ordinary *dividends,* once passed, are not made up, but CUMULATIVE DIVIDENDS, which see above, remain due to be paid in the future.

property ∿. One consisting of a portion of corporate property paid to shareholders, instead of cash or corporate stock. It may be the securities of another corporation, such as a subsidiary company, government bonds held, etc. It is distinguished from a LIQUIDATION DIVIDEND, which see above, in that it is paid by a corporation which is continuing in business, not one being dissolved.

regular ∿. One which is declared and paid at regular intervals, usually quarterly, semi-annually, or annually, and in a uniform amount at each interval.

scrip ∿. One which is paid in SCRIP, or in other words, in a promissory note, which is due to be paid at some future date. Thus, it is a form of DEFERRED DIVIDEND, which see above.

security ∿. See PROPERTY DIVIDEND, above.

stock ∿. One paid in the stock of the corporation, rather than in cash. Such a *dividend* may be paid, for example, when the corporation wishes to conserve cash for future expansion. Such *dividends* may also be paid when the stockholders wish to avoid taxable income from the corporation.

unearned ∿. One, the payment of which reduces or impairs the capital of the corporation. Such *dividend* payments are unlawful. A *dividend* is not *unearned,* however, if it is paid out of previous earnings held in surplus, but not included in the capital of the corporation.

year-end ～. One paid at the end of the corporate fiscal year, the amount of which depends on the total earnings of the corporation during the year. A *year-end dividend* is actually a form of EXTRA DIVIDEND, which see above, but some corporations make a regular practice of paying conservative REGULAR DIVIDENDS, which see above, and paying *year-end dividends* of varying amounts every year.

dividend warrant. See under WARRANT (2).

dock. Literally, to cut short, or to cut to a stump. Hence, to shorten, diminish, or withhold. Hourly wages, for example, may be *docked,* or reduced, as a penalty for lateness, or wages based on output may be *docked* for low quality of work. The term is seldom used today in any other context.

document. Originally, a lesson, warning, or demonstration; hence, anything which tends to prove or demonstrate facts, or to serve as evidence. More specifically, as used today, any written instrument containing facts, figures, designs, or other information, which may be used as evidence or proof. Examples include contracts, deeds, affidavits, official records, etc.

documentary bill. See under BILL OF EXCHANGE.

documentary draft. See under DRAFT.

documentary instructions. In foreign trade practice, a term for the written agreement between an importer and a foreign exporter covering the disposition of the various documents relating to a shipment, and the disposition of the goods themselves. For example, the instructions may call for delivery of the goods upon acceptance of the draft or bill, or they may call for immediate payment before the transfer of the remaining documents and the goods.

dodger. In advertising slang, a term for a small HANDBILL, designed to be distributed on the streets, or perhaps from door to door. It is also sometimes known as a throw-away. A FLIER (2).

doing business as. A term used in credit reference books, business listings, and some legal records, before the TRADE NAME under which a business operates, indicating that the name is not part of a corporation title, or of a registered trade mark.

dole. Originally, a share or portion, especially a small portion. Hence, in modern usage, a charitable allowance or distribution. There is a sharp distinction between unemployment allowances based on insurance, and those which are purely charitable, and only the latter, strictly, are a *dole.*

dollar. The standard monetary unit in the currency of the United States. The name is originally derived from the Bohemian town of Joachimsthal, in which *Joachimsthaler guldens* were first minted. The coins came to be known as *thaler,* and in English as *dollars.* As established by the International Monetary Fund in 1946, the United States *dollar* is worth 0.88671 grams of fine gold, or 35 *dollars* per troy ounce of gold. Gold *dollars,* however, are no longer minted. The silver *dollar* weighs 412.5 grains, consisting of 371.25 grains of pure silver and 41.25 grains of copper-base alloy metal. The *dollar* most commonly in actual use is the silver CERTIFICATE (2), which represents one *dollar* in silver on deposit in the United States Treasury. Several other countries, including Canada, Liberia, etc., also use a *dollar,* based more or less on the United States *dollar,* as their standard monetary unit.

dollar averaging. In the securities trade, the name for the practice of buying a fixed dollar amount of a given security at regular intervals. Under such a plan, more shares of the security are bought when prices are low, and fewer shares when prices are high, so that the average price paid for all of the shares bought tends to be less than the average market price for the security over the period of purchase. *Dollar averaging* is frequently used by INVESTMENT COMPANIES, insurance companies, trust funds, and other regular buyers of securities, and is also used by individual investors. It is the method followed, for example, in the MONTHLY INVESTMENT PLAN, and in investing in most mutual fund investment companies. See also AVERAGING.

dollar-a-year man. A term for an executive or consultant, especially one serving the government, who serves without compensation, or for nominal compensation. Such executives may serve, for example, in time of war or other emergency, in those agencies dealing with industrial mobilization, price control, or other government activities relating to business. Originally, a nominal payment, such as one dollar per year, was paid to such men, since there was no provision for completely voluntary service. Now, however, there is a regular means for accepting services without compensation, and the government advisers and consultants who serve on this basis are known as W.O.C.s.

dollar bloc. In international finance, the term used to describe the group of nations which have aligned their currencies and foreign exchange operations with the United States DOLLAR.

dollar bond. See under BOND (1).

dollar exchange. See under EXCHANGE (4).

domain. Originally, belonging to a lord or a feudal proprietor. Now, the complete and absolute ownership of land, or of the title to real property. Also, any lands held in such complete ownership. See also EMINENT DOMAIN.

public ∼. All those lands which are owned directly by the government, especially the federal government. The term includes both those lands which have not yet passed into private ownership, and those which have been reacquired by the government, under CONDEMNATION or other proceedings. The *public domain* of the federal government is sometimes known as the national *domain*, to distinguish it from the public lands of states or subdivisions of states.

domestic. As used in business, originating, transpiring, or destined for delivery in, the same state or country, as distinguished from FOREIGN or INTERNATIONAL, which imply the involvement of two or more states or countries. See each of the following under the principal listing: ∼ BILL OF EXCHANGE; ∼ CORPORATION; ∼ EXCHANGE (4).

domestic commerce. As generally used, COMMERCE and TRADE (2) within the boundaries of the country, as distinguished from FOREIGN COMMERCE, which is between two or more countries. The term may refer either to commerce between the states, or to commerce entirely within the boundaries of one state. See also INTERSTATE COMMERCE, INTRASTATE COMMERCE.

domestic exports. In foreign trade statistics, one of the two categories in which EXPORTS are classified. *Domestic exports* are those of goods originally grown, produced, or manufactured in the United States, as distinguished from RE-EXPORTS, the other category, which are goods originally imported and again exported without any substantial change in their nature or degree of processing.

domestic money order. See MONEY ORDER, POSTAL.

domicile. In general, the place in which a person has established his permanent and fixed abode, as distinguished from any temporary or transient abodes which he may maintain. In business, the state in which a company is originally organized, and under which it holds its charter or other authorization to do business. A corporation may only be *domiciled* in one state, but it may form associated

or subsidiary corporations with *domiciles* in other states. Sometimes, *domicile* is distinguished from RESIDENCE in that a person may have only one *domicile* at a time, but several residences.

domiciled bill. See under BILL OF EXCHANGE.

donated stock. See under STOCK (1).

donee. In law, the name for the recipient of any donation, gift, or BEQUEST.

donor. In law, the name for the person who makes a donation, gift, or BEQUEST.

door-to-door selling. See HOUSE-TO-HOUSE SELLING.

dormant partner. See under PARTNER.

double daylight saving time. See DAYLIGHT SAVING TIME.

double-eagle. A gold coin, worth twenty dollars, which formerly circulated in the United States. See also EAGLE.

double-entry. The name for the system of BOOKKEEPING or ACCOUNTING in which every transaction is eventually entered in two accounts, once as a CREDIT and once as a DEBIT entry. This is done on the principle that every transaction has a twofold aspect, and involves the exchange of one good or service for another good or service. A sale, for example, is viewed as both a sale of goods and a receipt of funds, payroll expenses as both an expenditure and a receipt of services, etc. In modern accounting systems, the transaction is first entered once in the JOURNAL, VOUCHER REGISTER, or other BOOK OF ORIGINAL ENTRY, and then transferred or POSTED to the appropriate two accounts in the LEDGER. See also SINGLE-ENTRY.

double indemnity. See ACCIDENTAL DEATH BENEFIT CLAUSE.

double-liability stock. See under STOCK (1).

double-name paper. See COMMERCIAL PAPER, TWO-NAME.

double-page spread. In advertising, an advertisement which cover two facing pages in a newspaper, magazine, or other publication. It is also sometimes known simply as a double-spread, or as a double-truck advertisement.

double standard. See BIMETALLIC STANDARD.

double taxation. The practice of taxing the same wealth, income, or property twice. For example, under present tax laws, corporate income is taxed twice; once as corporate profit and once as dividend income to the stockholders. Similarly, it is possible for a legacy to be taxed once through a federal estate tax and once through an inheritance tax of a particular state. See also TAX (2).

double-truck advertisement. See DOUBLE-PAGE SPREAD.

doubtful asset. See under ASSET (2).

doubtful title. See under TITLE (2).

dower rights. The rights which a widow has to a share of the estate of her late husband, either under common law or under the statutes of the particular state. The laws of the various states differ widely as to the amount to which the widow is entitled, and to the circumstances under which she may claim her *dower rights*. Generally, she is entitled to a minimum share, such as one third of the residuary estate, in the absence of more specific or more generous provisions. See also ESTATE (1), DOWER; STATUTE OF DISTRIBUTION.

downgrading. In personnel relations, the organized reduction in rank or demotion of employees. This may occur, for example, as a result of a reduction in force, so that employees with high seniority are required to take lower rated jobs to remain on the payroll. It may also result from an organized plan to upgrade the requirements for certain positions, so that the employees presently holding the positions are automatically demoted to a lower rating. See also UPGRADING.

down payment. A partial payment, made at the time of purchase, to secure the agreement. An amount of money paid by a buyer to a seller at the time of purchase, as part of an agreement providing for the payment of the balance of the total price in one or more later INSTALLMENTS. Title to the goods purchased may or may not change hands at the time the *down payment* is made, depending on the particular form of sales agreement, but possession of the goods usually does change hands. A *down payment* may or may not be forfeit if the sale is not completed, also depending on the particular agreement. See also EARNEST.

downstream. In business usage, a term for any transaction or operation that proceeds from a higher or senior level to a lower or junior level. For example, a downstream loan is one made by a parent company to a subsidiary, such as a loan made by a HOLDING COMPANY to one of the operating companies it holds. See also UPSTREAM.

draft. 1. A preliminary or tentative text of any literary work, document, or other writing. A text referred to as a final *draft* is usually one which is in final form as far as the content is concerned, but not as far as the formal presentation or writing is concerned.

2. In banking and finance, an order drawn by one person upon another, calling for payment of money to a third person. Thus, a BILL OF EXCHANGE and a CHECK are both forms of *draft*. In business usage, however, a *draft* is an order payable within the United States in dollars, while a bill of exchange is an order which may be payable in a foreign country, or in a foreign currency. Similarly, a check is commonly known as a *draft* only if it is drawn by one bank upon another. The principal types of *drafts* are listed and defined below.

bank ~. One drawn by one bank on another bank, and payable on demand. It is used to transfer funds between banks, and to settle outstanding balances between banks.

clean ~. One which has none of the documents covering a shipment attached to it, as distinguished from a DOCUMENTARY DRAFT, which see below.

demand ~. See SIGHT DRAFT, below.

documentary ~. One to which the various shipping documents on a domestic shipment are attached, including, usually, the bill of lading, insurance certificate, and any other papers or certificates required. See also BILL OF EXCHANGE, DOCUMENTARY.

sight ~. One which is payable immediately on presentation, or on demand. In some states, however, the law requires that a specified number of DAYS OF GRACE be allowed for the payment of any negotiable instrument, including a *sight draft*. In effect, a *sight draft* on a bank is a CHECK.

time ~. One which is payable a fixed number of days AFTER SIGHT, or after presentation for ACCEPTANCE, but not a fixed number of days after it is drawn. The number of days after sight must be specifically mentioned in the *draft* at the time it is drawn.

dram. 1. A unit of weight in APOTHECARIES' MEASURE, equal to one eighth part of an OUNCE, or one ninety-sixth part of a POUND. It contains 3 SCRUPLES, or 60 GRAINS, and is the equivalent of 3.8879 GRAMS in the metric system.

2. A little-used unit of weight in AVOIRDUPOIS MEASURE, equal to one sixteenth part of an OUNCE, and the equivalent of 1.7718 GRAMS in the metric system.

3. A unit of liquid capacity, equal to one eighth part of a fluid OUNCE. It is used primarily in the preparation of medicinal prescriptions.

draw. Originally, to outline, or to frame, and hence, to prepare, or put into the proper form. To *draw* a CHECK or DRAFT, for example, is to prepare or write out the terms and amount of the instrument. It is universally understood that an instrument is *drawn* by the person who is giving the order to pay, and who signs the instrument. It is *drawn* upon the party who is to pay out or turn over the funds to the third party named in the instrument. See also DRAWER; DRAWEE.

drawback. In shipping usage, a REFUND paid to a shipper when a mistake has been made in calculating the freight charge on a shipment. Strictly speaking, a *drawback* is distinguished from a REBATE in that it is returned as the result of an overcharge, while the latter is frequently a method of reducing the charge below that called for by the scheduled rates. Similarly, in customs usage, a *drawback* is a return or refund of part or all of an import tariff when the goods are re-exported.

drawee. The person or institution upon whom an instrument is DRAWN. The person who is ordered, in a check, draft, or bill, to pay money over to the person named. The funds paid over need not be those of the *drawee;* in fact, they are usually those of the DRAWER, on deposit with the *drawee.*

drawer. The person who DRAWS an instrument upon another. The person who orders, in a check, draft, or bill, that money be paid over to a third party by the DRAWEE. Usually, the *drawer* orders that his own funds, which are being held by the drawee, be paid out. In some types of transactions, such as when he draws a check to "cash," or makes a bill payable to BEARER, the *drawer* may also be the person to whom the money is paid.

drawing account. A term for the account or credit established by a business, against which a salesman, employee, or principal of a business may make withdrawals. Companies frequently establish such *drawing accounts* for their salesmen, on the basis of commissions anticipated or earned. A salesman who is compensated on a *drawing account* basis is sometimes said to be on draw against commissions.

drawn bond. See under BOND (1).

drayage. A term for the charge made for transporting goods locally to or from shipside, or to or from a rail freight terminal. Essentially, it is the same as CARTAGE.

drive-in. The term used for any business establishment which is so designed that a customer is able to drive his automobile onto the property of the establishment and conduct his business while remaining in the car. A *drive-in* bank, for example, may have a special teller's window to which the customer drives, while a *drive-in* restaurant serves food to the customer in his car. A *drive-in* theater is one in which the patron is able to watch a motion picture or other entertainment while seated in his car.

drop. In some lines of trade, a term used for a pattern or model which has been discontinued, or dropped from the product line. Such items are frequently disposed of at reduced prices, or used as special low price promotional items in sales. See also CLOSE OUT (2).

drop shipment. In distribution, a term for a shipment of goods made directly from a manufacturer to a dealer or industrial consumer, on the order of a wholesale distributor. Though the order goes directly from the manufacturer to the customer, the wholesaler takes title to the goods during shipment if he would normally do so on shipments made to him. When an appliance retailer, for example, is able to order an entire carload of appliances, they are usually shipped directly to him as a *drop shipment,* though the wholesaler through whom he places the order earns his usual profit on the transaction. The dealer's gain is in the lower freight charge on the shipment.

drop shipper. In business usage, the name for a wholesale distributor who regularly takes orders for goods which are to be delivered by the manufacturer directly to the wholesaler's customers by DROP SHIPMENT. A *drop shipper* is distinguished from a manufacturer's agent in that he takes title to the goods during shipment, and provides all of the services of a wholesaler, including billing, collection, dealer service, etc., though he does not take possession of the goods. He is sometimes known as a desk jobber. See also AGENT, MANUFACTURER'S.

drummer. In business slang, a traveling salesman, or COMMERCIAL TRAVELER. Originally, one who went about drumming up trade for his employer's products.

dry goods. See GOODS (2).

dry measure. A system for measuring the volume of various dry commodities, or the capacity of containers for such commodities. It is used for measuring fruits, vegetables, grains, etc. The system is based on a PINT of 33.60 cubic inches, with 2 pints equal to one QUART, 8 quarts equal to one PECK, and 4 pecks equal to one BUSHEL. The dry pint and quart are slightly larger in volume than the measures with the same names in liquid measure.

dry trust. See under TRUST (1).

dual union. See under UNION.

due. Originally, deserved, just and proper; hence, owed. Strictly, that which is *due and payable* is presently payable, but that which is *due and owing* is owed but not yet payable. As used alone, however, the term is usually taken to mean *due and payable,* or MATURE.

due bill. See under BILL (6).

due date. The term for the date on which a debt or obligation, especially one evidenced by a note or bill, becomes payable. The maturity date of a debt.

due process. See PROCESS (1).

dummy. Literally, a sham, or false person. A term used for a person who serves in place of another, or who serves temporarily until the proper person is named or is available to take over. When a corporation is newly organized, for example, it is common practice to name several *dummy* directors to meet the legal requirements for organization. These are replaced by directors elected by the shareholders after the corporation stock has been distributed. Similarly, in real estate trading and other transactions, it is common for *dummy* owners to take temporary title to property so that the identity of the actual buyer is not known to the seller.

dumping. In general, the practice of selling large quantities of a product at a very low price, especially to gain an advantage in a market. In international trade, in particular, it is defined by federal law as the sale in the United States of foreign goods below their cost of production. The Tariff Commission is instructed to watch for such actions, and the country engaging in *dumping* is subject to punitive tariff action. See also TARIFF, ANTI-DUMPING.

dun. To make insistent demands for the payment of a debt. To press a debtor for payment. The term derives from the practice, in medieval England, of crying the names of delinquent debtors through the streets, while beating a drum, ringing a bell, or otherwise creating a din, or *dun.*

dunnage. Any material used in a ship's hold or in a freight car, usually wood, mats, coarse straw, etc., to keep the cargo from shifting or from being damaged in motion. When a freight shipment requires special or additional *dunnage,* the usual practice is for the railroad to charge for this by weight at the same rate as that charged for the goods themselves.

duodecimo. See under BOOK SIZES.

duopoly. In business, the ownership or control of enough of the source of supply of, or market for, a product by two companies to stifle competition, control prices, or otherwise restrict trade. Strictly, a *duopoly* is distinguished from a MONOPOLY (2) in that two companies exercise control, instead of one.

duplicate. Literally, a double. An exact copy or counterpart of a document or instrument. It is usually a second printed copy, filled in where necessary with the same information, or a facsimile prepared by any of various duplicating processes. Law or accounting practice requires that many common business instruments, such as invoices, bills of exchange, etc., be prepared in *duplicate.*

duplication of readership. In magazine circulation, the degree to which the circulation of two or more magazines reaches the same readers, so that advertising placed in all of the magazines concerned is seen more than once by some of the reading audience. It is a usual aim, in selecting magazines as advertising media, to avoid *duplication of readership* as far as possible.

durable goods. See under GOODS (3).

duress. In law, any unlawful use of force, the threat of force, fear, or deceit to deprive a person of the exercise of his free will. *Duress* used by one party to an agreement against the other invalidates the agreement under law.

Dutch auction. See under AUCTION.

duty. Originally, any payment owed, especially one owed to a government. As used currently, any tax payment collected on the import or export of goods. Under Article I of the Constitution, no tax on exports may be levied. Strictly speaking, a *duty* is the actual tax collected, while a TARIFF is the schedule, basis, or rate of taxation. Thus, in this text, the various classifications and types of tariffs or *duties* are listed and defined under TARIFF, which see.

dwt. See PENNYWEIGHT.

E

each way. An expression used in the trading of stocks and commodities, meaning on both the buying and selling side of the transaction. Thus, when a broker charges a commission of 2 percent *each way,* he receives 2 percent from one party for selling the items and another 2 percent commission from the other party for buying.

eagle. The name for the ten dollar gold coin which formerly circulated in the United States, and was one of the basic coins of the monetary system. Its name derived from the likeness of the American *eagle* which appeared on the coin. The *eagle* was 1.05 inches in diameter, .60 inches thick, and 258 grains in weight. A *double-eagle* was a 20 dollar gold coin, a *half-eagle* five dollars, etc.

earmark. Originally, and literally, a mark put on the ears of sheep to distinguish them from those of other owners. Thus, any mark put on a thing to distinguish it or mark it aside, or the act of setting something aside for a specific purpose. For example, funds in a corporation's cash reserve may be *earmarked* for any of a number of special purposes.

earned. Literally, received in exchange for work done, or for services rendered, or for goods provided. Money which is *earned* is distinguished both from that which is received as a gift, and from that which is received for work, services, or goods to be provided in the future. See each of the following under the principal listing: ∼ INCOME; ∼ PREMIUM (2); ∼ SURPLUS.

earnest. Money paid by one party to a bargain to another, to bind the bargain between them. A prospective purchaser, for example, may pay an *earnest* to the seller, which binds him to keep the goods a reasonable time, and which at the same time binds the purchaser to pay for the goods and accept them. If and when the sale is completed, the *earnest* usually is considered a partial payment on the total price. If the bargain is not completed, the *earnest* is forfeited. The money so paid is called *earnest* money, or in European usage, handsel.

earning power. The capacity to gain or profit, or to return a profit; the productive capacity of a business or an investment.

earnings. 1. In general, income which is gained or merited by labor, service, or performance; a reward, wage, salary, pay or compensation. In this sense, *earnings* is used to distinguish the reward for personal effort from a return on investment.

2. The receipts from operations of a business enterprise; the operating profit of a business. See also INCOME; PROFIT.

gross ∼. The total earned income of a business, before the deduction of any operating expenses or taxes, but not, strictly speaking, including any income from investments. It is also called the gross operating income.

net ∼. The operating *earnings* of a business, after the deduction of operating expenses. *Net earnings* may be measured before the deduction of income taxes, or after taxes. It is also called the net operating income, or net operating profit.

earnings statement. See INCOME STATEMENT.

easement. A liberty, right, or privilege, apart from ownership and without profit, granted to the owner of one parcel of land with respect to the land of another. Examples of *easements* are light and air, providing that light will not be obstructed by construction on adjoining land; access, providing that entrance and exit to the property will not be blocked; etc.

private ∼. An *easement* concerning a privilege restricted to one or a few, such as one to light or access, as above.

public ∼. An *easement* concerning a privilege vested in the general public, such as an *easement* of passage, or of navigation of a stream.

easy. In financial usage, and in the securities and commodity trades, a term used to describe the condition of the market when supply tends to exceed demand. Thus, *easy* money is money borrowed at a low rate of interest, due to the fact that the supply of loanable funds exceeds the demand for loans. Similarly, the securities or commodities market is said to be *easy*, or to *ease*, when prices tend to decline in quiet trading. See also MONEY, EASY.

easy payment plan. See INSTALLMENT PLAN.

economic lot size. The term for that number or amount of a product which should be manufactured or purchased at one time to minimize the total cost involved, taking into account direct and indirect costs of manufacture or purchase, the costs of storage space, interest on the capital tied up in the product, etc.

economic strike. See under STRIKE.

economic unemployment. See UNEMPLOYMENT.

effective date. The date on which, or as of which, a contract or agreement goes into effect; as, for example, the *effective date*, or starting date, of an insurance contract.

effective rate. See YIELD.

effects. In law, strictly, personal estate or personal property, but sometimes held to include real estate or other real property. Because of the inexact nature of the term, it is usually inadvisable to use it in such documents as wills, deeds, etc.

efficiency. 1. In engineering and physics, the ratio of useful work obtained from a machine, operation or individual, in relation to the energy applied; the ratio of output to input. Thus, in measuring any business operation or work, it is the ratio of output, as measured in any of several ways, to input, measured in comparable terms. See also WORK MEASUREMENT.

2. In general usage, the quality of competence, capability, effectiveness or productivity; the ability to produce the desired results; effectiveness.

efficiency expert. One whose work is to study the management and methods of a business, for the purpose of increasing its efficiency of operation and its productivity. Today, the *efficiency expert* as such has largely disappeared, and this work is considered to be part of the profession of management engineering or industrial engineering.

elastic currency. See under CURRENCY.

elasticity of demand. The manner in which the DEMAND (1) for a commodity or product varies in relation to its price. When the amount of a commodity that people will buy increases or decreases very little as the price falls or rises, the commodity is said to have an *inelastic demand*. Conversely, when demand rises or falls sharply as the price becomes lower or higher, the demand is said to be highly *elastic*. The *elasticity of*

demand for the same product may be different at one price level than at another, and may change from time to time. In general, those products which are considered necessities or staples tend to have *inelastic demands*, while those in the luxury class have very *elastic demands*. Certain products, under certain conditions, may have a negative *elasticity of demand*, meaning that their demand decreases as their price falls, or increases as the price rises.

elasticity of supply. The manner in which the SUPPLY of a commodity or product varies in relation to its price. When the amount of a commodity that producers will supply increases or decreases very little as the price rises or falls, the commodity is said to have an *inelastic supply*. Conversely, when supply rises or falls sharply as the price becomes higher or lower, the supply is said to be highly *elastic*.

election. In business usage, a free choice, such as of a method of accounting for tax purposes, or of inventory evaluation; also, a choice of a remedy at law, by a plaintiff or complainant.

electrolytic plating. See ELECTROPLATING.

electromotive force (E.M.F.). The force or pressure under which electricity flows through a circuit. It is measured in VOLTS.

electronics. The science and technology dealing with the flow of electrons, such as from the filaments of an *electronic* vacuum tube, and with devices whose operation depends on this principle, including radio, television, radar, computors, etc.

electroplating. A method of plating out certain metals, including tin, copper, zinc, etc., on other metal surfaces. The object to be coated is placed in a bath containing the plating metal in an electrically conductive chemical solution, called the electrolyte. A bar or rod of the plating metal is also inserted, and when an electric current is made to flow from the object (the cathode) through the electrolyte to the plating metal (the anode), the metal in the solution plates out onto the cathode and is continuously replaced in the solution by metal from the anode. *Electroplating* produces an extremely uniform, smooth and polished coating. It is also known as electrolytic plating, galvanic plating, or GALVANIZING.

eleemosynary. Devoted to charity or alms; with a charitable purpose. See, for example, CORPORATION, ELEEMOSYNARY.

elevator certificate. A receipt issued by a grain elevator or warehouse for goods or grain stored therein. It is also called an elevator receipt. See also WAREHOUSE RECEIPT.

eligible bond. See under BOND (1).

eligible investment. A security or other income producing investment which is considered sufficiently sound for the funds of savings banks, trust funds, etc. Many states prescribe the types and classes of investments which are eligible for such institutions chartered within the state. See also BOND (1), ELIGIBLE; LEGAL LIST.

eligible paper. See under COMMERCIAL PAPER.

em. See TYPE SIZE.

embargo. 1. Strictly, a proclamation or order, such as might be issued in time of war or emergency, prohibiting the departure of ships from ports, or of the export of certain types of goods, or of shipments to specific countries. Thus, an *embargo* is distinguished from a BLOCKADE, which is directed against the importing state or area. In peacetime, an *embargo* may be placed on freight shipments by a railroad, due to a shortage of equipment, a strike, or to other conditions.
2. Loosely, any prohibition, such as one placed on the movement of specified goods in interstate commerce, or of trade with an enemy nation. For example, an *embargo* may be placed on interstate shipments of certain fruits or plants.

embarrass. To cause, or to result in financial difficulties. Thus, to be financially *embarrassed,* is generally understood to be short of funds or of resources.

embezzlement. In law, the fraudulent appropriation or conversion to one's own use or benefit of money or property entrusted to one by another, or otherwise in one's lawful possession. Thus, *embezzlement* is distinguished from LARCENY in that the property involved is already in the criminal's rightful possession. The term is believed to derive from the practice of trimming coins, by bankers, moneylenders and others who held them in trust, with a bezel or chisel.

embracery. In law, the offense of attempting to influence a trial jury by promises, persuasions, gifts, entertainment, etc., to reach a verdict favorable to one side or the other.

emergency. Any unexpected situation, state of affairs, or occasion for taking action. A sudden and pressing necessity for acting, as distinguished from a chronic situation which might call for the same action.

emergency facility. Any plant, equipment, or other productive facility acquired or built for use in fulfilling a national defense or war production contract or obligation. As so defined under federal regulations, such a facility may be entitled to a special tax concession, consisting of amortization of the total cost over a five year period instead of over the normal expected life of the facility.

E.M.F. See ELECTROMOTIVE FORCE.

emigration. The act of removing one's person from one country to another, with the intention not to return. Strictly, *emigration* is concerned only with the physical removal of one's person, and not with the abandonment of one's citizenship, which is known as expatriation. See also IMMIGRATION.

eminent domain. The power of the state to take over private property for public use, usually, but not necessarily, upon just remuneration. The power may be exercised by municipalities, and may be delegated to public corporations, such as port development authorities, transit authorities, etc.; or to public utilities, such as power transmission companies, public carriers, etc. *Eminent domain* should not be confused with the public DOMAIN or national domain, which are the lands owned directly by the government and which have not yet passed to private ownership, or which have been reacquired by the government. See also CONDEMNATION.

emit. To issue, put out, or put into circulation; as, for example, currency, notes, or other instruments.

emolument. Any gain or income from a position or office held. The term includes salary, wages, fees or other compensation, and usually refers to public offices.

employ. To engage the services of, or to hire another, or to entrust another with the management of one's affairs. Also, to use, as a tool, or a particular method.

employee. One who is hired or engaged to work for or perform services for another, on a continuous basis. He is distinguished from an AGENT in that he does not act for his employer, and from an INDEPENDENT CONTRACTOR in that he is fully under his employer's control. It is customary to distinguish *employees* from the officers or principals of a business, who may also, literally, be *employees* of the company. See also SERVANT.

employee benefit. See FRINGE BENEFIT.

employee publication. See HOUSE ORGAN.

employee stock ownership plan. Any of various plans, sponsored by an employer, under which employees of a corporation are assisted in purchasing the stock of the company in which they work. Under some plans, the company pays part of the cost of the stock, or offers it at a special price, while under many plans the company's part consists merely of enabling the employee to pay for the stock through small regular deductions from wages or salaries.

employees' association. In general, any organization of the employees of a company. More specifically, such an organization set up for the purpose of promoting employee welfare and working conditions. See also UNION.

employer. A person, organization, or other that employs or hires one or more persons to work or perform services for wages or salary. In special context, the PRINCIPAL of a business firm.

employers' association. A voluntary association of companies employing workers in a particular industry or geographic area, usually organized for the purpose of joint collective bargaining with the employees' representatives, or for the handling of other common problems.

employer's liability. The enforceable responsibility of an employer for injury suffered by an employee during or arising out of his regular duties or employment. See also WORKMEN'S COMPENSATION LAW; INSURANCE, CASUALTY AND LIABILITY.

Employers' Liability Act. The federal law defining and limiting the extent of an employer's liability for injuries to employees occurring in the course of employment. The act abolishes the common-law concept that an employer is not liable for injuries due to the negligence of a fellow-employee. It is the basis for the various state WORKMEN'S COMPENSATION LAWS.

employer's liability insurance. See under INSURANCE, CASUALTY AND LIABILITY.

employment. In general, the state of being employed, or of having regular, paid work. As used in government statistics, the total number of persons who are employed, or who are working at present in paid positions. The *employment* may be regular or permanent, or it may be temporary, or it may be casual, as long as the person is working at the date for which the figure is reported. In certain statistics, persons who have regular positions, but who are on temporary FURLOUGH and waiting to return to work on a given date, are considered to be employed though not literally working. See also UNEMPLOYMENT.

employment agency. An agency formed for the purpose of finding positions for persons seeking employment, and of finding prospective employees for employers attempting to fill vacant positions. Private agencies usually charge the employee a fee for their service, such as 2 or 3 percent of the annual wages.

Many states maintain state employment services in connection with their unemployment insurance plans.

emporium. From the Greek, a trading place, or commercial center. Thus, in frequent usage, a general store or department store. Many American department stores, in fact, have adopted the name "The Emporium," as descriptive of their activities.

en bloc. As a whole, as a unit; in one group rather than separately. Thus, a trader may sell his holdings of a stock *en bloc,* or a group may agree to act *en bloc.*

encroachment. In law any thing, such as a wall, fence, hedge, curbing, or driveway, which illegally infringes on the property of another, or on the public right of way. More generally, any act or behavior which infringes or limits the rights of others.

encumbrance. Any claim, right, or interest in land or other property, which, while it depreciates its value, does not prevent its transfer or sale. Examples are unpaid tax claims, mortgages, leases, and dower rights. It is common practice for the buyer of property to require the seller to warrant that the property is free of any *encumbrances.* The word is sometimes spelled *incumbrance.*

ending inventory. See under INVENTORY.

endorse. Literally, from the Latin, to write on the back. Hence, in business, to write one's signature on the back of an instrument for the purpose of transferring to another the rights or interest it conveys. For example, the person to whom a check or note is made payable may make it payable to another, or to bearer, by *endorsing* it on the back. Under some circumstances, a person may *endorse* an instrument, such as a copy of an invoice or packing slip, to indicate receipt of a shipment.

endorsed bond. See under BOND (1).

endorsement. 1. In insurance, a change or addition to a policy or contract, which is indicated by an attachment, signed by an agent or officer of the insurance company. It is known informally as a RIDER. For example, the EXTENDED COVERAGE clause is usually added to a fire insurance policy by attaching an *endorsement,* and the face amount of a group term life insurance contract is similarly often increased by use of a rider or *endorsement.*

2. In commercial law, the only recognized method of transferring title to a negotiable instrument, by writing one's name on the back of the instrument. This signature, which may be accompanied by conditional or restrictive wording, transfers from the original

payee of the instrument to another person, or to bearer, the right to receive the amounts represented by the instrument. Unless otherwise specified, the person who gives an *endorsement* automatically warrants that he has good title to the instrument, that it is genuine and proper, that he knows of nothing that will impair its validity, and that all prior endorsers were competent to do so. In so warranting, the endorser accepts the liability of making payment on the instrument if the original maker or the prior endorsers fail to do so. The various types and degrees of *endorsement* are listed and defined below.

absolute ∼. One by which the endorser passes along all of his rights in the instrument, and retains no responsibility to pay the amount due unless the original maker and all prior endorsers fail to do so, and he is duly notified of this.

accommodation ∼. One given by a person who is not the payee of the instrument, but who adds his name to it merely to make it more acceptable to others. By adding such an *endorsement,* however, a person takes on full liability for payment of the instrument. See also ACCOMMODATION.

blank ∼. See ENDORSEMENT IN BLANK, below.

conditional ∼. One in which there is some condition as to the endorser's responsibility for payment of the instrument. For example, a check may be endorsed to be paid after delivery of the merchandise for which it is the payment.

∼ **in blank.** One which contains only the name of the endorser, and which specifies no particular payee. In effect, it is an *endorsement* to bearer, and makes the instrument payable to any holder without further *endorsement.* This form of *endorsement* is commonly used on a bank check which is passed along to another person.

∼ **in full.** One which includes the name of a specified payee, such as "Pay to the order of John Doe." Such an *endorsement* requires a specific *endorsement* by John Doe for further transfer.

general ∼. One which contains the name of the endorser only, and does not transfer title to any particular party; an ENDORSEMENT IN BLANK, which see above.

irregular ∼. One which differs in form from an ordinary *endorsement,* such as one given by a person who is not the payee of the instrument; an ACCOMMODATION ENDORSEMENT, which see above.

joint ∼. One containing two or more names, when the instrument it transfers has been originally made payable to two or more persons jointly.

qualified ∼. One in which the endorser puts some qualification on his further liability for payment of the instrument, or denies it altogether. For example, a retailer may endorse the promissory note of his customer to a bank or sales finance company WITHOUT RECOURSE, meaning that in the event the note is not paid, the bank may not turn to the retailer for payment.

restrictive ∼. One which tends to limit the further negotiability of the instrument. For example, a check being endorsed for deposit in a personal bank account may be so noted, so that it may not be further transferred until it has first been deposited and credited as directed.

special ∼. One which specifies the person to whom the instrument is being transferred; an ENDORSEMENT IN FULL, which see above.

endorser. One who transfers his title to an instrument by writing his name on the back. Also, one who adds his name to the back of an instrument to make it more acceptable to others.

accommodation ∼. One who adds his name to an instrument which is not payable to himself, merely to make it more acceptable, and to strengthen the endorsement of another. See also ACCOMMODATION.

∼ **for value.** One who receives a valuable consideration for his endorsement, or for adding his name to an instrument.

endow. To make a permanent provision for some specified person or purpose, through the bequest, bestowal, or gift of money, or of an income. For example, a donor may *endow* a university or college by presenting it with a fund to be spent for specified or general purposes over a period of time.

endowment. The sum of money or fund bestowed on a person or institution for permanent use; a BEQUEST. For example, an *endowment* fund bestowed on a university may provide for its general needs for as long as the fund lasts.

endowment insurance. See under INSURANCE, LIFE, ACCIDENT, AND HEALTH.

engage. 1. To employ, or to hire; to arrange for services or labor, as through a contract.

2. To bind or pledge, whether by promise or contract; to commit or oblige one's self or someone to do or not do something. More broadly, to undertake, take part in, or embark on a venture, such as a business or trade.

engine. Strictly speaking, for example as defined in the Employers' Liability Act, any ingenious or skillful contrivance used to effect a purpose. In common usage, however, the term is restricted to machinery designed to produce energy or motive power.

engross. To buy up or secure enough of a commodity to obtain a monopoly, so as to resell at high prices. To CORNER the market.

enjoin. Strictly, to command or direct. To require a person, such as by an INJUNCTION or other order or decree, to perform, or to abstain or desist from performing, some act. For example, a court may *enjoin* a company from engaging in a practice until its legality or propriety can be tried and determined on its merits.

entail. In law, to limit or curtail the succession to property by the ordinary rules of inheritance; to direct or establish an order of inheritance other than through the usual sequence; to create an ESTATE IN TAIL.

enter. 1. To write down, record, or register, as, for example, to *enter* a transaction in a journal or account book.
2. To start or engage in, as to *enter* a profession, or to *enter* an agreement or partnership arrangement.

enterprise. Any undertaking, especially in commerce; a concern, firm or company; a project or venture, especially one involving financial risk and uncertainty. Also, initiative, spirit, or creative energy; the willingness to undertake a risk.

entire. Whole, without division or diminution; complete. See each of the following under the principal listing: ∼ CONTRACT (1); ∼ DAY.

entire tenancy. See TENANCY BY THE ENTIRETY.

entrapment. The act of a law officer or agent in inducing a person to commit a crime or violate a law, for the specific purpose of creating an opportunity to bring charges against the person. For example, forcing a bribe on an employee or official, then bringing charges, is *entrapment.*

entrepot. Originally, from the French, an intermediate port. Hence, a warehouse for the storage of imports or goods in transit, from which they may be re-exported or shipped to a final destination.

entrepreneur. From the French, one who takes part in, or undertakes. In economic theory, a person who undertakes, initiates, and operates a business enterprise. In common usage, the term has come to mean one who operates a small-scale business, such as a farmer or retailer; a proprietor.

entry. 1. In accounting, a recording or posting of the facts of a transaction in an account or account book. Those books in which such *entries* are first made are known as BOOKS OF ORIGINAL ENTRY, and are accepted as evidence for many purposes.

closing ∼. The *entry* used to summarize each income and expense account for transfer to a profit and loss account, in the preparation of a FINANCIAL STATEMENT at the end of an accounting period.
2. In foreign trade, the registration with the customs authorities of goods to be imported, together with the payment of the duty, if any. Also, loosely, the documents involved in this operation. See also BILL OF ENTRY.

E.O.M. (end of month). A term used in specifying TERMS OF SALE, always meaning the end of the month following the month of purchase, or the month in which the invoice is dated. For example, terms calling for payment *net E.O.M.* require that full payment is to be made by the last day of the month following the month in which the invoice is dated.

equal. Alike and uniform; exactly the same in quantity, weight or value. It is distinguished from EQUITABLE, which means just or fair in consideration of the circumstances, and from EQUIVALENT, which means of the same power, force or effect, but not necessarily alike or identical.

equalization. In taxation, an examination of the ASSESSMENTS on property made by the localities in a state, in comparison with actual property values. This is followed by the application of a percentage adjustment to the total assessed valuation of each locality, to bring about a statewide *equalization* between assessed and market values. Such a step is taken, for example, when state appropriations for schools, road construction and other local projects are based on the total assessed value of local property.

equation of exchange. In economic theory, a concept or identity which states that during a given time interval the amount of money in circulation, multiplied by the number of times it changes hands, is equal to the number of cash transactions times the unit prices at which these take place. The concept is most closely associated with the economist Irving Fisher.

equipment. In general, those industrial goods which are not consumed or used up during their useful life. Sometimes, it is distinguished from machinery, and limited to such things as small tools, industrial trucks, office furniture, etc. In another context, machinery is included in *capital equipment,* along with heating plants, power generators, etc., while other industrial goods are considered *accessory equipment.*

equipment bond. See BOND (1), EQUIPMENT TRUST; TRUST CERTIFICATE.

equipment note. See TRUST CERTIFICATE.

equipment trust obligation. See BOND (1), EQUIPMENT TRUST; TRUST CERTIFICATE.

equitable. Just, conforming to the principles of justice and right; fair and right in consideration of the existing circumstances; existing under the rules of EQUITY. See each of the following under the principal listing: ∼ ESTATE; ∼ LIEN; ∼ MORTGAGE.

equity. 1. A system of law based on the principles of justice and fair dealing, applied to settle the conflicting rights and claims of individuals apart from the remedies available under written law. In practice, the rules and precedents of *equity* are as firmly settled, though different from, those of the common law or legislation. See also COURT OF EQUITY.
2. In accounting and finance, the net investment which a person has in some enterprise, business property, etc. In a going business, the owner's *equity* is the difference between the total assets of the business and the total liabilities; the NET WORTH of the business. An owner's *equity* in mortgaged property, on the other hand, is the difference between the value of the property and the unpaid balance of the mortgage. Loosely, a security representing an ownership interest in the issuing company; a STOCK (1). See also CAPITAL (2), EQUITY.

equity annuity. See ANNUITY, VARIABLE.

equity capital. See under CAPITAL (2).

equivalent. Equal in value, force, power or effect, but not identical, and therefore not strictly EQUAL. For example, the price of a security quoted in pounds on the London stock exchange may be the *equivalent* of the price quoted in dollars on the New York exchange, but it is not equal.

erosion. The gradual eating away of land by the action of water, but not the sudden washing away, as by a storm. Under various rulings, the loss of land by *erosion* is not a catastrophe, and therefore not a casualty loss for tax purposes.

errors and omissions insurance. See under INSURANCE, CASUALTY AND LIABILITY.

errors excepted (or errors and omissions excepted). An expression frequently printed at the bottom of an invoice or statement of account, to give the renderer the privilege of correcting whatever errors or omissions may afterward be discovered, without affecting the validity of the invoice in general.

escalator clause. 1. In a sales contract, a clause providing that the price as quoted in the contract may be increased at the time of delivery if some other price, such as an index of the price of the contained materials, increases meanwhile. Such clauses are frequently inserted in sales agreements for heavy machinery, which often is delivered many months after the original order is placed. See also FLUCTUATION CLAUSE.
2. In a union wage agreement, a clause providing that wages will be automatically adjusted when there is a specified increase or decrease in the cost of living, usually as measured by the Consumer Price Index of the Bureau of Labor Statistics.

escape clause. 1. In an international tariff agreement, a clause providing that one nation may cancel a concession or lower tariff if, as a result of it, imports increase so as to cause or threaten to cause serious injury to a domestic industry producing similar or directly competitive products. Under present United States law, the Tariff Commission determines when a tariff rate has created such a condition, and notifies the President, who then, at his discretion, may suspend the concession or reduced tariff.
2. In a union agreement, a clause providing for an initial period, under a MAINTENANCE OF MEMBERSHIP clause, during which presently employed members may resign from the union.

escheat. In law, the reversion of property to the government, due to the lack of any person legally competent to inherit. Also, under the laws of several states, the reversion to the state of unclaimed property and wealth, such as the money in bank accounts the owners of which cannot be located after a specified period of time.

escrow. Originally a scroll, or document. An instrument of transfer or agreement placed in the hands of a third party, known as the DEPOSITARY, or *escrow* agent, to be delivered upon the performance of some condition, or the occurrence of some event, as agreed between the parties to the agreement. An instrument or fund so placed in the hands of a third party is said to be in *escrow,* and the agreement itself is an *escrow* agreement.

escrow deed. See under DEED.

establishment. As defined by the Bureau of the Census, a separate location at which a business is conducted, as distinguished from a COMPANY. Thus, a single company may operate several *establishments,* and in rare cases, several companies may jointly operate a single *establishment.*

estate. 1. In law, strictly, the interest or rights which a person has in lands or other real or personal property. More broadly, the total property and wealth which a person owns, both real and personal. Hence, the total property and wealth which a person leaves to his inheritors upon his death. See also FEE (2); TENANCY; TITLE. The principal types and classes of *estates* are listed and defined below.

absolute ∿. One in which ownership and title are full and clear, and not subject to conditions, qualifications, or challenges. A FEE SIMPLE.

conditional ∿. One which depends on the happening of some future event, whereby it may be created, enlarged, decreased, or wiped out. For example, an *estate* may be vested in an unborn child.

dower ∿. That portion, usually set at one-third, of a man's *estate* which passes to his widow upon his death, according to the STATUTE OF DISTRIBUTION in many states, in the absence of more specific and more generous instructions.

equitable ∿. The interest or rights which a person has in property which is held by another in trust for him, aside from any stated legal interest he may have in the property.

∿ for years. An interest in property which is held by virtue of a lease for a definite period of time; a LEASEHOLD.

∿ in common. See TENANT IN COMMON.

∿ in fee simple. See FEE SIMPLE.

∿ in possession. One in which the tenant, occupant, or holder has an immediate and present interest and right, though it may be a present right to future possession. It is also called an *executed estate* or *vested estate*.

∿ in tail. One in which the right of succession is limited, prescribed, or abridged in some way. For example, it may be one which is specified to pass to the lawful issue in each generation only, rather than to the heirs in general.

executed ∿. See ESTATE IN POSSESSION, above.

executory ∿. One, the full possession of which depends on some future event, or which will become certain at some indefinite future time.

joint ∿. See TENANCY, JOINT.

landed ∿. In general, a person's real property, including not only land itself, but the buildings, fixtures, equipment, and livestock that go with it, as distinguished from his PERSONAL ESTATE, which see below.

life ∿. An interest in property which is specified to last during the life of the tenant, or during the life of some other named person.

particular ∿. One in which there is an immediate, rather than a future, interest. More specifically, one in which there is only a present interest, such as an *estate* which

will pass to a previously specified other person on the death of the present tenant.

personal ∿. In general, all of the personal property which a person owns, including not only his household and personal goods, but money, securities, insurance, etc., as distinguished from his LANDED ESTATE, which see above.

residuary ∿. The remaining portion of the *estate* of a deceased person, which is not specifically disposed of in his will by BEQUEST, DEVISE, or LEGACY.

vested ∿. See ESTATE IN POSSESSION, above.

2. Historically, one of the three divisions of the feudal realm; namely, the clergy, nobility, and commons. The press is sometimes known, figuratively, as the fourth estate.

estate planning. The deliberate ordering and disposal of one's *estate* during life, including the making of a will, the purchase of life insurance, the transfer of property by gift, etc., in order to minimize loss through taxes and otherwise, and to maximize the benefits to dependents and beneficiaries.

estate tax. See under TAX (2).

estimate. A valuation or rating prepared without actually measuring, counting, or weighing the subject. It may be based on observation, experience, sampling, calculated judgment, etc., and carries the implied qualification of more or less, or approximately.

estimated tare. See under TARE.

estoppel. The exclusion, barring, or prevention of a person from alleging or denying a fact, as a result of his own previous actions or statements. For example, one's signature on a note of indebtedness serves as an *estoppel* to prevent his denial of the debt. Similarly, one who accepts property or goods WITH ALL FAULTS is *estopped* from seeking a future rebate for imperfections.

et al. From the Latin, a term meaning "and others"; the others usually being specified elsewhere in the document.

et ux. From the Latin, "and wife."

evaluate. To appraise, or establish a value; to determine the worth, amount, or capacity of something.

evening up. In the securities and commodities trade, an offsetting operation, such as the buying of securities by a trader who has sold short, or the sale of securities by a trader who has accumulated a balance in his own name, to even up his trading operations, and return his position to that formerly existing.

ever-normal granary. A concept in agricultural economic planning, under which surplus crops from good harvest years are stored, and released on the market in years of poor harvest. The crops are stored under government supervision, and loans made to the farmers against the value of the stored grain, until it is sold. This concept was the original basis of the federal crop loan program.

eviction. A dispossession from, or deprivation of property, especially under a court order or legal judgment. See also DISPOSSESS.

evidence. In law, any proof, or any factual material, presented to induce belief in, or acceptance of, a contention or disputed point. Hence, anything which tends to prove or disprove a point in question. *Evidence* may be *direct,* or dealing with directly observed occurrences or known facts, or it may be *circumstantial,* dealing with conditions or circumstances which may lead indirectly to a conclusion. *Evidence* may be given in the form of TESTIMONY or otherwise, such as by exhibit, and testimony may conceivably contain no *evidence.*

ex-. The Latin preposition meaning, in different contexts, from, out of, by, according to, formerly, or without. For example, consider the following:

ex-cathedra. Literally, from the chair, or throne. Hence, a statement from authority.

ex-coupon. After the current coupon has been detached, as on a coupon-bearing bond. See also BOND (1), COUPON.

ex-dividend. Without DIVIDEND; applied to the quoted price of a security during the time between the date of record of a dividend payment and the date the dividend is actually paid. Since the seller will receive the dividend though he no longer owns the stock, the sale price is reduced by the approximate amount of the declared dividend, and noted as such.

ex-dock (named port). A price quotation indicating that the stated price includes all costs of making the goods available at dockside, including freight, duty, etc. Sometimes quoted as *ex-quay.* See also FREE ON BOARD.

ex-interest. Without INTEREST; applied to the price of a bond after the date of record of an interest payment, but before payment is made. See EX-DIVIDEND, above.

ex-officio. Literally, from the office. By virtue of a position held, such as automatic membership on a committee because of an office held.

ex-parte. On behalf of one party or one side only; on the application of one party to a legal dispute, such as when a hearing is held at the request of one party only.

ex-(point of origin). A basis of price quotation under which the seller stipulates that the price applies at the point of origin of the goods, such as a mine, mill, factory, etc., and that the goods will be turned over to the buyer at this point.

ex-rights. Without RIGHTS. A sale of a security made with the understanding that the buyer will not receive a recently declared right granted to stockholders, such as the right to purchase additional shares at a favorable price.

exact interest. See under INTEREST (2).

examiner. See BANK EXAMINER.

exception. In law, a holding back or withdrawal of approval from some existing state of affairs. Also, a holding back to one's self of some existing right or privilege, rather than a contribution of it to a common lot. It is distinguished from a RESERVATION, which refers to a right to future enjoyment.

excess condemnation. The practice of taking more land or property, under a CONDEMNATION proceeding, than is actually needed for the project or operation in question. A railroad, for example, may be encouraged to build a new spur line into a presently unprofitable area by being offered more land, under condemnation proceedings, than is needed for the right of way. The excess land may then be sold off by the railroad to offset its costs of building and operating the spur line.

excess coverage clause. A clause used in some insurance policies, stating that the particular insurance shall be considered in *excess* of any other insurance carried against the same risk, in the event of a loss. For example, if a policy owner has two fire insurance policies, for $10,000 and $20,000, covering a particular property, and the second policy contains an *excess coverage clause,* a loss of $15,000 would be settled by a payment of $10,000 under the first policy and $5,000 under the second. In practice, however, since most policies came to carry such *excess coverage clauses,* losses came to be settled in proportion to the amount of insurance in each policy. This practice is now formalized by the use of a CONTRIBUTION CLAUSE, which states specifically that the policy will contribute to the coverage of each loss in proportion to the share of total insurance it represents.

excess insurance. Insurance which is designed to cover only that part of each loss which is in *excess* of a stated amount, or which is in *excess* of other insurance carried to cover the same risk. For example, a company that chooses to self-insure its WORKMEN'S COM-PENSATION risks may carry *excess insurance* with a lower limit fixed at the amount of loss the company feels it can afford to absorb on each claim. In this way, the company is protected against the risk of having to bear a very large cost in an unusual case. The *excess* principle differs from the use of a DE-DUCTIBLE CLAUSE in that it is normally based on insurance or self-insurance to cover the smaller losses, while the deductible clause is usually applied in cases in which the small losses can be absorbed as current expenses, without the need for insurance or a self-insurance reserve. See also INSURANCE; SELF-INSURANCE.

excess loan. A loan made by a bank to a single customer, in an amount which is in excess of the limitation set by law. For example, the National Bank Act provides that the total obligation of any one borrower to any national bank may at no time exceed ten percent of the bank's capital stock. Thus, in this case, and where state banking laws have similar limitations, an *excess loan* is unlawful.

excess profits tax. See under TAX (2).

excess reserve. See under RESERVE (2).

exchange. 1. Broadly speaking, the act of giving or taking one thing in trade for another; barter. Hence, commerce or trade, either in goods, currency, or negotiable instruments.

2. A market or meeting place where sales, purchases, or trades of particular commodities or securities take place, under definite rules of procedure. As defined by the Securities Exchange Act of 1934, an *exchange* is any organization, association, or group of persons, incorporated or not, which constitutes, maintains, or provides a market place or facilities for bringing together purchasers and sellers of securities, and includes the market place and facilities maintained by such an *exchange*.

commodity ~. One specializing in the buying and selling of one or more particular basic commodities, such as coffee, sugar, cotton, grains, etc. Such an *exchange* provides a means for determining market prices for commodities, and for establishing a FUTURES trade in the particular commodities.

securities ~. An *exchange* specializing in the buying and selling of various securities, including common and preferred stocks, bonds, warrants, rights, etc. The most prominent of these is the New York Stock Exchange, an unincorporated association of security dealers, traders and brokers, which provides *exchange* facilities in New York City, but which conducts business for buyers and sellers literally all over the world.

3. The value of one currency expressed in terms of another, or the ratio of the value of one currency to another. See PAR OF EX-CHANGE; RATE OF EXCHANGE.

4. The system or process by which commercial debts contracted at one time and place are discharged at some future date at another place, without the actual transfer of money from debtor directly to creditor; the use of negotiable credit instruments to facilitate the payment of debts arising out of commerce or financial operations. Also, the particular instruments themselves which are used in *exchange* operations, such as drafts, bills, acceptances, etc. Thus, one who buys and sells these negotiable instruments may be known as a dealer in *exchange*. See also COMMERCIAL PAPER.

bank ~. A trade term for instruments of *exchange*, such as bills, drafts, etc., issued and sold by a bank, and drawn on or payable by another bank.

cross ~. An *exchange* operation in which three or more places become involved in the settlement of a debt. For example, a person in New York who has an obligation to meet in London may find that due to the RATE OF EXCHANGE it is cheaper to purchase and forward a draft on Paris, which is then sold on the London market. See also ARBITRAGE.

direct ~. An *exchange* operation completed directly between two markets, without involvement of a third market, as in CROSS EXCHANGE, above.

dollar ~. An *exchange* instrument drawn in a foreign country and payable in the United States in dollars; also, an instrument drawn in the United States for a specified number of dollars, though it is to be paid abroad in the equivalent amount of foreign currency.

domestic ~. The settlement of commercial debts, by the use of negotiable instruments, within the United States; also, the instruments used in such operations, including checks, drafts, acceptances, etc. It is sometimes known as *inland exchange*.

fixed ~. The term for the situation in which *exchange* operations are quoted in the currency of the country in which the instrument is issued, but are payable in the currency of the country in which payment is to be made. For example, instruments drawn on London and purchased in New York are quoted in dollars, and the pound sterling is quoted in New York in a fluctuating amount of dollars. Hence, *exchange* on London quoted in New York is said to be *fixed exchange* in that the pound sterling is held fixed in quotations. See also MOVABLE EXCHANGE, below.

foreign ~. The settlement of commercial debts, by the use of negotiable instruments, between two or more different countries; also the instruments used in such operations, such as drafts, bills, acceptances, etc.

indirect ~. See CROSS EXCHANGE, above.

inland ~. See DOMESTIC EXCHANGE, above.

movable ~. The term for the situation in which *exchange* operations are quoted in the currency of the country in which the payment is to be made, rather than in that of the country in which the instrument is issued. For example, instruments drawn on Paris and purchased in New York may be quoted in francs, and are payable in francs in Paris. Hence, *exchange* on Paris quoted in New York is said to be *movable exchange,* in that the franc fluctuates or moves in the quotations. See also FIXED EXCHANGE, above.

pegged ~. Operations conducted under *exchange* rates which are fixed by one or both of the governments of the countries involved, by the purchase and sale of currency or by other manipulative operations.

exchange broker. See under BROKER (1).

exchange charge. In banking, a fee charged by some banks for handling a check or draft drawn on a bank whose notes or bills sell below par. Also, sometimes, a charge made for handling a check drawn upon the bank itself, but presented through the mail for payment, instead of through normal clearing channels. See also COLLECTION CHARGE.

exchange control. The application of control over foreign exchange transactions by governmental agencies. These may include the allocation of available foreign exchange credit among those applying for it, the establishment of fixed rates for the buying and selling of exchange, control over the actual transfer of gold and currency, and similar restrictions.

exchange current. In banking, a trade term for the current RATE OF EXCHANGE.

exchange jobber. See under JOBBER.

exchange rate. See RATE OF EXCHANGE.

exchequer. In England, the department of the government which has responsibility for the collection of revenues, their care and disbursement. It is similar to the Treasury Department in the United States government. Hence, a treasury in general, or a private supply of funds. Thus, when a businessman speaks of his *exchequer* being low, he means, in effect, that his private treasury is low in funds.

excise tax. See under TAX (2).

exclusion. In insurance, a statement in an insurance policy or contract specifying the conditions or situations in which the contract does not provide insurance, and the perils and persons not insured by the agreement. For example, a typical *exclusion* in fire insurance contracts provides that the insurance does not apply to property in the care or custody of the insured.

exclusive dealer. A DEALER who has secured the exclusive right to represent a particular manufacturer or brand name in a given territory, or in selling to a particular class of trade. Also, a dealer who has agreed to carry only one make or brand of product in a given class, to the exclusion of others. See also FRANCHISED DEALER.

exclusive dealing. An agreement or practice between a supplier and a customer under which the customer is required to obtain all of his needs for a given class of products from the one supplier, and is barred from buying any of the specified products from any other source. Such agreements are illegal under the anti-trust laws. See also TIE-IN SALE.

exclusive selling. A method of selecting dealers, distributors, or other sales outlets for a product or service, under which sales in any one territory or to any one class of trade are made only through one particular dealer or distributor, usually under a contract or FRANCHISE agreement. This form of selling is frequently used for major consumer goods, such as appliances and automobiles, and also sometimes for consumer soft goods, such as apparel, or for industrial machinery, but practically never for industrial supplies.

executed. In law, having been performed, or carried out; made, or put into effect. For example, an executed contract is one which has been carried out, according to its terms. See each of the following under the principal listing: ~ CONTRACT (1); ~ TRUST.

executed estate. See ESTATE (1) IN POSSESSION.

execution. 1. In law, the process of enforcing the payment of a judgment debt, usually by a sheriff or other officer named by the court. Also, the writ itself, directing the officer to enforce the payment.

2. The proper actions involved in completing an instrument or document, such as a contract, deed, will, etc. These acts include the signing, witnessing, sealing, etc. of the document.

executive. 1. Literally, one who carries out, or performs. Thus, in business, a person with responsibilities for making decisions and seeing that they are carried out. A head of a department, division, operation or company. The limitations of the term differ widely from company to company and writer to writer. In some cases, for example, employees with little or no actual responsibility for decision making may be considered junior *executives*.

2. In government, that branch which is responsible for the administration of the laws, and for the carrying out of legislative or judicial decisions.

executive committee. In business, a committee entrusted with the direct management of a business. It is usually made up of the principal officers of the business, and may be a sub-committee of the board of directors of the corporation. More generally, any committee entrusted with the management of the affairs of an organization, such as between regular meetings of the membership.

executive officer. As defined in various federal laws and statutes, an officer of a corporation who participates in its management, including the president, vice-presidents, secretary, and treasurer, and also such officers as chairman of the board, chairman of the executive committee, cashier, controller, etc., if they exist, as well as their assistants, if there are such. In the case of a partnership, all of the full partners are considered *executive officers*.

executor. In law, one who is charged by the maker of a will with the duty of carrying out its terms. In practice, two or more persons may be named to act as *executors* jointly. Local statutes vary, but the *executor* is generally responsible for the distribution of the various BEQUESTS and DEVISES, and for reporting on his administration of the estate to the proper authorities.

executor's bond. See under BOND (2).

executory. In law, not fully carried out; leaving something still to be done or put into effect; not yet absolute or complete. See each of the following under the principal listing: ~ CONTRACT (1); ~ ESTATE (1); ~ TRUST.

exemplary damages. See DAMAGES, PUNITIVE.

exempt. To relieve or excuse from some duty or task; to release from the provisions or restrictions of a law or regulation. Also, to be so relieved, excused, or released. For example, *exempt* funds in an estate are those, such as certain pensions, which are not subject to any claims against the estate.

exempted security. See under SECURITY (1).

exhaust price. In the securities trade, the term for the price at which a security bought on MARGIN will have to be sold to protect the interest of the broker or dealer. It is the price at which the security is worth only the difference between the amount deposited with the broker and the original purchase price of the security. For example, a stock bought at $50 per share, with only 30 percent margin, or a $15 deposit per share, will ordinarily be sold by the broker if it falls to a price of $35 or less, unless the buyer deposits additional margin. In this case, $35 is the *exhaust price*, or the price at which the buyer's interest in the security has been exhausted.

exhibit. 1. In general, any public showing or display, or something which is placed on display. In business, an *exhibit* is usually for the purpose of obtaining sales of the goods displayed, either at a general exhibition, or at the seller's own place of business.

2. In law, anything produced in court to support a contention or to aid in proving an alleged set of facts. An *exhibit* may be admitted as EVIDENCE, the same as testimony.

3. In general, any supporting or illustrative material submitted in connection with a report or recommendation.

exhibitor. In general, one who conducts an EXHIBIT, or who enters a display in an exhibitions, fair or other similar event. In particular, an owner, manager, or operator of a motion picture theater. Hence, in effect, one who retails motion pictures.

ex-im. See EXPORT-IMPORT BANK OF WASHINGTON.

exit interview. In personnel management, an interview conducted with an employee who is leaving the employ of a business, conducted for the purpose of determining, if possible, the reasons why the employee is leaving. In many personnel departments, such interviews are regularly conducted with all employees who leave voluntarily, in an attempt to discover, and thus to eliminate, the causes of employee turnover.

expansion. 1. The phase of a BUSINESS CYCLE during which business activity in general is rising in volume; the period from a TROUGH to a following PEAK, as contrasted with a CONTRACTION, which is the period from a peak to a trough.

2. Any increase or enlarging of the facilities of a business, in order to handle a larger volume of business. Also, the increasing volume of business itself. The opposite of a RETRENCHMENT.

expectancy (or expectation) of life. The average number of years which a person of a given age may expect to continue to live beyond his present age, as determined according to a MORTALITY TABLE. *Expectancy* is used as the basis for determining the premiums or charges to be paid for life insurance, annuities, pensions, or other contracts based on the expected age at death or the expected number of years from a given age until death.

expedite. In general, to quicken or to hasten along the progress or movement of something. To create conditions which permit and encourage the speedier completion of some project or operation. For example, to *expedite* the manufacture of a product might involve such steps as assuring the availability of raw materials, the assignment of sufficient labor, the proper maintenance of the machinery used, etc.

expediter. A person engaged to hasten or facilitate the flow of shipments of materials, either incoming or outgoing. For example, a materials *expediter* engaged by a manufacturer checks on the delivery schedules of suppliers, takes whatever steps he can to help the supplier meet his schedules, follows the goods while they are in transit, etc. An *expediter* for a railroad, on the other hand, takes steps to see that goods entrusted to the railroad for shipment, especially rush deliveries, are moved with proper speed and reach their proper destinations, to avoid the need for emergency handling, tracing of shipments, etc.

expendable. Normally consumed or used up in service, or treated as if it is so used up. Considered as a business expense, rather than as a capital investment. For example, cleaning supplies, small hand tools, light bulbs and many other items are considered as *expendable* in business operations, and charged to current expenses. On the other hand, under some conditions, such as the urgent need to fill a large order, equipment which would ordinarily be considered as capital equipment might be treated as *expendable,* in that it is not shut down for maintenance work, etc.

expenditure. In accounting and finance, the committing of funds, or the creation of a current LIABILITY, such as by making a purchase or using a service. It is distinguished from an APPROPRIATION, which is the authorization for spending and payment, and from a DISBURSEMENT, which is the subsequent elimination of the liability by the actual payment of cash or the writing of a check.

expense. 1. In general, any charges or costs incurred in the conduct of a business; the cost of carrying on a business, or of maintaining property, etc.

2. In accounting, specifically, any operating charge or cost which is applicable to a particular accounting period. Also, to charge an expenditure to the particular accounting period to which it applies. For example, labor costs are normally an *expense* to the period in which the work is performed. A capital equipment expenditure, however, is not an *expense,* but the depreciation charges on the equipment over its life are usually *expensed* to successive accounting periods. See also COST. The principal classes of business *expenses* are listed and defined below.

accrued ~. One which has been incurred during a particular period, but not yet paid. Examples might include wages, taxes, rent, etc. Depending on the accounting system being followed, such *expenses* may be charged to the period in which they are incurred, or to that in which they are paid.

administrative ~. One of a class of business *expenses,* usually including such items as office and executive salaries, postage and telephone, office supplies, etc.

current ~. One of those incurred in the regular daily operations of a business; any normal and continuing OPERATING EXPENSE, which see below. It is sometimes called a running *expense.*

factory ~. See MANUFACTURING EXPENSE, below.

general ~. One of a class of business *expenses,* usually including such items as executive salaries, rent, insurance, taxes, etc. These are frequently lumped with ADMINISTRATIVE EXPENSES, which see above, as *general and administrative expenses.*

manufacturing ~. One of a class of business *expenses,* usually including such items as material costs, equipment depreciation, labor, maintenance, fuel and power, etc., but excluding those costs not connected with manufacturing, such as SELLING EXPENSES, which see below.

non-operating ~. One which is not directly connected with the operations of the business, as distinguished from an OPERATING EXPENSE, which see below. Examples include interest on debts, reserves for taxes, etc. These are sometimes reported as *other expenses.*

operating ~. One of a class of business *expenses,* including all those *expenses* connected with the normal operations of the business, and hence excluding only such *expenses* as interest on debts. See also NON-OPERATING EXPENSE, above.

other ~. See NON-OPERATING EXPENSE, above.

out-of-pocket ~. A term for any direct *expense,* or for one requiring a direct outlay of cash, as distinguished from one which accrues on the account books of the business, such as a depreciation charge.

running ∼. See CURRENT EXPENSE, above.

selling ∼. One of a class of business *expenses,* usually including all the costs connected with the sale and distribution of the company's products, and hence including such costs as advertising, sales salaries, commissions, delivery, etc. Depending on the accounting system, such costs as packaging, storage of finished goods, etc., may be *selling* or MANUFACTURING EXPENSES, which see above.

expense account. 1. A statement or report of the expenditures made by an individual in the interests of a business, usually submitted periodically for the purpose of obtaining reimbursement for the money spent. To be on an *expense account,* as in the case of a traveling sales representative, implies that all approved expenditures will be reimbursed by the employer.

2. In accounting, any of various accounts maintained for recording the several classes of EXPENSES (2) of the business.

expense ratio. In insurance, the proportion of expenses, including selling and administrative costs, inspection costs, reserves against future losses, etc., to total premiums collected by an insurance company, or by a group of companies which set rates jointly. The total premium is divided into three parts in rate-making statistics; expenses, losses, and dividends for stockholders or policy holders. See also PREMIUM, NET; LOSS RATIO.

experience rating. In insurance, a method of determination of premium rates on various forms of insurance, based on the loss experience of the insured over a period of years. For example, in workmen's compensation insurance, the fewer accidents resulting in compensation payments that a company has over a period of years, the lower its annual premium cost would be under an *experience rating* system, also known as a merit rating system. Similar procedures are sometimes used to determine premium rates for fire insurance, transportation insurance, and other forms of business insurance, but usually only in cases involving relatively large premiums. The smaller cases are ordinarily MANUAL RATED, or charged a premium based directly on the rates established by the RATING BUREAU and published in a manual of rates. See also RETROSPECTIVE RATING.

experience table. See MORTALITY TABLE.

expire. In business usage, to come to the end of an allotted or specified time period; to lapse, cease, or terminate. For example, an annual liability insurance policy *expires* exactly one year after the first day it is in force, unless it is renewed beforehand.

explosion insurance. See under INSURANCE, CASUALTY AND LIABILITY.

export. To send goods out of a country or state, to other countries or states, either in the normal course of trade or as an individual act. Also, the item itself which is sent from one country or state to another. See also DOMESTIC EXPORTS; RE-EXPORTS. See each of the following under the principal listing: ∼ BOND (2); ∼ BROKER (1); ∼ CREDIT (3); ∼ LETTER OF CREDIT; ∼ QUOTA.

export association. An association formed by two or more companies exporting the same or similar products, for the purpose of coordinating their efforts, arranging to share the foreign market, setting prices to be charged abroad, and for similar activities. Since such domestic activities by American companies are specifically barred by the antitrust laws, the Webb-Pomerene Act was passed to permit American exporters to form such associations and to engage in specified activities connected only with their exporting operations, in order to be able to compete more effectively in the world markets with foreign companies. Hence, legally constituted *export associations* are frequently referred to as Webb-Pomerene associations.

export commission merchant. See EXPORTER, INDIRECT.

export declaration. A document required, under federal laws, covering each export shipment from American ports. It shows the name and address of the shipper, name and address of consignee, destination of goods, description of goods, quantity, value, and similar information. The information provided in the *export declaration* must conform with those laws and regulation under which the export to certain countries of specified items, such as war materials, critical raw materials, and other products, is forbidden.

exporter. In general, a person or company engaged in the business of selling and shipping domestic products abroad.

direct ∼. One who ships abroad, for sale, goods which he has manufactured, grown, or processed himself. Many manufacturers of automobiles, appliances, machinery and similar products are *direct exporters,* either through special export sales departments, or through export divisions or subsidiaries which handle the company's products exclusively.

indirect ∼. One who buys goods domestically and ships them abroad for sale. He may handle broad classes of goods, or may specialize in one or a few lines. An *indirect exporter* who buys goods on the order of foreign customers, for shipment to them, is known as an export COMMISSION MERCHANT.

Export-Import Bank of Washington. An independent bank, under federal charter, originally established in 1934. It makes loans to finance the flow of imports and exports, specializing in loans to both individuals and to foreign governments which are for worthwhile purposes but which are not met by private capital.

export license. A certificate issued by a federal agency, permitting an exporter to ship specified goods to a particular foreign country. Such a license might be required, for example, to make a shipment to a neutral country during war time, or to make shipments of military or critical materials to any country. In some cases, licenses may be granted covering only a certain quantity of a particular product over a period of time, under a system of export quotas.

export point. See GOLD POINT.

export rate. A FREIGHT RATE, such as for rail shipment, which is established to cover only goods intended for export, and which is usually lower than the regular rate for the particular goods and route. Such a rate may be established to encourage the use of rail shipment for export goods, or to encourage the use of the particular ports served by the railroad setting up the rate.

exports. Collectively, all of the goods which are EXPORTED from one country to all others. See also DOMESTIC EXPORTS; RE-EXPORT.

exposition. A large public exhibition; a fair. It is common for members of an industry, or companies in a particular region or country, to arrange an *exposition* of their products periodically, to attract new customers and stimulate sales.

ex post facto. Literally, in Latin, after the fact. The United States Constitution provides that no *ex post facto* law may be passed, meaning that no law may be passed which applies to events already occurred. For example, a law which makes the sale of certain products illegal cannot be used to convict a person for sales made before the passage of the law.

exposure. In insurance, the condition of being open to loss from some particular hazard or contingency. Also, as used in the insurance trade, the amount of money, or the insurable value, which is so exposed to loss. For example, a company may be said to have an *exposure* of $100,000 to fire loss, meaning that the insurable value of its property which may be damaged by fire is $100,000.

express. 1. In law, stated specifically, explicitly, and directly; not left to inference or to conclusion by implication. It is the opposite of IMPLIED. An *express* WARRANTY, for example, is one made in a direct statement by the seller of the goods which are warranted. See also each of the following under the principal listing: $\sim$ ACCEPTANCE (1); $\sim$ CONTRACT (1); $\sim$ TRUST.

2. In transportation, by the shortest, fastest, and most direct route; without intermediate stops. The opposite of LOCAL.

3. A system for the rapid transportation of personal property, parcels, and small freight shipments, through the use of special cars attached to fast passenger trains, or through the use of special space on passenger air flights. See also AIR EXPRESS; RAILWAY EXPRESS AGENCY.

express company. An organization engaged in the business of transporting personal property, parcels, and small freight shipments, and specializing in rapid transportation through special pickup and delivery service, and through the use of special cars attached to fast passenger trains, space on passenger air flights, etc. See also AIR EXPRESS; RAILWAY EXPRESS AGENCY.

express money order. See under MONEY ORDER.

extend. In accounting and bookkeeping practice, to multiply the unit price by the number of units, on an invoice, to obtain the total cost; to multiply hourly wages by the number of hours worked to obtain total wages due on a payroll record; or to perform similar multiplications of numbers by unit rates to arrive at dollar totals in business records.

extended. 1. With respect to an obligation or contract, a term indicating that it has been continued beyond the originally set date of maturity or completion, or has been kept in force beyond the date on which it would ordinarily expire. See, for example, BOND (1), EXTENDED; POLICY (2), EXTENDED.

2. In business, the condition existing when liabilities have grown far out of proportion to current assets. See also OVEREXTENDED.

extended coverage. In insurance, the extension of an insurance policy to provide insurance against hazards which are not covered by the basic policy. In fire insurance, for example, the standard *extended coverage* clause provides insurance against windstorm, hail, explosion, riot, civil commotion, aircraft and vehicle damage, smoke damage, and, in some areas, malicious mischief and vandalism. The premium charge for such *extended coverage* is usually set as a percentage of the normally applicable fire insurance rate for the property covered. See also INSURANCE, PROPERTY.

extended coverage insurance. See under INSURANCE, PROPERTY.

extended policy. See under POLICY (2).

extended term insurance. See under INSURANCE, LIFE, ACCIDENT, AND HEALTH.

extension. 1. A term for an agreement between a creditor and a debtor, providing that the creditor will not demand payment of the debt until some specified time after it matures or becomes due.

2. With respect to credit, the granting of borrowing privileges, or the privilege of making purchases without immediate payment.

external. 1. Outside the country; foreign. An *external* LOAN, for example, is one in which money is borrowed from abroad, and *external* trade or commerce includes the importing and exporting of goods from and to foreign countries.

2. Outside the company; in the general business world. For example, an *external* HOUSE ORGAN is a company publication distributed to customers, dealers, and others, as well as to employees.

extinguish. To wipe out; to settle, or to close out. The final payment on a loan, for example, *extinguishes* the debt or obligation. Similarly, a bank account or deposit is *extinguished* when the remaining balance is drawn out.

extortion. In law, the taking of something of value from another by force, or by the threat of force, or by fear of exposure. In a particular sense, it is the taking of anything by a public officer, from those with whom he deals, for his own private benefit, which is not due him as a right of his office.

extra. In Latin, additional. As used in various contexts, a term meaning additional, outside, beyond, abnormal, etc. See also INFRA; SUPRA.

extra dividend. See under DIVIDEND.

F

fabricate. To make, build, or manufacture. As generally used, to manufacture by assembling standardized parts, or by the further processing of already manufactured materials. For example, a fabricator of plywood is one who uses plywood to make finished furniture, and a fabricator of appliances is one who assembles standard parts and sub-assemblies into completed units.

fabricated materials. Industrial goods which have been processed beyond the state of RAW MATERIALS, and which will be further processed or assembled into finished goods. Examples include such things as metal shapes or tubing, plywood, laminated plastic, etc.

fabrication in transit. A term used in common carrier contracts, meaning the further processing of a product or material during a delay in shipment at some point between the originating point and the final destination. Such fabrication is permitted, with the goods still entitled to a through rate from originating point to destination. See also FREIGHT RATE.

face. In general, the surface of any written instrument, on which are written the pertinent facts concerning its purpose, such as the date, amount involved, the principals, terms, etc. Sometimes, the amount or value itself, which is specified on the face of an instrument.

face amount. The amount of money stated on the FACE of an instrument or contract, with no allowance for interest, discounts, etc. For example, the *face amount* of a life insurance contract or policy is the amount that will be paid in the event of death or maturity of the policy, not including any accumulated dividends, accidental death benefits, or other special provisions.

face par. See PAR.

face value. See under VALUE (2).

facility. In general, anything that promotes an action, operation, etc. In business, it is usually limited to physical plant, equipment, vehicles, etc. in common usage. An installation.

facsimile. From the Latin, made alike; an exact copy or reproduction. A *facsimile* signature, for example, is one which has been prepared by some mechanical or photographic process from an original signature.

fact-finding board. A group or committee appointed by a governmental or business agency to investigate and make public the facts concerning a dispute, accident, or other occurrence. The board's authority may or may not include the making of recommendations. Examples include the boards appointed to study labor disputes as provided for under the Railway Labor Act and other legislation, and the boards named to examine the causes of aircraft accidents.

factor. 1. A person or institution engaged in the commercial financing of the operations of other companies, especially in the textile trades. The *factor* typically purchases outright the accounts receivable of the company needing funds, and undertakes the collection of the accounts. The *factor* thus purchases the accounts WITHOUT RECOURSE, but usually makes a small charge for the risk assumed, besides an interest charge on the cash advanced, depending on the number of months the purchased accounts are still outstanding. Many *factors* also engage in making commercial loans, on accounts receivable or other collateral. See also ACCOUNTS RECEIVABLE FINANCING; SALES FINANCE COMPANY.

2. In the textile trade, a form of selling agent, who sells goods for others on a commission basis. The *factor* differs from a true AGENT in that he deals in his own name rather than in the name of a principal. He also differs from a true BROKER, however, in that he usually takes physical possession (but not title) of the goods he sells, rather than merely arranging for their sale. Many selling *factors* also engage in a form of accounts receivable financing, by making immediate payment to the seller of the goods and then assuming the responsibility of collecting from the buyer. In fact, this is the derivation of the usage of the term defined in (1) above.

3. Any element, constituent, circumstance or influence which produces a result; such as, for example, an expense *factor,* a *factor* of production, job *factor,* etc.

factorage. The commission or allowance paid to a FACTOR (2) for his services. Also, the business of factoring.

factor of safety. See SAFETY FACTOR.

factory. In general, any building or structure in which goods or materials are manufactured. The commercial, insurance, and other statutes of many states define the term variously, and these should be consulted for strictly legal purposes. *Factory* is a narrower term than PLANT, since a plant may be the place of operation of a non-manufacturing business, such as a warehouse, laundry, telephone exchange, etc.

factory burden. See OVERHEAD.

factory cost. See under COST.

factory expense. See EXPENSE (2), MANUFACTURING.

factory mutual insurance company. See under INSURANCE COMPANY.

factory price. See under PRICE.

factory sales branch. See SALES BRANCH, MANUFACTURER'S.

Fahrenheit scale. The thermometer scale of measurement in common use in the United States, named for its creator, G. D. Fahrenheit. On this scale, the freezing point of pure water at sea-level pressure is 32 degrees, and the boiling point 212 degrees. See also CENTIGRADE.

fail. 1. To be unable to meet normal business obligations; to become insolvent or bankrupt. See also FAILURE; BANKRUPTCY.
2. In general, to fall short of a desired or prescribed end, purpose or standard. For example, a concrete block may be said to *fail* at a given number of pounds of pressure, or a cable may *fail* under a weight of a given number of tons.

failure. The suspension or discontinuance of a business, resulting from the inability to discharge the financial obligations of the business. A failure may be *involuntary,* as the result of actions taken by the creditors of the business, or *voluntary,* in which case the initiative is taken by the business itself. See also BANKRUPTCY.

fair. 1. Originally, a holiday or festival. Thus, any public market or exhibition held at intervals, or on holidays, for the purpose of trading, bartering, or showing goods; an exposition or exhibition.
2. That which is just, equitable, or reasonable; such as a *fair* price, a *fair* value, a *fair* day's work, etc.
3. That which is average or moderate, neither very good nor very poor; such as when business is described as being *fair.*

fair employment practice. A policy of hiring, job assignment, advancement, etc., which is based strictly on merit and fitness, without regard to race, color, religion, or national origin; a non-discriminatory practice. Some states have passed Fair Employment Practice Acts, under which employment policies defined as discriminatory are forbidden, and under which a Fair Employment Practices Commission (FEPC) investigates charges of such discrimination and administers the act.

fair market value. See VALUE (2), MARKET.

fair trade. In general, a trade or business conducted under legal and ethical standards. Specifically, in common usage, the practice of selling merchandise at retail at prices specified by the manufacturer or wholesale distributor.

Fair Labor Standards Act. See WAGE-HOUR LAW.

fair trade law. A law passed by a state, providing that a manufacturer may legally set a minimum resale price for his products, which price must be observed by retail dealers or distributors. Many of these state acts provide for non-signatory price maintenance; that is, a dealer is bound to observe the minimum fair trade price even though he himself has not signed a contract to this effect with the manufacturer or distributor. In several states, the courts have declared such non-signatory provisions to be unconstitutional, and the matter is presently unsettled. In 1937, the federal government passed the MILLER-TYDINGS ACT, exempting such resale price agreements from the existing anti-trust laws and, in effect, giving interstate force to the state laws. In 1951, the Supreme Court declared the non-signatory feature of state laws as not being protected under this Act, and in 1952 the federal government passed the McGUIRE ACT, specifically exempting from anti-trust legislation the non-signatory provisions of such acts, and providing for their enforcement in interstate commmerce if they are provided for in the state laws. See also RESALE PRICE MAINTENANCE.

fair price. See under PRICE.

fair value. See under VALUE (2).

false advertising. As defined by the Federal Trade Commission Act, any advertising which is misleading in a material respect, including not only false representations as to the benefits or results of using the commodity advertised, or as to its contents, but also the failure to reveal any consequences which are likely to follow from its use. Under the law, false labeling is not considered *false advertising,* but is treated separately under the Pure Food and Drug Laws.

Fannie Mae. See FEDERAL NATIONAL MORTGAGE ASSOCIATION.

farm out. Originally, to let out for a term, at a rental charge, as farm land. Now, generally, to subcontract or delegate an item of work or a duty.

farm paper. A magazine or other publication aimed at farmers, as distinguished from trade papers, business papers, or general magazines.

F.A.S. See FREE ALONGSIDE.

fatal defect. See under DEFECT.

fathom. A maritime measure of depth, or of chain or cable, consisting of six feet. Originally, it was the length of a man's outspread arms.

fault. 1. In law, an improper act, breach, or omission, which comes about through negligence, and which is injurious to another.
2. A defect, blemish, or imperfection; for example, as in the sales contract term WITH ALL FAULTS, meaning without guaranty of absence of defects.

F.C.C. See FEDERAL COMMUNICATIONS COMMISSION.

featherbedding. The practice of requiring that more workers be employed than needed for a job, or of placing limitations on the amount of work which each worker may do. The railway unions, for example, at one time required that a fireman be included in the crew of a diesel locomotive, though none was required for the operation of the locomotive. Similarly, a building trades union might restrict the number of bricks a bricklayer may lay in an hour.

Fed. A nickname for the FEDERAL RESERVE SYSTEM, or for its Board of Governors.

federal aid. Assistance, particularly financial aid, granted by the federal government to the states or to localities. Such aid includes grants for highway and school construction, for general education costs, for housing, etc.

Federal Communications Commission. The independent federal agency, created in 1934, that regulates interstate and foreign commerce in communications by both wire and radio means. Its jurisdiction includes the telephone and telegraph services, radio, and television. It assigns wavelengths and channels to commercial and private radio and television broadcasters.

federal court system. The system of federal courts, established under the Constitution and under various laws. The chief court of the system is the Supreme Court of the United States, which has direct jurisdiction over cases involving treaties, controversies between the states, etc., and has appellate jurisdiction over all other federal courts. The United States Court of Appeals is the court of intermediate review and appeal between the Supreme Court and the various federal courts. There are eleven circuit courts of appeals, one in each of ten districts and one for the District of Columbia. There are 84 Federal District Courts, which are the courts of original trial in the federal court system. The decisions of these courts may be appealed to the circuit court of appeals for each district, and ultimately to the Supreme Court.

federal credit union. See under CREDIT UNION.

Federal Deposit Insurance Corporation. A public corporation established by the Treasury and the Federal Reserve System to insure bank deposits against the inability of the bank to pay. All deposits, whether savings, checking, or otherwise are eligible, up to a limit of $10,000 per account. Deposits in savings and loan associations are insured through the Federal Savings and Loan Insurance Corporation, a similar organization.

Federal District Court. See FEDERAL COURT SYSTEM.

Federal Home Loan Bank. One of eleven regional banks, established originally in 1932, and owned jointly by the various SAVINGS AND LOAN ASSOCIATIONS, BUILDING AND LOAN ASSOCIATIONS, savings banks, insurance companies, etc. It makes loans to its member or owner organizations, to provide funds to be reloaned to the public as home mortgages, etc.

Federal Housing Administration. The independent federal agency, originally organized in 1934, and placed under the Housing and Home Finance Agency in 1947, which provides federal assistance in the financing of home mortgages. Its major activity is the insurance of both improvement and construction mortgages for homes.

Federal Intermediate Credit Bank. One of twelve district banks, originally established in 1923, to make loans to the BANK FOR CO-OPERATIVES and other organizations. The banks are government owned, but operate by selling short-term debentures, not with government funds.

federal labor union. See under UNION.

Federal Land Bank. One of twelve district

banks, originally established in 1916, to make long-term mortgage loans to farmers. The twelve banks are cooperative banks, owned by the National Farm Loan Associations throughout the country. They form part of the Farm Credit Administration.

Federal National Mortgage Association. The independent federal agency, originally chartered in 1938, and reconstituted in 1954 with new powers. Its principal activity is the purchase of mortgages from banks and other lenders, to create a revolving fund of money available for mortgage lending. It is popularly known as "Fannie Mae."

Federal Reserve Act. An act of Congress passed in 1913, and since amended several times. It provided for the establishment of the 12 Federal Reserve Banks, the Board of Governors of the Federal Reserve System, and for the supervision of the banking system in the United States. See also FEDERAL RESERVE SYSTEM.

Federal Reserve Advisory Council. A council consisting of one member from each of the 12 Federal Reserve Districts, selected annually by the Directors of the Federal Reserve Bank in each District. It meets in Washington periodically and confers with and advises the Board of Governors of the Federal Reserve System on business conditions and the general affairs of the banking system.

Federal Reserve Bank. One of the twelve banks established in each FEDERAL RESERVE DISTRICT. Each is owned by the member banks in the district, and serves these banks by holding their reserve funds, discounting COMMERCIAL PAPER, and making other loans. The banks issue the FEDERAL RESERVE NOTES, which are the most common form of paper currency in circulation. They are also empowered to make direct loans to business under certain conditions, but this power is not widely used.

Federal Reserve bank note. See under BANK NOTE.

Federal Reserve Board. The original central authority of the Federal Reserve System, supplanted under the Banking Act of 1935 by the Board of Governors of the Federal Reserve System. The present Board, however, is still informally called the Federal Reserve Board.

Federal Reserve city. One of the twelve cities in each of which is located a Federal Reserve Bank. The twelve cities, and the number of the Federal Reserve District for which each is the central city, are as follows: 1st, Boston, Mass.; 2nd, New York, N. Y.; 3rd, Philadelphia, Pa.; 4th, Cleveland, O.; 5th, Richmond,

Va.; 6th, Atlanta, Ga.; 7th, Chicago, Ill.; 8th, St. Louis, Mo.; 9th, Minneapolis, Minn.; 10th, Kansas City, Mo.; 11th, Dallas, Tex.; and 12th, San Francisco, Cal.

Federal Reserve District. One of the 12 numbered districts into which the country is divided under the provisions of the Federal Reserve Act. In each district there is a FEDERAL RESERVE CITY, in which is located the District Federal Reserve Bank.

Federal Reserve note. A form of currency, the most common now in circulation in the United States. These notes are printed by the Treasury and issued by the Federal Reserve System through its District Banks. *Federal Reserve notes* are obligations of the United States government, are redeemable in lawful money, and are full legal tender. They are issued in denominations of $5, $10, $20, $50, $100, $500, $1,000, $5,000 and $10,000. See also BANK NOTE, FEDERAL RESERVE.

Federal Reserve System. The financial institution or system, established by the Federal Reserve Act of 1913 to serve as a central banking system for the United States. The aim in establishing the system was to provide for a flexible currency, establish a network of central banks through the Federal Reserve Banks, provide an organized means for the rediscounting of commercial paper, and supervise the operations of the commercial banking system. The system consists of its Board of Governors, the Open Market Committee, consisting of the seven governors and five representatives of the Federal Reserve Banks, and the twelve Federal Reserve Banks, one in each Federal Reserve District. All national banks, and those state commercial banks that wish to join, are member banks of the *Federal Reserve System.*

federal savings and loan association. See under SAVINGS AND LOAN ASSOCIATION.

Federal Savings and Loan Insurance Corporation. See FEDERAL DEPOSIT INSURANCE CORPORATION.

federal specifications. The official specifications established for the purchase of supplies, equipment and material by the United States government, its departments and agencies. In some lines, these requirements have become the standards of acceptance, and it is common for suppliers to state that their goods meet *federal specifications.*

Federal Trade Commission. The independent federal agency, originally established in 1914, which administers and enforces the various federal anti-trust laws. It prevents false advertising, false labeling of non-food products, unfair competition, etc. See also WHEELER-LEA ACT.

fee. 1. A charge, such as one for admission or for services rendered, especially for services in one of the professions, for the services of a government or public official, or for the use of some government privilege or facility. The charges of doctors, lawyers, architects, etc., are examples of *fees*. See also HONORARIUM; RETAINER.

contingent ∼. One which is to be paid only upon the successful completion of some matter. A lawyer, for example, may agree to represent a client under an arrangement in which he will receive a stated percentage of any amounts recovered, so that if the suit is unsuccessful, there is no *fee* paid.

2. In law, an ESTATE or inheritance in land, derived originally from the term *fief,* or property. As used, a *fee* is a right or interest in real property. The principal types are listed and defined below.

conditional ∼. One that is either to begin or end on the completion of some condition, such as the coming of age of the person who is to receive it.

determinable ∼. One that may continue forever if undisturbed, but that is liable to be determined, or terminated, by the occurrence of some prescribed event, such as the birth of a male heir.

∼ simple. A term for an estate belonging to a man and to his heirs absolutely and unconditionally, as distinguished from a FEE TAIL, which see below.

∼ tail. A term derived from the same source as *tailor,* meaning an estate in land which is cut or limited to a particular class of heirs. See also ESTATE IN TAIL.

qualified ∼. One which is granted to a man and to certain of his heirs only, such as those living at the time of the grant.

feeder line. A name applied to a railroad, airline, or other common carrier, from which another, more important line, called a MAIN LINE or TRUNK LINE, receives passenger or freight traffic. A BRANCH LINE, serving less important cities and areas than those served by the main line.

felony. A general term for any serious crime, as classified or defined by state or local laws. Crimes less serious than *felonies* are usually classed as MISDEMEANORS, and the principal effect of the distinction is in the type of punishment permissible. A *felony,* for example, may call for a sentence in a penitentiary, while a misdemeanor may be punishable only by a shorter term in a local jail. Originally, in English law, a *felony* was any crime punishable by the forfeiture of land and goods.

fence. In slang, a receiver of stolen goods; one who arranges for the sale or other disposition of stolen goods.

fiat. From the Latin, literally, let it be done. A formal command, order, or DECREE of a judge or some public officer, for the purpose of permitting or forbidding some act or process. A governmental declaration or decree.

fiat money. See under MONEY.

FHA mortgage. See under MORTGAGE. See also FEDERAL HOUSING ADMINISTRATION.

fictitious freight. See FREIGHT, PHANTOM.

fidelity bond. See under BOND (2).

fidelity insurance. See under INSURANCE, SURETY AND FIDELITY.

fiduciary. 1. A person who is put in a position of trust; one on whom a trust has devolved, either by law or by voluntary act. A trustee, invested with the power and right to act for another.

2. Not secured by any COLLATERAL or deposit, but based on confidence, faith, or mutual trust. See each of the following under the principal listing: ∼ LOAN; ∼ MONEY.

fief. See FEE (3).

field. 1. The area of outside activities of a business, or of those activities which bring representatives of the business into contact with customers. These are distinguished from the activities which are carried on at the factory or at the home office of the company. For example, a *field* salesman, *field* office, *field* survey, etc.

2. The general marketing area, by function, trade, geographic description, or otherwise, in which a business operates. For example, a company may be in the retail *field,* in the construction *field,* in the rural selling *field,* etc.

field warehouse. A segregated storage area located on the premises of a manufacturer, processor, distributor, or other owner of goods, in which are stored goods which are under the control of an authorized employee of a public warehouse company. Since the goods are, in effect, in bonded storage, the owner can use the WAREHOUSE RECEIPT as collateral in obtaining financing. See also WAREHOUSE.

field warehouse loan. See under LOAN.

field warehousing. The activity of operating FIELD WAREHOUSE areas in the storage facilities of manufacturers and others. Generally, public warehouse companies, especially those with experience in operating bonded ware-houses, engage in this activity. The operation involves taking accurate inventories, protect-ing and safeguarding the goods, issuing them under proper authorization to the owner, etc. Also, the setting up of a field warehouse area by a manufacturer or other owner of goods, for the purpose of obtaining a WAREHOUSE RECEIPT to be used as collateral for financing.

FIFO (first-in-first-out). See under INVENTORY VALUATION.

fighting brand. See under BRAND.

file. 1. To deposit with the proper authority, as a registration, report, request for official permission to perform some act, etc.

2. To store in a *file* cabinet or similar accessible place.

fill. To supply the items requested. To execute, as of an order or requisition.

fill-or-kill order. See ORDER (4), IMMEDIATE.

final closing. See CLOSING DATE.

final decree. See under DECREE.

final injunction. See under INJUNCTION.

finance. 1. In general, the art, science, or system of dealing in, supplying, regulating or managing the money and credit of a nation, state, or private enterprise.

2. To provide or supply credit, money, or other resources to a business enterprise or private individual. See also FINANCING.

3. To obtain or procure money or credit as the basis for a business enterprise; to obtain working capital.

finance bill. See under BILL OF EXCHANGE.

finance company. Any of various types of finan-cial institutions, other than banks, in the business of making loans to businesses or to individuals. Those making loans to business are generally known as SALES FINANCE COM-PANIES, and those making loans to individual consumers are known as PERSONAL FINANCE COMPANIES. When the term is used alone, however, it usually refers to a personal *fi-nance company.*

finances. In general, monetary resources, in-cluding money, credit, balances due, etc.

financial incentive. See under INCENTIVE.

financial ratio. See OPERATING RATIO.

financial statement. An authorized statement of the assets and liabilities of a business organization, usually at the end of a fiscal period, prepared for distribution to stock-holders, creditors or others. See also BALANCE SHEET.

financing. Any one of several methods of ob-taining or supplying money or credit for a business enterprise or an individual. For example, INVENTORY FINANCING is the making of loans with inventory pledged as collateral, and ACCOUNTS RECEIVABLE FINANCING is the supplying of funds to a business in exchange for the assignment or outright sale of the assets represented by accounts receivable.

finding. 1. In law, a determination of the facts in a dispute. The DECISION of a court or semi-judicial body, when the question before it is one of fact.

2. In various industries and trades, a term used for the smaller or incidental parts used in production. Jewelers' *findings,* for ex-ample, are the backings, pins, settings, etc., used in the manufacture of jewelry, while *findings* in the shoe industry are the buckles, tacks, nails, grommets, laces, rubber, etc., used in the manufacture or repair of shoes.

fine. 1. A penalty requiring the payment of money, imposed by a court or similar body as prescribed by law.

2. Excellent, or of the highest quality, as of a note or draft backed by the highest quality of collateral or credit. See also PRIME.

3. Pure, or of a stated degree of purity. For example, *fine gold* is pure gold, with no alloying metal, and *fine silver* is at least 99.9 percent silver.

fineness. In reference to metals, coins, etc., the proportion of pure metal to alloying ingredi-ents. For example, the *fineness* of United States silver coins is *nine-tenths fine,* or 90 percent pure silver.

finished goods. In inventory terminology, man-ufactured items ready for sale, as distin-guished from WORK IN PROCESS and RAW MATERIALS (2).

fink. In labor usage, the term for a worker who is hired deliberately to replace an employee who is on strike. Thus, a *fink* is distinguished from a SCAB, a regular employee who does not join a strike. A STRIKEBREAKER.

fire insurance. See under INSURANCE, PROPERTY.

fire mark. Formerly, a metal plaque issued by a fire insurance company and attached to the face of a building, indicating that the building was covered by fire insurance issued by the particular company.

fireproof. Strictly speaking, incombustible, or made of incombustible materials; not in dan-ger from action by fire. Fireproof is the highest degree of resistance to fire, the lesser degrees, in generally recognized order of resistance being *fire-resistant, fire-retarding,* and *flameproof.*

fire-resistant. See FIREPROOF.

fire-retarding. See FIREPROOF.

fire sale. Specifically, a sale at reduced prices, of merchandise damaged or water-soiled in a fire. Loosely, any emergency sale or bargain sale. See also SALE (2).

firkin. A small cask or container, holding, in old English measure, one-fourth of a BARREL or nine imperial GALLONS.

firm. 1. Strictly, an unincorporated business carried on by more than one person, jointly; a partnership. The name or style under which such a business is carried on. Under law, a *firm* is not recognized as a separate person apart from the individuals operating it, as is a CORPORATION. In popular usage, any business, COMPANY, or concern, incorporated or not.
2. Unfluctuating, steady, not affected by market influences. Supported by an adequate demand to balance supply, as, for example, when prices are said to be *firm,* or when the market for a given commodity is *firm.*
3. Carrying an obligation to perform, deliver, or accept, as a *firm* bid, offer, price or contract. A *firm* offer is binding, if accepted within a specified period of time.

firm price. See under PRICE.

first and refunding mortgage bond. See under BOND (1).

first class. Of the highest or best quality available; of superior rank, grade, or degree; in excellent condition. See, for example, COMMERCIAL PAPER, FIRST CLASS.

first-class mail. See under POSTAL SERVICE.

first closing. See CLOSING DATE.

first cost. See COST, INITIAL.

firsthand. Obtained directly from the original producer, supplier or importer, rather than from a middleman or distributor. Also, new, as distinguished from SECONDHAND, or used.

first-in-first-out (FIFO). See under INVENTORY VALUATION.

first lien collateral trust bond. See under BOND (1).

first-line. The level of management supervision in direct contact with the workers or operators. Foremen, gang bosses, straw bosses, etc. are included in this category. It is also known as *front-line* management or supervision.

first mortgage. See under MORTGAGE.

first mortgage and collateral trust bond. See under BOND (1).

first mortgage bond. See under BOND (1).

first of exchange. The first, top, or original copy of a foreign bill of exchange, when it is prepared in a set of copies. The duplicate or carbon copies are known as the *second of exchange, third of exchange,* etc. The various copies are forwarded to the payee by different ships or planes, so that if one is lost or destroyed in transit the others will be received. The payment of any one copy automatically cancels the others. See also BILL OF EXCHANGE, FOREIGN.

first refunding bond. See under BOND (1).

firsts. In general, items or units of a commodity or product of the top grade, or without blemish or imperfection, as distinguished from SECONDS.

fiscal. From the Latin *fiscus,* a money-basket, having to do with the treasury or with revenue. Hence, by extension, having to do with money or financial affairs in general.
~ **agent.** An agent or representative, usually a bank or trust company, which serves as a depository for public or corporate funds, makes collections and disbursements, and performs other financial services.
~ **officer.** One charged with the collection and disbursement of funds; a TREASURER.
~ **period.** Any accounting period for which financial statements or reports are prepared, such as a fiscal year, quarter, etc.
~ **year.** Any period of twelve consecutive months selected as the basis for annual financial reporting, planning, or budgeting by a business or government. A company using the CALENDAR YEAR as its *fiscal year* is said to be on a calendar year basis, and any other is said to be on a *fiscal year basis.*

five-and-ten-cents store. See RETAIL STORE, LIMITED PRICE VARIETY.

five percenter. In business slang, a person who, for a commission usually set at five percent, offers his services and influence to attempt to secure government or other contracts for a business. Such activities are now illegal with respect to federal government contracts.

five-twenty. In the securities trade, a term for a form of BOND, especially a government bond, which is redeemable after five years, and payable at the end of twenty years. Similar bonds with different redemption and payment periods are known as TEN-FORTIES, etc. See also BOND (1), OPTIONAL.

fixed. Permanent or installed; recurring or continuing over an extended period of time. Definite, not fluctuating or subject to change; invariable. See each of the following under the principal listing: ~ ASSET (2); ~ BUDGET; ~ CAPITAL (3); ~ COST; ~ DEBT; ~ EXCHANGE (4); ~ INCOME; ~ LIABILITY (3); ~ PRICE.

fixed charge. In accounting, a charge against the company that becomes due in a regular amount at stated intervals. Examples include rent, interest, taxes, transfers to reserve funds etc. Thus, they are the charges which must be paid before the owners can participate in the gross profits of the business. See also COST, FIXED.

fixed fee. A term used in contracts, especially for construction work, in which part of the compensation is to be a fixed amount of money, rather than a fixed percentage of profit. The usual wording of the contract is COST-PLUS *fixed fee.*

fixed trust. See TRUST (1), NON-DISCRETIONARY.

fixture. 1. In law, any CHATTEL, or personal property, which is attached to real property in a permanent manner. Such *fixtures* are treated as BETTERMENTS, and become the property of the landlord, though they may have been added by the tenant. Examples include lighting, plumbing, heating and cooking equipment, etc.

2. In current business lease practice, any item of equipment or furnishing which a business may add to its rented space to enable it to better conduct its business. Examples include partitions, shelving, lighting, workbenches, storage bins, etc. Such *fixtures* may or may not become the property of the landlord, depending on the exact terms of the lease, and on state law. The terms of the lease should be examined carefully to determine who receives eventual title to *fixtures,* who is responsible for repairing damage to them, whether they may be removed by the tenant before the lease expires, etc.

flameproof. See FIREPROOF.

flat. In the securities trade, a term meaning without interest. When a bond is sold *flat,* for example, no charge for interest accrued to date is added to the amount paid by the buyer. Any interest accrued, in other words, is already included in the price quoted. Similarly, when a broker makes a loan on the basis of securities deposited, he is frequently able to borrow the money *flat,* or without interest.

flat price. See under PRICE.

flat rate. 1. A rate which is charged uniformly for every unit of goods or service, regardless of the number of units, frequency of use or purchase, etc. In advertising, for example, a *flat rate* may be set for classified advertisements, meaning that the same rate per inch is paid by all, regardless of the number of inches or the frequency of insertion. Similarly, a public utility may set a *flat rate* for sales of electricity above a certain amount, meaning that above that amount there is no further reduction in unit price regardless of the quantity consumed.

2. A rate or price offered which covers an entire transaction, or a group of related transactions, in one amount or rate, with the understanding that no additional charges or allowances are to be made. A purchaser of services which include printing, folding, inserting, and mailing of advertising material, for example, may obtain a *flat rate* covering the entire operation.

fleece. In business slang, to take money or property from an unsuspecting victim by unfair means; in other words, to shear a LAMB.

fleet. A number of ships, airplanes, motor vehicles, etc., operated together by a single operator, or owned by a single owner. In automobile insurance rates, for example, special reductions are usually allowed when a number of vehicles are operated as a *fleet* by a single insured person.

flexible budget. See BUDGET, VARIABLE.

flexible tariff. See under TARIFF (2).

flexible trust. See TRUST (1), DISCRETIONARY.

flier. 1. A speculative purchase or investment, especially one made by a person whose regular business is other than speculating in the particular commodity or security bought. For example, a person may decide to *take a flier* in wheat, or in oils, meaning that he will speculate in the wheat futures market, or in oil company securities.

2. In the advertising field, a HANDBILL; a single sheet of advertising or promotional matter designed to be handed out, placed under doors, inserted in mailings, etc. A DODGER.

flight of capital. In financial circles, a term for the heavy movement of funds and credit from one country to others, for reasons other than for normal financing of trade or investments. A *flight of capital* may take place, for example, because holders of funds fear that the domestic currency will be severely depreciated by inflationary policies, by political developments, or by other circumstances.

float. 1. To launch a new enterprise, or to arrange for new capital for an existing enterprise. For example, a new corporation may *float* an issue of stock to attract investors, or an existing business may *float* a loan, meaning that it arranges for borrowed capital, either by a public bond issue or by private negotiation.

2. In banking, the value of checks and drafts drawn but not yet collected; more specifically, the value of checks which have been presented at a first bank for collection, but are still in transit and not yet presented at the bank against which they are drawn.

3. In the securities trade, the portion of

a new issue of securities which has not yet been purchased by the public, and which is still to be absorbed by the market.

4. In land law, a term formerly used for a certificate authorizing entry to land which had not yet been specifically selected or located. Such certificates were issued, for example, to railroad companies which were surveying routes for new lines, so that they could lay immediate claim to the right of way as it was surveyed.

floatage (or flotage). The charge made for transferring railroad freight cars across water, such as rivers or harbors, on specially constructed barges or floats.

floater. The term for a type of insurance policy which covers the property insured at any location, within limits specified, not merely at its normal or fixed location. Such a policy may be issued, for example, to cover furs, jewelry, or other personal property which is normally carried about. See also INSURANCE, INLAND MARINE; POLICY, FLOATER.

floating. In various usages, not permanently fixed; not represented by fixed property or a fixed investment; available for investment or for lending. See each of the following under the principal listing: ~ CAPITAL (3); ~ DEBT; ~ LIABILITY (3); ~ STOCK (1).

floating conditions. Terms or clauses contained in purchase contracts involving shipment of the purchased goods by water, covering the responsibility for loading and unloading, the type of vessel and storage space to be used, etc.

floor. 1. In the securities and commodities markets, the trading place of an organized exchange. Hence, a transaction arranged on the *floor* is one made in open trading, as distinguished from one made off the *floor,* or by private negotiation. A *floor* TRADER is a BROKER who operates on the exchange *floor,* and who represents other brokers in active trading.

2. A minimum level set by regulation, law, or union contract for prices, wages, salaries, return on investment, etc., as contrasted with a CEILING, which is a maximum set. Minimum wage laws, for example, set *floors* for wages to be paid for various types of work.

floor trader. See under TRADER.

floorwalker. In retail stores, especially variety and department stores, an employee whose duty it is to circulate in the selling area, aiding customers, supervising sales clerks, and generally representing the store management.

flotage. See FLOATAGE.

flotation. The act or process of financing a commercial enterprise, or of launching an issue of securities. See also FLOAT (1).

flotsam. Goods from the cargo of a wrecked ship, or items of ship's equipment, found floating in the sea, as distinguished from JETSAM, which is deliberately thrown overboard to lighten the ship. Under maritime law, identifiable *flotsam* must be offered to the original owners in return for a SALVAGE payment, but that which cannot be identified, or is not claimed in a reasonable period is usually considered the property of the finder. See also LAGAN.

fluctuation clause. A clause sometimes included in a contract calling for future delivery over a long period of time, providing for automatic changes in the contract price if certain specified costs fluctuate or change meanwhile. In a contract for the purchase of imported goods, for example, the *fluctuation clause* may provide for automatic price increases if there are increases in shipping costs, insurance rates, tariffs, etc. See also ESCALATOR CLAUSE.

fluid. 1. In general, liquid, or flexible; rapidly changing or subject to rapid change. Market conditions are said to be *fluid,* for example, when prices are unstable and react strongly to external conditions.

2. In financial usage, LIQUID; in cash or easily convertible into cash; not FROZEN.

3. In measurement, liquid, as distinguished from dry measure. See, for example, OUNCE, FLUID; QUART, FLUID, etc.

flurry. In the securities and commodities markets, a short-lived disturbance or fluctuation in prices, which usually leaves prices essentially unchanged and has no lasting effects on price levels. The same term is used to describe similar fluctuations in interest rates or other prices. Also, a sudden but temporary increase in trading activity, with or without a disturbance in prices.

flush. 1. Full, or well-supplied, especially well-supplied with funds; rich, or solvent.

2. Straight, with no projections or indentations. In printing, for example, type set *flush* is with no paragraph indentations or marginal projections. In construction, brick laid *flush* is without any decorative projections or other surface irregularities.

fly-by-night. Literally, one who may disappear or abscond overnight. Hence, a business enterprise which is insufficiently financed or capitalized, and may easily fail, or which is established by inexperienced and irresponsible persons; any business which is not well-established.

fly-power. In the securities trade, a term for an ASSIGNMENT or ENDORSEMENT in blank, which, when attached to a particular stock certificate, permits it to be transferred without further action. An investor may leave several stock certificates with a broker, for example, and sign a *fly-power,* so that if any one of the stocks is sold the broker can fill in the name of the stock and make the transfer.

F.O.B. See FREE ON BOARD.

folio. 1. Originally, a leaf; hence a sheet or page in a manuscript or book. Also, the page number in a book, so that a book with unnumbered pages is said to be without *folio.*

2. In law, a unit used to measure the length of legal documents, and as a means of locating particular passages. In most states, a *folio* is fixed at 100 words.

3. See BOOK SIZES.

Food and Drug Administration. A federal agency, first established in 1930 as an independent agency, and now included in the Department of Health and Welfare. Its primary responsibility is the administration of the federal Food, Drug, and Cosmetics Act and other laws dealing with the contents, advertising, and labeling of food and drug products.

foot. 1. In linear measure, 12 inches or ⅓ of a yard. It is equal to 30.48 centimeters in the metric system. The term originally meant the length of an average human *foot.*

2. In accounting, to total up a column of figures and enter the total at the bottom or *foot* of the column.

3. In slang, to bear a cost, or to pay; as, to *foot* the bill for something, meaning to pay the costs.

foot-pound. A unit of energy or work, equal to the work done in raising a weight of one pound avoirdupois a distance of one foot against the force of gravity. To lift a weight of 6 pounds a distance of 2 feet, for example, requires 12 *foot-pounds* of work. The same measure is used to describe the work done in overcoming friction to move a weight horizontally. It is equal to 13,827 gram-centimeters, the corresponding unit in the metric system. See also HORSEPOWER.

for account of. 1. In an ENDORSEMENT, a term meaning that the amount is to be paid to the person whose name follows, or according to his instructions or directions. Thus, an endorsement *for account of* John Doe means that John Doe may re-endorse the instrument to another, as distinguished from an endorsement worded "Only to" John Doe, which cannot be further endorsed or negotiated.

2. A form of sale, especially an auction sale, in which the buyer or seller does not wish his name disclosed. In such event, the auction program may show that the sale is to be made *for account of* whom it may concern, and the record of the sale may show the purchaser in similar terms.

forbearance. In law, a voluntary delay or abstention in enforcing a right or demand, such as taking action against a delinquent debtor; a general leniency in pressing for collection of accounts due, or for performance of agreed obligations.

force. As used in the phrase *in force,* legally valid; not expired or cancelled because of a violation of terms; active, or effective.

forced. Involuntary; under the urgent need to raise funds; at a sacrifice. See each of the following under the principal listing: ∼ LOAN; ∼ SALE.

forced combination. In advertising, a term for a sale of advertising space in two newspapers, such as a morning and an evening paper under common ownership, under such conditions that it is impossible to buy space in the one without also buying space in the other. Such conditions of sale have been held to be illegal.

force majeure. In French, a major force; an irresistable force, or overwhelming circumstances, against which a person is not expected to take action or make a resistance; those dangers or accidents which are beyond human control. In an insurance policy, for example, the policy holder is usually required to take steps to protect and preserve the property insured, but he is not required to do so against a *force majeure.* See also ACT OF GOD.

for collection. A form of ENDORSEMENT on a check, note, or other instrument, not transferring title to the instrument, but merely authorizing the party named to collect the amount due for the endorser. See also COLLECTION.

forecast. A prediction of the future, or an estimate of the future based on reasonable assumptions, past experience, and current values. In business, *forecasts* of future sales, income, costs, capital needs, labor needs, etc., are essential parts of sound planning. See also BUDGET.

foreclose. In general, to bar, to terminate or shut off; to eliminate or do away with a right of redemption. To bring an action against a debtor who is in default, under which he is required to pay the debt in total or forfeit his right of redemption of the property put up as security. See also FORECLOSURE.

foreclosure. In law, an action or proceeding brought by a creditor against a debtor after the debtor has defaulted in payment on a secured debt or MORTGAGE. The purpose of the action is to compel the debtor to pay the debt in full or to forfeit his right to redeem the property, as provided for in the mortgage agreement. *Foreclosure* proceedings may also be brought, in some circumstances, for violation of the terms of a mortgage, such as the wrongful use of the property, as well as for default in payment of the principal or interest. The creditor, on gaining full possession of the property, may keep it, or may sell it in a *foreclosure sale,* depending on the circumstances and state laws. If the proceeds of the *foreclosure sale* exceed the amount of the remaining debt, the excess must usually be paid over to the debtor.

foredate. See ANTEDATE.

foreign. As used in business, a term which may refer to countries other than the subject country, or to states other than the subject one, or simply to any other place than the subject one. FOREIGN COMMERCE, for example, is commerce and trade with other countries, but a *foreign* corporation is one chartered in another state. In banking, *foreign* COLLECTIONS (2) are those outside of the local clearing house area. See also each of the following under the principal listing: ∼ BILL OF EXCHANGE; ∼ CORPORATION; ∼ EXCHANGE.

foreign commerce. In general, any commerce or trade between citizens of two or more different countries. Specifically, as defined by the Interstate Commerce Act, it is commerce between places in the United States and any place in a foreign country, or between places in the United States but through any foreign country. The term foreign trade is frequently used with the same meaning.

foreign exchange broker. See BROKER (1), EXCHANGE.

foreign freight forwarder. See under FORWARDER.

foreign money order. See MONEY ORDER, POSTAL.

foreign trade. See FOREIGN COMMERCE.

foreign trade zone. The name for a segregated, guarded area into which foreign goods may be imported directly without the necessity of going through CUSTOMS, or the payment of TARIFFS. In this zone, the goods may be stored, repackaged, assembled, combined with domestic materials, or otherwise processed, and then either re-exported or imported in the normal manner. If the goods are re-exported, there is no tariff charge, but if they are imported, the usual tariff must be paid. It is frequently called a free port, free trade zone, free zone, etc.

foreign value. As defined by the Tariff Act, the price at which any item imported into the United States is presently selling in its country of origin, plus the costs of preparing it for export. It is one of the two values used in determining the value on which import duties are to be based, the other being the UNITED STATES VALUE, which is essentially the price at which the item is to be sold in this country, less the costs of transporting it here.

foreman. In a manufacturing or operating company, the employee who is the direct representative of management at the operating level. He is the supervisor who directs the work of the ordinary employees, rather than that of other supervisors. In popular usage, he may be called a gang boss or straw boss, and may be formally known as a front-line or first-line supervisor.

forestalling. Originally, the act of intercepting a person on the highroad for illegal purposes. Currently, the act or process of buying or contracting for goods which have not yet reached the market, with the intent of reselling them later for a higher price. It is distinguished from ENGROSSING, which is the buying up of goods in the market, though both may be with the intent of CORNERING the market. Sometimes, but incorrectly, any purchase of goods in anticipation of a rise in prices, with the intent of selling at a profit, is known as *forestalling.*

forfeit. 1. To lose, as a penalty for some wrong, failure, or neglect; to give up as punishment or in forced payment.

2. Any property, right, interest, benefit, etc., which is taken from one person and given to another, as penalty for the violation of some duty, obligation, or law on the one hand, and as restitution or reward on the other. It is distinguished from a PLEDGE in that the thing taken was not originally deposited as security. The act of forfeiture differs from CONFISCATION in that the latter is the taking of property for public use and not through any fault on the part of the owner.

forge. To prepare an imitation of some written instrument, or to alter a written instrument, or to sign a false signature, for the purpose of fraudulently deceiving another person.

forgery. The crime of falsifying or altering a written instrument or signature, or of *forging*, for purposes of fraud. The only difference between *forgery* and COUNTERFEIT-ING is that the former is usually for the purpose of deceiving one person or a few particular persons, while the latter is the altering or falsifying of some public instrument, such as money, to deceive the public in general. Also, the document or writing *forged* is known as a *forgery*.

for honor. See ACCEPTANCE FOR HONOR.

forma. See PRO FORMA.

formal contract. See under CONTRACT (1).

form letter. A standardized form used for correspondence, when there are a large number of letters to be sent on a single subject and with the same or similar contents. The *form letter* may be in the form of a standard text with blank spaces to be filled in with the appropriate words or figures, or it may consist of a number of standard paragraphs from among which the appropriate ones are selected and typed out.

forthwith. As used in agreements, court orders, etc., a term meaning as soon as is reasonably possible; within a reasonably brief time; with no unnecessary delay.

forty. A term for a parcel of land containing *forty* acres; a QUARTER-SECTION of land again quartered into 1/16th of a SECTION. The *forty* is a common unit of land for trading, cultivating in a single crop, etc. A farmer, for example, may speak of planting grain on his north *forty*, using the south *forty* as pasture, etc.

or value. See HOLDER FOR VALUE.

or value received. See VALUE RECEIVED.

orward. 1. To ship goods by common carrier, especially to do so for the account of a customer, as a contractor or agent. To engage in business as a FORWARDER.

2. A term sometimes used to mean for future completion or execution. A *forward* purchase, for example, is one made at the present time, for future delivery and use.

orwarder. A person or concern whose business it is to receive goods for transport, and for services associated with transport, such as warehousing, packing and unpacking, consolidating and breaking down shipments, etc. *Forwarders* are of several types, the principal ones being listed and defined below.

carloading company. A *forwarder* specializing in the acceptance of LESS-THAN-CARLOAD shipments and consolidating them for rail shipment in CARLOAD lots. The *carloading company* charges shippers the regular less-than-carload rate, and makes its profit on the difference between the carload and less-than-carload rates. Similar companies handle shipments by highway truck in the same manner.

break-bulk service. A *forwarder* specializing in accepting full carload shipments at a terminal point, and breaking them down into smaller shipments for various destinations, which are then consolidated with other small shipments into carload shipments to the final destinations. The shipper pays the carload rate for the entire distance, and the *forwarder's* profit comes from a commission charged for the *break-bulk* operation.

foreign freight forwarder. One specializing in handling export and import shipments. The *forwarder's* services include arranging for cargo space, insuring the shipment, preparing, and processing customs documents, etc. Unlike domestic forwarders, *foreign freight forwarders* do not consolidate shipments, since cargo space on ships is usually not sold on a bulk rate basis.

packing and consolidating service. A *forwarder* specializing in receiving shipments from many small manufacturers in a local area, and shipping their products to the larger market cities in carload or truckload lots. Such services handle shipments from apparel manufacturers, furniture manufacturers, and other groups whose members tend to be concentrated in particular localities. They are also known as pool car services.

foul bill. See under BILL OF HEALTH; BILL OF LADING.

founders' stock. See STOCK (1), BONUS.

fourth-class mail. See POSTAL SERVICE, PARCEL POST.

fractional currency. See under CURRENCY.

franchise. 1. A special privilege granted by a government to an individual or a company, to perform some useful service, or to conduct some business of a public nature. For example, a bus company is granted a *franchise* to operate its vehicles on the city streets or state roads, and a utility company is granted a *franchise* to provide electricity or gas to the residents of an area.

2. In business, an agreement between a supplier and a retail or wholesale distributor, under which the former gives the latter the right to handle his product, under certain mutually agreed on conditions.

franchise clause. A clause sometimes included in automobile and other casualty insurance policies, providing that the insured will absorb all individual losses of less than a stated amount, but that the insurance company will pay the total amount of all losses over that amount. Thus, if the policy carries a $100 *franchise,* nothing will be paid for a loss of $75, but a loss of $125 will be settled in full. A *franchise clause* differs from a DEDUCTIBLE CLAUSE, which provides that the insured will absorb a stated amount of every loss, no matter what the size.

franchised dealer. A retail DEALER who handles the products of a supplier under the terms of a written agreement or FRANCHISE. Usually, the agreement provides that the dealer will have exclusive rights to handle the product in a given territory, that the supplier will provide certain advertising and other services, and so forth, in return for which the dealer will promote the product, maintain adequate stocks, install and service it as required, etc. See also EXCLUSIVE DEALER.

franchise tax. See under TAX (2).

franco delivery. In transportation, a term for a complete delivery of goods to a consignee, with all charges paid; in other words, a prepaid delivery.

frank. From the French, free. The privilege of sending letters or other matter through the mails free of charge, such as is granted to Congressmen. Also, to send letters under such a privilege. Members of Congress, for example, are provided with a supply of envelopes with their names on them, which may be used for the sending of *franked,* or free mail.

fraternal society. As defined under the statute adopted in many states, any corporation, society, order, or voluntary association, without capital stock, organized and carried on solely for the mutual benefits of its members and their beneficiaries, and not for profit, and having a lodge system with ritualistic forms and representative government, and making provision for the payment of benefits to its members and their beneficiaries. Aside from the social aspects, one of the most important services of such societies is the provision of insurance, death benefits, burial sites, and similar services for the members and their beneficiaries. They are also known as beneficial societies, mutual benefit societies or associations, etc.

fraud. Any false or deceitful practice or device, used for the purpose of depriving another person of his rights or property. Any false representation, or distortion of fact, such that one party to an agreement or contract is imposed upon thereby. In law, the elements of *fraud* are: 1) a false representation or concealment designed to mislead; 2) either guilty knowledge of the fact or gross carelessness; and 3) a deliberate intent and act of misleading the other party.

The discovery of *fraud* will nullify a contract. See also STATUTE OF FRAUDS.

fraudulent sale. See under SALE (1).

free. Depending on the particular context, without charge, without responsibility, without obligation, etc. As used in price quotations, for example, it means that the buyer assumes no costs or obligations for the goods up to a specified point, and assumes all after that point.

free alongside (F.A.S.). A term used in sale price quotations, especially for export, indicating that the price includes all costs of transportation and delivery of the goods alongside of the ship. The buyer is then responsible for having the goods loaded on board, and pays the costs of shipping from this point on. Prices on this basis are frequently stated as *F.A.S.,* or *free alongside ship,* at some named port.

free and clear. A term used in DEEDS and other documents conveying title to land or other property, indicating that the title being transferred is not burdened with any ENCUMBRANCE or LIEN.

free astray. In rail transportation, a term for a freight shipment which has gone astray, has been located, and has been shipped at no additional cost of the shipper to its original destination.

free coinage. The practice, formerly followed by the United States mint, of making into standard coins any amount of bullion, of the required fineness, and above a minimum amount, brought to it. Before the coinage of gold was stopped in 1933, the *free coinage* of gold was practiced at the mint. The *free coinage* of silver was an election issue over a long period of years, but was never established.

free currency market. See FREE MARKET.

free exchange rate. See RATE OF EXCHANGE.

free gold. The term for the gold held by the twelve Federal Reserve Banks in excess of their minimum reserve requirements, and therefore available for use on the world commercial markets if necessary or desired.

free goods. With respect to imports, the products and materials on which there is no tariff or duty charged, and on which there is no import quota set. These are usually goods which are needed by domestic industry but not available from domestic sources, such as, for example, chromium metal, carpet wool, etc.

freehold. In law, an ESTATE in land or other real property which has no definite or fixed termination date or condition, as dist guished from a LEASEHOLD, which is for a fixed or determinable period of time. However, a *freehold* may be contingent, in that it may be ended by some uncertain event at some uncertain time. State laws vary as to the exact definition and limitations.

freeholder. In general, a person who possesses land or property under a FREEHOLD. Under the laws of the various states, however, the term may have special meanings and restrictions.

free lance. Originally, a term for a knight or soldier of fortune whose services were available for pay to any ruler or government. Hence, today, any independent agent, who does not work continuously for any particular employer. Particularly, a writer or artist who works on individual assignments and sells his work to various publications, rather than working as a staff member for one particular publication.

free market. In general, any market or exchange in which buyers and sellers may operate without restrictions; an open market. More particularly, the *free currency market,* on which various national currencies are traded at their free, or real value, rather than at the value fixed by government edict.

free market value. See VALUE (2), MARKET.

free of all average. See under AVERAGE (3).

free of particular average. See under AVERAGE (3).

free on board (F.O.B.) A term used in sales price quotations, for both domestic and export sales, meaning, in general, that the seller assumes all responsibilities and costs up to the specific point or stage of delivery named, including transportation, packing, insurance, etc. The buyer takes over responsibility and costs at the same point. For insurance purposes, and in the event of settlement of any claims for loss or damage to the goods shipped, it is important to note that title to the goods changes hands at the named point, unless otherwise specified. A wide variety of particular *F.O.B.* terms are in use, the principal ones of which are listed and defined below. See also COST AND FREIGHT; COST, INSURANCE, AND FREIGHT.

~ **cars (named carrier at named point).** The seller pays all costs up to and including loading the shipment on the specified carrier, but the buyer pays the freight from the named point.

~ **factory.** The seller pays only the costs of preparing the goods for shipment, and the buyer is responsible for picking them up and for shipment. This is the generally understood meaning of *F.O.B.* when not otherwise qualified.

~ **(named point), freight allowed to (second named point).** The seller has title only to the first named point, but assumes shipping costs to the second point by allowing the buyer to deduct these costs from his invoice before payment.

~ **(named point), freight prepaid to (second named point).** The seller has title only to the first named point, but has prepaid the shipping charges to a second named point. In this and the above case, it is the buyer's responsibility to see that the shipment is covered by adequate insurance after he takes title.

~ **vessel (named port of export).** The seller assumes all responsibility and costs up to and including loading the shipment on board the vessel designated by the buyer. The buyer is responsible for the ocean freight and insurance charges.

~ **(named port of import in foreign country).** The seller assumes all responsibilities and costs, including freight, insurance, unloading, customs duties, etc., and turns the goods over to the buyer at the named port. The buyer is responsible only to take prompt delivery of the goods and to pay any costs from that point on.

~ **(named domestic point).** This is a non-specific term, generally meaning that the seller pays all costs up to delivery or loading in the named city. The use of the term should ordinarily be avoided, however, since it frequently leads to disputes over which party should bear the costs of loading and unloading and local delivery or pickup, and over which party is responsible for any loss or damage during unloading or loading operations, or while the goods are in temporary storage at the named point.

free overside. A term sometimes used in price quotations for export, meaning that the seller will pay all costs and assume all responsibility for the goods until the time at which they are unloaded onto the wharf or lighter at the point of importation in the foreign country. The buyer then pays all costs, including handling, customs duties, etc., beyond this stage of delivery.

free port. See FOREIGN TRADE ZONE.

free ride. In securities trade slang, a term for the practice of buying a security which is expected to rise, then selling it within a few days at a profit, before the date on which payment for the purchase is required. The speculator who does this is able to profit without putting up any of his own money, and thus gets a *free ride.* The practice is now illegal under the rules of the Securities and Exchange Commission and of the New York Stock Exchange, and a broker is required to obtain cash payment for the purchase before turning over the proceeds of the sale, in such a case.

free silver. A term used for many years as an election campaign theme in American politics, meaning, in brief, the demand for free and unlimited coinage of all silver presented at the mint, in a fixed ratio of value to gold. See also FREE COINAGE.

free time. In rail transportation, the period of time allowed by a railroad before a DEMURRAGE charge will be made for the use of a loaded freight car held by the receiver of a shipment.

free trade. As generally used, the unrestricted and unlimited trade between countries, with no quotas on imports or exports, and no import tariffs which are so high as to restrict the flow of commerce. Actually, the term is a relative one, with any lowering of restrictions on commerce considered a step in the direction of *free trade*.

free trade zone. See FOREIGN TRADE ZONE.

freeze. 1. To fix or stabilize at present rates or levels, or at some given point or level, or at a point or level in some fixed relation to another. For example, in time of war or national emergency, the federal government may take action to *freeze* prices, wages, rents, or the volume of some business activity, in order to prevent inflation, profiteering or other harmful effects of the general shortage of goods and services which exists at such a time. See also PRICE CONTROL.

2. To seize, impound, or otherwise render unavailable to the owners, by law or government action. For example, in time of war or national emergency, the federal government may *freeze* stocks of critical materials until they can be directed into the war effort, and may *freeze* the funds held in the United States by enemy aliens.

free zone. See FOREIGN TRADE ZONE.

freight. Strictly, the amount or charge paid by a shipper to a carrier for the transport of goods or commodities over the road, route, or facilities of the carrier. Also, loosely, the goods themselves transported by a carrier for another.

dead ~. The charges paid for dead or empty space by one who charters the use of a ship, car or truck and only partly fills it. Also, specifically, a charge payable to a ship owner when his entire vessel is chartered, but paid for on a weight basis, and the amount shipped does not total to a specified minimum.

fictitious ~. See PHANTOM FREIGHT, below.

~ allowed. A term used in price quotations, meaning that the seller will permit the buyer to deduct the cost of *freight* beyond a named point, but that title to the shipment passes at the named point. See also FREE ON BOARD; COST AND FREIGHT; COST, INSURANCE, AND FREIGHT.

~ collect. A term used on shipping documents and in price quotations, indicating that the buyer or consignee will pay all shipping charges. It is the opposite of FREIGHT PREPAID, which see below.

~ forward. A term used on shipping documents, indicating to the carrier that the charges are to be paid at the destination of the shipment by the consignee.

~ free. A term sometimes used in price quotations and contracts, meaning that the seller will pay all charges up to a named point, though title to the goods is in the hands of the buyer. See also FREIGHT PREPAID, below.

~ inward. In accounting, the charges paid on all shipments received by the company keeping the records.

~ outward. In accounting, the charges paid on all outgoing shipments by the company keeping the records.

~ prepaid. A term used in price quotations, meaning that the seller has paid the cost of *freight* beyond a named point to a second named point, but that title to the shipment passes to the buyer at the first named point. See also FREE ON BOARD.

phantom ~. A term for the excess of a standard *freight* or delivery charge paid by a buyer over the actual cost of the *freight* paid by the seller. For example, a manufacturer of automobiles may charge *freight* from Detroit on all shipments made, though some of the automobiles may actually be shipped from assembly plants which are nearer to the dealer who pays the charges. See also BASING POINT PRICING.

revenue ~. A term for goods which are carried by a railroad or other carrier for revenue, or income, as distinguished from the goods it may carry for its own use or convenience, such as coal, spare parts, etc.

freight absorption. In general, the payment by the seller of freight costs on shipments to buyers. More specifically, the amount of actual freight charges paid out by a seller which is in excess of the amount used in calculating delivered prices under a BASING POINT PRICING system. The courts have held that under certain circumstances, such *ab-*

sorption of charges by the seller is price discrimination, and illegal under the antitrust laws.

freight density. In railroad accounting and statistics, a measure of the relative usage of the road of a particular line, or of all railroads in an area. It is the total number of tons of goods carried one mile during the given period, divided by the number of miles of road operated, stated in FREIGHT MILES per mile. Similar measures are used for highway and air *freight density*.

freight equalization. The practice of charging a buyer the freight charge which he would pay from a nearer source of supply, rather than the actual costs paid by the seller. This situation arises under a BASING POINT PRICING system, for example, when the particular point used for a given buyer is nearer to him than the shipping point of the seller using the system. See also FREIGHT ABSORPTION.

freight forwarder. See FORWARDER.

freight mile. In common carrier traffic statistics, the equivalent of one ton of goods carried one mile. The total number of *freight miles* carried during a period is the total miles traveled by all shipments of goods over the particular route.

freight rate. The charge for transporting goods, or the scheduled rate at which such charges will be made, such as per pound, per piece, per mile, etc. More specifically, the term usually refers to the charges made by railroads for carrying goods in their cars, which are based on the commodities carried, the distance carried, the value of the goods, and the area or district in which they are carried. In the United States, there are three *freight rate* districts, the Official, Western, and Southern districts, which include the eastern, western, and southern states respectively.

> **class** ∿. A common rate charged for a number of different items in the same class, such as assorted furniture.

> **combination** ∿. One based on a combination of several factors or rates, such as one for goods carried over two roads in different rate districts.

> **commodity** ∿. One applying specifically to a named commodity, such as coal. These rates are often set at a lower and less profitable level than the rates for other goods and merchandise in general.

> **group** ∿. A uniform rate which is charged for shipments to and from a group of related or nearby points. See also ZONE RATE, below.

> **joint** ∿. One set by two or more connecting carriers for shipments from a point on the line of one carrier to a point on the line of another.

> **released** ∿. One which is based on a statement or release by the shipper that the goods shipped are worth no more than some minimum amount per pound. Under such a rate, the carrier is responsible only for the released value of the goods in the event of loss or damage, and the rate is therefore lower than would be charged if the goods were shipped at their true value. Such rates are frequently set for such valuable and breakable items as glassware, chinaware, etc., and the shippers who use such rates usually purchase special insurance to cover them in the event of loss.

> **zone** ∿. One set for shipments from any of a number of points in one zone or area to any of a number of points in another. In the case of RAILWAY EXPRESS or parcel post shipments, the rate for a shipment from a point to any other point which is more than a stated number of miles, but less than a second stated number of miles, distant from the point of origin.

freight release. A document, or an endorsement on a bill of lading, given by a ship charterer or similar party to the ship's officer, authorizing him to give up the named goods, the freight charges on them having been paid.

freight tariff. See FREIGHT RATE.

freight ton. See TON, MEASUREMENT.

frequency distribution. In statistics, a form or table in which are summarized all of the values in a given series of items, or distribution of observations. It is prepared by setting up a number of ranges or CLASS INTERVALS, and classifying each item or observation in the class interval in which it falls. Statistics on income, prices, and many other economic factors are usually presented in this form. See also HISTOGRAM.

frictional unemployment. See UNEMPLOYMENT.

friend of the court. See AMICUS CURIAE.

fringe benefit. Any one of a wide variety of non-monetary or indirect benefits which an employer may give his employees, in addition to regular wage or salary compensation. These include both those benefits on which an exact value can be placed, such as paid holidays and vacations, paid insurance and pension plans, etc., as well as those on which it would be difficult or impossible to place an exact value, such as recreational facilities, free refreshments, medical service, etc.

front foot. In real estate usage, one foot along

the edge of a property fronting on or abutting the public street or road, or a railroad, or the adjoining property. Real estate prices are frequently quoted in amounts per *front foot;* and real estate taxes or assessments for street improvement are frequently set in amounts per *front foot* on the street or road being improved. It is also known as an abutting foot.

front-line. See FIRST-LINE.

front office. In business slang, the executive or chief administrative offices of a company, or the persons in authority in these offices. Thus, an order from the *front office* is one coming down from the chief executive authority in the company. Also, sometimes, the administrative units of the company, as distinguished from the back shop, or manufacturing units.

frozen. Not readily available, due to external factors or due to governmental action; not readily convertible into cash; set at a fixed rate or level by government action. See also FREEZE; ASSET (2); FROZEN.

F.T.C. See Federal Trade Commission.

full contribution clause. A clause used in fire insurance policies in some states, providing that when there are more than one mortgage on the property insured, the insurance shall be used to pay the holder of the first mortgage until it is satisfied, then to pay the holder of the second mortgage, if funds are available, etc., rather than to pay all holders proportionately, or to be restricted to the first mortgage, as under a NON-CONTRIBUTION CLAUSE.

full coverage. In insurance, a term for any insurance which provides payment up to the full value of the property insured, or which provides protection against all losses with no exceptions or deductible amounts. See also DEDUCTIBLE CLAUSE; FRANCHISE CLAUSE.

full crew. In general, the number of workers required by contract, or considered necessary, to perform a given task. Particularly, the number of railroad employees required to man trains of different lengths and types, as stipulated in the *full crew* law. The principle has been broadly adopted by unions in various fields, such as the building and theatrical trades, in which union contracts frequently specify the number of men an employer must use, or at least the number of salaries he must pay, for a particular task. See also FEATHERBEDDING.

full employment. In economics, the condition said to exist when all qualified persons who are willing and able to work are either employed or have an opportunity for employment. See also EMPLOYMENT; UNEMPLOYMENT.

full endorsement. See ENDORSEMENT IN FULL.

full lot. See ROUND LOT.

full-paid stock. Seee under STOCK (1).

full partner. See under PARTNER.

full service. A term used in advertising, especially in transportation advertising, meaning that the advertisement will be displayed in all of the available exposures, such as all of the cars or buses of a given line, or all of the station platforms. A full run. See also HALF SERVICE; QUARTER SERVICE.

full-stock. See under STOCK (1).

fund. 1. To convert a debt, especially a short-term unsecured debt, into a long-term obligation, such as a BOND (1). For example, a company that floats a bond issue, and uses the proceeds to retire a number of its short-term debts, is said to be *funding* its outstanding debts. See also DEBT, FUNDED.

2. In accounting and finance, any amount of cash, or of assets quickly convertible into cash, which has been set aside or reserved for a particular purpose. More generally, especially in the plural, money or cash available for use. See also RESERVE (1); SINKING FUND; TRUST (1).

    general ~. One established for general purposes or expenditures, rather than for some special use. Schools, charitable institutions, etc., usually accept donations or grants for their *general funds,* as well as for special purposes.

    imprest ~. A term for a *fund* of cash, such as a PETTY CASH *fund,* set aside for expenditures and cash payments. It is usually necessary for the person in charge of the *fund* to obtain a receipt or voucher for each expenditure, to account for the cash disbursed from the *fund.*

    revolving ~. One which is established with a stated amount of cash, and which is regularly renewed by the repayment or replacement of the *funds* which are withdrawn or disbursed. A company or school, for example, may establish a *revolving fund* to make loans to employees or students, with additional loans made as the original ones are repaid.

funded debt. See under DEBT.

funded reserve. See under RESERVE (1).

funding. In general, the act or process of converting a short-term unsecured liability into a long-term obligation. In municipal and government finance, the process of providing for current expenditures out of anticipated future income by issuing long-term interest-bearing notes or bonds. Thus, a municipality making a heavy capital expenditure may *fund* the debt created by the expenditure by issuing long-term bonds against future tax receipts.

fungible goods. See under GOODS (3).

furlong. A measure of length, equivalent to one eighth of a MILE, 220 YARDS, or 40 RODS. The equivalent in the metric system is 201.17 meters. In surveyors measure, a *furlong* is 10 CHAINS or 1,000 LINKS.

furlough. In general a leave of absense. As used in business, it is usually a leave without pay, as distinguished from a VACATION, and may be due to a lack of work. Thus, a LAYOFF with a definite date set for returning to work is more correctly considered a *furlough*.

furnishings. As used in leases, insurance contracts, and other documents, any appliances or facilities provided either by a landlord or a tenant, the ownership of which usually passes to the landlord under state law. *Furnishings* are those things which are neither FURNITURE nor FIXTURES (2), but they are usually treated as fixtures, as in the common term *furnishings and fixtures*.

furniture. As used in leases, insurance contracts, etc., the movable equipment of a business which facilitates its routine operations, though not directly used in the operations. Thus the term includes desks, chairs, workbenches, tables, files, etc., but excludes machines, office machines, and similar operating equipment. See also FIXTURE (2); FURNISHINGS.

future goods. A term used in the Uniform Sales Act, meaning goods which have already been sold or contracted for, but which are not yet produced, or at least not yet in the final form called for in the contract.

futures. The system of buying and selling commodities, and sometimes securities, under contracts providing for the delivery of specific amounts of the commodity, of a specified grade, at a particular price, at some specified future date. Much of the trading in such basic commodities as wheat, corn, oats, cotton, coffee, sugar, etc. is carried on in such *futures* contracts. In actual practice, the particular agreement to deliver a specified amount of a commodity may be bought and sold many times over between the date that *futures* trading on commodities for delivery at a given date begins, and the arrival of the delivery date itself. The *futures* contract is the chief means of HEDGING (1), so a user of sugar, for example, might buy *futures* contracts to protect himself against a price rise, but resell the contract before the date for delivery. See also EXCHANGE, COMMODITY.

future sum. In banking and finance, the amount of money which a borrower agrees to repay for a note, bill of exchange, or other obligation. It is the net amount borrowed, or PRESENT PRICE, plus any interest or discount, and any service charges or other charges made. In the case of an interest-bearing note, the future sum is the PRINCIPAL (2) plus the interest, and in the case of a discounted note it is the PRINCIPAL itself.

G

gabardine. A tightly woven twilled material, which may be of cotton, wool, rayon, or a mixture. It is distinguished by a marked diagonal effect in the weave on the face side.

gage. A pawn or pledge; a deposit placed as security for the performance of some act. The word has the same derivation as wager and ENGAGE.

gain. In general, the increase in any amount or quantity, especially an increase in possessions or resources. In business, it is usually measured as the excess difference at the end of any period of time over the amount at the beginning of the period. Examples include the net annual *gain* in corporate assets, or in accumulated surplus. See also PROFIT.

gainful occupation. Any occupation or regular line of work for which a person receives compensation in money or in kind. In some statistical series, being engaged in a *gainful occupation* is the definition of employment.

gainful worker. A term formerly used in LABOR FORCE statistics by the Bureau of the Census. It described a person who normally followed a GAINFUL OCCUPATION, whether or not at the moment he was actually employed or seeking work. The term and the concept have both been dropped in current statistics.

gain sharing. See PROFIT SHARING.

gallon. A measure of liquid volume used in the United States and the British Commonwealth. It is divided into four QUARTS. The American *gallon* contains 231 cubic inches, and is equivalent to the older British wine *gallon*. The imperial *gallon* contains 277.42 cubic inches, or 1.201 American *gallons*.

galvanize. To coat or plate with zinc, either by galvanic plating, or ELECTROPLATING, or by dipping in a solution of molten zinc, using the so-called hot dip method.

gamma ray. An emission, similar to X-rays, produced by radioactive materials, or during nuclear fission.

gang boss. See FOREMAN.

Gantt chart. A graphic device, used to measure progress against a standard or schedule of performance. It is usually operated by increasing the length of a colored string or tape as the work is completed. The chart is named after its inventor, Henry L. Gantt.

garnish. Originally, to warn, or to summon; now used only as meaning to issue a GARNISHMENT.

garnishee. A person against whom a GARNISHMENT has been issued. One who holds money or property belonging to a defendant in a suit, or to a debtor whose property has been attached. A *garnishee* is forbidden to deliver or pay over the property until the suit is settled.

~ **order.** One issued by a court to a *garnishee,* commanding him not to pay or deliver any money or property to a debtor or a defendant, until a suit or action is settled.

garnishment. A legal proceeding, consisting of a warning, issued to a person who holds the effects or property of another, not to pay such money or transfer such property to the defendant in a suit, or to anyone else. Such a warning may be issued to a public warehouse, for example, in which a defendant in BANKRUPTCY proceedings has stored merchandise. See also ATTACHMENT.

gauge. 1. In railway usage, the distance between rails of track. Standard *gauge* in the United States and most countries is now 4 feet, 8½ inches. Broad *gauge* is 7 feet, and narrow *gauge* is 3 feet, 6 inches.

2. In hosiery manufacturing, a measure of the fineness of the knit. In full-fashioned hosiery, it is the number of needles in one and one half inches on the knitting machine. In seamless hosiery, *gauge* is measured according to the size of the needles, as in hand-knitting.

general. Not limited or SPECIAL, pertaining to all or to an entire class, rather than to particular or precise parts. However, it is not as broad a term as UNIVERSAL, which means all, without exception. See each of the following under the principal listing: ~ AC-

CEPTANCE (3); ~ AGENT; ~ AVERAGE (3); ~ CARGO; ~ CREDITOR; ~ DEPOSIT; ~ EXPENSE (2); ~ ENDORSEMENT (2); ~ FUND (2); ~ IMPORTS; ~ LEDGER; ~ LEGACY; ~ LETTER OF ATTORNEY; ~ LIEN; ~ MORTGAGE; ~ PARTNER; ~ PARTNERSHIP; ~ STRIKE; ~ TENANCY.

General Accounting Office. The federal agency, created in 1921, which audits and reviews the financial transactions of the federal government and reviews the expenditures of appropriations by federal agencies. It is an agency of Congress, established to review the activities of the executive branch. Its chief officer is the Comptroller General of the United States.

general average contribution. See AVERAGE (3), GENERAL.

general average loss. See AVERAGE (3), GENERAL.

general merchandise store. See under RETAIL STORE.

general mortgage bond. See under BOND (1).

general property tax. See under TAX (2).

general release. In law, a full and sweeping release, renouncing all claims whatever which the releasing party ever had, has, or may have against the other party. For example, such a release is given to an executor or administrator of an estate, or to a guardian or trustee, upon the completion of his duties.

gentlemen's agreement. A term for an informal or unwritten AGREEMENT, ostensibly based on the honor of the parties involved, to perform or refrain from performing some act or service. Actually, the reason for keeping the agreement informal and unwritten is frequently that it involves unlawful or unethical activities, such as CARTEL operations, RESTRAINT OF TRADE, etc.

geographic mile. See MILE, NAUTICAL.

geometric mean. See under AVERAGE (1).

German silver. An alloy of copper, nickel, and zinc. It has the general appearance of silver, but contains none, and probably did not originate in Germany.

gerrymander. The process of dividing civil or political subdivisions along other than their natural lines, in a way to accomplish some sinister or illegal purpose. Such a division may be made, for example, to assure a majority for one party in each of two districts, instead of in one; or to assure by the way in which school district lines are drawn that children of different races or cultures go to separate schools. The term is a combination of the name of Gov. Gerry of Massachusetts and the salamander, which contemporary political cartoonists saw as resembling the shape of the districts Gov. Gerry had created.

G.I. Originally, in military terminology, "general issue," meaning issued to all troops. Hence, anything military, or anything strictly according to regulations. Also, by association, a soldier, particularly an American soldier.

gift. In law, a voluntary transfer or conveyance, from one person to another, made gratuitously and not upon any CONSIDERATION.

  absolute ~. A gift made in the donor's lifetime, transferring absolute and irrevocable ownership of the property given.

  ~ in trust. A gift made in such a way that the donee has legal title to the property given, but not the beneficial ownership during the lifetime of the donor, or during some specified period. A person may give stock in trust to a son, for example, but retain the income during his own life.

  testamentary ~. A gift made in a will or testament, to be effective on the death of the donor.

gift certificate. A device used in retail merchandising, whereby a person, wishing to give another a gift, purchases a certificate or script having a stated exchange value in the store of purchase. The certificate may then be exchanged by the receiver of the gift for any merchandise desired.

gift tax. See under TAX (2).

gill. A measure of liquid or dry volume, equal to one-fourth of a PINT, or 4 ounces. It was originally a size of a wine glass.

G.I. loan. See SERVICEMEN'S READJUSTMENT ACT.

gilt-edge. Of the first or highest quality; first class. As applied to commercial paper, bonds, securities, etc., it implies that the investment they represent is "as good as gold," with virtually no risk of default.

gilt-edge security. See under SECURITY (1).

gimmick. Originally, in carnival slang, the control or brake used to manipulate a wheel of chance. By applying the *gimmick* the operator would attract a crowd by making it appear easy to win. Thus, in current usage, any trick or device used to attract interest or promote sales. The term, however, has lost its immoral or illicit implications.

gingham. A light cotton cloth, woven with a pattern of colored squares or checks.

give color. In law, to admit an apparent, or COLORABLE, right in the opposition case. For example, one party to a suit *gives color to* the arguments of the other by failing to deny statements made.

give-out order. See under ORDER (4).

glut. To satiate, or to fill to overflowing, in the manner of a glutton. Thus, to flood a market with more goods than it can readily absorb. A superabundance of a commodity, more than the market can absorb; a supply of any commodity greater than the effective demand for that commodity.

G.N.P. See GROSS NATIONAL PRODUCT.

go bail. See BAIL.

godown. A corruption of a Malay word, meaning WAREHOUSE. The term is widely used throughout the Far East for a commercial storage warehouse.

going concern. A business or corporation that continues to transact its ordinary business, and that will, it is expected, continue to do so. In accounting, a company's status as a *going concern* affects many basic procedures, such as those of valuation. Many legal points also hinge on whether a firm is actually a *going concern* at a particular time.

going price. See under PRICE.

going value. The value computed for the assets of a business as a going concern in active operation, rather than merely as items of property, as distinguished from the LIQUIDATION VALUE. Thus, *going value* includes such intangibles as the value of customer good will, etc.

going wage. The wage rate commonly paid in a given community for a specific type of work. See also PREVAILING WAGES.

gold. Specifically, the metallic element, but generally used as meaning *gold* coinage or BULLION. Fine, or pure, *gold* is known as 24-carat *gold,* the CARAT being one twenty-fourth part of pure *gold* in any alloy of *gold.* See also the following under the principal listing: ∼ BOND (1); ∼ CERTIFICATE (2); ∼ DOLLAR; ∼ NOTE (1).

gold brick. In business slang, a dishonest, fraudulent, or worthless scheme, business, or security, especially one which has been given a sound, honest or attractive appearance. The term and its usage derive from the practice of shrewd operators, who prepared false *gold bricks* which they sold to gullible persons as pure blocks of gold. In the armed forces, the term has come to mean a worthless, lazy soldier, one who shirks assignments.

gold certificate. See CERTIFICATE (2).

gold export point. See GOLD POINT.

gold import point. See GOLD POINT.

gold mine. In business slang, an extremely profitable venture; one which produces a steady flow of high profits.

gold point. The point or relative level in the RATE OF EXCHANGE between two currencies at which it becomes more advantageous to transfer gold than to buy or sell BILLS OF EXCHANGE in the open market. The *gold export point* for a country is the point at which it is advantageous to export gold, and the *gold import point* is that at which it is better to import gold. It is sometimes called the *gold shipment point.*

gold shipment point. See GOLD POINT.

gold standard. A standard or basis for a monetary system which recognizes gold as the basic medium of exchange and as the measure of value. In practice, a currency based on a *gold standard* is one with a basic monetary unit with a legally fixed value in gold of a specified fineness. Typically, under a true *gold standard,* there is free and unlimited coinage and movement of gold, redemption of gold at par in any other form of legal money, and the acceptance of gold as legal tender. Various countries have adopted so-called limited or restricted *gold standards,* under which one or more of these characteristics is missing.

go long. See LONG.

good. 1. Valid, sufficient at law, sound and acceptable, such as, for example, a *good* CONSIDERATION.

2. Responsible, solvent and able to pay; financially sound. For example, a bank may write or stamp *good* across the face of a check or draft, to certify that the drawer has funds on deposit to meet the obligation, and that it will be paid when presented.

3. A commodity. See GOODS.

good consideration. See under CONSIDERATION.

good delivery. In securities trade usage, a security properly signed, transferred, and in good physical condition. See also BAD DELIVERY.

good faith. Done with the honest intention to abstain from taking unconscientious advantage; with no intention to mislead or deceive; not prompted by self-interest. For example, a price reduction in *good faith* to meet competition is one made only for this reason, and with no ulterior or selfish motive, or with intention to harm a competitor or restrain trade. See also BAD FAITH.

good merchantable quality and condition. A phrase used in sales contracts, meaning that the goods to be supplied must be up to ordinary acceptable standards of quality, and in their customary sound state.

goods. 1. In law, any movable personal property, but not including livestock, and not including such intangible property as leases, etc. See also GOODS AND CHATTELS.

2. A term for textile products or fabrics which are still in the form of cloth, not made up into finished products, such as garments. The term is frequently used as *dry goods*.

3. In business in general, any manufactured or processed items; any merchandise or commodities handled in commerce. *Goods* are classified in several different ways in usage and in industrial statistics, the principal ones being listed and defined below.

capital ~. The equipment, machinery, etc., which is used in the production of other *goods*, or in providing a service, such as transportation or electricity. See also CAPITAL, FIXED.

consumers' ~. Those commodities and finished products which are bought and consumed or used by the general public, rather than by industry. They may be either DURABLE, NON-DURABLE, or SEMI-DURABLE GOODS, which see below.

convenience ~. Those CONSUMERS' GOODS, which see above, which are usually purchased at frequent intervals, and are relatively standard in nature, so that they are purchased at the most convenient source, with a minimum of shopping. Examples include newspapers, tobacco products, drug products, many grocery items, etc. See also IMPULSE GOODS; SHOPPING GOODS, below.

durable ~. Those products which are not normally consumed in use, and which are not further processed by their purchasers. Products with a relatively long useful life. Sometimes, a life of three years is considered to be the dividing line between *durable goods* and SEMI-DURABLE GOODS, which see below. They may be CONSUMERS' GOODS, which see above, such as appliances, furniture, etc., or PRODUCERS' GOODS, which see below, such as machinery and equipment.

fungible ~. In general, any product or commodity in which every unit is similar to every other or identical. Commodities made up of uniform, intermixed units, such as wheat, coffee, etc.

hard ~. In general, DURABLE GOODS, which see above. As used, however, the term usually refers specifically to consumers' durable *goods,* as distinguished from SOFT GOODS, which see below.

impulse ~. Those CONSUMERS' GOODS, which see above, which a person will usually buy only if they are on display and available, rather than as the result of a definite intention to purchase. The term is relative, so that many items of CONVENIENCE GOODS, which see above, are also considered to be

impulse goods. Examples include magazines, confections, beverages, etc.

industrial ~. See PRODUCERS' GOODS, below.

non-durable ~. Those products or commodities which are normally consumed in use, or which are further processed by purchasers. Products with a relatively short useful life. Sometimes, a life of six months is used as the dividing line between *non-durable goods* and SEMI-DURABLE GOODS, which see below. They may be CONSUMERS' GOODS, which see above, such as food, tobacco, etc., or PRODUCERS' GOODS, which see below, such as fuel, chemicals, etc.

producers' ~. Those products and commodities which are bought and consumed or used by industry, rather than by the general public. They may be DURABLE or NON-DURABLE GOODS, which see above, or SEMI-DURABLE GOODS, which see below. Examples include machinery, tools, raw materials, fuels, etc. They are sometimes called *industrial goods.*

semi-durable ~. In general, those products or commodities which are not immediately consumed in use, but which have a short useful life. Sometimes, a life of six months is considered the dividing line between *semi-durable goods* and NON-DURABLE GOODS, which see above, and three years as the dividing line between *semi-durable goods* and DURABLE GOODS, which see above. They may be CONSUMERS' GOODS, which see above, such as clothing, or PRODUCERS' GOODS, which see above, such as hand tools.

shopping ~. Those CONSUMERS' GOODS, which see above, for which a person will make a special shopping effort, rather than purchase at the most convenient source. *Goods* which are bought selectively, on the basis of price, quality, and features, which may differ widely from product to product. Examples include furniture, fashion apparel, automobiles, etc. They are sometimes called *specialty goods.*

soft ~. In general, those CONSUMERS' GOODS, which see above, which are essentially textile products, such as apparel, bedding, draperies, etc., and which are usually SEMI-DURABLE GOODS, which see above, as distinguished from HARD GOODS, which see above.

specialty ~. See SHOPPING GOODS, above.

goods and chattels. In law, all personal property, as distinguished from real property. The addition of the term CHATTELS extends the concept of PROPERTY to include such intangible items as claims, interests, leases, rights, etc.

goods in process. See WORK IN PROCESS.

good this month (week) order. See under ORDER (4).

good title. See under TITLE (2).

good (un)til canceled order. See under ORDER (4).

good will. In general, the benefits to a business arising out of its reputation, continued patronage, favorable location and similar intangible advantages. The value placed upon these intangible advantages in determining the value of the business. Good accounting practice does not permit a value being placed on *good will* in the preparation of financial statements, but it is frequently taken into account in determining a fair sale price for a going business. See also VALUE, PURCHASE.

go short. See SHORT (3).

go to protest. See PROTEST.

gouge. In business slang, to take an excessive profit, such as by overcharging or defrauding.

go under. To fail in business, to go bankrupt; to close down operations due to continued losses.

government. As an adjective, a term referring to the national or federal *government*. The terms MUNICIPAL, PUBLIC, STATE, etc., are usually used to refer to other than the national *government*. See each of the following under the principal listing: ∼ BOND (1); ∼ CORPORATION; ∼ DEPOSITORY.

government debt. See DEBT, NATIONAL.

grace period. See DAYS OF GRACE.

grade. A degree, position or ranking in a scale, classifying the size, quality, worth, etc., of commodities, merchandise, securities or other items which vary in these characteristics. A class of commodities, merchandise, securities, etc., of similar quality, size, worth or other characteristic. Also, to classify, score or rank the individual members of a group according to a present standard; to divide into *grades*.

graded tax. See under TAX (2).

graduated tax. See under TAX (2).

graft. Personal gain or advantage, especially monetary advantage, received or solicited because of one's peculiar position or influence. The acquisition of money or other things of value, through dishonest or illicit transactions, by one in a position of trust and confidence, especially a public employee or official.

grain. The smallest unit in the English and American systems of weight. In the AVOIRDUPOIS system there are 437.5 *grains* in an OUNCE, while in the TROY and APOTHECARIES'

weights, 480 *grains* equal one ounce. Originally, a *grain* was the weight of one dried *grain* of wheat, taken from the middle of the ear.

grain pit. The colloquial term for the place in the Chicago Board of Trade building where commodities brokers meet to transact business in the buying and selling of wheat and other grains. See also PIT.

gram. The basic unit of weight in the METRIC SYSTEM, now established as $\frac{1}{1000}$ of the standard kilogram. It was originally set as the weight of one cubic centimeter of pure water at its greatest density, or 4° centigrade. One *gram* is the equivalent of 15.432 GRAINS, or 0.03527 OUNCES, avoirdupois. See also METRIC SYSTEM.

grand. 1. As used in law, major; more important; as distinguished from PETIT (or PETTY). See, for example, LARCENY, GRAND; JURY, GRAND.

2. In slang, one thousand dollars.

grandfather clause. Broadly, any clause or condition which ties current or direct rights or privileges to previous or remote conditions or acts. For example, that portion of the Public Utility Holding Company Act of 1935 directed against companies having subsidiaries which themselves have subsidiaries was popularly known as the *grandfather clause*. Originally, the term applied to those clauses in the constitutions of several Southern states severely limiting the right to vote, but exempting those persons who had served in the armed forces of the United States or the Confederacy or their descendants. The general effect of such clauses was to deny the vote to the Negro population of these states.

grand jury. See JURY.

grand larceny. See LARCENY.

grant. To transfer real property by written DEED; to bestow, by a formal act. Also the transfer or bestowal itself. See also LAND GRANT.

grantee. One to whom a GRANT has been made; one who has received real property as the result of a transfer made in writing; the recipient of anything requiring a written evidence of title.

grant-in-aid. A sum of money given by a governmental unit or institution to another unit, institution or person, designated for a specified purpose, such as for roads or education, or for general use.

grantor. A party or person who makes a GRANT; one who transfers property or title to another by means of a written deed.

gratis. Literally, in Latin, as a favor. Hence,

free, without charge, without reward or compensation.

gratuitous. Freely given, without charge or compensation. Also, unsolicited or uncalled for, and hence unjustified. *Gratuitous* coinage is the free coinage of metal at government mints without charge. See also FREE COINAGE.

gratuitous contract. See under CONTRACT.

gratuitous deposit. See under DEPOSIT.

gratuity. A gift, usually of money, for a service rendered; a TIP.

graveyard shift. In a plant or other facility which operates on a 24-hour day basis, the workshift usually beginning at midnight and running until 8 a.m. It is sometimes known as the lobster shift.

gray market. The sale and purchase of scarce goods or commodities through practices which are non-standard and unethical, though technically legal, such as the payment of premium prices, the joint sale of wanted and unwanted items, etc. A *gray market* transaction is one which is a shade less illegal than one on the traditional BLACK MARKET.

great gross. Twelve GROSS, or 144 dozens.

greenback. The former United States paper money, issued originally during the Civil War, and so called because the back was printed in green ink. The *greenbacks* were later made redeemable in gold, and the last of them were recalled in 1934.

grievance. Anything which causes an employee or employer to be dissatisfied with some aspect of working conditions, wages, etc. Also, the complaint filed as a result of such dissatisfaction. Most union contracts contain clauses specifying the procedures to be used for handling *grievances*.

gross. 1. A measure of quantity, including twelve dozen, or 144.

2. To gain, to profit; to receive in total income, as, for example, to *gross* five hundred dollars per week.

3. Entire, whole, complete; before any deductions or allowances; great. See each of the following under the principal listing: ~ CHARTER; ~ EARNINGS; ~ INCOME; ~ NEGLIGENCE; ~ PREMIUM (2); ~ PROFIT; ~ RECEIPTS; ~ SALES; ~ TON; ~ TONNAGE.

gross margin. The difference between the total costs of goods sold and the net sales income of a retail or wholesale business, either in dollars and cents or figured as a percentage of net sales. For example, if a merchant pays $6,000 for goods over a period of time,

and sells them, after returns and allowances, for $10,000, his *gross margin* is $4,000, or 40 percent of net sales. The *gross margin* differs from the MARKUP in that it is the realized percentage of gain, while the latter is the intended percentage of gain.

gross national product. As defined by the Department of Commerce, the total market value of the goods and services produced by the nation's economy, before deduction of depreciation charges and other allowances for capital consumption. It includes the total purchases of goods and services by private consumers and government, gross private domestic capital investment, and net foreign investment. The *gross national product,* or G.N.P., is a widely used barometer of general business and economic activity.

gross profit ratio. See OPERATING RATIO.

gross weight. 1. Of packaged goods, the total weight, including contents and packaging material. The NET WEIGHT plus TARE and TRET.

2. Of a vehicle, the total loaded weight, including the vehicle weight and the weight of the load carried.

gross working capital. See CAPITAL (2) CIRCULATING.

groundage. A charge made in some ports for allowing a vessel to anchor.

ground rent. See under RENT (2).

grounds. In law, the basis or foundation for an ACTION or SUIT.

group banking. See under BANKING.

group insurance. See under INSURANCE, LIFE, ACCIDENT, AND HEALTH.

group rate. See under FREIGHT RATE.

growth curve. See OGIVE.

growth fund. See INVESTMENT COMPANY, MUTUAL FUND.

growth stock. See under STOCK (1).

grub stake. A contract or agreement under which one person provides provisions, tools, supplies, etc., to another, who prospects for and files claim to mineral bearing lands. The agreement usually provides that any benefits are to be shared, equally or otherwise, so that it represents, in fact, a form of special PARTNERSHIP.

guarantee. Strictly, to give a GUARANTY; infrequently, the one to whom a guaranty is given. Also, loosely, the guaranty itself.

guaranteed annual wage. See ANNUAL WAGE PLAN.

guaranteed bond. See under BOND (1).

guaranteed stock. See under STOCK (1).

guarantor. The person who binds himself by a

GUARANTY; the one who makes or gives the guaranty.

guaranty. An undertaking or contract to assume the liability for a debt, to perform a duty upon the default of another, or in general to give assurance that a thing will be done, or an obligation filled, as promised. As used in business, it is usually a promise that an item of equipment, machinery or goods will perform as claimed, contains the stated ingredients, or will last a stated period of time. Strictly speaking, a *guaranty* differs from a WARRANTY in that the latter is an absolute undertaking or assurance, and failure to perform may void the basic contract, while the former provides merely that the guarantor will be liable for the failure to perform.

guaranty bond. See under BOND (2).

guaranty company. An organization which, for a fee, provides the deposit or surety required on judicial bonds, fidelity bonds, etc. See also BOND (2); SURETY.

guardian. A person charged with the duty of caring for and managing the estate of a child, mental incompetent, etc. One appointed to care for the property of another; a TRUSTEE. See also WARD.

guardian's bond. See under BOND (2).

guild. An association of persons in the same trade, profession or business, aiming, by cooperation and regulation to promote their common interests. Originally, in England, the *guilds* were powerful groups, and played an important part in government. Currently, *guilds* are merely one particular type of trade, professional, or labor association.

H

habeas corpus. Literally, in Latin, you have
the body. The legal writ calling upon an
authority holding a person in custody to
produce that person before the court granting the writ. It is usually issued for the
purpose of ordering the release of a person
held pending indictment. The words by
which it is known are the opening words
of the original Latin legal text.

haggle. Originally a Scottish term, meaning
to cut or hack away. In current usage, it
means to argue or bargain over the terms
of a transaction.

hail insurance. See INSURANCE, PROPERTY.

half-dollar. The United States fifty-cent coin.
It is composed of 9 parts of silver to one
part copper, and weighs 12.5 grams.

half-eagle. A gold coin, valued at five dollars,
which formerly circulated in the United
States. See also EAGLE.

half-life. The period of time required for one
half of the contained radio-isotope in a
radioactive material to decay to a stable
form of the element. The *half-life* is the
usual method for measuring the relative
activity of radioactive materials.

half-section. See SECTION.

half service. A term used in advertising, especially in transportation advertising, meaning that the advertisement will be displayed
in one half of the available exposure locations, such as one half the cars or buses of
a particular transit line. A half-run. See also
FULL SERVICE; QUARTER SERVICE.

hall-mark. Traditionally, the official mark
stamped into articles made of gold or silver
at Goldsmiths' Hall in London, to attest
to the purity of the metal contained. Thus,
any mark of quality, or of claimed quality.

hand. 1. A measure of extension, traditionally
a hand's-breadth, equal to four inches. It
is currently used in measuring the height
of horses and some other animals, but for
practically no other purposes. A horse which
stands 15 *hands* at the shoulders, for example, is 60 inches or 5 feet high at that
point.

2. In textiles, the feel of a fabric. It is
an indefinite term, involving the resilience,
flexibility, weight, compressibility, etc., of
the fabric.

3. A term for a tied bundle of tobacco
or other leaf crop.

handbill. In advertising, a term for a small
printed announcement, designed to be delivered by hand. It is also known as a
DODGER, CIRCULAR, or FLIER (2).

handbook. Any manual, such as an instruction
book; a reference book or guidebook.

handle. In business usage, to trade in a commodity or class of merchandise. To buy and
sell, or transport, or distribute a commodity.
Also, to manage, or control; to direct activities.

hand money. See EARNEST.

handsel. See EARNEST.

hand-to-mouth. A term usually meaning
closely, with little or nothing to spare. For
example, a business that buys *hand-to-mouth*
buys only for its current needs, not for
future requirements.

harbor dues. Port charges, such as the fees
paid for the use of port or anchorage facilities; the GROUNDAGE.

hard cash. In popular usage, actual money,
either paper or coin, as distinguished from
credit or non-monetary property. Thus, one
who pays *hard cash* pays in full in money,
rather than on credit terms or in kind.

hard goods. See under GOODS (3).

hard money. See under MONEY.

hardness. See BRINELL HARDNESS; ROCKWELL
HARDNESS.

hard water. Water containing an excessive
amount of calcium or magnesium hydrox-
ides, and which therefore forms a hard
curd with soap, instead of lathering. In an
area in which the water supply is naturally
hard, most householders use either chemical
water-softeners, or wash with special syn-
thetic non-soap detergents.

hardwood. In general, any close-grained, dense
wood, specially suitable for furniture. Spe-

cifically, in forestry, the wood of any of the broad-leafed or deciduous, i.e. leaf-dropping trees, as distinguished from the evergreens.

harmonic mean. See under AVERAGE (1).

Harter Act. An act of Congress, passed in 1893, which provides that owners of vessels may not evade their responsibility for proper loading, equipment, supplies, and seaworthiness of their ships by any agreement with shippers; and that if a vessel is properly seaworthy, etc., the owners cannot be held liable for errors of navigation, dangers of the sea, acts of God, or any act or omission of the shipper.

hawker. One who goes about, in the public streets, offering goods for sale and attracting attention by crying out his wares; a PEDDLER. It is said that the name is based on the similarity of the *hawker's* hoarse cry to that of the hawk, while other authorities state that the original *hawkers* were peddlers of falcons.

hazard. In insurance any danger or dangerous condition which is associated with or surrounds the thing insured (the RISK), and which is likely to cause a loss. In general, *hazards* are grouped in three classes; physical *hazards*, such as construction, environment, manner of occupancy, fire prevention or protection, etc.; inherent *hazards,* or those naturally associated with the business or its methods of operation, such as the danger of dust explosion in a flour mill, or of fire in a sawmill; and moral *hazards,* such as those arising out of neglect, careless operation, or deliberate lack of precautionary measures. The insurance contract should define the particular *hazards* against which the risk is insured, and those which are not covered.

head money. See TAX (2), CAPITATION.

head of family. Generally, a person who maintains a family unit. He may not necessarily be a father or husband, but is any person who is responsible for at least one other person in his or her household. For example, a widow with children, or a bachelor supporting his parents, would each be a *head of family*. Under various state and federal laws and tax regulations, which may contain specific, limited definitions of the term, a *head of family* is entitled to various benefits and special considerations.

health insurance. See under INSURANCE, LIFE, ACCIDENT, AND HEALTH.

heaped bushel. See under BUSHEL.

hearsay. In law, evidence which is not first-hand, but which depends on the veracity of another, who is not under oath. Any testimony not based on actual experience, but on what one was told. Such evidence or testimony is ordinarily inadmissible in a court of law.

heavy market. In the securities and commodities trade, a term used to describe the condition in which supply exceeds demand, or outweighs it, so that prices decline.

hecto-. In the metric system, the prefix used for any measure which is equal to 100 times a basic measure; such as, for example, a hectoliter, hectogram, hectostere, hectare, etc.

hedge. 1. In the trading of commodities, or in similar activities, to take steps to offset a possible loss due to price changes by entering into a contract in the opposite direction. For example, a company buying sugar on long term contracts for use in production, may protect itself against possible lower sugar prices during the term of the contract by selling sugar on the FUTURES market. Then, if the price becomes lower, the profit on covering the future sale will offset the loss taken due to the long-term fixed purchase price. Similarly, the sugar seller, who has set a long-term price, may protect himself against a subsequent rise in prices by buying in the futures market. Then, if prices rise, he will profit by taking delivery of low-price sugar to offset the lost profits on his long-term sale.

2. In general, any action taken to offset or reduce a possible loss, such as the purchase of a security which is likely to rise under certain conditions, after buying one which is likely to fall in price under the same conditions.

hedge clause. A clause frequently inserted in the agreement for the underwriting of a new issue of securities, which gives to the UNDERWRITERS or to the issuing corporation the power to terminate the agreement at any time before the date of the public offering, or the delivery date, under certain conditions. Typical of these conditions are depressed prices for securities in general, or political, economic, or other conditions which are such that it would be inadvisable to proceed with a public offering of securities at the scheduled time.

heir. Any person who, by right of blood or by action of law, succeeds to or acquires all or part of the ESTATE of a deceased person.

    ~ **apparent.** An *heir* whose right of inheritance is secure, provided he outlives his ancestor; for example, a first-born son.

    ~ **at law.** An *heir* who is designated by

law to inherit, when a person has died intestate. For example, many state laws provide that widows and children have first claim on such estates, and are thus *heirs at law*.

~ **presumptive.** An *heir* who will inherit if the ancestor should die currently, but whose rights are not assured. For example, a brother or nephew, whose rights would be extinguished if a child should be born, is an *heir presumptive* to a childless person.

hereditament. In law, the term for any property which passes from a person to his heirs by DEVISE. Thus, it includes both land, and any rights or interest in land, such as leases, rents, etc. Personal property, strictly, passes from a person to his heirs as an INHERITANCE.

hidden asset. See under ASSET (2).

hidden tax. See under TAX (2).

high. In securities trading, the highest price paid for a security during a specified period; such as the daily *high,* weekly *high,* etc. See also CLOSE (4); LOW.

high finance. Any large scale financial operations or transactions; complicated financial dealings. In popular usage, a term describing a scheme involving large scale speculation, which will presumably produce extraordinarily large profits. Frequently the usage implies essentially unsound and even dishonest practices.

high grade. A term used with regard to securities and other investments, meaning of superior investment quality, with little or no risk attached, and a relatively assured income; a GILT-EDGE investment. It is the opposite of LOW GRADE.

highjacker. See HIJACKER.

high pressure. A term for any tactics making use of urgent, intense, energetic, or strongly persuasive methods. Examples include *high pressure* selling, *high pressure* advertising, etc.

high seas. In maritime law and contracts, the oceans beyond low water level. In general, international law governs all occurrences on the *high seas,* except that each country bordering on the ocean has exclusive jurisdiction, recognized by other countries, over the three miles of sea extending outward from the low water mark. Lakes and landlocked water in general are excluded from the term.

hijacker (or highjacker). In American slang, originally an armed thief who preyed on smugglers, bootleggers, etc. Hence, any thief who steals goods which have already been illegally come by, such as one who steals a truckload of stolen cargo from the original thief. More loosely, the term has come to be applied to any thief who steals goods in transit, especially in large quantities, regardless of whether the goods themselves are stolen goods.

hire. To purchase the temporary use of a thing, or to arrange for the labor or services of another at a stipulated rate. Also, the compensation paid for the thing or the labor temporarily engaged.

hiring hall. A form of EMPLOYMENT AGENCY, usually operated by a union, by an employers' association, by a public body, or jointly by a union and the employers in a field. Such joint *hiring halls* were used, for example, to provide new employees under CLOSED SHOP or PREFERENTIAL SHOP contracts. *Hiring halls* are still used in the maritime trades, and in such specialized fields as music, printing, etc.

histogram. In statistics, a graphic representation of a FREQUENCY DISTRIBUTION, in which the number of items in each class is represented by a bar or rectangle erected on the base, the width of the CLASS INTERVAL, and with a height proportional to the number of items falling in the class. As the number of class intervals is increased toward infinity, and the width of each bar accordingly narrowed, the *histogram* approaches the smooth frequency curve.

hoard. To collect or amass, and lay up or conceal, usually in secret, and simply for the sake of accumulating. To accumulate supplies of scarce or critical items in times of shortage, to such an extent that others are deprived of their rightful share. For example, during periods of war or other national emergency, it is common for some consumers to lay up or *hoard* excessive supplies of sugar and other imported staples.

hogshead. In general, any large cask or barrel. Specifically, a measure of liquid volume, equal to one fourth of a TUN, or two BARRELS, and containing 63 gallons. It is now seldom used, except to measure wine.

hold. In legal usage, to possess, especially by virtue of having legal title. As generally used, it is synonymous with OWN, so that one who *holds* stock is an owner of the stock.

holder. 1. In general, an owner; one who possesses with legal title.

~ **for value.** One who has given a valid CONSIDERATION for the thing he possesses.

2. As defined in the Uniform Commercial Code, one who possesses or holds for collection any negotiable instrument, such as a check, note, etc. One who holds an instru-

ment drawn, issued, or endorsed to him or to his order, or to bearer.

~ **in due course.** Any person who holds a negotiable instrument which he has accepted in good faith, on the assurance that it was regularly drawn, not overdue or dishonored, and with no defect in ownership on the part of the previous *holder* or endorser.

hold-harmless. An agreement, clause, or contract provision, stating that one party agrees to hold the other harmless, or without responsibility, for any injury, damage, loss, or other liability arising out of activities under the contract, regardless of the degree of actual responsibility or negligence involved. Such agreements, when broadly drawn, have been held not to be valid in the face of gross negligence on the part of the one *held harmless*. They are sometimes known as *save-harmless* agreements when these words are used in the text.

holding company. See under COMPANY.

holiday. In law, a day designated by statute for the whole or partial suspension of business, court activities, financial transactions, etc. In the United States, legal *holidays* are set by state legislatures, though Congress has set the official date on which Thanksgiving is to be observed. The following are now legal *holidays* in all states:
New Year's Day; January 1.
Washington's Birthday; February 22.
Independence Day; July 4.
Labor Day; first Monday in September.
Thanksgiving; fourth Thursday in November.
Christmas; December 25.

In addition, Election Day, Decoration Day, Lincoln's Birthday and Columbus Day are legal *holidays* in many states.

holograph. Any instrument or legal document, such as a will, deed, or grant, written entirely by the testator or grantor in his own hand. Such a document is recognized as valid without witnesses if it is otherwise properly drawn.

holographic will. See under WILL.

home office. The main, central or principal office of a business or other organization which maintains branch or subsidiary offices. The office located in the state in which the organization is chartered.

homeowners' insurance. See under INSURANCE, PROPERTY.

home port. Specifically, as defined by the United States Customs Bureau, the port in which the permanent registry document of a vessel is issued, and where subsequent sales, conveyances, mortgages, etc., of the vessel are recorded. For a private vessel which is not registered, it is the port in which it is permanently berthed, or in which the master or owner resides.

homestead. In general, the house and its adjoining land, belonging to a private homeowner. As used in various state laws, it is the minimum land and home which are exempted from forced sale to satisfy creditors. See also HOMESTEAD EXEMPTION LAW.

homestead exemption law. A statute, varying from state to state, but generally providing that a man's HOMESTEAD, that is, his house and surrounding land, is not included in his general estate for purposes of any forced sale to satisfy creditors, as long as the house is owner-occupied.

home store. See PARENT STORE.

homework. Any work done for an employer in the home of the worker. Such work is severely restricted or prohibited under present wage and hour legislation. See also SWEATSHOP.

honor. In general, to meet a claim or obligation when due. Specifically, to accept or pay an instrument of indebtedness, such as a note, check, or bill, under the terms and conditions prescribed. Hence, one who agrees to *honor* a note, or especially to *honor* another's signature on a note, agrees to pay the note as called for. See also DISHONOR; ACCEPTANCE FOR HONOR.

honorarium. In general a free gift or gratuitous payment, as distinguished from a payment for hire or compensation. In business usage, a term for a payment to a lawyer or other professional person for services rendered, particularly those for whom there is no fixed or established FEE.

Hooper rating. A measure of the audience for a particular radio or television program, as devised by C. E. Hooper.

horizontal. In business usage, consisting of two or more units which are at the same level of production or distribution, or are of similar type. Operating across a field or industry, rather than from top to bottom or from elementary to final stages; the opposite of VERTICAL. See each of the following under the principal listing: ~ AGREEMENT IN RESTRAINT OF TRADE; ~ INTEGRATION; ~ UNION.

horsepower. The standard unit for the measurement of power. It is the power or force required to lift 33,000 pounds one foot in one minute; expressed as 33,000 foot-pound per minute, or 550 FOOT-POUNDS per second. In comparing the claimed *horsepower* of two or more power units, it is important to note whether the rating is with or without accessory equipment in operation, direct or after passing through gears, etc.

hospitalization insurance. See under INSURANCE, LIFE, ACCIDENT, AND HEALTH.

house. In business slang, a firm or company, especially one engaged in mercantile or non-manufacturing activities, such as a *brokerage house, wholesale house, mail-order house,* etc.

household. In general, a family living together, or the place they occupy. As defined by the Bureau of the Census, it consists of the persons who occupy a single house, apartment, room, or other dwelling unit. Thus, an individual living alone, or an unrelated group of persons occupying a common dwelling unit, are considered *households* for census and statistical purposes.

house organ. The general term for one of a class of publications in the form of newspapers or magazines, issued by a business organization to further its own interests. It is also variously known as an employee publication, company magazine, etc. *House organs* are of two broad types: internal publications intended primarily for employees, and external publications intended for dealers, customers, stockholders, and other non-employee groups.

house-to-house selling. A method of selling at retail by calling directly on customers and prospective customers in their homes; door-to-door selling; CANVASSING. Companies which engage in this form of selling frequently describe themselves as DIRECT SELLING companies.

housing cooperative. See under COOPERATIVE.

huckster. In general, a petty retailer or peddler; one who will turn his hand to anything mercenary or profit-making. In business slang, one engaged in advertising or sales promotion work. The term is believed to be derived from HAWKER, or one who cries his wares.

hundredweight. A unit of weight defined as one-twentieth part of a TON. Hence, a *gross* or *long hundredweight* contains 112 pounds avoirdupois, and a *net,* or *short hundredweight* contains 100 pounds. It is roughly the equivalent of the European centner, or metric *hundredweight,* which contains 50 kilograms, or 110.23 pounds. It is sometimes called a cental or quintal.

hush money. In slang, money paid to assure the silence of the receiver; hence, a bribe.

hypothecation. A form or method of providing security or COLLATERAL for a loan, under which property is offered as collateral for the debt, but the lender is given neither title nor possession, but merely the right to order the property sold upon default, to satisfy his claim. It differs from a MORTGAGE, in that full title to the property remains with the borrower, and from a PLEDGE or PAWN in that the property is not actually deposited. A vessel may be *hypothecated,* for example, and yet used freely and profitably by the owner. Except for the physical deposit of the property with the lender, *hypothecation* is essentially a form of pledge, and has been held to be so by the courts.

I

I.C.C. See INTERSTATE COMMERCE COMMISSION.

identification mark. A mark, such as one used on imported goods, which identifies the shipper, or which serves to identify the country of origin.

ides. In the Roman calendar, the middle day of each month. It is the eighth day after the NONES, or the fifteenth day of March, May, July, and October, and the thirteenth day of other months. See also CALENDS

idle. Unused, unoccupied, unproductive, or unemployed. Examples include *idle* capital, *idle* capacity, or an *idle* worker.

idle time. See DEAD TIME.

if issued. See WHEN ISSUED.

illegal. Not legal; unlawful; contrary to or not permitted by law. See each of the following under the principal listing: ~ CONSIDERATION; ~ CONTRACT (1); ~ INTEREST (2); ~ PARTNERSHIP; ~ SALE (1); ~ STRIKE.

illicit. Literally, not permitted. Thus, prohibited; not allowed by law or custom; unlawful; such as, *illicit* trade, or an *illicit* relationship.

immediate. 1. At once, without delay; not deferred by an interval of time. It has been held by courts, however, that the term does not literally mean instantly, but that a reasonable period of time may elapse between one act and an *immediately* following act. See also ORDER (4), IMMEDIATE; ANNUITY, IMMEDIATE.

2. Not separated by any intervening object, cause, relation, claim, or right. See, for example, CAUSE, IMMEDIATE.

immigration. The act of coming into a country from another country, for the purpose and with the intention of establishing a permanent residence. See also EMIGRATION.

immovable. In law, any item of real property that cannot be moved, such as land, buildings, structures, trees, etc.

impair. To affect in an injurious manner; to make less useful; to diminish in quantity or value. For example, a law which by its terms materially changes or nullifies an otherwise proper contract is said to *impair* the contract. Article I of the Constitution provides that no state may pass such a law.

impairment. In a business sense, a weakening or lessening. For example, an *impairment* of capital is a reduction of capital through losses, distribution of dividends, etc. An *impairment* of credit is anything which results in a weakening of a company's credit position, or of its ability to pay its debts.

impartial chairman. In labor relations, a person who is chosen jointly by a union and the employers in an industry or trade, to perform such duties as the administration of collective bargaining agreements, the supervision of arbitration proceedings, and to act as mediator and chairman of contract negotiation meetings. The person chosen is usually someone who is outside the industry, with no interests on either side, but who by experience and ability can assist both sides in the day-to-day problems that arise out of collective bargaining.

imperial measure. The measures of volume, including the imperial PINT, QUART, GALLON, etc., used in the British Empire for both liquid and dry measure. In liquid measure, the imperial volumes are approximately 1.201 times the comparable American volumes.

imperial octavo. See under BOOK SIZES.

imperial ton. See TON.

implead. In law, to bring suit against more than one party; to add parties as defendents to an action.

implied. That which is not stated directly or expressly, but which may reasonably be inferred, or which follows as a necessary consequence from the conduct, actions, statements, and circumstances surrounding an event. See each of the following under the principal listing: ~ ACCEPTANCE (1); ~ CONTRACT; ~ PARTNERSHIP; ~ TRUST; ~ WARRANTY. See also EXPRESS.

import. To bring goods or merchandise into a country or state from another country, either in the course of trade, or as an individual act. Also, the item itself so brought into the country. See also EXPORT. See each of the following under the principal listing: ~ BROKER (1); ~ CREDIT (3); ~ LETTER OF CREDIT; ~ QUOTA.

import duty. See DUTY; TARIFF.

import gold point. See GOLD POINT.

import license. A license or permit, issued to an importer by an authorized government agency, permitting him to bring into the country certain specified amounts of specified merchandise, the importation of which would be otherwise barred or limited.

import rate. A FREIGHT RATE, such as for rail shipment, which applies specifically to imported goods. Such a rate may be set, for example, to encourage importers to use the port served by a particular railroad.

imports. The total or aggregate of all goods and merchandise brought into a country from other countries. As used, the term includes only those goods imported in the course of regular commercial trade.

general ~. In government statistics, the total *imports* for immediate use, on which duties are paid, plus those placed in bonded warehouses, on which the payment of duties is deferred. It is distinguished from IMPORTS FOR CONSUMPTION, which see below.

~ for consumption. In government statistics, the total of all *imports,* less those placed in bonded warehouses, plus withdrawals from bonded warehouses during the same period of imported goods on which duties are to be paid.

imposition. An enforceable tax or demand levied against goods, property, or activities by a competent taxing authority. Examples include TARIFFS and TOLLS.

impossible consideration. See under CONSIDERATION.

impossible contract. See under CONTRACT (1).

impost. A tax on imported items. See TARIFF.

impound. To seize and hold, or to place in legal custody, usually at the order of a court or law enforcement agency. Examples include *impounded* cash, *impounded* documents or records, *impounded* property, etc.

imprest fund. See under FUND (2).

imprimatur. Literally, from the Latin, let it be printed. The license or permission granted by the proper authority, giving permission to print and publish a book. Such permission is still required in some countries.

improved. With respect to urban property, land upon which a residence or business structure has been erected; as distinguished from UNIMPROVED property, which has not been built upon. With respect to agricultural land, *improved* property may be that which has been cultivated, or cleared for grazing, as distinguished from unimproved land, which is in its natural state.

improvement. 1. Any change made in property or in an aggregation of property whereby it is made more useful, or useful for other purposes, or more efficient, or in general of greater value. It is not merely a REPAIR or MAINTENANCE item. *Improvements* to property may include such things as the paving of a street, the erection of partitions in a store, the installation of lighting in a warehouse, etc. In insurance usage, *improvements* and BETTERMENTS are used synonymously.

2. In patent law, an addition of some useful thing or part to an invention, machine, device, article, or composition. An *improvement* patent may be obtained for such an addition, though the patent on the basic device may have expired.

improvement mortgage. See under MORTGAGE.

improvement mortgage bond. See under BOND (1).

improvements and betterments insurance. See under INSURANCE, PROPERTY.

impulse buying. Purchasing done by consumers of goods which are found on sale or on display, rather than of goods for which the particular shopping trip was planned, or goods for which a purchaser would have to ask. Impulse goods are goods or merchandise so purchased, as distinguished from shopping goods. See also GOODS (3), IMPULSE; GOODS (3), SHOPPING.

impulse goods. See under GOODS (3).

imputed. That which is ascribed, or assigned to a source. That which is attributed to a source, and estimated in amount.

~ cost. A derived or estimated cost, based on something other than actual cost records, such as may be assigned to an asset or expense item.

~ income. The value assigned to services or benefits which arise from the ownership of consumers' durable goods. The most common example is the estimated equivalent rental income which could be obtained from an owner-occupied dwelling.

~ interest. The estimated interest which is attributed to the capital invested in a business. See also under INTEREST.

~ negligence. Negligence charged to a person though it is not directly attributable to him, but to a person with whose fault he is chargeable.

~ notice. Notice which is held to have been given, though the actual notice was given to a person whose duty it was to repeat it to the person affected, as for example, his agent or attorney.

inactive account. See under ACCOUNT (3).

inactive market. A condition in the securities or commodities market in which relatively little trading occurs, as distinguished from an ACTIVE MARKET, which is characterized by frequent trading transactions. See also BROAD MARKET; NARROW MARKET.

inactive securities. See under SECURITY (1).

inactive stock. See under STOCK (1).

in and out. In securities trade slang, a term used to describe the actions of a speculator or trader who buys and then sells (or sells short and then buys) a security almost immediately, or in a very short interval. A trader who operates on this basis is said to be *in and out* of the market.

in ballast. A term descriptive of a vessel which leaves port with little or no cargo, and thus with BALLAST as her only load. A freight ship which has just unloaded its cargo at one port will often sail to a nearby port *in ballast* to pick up a new cargo.

in blank endorsement. See under ENDORSEMENT.

in bond. A term describing the situation in which goods are held under bond in a warehouse until they are released by the payment of import TARIFFS, excise taxes, or other charges. Under some circumstances, the goods may be processed while *in bond,* and released in a more finished form than that in which they were bonded. Alcoholic beverages, for example, may be bottled *in bond,* implying that they were placed under bond while in the cask, then held *in bond* after being bottled on the bonded premises. See also BONDED; WAREHOUSE, BONDED.

in bond price. A price quoted on goods held *in bond,* which does not include the tariff or tax which will have to be paid when the goods are released. The buyer assumes the cost of paying these charges when he buys at the *in bond price.*

in case of need. The term for a form of ENDORSEMENT used on a BILL OF EXCHANGE or other negotiable instrument, indicating that the person named will make payment on the bill if it is not met on maturity by the drawee, or named payer. The usual form of the endorsement is *"In case of need,* apply to A. (Signed, B)," meaning that if the bill is not paid, A has agreed to make payment for the HONOR of B, who is the original drawer of the bill, or perhaps an earlier endorser. The French expression *au*

besoin is sometimes used for this endorsement.

incentive. Anything which stimulates or incites to action or to greater effort; a motivating force.

    financial ~. An *incentive* offered to an employee or other person, in the form of money.

    ~ contract. A compromise between a COST-PLUS and a LUMP SUM contract basis, under which the contractor shares with the purchaser any savings which are brought about by the reduction of costs. See also CONTRACT.

    ~ system. Any method of paying wages, salaries, sales commissions, etc., under which the amount paid increases with the volume of production. There are almost an infinite variety of such systems, some based directly on the number of units produced, some based on the ratio of production to a standard, some based on a bonus for production over quota, etc.

    non-financial ~. An *incentive* in the form of welfare benefits, greater prestige, or other awards not in the form of money. Such *incentives* may be offered, for example, to a highly paid executive whose income tax rate is already so high that a direct monetary payment would add little to his net income.

inch. In linear measure, the twelfth part of a FOOT. It derives from the same Latin source as does OUNCE, which originally meant the twelfth part of a pound. In relation to the metric system, one *inch* equals 2.54 centimeters.

Inchmaree clause. A clause inserted in marine insurance policies following the litigation over the *S. S. Inchmaree.* The clause provides for payment in the event of loss or damage to the hull or machinery through the negligence of the master, crew or pilots, or through explosion, bursting of boilers, breakage of shafts, or through any latent defect in the machinery or hull, provided that such loss or damage has not resulted from lack of diligence by the owners or managers themselves. See also INSURANCE, MARINE.

inchoate. Newly begun or incomplete; unfinished or imperfect. For example, an *inchoate* contract is one which hasn't been executed by all those who are parties to it, and an *inchoate* instrument may be one not yet recorded or registered, if this action is called for.

incidence of taxation. The place, location, or stage of operations on which the effect of a tax falls. For example, if the net result of a manufacturers' EXCISE TAX is to raise the prices of the goods manufactured, the *incidence* of the tax is said to be on the purchase of the goods, or on the purchaser. See also TAX; TAXATION.

inclosure. In English law, the act of freeing land from the feudal system of common cultivation. The various *Inclosure Acts* of the late 18th and early 19th centuries put an end to the feudal system of land tenure in England, and resulted in a wholesale flight from the land to the towns, incidentally creating a labor force for the new textile and other factories.

income. In general, an increase in wealth or resources, measured in terms of money, which arises from the application of capital or of personal service, or both. It is usually measured in terms of the increase received or accruing over a given period of time. When modified in any of the ways listed below, the term may take on a specialized meaning. See also EARNINGS; PROFIT; REVENUE.

  accrued ∼. That *income* which is earned during a particular accounting period, such as sales commissions, interest, rent, etc., but which is not received during the same accounting period.

  deferred ∼. *Income* which is received in a given accounting or tax period, but which will actually be earned in a future period. Rents received in advance, payments under service contracts, or advance payments for goods not yet delivered are examples of such *deferred income*. The usual accounting practice is to enter the net total of such items on the balance sheet as liabilities, to balance the increase in cash assets resulting from the payments.

  earned ∼. *Income* derived from one's own efforts or labor, or through active participation in some business or venture, such as salaries, wages, or proprietors' withdrawals; as distinguished from UNEARNED INCOME, which see below, including dividends, rents, etc. In some states, and formerly in federal *income* tax regulations, *earned income* is taxed less heavily than unearned *income*.

  fixed ∼. An *income* the amount of which is fixed definitely and for a long period of time by law, contract, dividend rates, etc. Examples include pensions, long-term salary contracts, dividend *incomes*, etc.

  gross ∼. The total receipts of money by a business from all sources, before any deductions for costs of manufacturing and selling and other expenses. The total sales receipts, or the total of fees and charges collected are examples.

  net ∼. The net earnings or profits remaining to a business after the deduction of all costs of materials, labor, selling, and administrative and other expenses. *Net income* may be net before taxes or net after taxes, depending on whether *income* taxes on the business profits are taken into account.

  non-operating ∼. *Income* of a business which is derived from such sources as investments, the sale of real property, or any other transactions not directly connected with its regular business operations. Sometimes noted on *income* statements as *other income*.

  operating ∼. The profit on sales or other regular operations of a business, not including either profits or losses on investments or other non-operating factors.

  other ∼. See NON-OPERATING INCOME, above.

  unearned ∼. *Income* derived from dividends on investments, rentals on property, or other sources not involving the individual's personal efforts; as distinguished from EARNED INCOME, which see above. In some states, and formerly under federal income tax regulations, *unearned income* is taxed more heavily than earned *income*. Sometimes, in accounting usage, the term is a synonym for DEFERRED INCOME, which see above.

income basis. A method of calculating and reporting the rate of return on a stock or bond, based on the dividend and on the price paid for the security, rather than on its face or par value. For example, a bond paying 6 percent on its face or par value of $100, if bought at a price of $120 will return 5 percent on an *income basis*. See also YIELD; MATURITY BASIS.

income bond. See under BOND (1).

income in kind. See IN KIND.

income statement. A summary statement of the income and expenses of a business over a specified period of time, with an indication of the resulting profit or loss. The American Institute of Accountants has defined an *income statement* as an account or statement which shows the principal elements, positive and negative, in the derivation of income or loss, the claims against income, and the resulting net income or loss of the accounting unit. It is distinguished from a BALANCE SHEET, which reports the assets and liabilities at a given time. *Income statements* are also frequently known as profit and loss statements, earnings statements, operating statements, etc.

income statement account. See ACCOUNT (2), NOMINAL.

income tax. See under TAX (2).

incoming partner. See under PARTNER.

in common. That which is shared in respect to title, use, or enjoyment, without apportionment or division into individual parts; held by several for the equal advantage, use, or enjoyment of all. See, for example, TENANT IN COMMON. See also JOINT.

incontestable policy. See under POLICY (2).

inconvertible money. See under MONEY.

incorporate. 1. To include; to bring together into one body. For example, specific terms may be *incorporated* in an agreement.
2. To form a CORPORATION.

incorporation. The act of forming or creating a corporation; also, infrequently, the corporation itself.

incorporation certificate. See CERTIFICATE OF INCORPORATION.

incorporator. One who joins with others in forming a corporation. One who, with others, signs the articles or certificate of incorporation which a new corporation files with the state authorities.

incorporeal. In general, of no material substance; not physical in nature. In law, existing only as an immaterial creation, with no physical properties. Examples of such *incorporeal* legal creations are rights, interests, privileges, etc.

increment. In general, an increase or addition; a gain. An increase in value, such as of land or other property.

  unearned ∼. An increase in value that is not the result of any deliberate effort by the owner, but is due to some external cause, such as population growth, the advent of a railroad or highway, etc.

incremental cost. See MARGINAL COST.

incroachment. See ENCROACHMENT.

incumbent. The person who is presently in the possession of an office or position; the one legally and properly authorized to perform the duties of an office.

incumbrance. See ENCUMBRANCE.

indebtedness. The state of being in debt; also, the total amount of such debts. See also DEBT.

indemnify. To make a person safe from monetary loss or damage; to assure reimbursement in the event that a specified loss should occur. Also, to make reimbursement after a loss; to make good on a loss. For example, in a property damage insurance contract, the company agrees to *indemnify* the insurance buyer against loss from specified causes.

indemnity. 1. In insurance, an agreement under which one of the parties secures the other against loss from specified events or actions. Also, the payment made to cover a loss under such an agreement. Strictly speaking, an *indemnity* agreement is one providing specifically for payment to make good a loss, rather than for protection against the loss itself, or the replacement of the thing lost or damaged.
2. In law, a special act of a legislature, granting an exemption from prosecution for specified acts to certain persons, such as office holders, who may become involved in such acts in the course of their legitimate duties.

indemnity bond. See under BOND (2).

indent. A form of order, such as one sent abroad for goods to be imported, which is usually prepared in duplicate or triplicate. The name is derived from the old practice of cutting or *indenting* the edges of duplicate documents for identification purposes. A price quotation submitted, or an offer to buy at stated terms, is also referred to as an *indent* when prepared in duplicate or triplicate copies.

indent house. A term for an import agent or firm which imports goods on orders received from domestic buyers.

indenture. 1. In general, any formal document, contract, or agreement involving two or more parties. See also DEED, INDENTURE.
2. A contract of apprenticeship, binding one person to work for another for a fixed period of time.

independent. In business usage, a company or organization not belonging to a chain or to an association of companies. For example, an *independent* radio station is one not belonging to one of the major networks; an *independent* oil producer is one not associated with one of the integrated companies; and an *independent* grocer is one which is not a chain store.

independent audit. See AUDIT.

independent banking. See BANKING, UNIT.

independent contractor. A person who contracts to do a piece of work or perform a service using his own methods, rather than under the control and supervision of the one for whom the work is done. An *independent contractor* is distinguished from an EMPLOYEE principally by the degree of control or supervision exercised by the employer over the method of working and the conduct of the work, rather than merely over the results. For purposes of withholding taxes, unemployment insurance, etc., too great a degree of supervision may cause a contractor to be ruled an employee.

index number. In statistics, a computed measure used to demonstrate and compare relative changes. In business, index numbers are used primarily to measure changes over time, such as in the volume of business activity, the level of prices, etc. Typically, an index number is computed as the ratio between a number of selected quantities or prices in a present period and their level during a particular period in the past, known as the base period. The index is usually expressed as a percentage, with the level of the base period set at 100. See also CONSUMER PRICE INDEX.

index of industrial production. The index number, maintained and published by the Federal Reserve System, which is designed to measure the relative level of the volume of physical production in the United States. The index is divided into manufacturing and mineral operations, and is further divided into various categories of manufactured goods and minerals. The present index is published in relation to the average level during 1947 through 1949 as a base period.

indictment. An accusation found to be worth taking to trial, presented by a grand jury to a court.

indirect cost. See under COST.

indirect exchange. See EXCHANGE (4), CROSS.

indirect exporter. See under EXPORTER.

indirect labor. See under LABOR.

indirect selling. Selling to final users or consumers through wholesalers or dealers, rather than directly. See also DIRECT SELLING.

indirect tax. See under TAX (2).

individual proprietorship. See PROPRIETORSHIP.

indorse. See ENDORSE.

indorsement. See ENDORSEMENT.

in due course. A term used with regard to the payment of obligations, such as bills, time notes, etc., meaning at maturity, or when due.

indulgence. In business, the granting, as a favor, of an extension of time for the payment of a bill, the fulfillment of a contract, etc.

industrial. Dealing with or pertaining to industry or manufacturing, as distinguished from distribution or consumption. See each of the following under the principal listing:

~ ADVERTISING; ~ BANK; ~ DISTRIBUTOR; ~ STOCK; ~ UNION.

industrial accident. An accident or sudden occurrence arising out of work or operations, which results in the death or disabling of an industrial worker. See also ACCIDENT RATE.

industrial disease. A disease or disability characteristic of or peculiar to a particular industry. For example, silicosis, a disease caused by the inhalation of rock dust, was once an *industrial disease* of mining.

industrial goods. See GOODS (3), PRODUCERS'.

industrialist. In common usage, a person who owns, controls, or plays an important part in an industrial enterprise.

industrial life insurance. See under INSURANCE, LIFE, ACCIDENT, AND HEALTH.

industrial relations. The relations between management and employees, or employee groups, in industrial concerns. It includes the management of working conditions, collective bargaining, employee benefits, and so forth. It is generally considered a broader term than LABOR RELATIONS, which are concerned chiefly with collective bargaining. See also PERSONNEL RELATIONS.

industrials. In the securities trade, a term for the common STOCKS of manufacturing or trading companies, as distinguished from those of railroads, public utilities, etc.

industrial store. Any of various types of RETAIL STORES, operated by a company, such as a manufacturing, mining, or construction company, for the benefit of its employees. Frequently, the company employees are permitted to buy on credit, and have the accumulated amounts deducted from their wages. Formerly, it was sometimes the practice to pay employees in scrip redeemable only at the company store, but such practices are now illegal. Industrial stores are sometimes known as commissary stores, company stores, etc.

industrial union council. In the Congress of Industrial Organizations, an organization including all of the C.I.O. local unions in a city or metropolitan area. It was comparable to the CENTRAL TRADES AND LABOR COUNCIL of the American Federation of Labor, and since the unification of the two organizations, the two local organizations have also been united in many cities.

industry. 1. In general, all non-agricultural and non-distributive business activity. In this sense it includes manufacturing, processing, and mining.

2. Any distinct branch of business activity, in manufacturing, processing, or mining;

any group of companies engaged in the same type of operation, or concerned with the same group of products, such as the printing *industry,* textile *industry,* chemicals *industry,* etc.

industry-wide bargaining. See COLLECTIVE BARGAINING.

ineligible paper. See COMMERCIAL PAPER, NON-ELIGIBLE.

infant. In law, any person who has not yet reached the legally established age of maturity or adulthood. This varies from state to state, and sometimes between male and female persons. An *infant* who has reached the age of discretion but not yet the age of maturity is a MINOR.

infant industry. A term for a new, young, and growing industry or field of manufacturing in a country. As usually used, the term carries the implication that such an industry needs and deserves protection, such as tariffs on competing imports, subsidies of various sorts, etc.

inferior. Lower, subordinate, with less power; as, for example, an *inferior* court, or an *inferior* claim.

inferior court. See under COURT.

inflation. A sudden and sharp increase in prices, or a decrease in the value of money, brought about by an increase in the amount of money in circulation relative to the amount of goods and services available. *Inflation* may also be brought about by a shortage in the supply of desired goods, such as during a war, in the face of increased demand. See also DEFLATION.

informal contract. See under CONTRACT.

infra. In Latin, below. Beneath, under; also, sometimes, within or during. It is the opposite of SUPRA, or above; and sometimes of EXTRA.

infraction. Literally, a breaking. Hence, any breach or violation of a law, rule, contract, collective bargaining agreement, etc.

infringement. 1. In general, a breaking into, trespass on, or violation of the rights of another. For example, an employer who limits union activity among his employees may be committing an *infringement* on their rights under the union agreement.

2. In patent and copyright law, a violation of, or trespass on, the rights or privileges granted by a PATENT, COPYRIGHT, or TRADEMARK. Patent *infringement* consists essentially of the making, using, or selling for use or profit of an invention or design covered by a valid patent. In copyright law, an *infringement* is a close or exact copy of a

copyrighted work. However, to be judged an *infringement,* a work must include substantial portions of copyright matter, not merely a single brief extract. A trademark *infringement* consists of the unauthorized use of a trademark or trade name, or of an imitation of such a mark which is likely to confuse the public.

  contributory ∼. The intentional aiding of another to commit an *infringement* on a patented invention, such as by making component parts, assembling manufactured parts, selling accessory equipment to be used with the infringing device, etc. It is unlawful under the patent laws, and the contributory infringer is subject to the same penalties as a direct infringer.

ingot. Originally, a mold for casting metal; now metal in the form of a cast bar or brick, to be used for melting, storage, or transportation. There is no standard size or weight for an *ingot* of any particular metal; the weight of an *ingot* depends on the metal, the use to which it is to be put, and the custom of the caster or molder.

ingross. 1. To make a perfect and final copy of a document from a rough or preliminary draft. The final copy may then be executed and put into effect or use.

2. To ENGROSS.

inhabitant. In law, one who is a permanent resident of a country or place, rather than merely a temporary or transient resident. The laws of the different countries, and of the different states of the United States differ in detail as to the exact definition of an *inhabitant.*

inherent. Existing within a thing, rather than derived from some external power or cause. For example, an *inherent* weakness is one contained within the thing itself, and an *inherent* RIGHT is one which is inborn, not granted by an external source.

inherit. To take property as an HEIR; to receive something of value by right of descent from a deceased person.

inheritance. In law, the term for any personal property which passes from a person who makes a will to his heirs. Strictly, only personal and intangible property is inherited, while real property is passed by DEVISE, and is known as a HEREDITAMENT.

inheritance tax. See under TAX (2).

initial. 1. To sign with the first letters of one's names; to acknowledge, or approve by so signing.

2. The first one; the beginning, or opening thing or act. For example, the *initial* CARRIER of a shipment of goods is the one

who first receives the goods for transport. See also each of the following under the principal listing: $\sim$ COST; $\sim$ INVENTORY; $\sim$ LOSS; $\sim$ SURPLUS.

initialed check. See under CHECK.

injunction. A writ or order issued by a court, especially a court of equity, forbidding a person or corporation to do some act, or restraining him from continuing to do some act, which has been found to be inequitable and injurious. Ordinarily, an *injunction* is granted to prevent or to halt injury, not to provide redress for past injury.

    blanket $\sim$. One which forbids several acts at one time. For example, striking employees may be required to desist from several unlawful or injurious acts under the terms of a single *blanket injunction*.

    final $\sim$. One granted at the end of an action, after a court has determined the respective rights of the parties involved. It may make permanent the provisions of a TEMPORARY INJUNCTION, which see below.

    mandatory $\sim$. One calling on a defendant to do some positive thing, or to cease refusing to do it, or to remove obstructions he has set up to its being done. For example, a *mandatory injunction* may be issued against a landlord, calling on him to continue providing some service he had discontinued.

    temporary $\sim$. One granted on the face of the facts alleged in a case, usually for the purpose of halting an action while the rights of the parties are being determined. When it is for the purpose of preserving the rights of the plaintiff it is known as a *common injunction,* and when issued primarily to preserve the status quo pending a final determination is known as a *special injunction.* It is also sometimes called a *preliminary injunction.* See also RESTRAINING ORDER.

injunction bond. See under BOND (2).

injury. In law, any violation of the rights of others, or any wrong inflicted on others; any wrong or damage done to another's person, property or rights. See also TORT, which is an *injury* or wrong in equity, rather than under law or contract. See also LOSS; DAMAGE.

    personal $\sim$. One done to a man's person, such as a bruise or hurt received in an automobile accident. Also, in some cases, an *injury* to a man's standing or reputation.

in kind. Literally, in the same class or category. For example, a loan repayable *in kind* is payable in something equivalent to the thing loaned; a loan of merchandise repayable in merchandise, etc. Today, it is frequently taken to mean in any form other than money, such as in goods, service, or other object of barter.

    income $\sim$. Income received in the form of goods or services, rather than in money. Under the federal income tax laws, such income must be evaluated and included in reported income, though this provision is difficult to enforce.

    payment $\sim$. Non-monetary payment to employees, usually in the form of lodgings, food, or other services or goods, rather than literally in similar labor.

inland. A term meaning within the boundaries of a country or state; domestic, rather than foreign. *Inland* TRADE, for example, is trade or commerce within the borders of the country, excluding both export and import trade. Similarly, the term *inland* FREIGHT refers to shipments which are destined for domestic consignees, not for export.

inland bill of exchange. See BILL OF EXCHANGE, DOMESTIC.

inland exchange. See EXCHANGE (4), DOMESTIC.

inland marine insurance. See INSURANCE, INLAND MARINE.

innocent. In law, free of guilt; in good faith, ignorant of any wrongdoing or unlawful act. See for example PURCHASER, INNOCENT.

innovation. 1. Anything new or novel; a new or different method of doing something or of obtaining a result; a variation which is novel enough to be patented.

    2. See NOVATION.

inquest. In law, a body of men appointed to examine into a specified matter, such as, for example, a coroner's *inquest.* Also, in current usage, the inquiry or examination itself, conducted by a jury or other appointed body.

in re. A Latin term, originally meaning in fact, but as used, meaning in regard to; concerning; in the matter of.

in rem. In law, a Latin term meaning of a thing; against a thing; concerning property. For example, an ACTION *in rem* is one against property, rather than against a particular person.

inscription. In law, a form of accusation, under older civil law, in which the accuser agreed to suffer the prescribed punishment for the crime charged if the person he accused was found innocent. The purpose of this was to discourage loose accusations.

insert. In advertising, matter which is *inserted* along with other material, such as packaged goods, letters, invoices, etc. In magazine publishing, a page or section of matter prepared by someone other than the publisher, such as an advertiser, and *inserted* and bound into a regular issue of the magazine.

insertion. In advertising, a single appearance of an advertisement in a magazine, newspaper, or other medium. Advertising space rates are usually quoted at one price for single *insertions* and a lower price per *insertion* for multiple *insertions*.

inside director. See under DIRECTOR.

insider. In the securities trade, a term for a stockholder of a corporation who is also an officer or key executive. Also, a professional trader, as distinguished from a member of the investing public, who is known as an OUTSIDER, or LAMB.

insolvency. In general, the inability to meet one's just debts as they fall due; the condition in which one's total assets, if realized, would not be sufficient to cover one's total liabilities. However, the temporary inability to meet payments due to a shortage of ready cash is not necessarily a sign of *insolvency*, provided there are sufficient realizable assets to cover the debts. See also BANKRUPTCY; SOLVENCY.

insolvent. One who is unable to meet his debts; a person whose finances are in a state of INSOLVENCY; a BANKRUPT.

inspection. In general, the act of comparing something with an acceptable standard, to determine the amount, if any, of deviation from the standard. A purpose of *inspection* may also be to locate correctable defects so that the quality of the thing inspected may be brought up to standard by additional work. See also QUALITY CONTROL.

installation. 1. In general, the act of putting in place. For example, the ceremoney of putting new officers of an organization into office is known as an *installation*. The process of positioning, attaching, and otherwise making ready machinery or equipment is similarly its *installation*.

2. In industry, any place of operation; a FACTORY or WORKS; a place where machinery or equipment is installed.

installment. 1. One of several parts or portions, such as an *installment* of a continued novel in an issue of a magazine, or an *installment* delivery of part of a total shipment.

2. Specifically, a portion of a debt which is due and payable at a particular time, different from the time set for payment of other parts of the debt. See also each of the following under the principal listing: ～ BOND (1); ～ DEBT; ～ LOAN; ～ NOTE (1); ～ SALE.

installment buying. See INSTALLMENT PLAN.

installment credit. See CONSUMER CREDIT.

installment plan. A method of selling on credit, in which the total price of the goods is paid in stated amounts at fixed intervals over a period of time, sometimes after an initial down payment which is larger than the set installment. In such sales, the buyer usually signs a conditional sales contract, and receives a conditional bill of sale, under both of which title to the goods sold remains with the seller until the last installment is paid in full. *Installment plans* are frequently known as easy-payment plans, weekly payment plans, monthly payment plans, budget plans, etc. See also SALE, INSTALLMENT; BILL OF SALE, CONDITIONAL; CONDITIONAL SALES CONTRACT.

instant. In business correspondence, and in billing practice, the current month. The abbreviated form *inst.* is usually used. For example, reference to a letter of the 10th *inst.* means a letter dated the 10th day of the current month. Similarly, a note that payment of a bill is due on the 30th *inst.* means that it is due on the 30th or last day of the current month.

institute. 1. To begin, or to inaugurate; to put into action; as, to *institute* a legal suit.

2. In law, a person named in a will as technically an HEIR, but with instructions to pass the inheritance along to another, known as a SUBSTITUTE.

institution. 1. An organized association, such as one to promote an object or cause, usually public in nature; also, the building and property of such an association. In the corporate laws of most states, an *institution* is defined as being of a permanent nature, rather than merely temporary or transient.

2. In general usage, a custom or practice that has public or legal sanction, and may be included in the laws and regulations of the state. Examples include the *institution* of the free secret ballot, the *institution* of private ownership of property, etc.

institutional advertising. See under ADVERTISING.

in stock. On hand; available for sale or use; in inventory. See also OUT OF STOCK.

instrument. In law, any written or printed paper or DOCUMENT containing statements of fact, of sufficient authority to be used as proof or evidence. For example, an *instrument of indebtedness* is one representing a debt, and setting forth the facts and conditions involved, such as a BILL OF EXCHANGE, DRAFT, BOND, etc. See also NEGOTIABLE INSTRUMENT.

insufficient funds. A statement which a bank stamps on a check which it has received, when the account against which the check has been drawn does not have enough funds in it to meet the amount of the check. A bank will not make a partial payment on a check, so that a check may be rejected even though the drawer has an account and there are some funds in it. If there are no funds at all, the term NO FUNDS will be stamped, and if there is no account in the name of the drawer, the term used is NO ACCOUNT.

insurable interest. Any INTEREST which a person may have in property, or in the life of another person, such that loss or damage to the property, or injury or loss of life of the other person, would result in financial loss to the holder of the interest. For example, a business tenant has an *insurable interest* in the property he occupies; a supplier has an *insurable interest* in the business of his major customers; a corporation has an *insurable interest* in the life of one of its key executives.

insurance. Basically, a form of contract or agreement, called a POLICY, under which one party, called the INSURER, agrees, in return for a consideration known as a PREMIUM (2), to pay an agreed amount of money to another party, the INSURED, to make good for a loss, damage, or injury to something of value in which the insured has an INSURABLE INTEREST, sometimes called the RISK, as the result of some uncertain event called the HAZARD or PERIL. The premium may be paid in a single sum or in installments, the contract may be for a fixed period or until the happening of some event, the risk may be property, assets, income, or a human life. There are a great many particular types of *insurance,* but these may be generally classified into six broad fields, according to the types of companies that generally offer them. The six fields, which are separately defined, are LIFE, ACCIDENT, AND HEALTH; PROPERTY; CASUALTY AND LIABILITY; MARINE; INLAND MARINE; and SURETY AND FIDELITY. There are also several broad forms of *insurance,* cutting across several fields, which are listed and defined below. See also OVERINSURANCE; SELF-INSURANCE; UNDERINSURANCE.

all-risk ∼. Any of various forms of *insurance* protecting property from loss or damage from all causes, except those specifically listed in the policy. *All-risk insurance* is generally broader than COMPREHENSIVE INSURANCE, which see below, which usually covers causes of a specific class.

comprehensive ∼. Any of various forms of *insurance* which give protection against a variety of related hazards, either by listing the hazards covered or by listing those excepted. When *comprehensive insurance* covers a very wide range of hazards, it is sometimes known as ALL-RISK INSURANCE, which see above.

mutual ∼. Any *insurance* issued by a *mutual insurance* company; that is, by one which is owned by the *insurance* policyholders themselves. See also INSURANCE COMPANY, MUTUAL.

reciprocal ∼. *Insurance* written on the basis of a plan under which each insured is also an insurer of the others in the plan, so that he is responsible for a share of the total liability involved. Such *insurance* is written through a RECIPROCAL EXCHANGE, rather than through an INSURANCE COMPANY.

stock company ∼. Any *insurance* issued by an *insurance* company organized as a regular stock company. Except in the field of life *insurance,* by far the largest part of all *insurance* issued is *stock company insurance,* as distinguished from MUTUAL or RECIPROCAL INSURANCE, which see above. See also INSURANCE COMPANY, STOCK.

insurance, casualty and liability. A field of *insurance* including protection against a wide variety of miscellaneous hazards. Basically, these include liability which the insured may incur for any loss, damage, or injury done to others, and any loss, damage, or injury to the property or assets of the insured which is not normally covered by property *insurance.* Some of the principal types of *insurance* in this field are listed and defined below.

automobile ∼. Any of various forms of *insurance* protecting automobile owners against loss or damage to their vehicles, or against liability for loss or damage suffered by others as a result of operation of the vehicle.

contractual liability ∼. *Insurance* to protect persons or companies against liabilities they may assume as a result of contracts entered into. Such liability is usually excluded from the coverage of ordinary *liability insurance,* and must be insured against separately.

credit ∼. *Insurance* protecting companies against losses due to the failure of creditors to pay. In the usual form, the *insurance* company pays for losses on accounts overdue a specified period of time, and then attempts to collect the debts in its own name.

employer's liability ∼. *Insurance* to protect employers against liabilities arising out of injuries or death of employees, other than from causes covered by WORKMEN'S COMPENSATION INSURANCE.

errors and omissions ∼. *Insurance* to protect insurance agents, accountants, and others against liabilities arising out of errors they may make in work they do for their clients. See also PROFESSIONAL LIABILITY INSURANCE, below.

explosion ∼. *Insurance* that covers both loss or damage to owned property, and liability to others, arising out of the explosion or breaking of industrial machinery and equipment. It is sometimes called boiler and machinery *insurance*.

manufacturer's and contractor's ∼. The name for the form of PUBLIC LIABILITY INSURANCE, which see below, designed especially for the use of manufacturing and construction companies.

owner's, landlord's and tenant's ∼. The name for the form of PUBLIC LIABILITY INSURANCE, which see below, designed especially for the use of companies in the wholesale, retail, and other non-manufacturing fields.

personal liability ∼. *Insurance* to protect individuals against any liabilities they may incur as a result of their activities, their ownership of property, etc.

professional liability ∼. *Insurance* to protect doctors, lawyers, accountants, and other professionals against any liabilities they may incur as a result of their professional activities. It is sometimes known as malpractice *insurance*.

public liability ∼. Any of various forms of *insurance* to protect businesses against liabilities they may incur to persons other than their own employees, as a result of their business activities.

theft ∼. *Insurance* to provide for repayment for loss due to theft or burglary of owned property or valuables from insured premises.

title ∼. *Insurance* that protects against loss due to any defect discovered in a title to real estate. See also TITLE GUARANTY COMPANY.

workmen's compensation ∼. See directly.

insurance, inland marine. A somewhat misleading name for a field of *insurance* providing protection for goods or property while they are away from the owner's premises, and thus not covered by regular property *insurance*. This form of *insurance* is commonly known as FLOATER *insurance*, and the policies issued under it as floater policies, since the *insurance* floats with the property, following it wherever it may be located. The various forms of *insurance* available cover goods in commercial transportation on public carriers, in parcel post shipments, and in transit by other means. Personal property

is also covered, as are goods on consignment, leased equipment, property installed but not yet paid for, and so forth.

insurance, life, accident, and health. A broad field of *insurance* providing for payment in the event of loss of life, and also for disability and losses due to accident, sickness, and related causes. It is possible to obtain *insurance* covering only loss of life, or only disability due to accident or sickness, or a combination of both types. Some of the principal forms of *insurance* in this field are listed and defined below.

accident ∼. *Insurance* providing for payments in the event of accidental injury or death. The payment may be a specified amount for certain types of injuries, or a stated sum per week for a limited number of weeks.

business life ∼. Any of various forms of *life insurance* bought in connection with a business operation, usually to provide for needed funds in the event of the death of a principal, partner, or key employee of a business.

endowment ∼. A form of *life insurance* under which the amount of the *insurance* is paid to a beneficiary if the insured dies before a certain date, and is paid to the insured himself if he is still alive at that date.

extended term ∼. The name for the *insurance* provided under an ORDINARY LIFE INSURANCE policy, which continues for a stated period of time after the insured ceases to pay premiums.

group ∼. The term for any of various forms of *life, accident, and health insurance* which are purchased on a group basis, to cover the employees of a business, members of an organization, etc., under a single contract of *insurance*.

health ∼. *Insurance* providing for payments to cover loss of income, or medical and hospital expenses, or both, due to sickness incurred after the effective date of the *insurance*.

hospitalization ∼. *Insurance* providing specifically for the payment of hospital expenses, usually including board, certain medication, hospital services, etc., for confinements due to causes covered by the policy.

industrial life ∼. A form of *life insurance,* in which the amount of *insurance* is small, and the premiums are collected in small amounts at frequent intervals, such as weekly. It is so called because it was originally intended to provide a minimum of *insurance* for low-income industrial workers. It has now been replaced to some extent by SOCIAL SECURITY benefits.

limited payment ∼. A form of *life in-*

surance in which payments are made for a limited number of years, after which the insured remains protected for the remainder of his life, as distinguished from ORDINARY LIFE INSURANCE, which see below, in which premium payments are made throughout the life of the insured.

ordinary life ~. The basic form of *life insurance*, under which the insured pays a regular premium throughout his life, and a stated amount is paid to his beneficiary after death. Part of each premium payment is for pure or TERM INSURANCE, which see below, and part is used to increase the RESERVE VALUE of the policy. It is also known as straight life or whole life *insurance*.

renewable term ~. A form of TERM INSURANCE, which see below, providing coverage for a stated period of years, and with a provision that it may be renewed at the end of that period for another period of years, at a higher premium rate. It is also known as level premium term *insurance*, because the premium remains level for each period of years.

term ~. Any of various forms of temporary *life insurance*, providing *insurance* for a specified period of time only. The premium is for *insurance* only, and provides no RESERVE VALUE, so that *term insurance* is relatively inexpensive. It may be used to provide large amounts of *insurance* during a limited number of years, to provide *insurance* to guaranty the payment of a mortgage or debt, etc. The premium increases with age, either annually or after a fixed period of years.

surance, marine. A form of *insurance* covering loss or damage to vessels or to cargo or passengers, during transportation on the high seas. The hazards insured against are those commonly known as PERILS OF THE SEA, such as storm, collision, rocks, etc.; fire, and actions of the master or crew. The *insurance* is also known as *ocean marine insurance*, to distinguish it from inland marine insurance. The *insurance* may be purchased to cover a particular voyage, or for a particular period of time, or it may be purchased under an open policy, in which case the shipper reports periodically to the *insurance* company the value of the goods he has shipped and wishes covered. *Marine insurance* losses are divided into two types, called general average and particular average losses, which are settled under prescribed formulas. See also AVERAGE (3).

surance, property. A form of *insurance* designed to repay the owner of property for loss or damage due to a variety of hazards, including fire, windstorm, hail, lightning, vehicles, aircraft, riot, etc. It is commonly known as *fire insurance*, but the coverage is actually much wider in most cases. In modern *property insurance*, protection may be obtained against direct loss to property, against loss of income as a result of property damage, against loss of income due to property damage sustained by others, etc. The principal types of *property insurance* are listed and defined below.

builder's risk ~. *Insurance* covering loss or damage to property while it is still under construction. The protection also extends to building materials on the site. Usually, the amount of coverage increases over the term of the policy as the building nears completion.

business interruption ~. *Insurance* to cover loss of business profits while a business is unable to operate due to property damage. It is also available as *contingent business interruption insurance*, to cover losses due to property damage suffered by customers or suppliers. It is also known as *profits insurance*, and was formerly known as use and occupancy *insurance*, since the payment was considered to be for the insured's inability to use and occupy his property.

extended coverage ~. *Insurance* against loss due to hazards not covered in the basic FIRE INSURANCE, which see below. These hazards include windstorm, hail, explosion, riot, civil commotion, aircraft and vehicles, smoke damage, and sometimes, vandalism and malicious mischief. Additional *extended coverage* against other hazards is also available for dwellings and farms. The premium for *extended coverage insurance* is usually a stated percentage of the fire *insurance* rate.

fire ~. The traditional form of *property insurance*, providing protection against loss or damage to property due to fire or lightning. In the ordinary case, such *insurance* covers the actual cash value of the property, not its replacement cost or its stated value. But see also REPLACEMENT COST INSURANCE, below. See also VALUE, ACTUAL CASH.

homeowner's ~. A form of comprehensive *property insurance*, including not only FIRE and EXTENDED COVERAGE INSURANCE, which see above, but various other forms of *insurance*, such as liability, theft, etc., in a single policy. This form of *insurance* is not available in all states.

improvements and betterments ~. The form of *property insurance* which might be purchased by a commercial tenant, to cover the value of the fixtures, partitions, etc., which he has added to his premises, but which are not covered by the landlord's *property insurance* on the building itself.

leasehold ~. A form of *insurance* providing for payment of the difference between the rent paid on damaged property and the rent that must be paid for substitute quarters. This *insurance* is frequently bought by companies operating under favorable long term leases which could not be duplicated if new quarters must be found.

rent ~. *Insurance* to cover the loss of rental income on destroyed or damaged property.

rental value ~. *Insurance* to cover the cost of rented quarters when owned property has been destroyed or damaged. When the property is damaged beyond repair, the *rental value insurance* is usually settled for a calculated lump sum.

replacement cost ~. *Insurance* providing that any loss or damage will be paid for at the current cost of replacing the property, rather than at its actual cash value. Such *insurance* usually requires, however, that the insured property be replaced on the same site within a stated period of time, and is therefore not always considered advantageous. It is not available in all states.

insurance, surety and fidelity. A form of *insurance* providing protection against losses due to the dishonesty or lack of integrity of others, including employees, customers, and the general public. To a large extent, it is not strictly *insurance,* but a form of BOND (2) which is provided. The company agrees to indemnify the insured against losses due to the acts of the persons it has bonded, but also to repay losses due to acts by the general public. Typical losses covered by such *insurance* include loss by forgery, fraud, embezzlement, etc. A popular form of *surety and fidelity insurance* is the so-called 3-D policy, insuring against losses due to dishonesty, disappearance, and destruction. It covers losses of money or securities from any of a wide variety of causes, including fraud, theft, burglary, etc. See also SURETY.

insurance adjuster. See ADJUSTER (2).

insurance agent. See under AGENT.

insurance broker. See under BROKER (1).

insurance carrier. See INSURANCE COMPANY.

insurance certificate. See CERTIFICATE OF INSURANCE.

insurance company. In general, any company or association providing INSURANCE to the public or to limited groups, in any of the various fields of insurance. *Insurance companies* may be classified into several broad groups, regardless of the particular kinds

of insurance they provide. The most important of these classifications are listed and defined below.

assessment ~. A form of MUTUAL INSURANCE COMPANY, which see below, in which policyholders may be assessed for losses beyond the ability of the company to cover, as distinguished from a LEGAL RESERVE INSURANCE COMPANY, which see below. See also POLICY (2), ASSESSABLE.

direct-writing ~. One which solicits sales directly, either through its employees or by mail, rather than through agents or brokers

factory mutual ~. A type of MUTUAL INSURANCE COMPANY, which see below, specializing in providing property insurance on high grade industrial properties. Since the company restricts the type of risks it will accept it is usually able to charge lower rates than those charged by companies that accept average risks.

legal reserve ~. A MUTUAL INSURANCE COMPANY, which see below, especially in the life insurance field, which maintains a reserve against possible claims, as required under the appropriate statutes, and is therefore able to sell policies under which policyholders may not be assessed for losses, as distinguished from an ASSESSMENT INSURANCE COMPANY, which see above. See also POLICY (2), NON-ASSESSABLE.

multiple-line ~. One which is active in several different insurance fields, such as both property and liability insurance, or both casualty and fidelity insurance. In some states, *insurance companies* may be licensed in only one field, so that *multiple-line companies* are illegal in these states.

mutual ~. One organized as a mutual association in which each policyholder becomes a member. There are no stockholders and the company is managed by a board of directors or trustees who are named by the policyholders. All net profits of the company are returned to the policyholders as dividends or as rebates on future premiums. It may be either an ASSESSMENT or LEGAL RESERVE COMPANY, which see above See also RECIPROCAL EXCHANGE.

stock ~. One organized as a regular stock company, with stockholders who may not be policyholders. The operating profits of the company may be distributed entirely among the stockholders as dividends, or they may be partly distributed to policyholders. See also POLICY (2), PARTICIPATING

insurance dividend. See under DIVIDEND.

insurance management. In business, the branch of management which is concerned with protecting the company against loss by unforeseen or unpreventable occurrences. It includes the responsibility for decisions on what to insure, how to insure, and the amount of insurance to be purchased. It is a narrower concept than that of RISK MANAGEMENT, which includes not only insurance management, but safety management, the elimination of credit risks, and responsibility over other sources of preventable loss to the company.

insurance policy. See POLICY (2).

insurance warranty. See WARRANTY (2).

insured. In general, the person or party whose *insurable interest* is covered or protected by a policy of insurance. Strictly, in life insurance, the *insured* is the person on whose life or well-being the policy is written, whether or not he is the person who pays the premiums and controls the policy. The person who pays the premiums, receives the dividends, and to whose benefit the policy matures, if it is an endowment policy, is called the ASSURED. See also ADDITIONAL INSURED; NAMED INSURED.

insured account. See under ACCOUNT (3).

insured mail. See under POSTAL SERVICE.

insurer. In general, one who contracts to indemnify another, under the terms of a policy, for a loss suffered. An INSURANCE COMPANY.

intaglio. One of the three principal methods of printing, the other two being LETTERPRESS and OFFSET. In *intaglio* printing, the letters or illustrations to be printed are etched or engraved into the plate, so that the ink is retained where the plate material is etched away. In printing, the ink is first transferred to a drum or roll, and then to the surface to be printed. The rotogravure process and similar engraved printing processes are examples of *intaglio* printing.

tail. See ENTAIL; ESTATE IN TAIL; FEE TAIL; TAIL.

intangible. 1. In general, not corporeal, not capable of being touched; of no physical substance. In business, the term includes services, such as insurance, advertising, etc., which provide a value but which involve no physical products.

2. Financially, having no intrinsic or marketable value in itself, but representing value, such as bonds, securities, rights, etc. See also ASSETS, INTANGIBLE; PROPERTY, INTANGIBLE.

integration. In business, the process of combining into one corporation or complex of corporations several previously separate business operations. The purposes for such combination may be to gain advantages from coordinated operation, or to gain greater control over the market for products or the sources of supply for materials.

horizontal ∿. The combination of several business operations which are at the same general level of operation, such as the combination of a number of retail stores, or of several manufacturing companies making the same or similar products. *Horizontal integration* on a large enough scale may result in a monopoly over a given activity.

vertical ∿. The combination of several business operations which are at different levels of operation, such as a combination of raw material production with refining or manufacturing, or of manufacturing with wholesale or retail distribution. Where *vertical integration* results in unfair competition or in restraint of trade, it has been held to be a violation of the anti-trust laws. An example is the production of motion pictures, their distribution, and their exhibition in controlled motion picture theaters, by the same organization.

inter alia. A Latin term, meaning among other things. It may be used, for example, in a mention of one charge among others in an indictment.

inter alios. A Latin term, meaning among other persons. It may be used, for example, in mentioning one defendant among others in a legal action.

interchangeable bond. See under BOND (1).

interchangeable part. A part or component of a machine or other mechanical device which is so designed and manufactured that it may readily be substituted for the corresponding part in any similar machine. The principle of *interchangeable parts* is the basis of modern mass production and assembly, and thus of the industrial revolution itself.

intercompany. Literally, between companies; but as generally used, means between affiliated companies, or between parent and subsidiary companies. *Intercompany* sales, for example, usually refers to sales by one member of an integrated group of companies to another, such as by a raw materials producer to a manufacturing subsidiary, or by a component part manufacturing affiliate to an assembling affiliate.

interest. 1. In law, any right to the benefit from or enjoyment of property, except TITLE itself. As currently used, it includes a shared title, in which case each share is called an *interest*. A LEASEHOLD, for example, is an *interest* in the property leased. Similarly, a will may grant a *life interest* in property to one person, with title going to another on the death of the first. In this case, the first person may have the use of and income from the property during life, without actually holding title. See also INSURABLE INTEREST; VESTED INTEREST.

2. In finance, the price or compensation paid for the use of money over a period of time. It is expressed as a percentage of the amount of money borrowed or used for a period of time, usually a year. Hence, when it is said that the *interest* on a loan is 3 percent, with no other qualification, it means that the *interest* charge is on the basis of 3 percent of the principal amount of the loan per year, though the loan may be for a shorter or longer period. See also RATE OF INTEREST.

accrued ~. The amount of *interest* earned since the last regular payment, but not yet due and payable. For example, a bond on which *interest* is payable quarterly may be quoted for sale in the period between payments at a particular price, plus *accrued interest.* The term includes only *interest* currently earned, while *interest* which is overdue and as yet unpaid is ACCUMULATED INTEREST, which see below.

accumulated ~. *Interest* installments which have already come due and which are not yet paid. On most bonds, mortgages, and similar debts, *interest* is accumulated if not paid, but on income bonds and other debts for which it is specified that *interest* is paid only if earned, missed payments do not accumulate.

Boston ~. See ORDINARY INTEREST, below.

compound ~. *Interest* which is figured on previous *interest* which has become due and has been added to the principal amount. *Interest* on a savings bank account, for example, is compounded periodically, and each successive *interest* payment is figured on the total of the original principal and all the *interest* earned to date. Thus, if an amount of $100 is deposited at 3 percent *interest,* compounded annually, the *interest* payment the first year is $3; the second year is $3.09, or 3 percent of $103; the third year is $3.18, or 3 percent of $106.09; and so on. When an annual rate of *interest* is compounded more often than annually, the proportional amount of *interest* for the compounding period is used. For example, if *interest* at 4 percent per year is compounded quarterly, *interest* of 1 percent is added each quarter.

conventional ~. *Interest* which is set by the parties to a loan, and not fixed by law.

exact ~. *Interest* for periods less than a year, computed on the basis of the exact number of days in the period, as a proportion of the number of days in a year, rather than on the basis of the number of months or fractional months in the period. For example, *exact interest* for a three month period might be anywhere from $^{89}\!/_{365}$ to $^{92}\!/_{365}$ of the annual *interest,* rather than $^{3}\!/_{12}$. It is sometimes known as New York *interest.* See also ORDINARY INTEREST, below.

illegal ~. *Interest* charged at a rate higher than that permitted by law or statute for the particular type of loan; USURY.

legal ~. *Interest* charged according to a rate set by law for a particular type of loan.

New York ~. See EXACT INTEREST, above.

ordinary ~. *Interest* for periods less than a year, computed on the basis of standard months of 30 days and a standard commercial year of 360 days. For example, *ordinary interest* for a three month period is always $^{90}\!/_{360}$, or $^{3}\!/_{12}$, of the annual *interest,* regardless of the number of days in the months. It is sometimes known as Boston *interest.* See also EXACT INTEREST, above.

simple ~. *Interest* which is computed only on the principal amount, and not on previous *interest* amounts. *Simple interest* is usually paid out at the end of the period in which it is earned, but if it is accumulated it does not earn *interest* itself, as is the case with COMPOUND INTEREST, which see above.

3. Any group of persons or business concerns with common aims, often the dominant group in a particular industry or field of activity. For example, one may speak of the steel *interests,* the financial *interests* etc.

short ~. In the securities trade, the group of investors or speculators who have sold a particular stock SHORT. Also, in trade usage, the total number of shares of the stock which have been sold short by the group.

interest-bearing. Earning or paying interest as, for example, an *interest-bearing* note or other debt. A note is not *interest-bearing* unless it is specifically so stated on the face. See also NOTE (1), INTEREST-BEARING.

interest-bearing bond. See under BOND (1).

interest bond. See under BOND (1).

interest or no interest. A term used in some insurance policies, especially in marine insurance, indicating that in the event of loss or damage to the insured property the insurer will pay the amount named in the policy, whether or not the insured person has an INSURABLE INTEREST in the property; in other words, *interest or no interest.* Such terms are rare in the United States, but are common in policies written at LLOYDS on all types of risks, not merely marine risks. See also INSURANCE, MARINE.

interest policy. See under POLICY (2).

interest rate. See INTEREST; RATE OF INTEREST.

interest warrant. See under WARRANT (2).

interference. In patent law, a conflict existing between the claims of two or more patents, or between an existing patent and a new application. It may be, for example, that two independent inventions both depend on a particular device or principle for their operation, in which case the two are said to be in *interference*.

interim. In the meantime; provisional, or temporary. See each of the following under the principal listing: ∼ BOND (1); ∼ DIVIDEND.

interinsurance exchange. See RECIPROCAL EXCHANGE.

interlineation. Any writing between the printed or already written lines of an instrument. Such notations or writing may become part of an agreement or contract if acknowledged by all parties and appearing in all copies.

interlocking director. See under DIRECTOR.

interlocutory. Originally, said or pronounced in response, or during a proceeding. Hence, in law, pronounced in the course of a proceeding or action; provisional; not final. See also DECREE, INTERLOCUTORY.

internal. Pertaining to inner or domestic affairs or activities, such as of a company or country. See each of the following under the principal listing: ∼ AUDIT; ∼ HOUSE ORGAN; ∼ LOAN.

internal revenue. That part of the money income of the national government which is derived from impositions levied on domestic sources, including income, profits, manufactures, transportation, luxuries, and other services and activities. It does not include the income from tariffs, Panama Canal tolls and other external sources. See also TAX (2), INTERNAL REVENUE.

Internal Revenue Code. The codification of the federal tax laws, covering all internal taxes on income, stamp taxes, excises, etc. It was last thoroughly revised in 1954, but is continually subject to amendment and revision.

Internal Revenue Service. The division of the Treasury Department that is responsible for the collection of all internal taxes and duties, including income taxes, excises, stamp taxes, etc., and with the investigation and prevention of tax frauds. It is divided into nine regions and 64 districts, each of which is responsible for the collection of all taxes on activities within its geographic jurisdiction.

international. Between nations; originating or operating outside of the country; existing or operating in more than one country. See each of the following under the principal listing: ∼ STOCK (1); ∼ UNION.

international law. The entire body of laws governing the relations between independent nations, and between their citizens. It is not a fixed code, but includes all of the various conventions, treaties, agreements, codes, and so forth into which the several nations have entered, as well as established custom and precedent. Disputes between nations or citizens of different countries, which cannot be settled under domestic law or by negotiation may be referred to the World Court, at The Hague, in the Netherlands, which is recognized as the final arbiter in such disputes.

International Monetary Fund. The international organization, created in 1945, to promote international monetary cooperation. It acts to maintain an orderly and free system of foreign exchange, buying and selling currencies when necessary to maintain an equilibrium in the world currency market.

international money order. See MONEY ORDER, POSTAL.

international trade. The exchange of goods and services between nations. As used, it generally refers to the total of the goods and services exchanged among all nations, while the exchange between any particular nation and all others is known as that nation's FOREIGN TRADE, or FOREIGN COMMERCE.

interpolation. In general, a placing between. Thus, in law, it is the insertion of words or phrases into a document or instrument. In statistics, it is the estimation of amounts or values which lie between known values. This may be done by calculation, or by the use of a line or curve drawn between known values on a chart or graph.

interregnum. Originally, from the Latin, a period between rulers or administrations. As sometimes currently used, any intervening period of time.

interstate commerce. As defined by the INTERSTATE COMMERCE ACT, any COMMERCE between any place in one state and any place in another state, or between places in the same state through another state. Through various acts of Congress, Supreme Court decisions, etc., *interstate commerce* has come to include not only the trade in commodities, but any economic or financial activities between the states, such as transportation, communication, power transmission, securities trading, and so on. The power to regulate commerce among the several states is reserved to Congress by Article I of the Constitution.

Interstate Commerce Act. An act of Congress, originally passed in 1887 and amended several times since, which brought control of all common carriers engaged in interstate commerce under the INTERSTATE COMMERCE COMMISSION, which was created by the act. At one time, telegraph companies were placed by amendment to the act under the I.C.C., but when the FEDERAL COMMUNICATIONS COMMISSION was established, both telegraph and telephone wire service were placed under the new Commission, along with wireless communication service.

Interstate Commerce Commission. The independent federal agency, originally established in 1887, and given broader powers in 1906, which regulates rail, motor, and water traffic and commerce between the states. It establishes rates for interstate passenger and freight travel, prepares statistics on transportation, regulates the activities of carriers, forwarders, etc., and supervises the operation of freight pools and other services.

intervening cause. See under CAUSE.

intervening party. In law, the term for any person who has obtained the right to become a party to a pending legal action, though not one of the original parties to the action. See also PARTY.

inter vivos trust. See TRUST (1), LIVING.

intestate. The state of not having made a will. Hence, as used, a person who has died without leaving a valid will, or any other specific indication of his desires for the disposition of his property. The laws of the various states differ as to when a person has died *intestate,* and as to the disposition of his property in this event.

in the black. In business slang, an expression for the state of affairs when a business is operating at a profit, or when its profits have wiped out previous losses. The usage arises from the practice of using black ink to enter credit or income items in bookkeeping.

in the red. In business slang, an expression for the state of affairs when a business is operating at a loss, or when losses have wiped out previous profits and left the business in debt. The usage arises from the practice of using red ink to enter debit or expense items in bookkeeping.

in transit. On the way from one place to another; departed or put into movement, but not yet arrived or accepted at destination. Though it may be of great importance, under insurance or other contracts, to determine when goods are *in transit,* there is no complete uniformity among state laws and court rulings on the subject, so that it is necessary to include a clear understanding in any pertinent agreement.

intrastate commerce. As defined by various laws and statutes, COMMERCE or TRADE (2) transacted wholly within the boundaries of one state, as distinguished from INTERSTATE COMMERCE, which is between two or more states. A product which is manufactured, sold and used entirely within one state, for example, enters only into *intrastate commerce.*

intrinsic value. See under VALUE (2).

inure. Strictly, to take effect; to come into use. As used, to pass to the beneficial use of a particular person; to give the benefit or results of to a person. For example, the property of a deceased person *inures* to his heirs.

invalid. Not of binding force; null and void. Not founded on truth or fact. See also VALID.

invent. To produce something not previously known to man, or not previously in existence; to create or develop a new process or method of accomplishing some end. Strictly speaking, to *invent* is distinguished from to discover, in that the latter means to find something which existed but was unknown, such as a principle of physics, while the former always involves the creation of something new.

inventory. In general, a list of goods or property on hand. Also, the preparation of such a list of goods or property. In business, an *inventory* is a list of materials, work in process, and/or finished goods, together with the value of each item. For the various methods of determining this value, see INVENTORY VALUATION. The several types and methods of *inventory* are listed and defined below:

  beginning ~. The *inventory* counted on the first or opening day of a business period. Also, the value of goods in *inventory* on that day.

  book ~. One based on the stock of goods supposedly on hand, as shown by the record books in which additions to and deductions from *inventory* have been tallied, as distinguished from a PHYSICAL INVENTORY, which see below.

  closing ~. See ENDING INVENTORY, below.

ending ~. The *inventory* counted on the last or closing day of a business period. Also, the value of goods in *inventory* on that day.

initial ~. See BEGINNING INVENTORY, above.

opening ~. See BEGINNING INVENTORY, above.

perpetual ~. A method of keeping an *inventory* record by noting on STOCK RECORD CARDS each withdrawal from or addition to *inventory,* and keeping a running or perpetual balance. It is usual to adjust such a record from time to time by taking an actual count on PHYSICAL INVENTORY, which see below. A *perpetual inventory* is actually a form of BOOK INVENTORY, which see above.

physical ~. One prepared by making an actual physical count of all of the goods in stock. Because this is a laborious process, many businesses take PHYSICAL INVENTORY only once or twice each year, and depend on BOOK or PERPETUAL INVENTORIES, which see above, for accounting purposes in the intervening period.

inventory control. The process of maintaining inventories, whether of raw materials, goods in process, or finished goods, at the desired levels. This may be accomplished by determining the desired level of basic or normal stock, the rate of usage or sale, the ECONOMIC LOT SIZE for purchasing or manufacturing, the purchasing or manufacturing time cycle, and from these computing the level at which additional goods should be ordered or manufactured.

inventory financing. In general, the process of obtaining needed capital for a business by borrowing money with inventory used as collateral. The most common method is the use of the technique of FIELD WAREHOUSING, under which inventory on the company's own premises is placed under bond, and the WAREHOUSE RECEIPT on the goods used as the basis for a loan. Also, in a more limited sense, the borrowing of money for the specific purpose of investing in additional inventory.

inventory protection. The policy or practice of guaranteeing to dealers or distributors that they will not suffer any loss due to price changes on goods in stock. In some cases, this is accomplished by a flat guaranty that prices will not be changed for a given number of months. In other cases, the manufacturer simply agrees to credit to the dealer the difference between the new and old price on any goods held in inventory. This credit is usually granted by means of a

CREDIT MEMORANDUM, which the dealer may then use in payment for future purchases.

inventory reserve. See RESERVE (1), CONTINGENCY.

inventory turnover. See TURNOVER (1).

inventory valuation. The act or process of determining the value of goods in inventory. There are various standard and acceptable methods used in accounting practice, the principal ones of which are listed and defined below.

cost method of ~. The determination of *inventory value* by considering the price paid for each item, or its cost of production, as the present value. This method, or variations of it, is the one used almost universally by manufacturing companies and by most wholesale companies. One variation is the familiar COST OR MARKET, WHICHEVER IS LOWER, a method under which each item is valued either at the price paid or the price for which it could be sold, whichever is less. This is considered a more conservative basis than the strict *cost method.*

first-in-first-out method of ~. A variation of the COST METHOD, which see above, used by companies with large inventories of similar items or of uniform materials, so that it is difficult or impossible to determine the actual cost price of each item, or each portion of material in stock, as opposed to those which have been used or sold. Under this method, the assumption is made that the first goods received were the first used, or *first-in-first-out.* Thus, the goods in stock are assumed to be those most recently bought or made, and are valued at the most recent prices or costs, accordingly. It is frequently known by its abbreviation, FIFO.

last-in-first-out method of ~. A variation of the COST METHOD, which see above, which is an alternative to the FIRST-IN-FIRST-OUT method, which also see above. Under this method, the assumption is made that the latest goods received into stock are those used first, or *last-in-first-out.* Thus, the goods in stock at any time are assumed to be those first bought or made, and are valued accordingly. This method of *inventory valuation* is advantageous in a period of rising prices, since it avoids or minimizes any resulting taxable profits which would otherwise be based merely on inventory appreciation.

retail method of ~. The determination of inventory values by considering the intended selling price, or retail value, of each item, as its value. This method is widely used by retail stores, especially department stores. The usual practice is to mark each item or shipment with the intended selling price at the time it is received, and to use this amount as the value of the item until it is sold. Any sale made at less than the marked price is accounted for under the MARKDOWN item in the retail store accounting system.

invest. 1. In finance, to lend money on the basis of a long-term SECURITY (2), for the primary purpose of obtaining an income. More broadly, to place money in any venture, such as real estate, stocks, mining property, bonds, etc., primarily for the purpose of producing an income, rather than for profit on resale.

2. In law, to clothe with any right or benefit; to VEST.

invested capital. See under CAPITAL (2).

investing company. See INVESTMENT COMPANY.

investment. The act or process of investing. More generally, the property or rights in which money is INVESTED. To qualify as an *investment,* it is generally understood that a property, security, or other thing of value be of long term duration; that its value be relatively stable and well founded; that it produce a more or less regular income, or else that it have a reasonable certainty of appreciating in value over the long run. Thus an *investment* is sharply distinguished from a SPECULATION, which is liable to produce a large profit, but at a high risk of loss.

investment banker. An individual, partnership, or corporation, engaging primarily in the purchase of securities in large amounts, or blocks, or in the UNDERWRITING of security issues, and of reselling these securities to investors and the general public. The *investment banker's* primary source of income is the margin of profit between the price at which it buys securities from businesses and the price at which it resells them to the investing public, plus the service charges which it collects for its underwriting services. It does not perform the normal services of a BANKER, such as the lending of money, the accepting of money for deposit, and the exchange of currencies, except incidentally to its main services in dealing with securities. See also BANKING, INVESTMENT.

investment bill. See under BILL OF EXCHANGE.

investment bond. See under BOND (1).

investment broker. See under BROKER (2).

investment company. A financial organization, formed for the purpose of enabling individual investors to pool their funds with those of others, and to invest their collective funds in a diversified selection of investment securities. The company also provides management of the invested funds, selecting securities to buy or sell, reinvesting the income and profits which are left with the company, and so forth. Typically, the *investment company* issues shares of stock which it sells to the investing public, and invests the proceeds in a variety of securities, according to the chief purpose of the company. The principal classes of *investment company* are listed and defined below.

closed-end ∼. One with a fixed capital stock, or which issues new capital stock only infrequently. The proceeds of this capital stock are invested and reinvested in selected securities, and the value of each share of the company's stock is determined on the open market, in regular securities trading. See also OPEN-END INVESTMENT COMPANY, below.

mutual fund ∼. The popular name for an OPEN-END INVESTMENT COMPANY, which see below. The term *mutual fund* or *fund* frequently appears in the name of such a company, to indicate that it is formed by the mutual pooling of the investment funds of a large number of persons. Generally, such *mutual funds* are further known as common stock funds, growth funds, diversified funds, balanced funds, etc., depending on whether they invest primarily in common stocks, growth securities, a balanced mixture of stocks and bonds, or some other special class or diversified list of securities.

open-end ∼. One which does not have a fixed amount of capital stock, but continues to sell additional shares to the public as the demand requires. The shares of such companies are not traded on the securities exchanges, but may be bought only from the company, at the net asset value in investments represented by the shares, plus a LOADING charge to cover selling and administrative costs. Similarly, the shares can be sold only directly to the company at the approximate net asset value. See also CLOSED-END INVESTMENT COMPANY, above.

regulated ∼. One which has chosen, under the regulations of the Internal Revenue Code, to qualify for special tax treatment by distributing each year at least 90 percent of the income obtained from dividends and interest on its security holdings, rather than pay a higher tax on this income and reinvest it to increase the value of its own shares.

investment counsel. A person or company engaged for compensation in the business of advising others with respect to the investment of funds, especially in stocks and bonds. This advice may be given at one time, with respect to a particular plan of investment, or it may be given over a period of time, on a continuing basis. Several states regulate the activities of such counselors or advisors by law.

investment portfolio. In the securities trade, the term for the list or selection of securities and other assets held for investment purposes by an individual or company. The term derives from the fact that such securities are frequently kept in a portfolio, or folder designed for holding papers and records. The same term is frequently used for the list of outstanding loans, notes, bills, etc., held by a bank or commercial finance company.

investment trust. See TRUST (2); INVESTMENT COMPANY.

investment value. See VALUE, INTRINSIC.

investor. In general, one who uses his funds for the purchase or holding of securities or property, either for the interest or dividend income, or for the expected long-term appreciation of value. One who buys stocks and bonds primarily for income, rather than as speculations.

invisible supply. In the commodities trade, a term for those supplies of grain, cotton, or other agricultural products, which are not yet on the market. They may be in the hands of farmers, or being processed, or still unharvested. Such amounts are not included in the published statements on the VISIBLE SUPPLY.

invisible trade. That part of the trade between nations which is represented by the import and export of services, such as tourist travel, shipping charges, insurance payments, profit, interest and dividend payments, film rental and royalty fees, etc. It is distinguished from the VISIBLE TRADE, which consists of those tangible goods on which a customs valuation may be placed.

invoice. An itemized account of goods sent or services rendered, including, usually, a request for payment; a BILL (4). A complete *invoice* specifies the kind, amount, quality, and price of the goods or services, a description of the packages, the charges due on the shipment, terms of sale, method of shipment, and any other details required by the regulations or customs of the particular trade. It may be sent with the goods or separately. It is distinguished from a STATEMENT OF ACCOUNT, which is merely a summary of goods sent or services rendered over a period, and of payments received, and is not ordinarily a request for specific payment.

invoice back. In general, to charge back to a supplier, or to deduct from the amount paid, any difference between the amount charged and the proper amount as later determined. For example, a company may receive an invoice for a shipment, including an item for freight or postage prepaid. When the shipment arrives, however, the package itself may indicate that the transportation charge is less than that shown on the invoice. The customer may then *invoice back* to the vendor the difference between the stated and correct charges. Similarly, when a transaction has been submitted to ARBITRATION after the invoice has been paid, the buyer has the right to *invoice back* to the seller any reduction in the amount charged.

invoice register. In accounting, a BOOK OF ORIGINAL ENTRY used for recording the receipt of INVOICES on incoming shipments. It is usually divided into columns or sections for indicating the arrival of the goods themselves, and for distributing the charges on the invoice to the particular accounts involved, such as production materials, supplies, shipping costs, etc.

invoice value. See under VALUE (2).

involuntary. Against one's will or choice; by force or coercion; by order or by law; not VOLUNTARY. The laws of the various states differ as to what is an *involuntary* act, and when such an act is proper and legal. See each of the following under the principal listing: ∼ ASSIGNMENT; ∼ BANKRUPTCY; ∼ CONVERSION (3); ∼ DEPOSIT (2); ∼ TRUST (1).

involuntary servitude. In law, the condition of being forced to work for another, or to serve another, against one's will, whether or not for pay; forced labor. In the United States, *involuntary servitude,* except as punishment for a crime after conviction, is outlawed by the thirteenth amendment to the Constitution. See also PEONAGE.

iota. The Greek letter ι, the smallest letter in the Greek alphabet. Hence, a very small amount of anything; the smallest identifiable amount. The term jot has the same derivation.

I.O.U. A form of phonetic abbreviation for the phrase "I owe you." When accompanied by a date, a statement of a specific amount of money, and a valid signature, it constitutes a simple form of acknowledgement of a debt, and will be recognized as a valid memorandum of obligation. However, it is not negotiable, does not imply that interest will be paid, and is not itself a promise to pay at any specific time or place.

Irish dividend. See under DIVIDEND.

irredeemable. Not subject to being REDEEMED, or repaid. With no provision for repayment, or for exchange into other form of money or valuables. See, for example, BOND (1), ANNUITY; CURRENCY, IRREDEEMABLE.

irregular. Strictly, not according to rule. Not according to regular or ordinary practice or form. Also, not regular in the sense of not being uniform, periodic, or regularly recurring. In the securities trade, for example, the market is said to be *irregular* when some stock prices rise while others fall. See also DIVIDEND, IRREGULAR; ENDORSEMENT (2), IRREGULAR.

irrevocable. Not subject to being revoked, cancelled, withdrawn, or recalled. Not to be changed or terminated before the stated date of expiration. See also REVOCABLE. See each of the following under the principal listing; ∼ ASSIGNMENT; ∼ CREDIT (3); ∼ LETTER OF CREDIT; ∼ POWER OF ATTORNEY; ∼ TRUST (1).

island position. In newspaper advertising, a term for the position of an advertisement which is completely surrounded by editorial matter, rather than being placed next to other advertising matter or at one edge of the page. Such a position is considered to attract a high degree of reader attention, and is therefore desirable.

issue. 1. In law, a point in dispute; a fact in controversy between the two parties to a lawsuit. More generally, any controversy, as between the two parties in an election campaign, etc.

2. To send forth, or to put forth; to offer for circulation. Also, any class of securities or other obligations which are offered to the public at the same time. *Issued* securities are those put into the hands of the public. See also ACTUALLY ISSUED; NOMINALLY ISSUED.

issued stock. See under STOCK (1).

issue price. See under PRICE.

item. 1. Originally, in the Latin, also; a term used to introduce each new article or thing in a listing. Hence, by usage, the article itself; any single article or fact, especially of the sort entered on a list.

2. In banking practice, any financial instrument in which a bank deals, such as a check, note, draft, etc. A CITY ITEM, for example, is a term for a check or similar instrument drawn on a bank in the same CLEARING HOUSE area as that of the bank at which it is presented. See also CASH ITEM; OUT OF TOWN ITEM; COLLECTION ITEM.

itemize. To draw up a detailed list; to prepare a list of charges or costs, with the individual details shown. It is common, for example, for a contractor to submit an *itemized* account of his charges for work performed.

itinerant. Literally, wandering, or traveling; transient, with no fixed place of abode or work. Hence, an *itinerant* worker is one who goes from place to place to work, such as an agricultural worker who follows the harvests from place to place.

J

Jacquard weave. The type of weave produced on a Jacquard loom, in which threads of several colors or textures may be carried behind the surface of the fabric and brought to the surface as required for the pattern. The loom itself, invented by J. M. Jacquard, is controlled by an intricate system of perforated cards, arranged on a chain, which determine the particular threads to be brought to the surface at any time.

japanning. To coat a surface with a brilliant, hard varnish or lacquer to preserve the finish or to resist corrosion. This treatment is often used on painted or raw metal surfaces, as well as on wood.

jean. A variety of cotton twill fabric, woven in either solid colors or stripes, softer than drill. It is used principally in the familiar "blue jean" work clothing.

jerry-built. Originally, *jury-built*, from the same derivation as a *jury mast* or temporary mast on a ship. Thus any construction which is temporary, and not intended or expected to last for very long.

jetsam. Goods and merchandise from a ship's cargo, thrown overboard to lighten the ship, as in a time of danger, or to float the ship from a reef; that which has been JETTISONED. See also FLOTSAM; LAGAN.

jettison. To throw overboard a part of a ship's cargo, such as when the ship needs to be lightened to help weather a storm, or to float off a reef. To discard something of value for the general good, such as to cut off expenditures for one program, in order to conserve funds for others.

job. 1. Originally, a single amount or piece of work. Hence, any task, especially one carried through from beginning to end. Also, an occupation, especially one not requiring professional or highly skilled training.

2. To buy or sell goods or merchandise in lump amounts, rather than by detailed specification. More loosely, to act as a MIDDLEMAN or WHOLESALER in general. See also JOBBER; JOB LOT.

job analysis. In personnel administration, a complete analysis of all of the jobs or positions in an establishment, for the purpose of learning their requirements in terms of ability, and their relationships to each other and to the function of the establishment. It may be, for example, the basis for a program of JOB EVALUATION.

jobber. Originally, one who bought goods in JOB LOTS, for resale in smaller quantities. This specific qualification has largely disappeared in current usage, and the term is now synonymous with WHOLESALER in most trades in which it is used.

  exchange ~. A bank or banker who buys foreign exchange in large amounts, for resale to smaller banks and to individuals, earning a small profit or discount on the turnover.

  rack ~. A wholesale distributor of such items as notions, housewares, etc., who performs the additional service of placing the stock on the retailer's shelves, keeping the inventory records, etc. Often the title to the merchandise is kept by the *jobber* until the goods are sold. *Rack jobbers* operate typically in supplying supermarkets, drug stores and other types of retail outlets, which would not ordinarily find it profitable to carry housewares and similar items unless the costs of the services performed by the *jobber* are absorbed by him.

  wagon ~. A wholesale distributor who specializes in selling such items as prepared foods, cleaning supplies, etc., to large customers, such as hotels, institutions, restaurants, etc. Traditionally, the *wagon jobber* maintains no warehouse, but picks up bulk orders from the manufacturer and uses his wagon or truck to break down his customers' orders, thus providing essentially a break-down, delivery, and billing service. Today, however, many *wagon jobbers* also offer full wholesaler services if desired.

job classification. The arrangement of jobs into categories, following a JOB ANALYSIS, according to the kinds and degrees of skill

197

required; usually for the purpose of JOB EVALUATION.

job description. A more or less detailed description of the duties, requirements and other features of a job or position, for purposes of determining the rate of pay, for filling the position, etc.

job evaluation. A comprehensive determination of the relative worth and importance of all the jobs and positions in an establishment. A typical procedure involves the assignment of numerical values to various job skills and characteristics, and a totaling of the points for each job on the basis of a JOB ANALYSIS. A *job evaluation* program may be for the purpose of setting wage scales, for determining promotion requirements, for establishing incentives, etc.

job lot. A lot or order of goods, usually of miscellaneous kinds, sizes, styles, etc., made up by a manufacturer or distributor to be sold as a unit. At the end of a season, for example, an apparel manufacturer may collect all his remaining garments into *job lots,* for sale at a discount. See also JOBBER.

job order. An order or schedule, typically in a factory or shop, authorizing or directing the performance of specific work on a specified lot of materials. A *job order* usually accompanies each lot of materials released for production in a plant organized on a JOB SHOP basis.

job shop. A factory or plant which operates by carrying each order or piece through to completion, rather than on a continuous or mass production basis. Such operating methods are usually followed in the assembly of large or heavy equipment, the production of major castings, in foundry work, etc., and also in small factories which are organized more or less on a handcraft basis.

Johansson block. One of a set of hard steel blocks, familiarly known as "Jo-blocks," each of which has been ground and polished to a specified size within extremely narrow limits of tolerance. It is used as a standard thickness to test and set gauges, micrometers, and other measuring instruments.

joint. In combination, undivided, united; performed by, shared, or owned by, two or more persons in common. As applied to two or more associated persons or parties, it implies complete equality in action, power, interest, rights and obligations, rather than the dominance of one over the other. See each of the following under the principal listing: ∼ ACCOUNT (3); ∼ ADVENTURE; ∼ BOND (1); ∼ COST; ∼ ENDORSEMENT (2); ∼ FREIGHT RATE; ∼ MORTGAGE; ∼ NOTE (1); ∼ RETURN (3); ∼ TARIFF (1); ∼ TENANCY; ∼ TENANT; ∼ WILL.

joint agreement. In labor relations, a uniform agreement covering wages and working conditions, signed by all the unions and employers, or associations of employers, in an industry; also known as an industry-wide agreement. See also COLLECTIVE BARGAINING.

joint and several. A term used in instruments of indebtedness and other obligations, meaning that the signers or makers are bound jointly, and each one separately as well, to fulfill the obligation. In the event of default, suit may then be brought either against all the signers together, or separately against each for the whole obligation, until it is recovered. See also each of the following under the principal listing: ∼ CONTRACT (1); ∼ NOTE (1).

joint-and-survivor annuity. See under ANNUITY.

joint council. In a trade-union, a delegate body composed of representatives of several locals of the same international union in a given area. It is also known as a district council or joint board. Such *joint councils* are usually established for the purpose of negotiating JOINT AGREEMENTS with employers in a given industry in an area. The locals represented may be specialized by geographic area, by particular type of work performed, or by industry in which the work is done.

joint hiring hall. See HIRING HALL.

joint life annuity. See under ANNUITY.

jointly and severally. A phrase used in the signature section of an obligation, to indicate the JOINT AND SEVERAL liability of the various signers.

joint product. One of two or more finished products which are made as part of the same process, or using the same materials. Examples are fuel oil and gasoline, which are refined together from crude petroleum, or any of various chemicals which are normally produced in common processing with others. A *joint product* is distinguished from a BY-PRODUCT in that the latter is usually more or less incidental to the production of the principal product, while a *joint product* is the result of a process specifically designed to result in more than one finished product.

joint stock association. See JOINT STOCK COMPANY.

joint stock company. An association of individuals which is neither a PARTNERSHIP nor a CORPORATION, but which has some of the features of each. It resembles a corporation in that 1) its ownership is represented by shares of stock which are transferrable; 2) its existence is not affected by the death of any of the members; 3) its direction and management are in the hands of directors or governors elected by the member shareholders. However it is like a partnership in that 1) each member shareholder is personally liable for all the company's debts; and 2) the general law of partnerships governs the relationships between members. The laws of the various states differ as to the limits of the members' liability. Sometimes a joint stock association is distinguished from a *joint stock company* in that the former is under the common law while the latter is under statute.

joule. In electricity, a unit of work, or of energy expended. It is the energy expended by a current of one AMPERE, moving through a wire with a resistance of one OHM. It is roughly equivalent to three-fourths of one FOOT-POUND.

journal. 1. In accounting, a BOOK OF ORIGINAL ENTRY, formerly used as a means of recording all types of transactions, but now usually a specialized or subsidiary record for particular types of entries. Some of the more common *journals* used are the following:

cash disbursements $\sim$. May be either a petty cash record, or a form of check register, depending on the form of accounting used.

cash receipts $\sim$. A record of all money collections.

purchase $\sim$. Essentially an invoice register, showing the items purchased, the amounts and the accounts to be charged.

purchase return $\sim$. A record of purchases returned, kept as a step in charging back to the creditor the amounts no longer payable.

sales $\sim$. A record of sales, showing items sold, terms, purchaser, and perhaps an analysis or classification of sales.

sales return $\sim$. Used for recording returns, allowances and other deductions from gross sales.

2. A DAY BOOK; a record of the proceedings of a meeting or convention, or a personal record of events, such as might be kept by a military officer, ship's captain, etc.

journalize. To make the proper journal entries and accompanying account entries covering a business transaction; to record an event or transaction.

journal voucher. See VOUCHER.

journeyman. A member of a skilled trade or craft who has completed his apprenticeship and is qualified as being fully competent; as, for example, a *journeyman* printer or *jour-*

neyman plumber. See also APPRENTICE; MASTER.

judgment. The final decree, ruling, or sentence, handed down by a court or other tribunal or semi-judicial body, after hearing all of the evidence in a trial or other action or proceeding. See also each of the following under the principal listing: $\sim$ BOND (2); $\sim$ CREDITOR; $\sim$ DEBT; $\sim$ DEBTOR; $\sim$ NOTE (1).

judgment sample. See under SAMPLE (3).

judicial. Pertaining to, or part of, the administration of justice, or the practice of courts; as, a *judicial* proceeding. That which is ordered, sanctioned, prescribed or enforced by a court of law or a judge. See each of the following under the principal listing: $\sim$ BOND (2); $\sim$ SALE (1).

jump a claim. To illegally seize or take over a mining claim which has already been established by another. Hence, to wrongfully take over another's property or rightful sphere of operation in any field. See also CLAIM (2).

junior. Of lower standing or rank; of more recent date, younger or newer. Inferior in relation to that which is SENIOR in either of the above senses. See each of the following under the principal listing: $\sim$ LIEN; $\sim$ MORTGAGE; $\sim$ PARTNER.

junior board of directors. A device used in some corporations to enable the junior members of management to become familiar with the problems facing the corporation, and at the same time to enable top management to become familiar with the abilities of the younger men. The *junior board* is usually selected on a rotating basis, so that many have an opportunity to serve, and operates by making advisory suggestions to the officers and directors, after a thorough study of some problem in the company's operations. The practice of making use of a *junior board* or similar device is sometimes known as MULTIPLE MANAGEMENT.

junior lien bond. See under BOND (1).

jurisdiction. 1. In general, the power, right, or authority to hear and decide on an issue, and to enforce the decision reached. With respect to a court, it is the authority of the court, within specified limits, to accept, hear, and render decisions or judgments in legal actions and proceedings. The *jurisdiction* of a court may be restricted in several ways, including the nature of the offense, the amount of the claim involved, the residence of the litigants, etc.

2. Loosely, the geographic area within which a court, government, union, or other

organization or authority exercises power. It may be said, for example, that the *jurisdiction* of a state extends to three miles beyond low water along its shores.

jurisdictional dispute. A disagreement between two or more trade-unions over the right to bargain for workers in a certain line, trade, industry or geographic area. Such a dispute may arise, for example, between two craft unions each claiming jurisdiction over a certain type of skilled operation, or between a craft union and an industrial union, one basing its claim on the operation, the other on the industry in which it is performed. See also UNION.

jurisdictional strike. See under STRIKE.

jurisprudence. Broadly speaking, the science and system of applied justice, through the laws and the courts. More narrowly, the collective body of laws of a state or country, including both those laws relating to individual rights and those relating to the enforcement of these rights by the state authorities.

jury. In law, a body of men who are selected to investigate the facts of some matter, and to hear all of the evidence involved. They are sworn to find the true facts and to reach a proper decision or VERDICT. *Juries* are used in several types of actions. A *trial jury,* for example, hears the evidence in a regular civil or criminal case, while a *coroner's jury* meets to consider whether foul play is involved in the event of a death. A *grand jury* is named to hear the evidence presented by the state or by a district attorney, and to decide whether a strong enough case exists to hold a trial, in which case it hands up an INDICTMENT.

K

karat. See CARAT.

keelage. In maritime usage, the fee charged for permission to anchor a vessel in a harbor or roadstead.

keg. In general, a small barrel or cask. As a measure of volume, a variable amount, usually from ten to thirty gallons. As a measure of weight, used for nails, it is equal to 100 pounds.

key. See QUAY.

keyed advertising. Advertising which includes some special symbol by means of which it is possible for the advertiser to determine which publication prompted the reader's inquiry. The key may be a special street or box number, or a department to which the reply is to be addressed, or it may be a number or letter code included in the reply coupon if one is used. A reply addressed to Dept. K, for example, may mean that the inquirer saw the advertisement in publication K. See also ADVERTISING.

key punch machine. A device, with a keyboard similar to that of a typewriter, used for punching coded holes in the columns of a tabulating machine card. See also BUSINESS MACHINE.

keystone pricing. A form of nominal pricing, used in the jewelry trade, and usually signifying that the marked price is double the actual fair selling price. Thus, an item priced at $100 *keystone* is actually intended to sell for $50. The higher marked price is merely intended to make the customer feel that he is getting a bargain.

kickback. A portion of a fee, sales commission, or wages which is turned back to some agent as a bribe for the privilege of having earned the money. For example, a lawyer may be asked to *kick back* part of his fee, or a salesman may be asked by an unscrupulous purchasing agent to *kick back* part of his commission, or a worker may be required by a racketeering union official to *kick back* part of his earnings to retain his job.

killing. A sudden and large profit, such as might be made on a single transaction or speculative move. To *make a killing* on a stock speculation, for example, means to realize a large and quick profit, such as by buying low before a sudden rise, and then selling out.

kilo-. In the METRIC SYSTEM, the prefix used for any unit of measure which is one thousand times as large as a basic unit. It is now also frequently used for any unit which is 1,000 times as large as another, whether or not in the metric system. Examples include the kilogram, kilometer, kiloton, etc.

kilovolt. One thousand volts. See VOLT.

kilowatt. One thousand watts. See WATT.

~ hour. The amount of electrical energy consumed in one hour by an electrical device using current at the rate of 1,000 WATTS. It is the standard measure of electrical energy consumption, and the basis for ordinary charges for the use of electricity.

kin. Strictly, blood relations. The term has been held to include relatives by marriage, however, and the exact meaning for legal purposes may differ in different states.

next of ~. The closest blood relation. As generally used, the closest living relation to a deceased person. Legally, husband and wife are not *kin* to each other, and so are not each other's *next of kin,* but under state laws *next of kin* usually rank after spouse in precedence, so that the effect is the same. State laws vary as to the order in which persons holding various relationships to the deceased rank as *next of kin.*

kind. See IN KIND.

king. One who dominates, or is pre-eminent in some particular field; as, for example, a cattle *king,* railroad *king,* etc.; a MAGNATE, or TYCOON.

kip. 1. Originally, the hide of any of a number of young animals, such as calf, lamb, colt, etc. In current usage, the hide of medium age bovines, older than calf, but younger than full-grown cattle. In the commercial classification of hides, those weighing up to 15 pounds are calfskin, and those weighing 16 to 25 pounds are *kipskin*.

2. As a measure of weight, a load of 1,000 pounds.

kite. 1. To discharge an obligation by the expedient of incurring a fresh one. For example, a depositor in a bank may have issued a check which overdraws his account. To cover this, he makes out another check, cashes it somewhere and deposits the cash to replenish his account before the first check is presented. He now must cash still a third check to cover the second, and so on.

2. To raise the face amount of a check by forgery. One who *kites* a check, for example, may raise the amount from seven to seventy dollars by skillfully altering the letters and numbers involved.

3. Sometimes, in financial usage, a term for an ACCOMMODATION BILL.

knocked down. 1. Not assembled; as when furniture, machinery or equipment is shipped from the factory in a condition that requires the customer or dealer to assemble it for sale or use. Aside from any saving in labor, shipping goods *knocked down* can mean important savings in shipping costs from the more compact usage of freight car space, and sometimes from the lower shipping rate which is available.

2. A term used in auction selling to refer to the practice by the auctioneer of banging down his gavel when the highest price obtainable has been reached. This signifies that the item has been sold, or *knocked down* to the highest bidder.

3. In retail selling, a term used to describe the situation in which a seller has lowered, or *knocked down* his price in order to make a sale.

knot. A measure of speed at sea, equal to one nautical MILE (6,080.2 feet or 1.15 land miles) per hour. Also, loosely but incorrectly, a nautical mile itself. The term derives from the *knots* placed at measured intervals in the rope attached to a LOG which sailing ships dropped overboard to measure their speed. The number of *knots* in the rope that were paid out in a given period of time determined the speed. Thus, a ship is said to be making 8 *knots,* meaning its speed is 8 nautical miles per hour.

know-how. In business slang, technical ability or specialized skill in any field. Sometimes, the term is used to imply intuitive or intangible knowledge of a field, as distinguished from textbook knowledge.

kraft paper. From the German, for strength; a strong, coarse wrapping or bag paper made from unbleached (hence its usual brown color) sulfate-process woodpulp.

L

label. As defined in various statutes, anything, whether a piece of paper, printed statement, imprinted metal, leather, etc., which is either a part of or attached to some item of merchandise or its package, describing the nature of the product, the contents of the package, or indicating destination, origin, or price.

    descriptive ∼. A *label*, as required by law, which lists the contents or ingredients of a product or material.

    union ∼. An imprint placed on a product indicating that the item was manufactured by union labor, under union-approved working conditions.

labor. 1. In general, work, especially physical work as distinguished from mental work; any human effort toward constructive ends. Also, the workers themselves, collectively, as distinguished from MANAGEMENT in a business organization.

    common ∼. Those occupations or duties which are essentially manual and unskilled, which can be learned in a very short period of time, and which require little, if any, exercise of judgment. Also, the workers in a company engaged in such occupations. See also SKILLED LABOR, below.

    direct ∼. In cost accounting, those efforts which go directly into the production or manufacture of finished goods, or into the chief business of the company. Also, those workers engaged in such efforts, such as machine operators. See also INDIRECT LABOR, below.

    indirect ∼. In cost accounting, those efforts which do not go directly into production, but which go toward keeping the plant in condition to produce, including maintenance, storage, etc. Also, those workers engaged in such efforts. See also DIRECT LABOR, above.

    skilled ∼. Those occupations or duties which require a high degree of ability and skill, which call for a relatively long period of training, and which require a considerable degree of judgment. Also, the workers in a company engaged in such occupations. See also COMMON LABOR, above.

    unskilled ∼. See COMMON LABOR, above.

    2. Broadly, organized workers; their UNIONS or other representatives of their common interests. Those groups which claim to speak for the interests of working people.

labor bank. See under BANK.

labor contract. An agreement, arrived at by COLLECTIVE BARGAINING between an employer and his employees, as represented by a union, which covers wages, working conditions, and other factors involved in employment.

labor dispute. As defined by the National Labor Relations Act, any controversy concerning terms, tenure, or conditions of employment, or concerning the association or representation of persons in negotiating, fixing, maintaining, changing, or seeking to arrange conditions of employment, regardless of whether the disputants stand in the relation of employer and employee. Thus, a *labor dispute* may arise between an employer and his employees, between union and non-union employees, etc.

labor force. 1. As defined in current Bureau of the Census statistics, those members of the non-institutional civilian population 14 years of age or older who, at a given time, are either employed, unemployed and looking for work, or would be looking for work except for certain specified conditions. At one time, the definition was in terms of persons with GAINFUL OCCUPATIONS, whether they were working, looking for work, or doing neither. See also UNEMPLOYMENT.

    2. In general, the workers in any group, such as those at a particular plant, or in a particular community or area.

labor law. In general, any legislation, either state or federal, pertaining to workers, working conditions, or labor relations.

Labor-Management Relations Act. See TAFT-HARTLEY ACT.

labor organization. As defined by the National Labor Relations Act, any organization of any kind, or any agency or employee representation committee or plan, in which employees participate and which exists for the purpose, in whole or in part, of dealing with employers concerning grievances, labor disputes, wages, rates of pay, hours of employment, or conditions of work. See also UNION.

labor pirating. The practice of enticing workers from other employers, by offering them higher wages, better working conditions, or other advantages. It may be resorted to in a period of general labor scarcity, or to overcome a shortage of workers with particular skills.

labor relations. In personnel management, the area involving relations between an employer and his organized or unionized employees, covering both economic and non-economic aspects of these relations. It is one phase of the broader field of PERSONNEL RELATIONS.

labor spy. A person who is hired by an employer or an association of employers, for the purpose of operating under cover to obtain information about the plans and activities of the union representing their employees.

labor turnover. See TURNOVER (2).

labor union. See UNION; LABOR ORGANIZATION.

laches. In law, the omission or failure to assert a right for an unreasonable and unexplained length of time. A lack of activity and diligence, or a negligence in making a claim or enforcing a right, which makes present enforcement impossible. This rule is included in various statutes and contracts, to discourage the presentation of old or stale demands, and to protect those who act in good faith against such demands.

lading. Literally, a load. Thus, cargo or freight. See also BILL OF LADING.

lagan. Goods from the cargo of a ship which have been thrown overboard to lighten the ship in a time of peril, but to which a buoy or marker has been attached for possible future recovery. Under maritime law, such goods remain the property of the owner, and a finder is bound to return them upon payment of a reasonable SALVAGE charge. The term is sometimes used as ligand, or ligan, and is derived from the old French. See also FLOTSAM; JETSAM.

laissez faire. In French, literally, to leave alone. The economic policy or principle of non-interference in business and trade by government, based on the general belief that a free economic system operates best for the greatest benefit of all with a minimum of governmental control or regulation. The *laissez faire* philosophy is generally opposed to any restrictions on free enterprise, such as those which characterize the recent

movement toward a welfare state in most capitalist countries.

lamb. In securities trade slang, a person who is inexperienced in stock speculation, or who trades in an amateurish manner, as distinguished from a WOLF, who is a crafty, experienced trader.

land. As used in contracts, deeds, and other legal forms, the earth, soil, or ground, and that which is naturally upon it, such as trees, herbage, and water, but not structures, as distinguished from REAL ESTATE, which includes any improvements permanently attached to the land. See each of the following under the principal listing: ~ CONTRACT; ~ LEAGUE; ~ TAX (2).

land bank. See FEDERAL LAND BANK.

landed estate. See under ESTATE (1).

landed price. See under PRICE.

land grant. A donation of public land by one government to a subordinate government, or to a public body, a corporation, or an individual. For example, the federal government made *land grants* to the states for educational purposes, and to the railroads, to aid them in financing construction.

~ **college.** A state college or university originally established with funds raised by the sale of lands granted to the states by the federal government.

~ **railroad.** A railroad which was originally aided by a *land grant,* on condition that the federal government be granted free use of the railroad, or a reduced rate, known as a *land grant* rate or tariff.

landing notice. A formal notice sent by a common carrier, such as a steamship line, to the consignee of goods, stating that the goods are ready for delivery by the carrier at a designated place and time, upon payment of freight and other charges in the amount stated.

landlord. One who owns or holds property, either land or buildings or both, and LEASES it to another, the TENANT, for a definite period of time, at a stipulated charge, the RENT. A LESSOR.

land measure. The system of square measure used in the measurement of tracts of land, including ACRES, SECTIONS, etc.

land mile. See MILE.

land office. A local office of the General Land Office of the Department of the Interior, in charge of all public land, its survey, sale, and patenting. The *land offices* were first established by act of Congress in 1812. During the periods when public lands were available for claim and settlement, the *land* *offices* were the most important government offices in the settlement areas.

land-office business. In business slang, a booming or rushing business, similar to that done by the LAND OFFICES at the height of the land rush period.

Lanham Act. The federal law governing trademarks, passed in 1946 and since amended. It revised and codified all previous trademark regulations. See also TRADEMARK.

lapse. 1. In law, the termination of a right, privilege, or opportunity through failure or neglect in performance, or through the happening of some unforeseen contingency, or through neglect to exercise the right within a limited time. See also LACHES.

2. In insurance, the termination or discontinuance of an insurance policy, due to the failure to pay a premium when due, or within an allowed number of DAYS OF GRACE. See also INSURANCE.

lapsed. Having terminated, or having been discontinued under the conditions of a LAPSE. See, for example, LEGACY, LAPSED.

larboard. In older usage, the left side of a ship, facing forward; the PORT side. The opposite side from STARBOARD.

larceny. In law, the wrongful and fraudulent taking and carrying away by one person of the personal goods or money of another, without consent, and with intent to convert the property taken to the use of the taker. Strictly, it includes BURGLARY, ROBBERY, and THEFT, but excludes EMBEZZLEMENT, in that the last is the wrongful appropriation or conversion of property already in the custody of the embezzler. In some states, larceny is divided into grand and petit (or petty) larceny, according to the value of the property involved and the degree of punishment authorized by law.

last-in-first-out (LIFO). See under INVENTORY VALUATION.

last survivor annuity. See under ANNUITY.

last will and testament. The final written declaration of an individual regarding the disposal of his property upon his death. See also WILL; TESTAMENT.

latent defect. See under DEFECT.

law. In general, any body of rules or principles, made enforceable by custom, authority, or legislation, and used as rules of conduct or for the settlement of disputes within a nation, community or other group. Also, any one of such rules or principles. See also CIVIL LAW; COMMERCIAL LAW; COMMON LAW; CRIMINAL LAW; EQUITY; MARITIME LAW.

lawful money. See under MONEY. See also LEGAL TENDER.

lawsuit. See SUIT.

layaway plan. A form of INSTALLMENT PLAN selling under which the merchandise is put aside until all the payments are completed. See also WILL-CALL.

lay corporation. See under CORPORATION.

lay day. See LYING DAY.

layoff. As now generally understood, a termination of employment due to a lack of work. It is ordinarily intended as a temporary separation, until work is again available, but of course may become prolonged or permanent due to unforeseen conditions. *Layoff* is sharply distinguished from DISCHARGE, in that the former is due to conditions beyond the employee's control and the latter is usually for cause. It is also distinguished from FURLOUGH, which is for a short period of time, with a definite date of return.

l.c.l. See LESS-THAN-CARLOAD.

lead time. In purchasing, the time that must be allowed between the ordering of an item and its expected delivery. Similarly, in production scheduling, it is the time between the putting of a part or component into production and the time at which it is ready for the next operation.

league. A unit of linear measure, which has been defined differently at different times, but is now generally defined as equal to three MILES. The land *league* is equal to three statute miles of 5,280 feet each, while the marine *league* contains three nautical miles, of 6,080 feet each.

leap year. The year, occurring once in every four, to which is added an extra day in the month of February. This is done to bring the calendar in line with the actual period of revolution of the earth about the sun, which is roughly $365\frac{1}{4}$ days. *Leap years* are designated as all of those years which are divisible by four, such as 1956, 1960, 1964, etc., but excluding the century years, such as 1900, 2000, etc.

learner. A designation for a beginner in any work operation, but generally in one which requires a relatively short training period, rather than in a skilled operation which requires APPRENTICE training. Usually, lower rates of pay are set for *learners,* who then go on full wages or piece rates after becoming fully trained.

lease. A form of contract transferring the use or occupancy of land, buildings, space or equipment, in consideration of a payment in the form of RENT. It may be for life, for a fixed period of time, or for an indefinite period. The LESSOR gives the use of the property to the LESSEE.

mineral ∼. One covering a mining claim or oil-bearing property, giving the lessee the right to work the mine or extract the oil, for a rent which is usually in proportion to the amount of material withdrawn. There may be clauses restricting the amount of material to be withdrawn in a given period of time. It differs from an ordinary property *lease* in that the lessee is given ownership of the material withdrawn.

net ∼. One under which the lessee agrees to pay all or most of the expenses connected with operating the property, such as insurance, heat, utilities, decorating, maintenance, etc. Similarly, under a *net lease* for a motor vehicle, the user pays for all gasoline, oil, insurance, maintenance, etc.

percentage ∼. One, usually for retail selling space, under which the rent is based in whole or in part on a percentage of the total sales income of the leased space. It may provide, for example, that the rent is 6 percent of sales, or that it is a fixed monthly amount plus some smaller percentage of sales.

sub- ∼. One made by a lessee to a third person, for a shorter period of time than that covered by the basic *lease*. Strictly speaking, a *sub-lease* for the full period of time during which the lessee has control of the property is an ASSIGNMENT.

leased department. In department store selling, a department which is operated by an outside organization, on a contract agreement with the store. Often the *leased department* is operated by a chain organization that specializes in this type of selling, and presumably can run the department more efficiently and profitably than the store itself could do. Departments which are frequently leased include millinery, shoes, and similar departments selling merchandise calling for wide assortments of styles and sizes and requiring specialized knowledge of fashion trends, etc.

leasehold. An estate conferred by the terms of a LEASE; a TENANCY.

leasehold insurance. See under INSURANCE, PROPERTY.

leave of absence. In personnel management, a period of allowed time off from a job or position with the right of reinstatement preserved and with no loss of seniority. *Leave of absence* may be with pay or without pay, depending on the reason and on the type of work.

ledger. In accounting, the final book of entry for recording the financial transactions of a business, in which entries are made from the original books of entry, such as the JOURNAL, VOUCHER REGISTER, etc. The *ledger* is divided into a series of accounts, one for each type of transaction.

general ∼. The principal *ledger,* in which are posted the summary and controlling accounts of the business. It includes the various asset, liability, income, and expense accounts which go into making up the BALANCE SHEET and INCOME STATEMENT.

private ∼. The *ledger* in which are kept those accounts of a confidential nature, such as executive salaries, proprietor's withdrawals, profits on investments, etc.

purchase ∼. The ACCOUNTS PAYABLE *ledger,* in which are kept the records of dealings with individual suppliers.

sales ∼. The ACCOUNTS RECEIVABLE *ledger,* in which are kept the records of dealings with individual customers.

stock ∼. A book of record kept according to the corporate charter requirements of some states. It includes, typically, the names and addresses of stockholders, number of shares owned of each class of stock, etc.

subsidiary ∼. A *ledger* in which are kept various detail accounts which are later summarized in the GENERAL LEDGER, which see above, such as plant and equipment expense, inventory, etc.

legacy. Strictly, a BEQUEST or gift of money or personal property in accordance with the terms of a WILL. It is distinguished from a DEVISE, which is a gift of real property under a will. See also ESTATE.

demonstrative ∼. One which is to be paid out of a particular fund, or out of the proceeds of the sale of particular property. However, the will may specify that if the indicated fund or property doesn't produce sufficient means to pay the *legacy,* the rest may be taken from the general funds of the estate.

general ∼. One which is to be paid out of the general estate of the deceased, not out of any particular assets or source of funds.

lapsed ∼. One which is left or given to a particular person under a will, but which falls into the residuary estate due to the fact that the named person, or legatee, has died before the maker of the will. The law of the various states vary as to the treatment of such *legacies.*

residuary ∼. One giving all or a share of the deceased's personal estate, after all SPECIFIC LEGACIES, which see below, have been paid, and all expenses and debts satisfied. All residuary legacies are GENERAL LEGACIES which see above.

specific ∼. One which gives a specific identifiable article, or a particular fund of money. Also, loosely, one which specifies the amount or value, as distinguished from one which gives a share of an estate, as in a RESIDUARY LEGACY, which see above.

legal. Pertaining to, based upon, or enforced by law; established according to a law. See each of the following under the principal listing: ∼ BOND (2); ∼ CONSIDERATION; ∼ CONTRACT (1); ∼ DEBT; ∼ HOLIDAY; ∼ INTEREST; ∼ LIABILITY (1); ∼ RATE OF INTEREST; ∼ RESERVE (1); ∼ RIGHT; ∼ TITLE (2); ∼ TRUST.

legal bond. See BOND (1) ELIGIBLE.

legal investment for savings banks. A phrase used in the prospectus or sales literature for some bond issues, indicating that the bond is approved by the proper state agency for investment of savings bank funds. The use of the phrase is usually intended as a reassurance to potential investors that the issue is a sound one, and meets all legal requirements. See also LEGAL LIST.

legal list. A list prepared by the proper state agency, naming and describing those securities or investments which are approved for purchase by savings banks and trust funds. In most states, the list includes such securities as first mortgages on real estate, government obligations, and high grade corporate bonds.

legal person. See PERSON, ARTIFICIAL.

legal reserve insurance company. See under INSURANCE COMPANY.

legal tender. Any authorized currency or coinage that may be legally offered or tendered in payment of a debt, or in meeting any other obligation, public or private. A creditor does not have the privilege of refusing to accept such payment. Historically, *legal tender* in the United States consisted of gold and silver coins and notes backed by gold or silver. Minor coins, including nickels and pennies were *legal tender* only in small amounts, and many forms of bank notes were not *legal tender*. Since 1933, however, all coins and currencies of the United States, including Federal Reserve notes and other notes, are full *legal tender* with no restrictions. See also MONEY, LAWFUL; BOND (1), LEGAL TENDER.

legatee. One who receives personal property under a WILL; one to whom a LEGACY is given.

legation. A diplomatic delegation; also, the official residence of the diplomatic representative of one country to another; an embassy.

legitimate. That which is lawful; recognized or permitted by law; as, for example, a *legitimate* heir, or a *legitimate* occupation.

lend. To give up something of value to another, for a fixed or indefinite period of time, without giving up ownership, and retaining the right to get back the original thing or its equivalent. One who *lends* machinery or real estate, for example, may reasonably expect to get back the original property, but one who *lends* money or expendable supplies expects to get back an equivalent amount. Whether or not there is compensation is not material. *Lend* is the opposite of BORROW. See also LOAN.

lend-lease. A term first used during World War II to describe the supplying of war matériel, including ships, tanks, aircraft, munitions, rations, etc., to countries which were allies of the United States or which, before our entry into the war, it was considered necessary to aid. Technically, the items supplied were considered to be loaned to the countries aided, originally to avoid the terms of the Neutrality Act, but actually it was not expected that such things as munitions and aircraft would be returned.

less-carload. See LESS-THAN-CARLOAD.

lessee. The one to whom a LEASE is granted; the one who RENTS, or pays rent; a TENANT.

lessor. One who grants a LEASE; one who gives another the use of property in return for RENT; a LANDLORD.

less-than-carload. A term used in railroading to describe a shipment which is not large enough to make up a minimum CARLOAD. Such a shipment, or *less-than-carload* lot, is carried in the same car with other shipments, and may be transferred from car to car before it reaches its final destination, if other shipments for the same area are not available at the time of loading. Railroads charge a higher rate per pound for *less-than-carload* shipments than for carload lots. The term is frequently used as *less-carload,* and is commonly abbreviated as *l.c.l.*

less-than-truckload. A term for a shipment of highway freight which is not large enough to make up a minimum TRUCKLOAD. Highway freight carriers charge higher rates per pound for these shipments than for full truckloads. The term is frequently used as *less-truckload,* and is commonly abbreviated as *l.t.l.*

less-truckload. See LESS-THAN-TRUCKLOAD.

let. 1. To grant the use of; to lease or hire out.
   2. To award or assign, as a contract for

work to be done, or equipment to be supplied.

3. In law, an obstacle or hindrance, as in the phrase, "without any *let* or hindrance."

let in. To admit, or to accept; as, for example, a new partner in a firm or an additional party to an agreement.

letter. In law, a written instrument or document attesting to the granting of some power, right, or authority. See, for example, LETTER OF ATTORNEY; LETTER OF CREDIT; etc.

letter of administration. A document issued by a court, authorizing a person to administer the estate of another, who has died without leaving a will. Ordinarily, a near relative of the deceased will apply for and receive a *letter of administration,* but if he fails to do so, anyone with a legitimate claim against the estate may apply.

letter of advice. An instrument used in commerce, especially in foreign commerce, by means of which a consignor may notify a consignee that goods have been shipped; an agent may notify a principal that a sale has been made; a drawer may notify a drawee that a bill of exchange has been issued; etc. Depending on its terminology, a *letter of advice* may be confirmed or unconfirmed, revocable or irrevocable. It is frequently referred to simply as an ADVICE.

letter of attorney. A legal document under which one person authorizes another to act in his behalf. It may be a *special letter of attorney,* applying to a particular matter, such as a transfer of stock, or a *general letter of attorney,* applying to matters generally, or with specified exceptions. The authority granted is known as a POWER OF ATTORNEY.

letter of credit. A letter or advice from a bank to its agent or correspondent, requesting that a sum of money be made available to the person named in the letter, under specified conditions. Such a letter may be obtained for various purposes, and under various conditions, as described below.

circular ∼. See TRAVELER'S LETTER OF CREDIT, below.

commercial ∼. One purchased or obtained as a credit by a prospective buyer of merchandise, and forwarded to a branch or correspondent bank in the city in which the purchase is to be made. The seller of the merchandise is notified, and presents his DRAFT, together with the required documents of sale and bill of lading, to the correspondent bank to obtain payment. A letter may be opened, or obtained, to cover one transaction or several. In the latter case,

the seller presents his draft and the appropriate documents for each shipment made. The *letter of credit* is a common means of financing foreign trade, and eliminates the need of transferring actual funds to the foreign bank.

confirmed ∼. One on which the local correspondent bank gives its own guaranty or assurance that the seller's draft will be honored, if the issuing bank fails to do so.

export ∼. One sent by a local bank to an exporter or seller, notifying him that a credit has been opened in his favor by a foreign bank at the request of a foreign importer, and agreeing to honor the exporter's drafts for goods shipped under the letter.

import ∼. One sent by a foreign bank to a local exporter or seller, authorizing him to draw drafts on the foreign bank or its correspondent, against shipments made under the letter.

irrevocable ∼. One in which it is specified that the issuing bank will not withdraw the credit or cancel it before the date of expiration of the letter, except with the consent of the person to whom the funds are to be made available.

Oriental ∼. See AUTHORITY TO PURCHASE.

revocable ∼. One in which the issuing bank reserves the right to withdraw from the arrangement upon proper notice.

traveler's ∼. One purchased by a person intending to travel abroad, authorizing him to obtain funds, in local currency, at any of a number of listed correspondent banks. The traveler presents the letter at the local designated bank, signs a check drawn on the issuing bank for the amount he desires, and receives the funds. The local correspondent notes on the letter the amount issued and the amount still remaining, and forwards the check to the original issuing bank for credit to its account. Such a letter is sometimes called a *circulating letter of credit,* since it is addressed to any or all of the correspondent banks listed, and may be presented to one after the other.

unconfirmed ∼. One to which the local correspondent bank has not added its own guaranty of payment of drafts presented against it.

letter of delegation. In commerce, a letter authorizing another to collect an amount due. For example, a shipper may give a *letter of delegation,* accompanied by the bill of lading, to a bank in the consignee's city, authorizing the bank to make collection for the shipment, as correspondent.

letter of hypothecation. See HYPOTHECATION.

letter of indemnity. A letter which a shipper

may send to a carrier, freeing the carrier from any claims arising out of disputes over the condition of the goods when shipped, the number of packages delivered to the carrier, etc. Such a letter goes beyond the terms of the standard BILL OF LADING, and is therefore kept as a separate document when used.

letter of indication. A letter of identification, given by a bank to a traveler who purchases a LETTER OF CREDIT.

letter of license. A letter from a creditor or group of creditors, giving a debtor permission to continue to do business, or to pay his debts in amounts and under conditions specified. Such an arrangement between creditors and debtor is used to avoid forcing the debtor into bankruptcy.

letter of marque. Formerly, an authority or license given by a government to the owners of private ships in a time of war, permitting them to attack and seize enemy ships or property. Such letters were given to the owners of the American privateers which operated during the Revolution and the War of 1812. They were also known as *letters of marque and reprisal.*

letterpress. The most common of the three principal methods of printing, the other two being INTAGLIO and OFFSET. In *letterpress* printing, the characters to be printed are raised on a plate, so that they take the ink and transfer it to the surface to be printed. The printing plate may be flat, in which case the process is known as flatbed printing, or it may be a round cylinder, in which case the process is known as rotary printing.

letters patent. The name for the instrument by which the government grants special rights and privileges, under the PATENT and COPYRIGHT laws to an inventor or author.

letters testamentary. The written authority granted by a probate court to the person designated in the WILL of a deceased, called the EXECUTOR, to administer and distribute the estate of the deceased according to the terms of the will. It differs from a LETTER OF ADMINISTRATION, which is given to a person who administers the estate of one who has died without leaving a will.

level premium. See under PREMIUM (2).

level premium term insurance. See RENEWABLE TERM INSURANCE, under INSURANCE, LIFE, ACCIDENT, AND HEALTH.

leverage. In economics, and in securities trade usage, the property which something has of rising or falling a proportionately large amount in relation to some other factor. For example, a company with a high BREAK EVEN POINT will also usually have high *leverage,* meaning that a relatively small increase or decrease in volume will result in a large increase or decrease in profits. Similarly, a securities WARRANT (4) is said to have high *leverage* in relation to the stock in connection with which it is issued, since a relatively small price change in the stock will result in a large increase or decrease in the value of the warrant.

levy. To exact, raise, or collect, as a tax. Also, sometimes, the tax itself.

lex loci. From the Latin, local laws. A term frequently used in contracts and agreements, to indicate that the local applicable laws shall govern, where they are inconsistent with the contract terms. Depending on how the term is used, it may mean the local law of the place in which the contract is made, or the place in which it is performed. Usually, it is state law to which reference is made.

lex mercatoria. The laws of commerce; the branch of the COMMON LAW governing matters relating to trade and commerce, including shipping, insurance, negotiable instruments, sales, etc. The COMMERCIAL LAW.

liability. 1. In general, the condition of being bound or obliged, in law or equity, to do, pay, or make good something; any obligation one is bound to honor or perform.

    legal ~. One recognized by the courts or prescribed by law, such as those under contracts, workmen's compensation acts, etc.

    2. In accounting, the obligations of a business to its creditors, suppliers, customers, etc., as distinguished from those to its proprietors, partners or stockholders. The debts of a business, as opposed to its ASSETS.

    accrued ~. An obligation which has been incurred but not yet paid, such as rent, wages, taxes, or insurance due. In a business using ACCRUAL BASIS ACCOUNTING, these are entered as *liabilities* on the balance sheet to show the true state of the business.

    capital ~. A debt of a business represented by a bond or other security with a fixed, future payment date. It does not include the capital stock of a corporation. See also DEBT, FUNDED.

    current ~. An obligation of a business which is due and payable within the current fiscal year. Examples include accounts payable, notes payable, interest due on long-term debts, etc. Sometimes called a floating liability.

    deferred ~. An entry on the *liability* side of a balance sheet, to offset cash income received but not yet earned, such as deposits on contracts, advance payments on sales, advance rent received, etc.

floating ∼. See CURRENT LIABILITY, above.

3. Any debt or obligation of a person or business, monetary or otherwise.

contingent ∼. One which will come into definite existence only on the occurrence of some event. For example, the endorser of a note has a *contingent liability*, which will become fixed or actual if the original signer of the note should default.

direct ∼. One which is determined and undisputed, rather than being contingent or conditional.

fixed ∼. One in which the *liability* of the debtor is definitely established as to amount, time, etc., as in a mortgage or contract.

floating ∼. A term used for a *liability* which may vary in amount, such as the accounts payable of a business.

secured ∼. One in which the debtor's obligation may be met by the proceeds of a sale of property in pledge or in the hands of a creditor.

liability insurance. See INSURANCE, CASUALTY AND LIABILITY.

liable. 1. Bound or obliged by law or equity; compelled to make restitution for a loss; chargeable or responsible.

2. Exposed or subject to a particular risk, expense or penalty, which is more or less likely.

libel. In general, anything written or printed, and published or circulated, which is calculated to defame or injure a person's character or reputation, and bring about ridicule, hatred, or contempt. The various state laws and court interpretations differ as to whether the injury must be intentional and malicious or whether the effect is the key factor. It differs from SLANDER, which is oral defamation as contrasted to written.

criminal ∼. Any *libel* likely to excite a breach of the peace, either by the person libeled or by others. Also, *libel* committed with criminal intent.

liberal construction. An interpretation of a law, contract, regulation, etc., under which the strict letter of the document is enlarged or stretched to a broader or looser meaning than the original words. It is the opposite of a STRICT CONSTRUCTION, which sticks to the letter of the original document.

liberty bond. See under BOND (1).

license. 1. A non-transferrable permission, granted by a government or other authority to do something, or engage in some enterprise which is restricted or regulated by law. Examples include the permission to operate an employment agency, to drive a motor vehicle, to marry, etc.

2. Under patent law, an authority granted by the owner of a patent to another person, giving him the right to make, use or sell the patented item, design or process under stated restrictions. If no restrictions are placed on the grant, it is not a *license* but an ASSIGNMENT.

3. Any unusual or excessive freedom to act, regardless of the rights of others. It has frequently been pointed out in court decisions that statutes or constitutional provisions granting certain freedoms or liberties do not grant the *license* to exercise these in a way that injures others.

licensee. One to whom a LICENSE has been granted or issued.

license tax. See under TAX (2).

licensor. The person or authority granting a LICENSE to another.

lien. In law, the right or claim which a creditor has against the property of a debtor, under which he may detain or seize the property pending the payment of a debt, the completion of work or the fulfillment of some other obligation. It may be voluntary or contractual, set up by agreement between the parties concerned, or legal, provided for y statute. In either case, it is always against property, rather than against earning power. See also ATTACHMENT.

equitable ∼. One existing in equity, giving a creditor the right to have a fund or property of a debtor directed in whole or in part to the satisfaction of some claim or debt.

general ∼. One existing against property, due to an undischarged obligation of its owner, which may be totally unconnected with the property itself, or its use. It is distinguished from a PARTICULAR LIEN, which see below.

junior ∼. One which follows, or is subordinate to others in right of satisfaction, though not necessarily in point of time. See also PRIOR LIEN, below.

∼ **maritime.** The claim, under common law, and under some statutes and contracts, which seamen have against a ship and its cargo for unpaid wages.

mechanic's ∼. The *lien*, provided for by statute, which a contractor or worker who has constructed or repaired, or provided material for a building or improvement to property, has against the property, to secure him until he is compensated for the work done or materials supplied. It usually takes priority over other *liens* against the property.

particular ∿. One against a particular piece of property, in connection with some claim against the property itself, or work done on it. It may be provided for in statute, contract or common usage.

prior ∿. One which precedes others in right of satisfaction, though not necessarily in point of time.

second ∿. See JUNIOR LIEN, above.

senior ∿. See PRIOR LIEN, above.

special ∿. In effect, a PARTICULAR LIEN, which see above.

tax ∿. The claim which a government has against property for unpaid taxes levied on it or on its use. State laws vary widely regarding the nature and status of such *liens*. It may take effect as soon as the tax is levied, for example, or only after it has been unpaid for a stated period of time. Also, it may or may not be a PRIOR LIEN, which see above, over others.

vendor's ∿. In common law, the right which any seller has to retain possession of property which has been sold but not effectively delivered, until the purchase price is paid. In the event of a bankruptcy on the part of the buyer, for example, the unpaid vendor has an automatic *lien* on the goods undelivered or in transit, though title may technically have passed. Once the goods are delivered, however, this *lien* ceases to exist. Under some statutes, the seller of land has a *vendor's lien* on the property until full payment is made, even though the land is not undelivered. See also STOPPAGE IN TRANSIT.

warehouseman's ∿. The claim, provided for by statute, which a warehouseman has against property in his care, to meet his charges for services rendered.

life. As used in law, contracts, insurance, etc., the life span of a named or described individual. See each of the following under the principal listing: ∿ ANNUITY; ∿ ESTATE (1); ∿ EXPECTANCY; ∿ INSURANCE; ∿ INTEREST (1); TENANT FOR ∿.

life table. See MORTALITY TABLE.

LIFO (last-in-first-out). See under INVENTORY VALUATION.

lagan. See LAGAN.

light. Under the stated or required weight. For example, a shipment or delivery is said to be *light* when it falls short of the weight stated in the shipping documents, and a coin is *light* when it has been worn or abraded until it is below the standard or legal minimum weight.

lighter. A small ship, used for the loading or unloading of cargo from larger ships. It may be operated by a railroad serving a port, by a company specializing in such service, by a steamship line, etc., but in any case is classed as a common carrier.

lighterage. The business or service of operating a lighter; the charge made for such service.

ligne. 1. A unit of measure used for the diameter of small watch movements. One *ligne* is equal to 2.2559 millimeters, or roughly 1/11th of an inch.

2. A unit of measure used for ribbon, tape, and other narrow fabrics, as well as for buttons and other fasteners. In the United States, it is 1/11th of an inch.

limitation. In general, any restriction or limit placed on an amount or period of time. As used in the term STATUTE OF LIMITATIONS, it is the limited period of time within which some legal action must be taken or begun.

limited. 1. In railroading or other transport usage, a train which makes only a *limited* number of stops; a through train or express.

2. In Canadian and British usage, a term used in the name of a company to indicate that it is organized as a *limited* liability COMPANY, similar to an American corporation. Sometimes, in the United States, used in a firm name to indicate that it is a *limited* PARTNERSHIP.

limited liability. The liability which stockholders of corporations, limited partnerships, limited liability companies, banks, etc., have for the debts of the company. Usually, it is limited by statute to the amount of the holder's investment in the company. In some states, and under some conditions, however, the stockholders may be assessed for additional amounts to meet special classes of debts, such as to the depositors of a bank, or for the unpaid wages due employees of a defunct company. See also CORPORATION; PARTNERSHIP; STOCKHOLDER.

limited liability company. See under COMPANY.

limited line store. See RETAIL STORE, SPECIALTY.

limited order. See under ORDER (4).

limited partner. See under PARTNER.

limited partnership. See under PARTNERSHIP.

limited payment insurance. See under INSURANCE, LIFE, ACCIDENT, AND HEALTH.

limited price variety store. See under RETAIL STORE.

limited trust. See under TRUST (1).

line. 1. A field of endeavor or enterprise; a *line* of business, such as, for example, the insurance *line,* the textile *line,* etc.

2. A class or group of products or mer-

chandise, such as is carried by a wholesale or retail merchant. For example, a merchant may carry a *line* of shoes, or a *line* of tools. The term is sometimes used to mean the products of a particular company, so that a merchant may carry the *line* of the X Company.

3. In insurance usage, a type or class of insurance, or of insurance risks. Also, the amount of total liability which an insurer is willing to carry on a particular type of risk, or in a particular class of insurance.

4. In transportation, a transportation system, company, service or carrier, as a railroad *line,* steamship *line,* bus *line,* etc.

5. In business or management organization, the chain of direct command and operational responsibility, as distinguished from STAFF.

lineage. The amount of advertising or editorial matter included in a newspaper or other publication, usually measured in standard AGATE LINES.

lineal. In a straight line; direct. For example, *lineal* descent is from grandfather to father to son, etc.

linear measure. The system of measurement of length or distance.

line of credit. A fixed amount or limit of credit which is established for a customer or borrower by a business or bank. It is the amount of outstanding credit which may not be exceeded at any time; or sometimes, the amount which the customer may borrow, in partial amounts, over a period of time. See also CONTINUING AGREEMENT.

line of discount. The limited amount of the credit which a bank will extend to a retail dealer on the basis of his accounts payable, which he discounts with the bank. See also DISCOUNT.

line organization. That part of a business or military organization which has the direct responsibility for the operation of the organization. The responsibility in a *line organization* descends directly from superior to subordinate, from the top executive to the lowest rank-and-file member of the organization. It is distinguished from the STAFF organization, which exists basically to service the *line organization,* and has no command responsibilities.

liner. In maritime transportation, a vessel operating on a regularly scheduled route. It may be a passenger *liner,* a freight *liner* or a combination vessel.

line rate. In advertising, the charge made for advertising space in a publication when it is sold by the AGATE LINE, rather than in larger units, such as inches, pages, or fractional pages.

link. A measure of length in land measure. In standard surveyors' measure it is 7.92 inches, 1/100th of a CHAIN, or 1/1000th of a FURLONG. The engineers' *link* is equal to one foot, or 1/100th of a chain of 100 feet.

liquid asset. See under ASSET (2).

liquidate. 1. To wipe out, settle, or pay off, as a current debt or obligation.

2. To wind up, settle, or dissolve a business or an estate, by determining the assets and liabilities and apportioning the assets to cover the debts or obligations.

2. To convert into cash, as by sale of securities, or other investments, or rights.

liquidated damages. The amount which is agreed on beforehand by the parties to an agreement, which is to be paid in the event of a breach of the contract or agreement. It is not considered a PENALTY. See also DAMAGES.

liquidation account. See ACCOUNT (2), REALIZATION.

liquidation dividend. See under DIVIDEND.

liquidation value. See under VALUE (2).

liquidator. A person who is employed to settle the affairs of an estate or wind up a business. It is his business to realize as much as possible from the sale of the assets of the estate or business, to pay all costs incurred, and to meet the liabilities as far as the assets will cover.

liquidity. The relative degree to which an individual or business can meet its liabilities without the conversion into cash of any of its fixed assets; the relative proportion of total assets which are in cash or a form readily convertible into cash.

liquid measure. The system for measuring the volume of liquids.

list and discount pricing. The name for the system of pricing most widely used in the sale of consumer goods and many industrial goods, to retail and wholesale distributors. Under this system, the manufacturer establishes a list or nominal price, from which discounts of varying percentages are allowed to customers in different lines of trade, for purchases of varying amounts, for sale at different levels of distribution, etc. see also DISCOUNT (1).

listed. 1. In securities trade usage, entered on the register of securities which have been admitted for trading on a securities exchange, having met the requirements of the exchange for such listing. See also SECURITY, LISTED.

2. In real estate usage, placed or registered with a real estate agent for sale or rent.

listed security. See under SECURITY (1).

listed stock. See under STOCK (1).

list price. See under PRICE.

liter. The basic unit of liquid capacity or volume in the METRIC SYSTEM. It is established as the volume occupied by 1,000 GRAMS (one kilogram) of pure water at a temperature of 4° centigrade and at sea level pressure. One *liter* is the equivalent of 1.0567 liquid QUARTS, or 0.9081 dry QUARTS in English and American measure.

litigation. A contest or action brought in a court of law, in an attempt to obtain a judgment on some point under dispute; a SUIT.

little board. In securities trade usage, the American Stock Exchange (formerly the Curb Exchange), as distinguished from the BIG BOARD, or New York Stock Exchange.

little steel. A term referring to the smaller companies in the steel industry, or sometimes to all the companies in the industry except the United States Steel Company and its subsidiaries, or BIG STEEL.

little steel formula. A wage adjustment formula worked out by the War Labor Board during World War II to settle a dispute affecting the LITTLE STEEL companies. It was designed to bring wages into line with rising living costs and was the model for many similar settlements in other fields.

littoral. Belonging to the shore. Hence, *littoral* rights are similar to RIPARIAN RIGHTS, except that they apply to a sea or lake, rather than a river or stream. There is no sharp distinction, however, and the terms are sometimes used synonymously.

live. Not recorded or transcribed, but an original performance, as a *live* radio or television broadcast.

live storage. See under STORAGE.

living trust. See under TRUST (1).

Lloyd's. The center of the marine insurance industry in London. It is not an insurance company, but an association of insurance underwriters, who share in the risks offered for insurance, and follow uniform policies on rates, settlements, etc. In the present day, the *Lloyd's* underwriters will insure all forms of risks in all fields of insurance except regular life insurance. The name derives from the fact that the underwriters originally held their meetings and did business at *Lloyd's* Coffee House, which is no longer in existence.

Lloyd's Register. A compilation, with the full title of "Lloyd's Register of British and Foreign Shipping," listing, describing, and classifying for insurance purposes all British commercial ships and most other ships. A ship to be listed is built under inspection by surveyors for Lloyd's, and the owner pays a small fee for this inspection and listing. Various marks and signs are used to classify each ship registered as to its construction, age, condition, etc.

load center. See COST CENTER.

loading. 1. In insurance, the portion of the total premium charge on an insurance policy which is used to meet the expenses of selling and administering the policy, over and above the portion needed to meet the liability assumed by the insurer under the policy. See also PREMIUM (2).

2. In the securities trade, the charge added to the price of shares in an open-end INVESTMENT COMPANY or mutual fund, to cover the costs of selling the shares and administering the fund, over and above the asset value represented by the shares.

3. In cost accounting, the process of distributing overhead costs among operations or products.

load line. See PLIMSOLL LINE.

loan. Originally, something granted or lent, or which one was given the use of for a period of time, with no compensation or charge. Now, however, it is usually understood as something of value, such as money, borrowed at interest for a specified period of time. In business, *loans* may be classified in several ways, depending on the time of maturity, the type of security, the character of the lender or borrower, etc. The principal types are listed and described below.

    amortized ∼. One which is to be paid off during its term by periodic payments, as specified in the *loan* agreement.

    broker's ∼. One made by a bank to a securities broker to enable him to finance his own operations, including the sale of securities on MARGIN.

    call ∼. A *loan* which is payable on the demand or *call* of either the borrower or lender. From the borrower's point of view, an advantage of borrowing in this manner is that the money may be returned promptly when there is no longer a need for it, saving interest. On the other hand, the one who borrows on *call* must be prepared to repay the *loan* at any time.

    collateral ∼. One made on a note which has COLLATERAL placed as security. The collateral may be securities or any property of value. The interest rate on *collateral loans* may be lower than on other *loans,* since the risk is smaller.

commercial ~. As generally used, those *loans* made by banks and other lending institutions for terms running from 30 to 90 days. See also COMMERCIAL PAPER.

commodity ~. A term for one made with some form of commodity, such as cotton, wheat, sugar, etc., as collateral. Since the collateral is usually in the form of a WAREHOUSE RECEIPT for the commodity, such *loans* are frequently known as *warehouse receipt loans.*

day ~. One made to a securities broker, foreign exchange broker, etc., to finance his day-to-day operations. These are usually unsecured *loans,* and may be renewed from day to day if needed. They are also sometimes known as *morning loans* within the trade.

demand ~. One which may be repaid at any time, and on which the lender may demand payment at any time; a CALL LOAN, which see above.

deposit ~. One carried out by the setting up of a deposit in the borrower's name, against which he may draw checks. Usually, the bank making such a *loan* will require that the borrower keep a certain proportion of the *loan* on desposit at all times, which in effect results in a higher rate of interest on the money actually available for use. See also DEPOSIT, DERIVATIVE.

external ~. One made outside the country; a foreign *loan.*

fiduciary ~. An UNSECURED LOAN, which see below; one granted on the honor of the borrower.

field warehouse ~. One based on goods placed under pledge in a FIELD WAREHOUSE.

forced ~. In banking, the *loan* that arises when a depositor has made an overdraft, and is unable to make good the deficit in his account on notification. The bank is thus forced to make a *loan* to the depositor until he can cover the overdraft. In government fiscal operations, a *forced loan* is one in which the public or business is forced to participate, such as through payroll deductions, by being required to accept partial payment in interest-bearing notes, or by some other means.

installment ~. One which is to be repaid in installments over the term of the *loan.* It is usually evidenced by one or more installment notes. Also, as sometimes used, a *loan* made to cover an INSTALLMENT PLAN purchase. See also NOTE, INSTALLMENT.

internal ~. One made inside the country, not to a resident of a foreign country.

morning ~. See DAY LOAN, above.

participation ~. A large *loan* granted or participated in by several banks or lending institutions jointly. Sometimes known as a syndicate *loan.*

personal ~. The name for any relatively small *loan* made to an individual, either by a bank or PERSONAL FINANCE COMPANY. Such *loans* may be unsecured, or they may be secured by chattel mortgages or other collateral.

secured ~. One in which the lender's risk is reduced by the borrower giving him something of value as security that the *loan* will be repaid. In effect it is the same as a collateral *loan,* except that in the latter some form of negotiable security is usually given as collateral, while personal property is usually given as security for a *secured loan.*

short-term ~. One made for a period of less than one year, usually at a fixed rate of interest, and evidenced by a NOTE, ACCEPTANCE or some other instrument, as distinguished from a TERM LOAN, which see below

sight ~. See CALL LOAN, above.

term ~. A form of business *loan* which runs for a period of more than one year, but for a shorter period than the typical bond. It is usually an INSTALLMENT LOAN, which see above, and may run for a period of up to five years, but seldom for longer. See also SHORT-TERM LOAN, above.

time ~. One made for a fixed period of time, and which may not be repaid before the end of the period, or the maturity of the *loan,* as distinguished from a CALL LOAN, which see above.

unsecured ~. One made with no actual property placed as security or collateral. In one sense, however, the honor and financial strength of the borrower are the security for such a *loan.*

warehouse receipt ~. See COMMODITY LOAN, above.

loan and trust company. A form of incorporated banking institution, which is empowered by its articles of incorporation to accept and execute TRUSTS, to receive deposits of money and other property and issue obligations therefor, and to lend money on real or personal security. Such an institution, however, is not permitted to issue bills or notes to circulate as money, and does not perform many other functions of a commercial bank. See also TRUST COMPANY; BANK, COMMERCIAL.

loan shark. A person or organization that lends money at excessive and illegal rates of interest, especially to persons who are not eligible for ordinary loans. Such organizations are known to operate among longshoremen and other low-paid manual workers, for example, making loans at rates that amount to as much as 100 percent annual interest. In general, any unlicensed moneylender; a USURER.

lobby. To be active among legislators for the purpose of influencing legislation. Also, a person or organization carrying on such activity. Under federal law, and some state laws, persons who are engaged by corporations, associations or others to represent them among legislators, and to attempt to influence the passage or defeat of legislation are now required to register as *lobbyists.* The term derives from the fact that such activities were originally carried on primarily in the *lobby* or anteroom outside the legislative chamber.

lobster shift. In a plant or other facility operating on a 24-hour day basis, the workshift usually beginning at midnight and ending at 8:00 a.m. Sometimes known as the graveyard shift, or midnight shift.

local. 1. Limited or confined in activity or representation to one particular place or area, such as city or town and its vicinity. See each of the following under the principal listing: ∼ ADVERTISING; ∼ ASSESSMENT (1); ∼ UNION.
2. In transportation, a train, bus or other carrier serving all of the way stations along a given route, as distinguished from an EXPRESS, LIMITED, or through train, bus, etc.

local freight. In transportation, shipments made from an originating station to a way station of a freight train or route, or from way station to way station, as distinguished from THROUGH FREIGHT, which goes from the originating station of a freight train or route to the final or terminus station.

local government. Any city, town, village, county, school or road district, township or other administrative unit below the state level, which has a resident population occupying a definite area, and has the defined power to provide certain public services, levy certain taxes and assessments, etc.

local option. A privilege granted by state legislation to local governmental units, such as counties, towns, etc., to decide for themselves the policies to be followed on specified matters. For example, in some states, the decision on whether to license the sale of liquor is left to *local option* on the part of the individual counties.

local rate. In advertising, the rate which a newspaper or radio station charges for advertising placed by a local source, such as a retail store, as distinguished from the NATIONAL RATE, which is charged for advertising placed by a national or regional advertiser, usually through an advertising agency. The *local rate* is almost always lower than the national rate, to encourage advertising by local merchants and others.

lockout. A situation arising in an industrial controversy, in which an employer shuts down his operation as a protest against employee or union actions or demands, or to force employees to accept his own terms for employment. The distinction between a *lockout* and a STRIKE is important under labor relations legislation, and under the unemployment insurance laws, since workers may collect unemployment benefit payments while *locked out,* but not while on strike. It has been held by some courts that the refusal of an employer to submit a dispute to arbitration when the union is willing to do so, transforms a strike into a *lockout* and makes the workers eligible for benefits.

lock-up. In banking, a trade term for a note or other obligation which has been renewed; that is, on which the time for repayment has been extended beyond the original due date. The term is derived from the fact that the funds represented by the note were not delivered when originally due, but were withheld or *locked up* for an additional period of time.

loco price. See under PRICE.

locum tenens. In Latin, holding the place of. Hence, a substitute or deputy; one who acts for, or represents another during his absence or inability to act. It should be noted that the word lieutenant has the same derivation, through the French, and the same original meaning.

locus sigilli. In Latin, the place for the seal. The words, or the abbreviation *L.S.,* often appear on various legal forms and instruments at the end of the line or place for the signature. In some states, this takes the place of the seal previously required.

log. 1. A device used for recording the rate and distance of travel of a ship. Originally, it was actually a wooden *log,* which was dropped overboard at the end of a rope, so that the amount of rope paid out to the floating *log* in a given period of time was a measure of the ship's speed. Now, it is usually a device with vanes, which rotate at a speed proportional to the speed of the ship and thus indicate the ship's speed on an attached dial. See also KNOT.
2. An official journal of the events occur-

ring on board a ship. It includes dates, locations, and various entries required by law. Modern ships may keep several *logs*, including an engine room *log*, a navigation *log*, etc. By extension, any record of events or of progress, such as a record of experimental research, is now often called a *log*.

3. To punish a crew member for failure to perform a scheduled duty, missing a turn at watch, etc., by withholding pay for the time lost and by adding a fine equal to the pay withheld. This form of double penalty for time lost has now been largely discontinued in the American merchant marine. The term derives from the fact that the missed duty and the penalty were recorded in the ship's *log*.

logarithmic scale. In graphic presentation, a scale in which the logarithms of the actual values are used instead of the values themselves. On such a scale, changes of equal proportion or percentage are indicated by equal distances, regardless of the actual amounts or units involved. For example, an increase from 4 to 16 is shown by a line of the same length and slope as an increase from 100 to 400. It is sometimes called a RATIO SCALE, since it indicates equal ratios.

log-rolling. A term for the practice of including in one item of legislation several items or appropriations, each of which is important to a small number of legislators, to assure that all will vote for the measure. Sometimes, the term is used to refer to any exchange of favors or influence.

long. In the securities and commodities trade, the situation of owning or holding a given security or commodity in ample amounts; to hold more than one has contracted to deliver in the future. Ordinarily, a trader or speculator who goes *long* on a given security does so in the expectation that prices will rise and that he will be able to realize a profit. It is the opposite of being SHORT, or of selling a security or commodity which one doesn't own, in the expectation of being able to buy it in the future at a lower price to make the delivery.

long and short haul clause. The phrase used to describe the particular section of the Interstate Commerce Act which forbids a common carrier to charge a greater amount, in the aggregate, for carrying freight a shorter distance than it charges to carry the same freight a longer distance by the same route, in the same direction, under substantially the same conditions. See also LONG HAUL; SHORT HAUL.

long bill of exchange. See under BILL OF EXCHANGE.

long dozen. In informal usage, one more than a dozen, or thirteen items. It is sometime's also called a baker's dozen.

longevity pay. Extra compensation, either in a fixed amount or as a proportion of the amount already earned, which is paid on the basis of length of service. Members of the armed forces receive additional *longevity pay* for each period of service, and some civilian companies follow a similar practice of rewarding their long-time employees.

long haul. In railroading, the transport of freight over long distances, as distinguished from SHORT HAUL transport. The point of distinction between the two is relative, rather than exact. In passenger transport, the term sometimes refers to travel between major terminal cities, rather than from a way station to a terminal or vice versa.

long hundredweight. See HUNDREDWEIGHT.

long of exchange. In the financial trade, a phrase used to describe the situation in which a dealer or trader in foreign EXCHANGE has purchased and holds foreign bills in an amount exceeding the bills of his own which he has sold and which are still outstanding. In this condition, the dealer is said to be *long of exchange.*

long rate. In insurance, the reduced PREMIUM rate charged when a policy is purchased for a period of more than one year. For example, the premium for two years may be $1\frac{3}{4}$ annual premiums, for three years $2\frac{1}{2}$ annual premiums, etc. In this sense, the basic annual premium rate is known as the SHORT RATE. Such reduced premium rates are usually available on fire insurance, and on some types of casualty insurance. It is also known as a term rate.

long-term capital gain. See CAPITAL GAIN.

long ton. See under TON.

loss. 1. In accounting and finance, the portion of expenditures and other costs which exceeds income, when such is the case. It is the opposite of PROFIT, which is the excess of income over expenditures.

net ~. The final *loss,* after taking into account income from all sources and expenses and costs to the business of all kinds.

operating ~. The *loss* on sales operations only, taking into account only sales income and the costs of sales, and excluding other income and expenditures, such as interest, etc.

2. In insurance, the injury, damage, or diminution of value sustained by the insured in consequence of an accident or oc-

currence against which insurance has been purchased. Also, the amount payable on this account.

actual ∽. The real destruction of property, as distinguished from CONSTRUCTIVE LOSS, which see below. Also, in fire insurance, the actual cash value of the *loss* sustained.

consequential ∽. One which is not caused directly by the hazard or peril which is insured against, but which follows as an indirect consequence of such hazard. For example, property may be undamaged by a fire, but damaged by the activities of the firemen in extinguishing the fire. Such losses are usually covered in the same policy which covers the DIRECT LOSS, which see below.

constructive ∽. The *loss* resulting from injuries or damages that make insured property useless for its intended purpose, or that would require a greater expenditure to restore the property to useful condition than it was originally worth. Thus, property may sustain a greater *constructive loss* than the ACTUAL LOSS, which see above, and may be a *constructive* TOTAL LOSS, which see below, though not actually destroyed.

direct ∽. One which is directly traceable to the peril which the property is insured against. In fire insurance, for example, a *direct loss* would be one directly caused by fire, rather than by the action of the firemen in extinguishing the fire. See also CONSEQUENTIAL LOSS, above.

general average ∽. See under AVERAGE (2).

initial ∽. That portion of an insured *loss* which is borne by the insured, under a policy providing for such an arrangement. For example, in credit insurance, it is typical for the insured to absorb that part of each credit *loss* which is considered the normal risk of business. In other words, the *initial loss* in this case is considered a normal business expense, and only the excessive *losses* are considered insurable risks. See also DEDUCTIBLE CLAUSE.

partial ∽. One which involves only part of the property insured, or part of its value. Hence, it is any *loss* which is less than a TOTAL LOSS, which see below, either actual or constructive. Also, as sometimes used, a *loss* which is less than the total amount of insurance.

salvage ∽. In marine insurance, one which is settled by deducting the SALVAGE VALUE of the goods saved from the total amount of insurance covering the damaged goods. Thus, it is roughly the same as a

PARTIAL LOSS, which see above, in domestic insurance.

total ∽. One in which the property involved is totally destroyed, or loses all of its value. It may be either actual, that is, the result of the real destruction of the property, or it may be constructive, that is, the cost of restoring the property to its original state may be greater than the total value of the property.

loss leader. In retailing, an article deliberately sold below its cost, or at a margin too small to cover selling expenses, in an attempt to attract customers, and thus to secure sales of more profitable items. In some states, it is illegal to sell any product below its cost plus the normal expense of handling it, so that in these states *loss leaders* are outlawed. Under the federal Anti-Trust Laws, a *loss leader* used to injure competition is considered to be in restraint of trade and therefore illegal.

loss ratio. In insurance, the proportion of loss payments to premiums collected by an insurance company, or by a group of companies which set premium rates jointly. In fire, casualty, and similar forms of insurance, it is typical for the *loss ratio* to be only about one half, more or less, of premiums collected, the remainder being accounted for by selling and administrative costs, inspection costs, reserves against future losses, and profits or dividends to policy holders. See also PREMIUM (2); EXPENSE RATIO.

lot. 1. Originally, a counter or marker used to determine an outcome by chance. Hence, to decide by *lot* is to decide by chance or at random. See also LOTTERY.

2. In real estate usage, a parcel of land, especially one in an urban area, in which case it is a parcel with specific boundaries making up part of a city block. However, the term is sometimes also applied to rural land, as, for example, a wood *lot*.

3. A share or group of goods or merchandise which is to be handled jointly, or bought and sold together. In some industries, a *lot* is the same as a JOB, that is, a group of items which is processed together. For example, a batch of hosiery or other items which are put through the dyeing process together are said to be in the same dye *lot*.

4. In the securities and commodities trade, a specified number of shares, or a given quantity of a commodity, which are considered as a unit for trading purposes. The number of shares involved in a particular transaction. See also ROUND LOT; ODD LOT.

lottery. Any scheme for the disposition of property or rights, or the assignment of a duty, by chance. Usually, it involves the drawing of LOTS, or the selection, by chance, of numbered slips or cards which match the numbered slips held by those who are taking part in the *lottery*. In business, a *lottery* may be used, for example, to select the particular bond certificates to be redeemed or called, in the case of a callable bond.

low. In securities trading, the lowest price paid for a security during a specified period; as, the daily *low,* weekly *low,* etc. See also CLOSE (4); HIGH.

low grade. A term used with regard to securities and other investments, meaning of inferior investment quality, speculative, and with uncertain income possibilities. It is the opposite of HIGH GRADE or GILT-EDGE.

L.S. See LOCUS SIGILLI.

l.t.l. See LESS-THAN-TRUCKLOAD.

lucrative. Literally, yielding gain. As used, the term means highly profitable, or paying a substantial return. For example, a *lucrative* investment, profession, or line of business is one paying more than average profits.

lucre. Originally, from the Latin, gain. In common usage, money or profits, usually used in a derogatory sense, as in the classic phrase, *filthy lucre*.

luggage. In transportation usage, those items of BAGGAGE, or necessary personal property, which a traveler actually carries with him on a trip, rather than having it placed in a baggage compartment or car. Public car-

riers frequently put a weight limit on the amount of *luggage* and baggage which a traveler may carry without extra charge.

lump price. See PRICE, BLANKET.

lump sum. In a single amount; in one payment. For example, a *lump sum* sales contract is one calling for payment in a single amount, rather than in installments, and a *lump sum* life insurance settlement option is one calling for payment of the face value of the policy in one amount, rather than in payments over a period of time. Also, a fixed sum, as distinguished from a variable amount, as, for example, under a COST-PLUS agreement.

luxury tax. See under TAX (2).

lying day. One of the number of days required to load and unload a ship, as set out in a CHARTER PARTY agreement or other contract for hire of a ship. Ordinarily, the shipper is allowed a stated number of *lying days,* or lay days, after which a DEMURRAGE charge is made by the ship owner. Unless otherwise specified, only working days count as *lying days,* not week ends or holidays.

lynch law. The practice of inflicting summary or arbitrary punishment on alleged offenders, without formal legal or judicial processes. The term originated with a Capt. William Lynch, a justice of the peace in early Virginia, who became widely known for his treatment of suspects. In current usage, reference is frequently made to "Judge Lynch," but this is a purely imaginary character.

M

McGuire Act. See FAIR TRADE LAW.

machine. 1. Any contrivance used to augment or regulate force or motion. A combination of mechanical devices and powers to perform some function. Strictly, it is distinguished from a PROCESS, in which the desired result or effect is achieved by chemical means, or by the elements of nature, rather than by mechanical means.

    dangerous ~. In industrial safety terminology, a *machine* from the operation of which danger may be anticipated in the ordinary course of events, so that the employee operating it must be continually on guard.

    perfect ~. In patent law, a perfected invention, in the sense that it will successfully accomplish the intended results in a practical manner. It need not, however, be the most perfect way of obtaining the result.

    2. To cut, grind or otherwise remove metal from a metal surface, by the use of a MACHINE TOOL, such as a lathe or planer.

machine hour cost. In industrial cost accounting, the cost of operating one machine for one hour, including both direct and indirect charges.

machine tool. In general, any mechanically operated device for removing metal, such as from a rough casting or forging. Some of the standard machine tools include drills, planes, lathes, reamers, broaches, etc.

mach number. A measure of relative velocity. It is the ratio of the velocity of an object, such as an aircraft, to the velocity of sound in the medium in which the object is traveling. Thus, *mach-one* is equal to the velocity of sound, *mach-two* is twice the velocity of sound, etc. The measure is named after Ernst Mach, an Austrian physicist.

made-to-order. See CUSTOM-MADE; MAKE TO ORDER.

made work. An assignment or operation that fulfills no productive requirements, but which is merely for the purpose of spreading out or creating employment. For example, during a slow period in a factory, an employer may assign workers to cleaning up, polishing machines, etc., rather than lay off men and rehire them later.

madras. A fine cotton fabric, used for shirting and dresses, with a woven pattern, usually a strong stripe. It was originally named for the city of Madras, in India, from which it was exported.

magnate. Originally, from the Latin, a great personage. Thus, one who is prominent, or of great influence, especially in some field of business; as, an oil *magnate,* a Wall Street *magnate,* a steel *magnate,* etc.

magnum. A double-size bottle, for wine, champagne or liquor. It is nominally two quarts, but the actual containers often hold two-fifths of a gallon, or from 48 to 56 ounces.

mailable matter. Any material which is suitable or admissible for transmission by mail, according to law and postal regulations. It includes letters, cards, parcels, books, newspapers, advertising matter, etc., and excludes such things as explosives, incendiary material, obscene literature, etc. See also POSTAL SERVICE.

mailing list. Any list of names of customers, subscribers, prospects, etc. In direct mail advertising, it is the usual practice for advertisers to purchase such lists, or to rent their use, from organizations specializing in their collection and preparation.

mail-order. An order for merchandise which is received, and ordinarily filled, by mail. Also, the business of selling merchandise through such orders. See also ADVERTISING, MAIL-ORDER; RETAILER, NON-STORE.

mail-order catalog. See under CATALOG.

main line. In railroading, a principal route or track, as distinguished from a BRANCH LINE, spur line, or from terminal, switching, or other tracks; a TRUNK LINE. A rail line between two or more principal cities, or one which is heavily traveled.

maintain. 1. To keep up, to preserve in good condition; to keep unimpaired, or in good repair.

2. To support, or to supply with the means of support; such as to *maintain* a dependent.

3. To continue with, or to carry on; as, to *maintain* a nuisance, in local police regulations.

maintenance. 1. In general, the work of keeping up property or equipment in good and sound condition, or the cost of doing so. It is distinguished from the REPAIR of property or equipment, which involves restoring it to good condition, and from an IMPROVEMENT, which involves a change in the condition of the property. The distinction is important for tax purposes, since *maintenance* and repairs are treated as current expenses, while improvements must be amortized as capital expenditures.

2. In law, sustenance or support. As used in contracts, employment agreements, etc., the term usually includes both food and lodging.

maintenance of membership. A provision often appearing in union contracts, stating that employees who have joined the union must continue as members during the term of the contract. New employees are not required to join the union unless there is also a UNION SHOP agreement, but once they do voluntarily join they also must continue their membership during the contract.

majority. 1. The period of life beginning at full age; the age, as fixed by local or state law, at which one is considered able to manage one's own affairs. The age of majority for voting, signing contracts, marriage, etc., may be different within the same jurisdiction. See also MINORITY (1).

2. More than half, or the greater number, as in voting. But where there are more than two choices, the greatest number of votes is a PLURALITY, unless the winning choice actually receives more votes than all the others combined. Unless otherwise specified, a *majority* vote is considered to be of those voting, rather than of those present or eligible to vote. See also MINORITY (2).

make. 1. In general, to cause to exist; to form, fashion, create, or fabricate. In law, to create, prepare, and sign. To execute and perform, or agree to perform. For example, one who transfers his property to an assignee or trustee *makes* an assignment, and one who executes a note of indebtedness in favor of his creditor is said to *make* a note.

2. The BRAND, origin, type or style of some manufactured or processed item. The manufacturer's identifying name or TRADEMARK.

make default. To fail or be wanting in some legal duty. For example, to fail to appear in answer to a SUMMONS or SUBPOENA.

make good. 1. To fulfill or carry out an obligation; to indemnify, such as to *make good* a damage or loss.

2. To demonstrate capability, or to prove up to or fulfill expectations, as to *make good* in a position of responsibility.

make over. To transfer ownership, control, or title. To convey by preparing and signing a document.

maker. 1. The one who executes and signs a negotiable instrument, such as a promissory note, bill or check; hence the one who borrows and who is indebted to pay.

2. The manufacturer, processor or producer of goods or merchandise.

make the cash. A term used in retailing, to describe the process of determining whether the cash on hand, after receipts and payments, balances with the record of sales and payments. To check the cash balance.

make to order. To manufacture, produce, or finish a specific item at the customer's request or order, and according to the customer's specifications, as distinguished from manufacturing for stock. See also CUSTOM-MADE.

make-up wages. A sum paid to an employee on PIECE-WORK rates, representing the difference between actual piece-work earnings and guaranteed earnings at some minimum rate, such as a statutory minimum wage.

make-up work. Work done outside of regular work hours to make up for time lost due to absences. It is paid for at regular rates, not at overtime or week-end rates.

making-up price. See PRICE, SETTLING.

mala fide. Literally, in Latin, in bad faith; dishonestly. It is the opposite of BONA FIDE.

malfeasance. The performance or doing of some act which one had no right to do, or has agreed not to do, such as in public office. It is distinguished from MISFEASANCE, which is the improper doing of an act one has the right to do; and from NONFEASANCE, the failure to do some act one should have done.

malice. The consideration or doing of a wrongful act intentionally, without just cause or excuse. Under the laws of LIBEL and SLANDER *malice* is an evil intent or motive for the libel or slander committed, arising from spite or from ill will.

malicious. Done with MALICE; or with evil intent.

malicious damages. See DAMAGES, PUNITIVE.

malinger. To feign sickness or injury, usual

to escape assignment, duty, or discipline, or to collect compensatory benefits.

malleable. Capable of being drawn out or formed by beating or hammering. Lead and copper, for example, are extremely *malleable* metals in their pure states. *Malleable* iron is a form of cast iron containing relatively little carbon, and which may be formed by hammering.

malpractice. Professional misconduct; an unreasonable lack of skill or integrity in professional or fiduciary duties. The term is most often applied to medical practice, but it may also refer to accounting, law, or the other professions.

malpractice insurance. See INSURANCE, CASUALTY AND LIABILITY.

manage. To conduct, carry on, or have under control. To administer, direct, or control the affairs of a business or other organization.

managed currency. See under CURRENCY.

management. The act, art, or techniques of managing; or of controlling and exercising discretionary powers in the direction of an enterprise. The things that are done to guide, direct, and supervise the operation of a business. Also, the managers, supervisors and executives who direct affairs, collectively. See each of the following under the principal listing: PERSONNEL ∼; PRODUCTION ∼; SALES ∼; WELFARE ∼.

management stock. See under STOCK (1).

mandamus. From the Latin, literally, we command. A writ or command from a higher court to a lower court, public officer, corporation, or some individual, calling for some specific act to be done or not done. Usually, it calls for the performance of an act which is part of the regular duties of an office or position.

mandate. In law, a court order commanding the proper officer or authority to enforce a decree, judgment, decision, or sentence of the court.

mandatory injunction. See under INJUNCTION.

man-hour. A unit of measurement for such industrial factors as work done, accidents, productivity, costs, etc. Ten *man-hours,* in any of these measurements, is the time spent by ten men during one hour, or one man during ten hours, etc. Thus, the number of accidents per *man-hour,* for example, is the number of accidents occurring, divided by the total number of *man-hours* worked.

manifest. A written document, signed by the captain, carried by all merchant vessels, containing a list or account of the cargo, its destination, etc., for the use of customs officials and other port officers. It is distinguished from a BILL OF LADING, which is the document accompanying a specific shipment in the cargo.

manit system. An incentive wage plan, under which standard performance is measured in man-minutes (*manits*), and extra or bonus payments are made for *manit* production in excess of 60 per hour of work. See also INCENTIVE.

manpower. In general, the number of workers available or required for a given operation. Sometimes, especially when used as two words, the work effort of one man, calculated at one tenth HORSEPOWER.

manual. 1. Performed or operated by hand, or by physical force; without the aid of tools or machinery. See also LABOR, COMMON.
2. A book of instructions, list of prices or rates, etc., designed to be carried in the hand; a handbook.

manual rating. In insurance, a method of determining the premium rates on various forms of insurance, under which the particular person, company, or risk to be insured is charged a rate found under the appropriate heading in a manual prepared by the insurance company, or a RATING BUREAU, and based on the long-term experience with average risks. This method is usually used for smaller risks, with the larger risks being eligible for either EXPERIENCE RATING or RETROSPECTIVE RATING.

manufacture. 1. To make, produce, or fabricate, either by hand or by machine. In general usage, to do so on a large scale.
2. In patent law terms, an invention; anything requiring more than ordinary ingenuity and mechanical skill to perfect.

manufacturer. A person or organization producing finished goods from the raw material to the final product. One who employs capital, equipment and labor in the production or assembly of manufactured articles.

manufacturer's and contractor's insurance. See under INSURANCE, CASUALTY AND LIABILITY.

manufacturer's agent. See under AGENT.

manufacturer's brand. See under BRAND.

manufacturer's representative. A person or organization acting as a sales representative for a manufacturer, on a commission basis. A *manufacturer's representative* doesn't take title to the goods he handles, but may perform many of the services of a wholesale distributor, such as billing, arranging for shipment, etc. Usually, he represents several related but non-competitive lines of goods. See also AGENT, MANUFACTURER'S.

manufacturer's sales branch. See under SALES BRANCH.

manufacturer's store. A RETAIL STORE operated by a manufacturer, usually for the purpose of experimenting with marketing and promotional techniques, or of measuring consumer acceptance of new products.

manufacturing expense. See under EXPENSE (2).

manuscript. Literally, written by hand. As used, a *manuscript* is any instrument or document not mechanically printed, so that it may be either hand written or prepared by typewriter.

margin. 1. In accounting, the difference between the cost of goods sold and the total net sales income; the GROSS MARGIN or gross PROFIT.

2. In the securities trade, the amount of money a customer must deposit with a broker to cover the difference between the amount of credit the broker is permitted to extend him and the market value of the securities he purchases. Before World War II, brokers were permitted to require only 10 or 20 percent *margin,* but *margin* trading was abolished during the war, and *margin* requirements have been kept high since.

The difference between the *margin* requirement and the cost of the security is, in effect, a loan by the broker to the customer, with the security as collateral, and the broker charges interest on this loan. For example, if a customer buys 100 shares of stock selling at 40, so that the total cost is $4,000, and chooses to buy on *margin,* with requirements as 75 percent, he must pay the broker $3,000, and pay interest on the remaining $1,000, until either he pays the amount or sells the securities.

~ **account.** An account maintained with a broker by a customer who is trading on *margin* on the securities exchange.

~ **call.** A demand by a broker for an additional deposit on securities bought on *margin,* usually made when the market price of the securities has fallen, so that the collateral value of the stock against the loan made has decreased.

marginal. 1. In general, on the border line; doubtful. For example, a *marginal* business is one which operates on the border between profitable and unprofitable operations, so that any decrease in sales or income will force it out of business.

2. In economics, that which results from the addition of one more unit. Thus, the

MARGINAL COST is the cost of producing one additional unit, the *marginal profit* is the rate of profit that would be earned on one more unit produced or sold, etc.

marginal cost. In economics, the cost of producing or acquiring one additional unit or the next incremental amount of an item. In most manufacturing operations, the *marginal cost* continues to decrease as the volume of production increases, due to more efficient use of equipment, broader distribution of overhead costs, etc. Beyond a point, however, the *marginal cost* may begin to increase, due to overtime scheduling, the use of less efficient equipment, etc.

marginal credit. See under CREDIT (3).

margin of profit. See PROFIT.

margin of safety. In investment banking, the difference between the total price of a bond issue and the actual value of the property against which it is issued. In general, it is the excess of the market value of any collateral over the amount of a loan secured by the collateral. Also, sometimes, the excess of total earnings of a business over the amount needed to pay the interest on its outstanding loans.

marine contract. See under CONTRACT (1).

marine insurance. See INSURANCE, MARINE.

marine league. See LEAGUE.

maritime bill of lading. See under BILL OF LADING.

maritime law. The branch of law relating particularly to commerce and navigation on the high seas, and to the vessels and employees involved.

maritime lien. See LIEN MARITIME.

mark. 1. The identifying sign or character made by a person who is unable to write. The usual practice is for some third person to write the name of the one who makes the *mark,* together with the words, *his mark,* above or below the *mark.* See also SIGNATURE.

2. The sign put on goods by a manufacturer or distributor to identify their source. See also TRADEMARK; BRAND; LABEL.

3. Evidence or proof; as, for example, a *mark* of confidence, or *mark* of fraud.

4. To put a price or price tag on goods. See also MARKUP, MARKDOWN.

markdown. 1. Any reduction of price below the originally marked or intended selling price. In systems of retail accounting in which goods are priced as they are received, an item may be *marked down* before it is actually placed on sale, if it is offered for sale at a price below that which would usually be charged for such goods.

2. To decrease the valuation of assets, such as securities held, to reflect a reduction in their market value. See also WRITE DOWN.

marked check. See under CHECK.

market. 1. In general, a public time and place for buying and selling goods and services; a place or set of conditions in which buyers and sellers are brought together, either face-to-face or through some means of communication, and either directly or through agents, brokers, etc., for the buying, selling, or exchange of goods and services.

2. The demand or potential demand for a given commodity or product; as, the *market* for sugar, or the potential *market* for a new product.

3. The operation of the forces of supply and demand to fix the prices and the amount of trade in the exchange of goods, securities, etc. The activity of these forces is described in such terms as ACTIVE MARKET, BROAD MARKET, NARROW MARKET, INACTIVE MARKET, etc.

4. The *market* price, as in the phrase "cost or *market,* whichever is lower."

5. A store, such as a meat *market,* vegetable *market,* etc.

6. To distribute for sale; to move goods through the various steps from producer to consumer.

7. The securities exchange; the New York Stock Exchange and its associated institutions.

marketable. Of such a nature that it may be sold in an open market; in fit condition to be offered for sale. See also MERCHANTABLE.

marketable security. See under SECURITY (1).

marketable title. See under TITLE.

marketing. The total of all the phases of business activity directed toward, and resulting in the flow of goods from the original producer to the final consumer. In the broad sense, this includes not only selling, but advertising, packaging, research, and other non-manufacturing activities. See also DISTRIBUTION.

marketing cooperative. See under COOPERATIVE.

marketing plan. A comprehensive program devised by a business organization, covering all the methods and procedures involved in marketing the products or services of the company.

marketing research. The gathering, recording, analysis and interpretation of the facts involved in problems arising out of the marketing of goods or services, from producer to consumer. It includes the study, among other things, of the relationships between production and consumption, the preparation

and packaging of goods, their physical distribution, wholesale and retail selling, the nature of the market for the goods, and so forth. It is a much broader field than MARKET RESEARCH, which is involved solely with the study of the market for the goods.

market letter. A circular letter or bulletin, prepared and distributed by a securities dealer or analyst, which usually contains information about individual securities and about the trend in the market and the factors influencing it. Such a letter may be distributed free to the dealer's customers, or it may be sold on a subscription basis.

market offering. In the securities trade, an offering of securities, such as an additional issue, or those previously closely held, in which the offering price is represented to be the prevailing market price.

market order. See under ORDER (4).

market-out clause. A clause sometimes inserted in a securities underwriting agreement, by which the underwriter, who agrees to sell the issue of securities at a stated price within a given period of time, reserves the right to terminate the agreement if unfavorable market conditions should arise.

market planning. The process of setting up company objectives for marketing activity, and of determining and scheduling the steps necessary to achieve these objectives. Sales planning.

market potential. The expected or possible sales of all makes or brands of a commodity or product, or of a group of products or services in a specified market. It differs from a SALES POTENTIAL, which is the potential sale for the products of one company.

market price. See under PRICE.

market research. An area of MARKETING RESEARCH, which is concerned with measuring the extent and nature of the market, and determining its characteristics.

market value. See under VALUE (2).

markon. The amount which a dealer or merchant adds to his cost of merchandise to cover his costs of doing business and provide for a profit. The cost of goods, including freight, plus markon, equals selling price. *Markon* is sometimes distinguished from MARKUP in that it is figured in dollars and cents, while the latter is a percentage. See also GROSS MARGIN.

markup. 1. The percentage by which a merchant increases the cost of goods to arrive at his selling price. The retail *markup,* or *markup* on retail, is the difference between the cost price and selling price figured as a percentage of the selling price, while the *markup* on cost is the same difference figured as a percentage of the cost. For example, if an item is purchased for $6.00 and priced to sell for $10.00, the *markup* on retail is 40 percent, and the *markup* on cost is 66⅔ percent. *Markup* differs from MARKON in that it is a percentage, not actual dollars and cents, and from GROSS MARGIN in that it is an intended percentage of gain, while the latter is the realized percentage of gain.

2. To increase the valuation of assets, such as securities held, to reflect an improvement in their market value. See also WRITE UP.

marline rate. A contraction of the term market line rate. It is a coined term for a measure of advertising effectiveness, based on the cost per AGATE LINE of advertising space, in relation to the total dollar volume of sales volume in the market reached by the particular publication. It is used as a basis of comparison between the effective cost of advertising in different media.

marshal. 1. A federal officer who is assigned to a local district to carry out the orders of the federal courts and other agencies of the national government in the district. The *marshal* is roughly the equivalent of the sheriff, who operates on the state level.

2. To arrange or rank in order, to place in order of priority. For example, to *marshal* the assets in an estate is to arrange the property and wealth in the estate in order, so that all of the creditors, heirs and other claimants may receive their due proportion. Similarly, to *marshal* claims against an estate or a bankrupt is to rank the claims in the proper classes and order of priority, so that each will receive the maximum proper satisfaction.

mart. A market or market place; a trading center; a place where goods are publicly bought and sold.

martial law. A system of law effective only in time of war, emergency, or civil disorder; the emergency rulings made by the military commander in charge of an area for the purpose of restoring or maintaining order and public safety. It is distinguished from military law, which is the organized law governing those who are regularly under the jurisdiction of the armed forces. See also ARTICLES OF WAR.

Mason-Dixon line. The surveyed line between the colonies of Pennsylvania and Maryland, originally run by the surveyors Charles Mason and Jeremiah Dixon, to help settle a dispute between the Pennsylvania colony and Lord Baltimore. It has become traditionally recognized as the dividing line between the North and South along the eastern seaboard.

Massachusetts trust. See under TRUST (3).

mass production. The manufacture or processing of very large numbers of identical items, particularly by the use of machinery, and frequently involving the use of assembly line methods. The *mass production* industries are those characterised by this type of production, including the automobile industry, low-priced apparel industries, etc., as distinguished from such industries as fine furniture, machine tool building, construction, etc., in which production is usually carried out on each article separately.

master. 1. In general, the person in position of command, authority, or direction. A ship's *master,* for example, is the captain or commanding officer.

2. The one to which others are subsidiary; the one which serves as a pattern or model. For example, a *master* set of plans is the one from which the plans for details, components or subsidiary parts are adapted.

3. A skilled worker who has reached the highest degree of skill and experience in his trade or craft, and who supervises the work of JOURNEYMEN and APPRENTICES. For example, a *master* printer or *master* plumber.

master agreement. A labor agreement worked out between a union and the leading employers in an industry or an employers' association. It becomes the essential guide for all subsidiary agreements between the union and individual employers in the same industry or craft.

master and servant relationship. In law, the relationship between one who employs another and the one who offers his services or labor for a consideration. It differs from the relationship between a PRINCIPAL and an AGENT or INDEPENDENT CONTRACTOR in that the master is considered to have continuous control over the manner in which the employee or servant performs the work, not merely in the results.

master in chancery. An assistant to a judge in a court of EQUITY or CHANCERY, who examines cases, takes preliminary testimony and makes reports and recommendations to the judge in cases of equity.

master policy. See under POLICY (2).

matched order. A form of securities exchange manipulation, whereby two or more dealers or speculators conspire to create the impression of an active market, or attempt to raise the price of a security. Each party places an order to buy and sell the same security, so that when the transaction is completed no stock has actually changed hands. This maneuver, which results in what is known as a WASH SALE, is now outlawed under the Securities Exchange Act of 1934. See also CHURNING.

material. 1. Relating to matter and substance, content, or physical existence, rather than to form or emotion. For example, a *material* objection is one to the content of a statement or evidence, and a *material* alteration is one to the substance of a thing.

2. Important or critical; having influence or effect on the outcome; substantial. For example, a *material* charge or allegation is one, which, if withdrawn or disproved, would alter the basis of a case.

materials. The things needed to do a piece of work, particularly those which are to be incorporated in the final product. There is no sharp definition agreed on as to the exact limits of the term. In contracts calling for one or the other parties to supply all *materials,* for example, interpretations have differed as to whether these include such things as fuel, cleaning supplies, packing, and so forth. It is therefore best to specify such matters in the agreement. See also RAW MATERIALS.

materials handling. The area of business operation concerned with the movement of materials, supplies, and products through the various stages of production, distribution, and storage. It does not include the transport of materials from place to place by carrier, but does include their loading and unloading. *Materials handling* equipment includes a wide variety of devices, from simple wheelbarrows to elaborate conveyor systems, pipelines, etc.

material value. See VALUE (2), ACTUAL CASH.

matured. With respect to any obligation, such as a note, bill, bond, etc., the term indicating that it has become due and is payable, or has reached the end of its full term.

matured bond. See under BOND (1).

maturity. The time fixed for the payment of any obligation, such as a note, bill, bond, etc., which has a definite time of payment included in its terms. When an obligation has run its full period, and has become due and payable, it has reached *maturity.* See also YIELD TO MATURITY.

maturity basis. A method of calculating the rate of return on a bond or similar obligation if it is held until maturity, based on the dividend or interest received and the price at which the bond will be redeemed at maturity. For example, a bond bought at

$120, and paying $6 in interest, or 5 percent on the basis of its purchase price, is said to pay 6 percent on a *maturity basis* if it will eventually be redeemed for $100. See also YIELD TO MATURITY; INCOME BASIS.

maximum. The greatest amount, or highest degree or level attained or attainable. An upper limit set by law or regulation, such as a *maximum* price.

mean. An AVERAGE (1).

mean deviation. See DEVIATION (3).

means. 1. Financial resources; money, property, wealth or other assets. A man of *means* for example, is a person of substantial wealth.

2. In general, the instrument, method, or agency by which something is achieved or accomplished.

means test. A test for unemployment benefits, relief, or other charity, in which the applicant's total wealth is taken into account in determining his eligibility, rather than simply his earnings, or lack of earnings. The term has now been extended to other fields, so that, for example, a scholarship which depends on financial need as well as scholastic ability is said to have a *means test* attached.

measure. 1. A law, statute, or act of a legislature, or a proposed law or act. Originally, a step taken, an action.

2. Any of various systems of measurement; as, for example, dry *measure,* cubic *measure,* nautical *measure,* etc.

3. A unit or vessel of standard capacity or quantity, used to *measure* out various amounts or quantities. In different fields, a *measure* of something may be the amount contained in a standard measuring unit, which is understood among those in the trade. In the dairy industry, for example, a *measure* is usually understood to be equal to one cup of eight ounces.

measured day rate. An hourly wage rate which is periodically set and adjusted according to the employee's average measured and recorded efficiency of production during each day of a previous base period, usually the immediately preceding period.

measurement goods. In shipping usage, a term for goods or commodities for which freight charges are based on cubic measurements, rather than on actual weight. For some light goods packed in bales, for example, 40 cubic feet is reckoned as the equivalent of one ton in figuring freight charges. See also TON, MEASUREMENT.

measure of damages. In law, any of several established rules of law according to which compensation is to be estimated and awarded in cases involving claims for DAMAGES. The laws of the various states differ as to the particular acceptable *measures of damages,* but these usually include compensation for services, restitution for wrong done, indemnity for loss, punishment for malicious or intentional act, etc.

measure of value. Anything with which several different things may be compared, to measure their relative worth. Any common property of two or more things which, by comparison, can yield a measure of their relative worth. The most common *measure of value* is, of course, money. But for common stocks, for example, dividend yield is one principal *measure of value.*

mechanic. In general, anyone who works with tools, or who works on a machine. In industry, the term usually refers to one who makes, repairs, maintains or adjusts machinery or equipment, rather than one who merely operates a machine.

mechanical patent. See PATENT.

mechanic's lien. See under LIEN.

median. See under AVERAGE (1).

mediation. Literally, the act of coming between. A process in which a disinterested third party acts to settle a dispute between two contending parties, by bringing them together to discuss their differences, and to compromise them on a basis acceptable to both. It is frequently resorted to to settle labor disputes, but also is used to settle any disputes over contract terms, compensation, etc. *Mediation* is sometimes distinguished from CONCILIATION in that a conciliator takes an active part in the discussion and makes recommendations for settlement, whereas a mediator acts simply as a go-between to bring the parties together and to keep them together until a settlement is reached. See also ARBITRATION.

medical expense insurance. See under INSURANCE, LIFE, ACCIDENT, AND HEALTH.

medium. A method, channel, or agency of communication, such as a newspaper, magazine, radio, television, etc. The term is usually used in the plural as *media.* See, for example, ADVERTISING, MEDIA; ADVERTISING MEDIUM.

medium of exchange. Anything which is useful in facilitating the exchange or transfer of one thing for another; anything which has a value measurable in relation to several different things, so that it can serve to effect their exchange by providing a common basis of measurement. Common examples include money, notes, checks, etc.

meet. To settle; to make payment; especially within the period or at the time specified; as, to *meet* a payment, *meet* a bill, *meet* a payroll, or *meet* a dividend.

melon. In business slang, a large surplus or profit; a large extra distribution to stockholders, such as might be the result of the liquidation of a subsidiary company, an especially profitable period of operations, etc. See also CUT A MELON.

member bank. See under BANK.

member bank reserves. See RESERVE (2).

member firm. In the securities trade, a firm of securities dealers or brokers, at least one member of which is an admitted member of a particular securities exchange.

memorandum. In general, something to be remembered; an informal note or reminder as a record of some act or event. In business an instrument or statement intended to provide a record of a transaction, rather than to serve as a basis for action. See each of the following under the principal listing: ~ BILL (4); ~ CHECK (1); ~ SALE (1).

memorandum clause. In marine insurance, a term for a clause inserted in policies, releasing the insurance underwriter from liability for damage to insured cargo from specified causes, such as damage to especially perishable foodstuffs by salt water, sea air, weathering, etc.

mercantile. In general, pertaining to merchants and to their business activities; applicable to trade, and to the buying and selling of goods and services. It is virtually a synonym for COMMERCIAL.

mercantile agency. An organization which collects data on the credit, financial strength, general business reputation, etc., of merchants, individuals and other customers or businesses, as an agent for its subscribers or members. Some *mercantile agencies* specialize in particular lines of trade or in particular areas, while others are general in their coverage. Some are organized as cooperative ventures by suppliers in a given field, or as adjuncts to trade associations, and some are strictly profit-making business organizations. See also CREDIT RATING.

mercantile bill. See BILL OF EXCHANGE, COMMERCIAL.

mercantile paper. See under COMMERCIAL PAPER.

mercenary. Literally, for a reward; for hire; hence, out of a desire for money. A person whose services are available for hire, such a professional soldier, is a *mercenary.* Similarly, a public official or other person whose favor can be purchased, is called *mercenary.*

merchandise. 1. All the commodities, goods and other articles of commerce that merchants may buy to resell, at wholesale or retail. The term does not include real estate or services, but is restricted to tangible goods which are held for sale, not as private property. As generally used, it is understood to exclude foods, beverages and other products which are immediately consumed in use.

2. To plan for the effective sale of goods, by arranging to present the right styles, prices, size assortments etc., at the right times to the buying public. To analyze past sales patterns for the purpose of determining which assortments of goods to offer for sale at particular times. See also MERCHANDISE PLANNING.

3. To promote the sale of goods or services; to coordinate advertising and selling operations to increase the sale of goods. For example, the use of reprints of magazine advertisements as point of sale material in retail stores, or the use of promotional sales techniques to sell services which are ordinarily not sold in this manner, are illustrations of *merchandising* in this sense.

merchandise planning. The analysis, planning, and execution of sales programs, including the choice of items, prices, styles, sizes and other characteristics of the goods, and the proper seasonal timing of purchases, inventory and sales presentation. *Merchandise planning,* or merchandising, is one part of the planning for profitable retail operation, the other part being the successful administration of selling and other expenses.

merchandiser. 1. An employee or executive whose work it is to MERCHANDISE the products or services of a company, either in sense (2) or sense (3). An expert salesman or promoter.

2. A fixture for promoting the sale of packaged goods in retail stores by making full assortments of sizes, styles, colors, etc., available for selection by the customer. It usually consists of a series of racks, bins, or divided shelves, in a unit designed either to stand on the floor or rest on the top of the selling counter. See also SELF-SERVICE.

merchant. 1. Literally, one who trades; a person who buys and resells goods for profit; a WHOLESALER or RETAILER.

2. Pertaining to trade, or to the buying and selling of goods; used in trade, or taking part in trade. A *merchant* seaman, for example, is one serving on a commercial or *merchant* ship, *merchant* PIG IRON is iron intended for sale to foundries and other processors, rather than for use by the company making it.

merchantable. In general, capable of being sold in the market; fit to be offered for sale. The word has specific meanings in the laws of the various states, which provide that goods must be in *merchantable* condition. See also MARKETABLE.

merchantable quality. See GOOD MERCHANTABLE QUALITY AND CONDITION.

merchant marine. In general, the total of the privately owned and operated ships of a nation; more particularly, those ships which are operated to carry cargo or passengers, or both, for profit. Private pleasure craft are ordinarily not considered to be part of the *merchant marine.*

merchant's rule. A procedure for the partial settlement of debts, usually used for debts of less than one year maturity, and sometimes used for debts of more than one year maturity when state law doesn't specify the application of the UNITED STATES RULE for these debts. Under the *merchant's rule,* the principal amount is considered to earn interest until the final settlement, or until the end of the first year, if this is sooner. Each repayment is also considered to earn interest from the date it is made until final settlement or until the end of the first year. The amount still due at any time is thus the amount of the loan plus interest, less the amounts repaid and the interest earned on them. On a debt for longer than one year, the amount still due is figured at the end of each year, and interest is added in each succeeding year only on the amount still due at the beginning of the year.

merchant wholesaler. See under WHOLESALER.

merger. In law, the absorption of a smaller estate by a larger one, and the extinguishment of the smaller one. In business, the fusion of one or more lesser companies into a larger one, by any of several means. The larger company may buy all of the outstanding stock of the smaller, for example, or it may give shares of its own stock in exchange for the shares of the *merged* company, or it may buy all of the assets of the smaller company, after which the shareholders of the smaller company usually vote to dissolve the remaining corporate shell. Strictly speaking, a *merger* is distinguished from a CONSOLIDATION, in which two or more equally important companies are dissolved into a completely new company, with none of the original companies surviving.

merit increase. A wage increase which is granted to an individual worker only when earned by greater proficiency or quality of work, rather than as a result of seniority, or due to increased output by the group as a whole. Some companies may specify the maximum amount and maximum frequency of *merit increases,* while others may leave the matter entirely to the discretion of each supervisor.

merit rating. 1. An organized and methodical plan for measuring the performance of the individual employee over a specified period of time, such as a year or half-year. In the typical plan, several factors are chosen as measuring performance, and numerical values are given to the worker's achievement in each of these factors. The values used may be determined by use of a scale, by check list, by comparison with one or more other workers, etc.

2. In insurance, an EXPERIENCE RATING.

metallic money. See under MONEY.

meter. The basic unit of length in the METRIC SYSTEM of linear measure. As originally conceived, it was to be one-ten millionth of the distance from one of the poles of the earth to the equator. As now used, it is the length of a standard metric bar, at the temperature of melting ice, at sea level atmospheric pressure. It is the equivalent of 39.371 inches, 3.281 feet, or 1.0936 yards in the English linear scale.

metric system. The system of weights and measures originally devised at the time of the French Revolution, and now in standard use in most countries not using the English system of weights and measures. The entire system is based on four principal units, and their decimal multiples and decimal parts. The four basic units are the METER as a measure of length; the LITER as a measure of volume; the GRAM as a unit of weight; and the ARE as a unit of land area. Each of these are combined in multiples of ten, one hundred, one thousand, etc., designated, respectively, by the Greek prefixes DECA, HECTO, KILO, etc.; and subdivided into tenths, hundredths, thousandths, etc., designated by the Latin prefixes DECI, CENTI, MILLI, etc.

metric ton. See under TON.

metropolis. Originally, from the Greek, a mother-city; a city or city-state from which colonies were sent out. As currently used, any large central city, especially one surrounded by smaller towns.

metropolitan area. See STANDARD METROPOLITAN AREA.

middleman. In general, an intermediary, a go-between; hence, an AGENT, BROKER, or WHOLESALER. In current usage, the term is used only in a broad sense, meaning any person who performs a function between the producer and consumer of goods. This may include transportation, storage, wholesale or retail distribution, etc.

middle management. In general, the group or class of junior executives and senior supervisory personnel in the direct line of authority and communications between the top levels of management and the first-line supervisory personnel. It has no exact limits, but generally includes division and department heads, staff specialists, etc.

midnight shift. In an industrial plant or other facility operating on a 24-hour day, the work shift beginning at midnight, and usually ending at 8 a.m. It is usually known as the LOBSTER SHIFT or GRAVEYARD SHIFT.

mile. A standard unit of linear measure or geographic distance, originally equal to 1,000 paces, or about 1,620 yards. The English and American mile is the equivalent of 1,760 yards, 5,280 feet, 320 rods, or 8 furlongs. Also known as the *statute mile,* or *land mile.*

nautical $\sim$. The standard measure of distance by sea or air, originally established as one minute (1/60 of a degree) of longitude at the equator, and now fixed as 6,080 feet. The *nautical mile* is sometimes confused with the KNOT, which is actually a rate of speed of one *nautical mile* per hour. Also known as the *admiralty mile, geographic mile, air mile,* or *sea mile.*

mileage. 1. In general, length or distance measured in miles. For example, car *mileage* is the total number of miles travelled by a particular freight or passenger car, or by all of the cars of a railroad. Similarly, track *mileage* is the total number of miles of track operated by a railroad, air route *mileage* is the total number of miles of flight routes operated by an airline, etc.

2. An allowance or rate of compensation for travel expenses, based on the number of miles travelled. For example, an employee who travels occasionally may be given a *mileage* allowance for each trip to cover fares, meals, etc., en route. A salesman who operates his own car on company business may be given a *mileage* allowance to cover his costs for gasoline, maintenance, depreciation, etc.

3. A charge or rate based on the number of miles goods are carried, a vehicle travels, etc.

milestone. Originally, a marker used on a road or highway to mark off each mile of distance between cities or other points. Now, any major point or stage of progress which is reached and passed, such as an anniversary, a level of production or sales, a number of customers, etc.

military law. See ARTICLES OF WAR.

milk. To manipulate a business or a fund in such a way as to drain off profits or the value of an investment to the personal advantage of the one doing the manipulating, but to the long-run detriment of the interests of the business or the fund. For example, an executive who draws an excessive salary from the business he manages is *milking* the business, and a trustee who takes excessive expense charges from a trust fund in his care is *milking* the fund.

mill. 1. In industry, to remove material from a piece of work, especially metal, by grinding or cutting. Also, a machine designed to grind or cut material.

2. A plant or factory in which material is ground, cut, or otherwise worked on. More generally, any factory. In the textile field, for example, plants engaged in spinning, weaving, knitting, and other operations are all referred to as *mills.*

2. In the United States, a fractional money of account, equivalent to one-tenth of a CENT. It is used in some price quotations and tax rates, but not in general trade.

Miller-Tydings Act. See FAIR TRADE LAW.

milli-. In the METRIC SYSTEM, the prefix used for any unit of measure which is one one-thousandth of a basic unit. It is now also frequently used for any unit which is one one-thousandth of another, whether or not in the metric system. Examples include the milligram, millimeter, millivolt, etc.

mill net price. See under PRICE.

mill run. See RUN-OF-MILL.

mineral lease. See under LEASE.

mine run. See RUN-OF-MINE.

minim. A unit of liquid measure in the apothecaries' measure, equal to one 60th of a fluid DRAM, or one 480th of a fluid OUNCE. It is used almost exclusively in the measurement of chemicals or prescription components.

minimum. The least amount, or the lowest degree or level attainable or permitted. A lower limit set by law or regulation, such as a MINIMUM WAGE.

minimum charge. A basic charge or cost that must be paid for a service, even though on a per unit, per hour, or similar basis the amount of the charge would be less. A utility company, for example, may have a monthly *minimum charge* for electricity or gas, regardless of the amount consumed, and a trucking company may make a *minimum*

charge for LESS-THAN-TRUCKLOAD shipments, when the weight of the shipment is below a specified amount.

minimum resale price. See RESALE PRICE MAINTENANCE.

minimum wage. The lowest permitted hourly wage rate, established by a WAGE-HOUR LAW, or by the terms of a union agreement. It may be a general minimum, applying to all types of work, or a specific one, applying particular *minimum wage* rates to different types of work. See also WAGES.

mining claim. See under CLAIM (2).

mining lease. See LEASE, MINERAL.

mining partnership. See under PARTNERSHIP.

minor. 1. Relatively less important; inferior or subordinate to another thing or class of things. See, for example COIN, MINOR.

2. A person who has not yet reached the age of MAJORITY; who is not yet an ADULT. For most legal purposes, a person who is under 21 years of age, but under the criminal laws of the several states the age varies, and may be 16 or some other age. See also INFANT.

minority. 1. The status of being a MINOR (2). The condition of one who has not yet reached the age of MAJORITY, which may differ from state to state.

2. Less than half, as in voting. There may be more than one *minority* vote, depending on the number of choices or candidates for each of which less than half of the voters cast their choice. Unless otherwise specified, a *minority* vote is considered to be of those voting, rather than of those present, or of those eligible to vote.

mint. 1. A place or plant in which money is coined under government authority. In the United States, metallic coinage is manufactured in several *mints,* and paper currency is manufactured in the Bureau of Engraving in Washington, D. C. Also, to make or stamp out coins.

2. New, or unused; in the original condition. A stamp which is unused and still has the original mucilage on its back, for example, is said to be in *mint* condition.

mint mark. The identifying mark placed on a coin at the time of manufacture to indicate the particular mint in which it was made. A coin made at the Denver mint carries a small letter D, for example, and one made at the San Francisco mint a small letter S.

mint par. See PAR OF EXCHANGE.

mint remedy. In U.S. Treasury practice, a term for the tolerance or allowance which will be made in the acceptance of coins which have been reduced in weight by abrasion. When gold coins circulated, for example, only a coin which had lost not more than ½ of 1 percent of its weight in 20 years of circulation was accepted at full face value by the U.S. Treasury. At present, there is no specific limit for silver coins, which will be accepted at full face value until their identification is obliterated. Also, the small allowance which is made for a difference in the fineness of the metal used in coins.

minute. 1. As a measure of time, one 60th part of an hour, or 60 seconds. As a measure of latitude or longitude, one 60th part of a degree.

2. A record of what has occurred, such as at a meeting, or assembly. Usually used in the plural. Corporate charters usually require that *minutes* be recorded and kept of all meetings of the stockholders and of the board of directors.

misappropriate. To take wrongly and fraudulently, especially to take things or money entrusted to one's care. For example, a TRUSTEE may misappropriate funds from a TRUST in his care.

misbrand. To label or mark a product in any false or misleading fashion, such as to indicate that it is of a higher grade than is the case, or that it is the product of another manufacturer. Such action is, of course, a violation of state and federal laws.

misdemeanor. In law, any criminal offense which does not amount to a FELONY in the particular state in which it occurs. Generally, the significant distinction is that a felony will be punished by a term in the state penitentiary, while a *misdemeanor* is punishable only by a shorter term in a local prison.

misfeasance. The failure to perform properly some lawful act or duty, such as the failure to carry out an order properly, or the performing of some duty without proper notice to those concerned. It is distinguished from MALFEASANCE, which is the performing of wrongful acts, and from NONFEASANCE, which is the complete omission or failure to perform duties.

misrepresentation. Generally, any statement of alleged fact which is untrue, or partly untrue, or which is so stated as to lead to false conclusions. For example, a false description of the condition of property in an insurance application, which would lead to the wrong premium being charged, is clearly a *misrepresentation*. In the eyes of the law, a *misrepresentation* may be innocent, that is, the person committing it may believe the statements to be true and correct; it may be negligent, that is, the committer may have no real knowledge of the truth or falsity of the statements made; or it may be fraudulent, that is, it may be made with full knowledge and intent to deceive.

missionary. In business, a representative of a manufacturer or supplier who visits his employer's customers, or the customers of distributors of his employer's products, for the purpose of stimulating goodwill and promoting sales, without making sales directly. He may, for example, train salespeople, set up displays, teach employees how to use the product, etc. The use of the term is believed to have originated in the liquor trade.

mistake. In law, an act or conclusion which is unintentional and based on ignorance, rather than on negligence or fraud. A *mistake* may or may not destroy the validity of an agreement or contract, depending on the circumstances and on the terms of local statutes. However, in the event of a loss or injury, the person committing the *mistake* is liable for damages, even though there is no gross or criminal negligence involved.

mixed. Containing or referring to things of more than one type or class; compounded of several elements which are still identifiable, rather than completely dissolved or fused together. See each of the following under the principal listing: ~ CURRENCY; ~ NUISANCE; ~ POLICY (2).

mode. See AVERAGE (1).

model. In general, a representation of an object or design, usually on a reduced scale; a copy, pattern, style, or design; anything to be copied or reproduced.

model law. One proposed for adoption by the several states by the United States Commissioners on Uniform Laws, or by a trade association or other group, but not of broad application or sufficient urgency to be recommended as a UNIFORM LAW.

moiety. In general, one of two equal parts; a half. More particularly, an undivided half interest in anything, as in a joint tenancy or estate. See also JOINT.

moisture content. As used in contracts, the moisture which a product, such as flour, wood pulp, cotton, etc., naturally absorbs during storage or transportation. Most contracts are based on dry weight, which is calculated in such cases as the actual weight less a percentage allowance for *moisture content*.

monetary standard. The particular standard of value established by law as the basis of the money of any country. In modern times, most countries have adopted either gold or silver, or the money of another country which is based on gold or silver, as the *monetary standard*.

monetary unit. The basic unit of measure for the money of a country, in terms of which all of its coins and currency are defined. In the United States, for example, the *monetary unit* is the DOLLAR, while in England it is the POUND STERLING.

monetize. To adopt as money, or as the basis for a system of money; to make legal as money. When congressmen from silver-mining states demanded the *monetization* of silver, for example, they were asking that the dollar be defined in ounces of silver, and that silver be freely coined. See also DEMONETIZE.

money. Originally, from the Latin, coins stamped in the temple of Juno Moneta, which was the Roman mint. Now, any circulating MEDIUM OF EXCHANGE which is widely accepted as a standard of value. Strictly speaking, it includes the coins and currency issued by a government, but more generally it includes all of those things which are readily accepted in payment for goods and services or to settle debts, such as CHECKS, DRAFTS, NOTES, etc. The chief types and classes of *money* are listed and defined below. See also each of the following under the principal listing: BOOT ~; CALL ~; DISPATCH ~; EARNEST ~; PURCHASE ~; SMART ~; TIME ~.

base metal ~. Coins made of metals less valuable than gold or silver. In the United States, for example, the CENT and the NICKEL are in this class.

cheap ~. See EASY MONEY, below.

commodity ~. The term for any metallic *money* whose intrinsic value as metal is the same as its face value, as distinguished from TOKEN MONEY, which see below. Currently, none of the regularly circulated United States coins of less than one dollar in value are COMMODITY MONEY, in this sense.

convertible ~. That *money* or paper currency that is convertible into gold or silver coins or bullion, and for which a reserve, equal to all or part of its face value, is maintained in gold or silver. The SILVER CERTIFICATE is an example of such *money*.

easy ~. *Money* borrowed at a low rate of interest, or available for loan at low interest rates. *Money* is said to be *easy* when the supply of loanable funds equals or ex-

ceeds the demand for loans. It is also called cheap *money*. See also TIGHT MONEY, below.

fiat ~. Paper *money* which has value only by fiat or decree of the government which has issued it, since it is backed by neither gold nor silver. The GREENBACKS issued during the Civil War, for example, were originally *fiat money*, though later made redeemable in gold.

fiduciary ~. That which is not fully backed by gold or silver, but which keeps its value because of the trust and confidence of the public in the government.

hard ~. In one sense, *money* fully backed by gold or silver, as distinguished from *money* backed in whole or in part by the credit of the government. Also, *money* which is borrowed or is available for loan only at high rates of interest, also known as TIGHT MONEY, which see below.

inconvertible ~. That which is not convertible into, or redeemable in gold or silver, but only in other *money* of the government. It is, in effect, simply a promise to pay on behalf of the government, or other issuing agency. FEDERAL RESERVE NOTES are in this class.

lawful ~. Any *money* declared by the government to be LEGAL TENDER; any *money* issued by a proper authority and backed by law, as distinguished from counterfeit *money*, or from any informal medium of exchange.

paper ~. In general, any CURRENCY, as distinguished from coinage, including BANK NOTES, DRAFTS, MONEY ORDERS, etc. Sometimes, the term is used loosely and incorrectly as a synonym for FIAT MONEY, which see above.

metallic ~. In general, the authorized coins of a country, as distinguished from the PAPER MONEY, which see above.

rag ~. In business slang, any depreciated paper *money*, such as, for example, the United States GREENBACKS, which sold at a discount from their face value before they were made redeemable in gold.

tight ~. In general, *money* which is difficult to borrow except at high rates of interest, as distinguished from EASY MONEY, which see above. Also, the description of the general condition said to exist when interest rates are high and *money* is difficult to borrow.

token ~. The term for all legal coins, the precious metal content of which is less than their face value, but which are still LEGAL TENDER. Currently, all of the generally circulating coins of the United States of less than one dollar in value are *token money* in this sense.

wildcat ~. Originally, the paper *money* issued by the wildcat banks of backwoods Wisconsin, which were so inaccessible that their bills could not be presented for redemption. Today, any paper *money* issued by a bank which is no longer able to redeem it in full, or whose liquidity is doubtful. See also BANK, WILDCAT.

money bill. In legislation, a BILL (3) dealing with the raising of revenues. Under Article I of the United States Constitution, all such bills must originate in the House of Representatives, but may be amended by the Senate.

money broker. See under BROKER (1).

money in circulation. As generally defined in economic statistics, all currency and coinage not held by the Federal Reserve Banks or the U.S. Treasury. It includes both that held by individuals and that held by banks as cash reserves. The phrase CURRENCY IN CIRCULATION is sometimes used with the same meaning.

money lender. See PAWNBROKER.

money market. In general, any place or system for dealing in short-term loans, negotiable instruments, etc. Also, the general machinery for handling the supply and demand of short-term loanable funds, as distinguished from the CAPITAL MARKET, which handles long-term funds and investments.

money of account. Any of the monetary units, or their multiples or subdivisions, which are authorized by law for use in reckoning value in all transactions or accounts. A unit of *money of account* need not be one that is actually issued. In the United States, for example, the MILL is part of the *money of account* but is not issued. In England, the guinea is only a *money of account* today, there being no coin of this value in use.

money order. A form of credit instrument used primarily for the transfer of money from one individual to another in a distant place without the necessity of forwarding cash. It is, in effect, a DRAFT drawn by the issuing bank or other institution on another, for the amount paid in by the purchaser of the order. The purchaser then forwards the order to the person in whose name it is made out, who may then receive its value at the place on which it is drawn. The principal classes are the following:

bank ~. One sold by a bank or banking institution, which may normally be cashed at any other bank, at home or abroad. It is similar to a cashier's check, except that it is sold to the general public, rather than only to customers of the bank. See also CHECK (1), CASHIER'S.

express ~. One sold by an express company and payable at any of its offices to the named person.

postal ~. One issued by a local United States Post Office, and payable at another post office. One payable at a post office in this country is known as a domestic *money order,* while one payable at a post office of another country, under an agreement between the two countries, is known as a foreign or international *money order.*

telegraphic ~. One issued by a telegraph company, and payable at one of its offices. Instead of being mailed to the person to whom it is to be paid, the order is sent by telegram, on a special form provided for the purpose.

money rate. The financial market term for the rate of interest at which money is available for short-term loans. Usually there is one rate for CALL MONEY; that is, money which must be returned on the demand of the leader, and one for TIME MONEY; that is money loaned for a specified period of time, such as 30 or 90 days. The rate for call money is ordinarily a little lower than that for time money.

money supply. In economics, the total of money outside of banks plus credit in the form of demand deposits, and sometimes plus time deposits. It is, in effect, the sum of the cash and credit immediately available to business and the public.

monger. A trader or seller. Today, the word is used only in combination with limiting or descriptive terms, such as *fishmonger, ironmonger,* etc. It is frequently used in a derogatory sense, as in *scandalmonger, admonger,* etc.

monometallism. An infrequently used term for a monetary system in which only one metal, such as gold or silver, is the basis of the monetary standard of the country, as distinguished from BIMETALLISM, in which both gold and silver are part of the monetary standard.

monopoly. 1. In general, an exclusive right or power to carry on a particular activity, such as to make a specified product, supply a service, and so forth. A PATENT, for example, gives an inventor a *monopoly* over his invention for a period of years. A state may give a *monopoly* over the supply of electric power to a given utility company for an area.

2. In business, the ownership or control of enough of the supply of or market for

a product or service to stifle competition, control prices, or otherwise restrict trade. Strictly speaking, a *monopoly* exists when a single company exerts such power, and control by two companies is a DUOPOLY, that by a few companies an OLIGOPOLY, etc.

month. The basic period of time into which the year is divided. Unless otherwise specified, the term means a calendar *month*, one of the *months* in the Gregorian calendar. When a period of a *month* from date is mentioned in a contract or agreement, the period until the same day of the next *month* is meant. When a business *month* is referred to, a period of 30 days is meant, as, for example, in the computation of ordinary interest. See also INTEREST, EXACT; INTEREST, ORDINARY.

monthly investment plan. The name for a plan devised by the New York Stock Exchange, and available through most securities brokers, under which investors may buy regular monthly amounts of one or more designated securities. The amount invested periodically need not be the price of an exact number of shares of stock, since fractional amounts are credited to the account of the investor. Since the amount invested remains steady, regardless of price fluctuations, the rate of share purchase may go up or down, and the plan is actually a form of DOLLAR AVERAGING.

moonshine. Any alcoholic liquor produced illegally; that is, by the light of the moon. More broadly, any illegal alcoholic liquor, whether produced illegally in this country, or produced legally elsewhere but smuggled into this country to avoid payment of import duties. See also BOOTLEG.

moot. In law, debatable or unsettled; not covered or made clear by previous cases or decisions. Thus, a *moot* point is one concerning which there is no uniform or clear-cut opinion.

moral hazard. See HAZARD.

moral obligation. See under OBLIGATION (1).

moratorium. In general, a period of delay granted by law or by executive action, during which a debtor or a class of debtors is not required to meet obligations which fall due. More specifically, an emergency act of a legislature authorizing a bank or all banks to suspend or defer making payments for a given period. See also BANK HOLIDAY.

morning loan. See LOAN, DAY.

Morris Plan Bank. See BANK, INDUSTRIAL.

mortality table. In statistics, one of a set of tables, showing for each age the expected death rate, the average number of years of

expected continued life, etc. Separate tables have been prepared for major groups in the population, such as white males, etc. In life insurance, such tables are used to determine the proper premiums to be charged for insuring the lives of persons in the various age groups. Sometimes known as an experience or life table. See also EXPECTANCY OF LIFE.

mortgage. A written conveyance of TITLE to property, but not its possession, to secure the payment of a debt or the performance of some obligation, under the condition that the conveyance is to be void upon final payment or performance. It is distinguished from a LIEN in that the creditor has actual title to the property, rather than merely a claim against it, and from a PLEDGE in that the debtor keeps possession of the property instead of depositing it. The various types of *mortgage* are listed and defined below. See also BOND.

adjustment ∼. See IMPROVEMENT MORTGAGE, below.

amortized ∼. One which provides that each payment reduces the principal of the *mortgage* as well as covering interest on the amount still due. The payments are usually specified to be regular and equal, so that the early payments are mostly interest, while the later ones are mostly principal. Most real estate *mortgages* are of this form.

blanket ∼. See GENERAL MORTGAGE, below.

chattel ∼. One on CHATTELS, or personal property, rather than on real property. This form of *mortgage* is usually used in the sale of automobiles and other major consumer items. It differs from a conditional sale in that title to the property is first transferred to the buyer and then taken back by the seller, or perhaps by a bank or finance company, rather than remaining in the seller from the beginning. In either case, however, the buyer doesn't receive full title until the final payment is made. See also SALE, CONDITIONAL; DEED OF TRUST.

closed ∼. One under the terms of which neither the amount of property mortgaged nor the amount of indebtedness may be changed during its existence. See also OPEN END MORTGAGE, below.

development ∼. One issued to raise funds for the development of a business, such as to buy additional equipment for a common carrier or local transportation company. The *mortgage* itself is usually on all of the property of the company, not merely on the equipment purchased.

direct reduction ∼. See AMORTIZED MORTGAGE, above.

equitable ∼. One existing in EQUITY, but

not evidenced by a formal agreement. A transfer of property to secure a loan, but without written documentation.

FHA ∼. One on housing, the repayment of which has been insured in whole or in part by the FEDERAL HOUSING ADMINISTRATION.

first ∼. That one which is prior to all others on the same property in order of claim, though not necessarily in time. It does not take precedence, however, over such prior liens as a mechanic's lien. See also LIEN, MECHANIC'S.

general ∼. One which covers all of the fixed property of a company, rather than specific buildings or equipment. Sometimes known as a blanket *mortgage*.

improvement ∼. One taken to finance improvements to property. The *mortgage* itself may be a JUNIOR MORTGAGE, which see below, on all of the property, not merely on the improvements made. Also known as an *adjustment mortgage*.

joint ∼. One issued jointly by two or more companies, and for which both are liable. Two companies which buy the property of a third for joint operation, for example, may issue a *joint mortgage* to finance the purchase.

junior ∼. One, such as a SECOND MORTGAGE, which see below, which is specified to be subordinate in its rights and claim to other *mortgages* on the same property, such as a FIRST MORTGAGE, which see above. See also SENIOR MORTGAGE, below.

open end ∼. In general, one which permits the mortgagor to borrow additional funds without making a new *mortgage*. It may permit a raising of the total amount of the *mortgage*, or the borrowing of additional funds after the total outstanding has been reduced by repayments, or it may have a face value of more than the initial amount borrowed, so that the total may be added to without a new authorization.

overlying ∼. A term referring to one which is subsequent in claim to another *mortgage*, such as a SECOND MORTGAGE, which see below, to a FIRST MORTGAGE, which see above. A JUNIOR MORTGAGE, which see above. See also UNDERLYING MORTGAGE, below.

purchase money ∼. The term for one given by a buyer of real estate, who has made an initial payment. The buyer receives title on the basis of his payment, then immediately transfers it back to the seller or to a bank as security for the unpaid balance of the price.

real estate ∼. One given on real estate, including both land and buildings. In some states, the laws covering such *mortgages*

provide that the transfer of title under the mortgage is actual, and that the creditor may take possession directly in the event of default. In the majority of states, however, the law treats the transfer of title more as a lien, and the creditor must bring a FORECLOSURE action and place the property for sale in the event of a default. Persons buying property under a *mortgage* should become familiar with the particular laws of the state involved.

second ∼. One that follows in order of claim to a FIRST MORTGAGE, which see above, on the same property. In the event of default, the laws of the various states differ as to the rights of the holder of a *second mortgage,* but in general he receives no payment until the claims of the first *mortgage* are satisfied.

senior ∼. A term for a *mortgage* which has precedence over another *mortgage* on the same property, though there may be, in turn, a *mortgage* which is *senior* to it. The term is relative, and does not describe the claim of a *mortgage* except in relation to a particular other *mortgage*. See also JUNIOR MORTGAGE, above.

underlying ∼. One which is prior in claim to one or more other *mortgages* on the same property; a SENIOR MORTGAGE, which see above. See also OVERLYING MORTGAGE, above.

mortgage bond. See under BOND (1).

mortgagee. The creditor or lender, to whom a mortgage is made or given.

mortgagee clause. In fire insurance policies, a clause covering the interests of the mortgagee in the event of loss, and providing for a distribution of the contribution to make up the loss in the event that the mortgagee has insured the property separately. See also INSURANCE, PROPERTY.

mortgage note. See under NOTE (2).

mortgagor. A debtor or borrower who gives or makes a mortgage to a lender, on property which the mortgagor owns.

mortmain. Literally, from the French, a dead hand. A term applied to property, such as that bought and held by a religious institution not for its own use, which is said to be controlled by a dead hand. Some states have laws restricting such ownership of property.

most favored nation clause. A clause, frequently included in commercial treaties between countries, providing that any and all concessions, privileges, advantages, or favors granted by either party to other nations must automatically be granted to the other party to the treaty, so that it receives the same privileges as the *most favored nation*. For example, a tariff reduction given by a country to any one country must also be given to all countries with which it has treaties containing such a clause. A privilege or advantage given in return for a consideration, however, need not be given to all other countries.

motion study. In industrial engineering, a detailed scientific analysis of the hand and body movements made by an employee in performing a particular task, for the purpose of determining more efficient methods for doing the same work, or to evaluate the task for wage purposes. Special photographic equipment is frequently used in such studies. See also TIME AND MOTION STUDY.

motor carrier classification. See CLASSIFICATION OF MOTOR CARRIERS.

movable. In general, that which can be changed from one location to another, though not necessarily portable, in the sense that it can be personally carried from place to place. In a contract, reference to *movables* usually means personal property, as distinguished from real property.

movable exchange. See under EXCHANGE (4).

move. In business usage, to dispose of, or to sell. The term is usually used to refer to an entire stock of goods, rather than to individual items.

multiple correlation. See under CORRELATION.

multiple insertion rate. In newspaper, magazine, and similar advertising, the scale of rates charged for advertising space for an advertisement that is to be run more than once. The rate is usually based on a sliding scale, with the charge per insertion decreasing as the number of scheduled insertions increases. See also ONE-TIME RATE.

multiple-line insurance company. See under INSURANCE COMPANY.

multiple listing. The procedure of placing or listing property which is to be sold or rented with several different real estate agents or brokers at the same time, rather than exclusively with one agent. Also, in some areas, an arrangement among local real estate agents under which the listing of property with one member of a *multiple listing* association automatically lists it with other agents who are members of the association.

multiple management. The term for a form of employee participation in company management, under which the members of top management are assisted in the formulation and execution of policy by committees of employees. These may be senior or key personnel, or they may be selected by the other employees as their representatives. The committees may be known by such names as JUNIOR BOARD OF DIRECTORS, junior management committee, etc.

municipal. As used in business, referring to a city, town, village, school or road district, or any political or administrative division smaller than a state or county. In the plural, a term used in the securities trade for all bonds of *municipal* or local governments. See each of the following under the principal listing: $\sim$ BOND (1); $\sim$ CORPORATION.

muniment. In general, anything which protects or enforces. Hence, a *muniment* of title is any document or instrument containing evidence or proof which may be used to support a claim to title of property.

mutual. Recriprocal; common between two or more parties; in friendly association. See each of the following under the principal listing: $\sim$ CONSIDERATION; $\sim$ INSURANCE; $\sim$ INSURANCE COMPANY; $\sim$ WILL.

mutual benefit society. See FRATERNAL SOCIETY.

mutual fund. See under INVESTMENT COMPANY.

mutual loan association. See SAVINGS AND LOAN ASSOCIATION.

mutual savings bank. See under BANK.

N

naked. Incomplete, lacking in some essential part, element or condition, and therefore invalid. For example, a *naked* CONTRACT is one in which there is no consideration involved. Also, unbalanced, or unilateral; for the benefit of only one party or principal. See each of the following under the principal listing: ~ CONTRACT (1); ~ POWER; ~ TRUST (1).

name bond. See under BOND (2).

named insured. In insurance, the person named in an insurance policy as the one who is specifically protected by the policy, usually the person with whom the contract is made or to whom the policy is issued. By definition, however, a policy may extend the term *named insured* to cover one or more other persons, such as the wife of the *named insured*. See also ADDITIONAL INSURED.

Napoleonic Code. The system of law, based on the French law, and differing in several important respects from the English COMMON LAW, which is the basis of the statutory law of the state of Louisiana. In the event of any legal proceedings, contractual relations, or other matters concerning or domiciled in Louisiana, it is important to consult the local statutes, which may differ from those of other states.

narrow fabric. In the textile trades, the term for ribbons, tapes, laces, belting and other fabrics which are woven in a narrow width, rather than cut to width. Generally, 18 inches is the arbitrary width below which fabric is considered to be narrow fabric.

narrow gauge. See GAUGE (1).

narrow market. In the securities trade, a term used to describe a condition in which trading is dull, light or inactive. It may apply to the market as a whole, or to a class of securities, such as steel industry shares. See also ACTIVE MARKET; BROAD MARKET; INACTIVE MARKET.

national. In general, pertaining to the country as a whole, rather than to any one state or region. As used with respect to government, it refers to the government of the United States, or the federal government, rather than to those of the several states. See each of the following under the principal listing: ~ ADVERTISING; ~ BANK; ~ BANK NOTE; ~ BRAND; ~ DEBT; ~ UNION.

National Bank Act. The act of Congress, passed in 1863, providing for the incorporation of banks under federal supervision. The act has been amended many times, and the national banks it established have become part of the Federal Reserve System. See also FEDERAL RESERVE ACT.

national bank call. See BANK CALL.

national bank examiner. See BANK EXAMINER.

National Bankruptcy Act. The federal law governing the conditions under which a person or business may be declared BANKRUPT, and specifying the procedures to be followed in BANKRUPTCY actions. It is important to note that bankruptcy is a procedure under federal law, that the REFEREE or other appointed official is a federal agent, and that a violation of the bankruptcy act may result in imprisonment in a federal penitentiary.

National Bureau of Standards. The federal agency, in the Department of Commerce, which establishes and maintains the physical standards for the basic units of measurement. It also does basic research in the physical sciences, develops new instruments and equipment for the federal government, and undertakes other scientific activities.

national domain. See DOMAIN, PUBLIC.

national income. In economic statistics, the total net money value of all goods and services produced in the country during the year. It may be computed as the total gross income of all producing units, less the money value of all purchased goods and materials, and after allowing for inventory change, depreciation and obsolescence. Alternatively it is equal to the total income, in money and in kind, distributed to indi-

236

viduals and groups of individuals, including salaries, wages, dividends, interest, entrepreneurial withdrawals, net rent and royalties, plus business savings. See also GROSS NATIONAL PRODUCT.

nationalization. The taking over of the ownership or control, by a national government, of property, natural resources, industry, etc., which has previously been privately owned or controlled. The government may pay compensation for the property taken, or it may issue interest-bearing bonds in place of the stock taken over from shareholders, or, in some cases, it may simply confiscate the property.

National Labor Relations Act. (Wagner Act). The federal law first guaranteeing to employees in interstate commerce the rights of self-organization, collective bargaining, and freedom of activity. The act defined certain unfair labor practices, such as interfering with the right to organize, intimidating employees before a collective bargaining election, discriminating against union members in personnel practices, etc. It created the NATIONAL LABOR RELATIONS BOARD to administer the act. In 1947, the act was broadly amended by the LABOR-MANAGEMENT RELATIONS ACT, known as the TAFT-HARTLEY ACT.

National Labor Relations Board (NLRB). The federal agency, established under the WAGNER ACT, and continued under the TAFT-HARTLEY ACT, to administer the act. The Board conducts elections to determine collective bargaining representation, investigates charges of unfair labor practices, orders them halted when necessary, and so forth. The present Board has five members and a General Counsel who is in effect the executive officer for the Board.

National Mediation Board. The independent federal agency, established in 1934, which operates under the Railway Labor Act. It acts to mediate disputes between railroads and their employees, and now acts for the airlines, express companies, and air express as well.

national rate. In advertising, the rate which a newspaper or radio station charges for advertising which is placed by a national or regional advertiser, such as a widely distributed branded product, as distinguished from the LOCAL RATE, which is charged for advertising placed by a local source, such as a retail store. The *national rate* is almost always higher than the local rate, to encourage advertising by local merchants and others.

national wealth. In economics, the money value of the total national stock of both private and public goods, including land values.

natural business year. The twelve-month period or fiscal year which is determined to be the best for representing the progress and condition of a business. It is usually chosen as the annual period ending at a time when both accounts payable and receivable are at a low point, such as at the end of the selling season, or during the least active period of business activity. See also FISCAL YEAR.

natural person. See under PERSON.

natural premium. See under PREMIUM (2).

nautical mile. See under MILE.

naval stores. The general name for the products which are derived from the tars and extracts of trees of the evergreen family, including turpentine, rosin, pitch, and other substances. They were originally so called because they were used primarily for caulking vessels and other marine applications.

navigable waters. In this country, those inland waters which afford a usable channel for commerce. The definitions included in state laws vary widely; for example, as to whether passage for any vessel or strictly for commercial vessels is included. In English common law, any waters subject to the ebb and flow of the tides, so that a river or stream is considered navigable as far upstream as it is affected by the tides.

nearby. With respect to FUTURES trading in commodities, a term referring to a CONTRACT MONTH which is relatively near, so that commodities sold under the particular contract will soon be delivered. It is the opposite of DISTANT, which refers to a contract month still a considerable time in the future.

necessity certificate. See CERTIFICATE OF NECESSITY.

neglect. In law, the omission or failure to do an act, or perform a duty; usually, but not necessarily, due to carelessness or lack of attention.

negligence. In law, the omission to do something which a reasonable, careful and prudent man, following ordinary considerations, would do under the circumstances. There are various degrees and types of *negligence* recognized in statutes; the principal ones of which follow:

   actionable ∿. Breach or non-performance of a legal duty, through neglect, resulting in damage or injury to another. *Negligence* which may lead to an action at law.

   comparative ∿. A doctrine of law according to which the relative *negligence* of the parties to a suit is compared, and rated as to whether it is SLIGHT, ORDINARY, or GROSS NEGLIGENCE, which see below. The recovery of damages is permitted, under this doctrine, when the *negligence* of the plaintiff is no more than slight and that of the defendant is gross, but is refused when the relative degrees of *negligence* are slight and ordinary, or ordinary and gross. In some courts, the amount of damages awarded may vary according to the relative degrees of *negligence* of the parties.

contributory ∼. The doctrine of law, followed in most states, according to which any want of care, however slight, on the part of the injured party, prevents the recovery of damages if it contributed toward the injury.

criminal ∼. An act of *negligence* which converts an otherwise lawful act into a crime. For example, *negligence*, if proven, will convert a simple automobile accident into vehicular homicide.

gross ∼. The degree of lack of care which shows a reckless disregard for life and safety; or which indicates a conscious indifference to the rights of others.

ordinary ∼. The failure to exercise ORDINARY CARE; the want of the degree of care which a reasonable man would show; inadvertence.

slight ∼. The failure to exercise the care and vigilance of an extraordinarily prudent man.

wanton ∼. In general, reckless *negligence; negligence* in which a person is aware that his acts are likely to cause injury, but still persists in them.

willful ∼. Essentially a contradiction in terms, implying a degree of *negligence* even stronger than gross. Thus, a person guilty of *willful negligence* must be deliberately bent on risking injury to himself or to others.

negotiable. In such a form that full legal title and the right of resale is transferred to another party merely by ENDORSEMENT, or by proper delivery. Instruments may be *fully negotiable, conditionally negotiable* or *non-negotiable,* depending on their terms and on the applicable laws. See also NEGOTIABLE INSTRUMENT. See each of the following under the principal listing: ∼ BILL OF EXCHANGE; ∼ BILL OF LADING; ∼ BOND (1); ∼ NOTE (1).

negotiable instrument. Any written evidence of indebtedness which may be freely transferred by ENDORSEMENT or by delivery. The commonest forms are checks, bills of exchange, drafts, promissory notes and some types of bonds and securities. According to the Uniform Negotiable Instruments Law, a truly *negotiable instrument* must be in writing and signed by the maker; contain an unconditional promise to pay a fixed sum, either on demand or at some specified time; and be payable to bearer or to order. However, it need not be dated, and need not name the transaction that gives rise to it.

negotiate. To transact business, or to reach a settlement or agreement, by mutual bargaining and discussion.

negotiated instrument. A NEGOTIABLE INSTRUMENT which has already passed from the original maker to another for value, or from the holder to others. In general, an instrument which has been put into commercial trade or circulation.

negotiation. 1. The discussion, deliberation or bargaining over the terms of an agreement, contract or settlement which takes place between the parties before the final terms are reached. For example, the COLLECTIVE BARGAINING which leads to a labor union contract.

2. The act by which a negotiable bill, note or other instrument is put into circulation, by being passed from the original holder to another.

net. 1. Free and clear of anything extraneous; after all deductions, such as discounts, allowances, taxes, expenses, etc. The opposite of GROSS. See each of the following under the principal listing: ∼ ASSETS; ∼ COST; ∼ EARNINGS; ∼ INCOME; ∼ LEASE; ∼ LOSS; ∼ PREMIUM (2); ∼ PRICE; ∼ PROCEEDS; ∼ PROFIT; ∼ RETURN; ∼ SALES; ∼ TON; TONNAGE.

2. The gain or profit itself; as in the phrase, "he *netted* $100 on the sale."

net asset value. The total market value of all of the assets of a company (especially of an INVESTMENT COMPANY all of the assets of which are in securities) less total liabilities. In the case of investment companies or funds, this total is usually expressed in dollars per share of fund stock.

net cash. See TERMS OF SALE.

net paid circulation. See CIRCULATION (3), PAID.

net pricing. The practice or policy of quoting the prices of goods for sale to retail or wholesale distributors at the actual price to be charged, rather than at a list or nominal price, from which a discount is allowed. Net pricing is the established method of pricing in some lines, such as industrial supplies, and is followed by many individual companies in other lines in which LIST AND

DISCOUNT pricing is more common. See also PRICE; DISCOUNT (1).

net purchases. In accounting, a term including the cost of purchased goods, plus inbound freight charges, and less returns, allowances and rebates. Cash discounts for prompt payment are sometimes treated as a deduction from gross purchases, but more often are considered as a reduction in price.

net weight. The weight of packaged goods, including only the weight of the contained goods, after allowing for or removing the weight of the container, packaging, wrapping, etc. See also TARE.

net worth. In accounting and finance, the excess of total assets over total liabilities. Thus, it includes both CAPITAL and SURPLUS, and represents the net EQUITY of the owners of the business, whether proprietors or stockholders.

tangible ∼. The *net worth* or equity in a business, figured only on the basis of tangible assets, and excluding such assets as good will, patents, etc., which are sometimes carried on company balance sheets. The *tangible net worth* is a basic guide in credit appraisal practice.

never-out. In retailing, an item or class of merchandise which is in steady demand, and which is therefore always kept in stock. Thus, an item on which a minimum stock level or reorder point is maintained. See also RUNNER.

new. Unused, not previously involved; not previously sold. Not as old as others of the same class or type. In patent law, novel and previously unknown; never before combined in exactly the same way.

New York Curb Exchange. See AMERICAN STOCK EXCHANGE.

New York interest. See INTEREST (2), EXACT.

New York plan. See TRUST CERTIFICATE.

New York Stock Exchange. The principal securities exchange in the United States, originally established in 1792, and reorganized under its present name in 1863. Membership in the exchange is limited to a fixed number of brokers, so that there is a high monetary value to a membership or SEAT on the exchange. It is an unincorporated, voluntary, membership association.

next of kin. See under KIN.

Nichrome. A trade name for an alloy containing iron, nickel and chromium, which has a high resistance to electricity and is therefore used in heating elements of electric appliances.

nickel. 1. A silver-like metal element, used for plating, and in alloys of steel, copper and other metals.
2. The official United States five cent coin. It is actually composed of 75 parts *nickel* and 25 parts copper.

Nielsen Index. A method of measuring and rating radio and television program audiences, developed and prepared exclusively by the A. C. Nielsen Company.

night. In statutes, frequently established as the period from 9:00 p.m. to 6:00 a.m., or a similar period of time. In common law, generally, the period after sundown and before sunrise, during which it is too dark to distinguish or discern objects clearly. When the term is important in a contract or agreement, it should always be clearly defined or limited. See also DAY.

night shift. Any work shift which requires employees to work during the night or evening. For example, a shift running from four p.m. to midnight, or from midnight to eight a.m. The latter hours are sometimes referred to as the GRAVEYARD or LOBSTER SHIFT.

nil. Nothing; of no amount; of no value.

ninon. A smooth, closely woven sheer fabric, usually of silk, rayon or nylon, used for curtains, etc.

nip. A small bottle for alcoholic beverages, usually containing 4 or 5 ounces.

nisi. Literally, in Latin, unless. For example, a DECREE NISI is one which will become fully effective at a future time unless some specified event occurs, or unless the situation changes in some prescribed way, or unless the person affected submits a successful appeal.

NLRB. See NATIONAL LABOR RELATIONS BOARD.

no account. A term stamped on a rejected check or draft by a bank when the drawer or issuer does not maintain an account at the bank. The term is distinguished from NO FUNDS or INSUFFICIENT FUNDS, which are used when the drawer has an account but cannot cover the check.

no arrival no sale. A term used in import contracts, meaning that if the purchased goods do not arrive in this country, the buyer is not liable for the purchase price. In other words, it states that the sale is to be completed on arrival of the goods, not at the time and place of shipment.

noble metal. One of the metals, such as gold, silver, platinum, or palladium, which is not attacked by the acids, except aqua regia, and which generally does not corrode on exposure to air.

no funds. A term stamped on a rejected check

or draft by a bank when the drawer or issuer has an account at the bank, but there are *no funds* to cover the check. This term is distinguished from INSUFFICIENT FUNDS, and from NO ACCOUNT, both of which are also reasons for rejection.

noibn. "Not otherwise indexed by name." An abbreviation used in freight commodity classifications and other schedules as a residual classification for miscellaneous items.

noil (or noils). The short wool fibers which are combed from WORSTED yarn during manufacture.

nolle prosequi. A Latin phrase meaning will not further prosecute. It describes a step taken by a prosecutor or plaintiff, indicating that an action or charge will not be pressed, but not admitting the innocence of the defendant. In such situations, a case is said to be *nolle prossed*.

nolo contendere. In Latin, means I will not contest it. It is a form of plea in a criminal case, which is in effect a plea of guilty, and on the basis of which sentence may be passed. In so pleading, the defendant admits to the facts of the case, but doesn't admit his formal guilt of a crime. The plea is resorted to primarily when a guilty plea would affect other interests, such as a contract, insurance, etc.

nominal. Literally, by name. In name only, titular; not actual, or in actual practice. Of no real value, or of very small value. See each of the following under the principal listing: ∼ ACCOUNT (2); ∼ ASSET (2); ∼ CAPITAL (2); ∼ DAMAGES; ∼ PARTNER; ∼ PRICE.

nominally issued. A term applied to securities which have been signed and certified and placed in a special fund or with the proper officer preparatory to issue, but which have not been ACTUALLY ISSUED.

nomograph (or nomogram). A diagram or graph, consisting of three or more scaled lines, so arranged that a formula or equation involving two or more independent variables may be solved by laying a straight edge across the scales on two or more of the lines at points representing the values to be entered in the formula. The solution may then be read from the value on the last scaled line at the point at which it is crossed by the positioned straight edge.

non-acceptance. The act of a buyer or consignee in refusing to accept delivery of goods or merchandise, for what he considers valid reasons. These may include damage or defects in the goods, failure to match the invoice description, etc. The neglect or refusal of a drawee or payer to accept a bill or draft when it is offered for ACCEPTANCE.

non-assented stock. See under STOCK (1).

non-assessable policy. See under POLICY (2).

non-assessable stock. See under STOCK (1).

non-callable bond. See under BOND (1).

non compos mentis. Literally, in Latin, not of sound mind. In law, not capable of making sound or responsible decisions. The term refers to idiots, the mentally deranged, chronic alcoholics, etc., who have no legal right to engage in contracts, and who are not responsible for any undertakings they may make.

non-contribution clause. A clause used in fire insurance policies in some states, providing that the proceeds of the policy shall be used to cover only the interests of the owner of the property and the holder of the first mortgage, if any. It is distinguished from a FULL CONTRIBUTION CLAUSE, which provides that any amounts left after the satisfaction of the first mortgage shall be used to pay the holder of a second or other mortgage.

non-contributory pension. See PENSION PLAN.

non-cumulative stock. See under STOCK (1).

non-detachable warrant. See WARRANT (4).

non-discretionary trust. See under TRUST (1).

non-durable goods. See under GOODS (3).

non-eligible paper. See under COMMERCIAL PAPER.

nones. In the Roman calendar, the eighth day before the IDES, or middle day of each month. Hence, the seventh day of March, May, July and October, and the fifth day of other months. See also CALENDS.

nonfeasance. In law, the failure to perform some act which one had agreed to do, or was bound to do, or ought to do, as in public office. It is distinguished from MALFEASANCE, which is the doing of an act one has no right to do, and from MISFEASANCE, which is the improper doing of an act one has the right to do properly.

non-financial incentive. See under INCENTIVE.

non-interest-bearing. Bearing or paying no interest, as, for example, a loan made on a personal basis, or a note issued for such a short period of time that interest isn't computed. See also BOND (1), NON-INTEREST-BEARING.

non-mailable. Not admissable to the United States mails, because of size, nature of contents, or moral character, as defined in the postal regulations. For example, parcels which are larger than a specified length or girth, any explosive or inflammable matter, or any obscene literature are all *non-mailable*. See also POSTAL SERVICE.

non-marketable security. See under SECURITY.

non-member bank. See under BANK.

non-negotiable. In such a form that title cannot be transferred by delivery or by endorsement. See also NEGOTIABLE. See each of the following under the principal listing: ∼ BILL OF EXCHANGE; ∼ BOND (1); ∼ NOTE (1).

non-operating expense. See under EXPENSE (2).

non-operating income. See under INCOME.

non-participating policy. See under POLICY (2).

non-performance. The failure, omission, refusal, or neglect to do some act which one has agreed to do, for example, under a contract. Such failure may void the contract, or may make the person who has not performed liable to legal action. See also PERFORMANCE.

non-profit corporation. See under CORPORATION.

non-redeemable bond. See BOND (1), NON-CALLABLE.

non-resident. In law, one who doesn't dwell, or have a settled residence in a given jurisdiction. In many states, for example, *non-residents* pay an income tax on a different basis than do those who are RESIDENTS of the state, or who maintain their principal dwelling therein.

non-scheduled airline. See under AIRLINE.

non-stock corporation. See under CORPORATION.

non-store retailer. See under RETAILER.

non-value bill of exchange. See under BILL OF EXCHANGE.

non vult. From the Latin phrase, *non vult contendere,* he will not contest. A plea made on behalf of a defendant, similar to a plea of NOLO CONTENDERE, and essentially a plea of guilty to the charges.

non-waiver agreement. In insurance, an agreement between an insurer and insured, after a loss or damage, providing that neither of them waives any rights or admits any liability by permitting an immediate inspection and evaluation of the damage. Without such an agreement, it might be held that the insurer admits the existence of an insured loss by undertaking such an evaluation.

non-woven fabric. A fabric or cloth, such as felt, which is made by pressing fibers together, with a binder, rather than by weaving or knitting.

no par value stock. See under STOCK (1).

no protest. A term stamped or marked on a draft or promissory note, indicating that the note is not to go to PROTEST if not paid when due. This may be done so that the bank or other collection agency will not charge a protest fee if the draft or note is not paid.

norm. A set standard of normal or desired production or other accomplishment; a model or average.

normal. According to the established behavior or procedure; not deviating from the standard or regular pattern; within the limits established for acceptance; according to nature.

normal distribution. In statistics, the distribution of a large number of observations on a variable which is randomly determined. The curve which envelops this distribution is known as the normal curve. For example, if a large number of coins are simultaneously tossed a great many times, the frequency of heads (or tails) will be a *normal distribution*. Similarly, if the length of a manufactured part is determined, within limits, by a number of RANDOM factors (such as metal content, tool speed, tool sharpness, etc.), the measured sizes of a large number of similar parts will form a *normal distribution*.

normal stock method. See INVENTORY CONTROL.

Norris-LaGuardia Act. The federal law, passed in 1932 and known technically as the Federal Anti-Injunction Act, which limited the rights of the courts to issue injunctions in cases of labor disputes. Though the Clayton Act officially declared that labor organizations did not come under the anti-trust laws, the courts had gradually narrowed this exemption, and had begun to issue restraining injunctions against unions in many situations. The *Norris-LaGuardia Act* clarified the conditions under which injunctions could not be issued in labor disputes. It also declared that agreements by employees not to join, or to leave a labor organization as a condition of employment (YELLOW DOG CONTRACTS) were not enforceable in a federal court.

nostrum. Literally, in Latin, ours. A proprietary medicine or remedy, the formula for which is kept secret. Hence, a quack remedy. Now, more broadly, any scheme or cure-all solution to a social or economic problem.

notary public. A person licensed as a public officer for the purpose of attesting or certifying to the validity of signatures on documents requiring such certification. The *notary's* certification, which he gives by signing and stamping his official seal, attests that the document was signed in his presence, but states nothing concerning the truth or accuracy of the statements contained in the document.

note. 1. Any of various forms of credit instruments, consisting essentially of a written, unconditional promise to pay a sum of money at some specified future date to a named person, or to order, or to the bearer. The general term is *promissory note,* but there are many variations and modifications, the principal ones of which are listed and defined below.

accommodation ~. See ACCOMMODATION PAPER.

bearer ~. See NEGOTIABLE NOTE, below.

blue ~. A term sometimes used for a DEMAND NOTE, which see below. It is so called because this type of *note* is frequently printed on blue paper to make it easily distinguishable from a TIME NOTE, which see below, which is usually printed on white paper.

call ~. See DEMAND NOTE, below.

circular ~. One issued by a dealer in foreign exchange, and payable by any foreign correspondent of the dealer. Thus, it is a form of LETTER OF CREDIT.

cognovit ~. See JUDGMENT NOTE, below.

collateral ~. One the payment of which is secured by a pledge of COLLATERAL, such as securities or something else of monetary value. See also SECURED NOTE, below.

coupon ~. An INTEREST-BEARING NOTE, which see below, the interest on which is payable by means of coupons attached to the *note,* which are detached and presented for payment.

demand ~. One which is payable on presentation, or on demand by the holder. It is also payable at the option of the borrower at any time before it is presented. It is also commonly known as a *call note.* See also TIME NOTE, below.

equipment ~. See TRUST CERTIFICATE.

gold ~. A term for a *note* specifying payment in gold. Such *notes* have not been legal in the United States since 1934.

installment ~. One of a series of *notes,* issued to cover a single obligation, with maturity dates occurring at regular intervals. Thus, a $10,000 loan might be repaid by a series of *installment notes,* for $1,000 each, due at the end of one, two, three, etc., years. These are sometimes known as serial *notes.*

interest-bearing ~. One on which there is a regular interest charge, payable either periodically or at maturity. Not all *notes* are interest-bearing. Some are DISCOUNTED, and many are for loans without interest.

joint ~. One which is signed by two or more parties, so that the signers undertake the responsibility to pay it at maturity as a JOINT obligation.

joint and several ~. One signed by two or more parties, in which it is specified that the signers have JOINT AND SEVERAL responsibility for its payment, so that they may be sued together, or any one separately, for its payment.

judgment ~. One to which is attached a WARRANT OF ATTORNEY, authorizing the creditor to enter a JUDGMENT against the debtor in case of non-payment without the necessity of special court action. It is sometimes called a *cognovit note* from the opening Latin words of the warrant of attorney.

mortgage ~. One which is secured and evidenced by a mortgage, usually a chattel mortgage on personal property. Such a *note* might be given, for example, to cover all or part of the purchase price on an item of personal property bought, with the property itself mortgaged to secure the *note.*

negotiable ~. One on which the right to receive payment is transferable by endorsement, or which is payable to bearer. A *note* is made negotiable by being made out to the order of a person, rather than directly to the person himself.

non-negotiable ~. One which is not transferable, as distinguished from a NEGOTIABLE NOTE, which see above. It is made out to the name of a particular person, rather than to order or to bearer.

promissory ~. In general, any written promise to pay. It may be negotiable or non-negotiable, secured or unsecured, interest-bearing or without interest, etc. It differs from a BOND (1) primarily in that it is a direct agreement between the two parties to it, rather than a formally issued certificate which is sold by one party and bought by the other. The laws of the various states may prescribe other legal differences.

renewal ~. One which takes the place of a *note* which has matured without being paid, usually by agreement when the maker is unable to pay.

secured ~. One the payment of which is secured, by a pledge of collateral, by a deposit, by a mortgage, or by some other form of valuable security.

serial ~. See INSTALLMENT NOTE, above.

sight ~. See DEMAND NOTE, above.

stock ~. In the securities trade, a term for a COLLATERAL NOTE, which see above, the collateral for which is in the form of securities, including both stocks and bonds.

time ~. One which is due and payable at some specified date in the future, or some specified period of time after a named date such as ninety days from date. A *time note* may not be repaid in advance at the option of the borrower, without the consent of the creditor. See also DEMAND NOTE, above.

unsecured ~. One which is simply an obligation to pay the principal and interest, if any, with no security other than the word and integrity of the borrower. In the event of the bankruptcy of the debtor, the holder of an *unsecured note* comes after all secured creditors in order of payment.

2. In the securities and commodities trades, a *note* or memorandum from a broker or dealer to his client or customer, reporting the subject, terms, and other details of a purchase or sale made for the customer.

bought ∼. One delivered by a broker to his customer reporting the purchase of securities or commodities in the customer's name and account, listing the price, total amount paid, commissions, taxes, etc., and the total amount due the broker.

sold ∼. One delivered by a broker to his customer reporting the sale of securities or commodities for the account of the customer, listing the price, total amount received, taxes, commissions, etc., and the net amount credited to the customer's account. *Sold notes* are usually printed in red, to make them readily distinguishable from BOUGHT NOTES, which see above, which are printed in black.

3. A general term for various forms of paper money, which represent promises to pay on behalf of the issuing government, bank, or other institution. Examples include BANK NOTES and FEDERAL RESERVE BANK NOTES.

note broker. See under BROKER (1).

note of hand. See NOTE (1), PROMISSORY.

notes payable. In accounting, those current liabilities which are represented by promissory notes, or other instruments of short-term indebtedness. Strictly speaking, these do not include liabilities arising out of purchases or other current expenditures, which are properly included under ACCOUNTS PAYABLE.

notes receivable. In accounting, those current assets which are represented by promissory notes or other instruments of short-term indebtedness. Strictly speaking, these do not include assets arising out of the normal sale of goods or services, which are properly included under ACCOUNTS RECEIVABLE.

note teller. See TELLER.

notice. Information given, or observation, leading to a knowledge of the pertinent facts. In law, *notice* of facts may be actual, in that it was given as such, or constructive, in that it was available to the person affected, and could easily have been observed or obtained. For example, if a public road is to be closed, posting a sign to this effect on the road itself is considered constructive *notice* to all concerned. *Notice* may also be express, in that it is directly given, or implied from the circumstances or the actions of the parties concerned.

notification. In ACCOUNTS RECEIVABLE FINANCING, the act of notifying the debtors that their accounts have been sold to a FACTOR (1) or other financial agency.

not otherwise indexed by name. See NOIBN.

novation. The substitution of a new debt or obligation for an old one. Also, the substitution of a new creditor for the former creditor, or a new debtor for the former debtor, in an obligation. A creditor may always assign his rights to a debt to another, and this is the basis of all FACTORING and ACCOUNTS RECEIVABLE FINANCING. A debtor, however, may not substitute another debtor without the consent of both his creditor and the substitute debtor. For example, a person who is a debtor to one person and a creditor to another, may transfer his rights as a creditor to his own creditor, with the permission of both the debtor and creditor involved. See also SUBROGATION.

NRDGA. The National Retail Dry Goods Association, the trade association of department and specialty stores.

nude. See NAKED.

nuisance. Any unreasonable or unlawful use by a person of his own property, or any improper or unlawful personal conduct, which interferes with the rights of others or of the public, and which produces interference, annoyance, hurt, or damage. The damage may be to an individual, or to real property. Examples include factory smoke, unclean premises, unsightly property, etc. The person permitting or causing such conditions is said to maintain a *nuisance*.

attractive ∼. One which is likely to be especially attractive, particularly to small children. Such a nuisance is unlawful even though it would not normally cause harm or damage to the general public, or to reasonably prudent adults. Examples include vacant buildings, open excavations, construction work, etc., unless properly protected or guarded.

private ∼. One which does harm to one or more individuals, as individuals.

public ∼. One which does harm to most or all of the residents of a vicinity, or of the persons coming in contact with the existing conditions. A *nuisance* may be both public and private, in which case it is known as a *mixed nuisance*.

null. Invalid; of no effect; as if not existing. The term is usually used in the phrase *"null and void,"* meaning of no legal force, or voidable as a result of its invalidity.

nuncupative. Announced; publicly stated or declared. See, for example, WILL, NUNCUPATIVE.

O

OASI. See OLD AGE AND SURVIVORS' INSURANCE.

oath. Literally, a calling on God to witness the truth of a statement. More commonly, a formal affirmation of the truth concerning some matter, taken or executed before a proper official, who attests to the fact that the *oath* was taken. In most states, those who for religious or conscientious reasons will not swear an *oath* are permitted to AFFIRM the truth of their statements.

obiter dictum. From the Latin, that which is said along the way. A remark made or an opinion expressed by a judge, incidental to a decision being rendered, but not bearing directly on the question being settled. These *obiter dicta* are not the binding rulings of the court, but some of the more important *dicta,* especially those of Supreme Court justices, have been frequently cited in arguments and decisions in later cases.

obligation. 1. In general, any binding duty either assumed by or enforced upon a person. The *obligation* which the OBLIGOR engages or binds himself to perform may be to do or not do some act or to pay an amount of money. *Obligations* are classified in various ways, of which the following are the principal ones: An *obligation* may be—
   contractual or *moral;* that is, it may arise out of the terms of a contract or agreement, or it may rest on conscience, natural justice or ethical considerations.
   determinate or *indeterminate;* that is, it may call for doing or paying a specific thing, such as delivering a particular horse, or it may call for delivering any one of a class of similar things, such as any horse.
   divisible or *indivisible;* that is, it may be divided, either among two or more obligors or obligees, or it may require that the entire obligation be paid by or to a single person and not transferred to another.
   express or *implied;* that is, it may be stated in direct terms, or may follow by inference from a law, the terms of a contract, etc.
   heritable or *personal;* that is, it may be enforceable against or collectable by heirs,

or it may be only between the original obligor and obligee. But an *obligation* may be *heritable* on one side and *personal* on the other.
   joint or *several;* that is, two or more obligors may bind themselves together to perform or pay it, or they may each bind themselves separately to fill the total obligation.
   natural or *civil;* that is, it may continue after the legal statute of limitations has expired, or it may be wiped out by the expiration of the limitation period.
   perfect or *imperfect;* that is, it may be recognized, sanctioned and enforced by law, or it may be moral only, with no force of law.
   personal or *real;* that is, it may bind the obligor himself, personally, or it may bind real estate or other real property, as when the obligation is an easement against property.
   penal or *single;* that is, it may have a penal clause, calling for some punishment if the obligation is not performed, or it may have no penalty attached.
   primary or *secondary;* that is, it may be the principal object of a contract, or it may be incidental to it. For example, the *primary* obligation undertaken in a sales contract is to transfer and deliver, while the *secondary* one is to pay damages for not doing so.
   simple or *conditional;* that is, it may not depend on the occurrence of another event, or it may be dependent on an uncertain event's occurrence.
   2. A written instrument, setting forth the terms of an agreement by which one is bound to do some act or pay some amount. In commerce, it may be an acceptance, contract, note, etc.

obligee. The person or party in whose favor an OBLIGATION is assumed by another; for example, a creditor.

obligor. The person or party who engages or binds himself, or is bound, to perform an OBLIGATION.

obsolescence. With respect to an asset, the loss in value brought about through improvements in technology, changes in public taste, or a falling off in demand for the products manufactured. It is distinguished from DEPRECIATION, which is a loss of value due to normal wear and tear and the ravages of time.

occupancy. In law, taking possession for one's own use of property which previously had no owner, with the intent of establishing ownership through continued possession and use. In general, it is possession through use, rather than constructively. For example, in insurance contracts, *occupancy* of the insured property means its use, not necessarily continuously, but as a place of usual return. See also TITLE (2).

occupancy ratio. In housing statistics, the percentage of available dwelling units that are occupied, so that full occupancy is a ratio of 100. The *occupancy ratio* is also 100 minus the VACANCY RATIO.

occupation. 1. The taking of possession, under a right of OCCUPANCY, or with the intent of claiming ownership.

2. In general, any activity by which one earns one's livelihood; a trade, profession or business; employment.

occupational disease. Any disease which is definitely linked to the working conditions of a given occupation. Usually, it is one which results from continued exposure to a given set of conditions. For example, silicosis, which is caused by the continued breathing of stone or rock dust, is an *occupational disease* of quarry workers, miners, and drillers.

occupation tax. See TAX (2), FRANCHISE.

occupy. In general, to hold in possession; to keep for use. In insurance, specifically, it means to put to actual use for the purpose for which the property was intended. Thus, UNOCCUPIED property is not necessarily VACANT, but is not being used as intended. For example, a dwelling used for storage is not *occupied* as a dwelling.

occurrence. Any happening or event, whether expected or predictable or not, as distinguished from an ACCIDENT, which is unforeseen and unexpected.

ocean bill of lading. See under BILL OF LADING.

ocean marine insurance. See INSURANCE, MARINE.

octane. 1. In chemistry, one of a class of hydrocarbons with 8 atoms of carbon in its molecule. One of these, iso-octane, is used as a standard for measuring the quality of gasoline.

2. A standard for measuring the "antiknock" qualities of gasoline. The *octane* number of any particular gasoline is the equivalent power or quality that would be obtained from a mixture containing the necessary percentage of pure iso-octane. Thus, a gasoline rated at 80 *octane* has the equivalent anti-knock qualities of a mixture containing 80 percent iso-octane. Theoretically, a 100 *octane* gasoline is an ideal fuel, but modern gasolines, through the use of various additives, have ratings of over 100 *octane*.

octavo. See under BOOK SIZES.

octodecimo (eighteenmo). See under BOOK SIZES.

odd lot. In the securities and commodities trades, an amount smaller than the usual and normal unit of trading, as distinguished from a ROUND LOT, which is a multiple of the trading unit. Examples of *odd lots* are less than 100 shares of stock, less than $1,000 in bonds, less than 30,000 pounds of cocoa, etc.

odd lot broker. See under BROKER (2).

off. In business slang, lower or less active. For example, prices are *off* when they are lower, but the volume of securities trading is *off* when fewer shares are traded.

offer. In general, any proposal to do or not do something, submitted by one person to another for acceptance or rejection. In the law of contracts, an *offer* is not complete unless and until it is known by the person to whom it is made. Hence, an *offer* made by mail, for example, is not actually made until it is received. An *offer* may be either oral or in writing, or may even be a sign, as the signal given by a bidder at an auction, as long as it is mutually understood by both parties. It may be conditional, that is, subject to the acceptance of stated conditions by the acceptor, or it may be unconditional. It may be firm, that is, binding on the maker if accepted within a given period, or free, being subject to some condition such as the prior sale of the goods offered, etc. See also CONTRACT.

offered price. See PRICE, ASKED.

offering. In the securities trade, a term used to indicate an issue of bonds or other securities offered for sale to the public. For example, the press may report the total of daily bond *offerings*. See also MARKET OFFERING; SECONDARY OFFERING.

office. 1. In political terms, public employment in a position of trust, or the position so held. A continuously performed public duty.

2. Any place for the regular conduct of business, especially the clerical, administra-

tive, or executive operations of a business. See also HOME OFFICE.

office copy. In general, a copy or transcript of any document or other material retained for office use. In law, a copy of a document made by an officer of the court or other public officer.

office machine. Any mechanical device, such as a typewriter, dictating machine, adding machine, duplicating machine, etc., used to expedite the flow of work in business offices.

officer. In a corporation, one of the key management positions, as provided for in the corporate charter. Under most state corporation laws, every corporation must have at least a PRESIDENT, SECRETARY, and TREASURER, and most corporations have in addition one or more VICE-PRESIDENTS. The corporate charter, following the state law, provides for and regulates the choosing, term of office, powers, duties, and compensation of the *officers*. Usually, the *officers* are appointed by the corporation DIRECTORS, acting for the stockholders.

official bond. See under BOND (2).

official exchange rate. See under RATE OF EXCHANGE.

off-premise clause. A clause used in household fire, theft, and similar insurance contracts in those states where it is permitted, providing that the insurance covers a limited amount of property, usually 10 percent of the total insured, when it is temporarily located off the premises named in the policy.

off-premise sale. A term used in liquor sale legislation and regulations, referring to the sale of alcoholic beverages in bottles or cans for consumption elsewhere than on the premises of the establishment where sold. See also ON-PREMISE SALE.

offset. 1. To counterbalance or neutralize; to post an entry to a business account which restores its balance, or which counters the effect of a previous entry. Such an entry is known as an *offsetting* or balancing entry.
2. One of the three principal methods of printing, the other two being INTAGLIO and LETTERPRESS, in which the ink is first transferred from an etched or sensitized master to a rotating drum and then to the paper or other surface being printed. The master may be a lithograph, an etched metallic plate, or a sensitized photographic plate, in which case the process is known as *photo-offset*.

ogive. In statistics, a graphic curve commonly known as a growth curve. It is the curve describing the total amount of any factor which increases at an increasing rate until a particular stage of growth, and then increases at a steadily decreasing rate. It is sometimes called an S-curve, because of its characteristic shape.

ohm. The basic unit of electrical resistance. A conductor has a resistance of one *ohm* when a current of one AMPERE flows through it at an electrical pressure of one VOLT. The relationship is *ohms* equals volts divided by amperes.

O.K. An abbreviation or symbol, of doubtful origin but widespread use and acceptance. Both traditionally and through various court rulings, it means correct, seen and approved, accepted, satisfactory, etc.

Old Age and Survivors' Insurance (OASI). A system of social insurance, established under the Federal Social Security Act, and providing for retirement pensions, widows' and dependents' pensions, death benefits, and other payments aimed at helping establish the financial independence of those who no longer work, or who have lost the income of the family wage-earner. See also SOCIAL SECURITY.

oligopoly. Literally, from the Greek, few sellers. In economics, a situation in which a few companies or sources control or dominate the market for a product or service. See also MONOPOLY.

olographic. See HOLOGRAPH; WILL, HOLOGRAPHIC.

omission. In law, the neglect or failure to perform some required or promised act. It is distinguished from the wrongful performance of the required act, and from the performance of an uncalled-for act.

omnibus. From the Latin, by all, or for all; covering two or more independent matters or parties. For example, an *omnibus* bill in a legislature is a measure including several independent matters, or the appropriations for several independent agencies.

omnibus clause. In insurance policies, particularly in automobile and other liability policies, a clause extending the definition of INSURED to cover persons other than the named insured, under prescribed conditions.

on account. A term meaning in partial fulfillment of an obligation, such as, for example, a payment made *on account* to partially liquidate an outstanding debt, as distinguished from a payment of the debt in full.

on a scale. In the securities trade, an expression for a system of buying or selling in which an investor buys or sells equal amounts of a given stock at prices which are spaced by a constant interval, as the market price rises or falls. For example, an in vestor who buys 100 shares of a stock at a price of 50, another 100 shares at 48, more at 46, 44, and so on, is said to be buying *on a declining scale*. Similarly, one who makes successive sales at uniformly higher price intervals is said to be selling *on a rising scale*. In either case, the purpose of the maneuver is to take advantage of the falling or rising prices without running the risk of waiting too long to buy or sell, as the case may be.

on call. 1. In general, a synonym for ON DEMAND, meaning payable or deliverable on request or notification. See also LOAN, CALL; CALL MONEY.

2. In the cotton trade, a term describing a type of transaction in which goods have been sold, but the price has not yet been fixed. The agreement provides that the price must be fixed on or before the date of *call*, or settlement.

on consignment. See CONSIGNMENT.

on demand. Payable *on demand* or on presentation, as a bill of exchange or draft. See also NOTE, DEMAND; LOAN, DEMAND.

one-day loan. See LOAN, DAY.

one-name paper. See COMMERCIAL PAPER, SINGLE NAME.

one-price policy. The announced policy or practice of offering goods for sale at one price only, to all classes of customers. Under such a policy the price for a particular item is the same regardless of the number purchased, the terms of sale, the type of business of the buyer, etc.

one-price store. See RETAIL STORE, LIMITED PRICE VARIETY.

onerous. Burdensome, placing an undue burden; imposing hardship, or oppressive. An *onerous* duty, for example, is one which it will be a hardship to perform or carry out. In law, imposing a real burden in return for benefits received. Hence, it means good or valuable, as, for example, an *onerous* CONSIDERATION, which is distinguished from one which is merely a token.

one thousand hour clause. The popular term for that section of the FAIR LABOR STANDARDS ACT which provides that working schedules may be set without regard to the regulations covering daily and weekly maximum hours, providing that no employee works more than 12 hours in one day, 56 hours weekly or 1,000 hours in any consecutive 26 weeks. This clause is meant to regulate the hours of those workers or specialists, the nature of whose work requires that they be on duty longer than the 8 hours daily or 40 hours weekly which are the basic maximums set by the act. See also TWO THOUSAND HOUR CLAUSE; BELO PLAN.

one-time rate. In newspaper, magazine and similar advertising, the rate charged for advertising space for an advertisement that is placed for only one insertion. It is higher than the MULTIPLE-INSERTION RATE, which is usually set on a sliding scale discount, based on the number of insertions.

on margin. See MARGIN.

on memorandum. See MEMORANDUM.

on or about. A phrase frequently used in business or commercial agreements, but with no definite or restricted meaning. As commonly understood, it means approximately on a given date, and not substantially before or after. The term is mostly used to avoid a definite commitment or promise concerning a future occurrence, such as a delivery, the opening of a store, etc.

on order. 1. Ordered from a source but not yet received. Where notice of shipment is usually given, it may have the more restricted meaning of ordered but not yet shipped, so that ordered goods may be either *on order*, IN TRANSIT, or on hand.

2. Subject to order. Shipped without a definite consignee being named, such as is done with grain, some perishable foods, empty food cans at the height of the packing season, etc. The consignee is named while the goods are in transit, or in temporary storage en route, and the railway bill of lading is turned over to the consignee as a basis for taking delivery of the goods.

on-premise sale. A term used in liquor sale legislation and regulations, referring to the sale of alcoholic beverages for consumption on the premises of the establishment where sold. The sale may be in bulk, or in a package that is opened for consumption. See also OFF-PREMISE SALE.

on the books. In popular usage, amounts owed by credit customers to a business; the amounts of accounts receivable carried.

on-the-job training. The training or education of an inexperienced worker or apprentice directly at the work, where he uses the actual tools, materials, methods, and equipment with which the work is done, but under the supervision of an experienced or skilled worker or supervisor.

open. 1. To begin, or to create. For example, a bank may *open* a line of credit for a customer, making credit available to him. The price at which a stock is traded in the first transaction of the day is known as the *open* price. See also CLOSE.

2. Current; without a definite closing or

finishing date. Without restriction as to time, or other terms or qualification. See each of the following under the principal listing: ~ ACCOUNT (4); ~ CORPORATION; ~ CREDIT (3); ~ ORDER; ~ POLICY (2).

open-end. With no definite limit as to duration, as to amount, or as to other conditions or qualifications. Deliberately left open or indefinite. See each of the following under the principal listing: ~ CONTRACT (1); ~ INVESTMENT COMPANY; ~ MORTGAGE.

opening inventory. See INVENTORY, BEGINNING.

opening price. See under PRICE.

open market. 1. In general, a MARKET which is open to the public, or free to all buyers and sellers, as distinguished from one which is restricted, or closed to all but a specified class or group. See also FREE MARKET.

2. A term referring to a type of operation of the Federal Reserve Bank, designed to influence the cost and availability of commercial credit. The operations consist of the buying or selling of government obligations and other high-grade securities or commercial paper in the *open market*. By adding to the supply of paper, the Bank can cause the interest rate to become lower, and similarly, by buying up securities, the Bank can bring about a slight rise in rates, or halt a decline.

open market rate. The interest or discount rate for loans, or for the resale of commercial paper in the open or free commercial market. Sometimes called the open rate.

open order. See under ORDER (4).

open shop. A shop, factory or other place of employment in which individual employees are neither required nor forbidden to be members of a labor union. A shop in which the employer does not recognize the union as the sole representative of the employees for collective bargaining, though he may deal with the union with regard to its members. See also CLOSED SHOP; UNION SHOP.

open stock. A term used in retail and wholesale trade, especially in the chinaware, silverware and glassware trades, indicating that a given pattern or product will be kept available for a relatively long period of time, and that it may be purchased by the individual piece, to add to a set or to replace broken pieces, as well as in sets or settings. There is no fixed time period for which an item must be kept available to be legitimately described as *open stock,* but the implication is that it will be kept perpetually available is seldom intended seriously.

open to buy. In retail merchandising, the state of being able or authorized to purchase additional goods. As commonly used, the term refers directly to the amount of money which the buyer is authorized to spend, usually based on his planned purchases for a given period, less the commitments already made and goods on hand. A buyer may speak of having a certain amount of *open to buy* in each of several different classifications of merchandise, indicating that he is free to commit himself for additional purchases up to these amounts.

open trade. In the securities and commodities markets, a speculative transaction that has not yet been closed. For example, when a security is sold short, the transaction is an *open trade* until the purchase of the same security has been made to cover the sale. Similarly, when a purchase contract for a commodity has been made with the intention of reselling the commodity before delivery, the transaction is an *open trade* until the resale has been made. See also CLOSED TRADE.

open union. See under UNION.

operating. Concerned with the principal operations or line of business, or with business activities. Dealing with manufacturing or distribution, rather than with financial operations. See each of the following under the principal listing: ~ BUDGET; ~ COMPANY; ~ EXPENSE (2); ~ INCOME; ~ LOSS (1); ~ PROFIT; ~ RESERVES (1); ~ SURPLUS.

operating cost. See EXPENSE, OPERATING.

operating cycle. In a business organization, the average period of time between the acquisition of goods or materials and the final conversion of these items into income, through manufacture and sale or through resale. See also TURNOVER.

operating ratio. Any one of a number of ratios or relationships commonly used to measure the profitability or soundness of a business, or to analyze its financial soundness. The data for such ratios are usually drawn from the annual FINANCIAL STATEMENT and INCOME STATEMENT of the business. A wide variety of ratios are used in different fields, and Dun & Bradstreet, Inc. the MERCANTILE AGENCY, collects and publishes data on 14 different ratios for various lines of business. Some of the more common measures used in business, such as TURNOVER, the SAFETY FACTOR, the COLLECTION PERIOD etc., are actually operating ratios. Two of the more important ratios, which are applicable in all lines of business, are the CURRENT RATIO, which is the ratio of total current assets to total current liabilities, and the *gross profit ratio,* which is the ratio of total operating costs to total gross sales.

operating results. The accounting figures reflecting the results of business operations for a given time period. Included are such items as the average cost of goods sold, average selling costs, gross margin, markup, net profit, etc. Trade associations and other agencies frequently prepare reports of average or typical *operating results* for large numbers of retail stores or other businesses in given classifications.

operating statement. See INCOME STATEMENT.

operative. 1. In general, one who works for another for wages; a worker. As commonly used, a worker who operates or tends a machine, especially MILL machinery of one sort or another; a mill hand.

2. In force, or effective. The *operative* clause or section of an agreement is that which puts the particular transaction or other subject of the agreement into operation or effect.

operator. 1. In industrial usage, a worker who operates a machine. In the textile and apparel industries, especially, an *operator* is one who operates a spinning or weaving machine, a sewing machine, etc.

2. A person or company engaged in coal mining operations; a mine *operator*.

3. A professional trader or speculator; one who makes his living by taking advantage of rising or falling market prices. At present, the term is often used in a derogatory sense, as a schemer, and may imply activities bordering on the illegal, as in the phrase a fast *operator*.

opinion. The concluding statement by a judge or by the court in a civil case, covering the legal questions involved, and explaining the basis on which the JUDGMENT of the court is based.

    concurring ∼. One delivered by an individual judge or a number of the member judges of a court, agreeing with the majority view, though perhaps based on different grounds and reasoning.

    dissenting ∼. One delivered by an individual judge or a minority of the court, announcing a disagreement with the majority view and giving the reasons involved.

    per curiam ∼. One delivered in the name of the entire court, without any one particular judge being named as the author. This form is frequently used for brief opinions, especially those in which the court is unanimous.

option. 1. A privilege to buy or sell, receive or deliver property, given in accordance with terms agreed upon, and usually for a consideration or price. In one case, for example, a prospective buyer may pay for the privilege of accepting delivery or not, as he may decide, within a stated period of time. In another case, a seller may pay for the privilege of delivering or not, as he may decide. The buyer who obtains the privilege of buying the property or not is said to take an *option,* and normally other offers to buy may not be considered while the *option* is in effect. If the buyer does not exercise his *option* to buy, he usually forfeits his *option* payment, but if he decides to buy, this is included in the price.

2. In the securities and commodities trade, the purchased privilege of receiving or delivering a specified security or commodity, in specified amounts, at a specified price, at some future time. See also PUT; CALL; STRADDLE.

3. In life insurance, the privilege of an insured person or a beneficiary to choose the method or form of payment of the proceeds of an insurance contract. For example, typical *options* for the payment of the principal of a life insurance contract include a single, or lump-sum payment, a fixed number of payments of a certain size, or a life annuity of a stated annual amount.

optional bond. See under BOND (1).

optional dividend. See under DIVIDEND.

option contract. See under CONTRACT (1).

oral. By word of mouth; in spoken words only; not reduced to writing. Frequently *oral* and VERBAL are used synonymously, but the latter term may also include written statements which are informal, such as memoranda. See also CONTRACT (1), PAROL.

oral partnership. See under PARTNERSHIP.

order. 1. In law, a command by a court, by a judicial or public officer, or by some commission, board or other public body, or by any other person or body duly authorized to issue such a command. See also DECREE.

2. In business and commerce in general, any request or command to deliver, sell, receive or purchase goods or services. In this usage, an *order* is also a commitment on the part of the person making the request or giving the command. An *order* to deliver goods, for example, also commits the person giving the *order* to receive or accept the goods so ordered.

3. In relation to negotiable instruments, the direction prescribing the one to whom payment is to be made. The usual phrase in which this direction is given is "pay to the *order* of —." This may appear on the face of the instrument itself, or in an endorsement.

4. In the securities and commodities trade,

a direction by a person, or by another dealer or broker, to a commodities or securities dealer or broker, calling on him to buy or sell according to the specific directions included in the *order*.

carte blanche ~. One conferring on a broker an unlimited authority to buy or sell securities in the name of the one giving the *order*.

cross ~. One calling on a broker to buy and sell the same security. Under the rules of the New York Stock Exchange, a broker receiving orders from two customers to buy and sell the same security may not pair the one against the other, but must place *orders* with the floor brokers for each transaction. A fictitious *cross order,* entered for the purpose of creating a market for a security, is known as a MATCHED ORDER, or WASH SALE.

day ~. One directing a broker to buy or sell a security at a given price, to remain in force only during the trading day on which it is given. If the transaction cannot be executed or completed at the specified price before the close of the market, it is automatically cancelled.

discretionary ~. One in which the customer gives authority to the broker to buy or sell a security at what the latter considers the best or most profitable price. Many brokers will not accept an order in this form.

fill or kill ~. See IMMEDIATE ORDER, below.

give-out ~. One that has been received by a broker and has been turned over or given out by him to a specialist or other broker for execution.

good this month (week) ~. One directing a broker to buy or sell a security at a given price, which is to remain in force during the remainder of the week or month in which it is given. If it cannot be executed at the specified price during the named period, it is automatically cancelled at the end of the period and must be renewed, if desired.

good (un)til cancelled ~. One directing a broker to buy or sell a security at a specified price, which is to remain in force either until it can be executed or until the customer cancels or changes it. It is commonly referred to in the trade as a *G-T-C order*.

immediate ~. One directing a broker to buy or sell a security at a specified price immediately. If the *order* cannot be filled or executed at the specified price immediately, it is automatically cancelled, or killed. Hence, it is commonly known in the trade as a *fill or kill order*.

limit ~. One directing a broker to buy a security below or at a specified price, or to sell a security above or at a specified price. Hence, it is an *order* in which the customer puts an upper limit on the price he will pay or a lower limit on the selling price he will accept.

market ~. One directing a broker to buy or sell a security at the prevailing market price at the time the *order* is entered. Such an *order* is to be executed immediately, or as soon as a transaction can be arranged.

matched ~. See directly.

open ~. One that is to be held in force or open until it is either executed or cancelled. Hence, a GOOD (UN)TIL CANCELLED ORDER, which see above.

split ~. One directing a broker to buy or sell a security partly at one specified time or price, and partly at another time or price.

stop ~. One directing a broker to buy or sell a security when it reaches a specified upper or lower limit price. For example, if a security has been purchased at a price of 100, a *stop order* may be given to sell it when it reaches, say 105 (to take a profit) or when it falls to, say 98 (to minimize loss), or both. Similarly, when a security has been sold SHORT, at a price of 50, an *order* may be given to buy to cover at a price of 47, to take a profit, or at a price of 52, to minimize loss. When such an *order* is placed to minimize or stop a loss, it is known as a *stop-loss order*.

order bill of exchange. See BILL OF EXCHANGE, NEGOTIABLE.

order bill of lading. See under BILL OF LADING.

order blank. An order form; a business form on which the details of an order are recorded.

order instrument. A negotiable instrument which is made payable to ORDER (3).

ordinance. Strictly speaking, a ruling which puts things in order, or which disposes of things. As commonly used, any of the regulatory actions of a local or municipal legislative or administrative body. Typical municipal *ordinances* affecting business cover such subjects as waste removal, retail store hours, outdoor advertising, etc.

ordinary. Normal; according to usual custom or procedure. Common; without special rank or quality. As used in many business terms it may have any of a number of specific meanings, depending on usage in the particular field. See each of the following under the principal listing: ~ ANNUITY; ~ IN

TEREST (2); ~ NEGLIGENCE; ~ PARTNER-
SHIP; ~ STOCK (1).

ordinary care. A term frequently used in contracts, agreements, insurance, etc., meaning
the amount or degree of care which would
ordinarily be exercised by a reasonable and
prudent person, or by a person in the care
of his own property.

ordinary life insurance. See under INSURANCE,
LIFE, ACCIDENT AND HEALTH.

organization chart. A chart or diagram which
outlines or describes the functional relationships in a business, and the flow of responsibility and authority through the organization. It usually lists all of the principal
departments, officers and executives, and
shows, by means of connecting lines, the
relationships of each to the others.

organization expenses. Those costs and expenses which are incurred by a corporation
in the process of organization. They include
such expenses as legal fees, incorporation
fees, stock stamp taxes, costs of printing
shares, prospectuses and other documents,
promotional and underwriting costs, etc. In
approved accounting procedures, these costs
are usually charged off against surplus over
the first few years of the corporation's life,
with the remainder carried as a deferred
expense on the asset side of the balance
sheet. This is done as a practical matter
even though in theory the *organization
expenses* are of benefit to the company during its entire life, and should therefore be
considered as fixed assets and depreciated
over an infinite, or at least very long period
of time.

Oriental letter of credit. See AUTHORITY TO
PURCHASE.

original bill. See under BILL OF EXCHANGE; BILL
OF LADING.

original cause. See under CAUSE.

original cost. See under COST.

original entry. The first record of a business
transaction made in the books or records
of account of a company. Since such entries
frequently become points of evidence in
legal actions, it is important that they be
made in the proper book of accounts, in the
course of business, and by a person authorized to do so. Each entry should be properly
itemized and extended, to avoid confusion
in interpretation. Sales, purchases, payments
received and made, etc., are examples of the
kinds of transactions which must be recorded as *original entries.* See also BOOK
OF ORIGINAL ENTRY.

origin certificate. See CERTIFICATE OF ORIGIN.

ormolu. An alloy of copper and zinc with the
appearance of gold, used for imitation
jewelry.

ostensible partner. See under PARTNER.

other expense. See EXPENSE (2), NON-OPERATING.

other income. See INCOME, NON-OPERATING.

ounce. 1. A unit of weight in avoirdupois,
troy, and apothecaries' weights. In avoirdupois weight, one *ounce* is one-sixteenth of
a pound, or 437.5 grains. It is the equivalent of 28.35 grams in the metric system. In
troy and apothecaries' weight, one *ounce* is
one-twelfth of a pound, or 480 grains. It is
the equivalent of 31.10 grams in the metric
system. One *ounce* avoirdupois is equal to
0.91146 *ounce* troy, and one *ounce* troy is
equal to 1.097143 *ounce* avoirdupois.
  2. A unit of liquid measure, one-sixteenth
of a pint, 8 fluid drams, or 1.8047 cubic
inches. Traditionally it is the volume of one
ounce, by avoirdupois weight, of water, but
as standardized it is 1.0402 *ounces* avoirdupois.
  3. A unit of dry measure, one-sixteenth
of a dry pint, or 2.10002 cubic inches. Note
that one liquid *ounce* does not fill one dry
ounce of volume.
  4. As a measure of textile fabrics, it is
the weight, in *ounces* avoirdupois, of one
linear yard of the fabric, of a standard width.
In the United States, this width has recently
been newly standardized as 36 inches for
most fabrics.
  5. As a measure of leather, it is equal
to 1/64th of an inch in thickness, based on
the traditional assumption that one square
foot of standard grade leather of one *ounce*
weight will be this thick.

outbid. To offer a higher price for something
which is for sale at auction than that
offered by other bidders. Also, to offer to
perform work or provide materials at a
lower cost than any other supplier. In the
former sense, to *outbid* is to overbid; in the
latter case it is to underbid. See also BID.

outdoor advertising. See under ADVERTISING.

outgo. In business usage, any disbursement;
expenses or costs of doing business. Roughly,
INCOME less *outgo* equals PROFIT.

outlawed. In legal usage, barred by the
STATUTE OF LIMITATIONS. For example, a
creditor who delays too long in taking action
in the courts to collect an unpaid debt will
find that his claim has been *outlawed* by
the statute.

outlaw strike. See under STRIKE.

outlay. In general, an expenditure, particularly
an expenditure of cash funds. In financial

usage, it is specifically the full amount of a loan made, or of a bill which is purchased, before deduction of the DISCOUNT, if any.

outlet. In general, a channel of distribution, usually one for the products of a particular manufacturer. As used in retailing, a store specializing in the liquidation of excessive or distressed stocks, discontinued, obsolete and surplus goods, broken lots and assortments, etc. See also DISTRESSED GOODS.

out of court. Separate from the regular procedure of a court; taking place directly between the contending parties, without the aid or authorization of the court. For example, a plaintiff and defendant may reach an *out-of-court* settlement of a suit, as a result of which the suit is withdrawn. Strictly speaking, an *out-of-court* settlement is not binding upon a court, but in practice permission is always given to withdraw the suit.

out-of-pocket expense. See under EXPENSE (2).

out of stock. Not presently in inventory, or available for sale or use. When it is said that a particular item is *out of stock,* the implication is that the item is usually carried in regular inventory. See also IN STOCK.

out-of-town check. See under CHECK (1).

out-of-town item. In banking, the term for a check, draft, or other item presented for deposit or collection, which is not collectible at a bank within the territory covered by the local clearing house with which the bank receiving the item is associated. Frequently, a bank will accept such instruments only as COLLECTION ITEMS, meaning that they will not be credited until they are collected. There may be a charge for the collection of out-of-town items in some cases. See also CITY ITEM.

output. The total amount of goods or material which has been or can be manufactured in any given period of time; production. When the word is used to refer to the *output* of one or more plants during a particular past period of time, it means the actual amount produced. As sometimes used, however, referring to the *output* of a plant or plants in general, it means the normal capacity of the production facilities. When it is said, for example, that a distillery has an *output* of a particular number of barrels per month, it is meant that this is the normal production of the distillery, not necessarily its actual volume of production.

outside. As used in business, not a member of a regular organization; not registered on a local exchange. See each of the following

under the principal listing: ~ BROKER (2); ~ DIRECTOR; ~ SECURITY (1).

outsider. In securities trade slang, an investor or speculator who is not a professional trader; a LAMB. Also, as sometimes used, a stockholder who is not connected with a corporation as an employee or director, as distinguished from an INSIDER, a stockholder who is connected with the corporation.

outstanding. 1. With respect to a debt, account, or other obligation, not paid or settled; not discharged; uncollected. An *outstanding* obligation may be not yet due, due, or overdue.

2. With respect to corporate STOCK, issued and in the hands of stockholders, as distinguished from stock which has not yet been issued, or which has been issued but repurchased and held by the corporation.

outstanding debt. See under DEBT.

outstanding security. See under SECURITY.

outstanding stock. See under STOCK (1).

outward. As used in business, a synonym for EXPORT. *Outward* trade, for example, is the total of goods and services shipped to other countries, and *outward* charges are the costs of shipping exported goods.

overage. An excess amount; a surplus; the opposite of a SHORTAGE. When a physical inventory shows more goods on hand than have been carried on the accounts, for example, the excess is called an *overage.* Similarly, a shipper may deliberately include an *overage* in a shipment to allow for possible loss or shrinkage en route.

over and short account. In inventory accounting, an account in which OVERAGES and SHORTAGES are recorded, as balancing entries, to reconcile the inventory records with the results of physical inventory counts.

overbought. 1. The condition of having purchased more than is needed to meet requirements. However, as used, the condition does not necessarily result from excessive buying, but may be the result of shrinking needs or resale volume.

2. In securities trade usage, a condition in which the demand for securities at existing prices has been filled, so that prices tend to drop.

overcapitalize. See CAPITALIZE.

overdraft. A check written for an amount greater than that which the signer has on deposit. Under most circumstances, an *overdraft* will be stamped INSUFFICIENT FUNDS, and returned by the bank. In the case of a very good customer, however, the bank may honor the check, in which case the payment in excess of the deposit is actually a form of loan to the depositor, on which the bank may make an interest or service charge.

overdue. Past due; outstanding and still not paid at the time when due to be paid. *Overdue* accounts are frequently classified according to the number of days, weeks or months for which the debt has been outstanding. See also AGING.

overextended. In business, the condition in which the current assets of a company are far exceeded by its liabilities. Under such conditions, bankruptcy usually follows unless the company can somehow arrange to settle its debts or raise additional cash from its fixed assets.

overhead. The general term for those costs of operating a business other than the direct costs of materials and labor. *Overhead* costs are typically defined as those which would continue regardless of the volume or level of operations. In another sense, they are those costs which cannot be directly charged to any particular phase or division of the business. Examples include administrative and executive salaries, rent, insurance, maintenance, depreciation, etc. *Overhead* is frequently classified as factory, office, administrative, or sales *overhead* according to the area in which it arises. Other names for the same type of costs include burden, general expense, etc.

overhead price. See PRICE, ALL-AROUND.

overinsurance. Insurance against property damage which is in excess of the possible amount of loss. It is seldom deliberate, since it has no advantages and adds to the cost of insurance. It may result, however, from a faulty evaluation of the property insured, or from an over-cautious attitude on the part of the insurance buyer. In a few cases, an unscrupulous person may deliberately *overinsure* property in the hope of misleading a prospective purchaser, or in the hope of collecting an excessive settlement from the insurance company in the event of loss. See also INSURANCE, PROPERTY.

overlying bond. See under BOND (1).

overlying mortgage. See under MORTGAGE.

overnight. As usually used in business agreements and transactions, occurring within, or lasting for, or to be concluded in, the next 24 hours, or before the end of the next day. For example, a contract calling for *overnight* delivery, without other qualifications, is understood to require delivery before the end of the next business day, and one permitting *overnight* storage without charge

calls for the goods to be removed by the end of the next day, or by some specified removal time the next day.

overproduction. Excessive production, beyond the amount scheduled, or beyond the amount needed to fill requirements. In a broad economic sense, it is production beyond the amount that the market will absorb at current prices. It is frequently said that *overproduction* and underconsumption are essentially the same thing.

oversold. 1. In business, the condition existing when a producer has committed himself to deliver more of a commodity than he will be able to supply within the time specified for delivery. In the textile industry, mills will usually continue to accept orders for each season's scheduled production until they are *oversold,* before closing or withdrawing their products from additional sale, since they know that there will be a certain proportion of cancellations. See also SOLD UP.

2. In the securities trade, a term for the condition of a particular stock when the SHORT INTEREST in it is excessive in relation to the number of shares outstanding. In this condition, the attempt to cover the short sales will force a rise in prices.

oversubscribe. In the initial sale of securities, to offer or contract to buy more shares or bonds than are being offered for sale. An issued is said to be *oversubscribed* when the total number of offers to buy received are in excess of the total number of units for sale. See also SUBSCRIBE; UNDERWRITE.

overstock. Inventory on hand in excess of what is needed to meet normal requirements, or is in excess of the amount planned. Also, to acquire such excessive inventory by purchasing activities.

overt. Open, public, observable; the opposite of COVERT, or hidden. An *overt* act is one which is open and actual, rather than merely an intention not carried into action.

over the counter. In the securities trade, a term referring to the trade in securities which are not listed on a major securities exchange, but are traded in direct negotiations between buyers and sellers, or their representatives. It derives from the fact that these securities are traded on a face-to-face, or *over-the-counter* basis. In the actual operation of *over-the-counter* trading, a trader who specializes in a particular security arranges for all transactions, either by bringing buyers and sellers together, or by buying and selling the security for his own account. In this case, he usually buys at the BID PRICE and sells at the ASKED PRICE, making his profit on the small spread between these two prices.

over-the-counter stock. See STOCK (1), UNLISTED.

over the road. A term used to describe transportation between cities, especially by motor carrier, as distinguished from local transportation. A trucking company providing service between two or more cities is known as an *over-the-road* carrier.

overtime. In general, any work beyond normal or scheduled working hours. As presently defined by the Wages and Hours Division, any work beyond eight hours on one day, or beyond forty hours in one week. *Overtime* pay is compensation at a premium rate for work done during *overtime* hours. By law, the minimum rate of *overtime* pay is one-and-one-half times the regular hourly rate.

owe. Strictly speaking, to be bound to do something, or to have an obligation to someone. To be obliged to pay or repay an amount of money, or to perform some service; to be indebted.

owing. With respect to a debt, unpaid but not yet DUE. The phrase *due and owing* is frequently used to describe a debt which is currently outstanding and not yet overdue. On the other hand, the term *owed* is sometimes used to describe an overdue debt.

own. To possess legally, under good TITLE; to have as one's *own*.

ownership. The exclusive right which a person has to his belongings, or to those things he holds under good TITLE. Ownership is more than mere possession, and in fact exists independently of possession, so that a person may own what he does not physically possess.

owner's, landlord's, and tenant's insurance. See under INSURANCE, CASUALTY AND LIABILITY.

owner's risk. A term used by common carriers in contracts for the transportation of goods, relieving the carrier of responsibility for loss or damage to the goods from a wide variety of causes. Because this clause is widely used in transportation contracts, shippers frequently buy *owner's risk* insurance, to protect them in the event of loss. See also INSURANCE, INLAND MARINE.

P

pace. A measure of distance, of varying length, but most usually considered to be two and one-half feet, or 30 inches.

pack. 1. To deceive by false appearances; to counterfeit or delude; to unbalance or bias. Thus, to *pack* a jury is to include biased or easily influenced persons deliberately, with the intent of influencing the verdict or of obtaining a false conviction or acquittal.

2. To add fictitious or inflated items to the total cost of an item, so that an equally fictitious discount can then be granted without reducing the actual price. The inflated price charged is the *packed* price, sometimes called the loaded price, and the amounts added are known as the *pack*.

package. 1. In general, any CONTAINER or wrapping in which things are packed for shipment, such as a box, bale, bag, bundle, crate, etc. Also, the collection of goods itself, which has been made ready for shipment. Specifically, under the Pure Food and Drug Act, it is the immediate container in which an item is to be bought or used by the public, whether a box, bottle, tube, etc., not the outside wrapping or shipping container.

2. Any collection of articles, benefits, rights, merchandise, services, etc., which are offered for sale or provided as a unit. For example, a collection of benefits may be included in a union contract as a *package;* a series of radio or television programs may be sold to sponsors as a *package;* or a group of hazards may be insured against in a single insurance policy as a *package*.

package goods. In retailing in general, goods which are bought and sold by the retailer in prepared packages, as distinguished from those items which he either buys in bulk and packs himself, or buys in bulk and re-sells in bulk or in portions. In liquor retailing, specifically bottled liquors, as distinguished from those sold by the glass. Thus, a *package* store is one in which bottled liquor is sold.

packer. 1. In general, a person or company en-gaged in preparing goods for shipment or sale.

2. A company engaged in the business of slaughtering cattle and other meat animals, and preparing the carcasses for sale to the wholesale and retail butcher trade. Some *packers* also put up prepared meat products in cans and other containers.

packer's brand. See under BRAND.

packing and consolidating service. See under FORWARDER.

packing house. 1. An establishment for slaughtering cattle and preparing the carcasses for market. See also PACKER (2).

2. In commercial usage, a freight consolidator and FORWARDER, specializing in receiving small shipments, which he then consolidates or packages into carload or truckload shipments to a single consignee or single city. These services are used especially by the apparel manufacturing trades, and similar groups characterized by many small manufacturers selling to many customers located in the larger cities.

packing list. A list of the contents of a shipping package, which, for purposes of rail or truck shipment is usually placed in a special envelope on the outside of the package, available for inspection. The *packing list* includes the detailed contents, weight, and other required information. See also WAYBILL.

pad. Literally, to fill or stuff. Hence, to *pad* a payroll is to add unneeded workers, or even to add fictitious names; to *pad* an account or bill is to charge for goods or services not delivered, or to charge more than the actual price.

paid circulation. See under CIRCULATION (3).

paid-in capital. See CAPITAL (2), SUBSCRIBED.

paid-in surplus. See under SURPLUS.

paid-up capital. See under CAPITAL (2).

paid-up policy. See under POLICY (2).

paid-up stock. See STOCK (1), FULL-PAID.

palladium. A soft, whitish metallic element, closely related to platinum, used as an alloying metal with gold and in various chemical processes.

pallet. A portable platform, usually made of wood, on which boxed or bagged goods are stacked for storage or shipment. The platform is raised from the ground, permitting the load to be raised and transported by use of a fork-lift truck or other *pallet* lifting device. When properly loaded, *pallets* of goods can be stacked one above the other to make maximum use of stacking space. As tentatively set by the Federal Bureau of Standards, standard *pallet* sizes are 40″ x 32″, and 48″ x 40″, both 5 inches high. *Pallets* may be one-faced or two-faced, and may be designed so that they can be entered from two opposite sides or from all four sides.

pallet load (or **palletized load**). Boxed or bagged goods loaded on a pallet, and usually bound in place with flat steel strapping or baling wire. Such a load may be stored, shipped, and stacked entirely by the use of mechanical materials handling equipment, with no manual handling, loading, or unloading. First widely introduced during World War II by the armed forces, the PALLET and *pallet load* have literally revolutionized materials handling. It is sometimes known as a unit load.

palm off. To impose by fraud; to pass off an imitation by deceit; to pass a counterfeit. To attribute to one manufacturer or source goods or merchandise which are actually the product of another, inferior source.

palpable. That which is easily perceptible, plain or obvious. A *palpable* fraud, for example is one which is easily recognized as such.

panel. The list of names from which a jury is to be chosen. More broadly, a group or list of persons used to test the acceptance of a new product, or to check the uniformity of taste or quality of an existing product, or for some similar purpose related to product development or marketing. Also, an established group or sample of persons whose behavior or opinions are checked from time to time as representative of those of the population. See also SAMPLE; CONSUMER PANEL.

panic. A sudden, widespread and unreasoning fear of the collapse of trade, and more particularly of the financial structure of the country, resulting in wild selling of securities, withdrawal of bank deposits, conversion of property into cash, etc. A *panic* may or may not lead to or be accompanied by a DEPRESSION.

paper, commercial. See COMMERCIAL PAPER.

paper credit. See under CREDIT (3).

paper money. See under MONEY.

paper profit. See under PROFIT.

paper standard. A monetary system which is based on paper money which is not convertible into gold or other commodity of intrinsic value. See also MONEY; GOLD STANDARD.

papier-mâché. A material used for molding, made of wetted paper and paper pulp, mixed with a binding material such as glue, paste, or rosin.

par. 1. From the Latin, equal, equality. Strictly, a condition of equality between the face or nominal value and the market value of a share of stock, bond, bill of exchange, currency, or other instrument. Thus, if a stock sells on the market for its face value it is *at par,* if it sells for more than its face value it is *above par,* and if for less, it is *below par.* In common usage, *par* is taken to mean the face value itself, rather than the relationship. See, for example, VALUE (2), PAR.

2. A standard of performance; a quota. Commonly used in golf to refer to the standard or expected number of strokes required to complete each hole, it is now widely used in business to refer to any standard, normal, or expected performance.

paramount. Above, superior, prior, higher. For example, a *paramount* title, *paramount* equity, etc.

parcel. 1. Generally, a small package, such as one that can be easily carried. More particularly, a collection of items making up a single shipment or a single purchase lot.

2. In real estate, a portion of land lying within defined boundaries. Originally, a portion of an estate.

3. To divide up into portions, as to *parcel* out an estate of land; or to *parcel* out a work assignment.

parcel post. See under POSTAL SERVICE.

parchment. Sheep skin or similar animal hide prepared by special processes for writing. I is so called after Pergamus, in Asia Minor where it originated. Also, any of several paper products made in imitation of the real animal product.

pardon. In law, an act of grace, exempting one who has been found guilty of a crime from any further penalty or punishment, and obliterating his guilt. It is distinguished on the one hand from PAROLE, which is a conditional exemption and may be withdrawn and on the other hand from COMMUTATION which shortens a sentence but does not relieve guilt. It is also distinguished from AMNESTY, which is a *pardon* granted *en masse,* and usually refers to crimes against the state security.

parent. In law, one who begets children; a father or mother. The statutes of some states include step-mother or step-father, or an adopting *parent.* But one who is defined by statute as standing *in loco parentis* (in place of a parent), such as a guardian, is by definition not a *parent.*

parent company. See under COMPANY.

parent store. The term for a RETAIL STORE which is the main or principal one of a group of stores, or for a store that owns or operates one or more BRANCH STORES. It is sometimes known as a home store.

pari passu. From the Latin, literally, by equal steps. Moving or progressing together; without preference or order of precedence; of the same order of standing. For example, creditors *pari passu* receive equal and simultaneous payment out of the same fund, without precedence over each other.

parity. Equality in price, value, quality, rate, or other factors. *Parity* exists between prices in two markets, for example, when the price in one market is equal to the price in the second plus the cost, if any, of transporting goods from the one to the other. Similarly, *parity* exists between two currencies when they are exchangeable for each other at the par or official rate of exchange. See also PAR.

parity ratio. The ratio between the index of average prices received by farmers for their crops and animals, and the index of prices paid by farmers for the things they buy. Prices received for agricultural produce are said to be at 80 percent of *parity,* for example, when their average price is at 80 percent of the index of prices paid by farmers, using the same time period as a base. In federal statistics, the indexes of prices received, prices paid, and the *parity ratio* are calculated on a base of the average 1910 to 1914 prices.

parochial. Originally, within, or limited to, a single parish. Now, in one sense, any institution that is religious in nature, such as a *parochial* school. In a second sense, limited, narrow, restricted, or doctrinaire; as, a *parochial* point of view.

par of exchange. The precisely equivalent amount of money in one currency which will exchange at the official rate for a given amount in a second currency, or the amount of each which will exchange for a fixed amount of some commodity of intrinsic value, such as gold. When two currencies exchange at this rate in the open market, they are said to be at PAR. The *par of exchange* is sometimes called the mint *par of exchange,* or the mint par. See also RATE OF EXCHANGE.

parol contract. See under CONTRACT (1).

parole. In law, a conditional act of grace, exempting a person from further punishment for a crime of which he has been found guilty. A *parole* may be granted at the beginning of a sentence or after it has run for part of its term. In either case, the exemption is based on the good behavior of the person released, and may be withdrawn at any time. See also PARDON.

partial. Applying only to one part of something; not complete; secondary, or subordinate. See also TOTAL. See each of the following under the principal listing: ∼ ACCEPTANCE (3); ∼ CONSIDERATION; ∼ CORRELATION; ∼ LOSS (2); ∼ WILL.

partial average. See AVERAGE (3), PARTICULAR.

participating. Taking part in, sharing. As used in various business terms, it usually means sharing in income or profits. See each of the following under the principal listing: ∼ BOND (1); ∼ POLICY (2); ∼ STOCK (1).

participation. In some forms of casualty insurance and health insurance, a provision under which the insured person shares, or participates in, each loss covered by the insurance. Usually, the *participation* is for a specified percentage of each loss, sometimes figured after a deducted amount which is completely absorbed by the insured person. For example, under a policy providing for 25 percent *participation,* after a deduction of the first $50 of loss, a loss of $150 will be settled for $75, a loss of $450 will be settled for $300, etc. *Participation* is sometimes known as coinsurance, but the correct term is preferred, to avoid confusion with true COINSURANCE.

participation certificate. See CERTIFICATE OF PARTICIPATION.

participation loan. See under LOAN.

particular. As used in various business expressions, a term meaning not general, restricted, special, or specific. See each of the following under the principal listing: ∼ AVERAGE (3); ∼ ESTATE (1); ∼ LIEN.

particular partnership. See PARTNERSHIP, SPECIAL.

particulars, bill of. See BILL (1).

partition. In law, a division of property among those who are its co-owners, joint owners, or owners in common, so that it is thereafter held by them separately. Usually, any sort of property may be *partitioned,* with such exceptions as a HOMESTEAD, and, in some states, property held jointly by a husband and wife. A common instance of a *partition* of property is among heirs who have inherited jointly.

partner. One who enters into a relation of PARTNERSHIP with one or more others, for the purpose of carrying on a trade, business or enterprise together; a member of a FIRM or partnership. For the various types of *partner,* see below.

active ∼. One who takes an active and working part in the business with which he is associated, as distinguished from a SILENT PARTNER, which see below.

actual ∼. One whose name appears in the firm title as a member of the partnership, and who in fact participates in the business and its profits, as distinguished from an OSTENSIBLE PARTNER, which see below.

continuing ∼. One of the *partners* who remain in a firm after one or more others have retired or withdrawn. The *continuing partners* are jointly and individually liable with the retiring *partners* for the debts of the old firm.

dormant ∼. One who by agreement participates in the profits of the firm, but who takes no part in the activity or control of the business, and whose name does not appear as a member in the firm title. He differs from a SILENT PARTNER, which see below, whose name is included in the firm title.

full ∼. One who receives a full and equal share of the firm's profits; a GENERAL PARTNER, which see below.

general ∼. One who participates in the business, and who receives a full and equal share of the profits. He is liable for the debts of the partnership without limitation, as distinguished from a SPECIAL PARTNER, which see below.

incoming ∼. One who enters an already existing partnership. He is not liable for the debts of the previous partnership unless he agrees to be so.

junior ∼. One, usually a newer or younger member of the firm, who does not receive a full share of the profits, nor exercise equal authority in controlling the business.

limited ∼. A SPECIAL PARTNER, which see below. Also, sometimes, one, such as a JUNIOR PARTNER, who receives only a limited share of the profits of the firm.

nominal ∼. One whose name appears in the firm title for whatever benefit it brings the firm, but who in fact is not a *partner.* Under some statutes, he may be held fully liable for any damages done to an innocent third party by the deception.

ostensible ∼. One whose name appears in the firm title but who in fact and deed is not a *partner,* as distinguished from an ACTUAL PARTNER, which see above. A NOMINAL PARTNER, which see above, is an *ostensible partner* for deceptive purposes.

retiring ∼. One who withdraws or retires from a partnership. Generally, they are liable for all of the debts of the firm before their retirement, but not those assumed afterward.

secret ∼. One whose interest in a firm is withheld from the general public and from the firm's customers, but who participates in the firm's profits.

senior ∼. A GENERAL PARTNER, which see above.

silent ∼. One who invests money in a firm, but who takes no active part in the business, though his name appears as a member of the firm and he is fully liable for its debts. Businessmen frequently take their wife or other member of the family into a business as a *silent partner* to share in the profits.

sleeping ∼. See SILENT PARTNER, above.

special ∼. One who invests in a limited PARTNERSHIP. He takes no part in the business, and receives a limited share of the profits. Under most state laws, he is liable for the firm's debts only up to the amount invested by him.

working ∼. A GENERAL PARTNER, which see above. Also, sometimes, one who does not invest money in a firm, but who contributes his skill, experience, and labor instead.

partnership. A form of business organization under which two or more persons associate as principals, and contribute their property, skill, experience, and labor to carry forward some trade, business, or other enterprise, and to share in its control, profits, and risks. Under most state laws, the following features characterize a *partnership:* It may be dissolved by mutual agreement, the death of a partner, the transfer of one or more partners' interests, or a general assignment of its assets. The acts of each partner fully bind the firm, and each acts as both principal and agent to the others, fully binding them by his acts, and being fully bound by theirs in turn. Each is thus fully liable for the debts of the firm. Various forms of *partnership* agreement, which are valid in many states may modify the relationships and liabilities of the partners, as described below.

general ∼. One in which the several partners share equally and fully in the risks profits and liabilities, whether or not they contribute equally to the capital of the firm.

illegal ∿. One formed to engage in acts which are forbidden by law, or one in which one or more of the partners is disqualified to engage in the business of the *partnership*.

implied ∿. One which, while not based on a formal written agreement, will be found to be a *partnership* by a court from the actions and conduct of the associated persons.

limited ∿. One existing under statute, which has both general and special partners. The former actually conduct the business, and have the full liability of partners. The latter take no part in the business, but merely invest capital, and their liability is limited to the amount of their investment. The share of the profits for the special partners is usually limited to a percentage return on their investment.

mining ∿. A special form of *partnership*, recognized in some states, with some of the features of a JOINT STOCK COMPANY. The shares of the *partnership* are transferable, and the *partnership* is not dissolved by the death of one of the partners. The form was originally developed to provide a practical form of business relationship for the prospecting and mining of precious metals.

oral ∿. One existing on the basis of an oral agreement between the parties only.

ordinary ∿. One which exists in the ordinary sense; not a LIMITED or SPECIAL PARTNERSHIP. Also, as sometimes used, one which exists by virtue of long-continued usage and action as such, rather than on the basis of a specific written agreement.

particular ∿. See SPECIAL PARTNERSHIP, below.

∿ **at will.** One entered into by the several partners with the understanding that it may be dissolved at any time by the withdrawal of one or more of the partners at their own option, without being liable to the other partners for their withdrawal.

secret ∿. One in which the membership of one or more of the partners is not disclosed to the general public.

special ∿. One formed to engage in some special or particular branch of business, or to engage in one particular venture or effort. In some states it is known as a particular partnership.

universal ∿. One in which each member contributes his entire property, and in which all profits are distributed equally, regardless of the relative size of the contributions. Many of the religious cooperative communities, such as the Shaker communities, were of this nature.

partnership agreement. The agreement setting forth the conditions and terms under which a partnership is formed. It usually is in the form of written articles of partnership, but it need not be. It may be expressly stated or it may be implied from the actions of the partners and from the circumstances attending their acts.

partnership association. A little-used form of business organization, with some of the features of a PARTNERSHIP and some of a JOINT STOCK COMPANY. Its main features are the limited liability of the participants, the transferable nature of the shares, and the requirement that new members be approved by the others. It is recognized as a separate form of organization in some states, while others treat it as either a partnership or a joint stock company.

partnership insurance. See INSURANCE, LIFE, ACCIDENT, AND HEALTH, BUSINESS LIFE.

part-paid stock. See under STOCK (1).

party. 1. In general any person or group taking part in performing an act, or with a direct interest in some act, affair, contract, negotiation, etc. For example, one who encourages another to commit some act, and who benefits from so doing, may be held to be a *party* to the act.

2. In law, one who has a part or interest in a legal proceeding; one by or against whom a lawsuit is brought; a plaintiff or defendant in a legal action. In an action in which the interest of a person not originally a plaintiff or defendant may become involved, the person may be declared a *party* to the action, either at his own request or by the action of the court. For example, in a case involving the validity of a patent, a licensee of the patent-holder may be declared a *party* to the action.

par value. See PAR (1); VALUE (2), PAR.

par value stock. See under STOCK (1).

passbook. A book provided by a bank for its depositors, in which a record of transactions is kept; a bankbook. A savings account passbook is normally used to record deposits, withdrawals, interest earned and credited, and the current balance. A checking account passbook, now less frequently used, is primarily provided as a receipt book for depositors. It is now more customary to provide a receipted deposit slip or other special receipt for deposits.

passed dividend. See under DIVIDEND.

passenger. Any person whom a CARRIER has agreed, directly or by implication, to carry from one place to another, whether for payment of a fare or not. It has been held that a person is a *passenger* while waiting or embarking at a regular starting point or while alighting at a regular terminal, or using the facilities at either place, as well as when actually in transit. The term includes, therefore, not only ordinary ticketholders, but children riding free, those travelling by courtesy, a person about to buy a ticket at a regular embarking point, etc. With respect to a private vehicle, anyone riding with the permission of the owner or operator, whether or not for pay, is a *passenger*.

passenger density. In railroad, airline, and other common-carrier accounting and statistics, a measure of relative passenger traffic. It is the total number of miles all passengers were carried during a period, divided by the total number of miles of route operated, stated in PASSENGER MILES per mile.

passenger mile. In transportation statistics, a unit of traffic measure equal to the transport of one passenger over one mile of route. The total number of *passenger miles* for a specified period over a specified route is the sum of the distances traveled by all passengers during the period.

~ **cost.** The average cost of carrying one passenger for one mile. It is computed by dividing total passenger travel costs for the period by total passenger miles traveled.

passive bond. See under BOND (1).

passive trust. See TRUST (1), DRY.

passport. Originally, a document giving a vessel permission to leave a port or harbor; a clearance. In general, any document giving freedom to travel or move about; a safe-conduct. More particularly, a document given by a government to its citizens, verifying their citizenship, so that they will be free to leave the country and re-enter without challenge, and will have identification while traveling abroad.

patent. 1. Evident, manifest, openly seen. For example, a *patent* DEFECT is one which is visible, or which can be discovered by a simple inspection.

2. In general, a grant of privilege, property or authority by a government to one or more persons.

3. Particularly, a grant by a government to an inventor, securing to him the exclusive right to make, use or sell his invention for a period of years, in the United States 17 years. Strictly speaking, the right given is to exclude others from making, selling, or using the invention, but the inventor may LICENSE others to do so. A *mechanical patent* covers any new machine or device, a *process*

patent covers a new method or procedure for achieving a result, and a *design patent* covers a new and ornamental design for an article of manufacture. *Design patents* are applied for in the same way as the others, but are granted for periods ranging up to 14 years, depending on the fee paid. The *patent* right becomes part of the estate of the holder, and passes to his heirs if it has not expired, or if he has not ASSIGNED it to others during his life. See also ASSIGNMENT; INFRINGEMENT.

patent defect. See under DEFECT.

patent medicine. See PROPRIETARY.

patron. Originally, from the Latin *pater,* or father, a protector, supporter, or benefactor. Now, in business usage, a customer or client; one who deals regularly with a business establishment.

patronage. 1. The customers, collectively, of a business; the business or trade which regular customers bring.

2. The right or privilege of making appointments to public office; more broadly, any political honor or favor dispensed, or the dispensing itself.

patronize. In business usage, to be a regular customer; to deal with or do business with; to be a client.

pauper. A person who is without funds or means of support; one who is so poor he must be supported at public expense. In certain circumstances, one who declares himself a *pauper* may be permitted to sue, or to defend a lawsuit without being chargeable for the costs. Also, one who declares himself to be a *pauper,* and who assigns whatever property he may have, may be discharged from BANKRUPTCY by a court.

pawn. A PLEDGE, in the form of goods or property, left as security for a debt, or for the fulfillment of an obligation; a BAILMENT. Also, the act of pledging something for the purpose of obtaining a loan.

pawnbroker. One who is in the business of lending money against the security of personal property left with him as a pledge or PAWN; a licensed BAILEE. In most places, he is required to keep a record of the name of the borrower, date, amount loaned, the terms and period of the loan and a description of the pledge, and to give the borrower a receipt with the same information. This is both for the protection of the borrower, and for the benefit of the police in the tracing of stolen goods.

pay. To discharge a debt, to disburse funds for compensation; to remunerate for services rendered. Also, the compensation or remuneration given for services rendered, especially when given in a fixed and regular amount, such as SALARY or WAGES. See also CALL-BACK PAY; CALL-IN PAY; LONGEVITY PAY; SEVERANCE PAY; VACATION PAY.

payable. Capable of being paid; eligible to be paid; due to be paid at this time. In the last sense, *payable* implies that the obligation is due at the present or indicated time, as distinguished from OWING. An instrument may be designated as *payable* in various ways or under different conditions. See each of these under the principal listing: ~ AFTER DATE; ~ AFTER SIGHT; ~ ON CALL (1); ~ ON DEMAND; ~ TO ORDER; ~ WITH EXCHANGE.

pay-as-you-go. Any system of meeting costs or expenses as they occur, or out of current earnings. For example, a *pay-as-you-go* tax plan is one in which taxes on income are paid at the time the income is earned, rather than in the following year, and a *pay-as-you-go* capital expenditures budget is one which allows only for those projects which can be financed out of current earnings, without incurring long-term debt.

payee. The person or organization in whose name a check, draft, bill, note or other obligation is made payable or drawn. In a broad sense, any person to whom money or other obligation is paid.

payer. The person or organization designated in a negotiable instrument or obligation as the one that will make payment; the MAKER (1). In a broad sense, any person who pays money or discharges an obligation.

paying. Offering a compensation, worth while; offering a profitable enough return to warrant carrying through, as a *paying* proposition.

paying teller. See TELLER.

payload. In general, that part of the total load carried by a vessel, car, or aircraft that produces revenue; the CARGO. When used in rating a particular type of vessel, car, or aircraft, it is the maximum weight of revenue cargo that can be carried.

payment. The discharge of a debt or obligation, or the fulfillment of an agreement. The discharge need not be in the form of money, but may be the delivery of goods, the performance of a service or of labor, etc. A transfer from a debtor to a creditor in accordance with the terms of an obligation.

payment bill. See under BILL OF EXCHANGE.

payment for honor. The payment of a draft or bill by someone other than the one on whom it is drawn, after the latter has defaulted, when the purpose of the payment is to save the honor or credit of the original drawee. The payment creates a new obligation, which the defaulter is expected to discharge to the one who has paid. See also ACCEPTANCE FOR HONOR; DISHONOR; HONOR.

payment in kind. See under IN KIND.

payment stopped. See STOP PAYMENT.

payment supra protest. See SUPRA PROTEST.

payroll. 1. The total amount of money owed by a business organization to its employees for work done during a specified period. As used in this sense, the term is usually qualified to indicate the period covered, as, the weekly *payroll*, monthly *payroll*, etc.
2. The list of employees who have earned pay during a period, with the amounts due to each for work performed.

payroll tax. See under TAX (2).

peak. A maximum, or the highest point reached during a given period. For example, the *peak* of agricultural employment is reached during the summer months each year, and *peak* prices are usually obtained when the supply of a product is at its shortest for a period.

peck. A dry measure of capacity, equal to one fourth of a bushel, two gallons, eight quarts or sixteen pints. It is equivalent to 8.8096 liters, in the metric system.

peculation. The unlawful appropriation of public funds or property, by one with whom they have been deposited, or to whose care they have been entrusted. Thus, it is a form of public EMBEZZLEMENT.

pecuniary. Monetary; relating to money or monetary instruments or systems. It is sometimes used to distinguish between financial or monetary rewards and those which can't be measured directly in money, or which are *non-pecuniary*.

peddle. To travel from place to place selling small wares or articles of merchandise. The origin of the term is not clear, but it apparently is derived from the same source as petty, and carries the implication of selling in a trifling or ineffective manner. A *peddler* or *pedlar* is one who *peddles*.

peg. To fix or stabilize the price of something, such as a security, commodity, or currency; to keep a price stationary. This may be done by regulation, or by manipulating the market or trading mechanism. For example, the federal government may *peg* the price of gold by offering to buy all that is presented at the stated price, or speculators may *peg* the price of a stock by engaging in frequent buying and selling operations at the desired price. Such *pegging* of a security price is now outlawed except as done in accordance with the regulations of the Securities and Exchange Commission.

pegged exchange. See under EXCHANGE (4).

penal. Punishable; dealing with or relating to punishment or penalties. For example, the *penal* code is the body of law dealing with punishable crimes, and prescribing penalties, and a *penal* offense is one which is punishable under law.

penalty. A punishment, fine, forfeiture or damages imposed for having done or not done something, in either case having acted unlawfully or not in accordance with an agreement.

   ~ **bond.** See under BOND (2).

   ~ **clause.** A clause sometimes inserted in a contract, specifying that a sum of money is to be paid by the party at fault in the case of non-fulfillment of the conditions of the contract. Also, that clause of any law or regulation which specifies the *penalty* to be imposed for its violation.

   ~ **rate.** A higher rate of pay in effect under specified conditions, such as for weekend work, hazardous duty, etc.

pending. 1. In process, not yet decided or determined; begun but not yet completed, as *pending* legislation, which has been introduced but not yet acted upon.

   2. Awaiting, or awaited; imminent. For example, payment may be withheld *pending* the arrival of goods.

penny. A CENT; adapted from the British *penny,* which was the roughly equivalent minor COIN.

penny stock. See under STOCK (1).

pennyweight. A unit of weight in troy measure, equal to 24 grains, or one-twentieth of an ounce. It derives its name from the old English silver penny, the standard weight of which was the same. Abbreviated *dwt.*

pension. In general, any allowance or payment to a retired person, for previous services rendered, by an employer or the government. The payments may be made either to the retired person only, or to his survivors.

pension plan. In business, a plan established and maintained by an employer to provide in a systematic manner for the payment of regular pension amounts to retired or disabled employees. The plan may be set up by the employer alone, or jointly with a union as part of a collective bargaining arrangement. The plan itself may be more or less informal, with payments determined individually in each case, or it may be actuarial, with payments based on prescribed contributions, age on retirement, length of service,

life expectancy, etc. The contributions to the pension fund may be made by the employer and employee together, in which case the plan is a contributory one, or they may be made by the employer alone, in which case it is non-contributory. Under some plans, the employee obtains an interest in the share of the fund intended for his pension, and may withdraw all or part of his share under stated conditions. In such cases, the plan is said to include VESTING, or to be a vested plan.

peonage. INVOLUNTARY SERVITUDE. Specifically, forced labor to work out a debt or obligation. Sometimes, the term is applied to the practice of hiring out convicts for labor. *Peonage* as such is outlawed in the United States.

people's bank. See CREDIT UNION.

per. In Latin, by; by means of; through; on account of. Also, as sometimes used, for each one; in each period.

   ~ **annum.** In each year, during each year, by the year, annually.

   ~ **capita.** Literally, by the head. For each one; individually; to or from each person.

   ~ **cent.** Parts in each hundred. A proportion expressed in terms of hundredths.

   ~ **curiam.** Literally, by the court. An opinion or decision delivered jointly by the members of a court, or by the presiding judge.

   ~ **diem.** By the day. An allowance, payment, charge or rental set on a daily basis. A *per diem* expense allowance is usually one given in lieu of paying actual expenses incurred.

   ~ **se.** By itself; in or of itself; taken alone; inherently.

percentage. Strictly, a percent, or proportion in hundredths, as a rate. For example, interest charged at 5 percent of the capital is a *percentage* interest rate, as distinguished from one quoted in actual dollars. More loosely, any proportion, or any amount expressed as a proportion of another, is said to be a *percentage*.

percentage distribution. A FREQUENCY DISTRIBUTION or table in which the percentage of the total number of items falling within each interval is given, rather than the actual number of items.

percentage lease. See under LEASE.

perch. 1. A unit of linear land measure; equal to one ROD, 5½ yards or 16½ feet.

   2. A unit of cubic measure, especially for masonry work. It is the volume one ROD long, 1½ feet wide and 1 foot deep, or 24¾ cubic feet. In some states it is fixed as 25 cubic feet.

3. In land measure, one square ROD, 30¼ square yards, or 1/160th of an acre.

per curiam opinion. See under OPINION.

perempt. To cut off, or bar further action or appeal, especially by ones own actions. In general, to close off, to make final.

peremptory. Final, absolutely final; not permitting of question; barring further action. Also, arbitrary, with no cause needed or shown. For example, a *peremptory* challenge of a juror in a court trial is an objection to a juror made for no stated reason, but as one of a permitted number of such *peremptory* or arbitrary challenges or objections.

perfect. 1. Complete in every detail, and with no legal defects. Hence, not open to dispute or challenge; enforceable at law. For example, a *perfect* TITLE.
2. Finished and complete, with no defects that impair its intended use. For example, goods are considered delivered in *perfect* order if they have no defects relating to their use or appearance.

perfect machine. See under MACHINE.

perform. To execute, or carry out; to fulfill or accomplish according to the terms of an agreement, or as ordered by another.

performance. In general, the keeping of a promise or agreement; the doing, by one party to an agreement, of that which he agreed to do; the accomplishment under an agreement or order of that which was to be accomplished.

performance bond. See BOND (2), CONTRACT.

performance standard. See under STANDARD.

peril. In insurance usage, the HAZARD or contingency insured against; the potential cause of loss or damage. For example, fire, storm, shipwreck, etc., are all *perils* against which insurance may be obtained. See also INSURANCE.

peril of the sea. In marine insurance, a natural or accidental danger which a ship may meet on a voyage. As generally interpreted, the term includes storms, waves, winds, rocks and shoals, collisions, and other sources of loss or damage arising from the natural elements or from pure accident. See also INSURANCE, MARINE.

peril point. Under the Trade Agreement Extension Act of 1951, the point at which a reduction in a tariff threatens to do serious injury to a domestic industry producing like or competitive products. The federal TARIFF COMMISSION is charged with submitting reports on such situations to the President, making recommendations for raising the tariff, removing the tariff concession, or taking other appropriate action. The President may either follow the Commission's recommendation, or decline to. If he declines, however, he must justify his decision in a report to Congress. Congress has no veto power over the President in these matters, so that he is free to carry out or continue the reduction if he still desires to do so.

periodic. Occurring at fixed, regular, intervals of time, or existing for the duration of regular periods of time. For example, a contract calling for *periodic* payments will usually also specify the particular period of time, or interval, such as a month, between payments.

perishable. As usually used, subject to rapid decay unless properly stored and protected. Sometimes, subject to easy destruction by any means; delicate.

perjury. In law, the willful assertion as fact or knowledge of something known to be false. *Perjury* is deliberate falsification under oath, whether in oral testimony, an affidavit, deposition, or other sworn statement. For example, a false statement in a tax return or customs declaration is *perjury*.

permanent. Enduring, not temporary, but not necessarily PERPETUAL. Not easily subject to change; established with the intent to remain fixed and unchanged. A person's *permanent* abode, for example, is that place of residence which he has no intention of changing or abandoning, though he may reside at other places from time to time.

permanent investment. The term for a fund which is kept continually invested over a long period of time. It is not necessarily kept invested in the same securities, but may be invested and reinvested over the period of time.

permissive. Allowed, or allowing. Not strict and narrow, but subject to variation. For example, a *permissive* adjustment clause in a union agreement may permit either party to reopen the question of wage rates in the agreement at any time that certain specified conditions have changed.

permit. 1. In general, to allow; to grant a license or authority.
2. Any license or warrant given by the proper authority, empowering a person to do some lawful act, but one which is regulated and not allowed without such license or authorization.

permit card. In labor union practice, a card or other written permission issued by a union to a non-union employee, permitting him to take temporary employment with an employer who has signed a CLOSED SHOP contract with the union. Such a permit may be given, for example, when the union is unable to fill a vacant position from among qualified union members.

permutation. 1. In law, the exchange or substitution of one thing for another, especially of a movable thing. It does not imply any deception or fraud, unless such exchange is expressly not permitted.

2. In mathematics, the process of changing the order in which a number of things are arranged; hence, any one of such possible orders of arrangement. It is distinguished from a combination of things, which is a number of things taken together, regardless of the order. For example, there are only three combinations of two numbers which can be found in the numbers 1 through 3 (1 and 2, 2 and 3, 1 and 3), but there are six *permutations* (12, 21, 23, 32, 13, 31).

perpetual. Never ending; continuous, without interruption; unlimited in time or duration. See each of the following under the principal listing: ∼ ANNUITY; ∼ INVENTORY; ∼ TRUST (1).

perpetual bond. See BOND (1), ANNUITY.

perpetuity. A term for a particular form of trust fund, for beneficial or charitable purposes. Despite the name, such trusts do not run forever, but for periods which are usually fixed by statute, and in any case for not longer than the charitable or other need exists. See also TRUST (1), PERPETUAL.

per procurationem. A Latin phrase, meaning, in literal translation, as an agent, and roughly converted in current usage into the term PROXY. When an agent signs a document in place of his principal, the words *per procurationem* or the abbreviation *p. proc.* are usually added.

perquisite. Originally, something which is sought out; later, something which is come by, which is in addition to regular pay or compensation. Products or services provided by an employer in addition to money wages, especially those which are considered to be customary for a particular type of work, such as free transportation for railroad employees, meals for restaurant employees, etc. In a particular sense, the compensation, rights, and other benefits which attach to a public office.

person. In law, a being or creature, human or artificial.

artificial ∼. An association of individuals, cloaked by statute with the rights and obligations of a NATURAL PERSON, which see below.

The term includes corporations, partnerships, boards of directors or trustees, etc. Thus, in the United States, all laws and statutes containing such phrases as "No *person* shall . . ." apply equally to individuals and to *artificial persons.*

legal ∼. An ARTIFICIAL PERSON, which see above.

natural ∼. A single human individual. Depending on the context, the term may mean literally any human, or any individual meeting certain qualifications, such as adulthood.

personal. In general, related to individual persons, or to people, rather than to inanimate things. See each of the following under the principal listing: ∼ ESTATE; ∼ INJURY; ∼ LOAN; ∼ PROPERTY; ∼ SAVINGS; ∼ SECURITY (2).

personal consumption expenditures. As defined by the Department of Commerce, and as used in NATIONAL INCOME statistics, the total market value of the purchases of goods and services by individuals and by non-profit institutions, plus the value of food, clothing, housing, and services received as income in kind. The total includes the rental value of owner-occupied dwellings, but excludes purchases of dwellings, which are classified as capital expenditures. The figures as published are on a net basis; that is, expenditures for such things as insurance are included only to the extent that premiums exceed benefits, etc. *Personal consumption expenditures* plus personal savings equal disposable personal income. See also INCOME; SAVINGS.

personal finance company. A financial institution organized for the purpose of making small loans to individuals, usually to finance the purchase of consumer goods, or for general use. The loan made may be unsecured, or may be secured by a chattel mortgage on an automobile, household goods, or other personal property. Loans are usually made for periods of from six months to three years, and the terms of the loan usually call for payment in equal monthly or quarterly installments over the life of the loan. These companies are also frequently called small loan companies, personal loan companies, etc. See also COMMERCIAL FINANCE COMPANY; LOAN, PERSONAL.

personal holding company. See under COMPANY.

personal income. In government statistics, the total of income received by individuals from all sources, including payments from government and from business, but excluding transfer payments among individuals. It is the total of wages, salaries, other labor income, proprietors' and rental income, interest, dividends, and other payments received by individuals and unincorporated business proprietors.

personal liability insurance. See under INSURANCE, CASUALTY AND LIABILITY.

personal property tax. See under TAX (2).

personal service corporation. See under CORPORATION.

personalty. A term for personal property. See PROPERTY, PERSONAL.

personnel management. The branch of business management concerned with the administration and direction of all of the relations between a company and its employees, including the recruiting of new employees, training, testing, promoting, and supervising employees, etc., as well as the administration of all PERSONNEL RELATIONS.

personnel relations. The broad field of business administration involving the relations between a company and its employees. It includes not only LABOR RELATIONS, which deals with working conditions, wages, and similar areas, but the human and welfare aspects of the relations between management and the employees as well.

per stirpes. Literally, in Latin, by the roots. A legal phrase used to indicate that the descendants of a deceased ancestor are to share in his estate proportionately, according to the rights of representation and inheritance as established by law, and not as individual inheritors. In the various states, for example, the law prescribes the particular share of an estate to which a widow, child, grandchild, or other relative is entitled in the absence of a specific will, as a *per stirpes* inheritance.

petit. Small, minor, lesser, as opposed to GRAND. The term is sometimes used as petty. See, for example, LARCENY, PETIT (PETTY).

petition. A formal, written request or application, calling on an authority to redress a wrong, to grant a special favor or privilege, etc. The *petition* is a recognized means of bringing a matter to the attention of the courts or the government, or of initiating legislative action. In some states, for example, a *petition* with the required number of signatures may be used to force the question of the recall of an elected official to be placed on the ballot at an election.

petition in bankruptcy. The form in which a person applies for a declaration as a BANKRUPT; the form used by creditors to force a debtor into BANKRUPTCY.

petitioning creditor. See under CREDITOR.

pettifogger. A lawyer, or sometimes any professional practitioner, who carries on a petty, underhanded or disreputable business; one who takes on tainted cases; a SHYSTER.

petty cash. In accounting, a revolving cash fund, withdrawn from the general cash account and made available for small purchases and other expenditures which are too small to warrant full accounting treatment. In most companies there is a limit, varying with the activity and size of the company, on the maximum amount of a single disbursement from the *petty cash* fund. The fund is typically used for such expenditures as local travel, stationery, supplies, etc. Payments from the fund are made on the basis of a simple voucher, signed by the person withdrawing the money and countersigned by the person authorized to approve disbursements.

phantom freight. See under FREIGHT.

Philadelphia Plan. See TRUST CERTIFICATE.

photo-offset. See OFFSET (2).

physical inventory. See under INVENTORY.

pica. A printer's measure of width, or of line length, equal to 12 POINTS (2), or 1/6th of an inch. Also a TYPE SIZE, 12 points high, and thus printing 6 lines to the inch.

picket. Originally, a detachment or line of troops set out to observe the enemy or serve as sentries. Thus, in a labor strike, a union member who is posted outside the struck establishment to notify other workers and the public that a strike is in progress, and to discourage them from entering. In some cases, a union member posted to notify the public that an establishment is UNFAIR TO UNION LABOR.

pickup service. In freight transportation, the collection of shipments by a carrier from places of business or residences. In some cases, this may be a free service of the carrier, forwarder, or express service, and in others it may be at a fee. Where *pickup service* is not provided, the shipper is expected to deliver the shipment to the freight terminal, or arrange for its delivery. See also CARTAGE.

piece goods. In the textile trades, those items which are sold to the retail trade by the piece, such as towels, sheets, handkerchiefs, blankets, curtains, etc., rather than by the yard. See also YARD GOODS.

piece work. A system of wage payments based on a measure of unit output, rather than on time worked. In apparel manufacturing, for example, most work is paid for on a *piece* *work* basis, such as the number of patterns cut, the number of seams sewn, buttons attached, etc. Most INCENTIVE plans involve *piece work* payments to some extent. See also TIME WORK.

piker. Originally, a petty gambler or "freeloader" who frequented the turnpikes or tollroads on which the wealthy traveled. Thus, anyone who tries to avoid paying his own way, or spending his own money, especially by petty tactics. Also, still, a petty gambler.

pilferage. Originally, plunder, spoilage, or pillage. As used currently, stealing, especially stealing small amounts of stored goods, or of supplies.

pilotage. The charge or fee collected by harbor or river pilots for their services in conducting ships in and out of port, or through other channels requiring special care and knowledge.

pilot plant. A test plant, or experimental plant, designed and constructed to test out a new production process, or to develop methods for manufacturing a new product. A *pilot plant* is more than a laboratory, since it is designed to reproduce the conditions that will exist in the full scale plant during actual production operations.

pint. A unit of measure of both liquid and dry capacity. One PINT liquid contains 16 fluid ounces, one-half a liquid quart, or 28.875 cubic inches. One dry PINT contains 16 dry ounces, one-half a dry quart, or 33.60 cubic inches. The British imperial PINT contains approximately 20 fluid ounces, or 34.68 cubic inches.

pipe. A measure of liquid capacity, used for wine and sometimes for olive oil. It varies from country to country in exact quantity, being 3 BARRELS, or 93 GALLONS in the case of Spanish and Portuguese wines, and 4 barrels, 2 HOGSHEADS, ½ TUN, or 126 gallons in American and English usage; a BUTT.

piracy. Originally, robbery by force on the high seas. In current usage, any of various unethical or extra-legal activities, such as the appropriation of a design or copyright work of art or literature without payment or credit; INFRINGEMENT.

pit. In the commodities trade, the name for the special section of the trading floor of the Chicago Board of Trade devoted to trade in each of several particular commodities. Each such area is generally circular in shape, with an inner trading area surrounded by a higher platform, each area roughly corresponding in function to the trading posts of the New York Stock Exchange. There are four such *pits,* for trade in wheat, oats, other grains, and provisions. In a broader sense, the grain trade in general.

pit trader. See under TRADER.

place. 1. To arrange for, or to dispose of; to make, or settle. For example, a borrower *places* a loan, a customer *places* an order, etc.

2. To arrange for, or to find, a position of employment for a person.

placement. 1. The activity of finding employment for persons, either as an employment agency or through a company organization.

2. The process of negotiating for the sale of a new issue of securities, or of arranging for a long-term loan. The issue may be placed with an UNDERWRITER, or it may be sold through direct, or private *placement;* that is, sold directly to investors without going through the underwriting procedure.

plagiarism. The act of appropriating for one's own purposes the literary or artistic composition of another, or of passing off the creative ideas of another as one's own. It is illegal under the federal copyright laws, and under the statutes of most states.

plain bond. See BOND (1), DEBENTURE.

plaintiff. In law, the complainer; the one who brings an action or suit against another to obtain satisfaction or redress. The opposite of DEFENDANT.

planned economy. In economic theory, a state in which the allocation of resources, including land, labor, and capital, is under the direction of the state. In a fully *planned economy* all economic activity is at the discretion of the state, but the term is also applied to economic systems in which the state regulates only some key activities, such as investment, the allocation of scarce materials, consumer prices, etc.

plant. 1. A manufacturing establishment; the income-producing equipment, machinery, and property of a business; a factory, mill, or works.

2. Production equipment in general, including machinery, major tools, the structures that house them, etc. The term *plant and equipment* includes all of the income producing assets of a company.

play the market. In securities trade slang, to speculate in securities or commodities; to buy and sell for a quick profit, rather than for investment.

plea. In law, the reply of a defendant in a civil suit, answering the matters of fact alleged by the plaintiff. A reply based purely on matters of law, such as a claim that the court has no jurisdiction in the case, is called a DEMURRER. In a criminal case, the initial statement by the defendant as to his guilt or innocence of the crimes charged.

plead. 1. To present a PLEA in a civil suit or criminal case; to answer an allegation or charge.

2. To conduct a legal case as a trial lawyer or advocate; to present the arguments on behalf of a client before a court.

plebiscite. Literally, a vote of the people. A direct vote by the electorate on an issue, which may be one ordinarily handled by the legislature. For example, many state constitutions require a *plebiscite* on such matters as bond issues, zoning changes, etc. A REFERENDUM.

pledge. 1. Any thing put up, or turned over to a creditor, as security for a loan; a PAWN. When the *pledge* consists of such things as securities, bonds, notes, etc., it is called COLLATERAL. A *pledge* differs from a MORTGAGE in that title to the thing *pledged* remains with the debtor. See also HYPOTHECATION.

2. To deliver something of value as security. In general, to make a promise by which one binds oneself to carry out some contract or agreement, whether or not secured by a deposit.

Plimsoll line. A line or mark placed on the side of a ship to indicate the safe depth to which it may be allowed to sink in the water when carrying a maximum load. Actually, it is usually a series of lines or marks, for fresh and salt water, for inland water, coastal waters, open seas, etc. It is named for Samuel Plimsoll, who was instrumental in putting an act preventing the overloading of merchant ships through the British Parliament. It is also technically known as the load line.

plow back. To reinvest earnings or profits in a business venture, rather than to pay them out as dividends to stockholders or as proprietor's withdrawals. The derivation, of course, is from the agricultural practice of plowing under certain crops to enrich the soil.

plug. In advertising slang, an advertisement; especially one inserted on a radio or television program. Also, in another usage, a free advertisement, or any favorable mention of a person or product, such as in newspapers, or in radio program material.

plunger. In securities trade slang, a reckless speculator; one who invests large sums of money in uncertain securities in the hope of reaping very large profits.

plurality. In an election, the excess of votes for the winning candidate over the vote for the next nearest candidate. When there are only two candidates, the winner's *plurality* is also his MAJORITY.

P.M. See PUSH MONEY.

point. 1. In the securities, commodities, and currency markets, a standard unit of price. The fixed amount or step by which price quotations are changed as prices rise or decline. On the stock market, for example, a *point* is one dollar per share in the price of a stock or bond. Price changes are noted in *points,* or in fractions of a *point,* so that a change of 1/8th *point* is a rise or fall of 12.5 cents in price. In the commodities market, one *point* is usually one cent per hundred pounds of a given commodity, and in the currency market it is usually one hundredth of one cent. A change in the price of the pound sterling from $2.7950 to $2.7960, for example, is said to be a ten *point* rise.

2. In printing, a measure of TYPE SIZE, equal to about 1/72 of one inch in type height, with a minimum allowance of space between lines. Thus, a type that prints nine lines to the inch is said to be eight *point* type.

point-of-purchase advertising. See under ADVERTISING.

pole. In land measure, an area equal to one square ROD or PERCH, or 30.25 square yards.

policy. 1. In general, any definite statement of the philosophy or purpose of a business, government, or other organization. A plan or course of action, based on such a philosophy or purpose. *Policy* decisions are those which change, interpret, or affect the basic plan or philosophy, as distinguished from administrative decisions, which are made to carry out *policy.*

2. In insurance, the name for the written contract between the insurer and the insured, setting forth the terms and conditions under which the insurance is issued, the particular property, risks, or hazards covered, the amount of insurance, the period, cost, etc. *Policies* are of many types, some of which are peculiar to specific forms of insurance, and others which are more widely applicable. The major types and classifications of *policies* are listed and defined below. See also INSURANCE.

assessable ~. One under which the policyholder may be held liable for any losses of the insurance company which exceed its reserves or its ability to pay. The *policies* of some mutual insurance companies and of some reciprocal insurance companies may be assessable, but under the statutes of many states, mutual companies may issue NON-AS-SESSABLE POLICIES, which see below.

blanket ~. One covering more than one named building or property, or the contents of more than one named building, whether the properties covered are at the same general location or widely separated. Contents covered under a *blanket policy* are insured when they are moved from one named building to another, such as from a warehouse to a factory, but not while in transit unless this is specified.

block ~. See FLOATER POLICY, below.

extended ~. In life insurance, one the coverage of which has been extended beyond the time after premiums are no longer paid, either to give the insured more time in which to pay, or under a contract specifically providing for extended insurance after premiums cease.

floater ~. One covering specified items, or a specified value of items, wherever they may be located. This form of *policy* is commonly used to insure personal property, such as jewelry, furs, recreational equipment, etc., which are carried about from place to place. When it covers the stock in trade of a business, such as the musical instruments which a dealer may lease out, or the jewelry which a dealer may deliver on approval, it is commonly known as a block *policy*.

incontestable ~. In life insurance, one which has been in force for a specified period of time, such as two years, and which therefore can no longer be contested, canceled, or challenged by the insurance company on the basis of the statements made in the application.

interest ~. One held by a person who has a true INSURABLE INTEREST in the property or life covered, as distinguished from a WAGER POLICY, which see below.

master ~. In group insurance, the single *policy* containing the agreement under which the entire group are insured. Each individual is given a CERTIFICATE OF INSURANCE as evidence of his coverage under the *master policy*.

mixed ~. In marine insurance, one covering a ship during all its voyages from one named port to another during a specified period, such as a year. Thus, it is a mixture of a TIME and VOYAGE POLICY, which see below.

non-assessable ~. One under which the liability of the policyholder is limited to the premium paid on his own policy, as distinguished from an ASSESSABLE POLICY, which see above.

non-participating ~. One under which the policyholder does not participate in any

division of the profits of the insurance company. Many stock insurance company policies are non-participating, with all profits being divided among the company stockholders. See also PARTICIPATING POLICY, below.

open ~. One covering a specified type of goods, or a specified location, but with the value of the goods or property covered left indefinite, or open. In marine insurance, for example, it may cover all shipments in a specified geographic area, with the actual amounts reported from time to time by the insured. See also REPORTING POLICY, below.

paid up ~. In life insurance, one on which all the premium payments called for have been made, or one which has been issued for a reduced amount of insurance in lieu of further premium payments on the regular *policy*.

participating ~. One under which the policyholder participates in the profits of the insurance company, either through direct dividends or through rebates on future premium payments. Practically all mutual insurance company *policies,* and some stock insurance company *policies,* are *participating policies.* See also NON-PARTICIPATING POLICY, above.

reporting ~. One covering a specified type of property at one or more specified locations, but with no set amount of coverage. The value of the property, such as goods in inventory, is reported by the insured to the company periodically, and the premium determined at the end of the year. See also OPEN POLICY, above.

term ~. One which gives protection over a specified period of time, and which expires at the end of that period. In life insurance, in particular, it is a *policy* which has no RESERVE VALUE.

time ~. In marine insurance, one covering a vessel for a specified period of time, wherever it is, rather than for a specified voyage or voyages. See also VOYAGE POLICY, below.

tontine ~. In general, one which has TONTINE features. Particularly, in life insurance, one of a class of *policies* under which the accumulated dividends and benefits are withheld until some stated time, then divided among the policyholders still surviving. Such *policies* are illegal in most states.

unvalued ~. One which is for a specific total amount of coverage, but under which the amount to be paid for the loss of each item of property covered is not specified in advance, but is to be determined after the loss or damage. See also VALUE (2), ACTUAL CASH.

valued ~. One under which the value of

each item insured is stated, and the amount to be paid in the event of total loss specified. Thus, there is no need for a survey or appraisal after loss, except to determine the extent of a partial loss. Such *policies* are not permitted for property insurance in some states.

voyage ~. In marine insurance, one covering a vessel for the duration of a particular voyage, no matter how long it may last, rather than for a specified period of time. See also TIME POLICY, above.

wager ~. One held by a person who has no legitimate INSURABLE INTEREST in the thing or person insured, and is thus, in effect, simply betting with the insurance company that there will be a loss under the *policy*. Such *policies* are generally illegal in the United States, but may be purchased through LLOYD's. See also INTEREST POLICY, above.

policyholder. The person who owns or possesses a POLICY (2) of insurance, whether or not he is the person whose life is insured, or the person whose property is insured. In most states, any person with a legitimate INSURABLE INTEREST may be a *policyholder* of insurance on a life or on property.

policy year. As used in insurance, the twelve month period commencing with the exact date and time of the beginning of an insurance policy, or with the anniversary of that date. Unless otherwise specified, a *policy year* is usually assumed to begin at 12:01 a.m., standard time, on the date specified.

political strike. See under STRIKE.

poll. 1. Originally, a head, and hence a person. A *poll,* in current usage, is a counting of heads, or a vote, as for example, the *poll* of a jury to determine a verdict. Also, a place in which voting takes place.

2. Shaved, as a head. Hence, smooth, or with clean edges, as a DEED POLL, as distinguished from an indenture deed.

poll tax. See under TAX (2).

pool. In general, any amount made up by common contributions, or any combination of persons or companies in which all contribute to the common fund of resources, or to the common effort. The purpose of a *pool* may be legitimate, as when companies join a shipping *pool* to save on freight charges, or it may be for illegal purposes, as when a *pool* is formed to stifle competition, control prices, or divide a market. See also CARTEL; TRUST (2).

pool car service. See FORWARDER, PACKING AND CONSOLIDATING SERVICE.

pooling agreement. In railroading, a contract or arrangement between competing railroads, providing for the *pooling,* or allocation of freight between the railroads, and a division of the profits. Such agreements are forbidden under the Interstate Commerce Act.

port. 1. In general, any place at which ships may arrive, unload cargo and passengers, and take on others. In modern usage, any place at which goods and passengers may be brought into a country or from which they may depart, whether by ship, railroad, aircraft, etc. An inland airport, for example, may be a *port* as far as the immigration and customs laws are concerned.

~ of entry. Any one of the *ports,* designated by law, at which federal customs officers are stationed for the inspection of incoming cargo and baggage, and the levying of import duties according to the tariff laws. The *port of entry* need not be the actual *port* at which goods enter the country, but may be the *port* or place to which they are brought for inspection.

2. In maritime usage, the left side of a ship, facing forward. It was originally so named because ships tied up on this side. In older usage, it was sometimes known as the larboard side. See also STARBOARD.

portal-to-portal. The term for a system of wage payments under which the employee is compensated for the travel time spent on company property, for washing-up and dressing time, etc., as well as for the time actually spent working. An employee on a *portal-to-portal* basis, for example, might punch a time clock at the plant gate on arrival and leaving, and be paid for all time spent on company property. The term first became prominent in connection with coal miners, who demanded and won pay for the total time they spent on mine property, rather than only for the time spent at the working face of the mine, as previously.

port authority. A government commission created to administer the flow of traffic, loading and unloading activities, dock and other facilities in the area of a port. The *port authority* may be created by a city, a state, or by two or more cities or states acting together. See also AUTHORITY.

port differential. In railroading, a difference in through freight charges on the same commodity or class of goods, going from a single point to two or more different competing ports. Such differential charges may be made on the basis of the costs or inconvenience of handling freight at one port, or to equalize the traffic load between more and less popular ports.

portfolio. See INVESTMENT PORTFOLIO.

position. 1. In the securities and commodities trades, a term used for the condition of the market, or for the condition and composition of a trader's inventory of stocks or commodity contracts. It may be said, for example, that the *position* of the FUTURES market for a given commodity is strong, meaning that there is a demand for the commodity. An investor may take a *position* in a given security or class of securities by investing heavily in the particular security, or by selling it short.

2. An employment situation; a job, especially one in administrative work, rather than in production.

position bond. See under BOND (2).

possession. 1. In law, the custody and control of anything, for purposes of use and enjoyment, regardless of ownership or title. Thus, *possession* may be either lawful or unlawful, and implies no right to the thing possessed.

adverse ~. The open *possession* and use of property for a specified length of time, in opposition to a title in dispute or claimed by another. Under the laws of various states, *adverse possession* of property for a specified long period of time, without objection being filed, may give the occupied some claim to the property thus possessed. This is loosely referred to as squatters' rights.

2. In general, a thing owned. In a will, for example, it is common for the testator to leave to a person "all my *possessions,*" meaning all the property, both real and personal, which he owns.

post. 1. Originally, from the Latin, a place or station, especially one for the changing of riders and horses in a dispatch system. Thus, to *post* a message or parcel is to dispatch it, especially through a regular POSTAL SERVICE. Similarly, a watchman's *post* is his regular station.

2. In Latin, after. Thus, *post meridian* time is time after noon, or *p.m.* Similarly, an instrument which is *post-dated* is one which is given a date later than the one on which it is actually executed. See, for example, CHECK, POST-DATED.

3. In accounting, to transfer an entry or record from a JOURNAL or other BOOK OF ORIGINAL ENTRY, to the appropriate account maintained in the LEDGER. Strictly, the original recording of an item in a journal is not a *posting*, but an ENTRY.

postal money order. See under MONEY ORDER.

postal savings system. A division of the United States Post Office, established to provide facilities for the depositing of savings at interest. Deposits made are evidenced by *postal savings* stamps, in amounts of less than one dollar, or by *postal savings* certificates, in denominations of from one to 500 dollars. Since the spread of mutual savings banks, savings and loan associations, and other savings facilities, the *postal savings system* has declined in importance, and total deposits have been shrinking in recent years.

postal service. The service provided by the United States Post Office. In general, it includes the collection, transportation, and delivery of mail of various classes. The several classes into which mail is divided are based on the nature of the material mailed, the speed of service desired, the value of the material, etc. The following are the principal classes of mail presently available through the *postal service.*

first-class mail. In general, all letters, postal cards, and similar matter containing personal messages or particularly directed matter, such as checks, documents, filled in questionnaire or report forms, etc. Generally, *first-class mail* must be sealed, but it has been ruled that if the material is eligible for *first class,* and the proper postage has been paid, it will be handled and delivered as *first-class mail* whether sealed or not.

second-class mail. The class reserved for newspapers and periodicals. Any such publications, to be eligible for *second-class mail* privileges, must be first entered at the post office as *second-class mail* material, and must bear a notice to this effect.

third-class mail. The class reserved for unsealed material of various sorts, not personally directed, and not weighing more than 8 ounces. Individual items eligible for this class include greeting cards without written messages, photographs, small parcels, etc. Items eligible for bulk mailing under *third class* rates include catalogs, circulars, bulletins, and other printed matter. When such matter is to be mailed in bulk, it must be sorted and bundled according to destination, and each piece must be marked "Sect. 34.66 P.L. & R.," referring to the section of the postal laws and regulations under which this form of mailing is made.

fourth-class mail. See PARCEL POST, below.

air mail. Any mailable matter, except that which may be damaged by freezing, may be sent by *air mail,* by paying the *air mail* rate and marking the item *via air mail.* Parcels weighing more than eight ounces are sent by air parcel post.

certified mail. A service provided to permit the mailing and receipted delivery of material which is of no intrinsic value. For a small fee, a receipt of delivery is provided, and there is no necessity to pay the minimum valuation insurance fee, as would be the case with REGISTERED MAIL, which see below.

insured mail. A service provided for the mailing of valuable items not eligible for first-class mailing. Both third- and fourth-class mail may be insured up to a limit of $200.

parcel post. A service provided for the mailing of parcels of more than eight ounces, and up to a limit of 20 or 40 pounds, depending on the classification of the office in which it is to be delivered. Parcels of eight ounces or less are sent by third-class mail. The charge for *parcel post* is based on the weight of the parcel, and on the zone to which it is mailed. The zone is determined according to distance from originating to destination post office. Technically, *parcel post* is fourth-class mail.

registered mail. A service provided for the mailing of valuable items by first class mail. The sender places a value on the item, and the post office will pay an indemnity if the material is lost or damaged in transit. For a small fee, a return receipt is provided, giving evidence of delivery. See also CERTIFIED MAIL, above.

special delivery. A service providing the immediate delivery of any class of mail, when it is received by the destination post office. *Special delivery* mail receives no priority handling, over and above that to which it is entitled by the class of mail used, until it reaches the destination office.

postdate. To mark with a date which is later than the actual one. An invoice may be *postdated*, for example, as a means of granting a customer a longer period to make payment. A check may be *postdated*, to prevent it from being cashed, but such a check is illegal, since it is actually a form of promissory note. See also ANTEDATE; CHECK, POSTDATED.

post diem. In Latin, after the day. A legal expression for an act done after the day set for its doing. For example, the payment of an overdue note is a *post diem* act. More particularly, it is any such act which alters the relationship created by the original default, or failure to act at the appointed time. Hence, not all late performances are *post diem* acts in this sense.

poster. A placard, or advertising sheet, especially one designed for posting or displaying in a public place. An advertising sign or public notice, affixed to a wall or outdoor billboard.

post exchange. A retail store for military personnel, located on an army post or air force base. Modern *post exchanges*, especially those located at overseas posts and bases, are complete retail establishments, catering not only to members of the armed forces, but also to their families and to civilian employees of the armed forces. The stores are familiarly known by the abbreviation, *PX*.

post facto. In Latin, after the fact. See EX POST FACTO.

potential. Literally, having power; hence, having the power to come into being. Possible or likely to occur, or to be achieved. See, for example, MARKET POTENTIAL; SALES POTENTIAL.

potential stock. See STOCK (1), UNISSUED.

potential supply. See VISIBLE SUPPLY.

pound. 1. A standard unit of weight in several systems of weight measure. In AVOIRDUPOIS measure, the *pound* contains 7,000 GRAINS, or 16 OUNCES of 437.5 grains each. In TROY and APOTHECARIES' MEASURE, the *pound* contains 5,760 grains, or 12 ounces of 480 grains each. The term derives from the Latin word for a weight. The *pound* avoirdupois is the equivalent of 1.2153 *pounds* troy.

2. The standard unit of currency in the English monetary system, and in many countries of the British empire and commonwealth. Originally the worth of one *pound* of silver coins, the English *pound* sterling is now established at 2.48828 grams of fine gold, and is equivalent to $2.80 in United States currency. The *pound* is divided into 20 shillings, which in turn are divided into 12 pennies each. There is no *pound* coin, but paper currency in denominations of one or more *pounds* are issued. See also STERLING.

power. In law, a right or authority; an ability or liberty of doing something. More particularly, a right or authority conferred by one person on another, giving the latter the right to act for the former, such as in disposing of property. A *power* may be NAKED, in the sense that the person given the *power* has no mutual or reciprocal interest in the welfare of the giver or of the property concerned. It may also establish a relationship of TRUST, where the necessary conditions exist. The laws of the various states differ as to the *powers* that may be granted, and the rights and responsibilities of one to whom a *power* is granted. See also POWER OF ATTORNEY; POWER OF SALE.

power of attorney. The power of authority by means of which one person authorizes another to act as his agent or ATTORNEY IN FACT. Ordinarily, such power is granted by means of a written instrument, and this instrument is commonly known as a *power of attorney*. Strictly speaking, however, the instrument itself is a LETTER OF ATTORNEY, and the authority it conveys is the *power of attorney*. Such a power may be general, applying to all matters in general for a specified period of time or until revoked, or it may be special, applying only to a particular transaction or class of transactions. It may also be irrevocable, as for example, the one given to the security broker in an ASSIGNMENT of a stock certificate.

power of sale. A clause sometimes included in a MORTGAGE or DEED OF TRUST, giving the holder or trustee the right to seize and sell the pledged property upon default in payments, or other violation of the conditions of the mortgagee. In states in which this clause operates, the holder may sell the seized property at public auction, after due notice, without going through special procedings to obtain this right. Also, in a will, a power given to the executor to sell or otherwise dispose of real property in the process of settling the estate.

practitioner. A person engaged in employment in a particular field, especially in one of the arts or professions, such as accounting, medicine, law, etc.

prayer. In civil law and equity, the name for that part of a pleading by the plaintiff which asks for the particular judgment or relief desired. Generally, it takes the form of a request for specific relief plus a request for whatever other relief the court may grant. This latter request is included to permit the acceptance of additional or alternative relief to that which is specifically requested.

precatory. Literally, in the nature of a prayer. A term referring to the words used in a request or supplication, or a statement expressing a wish, rather than a direction. Thus, in a will, a phrase such as "it is my wish and desire," is a *precatory* phrase, which will be considered as establishing an intent, though no express instructions are given. See also TRUST (1), PRECATORY.

precedent. Literally, that which goes before. In law, any previous case, ruling, or decision, which is considered as a guide to be followed in later instances of similar circumstances, or as an authority on which future rulings or decisions may be based. Strictly, a *precedent* serves the court as a guide, rather than as a limit to its power of decision.

precept. A command or a directing order in writing. Specifically, an order from an authority, such as a court, to a public officer to do something which is within his power. A WRIT directed at a public officer.

precious metal. In general, gold, silver, or platinum, as distinguished from all other metals, which are known as BASE METALS. The term is used especially with reference to metal used in coins.

précis. An abridgement, abstract, or summary. Especially, a summary of a letter or other short written document.

predate. To mark with a date which is earlier than the actual one, or than the date on which an instrument is effective. Since this term is easily confused in meaning with POSTDATE, the more precise term ANTEDATE is preferred in business and legal usage.

pre-emption. In general, the right to make a purchase before others. In U.S. land law, for example, the right of *pre-emption* was given to a settler, entitling him to buy the land he cleared and settled at a fixed, limited price, to the exclusion of others. Similarly, the present shareholders of a corporation may be given a right of *pre-emption* to buy a new issue of stock at a favorable price before it is sold to the public. See also RIGHT (1).

preference bond. See BOND (1), INCOME.

preferential rate. Any rate, such as a FREIGHT RATE, which gives a preference to certain classes of goods, passengers, or customers, over others. When such a rate is set arbitrarily, or with the intent of injuring competition or restraining trade, it is considered to be DISCRIMINATION, and is illegal under the anti-trust laws.

preferential shop. The term for a shop, plant or other place of employment in which, by agreement between the union and the employer, union members are to be given preference over non-members in employment Usually, the agreement provides that if a union member is available and qualified for the position, he must be employed. This is not the same as a UNION SHOP, in which all newly employed persons must join the union or a CLOSED SHOP, in which only union members are employed.

preferential tariff. See under TARIFF (2).

preferred. In general, having certain privileges or priorities; entitled to preference over other claims or interests; granted first consideration in payment. See each of the following under the principal listing: ~ CREDITOR; ~ STOCK (1).

preferred position. In advertising, any of various positions or locations for a newspaper advertisement which are presumed to give an advantage, and for which there is usual an extra charge. Examples include the first right hand page of the paper, the page opposite the editorial page, the outside back page, and other pages of particular papers, as well as certain positions on the page or on particular pages. When an advertisement is not specified for a *preferred position*, and the additional rate paid, the advertisement will be placed on a RUN-OF-PAPER basis, indicating that it will be placed wherever convenient for the newspaper.

prejudice. In general, a prejudgment, or a preconceived opinion. Thus, it is stronger than BIAS, which implies a leaning toward one opinion or conclusion. In law, it is any condition reducing the rights or interests of one party to a legal action or suit. The dismissal of a suit *with prejudice,* for example, means that the plaintiff loses the right to bring suit again on the same grounds. See also DISMISS (1).

preliminary injunction. See INJUNCTION, TEMPORARY.

premises. Originally, the things conveyed in a bequest, deed, or grant; hence, an estate, especially of real property, such as land or real estate. In modern usage, land and the buildings or structures on it. As used in workmen's compensation laws, and in liability insurance policies, it is all of the property owned by the employer or person insured, as described and limited in the policy.

premium. Anything paid or given as a bounty, reward, or bonus. Anything extra paid or given as an inducement, or any extra payment which is above the regular or face amount. Thus, a bond is said to sell at a *premium* when its market price is above the face value; extra wages for work on late shifts, or on difficult operations, is known as *premium* pay; and anything given with a product, such as a coupon, merchandise, etc., to encourage buyers, is a *premium*.

  self-liquidating ∼. 1. A *premium* made available with a consumer product, which pays for itself and involves no net expenditure by the seller, since a payment must be made for it which is at least as great as the cost of the *premium* to the seller.

  2. In insurance, the regular, periodic, amounts which are paid by the insured to the insurance company as the price for the insurance granted. The various types and classifications of *premiums* are listed and defined below.

  deferred ∼. One not paid in advance of the period covered, but paid in monthly, quarterly, or semi-annual installments during the year covered by the insurance policy.

  earned ∼. That part of a *premium* already paid which covers time that has elapsed since the beginning of the period covered by the *premium*. Thus, it is the portion of the *premium* earned by the insurance company to date, by the protection given. See also UNEARNED PREMIUM, below.

  gross ∼. The total premium paid, including both the NET PREMIUM, which see below, to cover the actual cost of the insurance, and the LOADING (1), which covers the selling and administrative costs and the company's profit.

  level ∼. One which is at a fixed and level rate for the life of the insurance policy, rather than increasing over time, as distinguished from a NATURAL PREMIUM, which see below. The *premium* on a whole life insurance policy, for example, is level for the life of the insured, and the *premium* on a five or ten year term insurance policy is usually level for the term of the policy. See also INSURANCE, LIFE, ACCIDENT, AND HEALTH.

  natural ∼. In life insurance, one which is paid on a renewable one year term basis, and which therefore increases from year to year in accordance with the increasing risk.

  net ∼. That portion of the total *premium* on an insurance policy which is actually needed to meet the risks involved. In life insurance, for example, it is the portion calculated to cover the actuarial risks of mortality. See also GROSS PREMIUM, above.

  single ∼. One which is paid in a single lump sum, at the beginning of the total term of a policy, or which is paid to purchase an ANNUITY.

  step-rate ∼. See NATURAL PREMIUM above.

  unearned ∼. That part of a *premium* already paid which is for the period of time not yet elapsed, during the total time covered by the *premium*. Thus, it is that portion of the *premium* which is not yet earned by the insurance company to date. In the event that the policy is cancelled, it will be returned after a deduction for administrative costs. See also EARNED PREMIUM, above.

premium annuity. See under ANNUITY.

premium loan. See AUTOMATIC PREMIUM LOAN.

premium money. See PUSH MONEY.

premium pay. See PREMIUM (1).

prepayment. In general, the payment in advance, or before it becomes due, of any debt or obligation. Particularly, the payment before maturity of a time BILL OF EXCHANGE.

presentment. 1. In law, an accusation handed up by a grand jury on its own initiative, rather than one based on a bill of indictment drawn up and presented to the jury.

  2. As defined by the Uniform Commercial

Code, a demand for acceptance or payment of a negotiable instrument, made upon the maker, acceptor, or drawee, by or on behalf of the holder of the instrument.

present price. In banking and finance, the amount of money, or the *price,* paid to a borrower for a note, bill of exchange, or other obligation. Thus, it is the face value of the note if it is interest-bearing, or the discounted value if it is a DISCOUNT (2) note. It is distinguished from the FUTURE SUM, which is the amount to be repaid by the borrower, including any interest, discount, service, or other charges made. See also NOTE; PRINCIPAL (2).

present value. See under VALUE (2).

president. In business, the chief executive officer of a corporation, responsible for the over-all policy of the corporation and the supervision of its activities. He is named by the corporate stockholders, acting through the board of directors of the corporation.

presumption. In law, that which may be presumed, or reasonably inferred, from the circumstances surrounding a matter in dispute, or which may be presumed as a matter of course. For example, the *presumption* may be made that an infant is incapable of crime. Some *presumptions* have become part of legal precedent or have been written into law. For example, adverse possession for the required period of time creates a *presumption* of title to property. See also TITLE (2), BY ADVERSE POSSESSION.

pre-termination agreement. An agreement between the parties to a contract, which is made a part of the contract, providing for the steps to be taken and settlements to be made in case the contract is cancelled. Such an agreement is frequently included in individual employment contracts between companies and executives. Typically, it may contain some provisions which are binding, and others which are subject to further negotiation at the time of cancellation.

prevailing price. See PRICE, GOING.

prevailing wage law. Any of various state or federal laws providing that the PREVAILING WAGES in an area or trade must be paid on any work done under government contract. An example of such a law is the federal BACON-DAVIS ACT. Controversy has frequently arisen in the past over the definition of the area to be considered in deciding the prevailing wage, under such laws.

prevailing wages. The WAGES or wage rates customarily paid for given services or classes of work in a particular geographic area or line of work; the going wages. These may be

higher or lower than the UNION RATE for the work, depending on conditions in the area or industry concerned.

price. In general, the monetary consideration which is given for the purchase of something. The amount of money for which something exchanges, such as in a market. More broadly, the amount of money which is either asked or received by an owner, or offered or given by a buyer, for any kind of property. In various usages, there are a wide variety of types and classifications of *prices,* the principal ones of which are listed and defined below.

    actual ∼. The *price* at which a particular transaction actually takes place, as distinguished from the BID and ASKED PRICE, which see below. The term is especially used in the securities trade.

    all-around ∼. One which includes all services and other extras, which may sometimes be charged for separately, as distinguished from a BASE PRICE, which see below. In some trades, it is known as an *overhead price.*

    asked ∼. The *price* which a seller asks for his property; the value a seller puts on property which is offered for sale. The term is used especially in the securities trade. See also BID PRICE, below, and BID AND ASKED.

    base ∼. One which is used as a base or starting point for other *prices,* which may include transportation costs, extra work, packaging, services, and other extras. In the steel industry, the *base price* for each category of finished steel is the *price* at a named city, such as Pittsburgh, and the extras may include shipping, cutting, additional rolling or shaping, etc. See also BASING POINT PRICING.

    bid ∼. The *price* which a buyer offers for property; the value a willing buyer puts on property which is offered for sale. The term is used especially in the securities trade. See also ASKED PRICE, above, and BID AND ASKED.

    blanket ∼. One which covers various classes or qualities of merchandise included in a single transaction. It is sometimes known as a *lump price.*

    ceiling ∼. One which is set as a maximum *price* by law or regulation, such as in time of war or other emergency resulting in shortages.

    closing ∼. In the securities trade, the *price* reported for the last transaction in a particular security on a given day. See also CLOSE (4).

    cost-plus ∼. One based on the cost of manufacturing or furnishing, plus an agreed amount or an agreed percentage of the cost. See also CONTRACT, COST-PLUS.

cost ∼. A term for the unit cost of goods held in inventory, for use or resale. It is not a true *price,* but a value, used for determining total inventory value, insurable value, etc.

current ∼. See GOING PRICE, below.

cut ∼. A reduced price; one which is below LIST or SUGGESTED PRICE, which see below; a special sale price.

delivered ∼. One which includes the cost of delivery, or a standard charge for delivery, as distinguished from a BASE PRICE, which see above, or a FACTORY PRICE, which see below. See also ZONE PRICING.

exhaust ∼. See directly.

factory ∼. The price quoted for goods at the factory gate, usually including packaging, but not including shipping costs. It is the opposite of a DELIVERED PRICE, which see above. See also FREE ON BOARD.

fair ∼. An abstract concept, but one frequently used in laws and regulations. As generally interpreted, it is a price that assures to a seller a reasonable return on his invested capital, and a reasonable profit on his sales volume.

firm ∼. One which is binding on the seller, if accepted within the fixed period of time specified in his offer at the particular price. See also OFFER.

fixed ∼. A definite or uniform *price;* one that is asked of all buyers. More particularly, a *price* set by a manufacturer for the resale of his product, which may not be undercut by resellers. See also RESALE PRICE MAINTENANCE.

flat ∼. In one sense, a FIXED PRICE, which see above, that is asked of all classes of customers. In another sense, a BLANKET PRICE, which see above, in that it is the *price* for a collection or assortment of goods or services. In the securities trade, a *price* without interest. See also FLAT; FLAT RATE.

going ∼. In general, the prevailing *price,* or current *price;* the MARKET PRICE, which see below.

in bond ∼. See directly.

issue ∼. In the securities trade, the *price* received for an issue of securities when it is first offered to the public. If the issue is sold through UNDERWRITERS, it is the *price* received from the underwriters, not the *price* paid by individual purchasers.

landed ∼. One on imported goods, including the cost of the goods themselves, freight, insurance, landing fees, tariffs, and any other charges or costs of placing the goods on shore at the port of entry.

list ∼. The published or marked retail *price* for merchandise. The catalog *price,*

from which the DISCOUNT (1) for each class of trade is computed.

loco ∼. One quoted on the basis that the buyer will accept delivery of the goods in their present condition, at their present location, and will pay transportation and other charges, if any.

lump ∼. See BLANKET PRICE, above.

making-up ∼. See SETTLING PRICE, below.

market ∼. The *price* currently being paid in transactions in the open market; the *price* a product or property would bring in a sale in a free and open market transaction.

mill net ∼. In the textile trade, the *price* actually received by the seller at the mill, after allowing for freight paid and other charges defrayed by the seller, which are included in the quoted *price.*

minimum resale ∼. See RESALE PRICE MAINTENANCE.

net ∼. The *price* actually paid or received; the LIST PRICE, which see above, less all discounts and allowances granted or taken.

nominal ∼. One quoted or reported for a commodity, security, currency, etc., in which there is actually no active trading, and therefore no MARKET PRICE, which see above. The *nominal price* is usually based on the most recent market *price,* or the *price* for a closely related item, etc.

offered ∼. Another term for ASKED PRICE, which see above.

opening ∼. In the securities trade, the *price* paid in the first, or opening transaction in a given security on a given day. See also CLOSING PRICE, above.

overhead ∼. See ALL-AROUND PRICE, above.

present ∼. See directly.

prevailing ∼. See GOING PRICE, above.

rendu ∼. One on imported goods, meaning that the *price* includes the cost of the goods themselves, freight, insurance, landing fees, tariffs, and the costs of delivering the goods direct to the buyer's place of business. In other words, it is an import delivered *price.* See also LANDED PRICE, above.

resale ∼. One set by a manufacturer for the resale of his product by dealers, such as under a state FAIR TRADE LAW. See also FIXED PRICE, above, and RESALE PRICE MAINTENANCE.

reserve ∼. At a public auction, the lowest *price* which a seller is willing to accept; the price below which he reserves the right to withdraw the goods from sale. See also UPSET PRICE, below.

retail ∼. The *price* of any commodity or merchandise in a sale to a final customer, especially through a RETAIL STORE, as distinguished from a WHOLESALE PRICE, which see below, or a FACTORY PRICE, which see above.

rock-bottom ∼. See ROCK-BOTTOM directly.

roll back ∼. Under a system of *price* controls, a CEILING PRICE, which see above, lower than prevailing *prices,* to which a seller is required to reduce, or *roll back,* his *prices.*

settling ∼. In the securities trade, the *price* at which brokers settle their outstanding transactions with each other, when they clear their balances.

spot ∼. In the commodities trade, a *price* quoted for immediate delivery, as distinguished from a *price* quoted on the FUTURES market. Also, a *price* at which actual deliveries have been made.

street ∼. In the securities trade, one quoted for a stock outside of the regular stock exchange trading process. Stocks in which there is no organized trading may be quoted at *street prices.*

suggested ∼. A final retail *price* suggested by a manufacturer for his product. It is usually the *price* that will provide the normal profit margin for the particular class of goods. However, the retail dealer is under no obligation to sell the product at the *suggested price,* as he frequently is when a LIST PRICE, which see above, is set.

support ∼. The *price* at which the government, or more particularly, the Department of Agriculture, stands ready to buy agricultural commodities as part of its crop support program. *Support prices* are generally set in relation to the PARITY RATIO. In other words the government will buy commodities at a given *support price* level in order to keep the parity ratio from falling below a stated level, such as 80 or 90 percent of parity.

to arrive ∼. In foreign trade, one quoted by a seller on goods already on the way to a buyer, usually including all costs up to the arrival of the goods and their delivery on shore. Unless otherwise specified, it is the same as the LANDED PRICE, which see above.

trade ∼. The price charged to dealers, after the deduction of all allowances and discounts, as distinguished from the LIST PRICE, which see above. See also WHOLESALE PRICE, below.

uniform delivered ∼. See directly.

upset ∼. In auction selling, the *price* set in advance by the auctioneer, below which he will not permit an item to be sold, but will *upset* the sale. In real estate auctions, in particular, it is frequently the *price* which will cover the mortgage or tax claim on the property being auctioned.

wholesale ∼. One at which goods are sold in bulk, or at which they are sold to RETAIL STORES or others for resale. In industries in which goods are sold direct from maker to dealer, it may be the same as the FACTORY PRICE, which see above.

zone ∼. One charged for goods throughout an entire zone, or geographic area, on a DELIVERED PRICE basis, which see above, though the cost of delivery is not the same throughout the zone. See also ZONE PRICING.

price control. The fixing or restricting of prices, especially by a governmental agency. In time of war or emergency, for example, to avoid serious inflation, the government may order prices to be held at their present levels, or may establish a series of formulas for setting maximum prices for goods and services. Such controls must be authorized by Congress before they can be applied by the government.

price cutting. The practice of offering goods for sale at prices below those regularly charged in the trade, or below those set or suggested by the manufacturer of the goods. Such *price cutting* is usually resorted to by a seller who wants to enlarge his share of the market. It frequently results in retaliatory *price cutting* by competitors.

price discrimination. As defined under various anti-trust laws, the practice of charging different prices for essentially the same product or service when it is sold to different customers, or in different markets. When the purpose or result of such *price discrimination* is to reduce competition or to injure competitors, either of the seller or the buyer, it is illegal under the anti-trust laws.

price fixing. See PRICE, FIXED; RESALE PRICE MAINTENANCE; FAIR TRADE LAWS.

price index. Any one of several measures used to show changes in the average level of prices, such as, for example, the CONSUMER PRICE INDEX. See also INDEX NUMBER.

price leader. See LOSS-LEADER.

price maintenance. See RESALE PRICE MAINTENANCE

price shading. See SHADE.

prima facie. Literally, in Latin, at first sight. Hence, on the face of things; according to appearances. *Prima facie* evidence is such that will tend to establish a fact in the absence of contradiction. A *prima facie* case against a defendant is the case based on the evidence at hand, or on the appearances of things, without any investigation beyond the surface.

primary beneficiary. See BENEFICIARY (2).

primary boycott. See under BOYCOTT.

primary market. The term for the market established for trading in a commodity in its basic form, or as it is originally sold, rather than in its processed or secondary form. The *primary copper market,* for example, is the market for newly mined copper, rather than that for copper products, or for scrap copper. In another sense, the most important or principle market for trading in a commodity. The Chicago Board of Trade, for example, is the *primary* United States *market* for grains.

primary obligation. In a contract, the essential obligation which a party to the contract undertakes, and the one from which other obligations flow or may be implied. It is the obligation which failure to perform may become the basis of a suit for damages. In a contract of sale, for example, the *primary obligation* of the seller is to deliver, and that of the buyer is to pay.

prime. First, and hence of first quality or rank. Also, first in the sense of coming before others in time, seniority, or importance. See, for example, BILL OF EXCHANGE, PRIME.

prime contractor. The CONTRACTOR who undertakes a basic agreement to perform work or supply goods or services, with the intention of making sub-contracts with others to do some or all of the actual work or supplying involved. In the construction of a building, for example, it is common for a *prime contractor* to undertake the actual building, arranging through subcontracts for the electrical work, plumbing, flooring, painting, and many other specific parts of the work.

prime cost. See COST, DIRECT.

prime paper. See COMMERCIAL PAPER, FIRST CLASS.

prime rate. See under RATE OF INTEREST.

principal. 1. In general, the chief, or most important person; the one with responsibility, on whom others depend. Hence, in business, an owner or operator of a business; a member of a partnership, or active stockholder of a close corporation. Also, a person who employs another as his AGENT. More generally, any person who is a party to a contract or agreement of any sort, or who is the subject of a contract, such as an INDEMNITY contract.

2. The original or face amount of a deposit, loan, or other amount of money on which interest is earned or paid. The face amount of a mortgage loan, for example, is the *principal* amount, and each periodic repayment may consist partly of interest and partly of *principal.* In the case of a DISCOUNTED (2) loan, the amount given the borrower is called the PRESENT PRICE, and the *principal,* or amount on which the discount is figured, is called the FUTURE SUM.

prior. Preceding others, either in time or rank,

or both; previously existing. See each of the following under the principal listing: ~ ART; BOND (1), ~ LIEN.

priority. In general, any precedence in rank, in order of claim, or in order of payment. The National Bankruptcy Act, for example, establishes the order of *priority* of claims of creditors upon the assets of a BANKRUPT. Similarly, in time of war, the GOVERNMENT may grant a *priority* to companies working on military contracts, to enable them to obtain scarce materials.

prior preference stock. See under STOCK (1).

private. In general, belonging to one person, or to a small group of persons; not open to the general public, or not involving the public interest. See each of the following under the principal listing: ~ BANK; ~ BRAND; ~ EASEMENT; ~ LEDGER; ~ NUISANCE; ~ PROPERTY; ~ SALE (1); ~ TRUST (1).

private debt. In national income statistics, a term for the net amount of gross corporate debts less duplicating corporate debt. Duplicating corporate debt is that which is owed by one member of an affiliated corporate system to another corporate member of the system.

private enterprise. See CAPITALISM; ENTERPRISE.

private placement. See PLACEMENT (2).

privilege. 1. In general, any advantage, benefit, favor, or immunity granted to one group over those granted to others. In business, for example, the stockholders of a company may be granted the *privilege* of buying additional stock in the company at a stated price, lower than the regular market price, for a limited period of time. See also RIGHT (1).

2. In the securities trade, a term for an option to buy or sell a stock; the various types of *privilege* include PUTS, CALLS, SPREADS, and STRADDLES.

privileged debt. See under DEBT.

probability sample. See under SAMPLE.

probate. In law, in general, any proof or testing. In relation to a WILL, the procedure in the proper court whereby the validity of the will is established through the presentation of the required proofs. The *probate* laws of the several states vary widely in application and detail. See also SURROGATE.

probate judge. See SURROGATE.

probation. Any period of testing, or of trial. In criminal law, a convicted person may be placed on *probation,* meaning that he is left at liberty, with his good behavior on trial. A new employee is often on *probation,* or in a testing period, before being made a permanent member of the staff.

proceeding. In law, any step taken in connection with an ACTION at law. As usually used, any steps taken in court, or any steps taken to bring an action into court. The term is used differently in particular contexts.

proceeds. In general, the amount realized from a transaction, such as, for example, the *proceeds* of a sale, which is the amount received by the seller, usually after the deduction of all allowances, commissions, etc. More particularly, the amount received by a borrower when his note is DISCOUNTED in advance, and thus the face value of the note less the discount. It is sometimes called the AVAILS.

process. 1. In law, any order or step taken by a court to compel compliance with its wishes, such as, for example, a SUMMONS, issued to compel attendance in court. More broadly, any or all of the proceedings or actions of a court, especially those taken to insure the rights of private individuals before the law. Due *process* of law, for example, means all of the legal steps and proceedings to which a person is entitled to protect his rights and property.

2. In industry, any method or art of accomplishing some desired end; any method of operation in manufacturing or creating some product. The Bessemer *process,* for example, is a method of converting iron into steel, and the Hall *process* is a method of refining aluminum. See also BATCH PROCESS; CONTINUOUS PROCESS.

process patent. See PATENT.

proctor. See PROCURATOR.

procuration. The act of naming another person to act as an ATTORNEY IN FACT, or as a PROXY. Also, the power granted by such an act, or the exercise of such power.

procurator. Originally, in Rome, an administrative officer who collected taxes, paid the local governmental expenses and otherwise represented the central power in a Roman province. Hence, in current usage, a person who represents or acts for another, as an ATTORNEY IN FACT, or as a PROXY. The term proctor is also sometimes used.

procurement. In business, the process or responsibility of obtaining materials, supplies, or services for any business operation, including the actual process of purchasing, the preparation of specifications, the submitting of invitations to bid, inspection of materials, storage, distribution, etc.

produce. In general, to create, or bring forth; to make, or manufacture. Also, that which is made or brought forth. In particular, agricultural products, especially vegetables or fruit, as distinguished from grains.

produce exchange. A specialized commodities EXCHANGE (2), in which agricultural products, such as fruits, nuts, field crops, etc., are bought and sold. Usually, such an exchange deals in both fresh and processed or packaged produce.

producers' cooperative. See under COOPERATIVE.

producers' goods. See under GOODS (3).

product. In general, that which is the result, or end, of any process of production or manufacture. See also BY-PRODUCT; JOINT PRODUCT.

production. Strictly, the act or process of creating or making something. In economics, *production* is sometimes defined as the creation of value by the addition of utility, including utility of form, time, place, or possession. In this sense, *production* includes distribution as well as manufacturing, and is distinguished from CONSUMPTION, or the using up of utility. As commonly used, however, the term refers to that part of a business operation concerned with the processing or fabrication of materials, or with manufacturing.

production and related workers. In employment statistics, a concept now used in the collection and reporting of data on factory employment to replace the previously used term of WAGE EARNER (2). It includes all nonsupervisory employees engaged in fabricating, processing, or assembling, inspection, receiving, storage, or shipping, maintenance, repair, other services, record keeping, etc. It includes working foremen, but not supervisory employees above the working foreman level.

production control. In manufacturing operations, the control of production and output through the careful, orderly, and systematic planning, scheduling, and routing of work, and through the issuing of the proper orders to the operating units to assure the effective coordination of men, machines, and materials.

production depreciation. See under DEPRECIATION.

production index. See INDEX OF INDUSTRIAL PRODUCTION.

production management. The branch or field of business management concerned with the production, processing or manufacturing activities of a company, as distinguished from the SALES MANAGEMENT of the company which is concerned with its marketing and distributing activities. The *production management* function usually covers the acquisition and storage of materials as well.

productivity. In general, the relationship of the amount of production to the effort required to produce it; the ratio of output to input for any system of production. The *productivity* of labor is usually measured in terms of the physical amount of goods produced divided by the total number of man-hours consumed in producing it; or in output per man-hour. It may also be measured in terms of the value of output, or in other units. Similarly, it is possible to measure the *productivity* of capital, by dividing output by the total amount of capital equipment used in producing it.

product planning. The process of designing, selecting, and obtaining the proper products for manufacture and sale. It includes not only product design, but the choice of styles, sizes, types, etc., of product, and the pricing of the product to assure the maximum profitable sales volume. In effect, it is the manufacturing counterpart of MERCHANDISE PLANNING.

profession. Strictly, something of which one professes knowledge. Any occupation requiring a high degree of knowledge, specialized training, and creative thought, as distinguished from one calling for technical skill alone. In current usage, the *professions* are considered to include law, medicine, architecture, engineering, accounting, etc.

professional. In one sense, a person who engages in some activity as his main occupation, as distinguished from one who engages in it occasionally, or as an amateur. A full-time securities trader, for example, is a *professional,* as distinguished from the typical member of the investing public, who is an occasional trader. In another sense, an employee whose work is primarily intellectual and creative, rather than routine or mechanical.

professional liability insurance. See under INSURANCE, CASUALTY AND LIABILITY.

profit. Broadly speaking, any advantage, gain, or benefit; any increase in material value. As used in business, that portion of income remaining after all expenses are paid, or the excess of business income over business expenses and costs. There are several bases for the measurement of *profit,* and several types of *profit* in business, the principal ones of which are listed and defined below. See also EARNINGS; INCOME.

anticipated ~. One foreseen or expected, but not yet realized or earned. For example, on the basis of expected costs and selling prices, it is possible to compute the *anticipated profit* from any volume of sales.

book ~. One existing in the books of account, but not yet realized. For example, a *profit* due entirely to an increase in the value of inventory held, which has not yet been sold to realize the *profit.*

clear ~. See NET PROFIT, below.

gross ~. In general, the amount realized from sales less the cost of the goods which were sold. The term is used almost exclusively in wholesale and retail distribution, and is usually taken as the difference between sales and costs, after allowing for inventory changes, but before taking expenses, such as salaries, rent, advertising, etc., into account. See also GROSS MARGIN, which is essentially the *gross profit* expressed as a percentage of net sales.

net ~. In general, the amount realized from sales less the cost of the goods sold and all expenses of operating the business. It may be measured before or after the deduction of taxes, and may be the *net operating profit,* or it may be the *net profit* after all expenses, including such non-operating expenses as interest on long-term debt. It is sometimes called *clear profit.*

operating ~. The *profit* arising from the regular operations of the business, not including the income and expenses related to interest payments, real estate operations, and other non-operating activities. See also INCOME, OPERATING.

paper ~. One which is potential, but not yet realized. For example, if an asset or security held has increased in value, it represents a *paper profit,* which may or may not materialize into an actual *profit* at some time in the future through the sale of the asset or security.

surplus ~. Those *profits,* or a rate of *profit,* greater than is normal or usual for a given line of business, or for a particular company in normal operations. In another sense, that *profit* which is transferred to SURPLUS, not distributed.

undistributed ~. The *profit* that is not distributed to the owners or stockholders of a business in dividends, but is retained. Such *profits* are subject to additional taxes under certain conditions.

profit and loss statement. See INCOME STATEMENT.

profiteer. One who takes excessive profits on his operations, especially one who does so by taking advantage of a wartime disaster, or a shortage of supply, or by dealing in the BLACK MARKET.

profit sharing. Any one of various systems under which the employees of a business receive a share of the business profits in addition to their wages. It frequently takes the form of a periodic distribution in cash of a substantial share of all profits, or of all profits above a fixed amount. In other systems, a share of company profits is credited to a fund, upon which the employees may draw, in proportion to their seniority and earnings, after retirement. In still other cases, the *profit sharing* is combined with an INCENTIVE SYSTEM, in which the profits resulting from increased productivity are distributed. This is sometimes known as gain sharing.

profit sharing bond. See BOND (1), PARTICIPATING.

profits insurance. See BUSINESS INTERRUPTION INSURANCE, under INSURANCE, PROPERTY.

profits tax. Any of various taxes on the profits of business, aside from the income tax, on the profit taken as income by the proprietor or stockholders of a business. See, for example, TAX (2), CORPORATE INCOME; TAX (2), EXCESS PROFITS; TAX (2), UNDISTRIBUTED PROFITS.

profit-taking. In the securities trade, the term for the sale, at a profit, of securities bought for speculative purposes. *Profit-taking* by a large number of speculative buyers at the same time, as frequently happens, may result in such an increase in the supply of the security that most of the increase in prices is wiped out.

pro forma. Literally, in Latin, as a matter of form. In accounting, a *pro forma* financial statement is one which combines two or more separate statements as if they represented the results of a single operation. When two corporations are merged, for example, it is common practice for the combined corporation to present a *pro forma* statement at the end of the first fiscal year after the merger, showing the results of the two companies as if they had been combined during the whole period covered. In another sense, a *pro forma* accounting report is one made up on the basis of previous transactions, to provide an estimate of the outcome of a proposed operation.

progressive tax. See under TAX (2).

prohibitive. In general, having the effect of forbidding or preventing some action. A *prohibitive* law, for example, is one that specifically forbids some act, such as the sale of narcotics. On the other hand, a *prohibitive* fee or charge is one that is so high as to have the effect of forbidding or preventing the use or purchase of that for which it is charged.

projection. In statistics, and in planning, an estimate of a future quantity, or of a quantity beyond the range of available data, on the basis of an extension of the observed re-

lationships. If income has increased at a rate of 3% per year for a number of years, for example, a reasonable *projection* for the future might assume a similar rate of increase. Similarly, if the ratio of profits to sales is known for a number of companies, a *projection* of the probable profits for another company in the same field may be made if its sales volume is known.

proletariat. Originally, the lowest, or propertyless strata of Roman society. In economics, a term sometimes used for the working class, or for those who earn their income by labor alone, as distinguished from the BOURGEOIS, or self-employed, and the CAPITALIST, or employing classes.

promise. Any declaration or engagement by which a person binds himself to do or not do something, whether for a consideration or not, and whether under law or not. A promise becomes a COVENANT if it is made a formal document, under seal if required.

promissory note. See NOTE (1).

promoter. Strictly, one who takes an active part in the formation or launching of a corporation or other business enterprise. He may do this by contributing capital, by securing additional capital from others, by lending his skills and abilities, etc. More loosely, any person who frequently suggests or organizes plans or schemes for obtaining large and quick profits. In certain fields, such as sports a *promoter* is a person who arranges for the presentation of events, and who brings the participants together to make the necessary contractual arrangements, for which he usually receives a share of the income or profits

promotion. 1. An advancement to a position of higher rank, or to one with increased responsibilities or prestige, usually with an accompanying increase in salary or wage. However, an increase in compensation alone without an advancement in position, is not *promotion*.

2. The activities connected with advancing, encouraging, or furthering any business venture, or increasing the sale or use of business product or service. See, for example, SALES PROMOTION.

promotional allowance. See ADVERTISING ALLOWANCE.

prompt. As used in business, without delay immediate. An invoice calling for *prompt* payment, for example, means that payment to be made immediately, with no period delay allowed. See also SPOT.

proof. 1. In law, that amount and quality EVIDENCE which produces certainty and assurance of the truth of a matter in dispute

Evidence which establishes fact, or contributes to the establishment of fact; conclusive evidence.

2. A measure of the alcoholic content of a liquid. The *proof* of any liquid mixture is twice the percentage of alcohol contained, by volume. Originally, *proof-liquor* is any liquid containing standard alcohol equal to one-half its volume, and this is now usually known as 100 *proof*, with other liquids measured in relation to this standard.

3. In general, any test, trial, or standard. In printing, for example, an impression taken from type before the regular production of printed material is called a *proof* sheet, and a preliminary print of a photograph is also known as a *proof*.

proof of loss. In insurance, a statement required from an insured person, stating the date and time of a loss, the amount of damage or loss, the circumstances, the names of any other insurance companies involved, and similar supporting data. Frequently, such a *proof of loss* statement must be sworn and notarized, since it may become evidence in any dispute over the amount of the award or settlement.

propensity to consume. In economics, a theoretical concept describing the relationship between consumption and income at any given level of income, and thus, also, of the relation between consumption and savings at any level of income. The concept was devised by J. M. Keynes, and forms an important part of his theories of economics and fiscal policies.

proper. In various contexts, fit, or suitable; acceptable, or in good order; right, or just. The term has different meanings in different particular fields of business usage.

property. Strictly, the exclusive and unrestricted right or interest which a person has in his belongings, whether lands or chattels. In current usage, however, the term has come to refer to the things themselves which are held, not the right to hold them. The various classifications of *property* which are recognized in law and usage are listed and defined below.

    intangible ~. Strictly, *property* which cannot be touched, or which has no physical existence. Examples include RIGHTS (2), CLAIMS (1), INTERESTS (1), etc., and such things as insurance, securities, etc.

    personal ~. In general, any *property* which is movable, or which is not land or inseparably connected with land, or an improvement on land. The term also includes all INTANGIBLE PROPERTY, which see above, whether related to land or not. There have

been numerous rulings concerning the classification of particular items as *personal* or REAL PROPERTY, which see below. See also CHATTEL.

    private ~. Any *property* owned or legally held by a private individual or by a corporation or association, as distinguished from PUBLIC PROPERTY, which see below.

    public ~. Any *property* belonging to the government, whether local, state, or federal, and any *property* dedicated to public use, whether or not the government strictly holds title.

    real ~. In general, land, including that which is naturally growing on it, and any improvements to land, including structures of all sorts, and that which is permanently or inseparably attached to such structures. The term is roughly synonymous with REAL ESTATE, in its broad usage.

    tangible ~. Strictly, *property* which is touchable, or which has a physical existence. Thus, the term includes all corporeal or physical *property,* whether REAL or PERSONAL PROPERTY, which see above, as distinguished from INTANGIBLE PROPERTY, which see above.

property dividend. See under DIVIDEND.

property insurance. See INSURANCE, PROPERTY.

property tax. See under TAX (2).

proportional tax. See under TAX (2).

proposal. In the preliminary negotiation of a contract or agreement, an offer or bid made by one of the parties for the consideration of the other. It is not an OFFER in the sense that its acceptance by the other party completes the agreement, unless the person submitting it specifies that it is such an offer. Otherwise it is to be taken merely as a basis for further negotiation and eventual agreement.

proprietary. Pertaining to private or exclusive ownership, or to private formulation or design. In general, referring to the status or rights of a PROPRIETOR. Specifically, with respect to products such as drugs, based on a private or patented formula or design, rather than on a standard or public formulation. In common usage, a *proprietary* drug is known as a patent medicine.

proprietary company. See under COMPANY.

proprietor. Generally, an owner. A person who has an exclusive right or interest in property or in a business venture. The property itself may be intangible, such as a patent. As used, a *proprietor* may be a sole owner, a member of a PARTNERSHIP or firm, or a principal owner of a close CORPORATION.

proprietorship. In general, ownership. As used in business statistics and general business terminology, a business organization which is completely owned, controlled and managed by a single individual, as distinguished from a PARTNERSHIP, which is owned by two or more individuals. It is sometimes known as an individual, single, or sole *proprietorship.*

pro rata. Literally, in Latin, according to the rate. In proportion to a total amount, or share. For example, if an agreement is cancelled before the end of the term for which payment has been made, a *pro rata* return of the payment may be made, in proportion to the unused or unexpired period of time remaining.

pro rata distribution clause. In property insurance, a clause frequently inserted in a policy covering several separate properties, providing that the amount of insurance in the policy shall apply to each property in proportion to the relation that the value of the individual property bears to the total value of all of the property covered. For example, three properties, each worth $50,000, may be insured under a single policy for $75,000. If the policy contains a *pro rata distribution clause,* a loss of $40,000 to one of the properties will be settled for only $25,000, since the insurance carried is considered to be $25,000 on each of the three properties. A loss of less than this amount will be settled in full. Thus, a *pro rata distribution clause* differs in effect from a COINSURANCE CLAUSE.

prorate. To divide or distribute proportionately, or in proportion to some established standard or scale. For example, it is common for trade associations to *prorate* the costs of the association according to the sales volume of the member companies.

prospect. In selling, a term for a possible, or prospective CUSTOMER. A person who has shown an interest in buying, or who has the necessary qualifications of becoming a customer or purchaser.

prospective. In general, looking forward, or applying to the future, as distinguished from RETROSPECTIVE, or applying to the past. For example, a *prospective* law is one designed to cover instances which may arise in the future, and a court may award *prospective* DAMAGES, to take into account further loss which may occur in the future as a result of a past action.

prospectus. A document issued by a company or public authority which is issuing or planning to issue stocks or bonds, describing the nature of the operation, the prospects for profit, and the nature of the particular securities, and inviting the public to subscribe.

Under the regulations of the Securities and Exchange Commission, the *prospectus* is the official offering of an issue of securities, and it must contain a full and honest disclosure of the company's status and prospects.

prosperity. In economics, a period of high levels of activity in business, characterized by high production, little unemployment, active consumer buying, an expanding credit structure, etc. It is the PEAK of the business cycle, as differentiated from DEPRESSION. In current usage, prosperity is a relatively stable and enduring period of high activity, as distinguished from a BOOM, which is a relatively unstable and short-lived expansion.

protection. In foreign trade, the policy of imposing high TARIFFS on imports that compete with products of domestic manufacture, with the purpose of giving the latter an advantage in the domestic market. This may be done with the avowed aim of preventing the destruction of the domestic industry, or to stimulate the growth of a presently weak or new domestic industry. See also TARIFF (2), PROTECTIVE.

protective committee. The name for a temporary committee of the security holders of a corporation, formed during a liquidation, reorganization, or other time of stress of corporation. The committee may be self appointed, or may actually represent a large proportion of the security holders. Its stated purpose is to protect the interests of the security holders, or of a particular portion or class of them, such as the preferred stock owners, mortgage bond owners, etc.

protective tariff. See under TARIFF* (2).

pro tem. From the Latin term *pro tempore,* for the time being. Hence, temporary, not permanent, substitute. For example, the majority leader of the United States Senate the president *pro tem* of the Senate, meaning that he acts as president, or chairman, during the absence of the Vice-President, who is the permanent president of the Senate.

protest. In connection with a promissory note, acceptance, or other credit instrument, a formal written notice, usually notarized, prepared by the holder of a note which has not been paid or accepted when presented. It states that the holder *protests* to the maker, endorsers, and other parties to the note, if any, against the fact that it has been DISHONORED, and declares that they will all be held responsible for its payment. When such a notice or statement is filed, the note is said to go to *protest.* There is usually a *protest* fee added by the holder to the amount of the note when it has gone to *protest.*

protocol. Originally, a brief, informal summary of the text of a document, preceding it and perhaps attached to the cover or flyleaf. Also, the informal minutes of a meeting or conference, especially those containing the substance of an agreement arrived at, which are initialed by the participants as being accepted, before being embodied in a formal treaty or agreement. More generally, pertaining to diplomatic documents in general, so that the *protocol* section of the Department of State is the one concerned with the technical preparation of treaties, their filing, etc. By extension, it is also the order or precedence of rank among heads of state and those who deal with heads of state; the etiquette of diplomacy.

proven reserves. With reference to crude petroleum, a term for the known and established supplies of petroleum underground, based on the estimated capacity of existing wells and explored fields. At any time, the *proven reserves* of petroleum may be sufficient for only a few more years of production, but in the past new supplies have generally been added to the *proven reserves* at least as fast as they are depleted.

provision for doubtful accounts. See BAD DEBT RESERVE.

proviso. A provision or condition, especially one which limits or restricts the application or effect of a document, such as a deed, lease, mortgage, etc.

proximate cause. See under CAUSE.

proximo. Literally, next. As used in invoices, TERMS OF SALE, etc., it means the next month after the month of the invoice, or after a named month if one is named. It is frequently abbreviated as *prox.,* so that a bill or invoice which is marked payable *10th prox.* is payable on or before the tenth day of the month following the one in which it is submitted. See also ULTIMO.

proxy. One who acts for another, or who represents another, as an ATTORNEY IN FACT. Also, the document by which such a representative is authorized to act. Specifically, in reference to voting at meetings of corporation stockholders, an authorization by a stockholder giving to the corporate management, or to a group opposed to the corporate management, the right to vote the shares held by the individual stockholder. A *proxy* may be limited to particular propositions to be voted on, or it may be general, giving the holder the right to vote the shares as he sees fit. See also PROCURATOR.

prudent man rule. The popular name for a provision included in various statutes and regulations, providing that trustees, or institutions managing trust funds, shall purchase only such securities and make such other investments as a *prudent man* would do, using his own funds. The trustee, under such a rule, is charged with exercising prudence, intelligence, and care in his investment activities for the funds he administers.

pseudo. A prefix meaning false, sham, spurious, or counterfeit. For example, a *pseudo*-contract is an agreement which has some of the appearances of a contract, but which is not a true and valid contract. The term is sometimes mistakenly used in place of QUASI, to mean partial.

public. Pertaining to the people in general, or to the community; open to or available to all the people, rather than merely to a few, as distinguished from PRIVATE. In another sense, pertaining to a government, or a governmental body. See each of the following under the principal listing: $\sim$ ACCOUNTANT; $\sim$ AUCTION; $\sim$ AUDITOR; $\sim$ AUTHORITY; $\sim$ CORPORATION; $\sim$ DEPOSITORY; $\sim$ DOMAIN; $\sim$ EASEMENT; $\sim$ NUISANCE; $\sim$ PROPERTY; $\sim$ SALE (1); $\sim$ WAREHOUSE.

public assistance. Any of various steps taken to make payments to persons or families in need of assistance. The federal government, through the Department of Welfare, provides *public assistance* under programs through which it gives financial assistance to the several states for aid to older persons, aid to the blind, aid to dependent children, and aid to those who are disabled.

publication. In general, the act of making public. Under COPYRIGHT law, it is defined as the act of making a work available to the public by selling, offering for sale, or distributing copies, not necessarily by formal publishing. Under the laws of LIBEL, it is the act of disseminating a statement, or making it known to one or more persons, by any means whatever. Thus, the dictation of a libelous letter to a secretary may constitute the *publication* of a libel, even if the letter is not later transcribed and mailed. The particular statutes of the various states vary widely as to the meaning of *publication* where it is required that rates, various notices, etc., be published.

public bond. See BOND (1), GOVERNMENT; BOND (1), MUNICIPAL.

public debt. See DEBT, NATIONAL.

publicity. In general, any actions taken to obtain public notice and attention for a product, person, or service. Any news or information about a product, service, or person which is disseminated without cost. *Publicity* need not be favorable, as long as it calls attention to the subject, and thus is not to be confused with true PUBLIC RELATIONS activities.

public liability insurance. See under INSURANCE, CASUALTY AND LIABILITY.

public relations. In general, the relations between any organization and the general public. The various actions and activities in which a company or organization engages to develop a mutual interest between the company and the social, economic, and political environment in which it operates. The steps by which a company attempts to create a favorable public attitude toward itself and its products.

public trust. See TRUST (1), CHARITABLE.

public utility. As usually understood, a private corporation which engages in the business of supplying some basic public service, such as water supply, gas, electricity, telephone or telegraph service, rapid transit transportation, etc. Such corporations usually operate under a government franchise and government regulation, and are granted a monopoly over the service they provide in the area in which they operate.

publisher. One who is in the business of manufacturing and selling literary works. One who is responsible for the printing, distribution, and profitable sale of a newspaper, periodical, or other literary work.

puffer. A person who is employed to submit fictitious bids at an auction, thereby puffing or increasing the final price obtained for the goods auctioned. He is also known as a BY-BIDDER.

puffing. In advertising, highly commendatory and exaggerated statements concerning a product, such as statements that it is the "world's best" or "best tasting" product. To the extent that such statements can be regarded as harmless boasting, they have been held not to constitute misleading advertising within the meaning of the laws against such advertising.

pump priming. In economics, a term for the action or process of stimulating business activity, or a recovery of business activity, by large scale government spending for public works of various sorts. The theory behind such spending is that it tends to "prime the pump" of business, which will be able to keep expanding on its own momentum after the initial impetus from the government spending.

punitive damages. See under DAMAGES.

purchase. Originally, in law, any means of acquiring property other than by descent. Thus, broadly, *purchase* includes the obtaining of property by sale, gift, lien, mortgage, etc. As usually used, however, it is the acquiring of property in an exchange for money, rather than by BARTER, which is an exchange for other goods. See also BUY. See each of the following under the principal listing: ∼ LEDGER; ∼ VALUE (2).

purchased paper. See under COMMERCIAL PAPER.

purchase money. In financial transactions, especially in the purchase of real estate, the initial payment of money made by a buyer to a seller, to secure the purchase, and to effect the transfer of title. The remaining amount of the total price may be covered by a mortgage or by notes. See also MORTGAGE, PURCHASE MONEY.

purchase order. A written authorization, signed by a designated employee, calling on a supplier or vendor to provide goods or services at specified prices, in specified amounts, at a designated time and place. Legally, a *purchase order* is an offer to buy, and a supplier or seller accepts its stated terms by making delivery or by agreeing to make delivery on the order.

purchaser. One who acquires title or an interest in property by the act of PURCHASE; a buyer.

   innocent ∼. The term for a person who acquires title or interest honestly, with no knowledge of any defect or infirmity in the title held by the person who sells. He is entitled to redress for any loss he suffers as a result of his purchase and its subsequent invalidation.

purchasing agent. An employee or officer of a company who is responsible for the buying of all of the needs of the company. His duties vary from company to company, but they usually include the evaluation of competitive or comparable products and services, the letting of bids and awarding of contracts, the continual testing and examination of new products and services, etc. They may also include the inspection and acceptance of purchased goods, the storage of goods on hand, the establishment of inventory levels and reorder points, the setting of specifications for purchased goods, etc.

purchasing cooperative. See under COOPERATIVE.

purchasing power. In general, the capacity or ability to purchase possessed by a person or group, as measured by income. With reference to money, the *purchasing power* of the dollar is the relative amount of goods and services that can be purchased with a dollar in a given period, as compared with some established base period. The *purchasing power* of the dollar falls as prices rise, and rises as prices fall. Thus, it is frequently measured as the reciprocal of a CONSUMER PRICE INDEX.

pure gold. See GOLD.

purposive sample. See under SAMPLE (3).

push money. In retail merchandising slang, a term for money paid by a manufacture or distributor directly to the sales personnel of a retail store, in an attempt to obtain extra sales promotion for the supplier's products. In the usual case, the *push money* is paid as an extra commission or bonus for each unit of the product sold by the sales-

person. It is frequently abbreviated as *P.M.*, and is sometimes known as premium money.

put. In the securities trade, a written agreement representing an option to sell a named security on or before a specified date at a given price. In effect, the buyer of a *put* option is betting the price he paid for the option privilege that the stock will go down in value. If it goes down more than the price paid for the *put,* he can sell at the option price and buy back at the lower market price to cover his sale, at a profit. See also CALL (1); STRADDLE.

put-and-call. See STRADDLE.

PX. See POST EXCHANGE.

Q

quadrant. In circular measure, one fourth of a circle, or 90 degrees.

qualified. 1. The condition of being fit or adapted for a specific type of work or assignment; possessed of the required qualities and abilities; prepared for or entitled to a position.

2. Limited, modified, or restricted. Altered by conditions. For example, an earlier statute may be *qualified* by a later one. See each of the following under the principal listing: ~ ACCEPTANCE (3); ~ ENDORSEMENT (2); ~ FEE (2).

qualified plan. A plan established by a company concerning employee pensions, profit-sharing, stock purchase, or other benefits, which meets the qualifications or requirements of the Internal Revenue Code. When a plan is considered qualified, the employer may deduct as expenses the contributions made to the plan in the year in which they are made, while the employee need not report them as income until the year in which he actually receives the benefit. For example, if a pension plan is qualified, the employer may deduct as business expenses his contributions to the trust fund set up under the plan each year, while the employees count as income only the payments they receive from the fund after retirement. The requirements for qualification are technical, and may be revised from time to time, so that the current regulations under the Internal Revenue Code should be consulted.

quality. Any attribute or characteristic that distinguishes one thing from others. A grade, or kind; a degree, standard, or rating of excellence or fitness.

quality control. The procedures, methods, or policies established by a producing company to control or maintain standards of production performance, so that the output and workmanship of a given operation will meet the company's requirements. When the methods of control are based on a systematic sampling of produced items, it is known as STATISTICAL QUALITY CONTROL.

quantity discount. See under DISCOUNT (1).

quantum meruit. Literally, from the Latin, as much as is merited. A term used to describe the principle of law providing that when a service is rendered without a specific agreement as to compensation, there is an implied promise by the employer to pay for the service as much as it is worth, or as much as is merited.

quarantine. A period of time, originally forty days, from which the name derives, during which a .vessel coming from a place where contagious disease is prevalent, is detained in harbor without being allowed to discharge its crew or passengers. Medical examinations are usually undertaken during this period. More generally, any means by which a person or thing is kept separated from the community, usually to prevent the spread of disease, but possibly for economic, political or other reasons. Also, the place or station at which vessels are detained during the *quarantine* period, and at which inspections and examinations are held.

quart. A unit of both liquid and dry capacity. The liquid *quart* contains two liquid PINTS, or 32 fluid OUNCES, and is one fourth of a GALLON. The dry *quart* contains two dry PINTS, and is one eighth of a PECK. The British imperial *quart* contains two imperial pints, and is one fourth of an imperial GALLON. It is 1.201 American liquid *quarts*.

quarter. 1. In general, the one fourth part of anything, such as a *quarter* year, *quarter* dollar, *quarter* section, etc.

2. In common business usage, any successive three months, or any period of 91 days. The year is considered to be divided into four *quarters,* referred to as the first, second, etc. The first calendar *quarter,* for example, consists of the months of January, February and March, while the first *quarter* of any FISCAL YEAR consists of the first three months of the particular fiscal year.

quarter-day. Traditionally, the first day of each calendar quarter of the year, on which payment of quarterly interest, rent, and other

286

periodic payments becomes due. The conventional *quarter-days* are thus January 1, April 1, July 1, and October 1. Among some corporations and in specialized lines of business, other days have been adopted as *quarter-days,* such as February 1, May 1, August 1, and November 1.

quarter-dollar. The official United States silver coin, equal to one fourth of a DOLLAR or 25 cents.

quarter-eagle. The United States gold coin, worth $2.50. It is no longer minted. See also EAGLE.

quarterly. Occurring once each quarter-year, or once each three months, as *quarterly* payments. Lasting for a quarter-year or for three months, as *quarterly* production.

quarter-section. A square fourth of a SECTION of land, containing 160 acres. A section is divided into *quarter-sections* by being divided laterally and vertically into equal parts.

quarter service. A term used in advertising, especially in transportation advertising, meaning that the advertisement will be displayed in one fourth of the available exposure locations, such as one fourth of the cars or buses of a particular transit line. A quarter-run. See also FULL SERVICE; HALF SERVICE.

quartile. In statistics, one of the three values in a ranked distribution of values or scores which divide the whole into four parts of equal numbers of elements. The *quartiles* are usually numbered from the lower to the higher values, so that, for example, the third *quartile* of a distribution of scores is the value that divides the top 25 percent of the scores from the rest of the distribution. The second quartile, counting in either direction, is the MEDIAN of the distribution. Sometimes, loosely but incorrectly, *quartile* is used to refer to the groups of values themselves, which each contain one fourth of the distribution. See also DECILE.

quarto. See under BOOK SIZES.

quash. To abate, annul, or make void. For example, to *quash* an indictment, or to *quash* a writ.

quasi. Literally, in Latin, as if. Analogous to, or resembling. Similar or resembling in certain characteristics, but not identical. It is distinguished from SEMI, which implies partly, in the sense of half developed; and from PSEUDO, which implies a false or sham similarity. For example, a *quasi*-judicial proceeding is one which follows some of the rules and practices of judicial proceedings, but not necessarily all of them. See each of the following under the principal listing: ~ CONTRACT (1); ~ CORPORATION.

quaternary. Containing or consisting of four parts, as a *quaternary* alloy, which contains four principal elements.

quay. A wharf or sea-wall built along the shore of the sea or harbor, for loading and unloading vessels. It is sometimes spelled key

quick assets. See ASSET (2), LIQUID.

quickie strike. See under STRIKE.

quid pro quo. In Latin, literally, one thing for another. In business, a mutual consideration; giving an advantage or concession in return for a similar favor. Tit for tat.

quintal. See HUNDREDWEIGHT.

quire. Originally, four sheets of folded paper. Specifically, as now used, 24 folded sheets of writing paper, or 24 envelopes. In printing papers, a *quire* is one twentieth of a REAM, or 25 sheets.

quit. In general, to leave, or to surrender up control or possession. To leave voluntarily from a job; a voluntary termination of employment. It is distinguished from a LAYOFF, which is an involuntary termination due to lack of work or some similar situation, and from a DISCHARGE, which is an involuntary termination for cause, such as incompetence, absenteeism, etc.

quitclaim. In law, a release given to one person by another, giving up some right of action, or a claim of title to some property. See also DEED, QUITCLAIM.

quittance. A release or acquittance, such as a release or DISCHARGE (1) from a debt or obligation.

quorum. Generally, the number or proportion of members that must be present in order for a body to act or to transact business. In a meeting of stockholders, for example, it is the number of voting shares that must be represented for the legal transaction of business. Unless otherwise specified, a *quorum* is usually a majority of those entitled to vote or to act. In any particular case, however, the number may be set by custom, agreement, or statute.

quota. In general, any proportionate share or part, such as the *quota* of immigrants permitted to enter from any one country each year under the Immigration Act. An assigned goal out of a total goal, such as a SALES QUOTA. In foreign trade, *import quotas* may be set, limiting the number or value of a given product, or the value of all products from a given country, which may be imported during a specified period. Similarly, *export quotas* may be established, limiting the amount or value of specific commodities which may be exported to particular countries during a time period.

quota sample. See under SAMPLE (3).

quotation. The statement, published or otherwise, of the current market price of something, such as a commodity, security, or service. Under certain circumstances, a *quotation* may be taken as an offer to sell at the price quoted.

quotation board. The board or bulletin in a securities broker's office, on which are posted the latest prices for selected securities or commodities. It is popularly known as a *quote board*.

quotidian. From the Latin, daily, or occurring every day. A *quotidian* assignment is one to be accomplished in a day, while a *quotidian* flood, for example, is one which occurs every day.

R

racket. In slang, any fraudulent or dishonest scheme for obtaining money; an illegal business operation. A racketeer is one who takes part in or lives by a *racket*. The derivation is uncertain, being thought by some to come from *racketing*, or living a noisy, lively, fast social life; and by others to come from *racking*, the process of stretching or straining a source of income beyond a reasonable return. See, for example, RENT, RACK.

rack jobber. See under JOBBER.

rack rent. See under RENT (2).

rag money. See under MONEY.

raid. In the securities trade, a concerted attempt by professional traders or others to depress market prices for a security. This is done, for example, by setting up prearranged or fictitious sales in the security below the market price.

rail bill of lading. See under BILL OF LADING.

rail bond. See under BOND (1).

railroad. 1. An enterprise established and operated to carry passengers and freight in cars on permanent rails. Also, the physical tracks, roadbed, right of way, cars, and other physical assets themselves. A railway is sometimes distinguished from a *railroad* in that the former is intended for passenger travel only, such as an urban street railway, while the latter is for regular passenger and freight use. In law, however, the terms are synonymous.
2. To force through to a decision with great and undue haste. For example, to *railroad* legislation is to rush it to a vote, while to *railroad* a defendant in a trial is to find him guilty and pronounce sentence with haste and usually for insufficient cause.

railroad classification. See CLASSIFICATION OF RAILROADS.

railway. See RAILROAD (1).

railway Express Agency. An organization, set up and owned jointly by the railroads, which handles shipments of goods sent express by rail. The agency provides pick-up and delivery service, and the shipments travel in special express cars attached to passenger trains, or in special trains made up entirely of express shipments. Thus, the service provided is much faster than rail freight, and compares with the mails. Charges are based on mileage, in zones, and on the classification of the goods shipped. The *Railway Express Agency* now also provides an AIR EXPRESS service, in conjunction with the airlines.

Railway Labor Act. The federal law, growing out of the Arbitration Act of 1888 and amended several times, which governs labor relations on the nation's interstate railroads. Those workers who are covered by this act are excluded from the terms of the National Labor Relations Act (Wagner Act). The act is administered by the National Railroad Adjustment Board, and by the National Mediation Board.

raise. 1. Any increase in value or amount, such as in wages or prices.
2. To increase the nominal or face value of a negotiable instrument by fraud. For example, to *raise* a check is to change the stated value of the check to a higher amount in an attempt to defraud the one on whom the check is drawn.

raised check. See under CHECK (1).

rake-off. In slang, a share, bonus, or commission received by one party to a transaction, especially one received or demanded illegally, or as a share of illegal profits.

rally. In the securities trade, a rise or recovery in the prices of securities or commodities after a decline, particularly after a sudden or steep decline.

ramie. An oriental plant yielding a fiber which may be processed into a yarn coarser than linen and much stronger. It is used for bagging, mats, and similar products requiring great strength and wear resistance.

random. In general, by chance, haphazardly; with no set pattern or method. As applied in various designations, it means run-of-the-mill, unclassified, or unsorted. For example, lumber in *random* lengths consists of pieces of varying length mixed together, and brick in *random* courses is laid in rows of uneven height.

random sample. See under SAMPLE (3).

range. 1. In general, the limits of possible variation, from the greatest to the least; the scope of possible events or results under given conditions.

2. In statistics, a measure of the dispersion of a distribution of values. It is the total algebraic difference between the greatest and the least items in an ordered series or frequency distribution.

rank correlation. See under CORRELATION.

rate. 1. A proportional or relative value or measure; a ratio or percentage. For example, the RATE OF INTEREST is the proportion of the value of capital that must be paid for its use; and the tax *rate* is the proportion of the value of a thing that must be paid in taxes.

2. To classify and rank with respect to particular qualities or characteristics. Thus, a *first-rate* item is one of the highest quality; and a credit *rating* is a classification based on eligibility for credit.

3. A price, charge, or fee, usually expressed as some proportion of the weight, number of units, dollar value, etc., of the thing for which the charge is made. For example, a FREIGHT RATE may be per hundred pounds, a telephone *rate* may be per call, an insurance *rate* per dollar of value, etc.

rate card. In advertising, a card issued by the publisher of a newspaper, magazine or similar medium, giving information concerning advertising rates, classifications, discounts, circulation, mechanical requirements, submission deadlines, etc.

rate discrimination. The application of different rates for two customers or classes of commodities, where the difference is not justified by differences in the cost of the service rendered. Where such discrimination tends to lessen competition, or give an unfair advantage, it is illegal under the anti-trust laws.

rate holder. In advertising, a term used for an advertisement which is run for the specific purpose of securing an advertising rate based on the number of insertions. An advertiser can frequently save money over the long run by placing a number of small advertisements in order to be eligible for a low MULTIPLE-INSERTION RATE on a few large-space advertisements.

rate of exchange. The actual and variable amount of the currency of one country which, at any given date, can be bought for a fixed sum in the currency of another country. The rate fluctuates from day to day, depending on the state of trade, the relative supply of the two currencies, and other factors. When the *rate of exchange* for one currency is above the PAR OF EXCHANGE, the rate is said to be favorable, and when it is below par, it is unfavorable.

free ∼. The rate at which currencies exchange for each other on the open or free market, as distinguished from the official, or nominal rate, which is established by the governments concerned, or by their central banks.

official ∼. The rate at which the monetary authority, or the central bank, of a country will buy and sell foreign currency in exchange for the currency of the country.

rate of interest. In general, the charge for borrowing money. The additional amount which must be paid for the privilege of using money, or for delaying a payment, calculated as a percentage of the total amount used, per unit of time. Unless otherwise specified, the *rate of interest* is always stated as the charge per year, regardless of the period for which the money is used. For example, if the interest charge on a loan of $100 for two months is $1, the *rate of interest* on the loan is said to be 6% (per year). In business there is no single *rate of interest*, but various rates, depending on the type of loan, the period of the loan, the character of the borrower, and the institution making the loan. See also INTEREST.

bank ∼. The prevailing *rate of interest* or discount charged at any one time by commercial banks on standard loans. It may be more closely specified, such as the *bank rate* on unsecured loans, on collateral loans, etc.

legal ∼. The maximum rate which may be set by statute for loans made by institutions within a state. Some states have established more than one legal maximum rate for different types of loans, and some have no *legal rate* at all.

prime ∼. The *rate of interest,* sometimes actually deducted in advance as a DISCOUNT, charged for the purchase of first class, or prime COMMERCIAL PAPER by the Federal Reserve Bank in each district. This rate, which is publicly established, tends to set the rate for all other forms of commercial interest payments in the district, and thus serves to control the flow of credit.

ratification. In law, an agreement to adopt as one's own an act performed by another. Such an agreement may be used as a means of imparting validity to an unauthorized act of another, such as an agent. The *ratification* may be either express, or implied from one's own acts.

rating. 1. An estimate of the financial strength or credit eligibility of a business enterprise, such as may be shown in a *rating* book of a credit *rating* agency, or other *rating* enterprise. Such *ratings* may be used not only to determine the amount of credit to be extended, but in the process of setting sales quotas and in other ways. Most *rating* systems are based on a combination of alphabetic and numerical rankings, so that, for example, AA-1 might be the *rating* for the top financial strength and top credit eligibility, and F-4 the *rating* for a company with the lowest ranking in both categories. In any particular system, of course, the significance of each *rating* is determined by the agency preparing the *rating*. See also CREDIT RATING.

2. In insurance, the basis of the premium charge made for an insurance policy. For the various methods of *rating* used, see EXPERIENCE RATING; MANUAL RATING; RETROSPECTIVE RATING.

rating bureau. An organization established jointly by the insurance companies operating in a state or region, which determines the insurance rates or premiums to be charged for insuring particular properties or classes of risks. The bureau operates by collecting statistical information on the experience with certain types of risk, and by inspecting the condition of properties to be insured. In some states, the activities of the *rating bureaus* are closely supervised under the state insurance laws.

ratio. A measure of the relation between two quantities of like items; a proportion. For examples of the *ratios* used in business, see EXPENSE RATIO; LOSS RATIO; OPERATING RATIO.

ration. Originally, an allowance, or fixed daily portion, such as the *ration* allowed to each soldier or seaman. Today, it is primarily a limited allowance of some scarce or critical commodity, which must be distributed under an allotment plan to assure equitable sharing of the available supplies. In time of war, for example, such items as sugar, gasoline, fats, and meat are usually among the first to be placed under a consumer *rationing* program.

rationalization. A term more widely used in England for the planned integration of all of the units in an industry. Such a plan, for example, might assign territories, production quotas, and shares of the market to each unit, for the purpose of maximizing the efficiency of production and distribution. In a period of war or national emergency, such a program of *rationalization* would be expected to eliminate waste and duplication. In normal times, however, *rationalization* is primarily a form of cartelization. See also CARTEL.

ratio scale. In graphic presentation, a scale chosen so that changes of equal proportion or *ratio* are indicated by equal distances, regardless of the absolute amounts involved. See also LOGARITHMIC SCALE.

raw materials. 1. In general, industrial goods which are to be used in manufacture, but which are still in a natural or unmanufactured state, except for the processing incidental to their preparation, packaging, or transportation.

2. From the point of view of the individual manufacturing company, any materials or goods with which the company starts its manufacturing process, whether they have actually been previously manufactured or processed, or are still in a raw or natural state.

rayon. A man-made textile fiber or continuous yarn, manufactured essentially from cellulose materials. Under present federal regulations, only the product made by the so-called viscose process may now be called *rayon,* while the similar product made by the acetate process is known as ACETATE. In use, the two types of fiber or yarn are frequently blended to obtain the best characteristics of each.

re. A Latin term meaning in regard to, relating to, in the matter of.

reaction. In the securities trade, a downward turn in securities prices, after a relatively sustained period of rising prices.

reacquired stock. See STOCK (1), TREASURY.

readjustment. A voluntary financial reconstruction or rehabilitation of a corporation which is in financial difficulties, undertaken by concurrence of the stockholders. It is distinguished from a REORGANIZATION, which is undertaken when the corporation or business is already in the hands of appointed receivers, or of its creditors.

ready. On hand, available; such as *ready* cash or money. Also, available, in the sense of receptive; such as a *ready* market.

ready-made. Made or manufactured in final form in anticipation of immediate sale to or use by any buyer, rather than a particular one. For example, a *ready-made* suit is cut and made to fit any person with the marked average measurements, and *ready-made* furniture covers are made to fit any piece of furniture of a given style. It is distinguished from made-to-order or CUSTOM-MADE, and from CUSTOM-TAILORED.

real. 1. In the law of property, those things which are in the class of LAND, rather than of personal property.

2. In law in general, those actions or causes which refer to things, rather than to people.

3. Tangible or physical, rather than intangible. See ACCOUNT (2), REAL.

4. Adjusted for changes in prices, or in the value of the dollar. See, for example, WAGES, REAL.

real estate. In common usage, real property, including both LAND and structures or improvements thereon, and any rights therein. Sometimes, but incorrectly, unimproved land. See each of the following under the principal listing: ~ BOND (1); ~ BROKER (1); ~ MORTGAGE; ~ TAX (2).

realization account. See under ACCOUNT (2).

realize. 1. To convert property or some asset into cash; to sell a claim or interest for money. In current usage, to receive or earn a return, whether from the sale of something or as profit on an investment.

2. In the securities trade, to sell a security for the purpose of obtaining the accumulated profit due to an increase in price. Thus, *realizing* is synonymous with profit-taking.

real property. See under PROPERTY.

realtor. A real estate BROKER. A member of any local association affiliated with the National Association of Real Estate Boards.

realty. Any real property; but in popular usage, real estate.

ream. The standard commercial measure by which paper is counted. A *ream* of printing paper, sometimes called a *printer's ream*, consists of 500 sheets, but a *ream* of writing paper is 20 QUIRES, or 480 folded sheets.

reasonable. As generally interpreted, that which an ordinarily prudent and reasoning man would do or say. That which is ordinary and usual, fit and proper, just and appropriate. In the making of rates, setting charges, measuring profits, etc., that amount which is neither so low as to be destructive of property or property rights, nor so high as to be injurious to the public.

reassurance. See REINSURANCE.

rebate. Literally, to beat down, or to cut back. Hence, any deduction made from a stipulated amount, payment, or charge. In current usage, a *rebate* is distinguished from a DISCOUNT in that the former is not taken out or deducted in advance, but is handed

back after payment of the full amount. Under customs regulations, for example, import duties paid on goods which are later re-exported may be *rebated* in part or in full. *Rebates* paid on freight charges are sometimes known as DRAWBACKS.

rebill. In railroad freight practice, to issue a new freight WAYBILL at a junction point between two carriers.

rebuilt. As interpreted by various agencies and courts, for example for use in advertising, those manufactured products, such as household appliances, office machines, etc., which have been disassembled and reconstructed, with the replacement of worn and defective parts.

recapitalize. To change the capital structure of a corporation, such as by increasing or decreasing the amount of capital stock. The usual procedure is for the stockholders to agree to the change, and for the stock to be called in and reissued in the new amount.

receipt. A written acknowledgment of the receiving or acceptance of money, or of something of value. A written acknowledgment of the payment of a debt or obligation. Legally, a *receipt* is considered as merely a statement of fact, saying nothing concerning the obligation itself, or the purposes of the giver or receiver. Also, to give such an acknowledgment or *receipt*.

receipts. The things or amounts which are received or taken in. The *gross receipts* are the total taken in, before any deductions for expenses, and the *net receipts* are the *receipts* less all expenses connected with the business. See also INCOME; EARNINGS.

receivable. That which is due or collectible. In the plural, the total amounts which are due for goods sold, services rendered, or money loaned. See also ACCOUNTS ~; BILL OF EXCHANGE ~; NOTES ~.

receive. To take a thing into possession or control, to accept custody of something. The act may be CONSTRUCTIVE; that is, not actual, such as when a warehouse is held to have *received* goods when they have been accepted by its agent for shipment to the warehouse.

receiver. In law, an independent person, appointed by a court, to take charge of an enterprise, collect and receive funds, pay out necessary charges, etc. This is done for example when a party to an action should not do so, as in BANKRUPTCY, or is incompetent to do so, as in the case of a child.

~ **in bankruptcy.** A *receiver* specifically named to handle the affairs of a bankrupt business, to preserve its assets, and, if possible, arrange for continuance of the business, or else for its liquidation and payment to creditors.

receiver's bond. See under BOND (2).

receivership. The condition or state of being under the care or administration of a RECEIVER. Also, the rights, duties and obligations of one appointed to the position of receiver.

receiving teller. See TELLER.

recession. In economics, a period marked by a mild decline, or receding of business activity from its high level. As generally used and understood, the term implies a gradual decline and one of relatively short duration, milder than a DEPRESSION.

reciprocal. Mutual, involving an even exchange of rights, privileges, responsibilities, etc. See each of the following under the principal listing: ∼ AGREEMENT; ∼ CONTRACT (1); ∼ INSURANCE; ∼ TRADE; ∼ WILL.

reciprocal exchange. In insurance, an unincorporated group of companies who join together to insure each other against loss. Each member of the *exchange* is both insured and an insurer of the others. Technically, the insurance is provided through an ATTORNEY IN FACT, who represents the members of the *exchange* and manages its affairs. A *reciprocal exchange* is distinguished from a mutual insurance company in that it is not formally organized as a company, and in that the insurance is not provided by the company or association, but directly and jointly by the other members of the *exchange*. It is sometimes known as an *interinsurance exchange*. See also INSURANCE COMPANY, MUTUAL.

reciprocity. 1. In general, mutual cooperation or exchange. The granting by one party to another of some special consideration or privilege in exchange for an equivalent concession.

2. In foreign affairs, the granting by one country of certain privileges or advantages to the subjects of another, on the condition that its subjects shall receive the same privileges in return.

3. In business, the practice under which one company favors another in purchasing, on the understanding that it will receive, or continue to receive, the same preference from the other. The practice has been held to be discriminatory under the unfair competition laws in some cases, and is usually considered to be poor business practice in any event.

reckless. Literally, not reckoning with the consequences. In law and insurance, indifferent to consequences; with no regard to probable and foreseeable loss or damage. For example, one who operates a vehicle in a *reckless* manner may not be entitled to recover damages under some insurance policies.

reclamation. In banking, a term used for an amount that may be found to be due or owing by a bank as the result of an erroneous listing of the amount of a check on a clearing house balance. In such an event, the checks involved are laid aside for *reclamation,* that is for payment or collection of the amount due.

recognizance. In criminal law, an OBLIGATION given, under which a person recognizes that a duty, such as to appear in court at a specified date, exists, and agrees to carry it out. In this sense it differs from a BOND (2) in that a bond always involves some surety or pledge, while a person accused of a crime may often be permitted to remain free pending trial on his own *recognizance,* meaning that he puts his own word or good faith as surety.

recompense. A repayment, compensation, or reward, especially a payment made as a means of making amends for some loss or damage.

reconciliation statement. A statement of account prepared for the purpose of bringing into agreement the totals or balances of two accounts which show a discrepancy. For example, a *reconciliation statement* of all deposits and checks may be prepared when there is a discrepancy between the cash account and a bank statement.

reconsign. To CONSIGN anew. To change the original destination of a shipment, or the name of the intended CONSIGNEE, or both, while the shipment is still in transit. This might be done, for example, if the order is cancelled after shipment.

Reconstruction Finance Corporation (RFC). An independent government corporation originally established for the purpose of making direct loans to business. It was set up because of the general unavailability of bank credit during the 1930's for the very businesses that needed it most. Its loan policies became a matter of controversy, however, and it has now been liquidated. Some of its functions are now performed by such agencies as the SMALL BUSINESS ADMINISTRATION.

record date. The date as of which stock ownership is determined for the purpose of paying dividends. When a corporation announces the payment of a dividend, it usually specifies that it will be paid on a certain date, to stockholders of record on an earlier date. In other words, the dividend is paid to those who were registered as stockholders on the *record date.*

recorder of deeds. See REGISTER OF DEEDS.

recoup. 1. In general, to recover or make up a loss by a subsequent gain; to recover one's fortunes after a period of financial loss.

2. In law, to deduct or withhold a part of that which is due to be paid, as rightful compensation, or to recover a debt.

recourse. In law, the right of a person to whom a note or other obligation has been endorsed to recover payment from the endorser in case of default by the original maker. Hence, when an obligation, such as a retail installment note, is sold or discounted *without recourse,* the endorser or seller of the note does not retain any responsibility for its payment. See also WITH RECOURSE.

recovery. 1. In the securities trade, a term for a rise in prices after a period of decline. Also, by extension, any improvement in conditions in a particular business or in general.

2. The regaining or reclaiming of something of value, such as a right or property, or its equivalent value in money.

recruiting. The process of seeking and obtaining large numbers of prospective new employees, by solicitation, advertising, or otherwise, for purposes of reviewing and screening the persons recruited for possible employment.

redeem. Literally, to buy back. To regain possession of some thing, or to gain release from a pledge by paying an amount due or performing as promised. For example, one *redeems* a bond by paying the principal on maturity, but a pledge may be *redeemed* by appearing at some specified time, or performing some specified act.

redeemable bond. See BOND (1), CALLABLE.

redeemable currency. See CURRENCY, CONVERTIBLE.

redeemable stock. See under STOCK (1).

redelivery bond. See under BOND (2).

redemption. 1. In general, the right to REDEEM, or the act of redeeming. As a right, it may be exercised by any person who has pledged his property, who owes a debt, has taken a mortgage, who has sold his property conditionally, etc. State laws vary widely as to the terms and conditions under which the right may be exercised, enforced, assigned, lost, etc.

2. In finance, the repurchase of a bond, note, banknote, currency, or other obligation by a corporation, bank, or government, by paying its value to the holder. The payment is usually in legal tender, unless the obligation specifies that it is redeemable in gold, silver, or some other form.

redemption fund. See SINKING FUND.

"red herring" prospectus. In financial circles, the popular name for a circular or preliminary PROSPECTUS distributed by the underwriters of a securities issue before the effective date of the formal registration statement. The name is not used in the usual sense of being something intended to divert attention from the true state of affairs, but arises from the fact that the Securities and Exchange Commission requires each page of such a prospectus to carry, in red ink, a notice that the information contained is for information only, and is not to be considered an offer to sell, or the solicitation of an offer to buy, the securities described.

red ink. The ink used for negative, or reverse, entries in books or records of account. It indicates that the amount so entered is to be deducted from the total of the positive or BLACK INK figures. Hence, in an income statement, *red ink* indicates losses, and a business which is losing money is said to be "in the red."

rediscount. Literally, to DISCOUNT again, or for a second time. To sell or discount a negotiable instrument which has already been discounted once. For example, a bank or sales finance company which has purchased or discounted the obligations of a retail dealer, may *rediscount* them by selling them to another bank or to the Federal Reserve Bank.

rediscount rate. The rate of interest charged for discounting a negotiable instrument which has been discounted once already. Specifically, the rate usually referred to is the rate set by the Federal Reserve Bank in each District for rediscounting first class or prime COMMERCIAL PAPER offered by member banks in the District. This rate tends to set the rate for all other commercial discount operations in the Federal Reserve District.

redraft. In general, a second draft or new copy. Specifically, a new DRAFT or BILL OF EXCHANGE which the holder of a protested bill draws on the original maker or endorsers for the amount of the bill plus any additional costs and charges.

red tape. Official routines or procedures, especially unnecessary or excessive procedures. The term derives from the *red tape* or ribbon traditionally used to tie up government documents and papers.

reduced rate contribution clause. See COINSUR-
ANCE CLAUSE.

reefer. In business slang, a refrigerated freight
car, motor truck, ship, or other freight
carrier especially refrigerated for carrying
perishable goods.

re-exchange. The charge made upon the drawer
of a negotiable instrument, especially a
foreign BILL OF EXCHANGE, which has been
dishonored on presentation, by the holder
of the bill when re-drawing a new bill. The
charge is to cover the loss and expense incurred through the failure to honor the bill,
but it is often stated in terms of a fixed
percentage rate of penalty, rather than
itemized.

re-export. The export, without basic processing
or alteration, of goods or commodities which
have been previously imported. In foreign
commerce statistics, EXPORTS are divided into
re-exports and DOMESTIC EXPORTS, which are
goods of domestic manufacture or growth
being exported.

referee. In general, one to whom something is
referred; an ARBITRATOR or umpire. In law, a
person appointed by a court, to whom a
pending action is referred for the taking
of testimony, resolving of points in dispute,
etc. The *referee* makes his recommendations
to the court, which in practice usually accepts them.

　∼ **in bankruptcy.** An officer appointed by
a court to carry out the administrative details in connection with a bankruptcy, such
as the appointment of a receiver, the determination of the rights and priority of claims,
the declaration of payments or dividends,
etc. Though strictly speaking his actions are
under the supervision and review of the
court, they are normally accepted by the
court without question.

referendum. A direct vote, especially one on
an issue referred to the electorate by their
representatives, or to stockholders in a corporation by the board of directors. For example, corporate charters normally provide
that a proposed change in the capitalization
of a corporation must be approved by the
stockholders in a *referendum*.

reform. In law, to change, correct, or amend
the terms of an instrument or agreement to
carry out or express its original intent. For
example, a court may *reform* the terms of
an insurance contract in which the actual
wording does not express the intent of both
the insurer and the insured at the time the
contract was made, and may then settle a
dispute under the contract on the basis of
the *reformed* terms.

refund. In general, any repayment of money
for any reason; a REBATE. More particularly,
a repayment of money which ought not to
have been paid, such as an overcharge, or
an estimated tax payment made in advance.
A *refund* is sometimes distinguished from a
REBATE in that it is the result of an overpay-
ment, while the latter is the return of part
of an originally stipulated amount.

refunding. The process or act of substituting
a new series of obligations in place of an
older issue, either before or at maturity of
the older issue. See also BOND (I), REFUND-
ING.

register. 1. Any book of accounts intended
primarily for keeping a record of internal
affairs or transactions. For example, a company operating on a VOUCHER SYSTEM may
keep a VOUCHER REGISTER for listing the
details of vouchers issued, and a bank may
keep a COLLECTIONS register in which are
listed the checks accepted for collection by
the bank.

　2. A list or record book maintained by a
corporation, containing the names of the
owners of the securities and obligations of
the corporation. Actually, the *register* may
be kept by the TRANSFER AGENT of the corporation. See also TRANSFER BOOK.

　3. A listing of ships names, their owners,
and their general descriptions, such as may
be kept by the collector of customs of a port,
or a marine insurance company. See, for
example, LLOYD'S REGISTER.

register check. See under CHECK (1).

registered bond. See under BOND (1).

registered company. One whose securities have
been registered or LISTED with one of the
principal securities exchanges, or with the
Securities and Exchange Commission. To be
registered, the company must meet certain
requirements dealing primarily with the disclosure of its capital structure and financial
strength.

registered coupon bond. See under BOND (1).

registered mail. See under POSTAL SERVICE.

registered mark. See under TRADE MARK.

registered tonnage. See under TONNAGE.

register of deeds. An officer, in some states,
who maintains a register for recording all
deeds, mortgages, and other documents relating to the ownership of real estate. In
some states, he is called the recorder of
deeds.

register ton. See under TON.

registrar. An officer or agent of a corporation,
often a bank or trust company, appointed
to keep a record of its securities, and to

certify that the name on each certificate issued is that of the owner of record. The *registrar* thus acts as a check on the transfer agent. It is also his duty to see that when new certificates are issued the old ones are cancelled and destroyed. See also AGENT, TRANSFER.

registration. 1. The listing of each certificate of the securities of a corporation on the register maintained for the purpose, giving the name of the holder, and noting any transfers of ownership.

2. The submission of the statement required by the Securities Exchange Act of 1934 of all issuers of securities, which must be provided before the securities may be offered for sale to the public in interstate commerce or through the mails. The *registration* statement is submitted to and approved by the Securities and Exchange Committee.

registry. The listing of a vessel under the name of the country whose flag it flies. For example, a ship of Panama *registry* is one registered under the maritime laws of the Republic of Panama. *Registry* need have no relation to the nationality of the owner of a vessel. Many American owned ships are listed under Panamanian or other *registry* for the advantages this may bring in terms of less stringent requirements for equipment, crew facilities, etc.

registry certificate. See CERTIFICATE OF REGISTRY.

regression. See CORRELATION.

regressive tax. See under TAX (2).

regular dividend. See under DIVIDEND.

regular lot. See ROUND LOT.

regulated investment company. See INVESTMENT COMPANY.

regular way. In the securities trade, a term designating a transaction in which delivery of the securities traded is to be made in the normal manner for that exchange, usually before the close of business on the third following day.

rehypothecation. In the securities trade, a term for the repledging by a broker or dealer of securities already left with him as a pledge by a customer. For example, a customer who buys securities on margin leaves them with the broker as a pledge against his margin loan. The broker, in order to finance his own activities, then pledges the same securities with a bank or other lender. This second pledging of the securities by the broker is known as *rehypothecation,* though neither of the pledges involved is a true HYPOTHECATION, since the securities are physically deposited.

reinstatement. 1. In insurance, the act of putting a policy holder back into the same position as he held before the policy was suspended or cancelled for non-payment, violation of terms, or for any other reason. When a policy is reinstated after it has lapsed for non-payment of premium, a penalty is frequently charged besides the premium itself.

2. In insurance, under a policy which provides that the amount of insurance shall be reduced by the amount of each loss paid, *reinstatement* is the raising of the total insurance to the original amount again by the payment of a required special premium. This type of policy is used only infrequently at present.

reinsurance. In insurance, a procedure under which an insurer contracts with another insurer to assume part of the risk the first has taken on. In other words, the reinsurer contracts to insure the first insurer against loss from some or all of the risks he has insured. There are several ways in which this may be done. For example, the reinsurer may agree to cover all losses above a specified amount on each contract, or he may agree to cover a proportion of every loss, or the total of all losses over a specified amount during a period, etc.

reject. In manufacturing, a unit or material which is spoiled and unusable, or which does not meet quality standards or engineering specifications. *Reject* material is distinguished from SCRAP (2), in that the latter is the intentional or unavoidable wastage which results from production, while a *reject* is an unintentional wastage of material or product

release. 1. In law, to abandon or concede a claim or right which one person may have against another. For example, one who is injured in an accident may *release* his right to further compensation or award from the responsible party, in return for a cash settlement or consideration. In the legal sense, *release* may be express or implied, and it may be for a consideration or not.

2. An instrument by which a person gives up his right with respect to some claim he may have. For example, when a photograph is to be used in illustrative or advertising material, it is customary to obtain a *release* from any person who is recognizable in the photograph, stating that the person gives up his right to any use of the photo, to further compensation, and to any claim for damage arising out of the intended use of the photo.

released rate. See under FREIGHT RATE.

release of mortgage. A written instrument, executed and delivered, by a mortgagee who has made the final payment on a mortgage, to the mortgagor. It sets forth the fact that the mortgage has been repaid in full, and when the mortgagor has filed it with the proper office, such as that of the register of deeds, it constitutes public notice that the mortgage has been discharged and is no longer a lien against the property.

reliction. An increase in the amount of a parcel of land by the permanent withdrawal of water, either a river or the sea. The person who owns the property thus enlarged is said to acquire title by *reliction* to the additional portion.

religious corporation. See under CORPORATION.

remainder. In law, an estate that begins upon the termination of a temporary estate which preceded it, both estates having been created by the same instrument. For example, a person, in his will, may give the use of property, or the income from an investment, to his wife for the rest of her life, and provide that the property itself pass to a child upon the death of the wife. The wife is said to have a LIFE ESTATE in the property, and the estate of the child is the *remainder*. It differs from a RESIDUE, which is the estate or inheritance remaining after specific bequests and claims have been satisfied. The term is also applied to the principal of a trust fund, which may pass to another party on the termination of a limited or temporary interest in it by a first party.

2. In the publishing trade, a stock of new books left in the hands of a publisher after sales have ceased or become unprofitable. Also, to dispose of such stocks at reduced prices.

remainderman. In law, a term for the person who is to receive full title to property after the termination of a temporary estate; the one who inherits by REMAINDER. Also, the person who, under a trust agreement, is to receive the principal of a trust fund upon the termination of a limited interest in it by another party.

remargining. In the securities trade, the furnishing of additional securities as collateral for a MARGIN loan, when the securities originally purchased on margin have declined in price below a stated percent of their market price at the time of purchase. Sometimes, the term is used for the payment of additional margin in cash under similar circumstances.

remedy. In law, the means or prescribed method by which a right is enforced; any relief to which an aggrieved party is entitled, with or without recourse to a tribunal.

remit. 1. Literally, to send back. As used in business, the term usually refers specifically to a payment forwarded from one person, to another, usually for goods purchased. Thus, an invoice for goods may bear the phrase, please *remit,* requesting payment.

2. To give up, pardon, or refrain from exacting. For example, a court may *remit* or waive a fine it has imposed in punishment.

remittance. A sum of money forwarded from one person to another, either by cash or negotiable instrument, usually in payment of an invoice for goods or services purchased.

remittance slip. A printed business form, designed to accompany a REMITTANCE to identify it. It usually includes a list of the invoices covered by the remittance, any discounts or allowances taken, and the amount enclosed. It may be in any of several forms. For example, it may be a stub attached by perforations to the check itself, or it may be a stub originally attached to the invoice, and separated for return with the check.

remonetization. The re-establishment of coins of a particular metal as legal tender, after they have for a time been removed from this status. Also, the re-establishment of a currency system as being based on metal, such as gold, after it has for a time been based merely on the good faith of the issuing government. See also DEMONETIZE.

removal bond. See under BOND (2).

remuneration. Compensation, payment, or reward, especially for services rendered.

render. 1. To give up, yield, or pay; to return, or to perform, as an obligation.

2. To make, cause, or result; to bring about. For example, changed conditions may *render* an agreement inoperative.

3. To state, or pronounce; to hand down, as, for example, to *render* a decision.

rendu price. See under PRICE.

renegotiation. Literally, to negotiate again; to review the terms of a contract, the costs and profits involved, with a view to adjusting the contract price. During World War II, the United States government provided, in contracts it signed for war materials, that after performance of the contract it could be reviewed to determine whether the profits realized had been excessive. Through this process of *renegotiation,* the government recaptured many millions of dollars of its original wartime expenditures.

renew. In general, to revive and to continue in force something that is about to expire or come to an end. For example, a lease which is about to expire may be *renewed* for another term; a loan which is about to fall due may be *renewed* for another period at the same interest; an insurance policy may be *renewed* for another period of years when the agreement expires, etc. Strictly, to *renew* an agreement is different from an extension, in that it involves making a new agreement, rather than continuing the old one.

renewable term insurance. See under INSURANCE, LIFE, ACCIDENT, AND HEALTH.

renewal. The act or process of renewing an agreement. With respect to a bond, note, etc., issued to replace one which has expired or matured. See also BOND (1), RENEWAL; NOTE (1), RENEWAL.

rent. 1. To take possession, or to occupy, under the terms of a LEASE. A TENANT *rents* property; a LANDLORD lets it out.

2. In economic theory, the share of created value which is attributable to LAND, as one of the three factors of production, the other two being LABOR and CAPITAL. Hence, it is the return on investment in land, or the compensation paid for the use of land. In modern usage, it is the fee paid under a LEASE for any real property, whether land, building, space, equipment, etc.

   ground ∼. The *rent* paid to an owner of property for the use of the ground, or land, including the permission to build on it.

   rack ∼. In law, an exorbitant or excessive *rent*. Specifically, the term is used for a *rent* charge which equals or exceeds the value of the property itself.

rental value. The reasonably expected income value of property if used for a specified purpose by a tenant. With respect to owner-occupied property, it is the reasonable rent which would be paid by the owner if he were occupying the property as a tenant. In federal statistics on consumer expenditures, the *rental value* of owner-occupied dwellings is included as being, in effect, an expenditure.

rental value insurance. See under INSURANCE, PROPERTY.

rentier. From the French *rentes,* a form of bond paying a fixed annual interest, any person who receives an annual income from investments, leases, etc. One whose income is primarily in the form of fixed interest or annuity payments.

rent insurance. See under INSURANCE, PROPERTY.

renunciation. In law, the act of abandoning a right or claim completely, without any reservation, or without transferring it to another.

reorganization. In general, an adjustment or revision of the capital structure of a corporation, usually involving the retirement of all outstanding securities, and their replacement by new securities. In particular, a *recapitalization* of a bankrupt corporation, under which the stockholders, bondholders, and creditors agree to surrender their interests and claims, and a new corporation is formed to settle the debts of the old and to carry on its business operations.

   ∼ committee. A committee of stockholders, bondholders, creditors, and the officers of a bankrupt corporation, formed for the purpose of taking charge of and carrying through the *reorganization* of the business.

repair. To take the necessary steps to restore property or equipment to good and sound condition, after it has deteriorated through age, decay, damage, use, or partial destruction. The *repair* of property is distinguished from its MAINTENANCE, which involves keeping it in the good condition which already exists, and from its IMPROVEMENT, which involves a change in the condition of the property, rather than its restoration to its original condition. The difference is important for tax purposes, since a *repair* is a current expense, while an improvement is a capital expenditure.

repairs. In accounting, the account under which the costs of repairing company property are entered. It is a division of the operating expenses account. See also EXPENSE, OPERATING.

reparation. In general, any payment made to redress an injury, or to make amends for a wrong done. As used, it is usually a payment made by one country to another for damages done during war.

repatriation. With respect to securities, the deliberate repurchase by the citizens of one country of securities of domestic corporations held by persons in another country. Actually, it is not the securities which are being *repatriated,* or brought home, but the control of domestic business.

repeal. With respect to legislation, the annulment of an existing law through the enactment of a new law, either revoking the old law, or containing new and inconsistent provisions.

replacement cost. See under COST.

replacement cost insurance. See under INSURANCE, PROPERTY.

replacement reserve. See under RESERVE (1).

replevin. In law, a form of action in which a person whose property has been wrongfully or illegally taken demands the return of the exact thing taken, not merely compensatory damages. Under the laws of most states, this action is the standard method for recovering property which is being unlawfully detained, either by an individual or by the state. See also BOND (2), REPLEVIN.

replication. In law, the reply of a PLAINTIFF to the DEFENDANT's answer to the original charges. The plaintiff makes his COMPLAINT, the defendant submits his PLEA, then the plaintiff has the opportunity to make a *replication.*

reporting policy. See under POLICY (2).

repossess. Literally, to possess again; to take back. As used in business, to recover goods for which a purchaser has failed to keep up installment payments as they fall due. The right to *repossess* is included in the conditional sales contracts and chattel mortgages under which installment sales are made. See also SALE (1), CONDITIONAL; SALE (1), INSTALLMENT; MORTGAGE, CHATTEL.

representation. 1. In a contract, the statement of the facts and circumstances on the basis of which the agreement is at least partly made, and which are assumed by both parties to the contract.

2. In an insurance agreement, the statements made by the insured to the insurer, which enable the latter to prepare the policy, and to determine the amount of risk and the proper rates. The *representation* made by the insured differs from the WARRANTY given, in that it need only be substantially and materially true, while the latter must be exactly and literally correct.

representative. In general, one who stands in the place of another; one who is authorized to act for another, such as an agent, trustee, executor, etc. In selling, a salesman, either one employed by the seller or operating as an agent. See, for example, MANUFACTURER'S REPRESENTATIVE.

reprieve. In law, a withdrawing of a sentence in a criminal case, especially a sentence of death, for a specified period of time. At the end of the period the sentence may be reinstated or further action taken. It differs from a PARDON, which is a complete cancellation of the sentence, and from a COMMUTATION, which is a reduction in the sentence.

reprisal. In general, the forcible taking of something by one person from another, in retaliation for a wrong done, or in satisfaction of an injury received. In the relations between countries, the action by one country of seizing the property of another, as a means of obtaining justice for alleged wrongs. See also LETTER OF MARQUE.

reprocessed wool. See under WOOL.

reproduction cost. See under COST.

repudiate. In general, to disclaim, or to renounce. One who *repudiates* a contract obligation, for example, refuses to perform something for which the contract calls. A government may *repudiate* its debts, in which case it refuses to pay all or part of its obligations.

requirement contract. See under CONTRACT (1).

requisition. In general, a formal request; an order or demand in writing. A *requisition* for materials or supplies, for example, is an order or request for delivery of the listed items. A *requisition* of goods or property by the government, such as in time of war, is a demand for delivery of the named property, with or without compensation.

res. The Latin word for things. The term is frequently used in legal terminology, meaning, in most cases, inanimate objects in general, rather than living persons.

resale. 1. In law, a second sale of goods which have already been once sold to another, but on which the first sale has not been completed, due to a default in payment or some other failure to fulfill the contract. In some sales contracts, the vendor retains the right of *resale,* and may require that the first buyer make up any deficit in the second sale price compared with the first.

2. In business generally, the sale of goods which have been purchased by the seller from another in essentially the same form. A contract for the sale of industrial supplies to a factory, for example, may specify that the supplies are not for *resale* by the buyer, but for his own use. Under state FAIR TRADE LAWS, manufacturers may set the price for *resale* of their products by distributors and dealers. See also PRICE, RESALE.

resale price. See under PRICE.

resale price maintenance. As defined by the Federal Trade Commission, any system of pricing for a trademarked, branded, or otherwise identified product, under which the manufacturer, brand owner, wholesaler, or other distributor prescribes by contract the minimum price at which the product may be resold by wholesale or retail distributors or dealers. Such contracts may be legally set under some state laws, and where these laws are in force, the federal FAIR TRADE LAW supports their enforcement when the product is moved in interstate commerce. In some states, the *resale price maintenance* agreement binds only those distributors who sign it, but in other states the signature of one dealer automatically binds all others. This latter form has been declared invalid by several state courts.

rescind. In law, to cancel, call back, annul, or abrogate a promise or agreement; to make void. Under the general law of contracts, any party who has been induced to enter a contract or agreement by fraud or misrepresentation has the right to *rescind* his acceptance of the agreement, provided he acts immediately on discovery of the fraud. This is sometimes known as the right of *rescission*.

rescript. 1. In American usage, an exact copy, or a duplicate, of any document or writing.
2. In older usage, a decree or ruling issued in reply to a question raised. A higher church official, for example, might prepare a *rescript* on a disputed or unclear point in reply to an inquiry from a lower official, after which the *rescript* would be the official position of the church on the matter in question.

research. In general, any systematic, diligent, and scientific investigation into the nature of occurrences or conditions for the purpose of establishing basic facts, or of discovering new principles, developing new methods or products, etc. In business, *research* may be engaged in to develop new products, to improve operating and production methods, to discover the nature of the market for a product, to determine the standing of a company in its market, and for many other purposes.

reservation. 1. In law, a holding back to one's self of a right or privilege. It differs from an EXCEPTION in that it refers to a right to the future enjoyment of something, while an exception refers to a thing that presently exists.
2. In general, something put aside, or held aside, such as a *reservation* of space or a seat on a railroad train or plane, or a *reservation* of time on a machine.

reserve. 1. In business accounting, an amount of money set aside from profits and other company funds, and transferred from surplus or undistributed profits to a special liability account. The purpose of setting up such a *reserve* account is to provide specific funds for meeting or offsetting those decreases in the value of company assets or those losses which, from the nature of the business, are known to be accumulating, or which are reasonably certain to occur in the future. Some companies may follow the practice of setting aside *reserves* for a wide variety of anticipated losses or costs, while others may establish little or no *reserve*, meeting such losses as they occur out of current income. The former is considered the sounder policy by most accountants. Under the 1954 Internal Revenue Code, companies may count certain transfers to *reserve* funds as expenditures when the transfer is made, or when the money is actually paid out, at the option

of the company. The typical purposes for which *reserves* are set up in business, and the various types of *reserve* funds, are listed and defined below.

contingency ∼. One set aside out of general surplus to meet contingent or uncertain losses, such as uninsured casualty losses, or shrinkage of inventory, which cannot be specifically identified in advance but which are still known to be likely to occur.

debt reduction ∼. One set aside out of current income for the specific purpose of reducing or redeeming outstanding debts. When such a fund is set up to accumulate money for the redemption of long-term debts at maturity, it is known as a SINKING FUND RESERVE, which see below.

depletion ∼. One set aside out of income by a company engaged in mining, oil well operation, timber cutting, or similar operations, to replace the assets which are reduced or depleted by normal company operations. The fund may be used periodically to acquire other assets, or for investment in other forms of business to diversify the company's operations. Under the 1954 Internal Revenue Code, a certain percentage of sales income may be set aside as a *depletion reserve* or allowance by such companies as a tax-free fund.

depreciation ∼. One used by some companies to accumulate the amount which is to be written off as depreciation of assets at the end of the accounting period. See also DEPRECIATION.

funded ∼. One which is invested in long-term interest bearing securities, rather than carried as part of the general cash assets of the company.

legal ∼. One which is required by law. A life insurance company, for example, may be required to retain a certain percentage of its funds as a *legal reserve* to meet its future policy claim obligations. A bank is required to hold a certain proportion of its deposits as a *legal reserve*, rather than use it to make loans. See also RESERVE (2), below.

operating ∼. One which is set aside out of operating income to meet those current expenses which cannot be identified in advance but which are bound to occur, such as freight overcharges, product loss and damage, minor injury and damage claims, etc. It is sometimes distinguished from a CONTINGENCY RESERVE, which see above, in that it covers expense items, rather than losses to assets.

replacement ∼. One set up to accumulate funds for the replacement of specific capital assets, such as production machinery, or plant buildings. A *replacement reserve* may differ from a DEPRECIATION RESERVE, which see above, in several ways. It is always intended for the actual replacement of the particular assets in connection with which it is accumulated, not merely as a transfer of funds from one account to another. It may be accumulated at a faster rate, due to expected obsolescence of the equipment, or accelerated wear and tear, than that set by the tax laws or other regulations for a normal depreciation fund. To the extent that a *replacement reserve* exceeds the annual allowance for depreciation it is not tax-deductible at the time the money is set aside.

sinking fund ∼. One set up for the purpose of redeeming long-term debts when they mature. The terms of the debt may call for the establishment of such a *reserve* fund. See also SINKING FUND.

statutory ∼. A LEGAL RESERVE, which see above.

tax ∼. One set aside out of income during the accounting period, to pay taxes based on business activity during the period but which are not due to be paid until the close of the period or later. Some companies may invest the *reserve* funds in TAX ANTICIPATION NOTES, so that the money tied up earns interest.

valuation ∼. One set aside to provide for a possible increase in the value of the company's assets, as a result of a VALUATION or APPRAISAL.

2. In banking, the percentage of a bank's total deposits which it is required to keep in lawful money, rather than use to make loans. The Federal Reserve Board sets requirements for the *reserves* which its member banks must keep on deposit with the Federal Reserve bank of their respective districts. State laws also set *reserve* requirements for banks chartered to do business within the state. In the Federal Reserve System, the heaviest *reserves* are required of member banks in the central reserve cities of New York and Chicago. Banks in other reserve cities are required to hold smaller *reserves,* and those in non-reserve cities, known as country banks, carry still lower *reserves.* See also FEDERAL RESERVE SYSTEM.

excess ∼. Those *reserve* funds of a member bank of the Federal Reserve System which are over and above the minimum requirement for its class of bank set by the Federal Reserve Board. The level of *excess reserves* in the banks in a region or in the country is a rough measure of the availability of bank credit in the area covered by the figures.

reserve bank. See FEDERAL RESERVE SYSTEM.

reserve city. One of the approximately fifty cities designated by the FEDERAL RESERVE BOARD for purposes of administering member banks and setting reserve requirements. See also FEDERAL RESERVE SYSTEM.

reserved surplus. See SURPLUS, APPROPRIATED.

reserve for bad debts. See under BAD DEBT.

reserve note. See FEDERAL RESERVE NOTE.

reserve price. See under PRICE.

reserve value. The value built up in a life insurance policy which has been in effect for a number of years. It is due to the accumulation of that part of the premium paid which is in excess of the premium required to provide pure, or term insurance. If the policyholder should surrender the policy, a SURRENDER CHARGE is deducted from the *reserve value* to determine the CASH SURRENDER VALUE of the policy.

residence. The place in which a person resides or lives; the dwelling unit which a person normally occupies. The various state laws differ on the definition of *residence* for purposes of voting, taxation, doing business in the state, etc. A person may have more than one legal *residences* for business or personal use, but may have only one voting *residence.* See also DOMICILE.

resident. A person who lives, works, carries on a business, votes, or is subject to taxes in a given place, depending on the particular law involved. A person may be a *resident* of several places at the same time for the same or different purposes, and may be considered a *non-resident* of a place for some purposes though he is a *resident* for other purposes. State laws differ considerably on the subject.

residuary. Pertaining to a RESIDUE, or remainder; that which is left over. The portion that is not specifically disposed of in any other way. See each of the following under the principal listing: ∼ ESTATE (1); ∼ LEGACY.

residuary clause. The term for the clause in a will in which the person making the will directs the disposition of that part of his estate which has not been otherwise disposed of through specific bequests. If a will should not dispose of any amounts remaining after specific bequests, they would be distributed according to the STATUTE OF DISTRIBUTION in most states.

residue. The remainder; a remnant after part has been removed or disposed of. For example, the *residue* of an estate is that part which remains after all expenses and debts have been paid, and after all specific bequests have been satisfied.

resource. 1. Wealth, or a source of wealth; an

ASSET. Anything of value belonging to a person or company; especially anything in the form of money, or that can easily be converted into money. The *resources* of a bank, for example, are the total of its deposits, capital, surplus, and undivided profits, or, in other words, the total of its assets less any operating liabilities.

2. In business, especially in retailing, a source of supply; a regular supplier. A department store, for example, usually has a number of regular *resources* or suppliers with which it deals for each category of goods it buys.

respondent. In law, a term for the defendant in a case at EQUITY. Also, in an appeal, the party who contends against the APPELLANT. Thus, the appellant and *respondent* stand in the same relationship as the PLAINTIFF and DEFENDANT.

respondentia. A term for the security which is put up against a loan under the process of HYPOTHECATION. More specifically, the cargo of a ship, which is thus placed as security, or hypothecated. Frequently, however, the term BOTTOMRY, which originally referred only to the ship itself as security, is used to refer to both the ship and its cargo. See also BOND (1), RESPONDENTIA.

responsible. In general, answerable, or accountable. Hence, in one sense, reliable, or qualified. A person who is financially *responsible*, for example, is one who is able to meet his obligations, and a *responsible* bidder is one who is qualified, both by financial resources and capability, to do the work for which he is bidding. In another sense, liable, or legally held accountable; obliged to pay a sum of money as a result of a judgment or other action. A husband, for example, may be held *responsible* for his wife's debts.

restitution. In law, the enforced return of something, or its equivalent value in money, to its rightful owner. A person who has been convicted of fraud or embezzlement, for example, may be required to make *restitution* of the funds he wrongfully obtained.

restraining order. In some states, a form of court order which the court may issue in an INJUNCTION proceeding, requiring the defendant to halt the disputed action until the question can be decided. The *restraining order* remains in force until the injunction is either granted or denied. In some states, however, a temporary injunction is granted in the same circumstances and for the same purposes.

restraint of trade. As defined under the antitrust laws, any action, by agreement or by a combination, which tends, or is calculated to eliminate competition, or to reduce or restrict free trade, or to create a monopoly, or to restrict prices, and so forth. See also COMBINATION IN RESTRAINT OF TRADE; AGREEMENT IN RESTRAINT OF TRADE.

restrictive endorsement. See under ENDORSEMENT (2).

resulting trust. See under TRUST (1).

retail. Originally, from the French, to cut off a small piece; to portion out in small amounts. Hence, to sell in small quantities, rather than in gross, or at WHOLESALE. As used, the term implies sale for final consumption, rather than for resale, or for further processing. In some trades, such as hardware, the distinction is sometimes made between sales in package lots and sales of less than an unbroken package, the former being considered at wholesale and the latter at *retail*.

retailer. A business which sells goods at RETAIL. As defined by the Bureau of the Census, a business establishment engaged primarily in selling merchandise directly to personal, household, and farm users. Under the Census definition, places of business operated by companies or membership clubs, and open only to their employees or members, such as a school cafeteria, factory store, or country club bar, are not included. See also RETAIL STORE.

  non-store ~. As defined by the Census Bureau, a *retailer* making sales at the customer's home, or at a place of business, or by MAIL-ORDER. The three principal types of *non-store retailer* are DIRECT SELLING or door-to-door distributors, merchandise VENDING MACHINE operators, and MAIL-ORDER distributors.

retailing. In general, the business of selling goods at RETAIL. Also, the skills, activities, special knowledge, etc., which make up the occupation or profession of selling at retail.

retail markup. See MARKUP.

retail method. See under INVENTORY VALUATION.

retail price. See under PRICE.

retail sales branch. See under SALES BRANCH.

retail store. As defined by the Bureau of the Census, a business establishment engaged primarily in selling merchandise directly to personal, household, and farm users, at RETAIL. In present census usage, the term does not include establishments primarily providing a service, such as shoe repair, laundry, etc., which are considered to be service establishments; nor does it include mail-order or direct selling businesses, which are classed as non-store retailers. See also RETAIL TRADE;

RETAILER. The several major types and classifications of *retail stores* are listed and defined below.

chain $\sim$. One which is a member of a group or association of stores which are similarly identified, and which may carry similar brands or makes of goods. The store may be a member of a true CHAIN, owned and operated by the same company as the other stores in the *chain*, or it may be a member of a VOLUNTARY CHAIN, as an independent store associated with others in common purchasing, promotion, and other activities.

department $\sim$. In general, one handling a wide variety of goods, which is divided into departments for purposes of purchasing, promotion, merchandising, and control. Specifically, as used in statistics, a store selling several varieties of apparel and other consumer soft goods, as well as home furnishings, as distinguished from a SPECIALTY STORE, which see below, which does not handle home furnishings.

five-and-ten cent $\sim$. See LIMITED PRICE VARIETY STORE, below.

general merchandise $\sim$. One of various types of stores carrying a combination of several classes of goods, such as apparel, dry goods, furniture, home furnishings, housewares, hardware, food, etc. It includes DEPARTMENT STORES, which see above, and VARIETY STORES, which see below.

limited line $\sim$. See SPECIALTY STORE, below.

limited price variety $\sim$. A form of VARIETY STORE, which see below, specializing in merchandise which can be sold at a limited number of prices, such as five cents, ten cents, one dollar, etc. Many such stores indicate this in their name, such as, five-and-ten, dime-to-dollar, etc. In current practice, however, such stores frequently carry goods in a wide price range, and are distinguished from DEPARTMENT STORES, which see above, more by their self-service features than by their selection of merchandise.

specialty $\sim$. In general, one specializing in a restricted or limited class or type of goods, as distinguished from a GENERAL MERCHANDISE STORE, which see above. Examples include floor covering *specialty stores,* childrens' wear *specialty store,* etc. Specifically, when not otherwise qualified, the term usually refers to a store specializing in apparel and other consumer soft goods, such as bedding, draperies, etc., as distinguished from a DEPARTMENT STORE, which see above, which also carries home furnishings.

variety $\sim$. One selling a wide variety or assortment of consumer goods, usually in a low and limited price range. It is characterized by a high degree of self-service, and open counter display of merchandise. Most variety stores are now members of chains of LIMITED PRICE VARIETY STORES, which see above.

retail trade. Broadly, the business of RETAILING. More particularly, the dollar volume of sales made by RETAIL STORES during a specified time period, or in a specified area. In current statistics, the Department of Commerce distinguishes between *retail trade,* which refers primarily to merchandise, and SERVICE TRADE, which consists primarily of consumer services, such as barbering, laundry, shoe repair, etc.

retain. Literally, to hold, to hold back, or to keep custody of. Hence, in business, to engage the services of a person, especially of a member of one of the professions, such as a lawyer, architect, or accountant, usually on a fee basis. Actually, services may be *retained* for a particular case or project, but the term has come to imply a continuing relationship.

retained earnings. See SURPLUS, EARNED.

retained income. See SURPLUS, EARNED.

retained risk. In insurance, the amount of the insurance on a given RISK or property which is covered by an insurance company on its own account, after part of the coverage has been reinsured. See also REINSURANCE.

retainer. The term for a fee paid to a professional person, such as a lawyer or architect, for his services. Also, the form of contract providing for the payment of such fee. A general *retainer* may cover any work that is done or required over a specified period of time, while a special *retainer* usually covers work on a particular case or project. Normally, one of the terms of a *retainer* agreement is that the person engaged will not accept similar or competitive work for any other employer during the period covered.

retire. 1. To withdraw from work or business, normally as the result of reaching a specified age. Many companies and government departments provide for voluntary *retirement* at a stated age, and for compulsory *retirement* at a stated later age. However, *retirement* may also be for medical or other reasons, and may take place at any age, as long as the person involved actually withdraws from activity with the intention of not returning. See also PENSION.

2. With respect to securities, or an obligation, to withdraw from circulation; to recall or redeem; to pay off completely. For example, the terms of a bond issue may provide that it may be *retired* before maturity

under certain circumstances, or a company may decide to *retire* all of its outstanding preferred stock after the need for it has passed. Similarly, a BILL OF EXCHANGE or other instrument is *retired* by being paid in full before or at maturity. See also BOND (1), CALLABLE; STOCK, PREFERRED.

retiring partner. See under PARTNER.

retrenchment. A cutting down, or cutting back. As usually used, a reduction or restriction in operations and the elimination of expenses in an attempt to reduce costs, or to conserve capital by bringing expenditures into line with income.

retrospective. Literally, looking backward; taking the past into account. Hence, a *retrospective* law is one which takes past events, acts, or behavior into account. Depending on the particular terms of such a law, it may be declared unconstitutional as EX POST FACTO legislation under Article I of the Constitution. See also PROSPECTIVE.

~ **appraisal.** One prepared as of some particular date in the past, and referring back to values and costs at the past time. Such an APPRAISAL would primarily be required to establish the previous value of property for taxation purposes, or in the settlement of an estate, when property is to be divided according to its value at the time of preparation of a will.

~ **rating.** In insurance, a RATING OR PREMIUM charge set at the end of the period covered by the insurance, and based on losses or claims during the period, as distinguished from an EXPERIENCE RATING, which is based on losses in the past. Such rating methods are sometimes used in WORKMEN'S COMPENSATION insurance when a company has enough employees to make its current experience stable enough to serve as a basis for premiums, and, rarely, for other forms of insurance involving large numbers of relatively small losses.

return. 1. A profit, yield, or earnings; the rate of profit on sales or on investment. See also RETURN ON INVESTMENT.

2. An item of merchandise brought back or sent back by a customer for refund, exchange, or credit toward a future purchase. In the calculation of net sales, such *returns* are deducted from gross sales. See also SALES.

3. A report or statement, especially a report of income, expenses, and taxes due, prepared by a taxpayer and forwarded with the required tax payment.

joint ~. One filed by a husband and wife, reporting the total income of both, and taking advantage of whatever deductions and allowances may be taken by persons so filing.

Under present federal income tax regulations, a husband and wife may file a *joint return* even though one of them actually earned all of the income reported.

separate ~. One filed by a husband or wife alone, reporting only his or her income and share of expenses. Under the federal income tax regulations, it may be advantageous for a husband and wife to file *separate returns* under certain special circumstances. In addition, the income tax laws of some states require the filing of *separate returns* in all cases.

return on investment. In general, the profit earned in relation to the value of the capital required to produce the profit. A concept used in business planning, under which the choice between alternative proposals for investment of a company's capital is made at least partly on the basis of the relative profitability of the various choices. The concept is similarly used to compare the profitability of different departments, or the profitability of the company at one time with its profitability at later and earlier times.

revalorization. A term for the re-establishment or restoration, in whole or in part, of the original value of the monetary unit of a country's currency, after it has previously been devalued.

revenue. The total INCOME of an operation, especially the total income of a governmental unit, from taxes, licenses, and other sources. With respect to non-governmental operations, *revenue* is sometimes used as income other than that from the sale of goods or merchandise. For example, the income of public utilities, railroads, etc., is frequently referred to as *revenue*.

revenue bond. See under BOND (1).

revenue freight. See under FREIGHT.

revenue tariff. See under TARIFF (2).

revenue stamp. A seal or STAMP placed on an article or container, or on a document, to indicate that a required tax has been paid. Such a stamp is required, for example, on alcoholic beverages, cigarettes, playing cards, and other products subject to excise taxes, and on various legal documents subject to transfer taxes. See also TAX.

revenue ton-mile. See under TON-MILE.

reverse split. In the securities trade, a term for a reduction in the number of shares of stock outstanding, with no change in the amount of capital, achieved by the calling in of all shares of stock and the issue of new shares at a rate of less than one share for each share of the old stock held. See also STOCK SPLIT.

reversion. In law, the return to an owner, or to an estate, of a portion of the property or estate which had been held by another under an ESTATE FOR YEARS, or some other form of estate which will terminate. Also, the right which the owner of the property has to property which is held under an estate which will terminate.

reversionary interest. Any interest or claim which a person may keep to property or income which has been assigned to another. For example, the grantor of a TRUST may insert a clause providing that he may revoke the trust under certain circumstances, and thus keep a *reversionary interest* in the property or assets of the trust. Such an interest may nullify the special tax treatment granted to a gift under the federal income tax laws. See also TRUST, REVOCABLE.

revocable. Subject to being withdrawn, cancelled, or revoked by the person granting or initiating the original instrument or privilege. See also IRREVOCABLE. See each of the following under the principal listing: ∼ CREDIT (3); ∼ LETTER OF CREDIT; ∼ POWER OF ATTORNEY; ∼ TRUST (1).

revocation. In general, the recall of a power, right, or authority originally conferred on an agent, attorney, licencee, etc. Also, the right which any person who makes an offer or proposal for an agreement or contract has to withdraw or revoke his proposal at any time before its definite ACCEPTANCE (1).

revolving. In financial arrangements, subject to constant or continuous automatic renewal without additional negotiation. For example, a *revolving* FUND of any sort is one made available in a specific original amount, but which is constantly renewed as it is used. A *revolving* fund may be established by a company to make loans to employees, with new loans made from the fund as others are repaid. See also CREDIT (3), REVOLVING; FUND (2), REVOLVING.

reward. Broadly, any compensation or pay for services rendered. As generally used, any special compensation for a service not included in normal activities. For example, a *reward* may be offered for the return of a lost article, for the capture of a criminal, etc.

RFC. See RECONSTRUCTION FINANCE CORPORATION.

rider. An addition or attachment to a document. In insurance, an additional clause, table, or schedule prepared in advance and attached to a standard insurance policy to increase or limit its coverage of specific risks, to increase the amount of the face value of the policy, or to add or remove any special provisions. By agreement between the insured and insurer, a *rider* becomes part of the policy itself. In legislation, an addition made to a bill being considered which is not directly related to the main purpose of the bill itself. See also ENDORSEMENT (1).

rigging. In the securities trade, the practice of manipulating or inflating the price of a stock by such devices as WASH SALES, CHURNING, the spreading of rumors, etc., so that the price bears no relation to the actual value of the stock. Speculators may act to create a *rigged* market in a particular stock in order to dispose of large quantities of it to unsuspecting purchasers at the inflated price.

right. 1. In the securities trade, a privilege given to a stockholder to purchase additional shares of the same stock at a fixed price for a given period of time. Typically, a corporation may issue *rights* to its stockholders when it wants to increase its capital stock without putting additional shares on the open market. The *rights* usually set a price below the current market price, and therefore have a value in themselves. They are normally transferrable, and are dealt in on the open market until their expiration date. Strictly, a *right* differs from a WARRANT (4) in that it gives the holder the privilege of buying additional shares of the same security, while a warrant may give holders of preferred stock the privilege of buying common stock, etc. Also, a warrant is usually issued along with the security to which it is attached, while a *right* is usually distributed at a later time.
2. In law, any power or privilege which an individual properly holds; any interest or claim in property which an individual may have. Such a power or privilege may exist in common law, or by statute, or both. See also INTEREST (1); CLAIM (1).

    legal ∼. The capacity or ability which any person has to act, or to control the actions of others, which has the assent or assistance of the state; any *right* which is recognized or created by statute, and which the state will enforce under its laws.

right in action. In general, any right to receive or to recover a debt or obligation, or monetary damages awarded. In legal usage, the evidence of such right, such as an invoice, bill, note, or other instrument, is also referred to as a *right in action*. The term CHOSE in action is sometimes used in legal terminology.

right of way. The right to cross or operate over the property of another, or over public property, which may be given to a person by law, or by a court decision. Also, the property itself, over which a railroad, for example, may be given rights or outright title, to enable it to cross what was formerly private property. More generally, any property on which a railroad line runs, including both the tracks and the flanking property on each side, whether or not originally acquired in an action to obtain a *right of way.*

ring. In business slang, any group or COMBINATION of individuals joined together in a transaction or other venture; especially such a group joined for the purpose of manipulating or controlling prices, or supply and demand in a particular field.

ringing out (or up). In the commodities trade, the practice among brokers and commission merchants of contacting each other periodically to settle or clear outstanding futures contracts by exchanging sale and purchase contracts among themselves before the contracts mature and become deliverable. For example, broker B may find that he has made an agreement to purchase in the future from broker A, and at the same time has made an agreement to sell the same commodity to broker C. Meanwhile, C may have agreed to sell the same commodity to broker A. In this case, the ring is complete, and the entire transaction can be cleared. If the ring is incomplete, however, most of the parties involved may still be able to clear up their commitments by the *ringing out* process.

riot. In general, any violent disorder or disturbance of the peace by a number of persons together. In some states, the law sets this number at three persons, in others at two persons. The traditional English *riot act,* which is frequently referred to, provided that any twelve or more persons who refused to disperse were guilty of a *riot.*

riparian rights. The rights which an owner of land bordering on a river or stream has, under the common law. These include such things as the right to fish the stream, to put watercraft on its surface, etc. Also, the right such a property owner has to any land or soil deposited by the action of the stream. The similar rights relating to property on the shore of a lake or other still body of water are known as LITTORAL rights.

risk. 1. In general, any element of uncertainty, or possibility of loss, which is inherent in any activity. The typical *risks* of business enterprise include price fluctuations, shifts in demand, the financial condition of customers, the ability to obtain materials, and so on.

2. In insurance, a term used with various meanings. Strictly speaking, it is the prospective amount of loss likely or possible from a particular danger or HAZARD. More loosely, the degree of such danger, as when a property is referred to as a high-grade *risk,* or an insured person is referred to as a poor *risk* due to the condition of his health. Hence, in insurance trade usage, the property or person insured. When an insurance company is said to refuse to carry a *risk,* for example, the meaning is that it has refused to insure a particular piece of property or a particular life, rather than that it has refused to insure any particular amount of *risk* or loss.

risk capital. See CAPITAL (2), VENTURE.

risk classification. See CLASSIFICATION OF RISKS.

risk management. In modern usage, that branch of management concerned with eliminating, minimizing, or insuring against all of the risks faced by a business in the course of carrying on its affairs, other than those which are the concern of management judgment itself. The duties of a *risk manager,* for example, may include safety, credit management, accident prevention, plant security, and so forth, aside from the actual purchase of the proper insurance where necessary. See also INSURANCE MANAGEMENT.

roadstead. An anchorage for ships, providing safe anchorage in protected waters, and access to shore, but not direct loading and unloading facilities. Ships anchored in a *roadstead* may be loaded and unloaded by LIGHTERS, or may wait for wharf facilities to become available.

robbery. In law, the felonious taking of personal property from a person's possession or immediate presence. Thus, *robbery* is a form of THEFT, and is distinguished from BURGLARY, which always involves breaking and entering a home or other property. See also LARCENY; EMBEZZLEMENT.

Robinson-Patman Act. The federal law, passed in 1936 and since amended, which further extends the coverage of the anti-trust laws. The principal sections of the act prohibit price discrimination between customers, unequal advertising or promotion allowances, price reductions or concessions not justified by costs, etc. The act also prohibits misrepresentative or misleading advertising, unreasonable sales inducements, and similar actions or practices likely to lessen free competition.

rock-bottom. In business slang, the minimum, the lowest possible level, or that below which one is not willing to go under any circumstances. A seller's *rock-bottom* price, for example, is the very lowest at which he will agree to sell his goods or services

Similarly, a contractor's *rock-bottom* bid or offer is the lowest at which he will agree to perform the work for which he is bidding.

Rockwell hardness. A standard method and scale for measuring the hardness or impenetrability of a metal. It is measured in proportion to the depth of penetration of a steel ball, or of a diamond pointed tool, under a specified controlled load. See also BRINELL HARDNESS.

rod. In surveyors' measure, a unit of length equivalent to 16½ feet, or 5½ yards. It is equal to one linear PERCH.

roll. Originally, a strip of parchment in cylindrical form, used for listing persons or things, or for official proclamations. Hence, any list of names or of objects. A tax *roll*, for example, may be a list of persons to be taxed, or a list of the taxable real property in a community, with its valuation or amount of tax due.

roll back. A term for an order by the government, such as might be issued during a period of national emergency, calling on sellers to reduce prices or profit margins to a level below that which prevails at the time the order is issued. It refers especially to an order to reduce prices back to the level prevailing at some specified previous date. See also PRICE CONTROL; PRICE, ROLL BACK.

rolling stock. In railroading, all of the wheeled property of a railroad, including not only passenger and freight cars, locomotives, and tenders, but also work cars, derricks and cranes on wheels, etc. In other words, the term includes any property of the railroad which will move on its own wheels on the tracks of the road.

rood. In land measure, one fourth of an acre, or 40 square RODS or PERCHES. It contains 1,210 square yards. A *rood* is almost exactly one tenth of a HECTARE, the metric land measure most commonly used on the European continent.

ROP. See RUN-OF-PAPER.

Rotary Club. One of a large number of local associations of business and professional people, established in many towns and cities throughout the world. Membership usually consists of one representative of each of the businesses, trades, and professions in the town. To accommodate additional members, however, it is common for local clubs to subdivide various trades and professions rather finely. The creed of *Rotary* is "He profits most who serves best," and the aim of the local clubs is to promote service, peace, and goodwill. The first club was formed in Chicago in 1905, and the various clubs are now members of *Rotary International*.

rotogravure. See INTAGLIO.

round lot. In the securities and commodities trades, the standard unit, quantity, or number of shares in which a security or commodity is normally traded. In the case of stocks, for example, a *round lot* is 100 shares; for bonds it is usually $1,000; in cocoa, 30,000 pounds, etc. See also ODD LOT.

round transaction. In securities trade usage, a transaction involving the sale of a lot of securities and the prompt reinvestment of the proceeds, or sometimes, the purchase of a security and the prompt sale of another or of the security purchased. In either case, a transaction which leaves the investor's total investment the same as before. It is also sometimes known as a round trade, or round turn.

route. In general, any established course, way, or road, such as that over which a shipment of goods is moved. In commerce, an established geographic order for the delivery of goods or services, or for the soliciting of sales. Such consumer goods or services as milk, baked goods, laundry, newspapers, etc., are commonly sold and delivered over regular *routes*.

route man. The term for a combination salesman and delivery man, who serves an established route or list of customers. A milk salesman, for example, who takes orders, delivers the milk himself, and then makes collections for the milk sold, is a typical *route man*. See also COMMERCIAL TRAVELLER.

routing. The process of directing a shipment of goods over a specified route and by specified carriers, or the directing of a work order through the various steps of processing, manufacture, or assembly. Also, the sequence of routes or processes themselves, through which the shipment or order is directed.

royal octavo. See under BOOK SIZES.

royalty. Originally, a right or prerogative granted by the crown to a person or company, especially a right over mineral lands. Hence, a payment made to the crown for the privilege of exercising such a right. As currently used, any payment made or demanded for some privilege or right. Examples include the payments made by mine or oil well operators to land owners under mineral leases, the payments made by licensees to the holder of a patent on a licensed invention, and the payments made by publishers to authors for the privilege of publishing and selling their works. The term is also used to describe the payments made by an employer to a union health or welfare fund, when these are based on the amount or value of production, such as the number of tons of coal mined, the number of phonograph records sold, etc.

rubber check. An expression for a bad check; that is, one which has been returned by a bank because there were insufficient funds on deposit in the account against which it has been drawn. The expression arises from the fact that the check has BOUNCED; that is, has been refused at the bank. See also INSUFFICIENT FUNDS; NO FUNDS.

ruin. The condition or state of a business which has become completely BANKRUPT, or which is in such poor financial condition that it cannot continue, whether or not formal bankruptcy proceedings are started.

rules of fair practice. Any of several sets of rules established by the members of particular industries or trades, as guides for the behavior of their members. Such sets of rules are usually drawn up under the sponsorship of the Federal Trade Commission, and are aimed at assuring that the members of the industry concerned will not violate the various anti-trust and unfair competition laws.

run. 1. To operate, administer, or to conduct a business, plant, or industrial process. A proprietor *runs* his business, and a machine operator *runs* his machine.

2. A continuous period of operation of a machine, process, or plant, or the continuous operation on a batch or lot of work pieces or materials. Also, the production turned out during such a continuous period of operation. When reference is made to a *run* of goods, for example, it means the goods turned out in the same continuous period of operation.

3. In banking, a sudden and heavy demand by depositors for their funds, prompted by rumors or by panic. Since a large proportion of deposits are out on loan at any one time, such a *run* may force a bank to close its doors temporarily.

runaway shop. In labor relations usage, the term for a business, plant, or factory which has been relocated to avoid signing a union contract, or to avoid the terms of state labor legislation. In the textile and apparel industries, especially, many such *runaway shops* have left the New England and Middle

Atlantic states over a period of years, and relocated in the South.

runner. In retail merchandising, the term for a best selling item, especially one which develops such a heavy sales volume that it is continually kept in stock. Any item which is continually in demand, and on which sales may be run frequently with assurance of satisfactory volume; a NEVER-OUT.

running account. See ACCOUNT (4), OPEN.

running day. See under DAY.

running down clause. See COLLISION CLAUSE.

running expense. See EXPENSE (2), CURRENT.

running inventory. See INVENTORY, PERPETUAL.

run-of-mill. In general, taken or offered as it comes from the normal output. Not selected, graded, or sorted; average or routine. A *run-of-mill* shipment of goods, for example, is one that includes all qualities of goods, as turned out by the particular factory or plant making the shipment. In some fields, however, *run-of-mill* has come to mean ordinary quality, with the better grades removed and sold separately. Similarly, a *run-of-mill* performance is one which is ordinary or mediocre.

run-of-mine. With regard to coal, or sometimes to other minerals, not sorted, graded, or selected; in mixed sizes and qualities, as produced at the mine. The term is sometimes used in price quotations and orders as mine run.

run-of-paper (ROP). In newspaper advertising, a term for advertising accepted with the understanding that it will be placed wherever convenient for the newspaper, rather than in any particular or specified position or section. As a matter of practice, most newspapers will attempt to place such advertising as requested by the advertiser, such as in the news, sports, or women's pages, but no promises to this effect are made. In another sense, when a newspaper states that color is available for use *ROP,* it means that color advertising will be accepted for any page in the paper, since all of the presses are equipped to print in color. See also PREFERRED POSITION.

run with. In legal usage, to be legally attached to, or to pass together with another right or obligation. It may be said, for example, that the obligation to maintain property *runs with* the title to the property, or that the privilege of using the waters of a lake *runs with* the ownership of land on its shores.

S

sabotage. The malicious destruction, waste, or damage of industrial property or equipment, or the obstruction and interference with normal operations, typically during an industrial dispute or strike. Such acts are, of course, illegal, and today are likely to be resorted to only by extremists, to enforce their demands. The term is said to derive from the practice of French workers, who used their wooden shoes, or *sabots,* to damage textile machinery during disputes in the early days of the industrial revolution.

sack. 1. An inexact measure of volume or of weight, which varies considerably from place to place and commodity to commodity. Generally, in this country, a grain *sack* contains 140 pounds, but it may be more or less.

2. In slang usage, to fire or discharge a worker. The term is usually used in the passive, as "he was *sacked,*" or "he got the *sack.*" The usage is believed to have originated in the early days of industrialization, when a discharged worker was literally given a *sack* in which to carry away his tools and belongings.

sacrifice. To sell at a loss, or at a great reduction in profit, usually for the claimed purpose of raising needed cash or of liquidating excess stocks. Hence, a *sacrifice* sale is one in which goods are advertised as selling far below their usual price, with the implication that the sale has been forced on the merchant by circumstances.

SAE. The Society of Automotive Engineers. The initials are used to designate various standards for motor oils, fuels, alloys, etc., which are set by the Society for the automotive industry.

safe deposit box. A box or compartment in the vault of a SAFE DEPOSIT COMPANY, or the safe deposit department of a bank or trust company, in which valuables may be stored for safekeeping. Boxes may usually be rented on a yearly basis by individuals, businesses, or other organizations.

safe deposit company. A corporation formed for the purpose of maintaining vaults for the deposit, storage, and safekeeping of valuables, in which individual compartments or boxes are rented to customers. The valuables usually stored in such vaults include jewelry, securities, valuable papers, etc.

safely landed. As used in marine insurance contracts, a term meaning landed without damage, and in the manner customary at a given port, within a reasonable time after arrival at the port.

safety factor. 1. In engineering, the extra strength allowed for in the design of a structure or part, beyond the greatest expected or permitted load. Hence, any allowance made in an estimate or forecast for unforeseen circumstances.

2. In finance, the ratio of total interest on funded debt to net income after payment of such interest. It is a measure of the adequacy of net income to cover charges against it. See also OPERATING RATIO.

safety margin. See MARGIN OF SAFETY.

safety of principal. In investment, the preservation of original capital, a factor in the choice of particular investments. By choosing a security which is not likely to depreciate in price, the investor obtains *safety of principal,* though usually in exchange for sacrificing higher income and opportunities for capital gains. See also INVESTMENT.

sag. In the securities and commodities trades, a slight decline or weakening in prices, such as might be due to a lack of adequate demand. Trading characterized by such mildly declining prices, due to lack of demand or selling pressure, is called a *sagging* market.

salable (or **saleable**). Capable of being sold. Fit or eligible for sale in normal trade, at usual selling prices; readily marketable.

salaried employee. As used in employment statistics and regulations, an employee whose compensation is based on fixed time periods, such as a week, month, or year, without regard to the actual hours worked or amount of work performed. The term is often loosely used to indicate an employee not eligible for overtime pay.

salary. Originally, the *salarium,* or salt allowance paid to Roman soldiers. Hence, any allowance or compensation paid for services over a fixed time period, typically for those services of an executive, professional, or clerical nature. It is distinguished from WAGES in that the latter are usually paid for skilled or unskilled labor, and are based on an hourly rate or on production; and from COMMISSIONS, which are paid on the basis of sales or profit volume. In many cases, however, the differentiation is not sharp and the three terms may be used synonymously.

sale. 1. A contract or agreement between two parties, known respectively as the seller or vendor, and the buyer or purchaser, by which the former, in consideration of payment, or the promise of payment, of a certain price in money, transfers to the latter title and possession of property. In law, a complete *sale* consists of two elements; the contract, including the offer, the price, the object of the *sale,* the acceptance of the offer, etc.; and the transfer itself of the property and title from seller to buyer, together with the payment of the agreed price.

A *sale* is distinguished from BARTER or EXCHANGE, which imply the transfer of property in exchange for property, while a *sale* is always for a money consideration. It is distinguished from a GIFT, in that a gift involves no consideration. A conditional gift may in fact be a *sale* if the conditions attached involve money and are sufficiently ONEROUS. It is distinguished from a BAILMENT in that this contemplates a return of the property or its equivalent to the bailor, while a *sale* is final. Similarly, it is distinguished from a RENTAL or LEASE, which provide for the temporary transfer of property but not its title.

absolute ∽. A *sale* which involves no conditions on the part of either the seller or buyer.

adjourned ∽. A *sale* the completion of which has been postponed to a future date by order of a court or a proper official.

as-is ∽. See SALE WITH ALL FAULTS, below.

bailment ∽. A form of conditional *sale* in which a bailee accepts property under an option to keep or to return the property. The *sale* may be completed by the bailee announcing his intention of adopting the purchase option, or by his failure to exercise the option to return the property within the time set. See also BAILMENT; SALE ON APPROVAL, below.

cash ∽. One in which payment is to be made in full in advance or on receipt of the goods. In some lines of trade, *sales* in which payment is made within some set billing period are considered *cash sales.* See also directly. See TERMS OF SALE.

conditional ∽. One in which the final transfer of title depends on the fulfillment of certain set conditions, such as the payment of a balance due, the acceptance of the goods, etc. A *conditional sale* is distinguished from a MORTGAGE in that under a mortgage the purchaser takes full title to the property, then places it as security for a loan, while under a *conditional sale,* title does not finally pass until the debt has been paid in full, or in some specified proportion.

consignment ∽. See SALE ON CONSIGNMENT, below.

forced ∽. A *sale* made without the consent of the owner, by virtue of a court order or similar action, such as under a foreclosure order. Such a sale usually results in a loss of value to the seller. At times, the term is used to describe a voluntary *sale* made at reduced prices to obtain capital or reduce inventories. See also SACRIFICE.

foreclosure ∽. See FORECLOSURE.

fraudulent ∽. A *sale* made for the purpose of defrauding creditors or assignees, by converting into cash property which would otherwise be used to satisfy their claims.

illegal ∽. A *sale* prohibited by statute on the grounds of being opposed to the public welfare and morals, or one in violation of laws governing weights and measures, taxes, gambling, etc. In general, if such a *sale* is made with intent and knowledge, the seller is liable to lose both the goods sold and the price received.

installment ∽. A form of CONDITIONAL SALE, which see above, in which the price is to be paid in regular and fixed installments, usually plus a service charge and interest. Full title does not pass until the full amount or a prescribed proportion of it has been paid, and the failure of the buyer to make an installment payment when due gives the seller the right to repossess the property. Local statutes vary concerning the exact rights of the buyer and seller under such circumstances.

judicial ∽. A *sale* made by virtue of mandate or order of a court, by an officer duly appointed for the purpose.

memorandum ∽. A form of CONDITIONAL SALE, which see above, in which the goods are delivered into the posession of the buyer but with the seller retaining title until the goods are inspected and either accepted or rejected by the purchaser. A *sale on memorandum* differs from an ordinary SALE ON APPROVAL, which see below, in that the agreement provides specifically for inspection. This form of *sale* is frequently used in commerce to encourage a buyer to order a new or not previously handled line of goods.

private ∿. A *sale* made by negotiation between a seller and buyer, rather than through the usual public notice, competitive bidding, or other means.

public ∿. A *sale* made in pursuance of a public notice, announcement, advertisement, or auction. State laws frequently require certain types of transactions to take place through *public sale*.

∿ and return. A form of CONDITIONAL SALE, which see above, in which the goods are delivered to the buyer and title passes, but with the understanding that the buyer may exercise an option to return any portion of the goods within a reasonable time and cancel their *sale*. It differs from an ordinary SALE ON APPROVAL, which see below, in that title initially passes at the time of delivery. The Uniform Commercial Code uses the phrase *sale or return* to describe this type of transaction, but the listed usage is more widely found in commerce.

∿ by description. A *sale,* such as by direct mail, in which there is an implied warranty that the goods delivered will correspond to the description of those offered for *sale*.

∿ by sample. A *sale* in which it is the understanding of both parties that the goods exhibited, upon which the *sale* is based, are representative of the goods to be delivered, and set the standard to which the delivery will conform. Such *sales* contracts are frequently used in commodities trading.

∿ in gross. A *sale* of an entire tract, or class of items, without regard to a specific quantity or weight. The agreement in such a *sale* may call for transfer of "all the fruit in a field," "all the cattle in a herd," "all of the inventory on hand," etc.

∿ on approval. A form of CONDITIONAL SALE, which see above, in which the *sale* becomes absolute if the buyer approves of or is satisfied with the goods. The approval may be constructive, as inferred from the fact that the goods are kept beyond some specified time or a reasonable period. It differs from a MEMORANDUM SALE, which see above, in that there is no specific provision for inspection, and from SALE AND RETURN, which see above, in that title does not pass on delivery.

∿ on consignment. An arrangement under which goods are delivered to a merchant with the understanding that he will not pay for them unless and until he sells them. Actually, such an arrangement is not a CONDITIONAL SALE, which see above, since the merchant is under no obligation to keep the goods, but is merely in the position of a BAILEE, until he sells the goods. Title to the goods passes only when they are sold to a final purchaser. See also CONSIGNMENT.

∿ on credit. A *sale* in which delivery is made and title passes, but full payment is deferred until some future time, usually with an interest charge on the unpaid balance. Strictly speaking, a *sale on credit* differs from an INSTALLMENT SALE in that transfer of title is not delayed pending payment.

∿ with all faults. A *sale* in which the buyer accepts the goods or property AS IS, with no guarantee of absence of imperfection, short of intentional fraud or misrepresentation on the part of the seller. Such *sales* are frequent in real estate dealings.

short ∿. See SHORT (3).

tax ∿. A *sale* of property by a tax-levying governmental unit, such as a municipality, after the property in question has been seized for non-payment of taxes. The money realized from the *sale* is used to make up the tax deficit, with any remainder going to the original owner of the property.

tie-in ∿. See directly.

voluntary ∿. A *sale* made freely, and under no constraints, by the owner of the thing sold. The opposite of a FORCED SALE.

wash ∿. See directly.

2. A special offering of goods at reduced prices; a BARGAIN (2); a CLEARANCE (3).

sale and lease-back. An arrangement whereby a company owning land, buildings, or capital equipment sells all or part of its property to a financial institution, charitable trust, or private investor, and simultaneously leases the property back under a long-term lease, usually for 20 to 50 years. From the point of view of the original owner, the purpose of such an arrangement is to obtain funds for working capital or expansion, and to convert its occupancy costs to rent, which is tax-deductible as a business expense. From the point of view of the investor, the arrangement provides a relatively safe investment at a favorable rate of return, since the lessee is usually willing to pay a generous rent. Normally, under a *sale and lease-back,* the lessee agrees to take a net lease; that is, he agrees to maintain the property, and pays such expenses as heat, utilities, taxes, insurance, etc. The lease contract may also include a renewal clause, and sometimes an option to repurchase the property. Under the 1954 Federal Tax Code, however, the inclusion of a repurchase option would convert the lease to a conditional SALE, and the tax advantages of the arrangement would be lost.

sale or return. See SALE (1) AND RETURN.

sales. 1. In accounting, the total money income received for goods and services sold. Depending on the accounting system followed, *sales* may be assigned to the time period in which the sale is made and the income earned, or to the period in which the payment is received.

    gross ∼. The total of *sales* income before deduction of any allowances or discounts granted, and before deducting the value of any goods returned.

    net ∼. The gross or total *sales* less returns, allowances, and discounts granted.

    2. In general, the process of disposing of the goods or services produced or acquired by a business organization, for money income. See each of the following under the principal listing: ∼ AGENT; ∼ ALLOWANCE (1); ∼ BUDGET; ∼ JOURNAL (1); ∼ LEDGER; ∼ RETURN (2); ∼ TAX (2).

sales account. See ACCOUNT (4).

sales bill. See under BILL OF EXCHANGE.

sales branch. A sales establishment maintained at a separate location by a manufacturer or distributor.

    manufacturer's ∼. An establishment set up by a manufacturer to handle the wholesale distribution of his product in a given territory or to a given trade. A *manufacturer's sales branch,* or factory *sales branch* usually performs the same services for the manufacturer and his customers as would an independent wholesale distributor.

    retail ∼. A retail establishment set up by a manufacturer or wholesale distributor, for demonstration or training purposes, to test new selling methods, or to serve as a yardstick for measuring the performance of regular dealers.

sales cost. See COST OF GOODS SOLD.

sales finance company. A business organization engaged primarily in the purchasing, at a discount, of the ACCOUNTS RECEIVABLE of other businesses, especially retail businesses with consumer installment accounts. The *sales finance company* then proceeds to collect the amounts due on the accounts it has bought, obtaining its income from the discount at which it purchased the accounts. The existence of such companies enables retail merchants to conduct a large volume of credit or installment sales without themselves tying up needed capital in the unpaid balances on the goods sold. They are also known as commercial credit companies. See also ACCOUNTS RECEIVABLE FINANCING; FACTOR.

sales forecast. An estimate of dollar or unit sales, for a specified product, territory, or class of sales, during some future period of time. The *sales forecast* for a particular company may be based on customer needs, salesmen's own estimates, industry trends, individual company sales growth, or a mixture of all of these and other factors.

sales management. That aspect or field of management concerned with the planning, direction, and control of the selling operations of a business organization, including the recruiting, selecting, and training of salesmen, the assignment and supervision of sale territories or market areas, the compensation and motivation of the sales force, and other matters relating to the successful sal of the company's products or services. I many companies, *sales management* also includes responsibility for advertising, market ing research, product development, an other related fields.

sales manager. The executive responsible fo the planning, direction, and control of th selling activities of a business organizatio especially the activities of the salesmen them selves. In larger companies there may b several *sales managers,* each responsible fo a particular region, product class, or type c customer.

salesmanship. The art of selling; the skill c ability of creating, on the part of potenti customers, a demand or desire for the pa ticular goods or services being sold, and translating that demand into an actual sal transaction.

sales potential. The expected or obtainable sal for the goods or services of a company, in given market, or during a given period time. It is the company's obtainable share the MARKET POTENTIAL, which is the expecte total of sales for all makes or brands of t product in the given market and time peric A *sales potential* may be an immediate short-range one, or it may be long-ran that is, the eventually obtainable level sales.

sales promotion. In general, all those activit by a company designed to increase its sa More specifically, those activities, other th selling itself, and other than direct adv tising, aimed at increasing sales. In this se it includes such activities as exhibitio special displays, the distribution of f samples, and similar efforts.

sales quota. An established sales volume g for a specified period of time, for particu products, salesmen, or markets. It may expressed in dollars or in product units. pending on its intended purpose, the *se quota* set may be the actually expec volume of sales, or it may be a higher amount, set as a goal or standard. In either case, the degree to which it is attained may be used as a means of measuring sales achievement, as a basis for sales compensation, or merely as a means of stimulating greater sales effort.

sales return journal. See under JOURNAL (1).

sales returns. See RETURN (2).

sales terms. See TERMS OF SALE.

salt. To make goods or a business offer appear to be more valuable or desirable by creating or implying false or inflated benefits or qualities. The term is derived from the practice of *salting* a claim, or the firing of a small quantity of gold into the surface of a vein of ore, using a shotgun, to make the claim appear richer to a prospective victim of a swindle.

salvage. 1. In general, that part of any property or goods which remains or has been saved after having been damaged or destroyed by wreck, fire, or other calamity.

2. In maritime practice, the allowance or payment made or claimed for saving a ship or its cargo from the perils of the sea, such as a wreck, fire, or storm. The amount of *salvage* awarded in a particular case may be determined by the maritime court on the basis of the value of the property recovered, and the amount of assistance rendered.

3. In insurance, any damaged property which is taken over by the insurance company after full payment of a claim, or which may be turned back to the insured in exchange for an agreed amount deducted from the claim settlement. Many companies prefer to keep possession of the damaged goods, rather than take full payment, in order to eliminate any chance of irregular or inferior units of their product finding their way onto the market as a result of the resale of the *salvage* goods by the insurance company.

4. In industry, any property or equipment which is no longer useful for its intended purpose, but which has more than SCRAP value. Such value is typically due to the fact that parts may be recovered and reused, though the equipment itself cannot be economically reconditioned.

salvage loss. See under LOSS (2).

salvage value. 1. In general, the residual value in any asset which is no longer useful for its intended purpose, but which has more than SCRAP value. The *salvage value* is usually dependent on the proportion of the asset which can be recovered and reconditioned for any future use. In accounting and tax practice, the estimated *salvage value* of an asset is normally deducted from its original cost before calculating the total and annual DEPRECIATION to be charged.

2. In maritime practice, the determined value of any property which has been salvaged at sea.

3. In insurance, the remaining value in property which has been damaged by an insurable cause. By agreement, the insured may keep possession of the property and the *salvage value* will be deducted from the claim, or the insurer will take over the property and dispose of it, paying the full claim.

salvor. In maritime law, the party who saves or helps save property from the perils of the sea, acting voluntarily or by request, rather than under contract for the purpose.

sample. 1. In general, a specimen of a large number of pieces, or of a large quantity of bulk material, representative of the total.

2. In business, frequently a trial amount or package specially prepared to introduce a new product or to promote its wider sale. See also SAMPLING (2).

3. In statistics, a relatively small segment of a population or universe, selected for the purpose of reaching conclusions concerning the various characteristics of the whole. In general, the effectiveness of a *sample* is measured by the extent to which it is reliable, in the sense that it gives a reasonably stable picture of the population, similar to the picture that would be shown by similarly drawn *samples;* and representative, in the sense that it includes all of the major elements found in the whole, in relative or known proportions. Various types of *samples* are used for different statistical purposes, the principal types of which are listed and defined below.

area ~. A form of PROBABILITY SAMPLE, which see below, in which the selection of groups to be sampled, and the individuals within the groups to be included in the *sample,* is done on a geographic area basis, through the selection of counties, towns, city blocks, and residences to be *sampled*.

judgment ~. The term for one in which the particular individual units included are selected on the basis of the judgment of the selector, rather than on the basis of chance or some systematic procedure. Such a *sample,* for example, might be composed of leaders of opinion, or persons who are known to have expressed average or typical views in the past.

probability ~. Any of various forms of RANDOM SAMPLE, which see below, in which different groups may be represented with different, but known probabilities or relative frequencies. The characteristic of all such *samples* is that within the selected groups, the probability of any individual being included in the *sample* is known or determinable.

purposive ~. One selected to meet a particular purpose, rather than to obtain a truly representative sampling of a population. Such a *sample,* for example, may be selected to include the most important members of a population, or those whose replies are most likely to be clear and forceful. See also JUDGMENT SAMPLE, above.

quota ~. One which is selected to be representative of a population by deliberately including individuals who have certain known characteristics, in the same proportion as these characteristics occur in the population. Since the individuals themselves are not chosen purely at random, such a *sample* cannot be scientifically analyzed with respect to its probable degree of accuracy or range of error.

random ~. One chosen in such a way that every member of the population, or every member of each sub-group included in the *sample,* has an equal opportunity to be included in the *sample* at every stage of the sampling process. Only when a *sample* or its *sub-samples* are chosen in this manner can the laws of probability be applied to measure the accuracy and range of error of the results obtained.

stratified ~. A form of PROBABILITY SAMPLE, which see above, chosen by dividing the population into groups, or strata, and selecting individuals at random within each strata. A *sample* may be *stratified* geographically, according to size of company, age of respondent, or according to some other objective criteria.

systematic ~. A variation of a RANDOM SAMPLE, which see above, in which individuals are selected by first arranging the population in some objective order, such as alphabetically or geographically, and then selecting every *n*th individual. Each individual has an equal opportunity of being selected before the sampling is begun, but not once it has started, so that a *systematic sample,* or *list sample* as it is sometimes known, is not truly a RANDOM SAMPLE.

sampling. 1. In statistics, the process of selecting and examining relatively small segments of a universe or population, for the purpose of reaching conclusions regarding the characteristics of the whole. See also SAMPLE (3).

2. In business, the practice of distributing free packages or trial portions of a new product, to introduce it to the market, to encourage prospective purchasers to find practical uses for it, or to encourage its wider sale in general. *Sampling* is an established practice in the consumer products field, and is also widely used in connection with drug products, industrial materials, etc.

sanction. 1. Originally, sacred, or inviolable. As commonly used, to approve, or to permit. For example, an act which is *sanctioned* by law is one which is approved or permitted, perhaps under stated conditions or restrictions.

2. In law, a penalty or punishment. For example, when one nation has violated a treaty or international agreement, other nations may invoke *sanctions* against it, meaning that they will take some form of punitive action, usually of an economic nature.

sans recours. See WITHOUT RECOURSE.

satisfaction. The discharge of a duty or obligation by the payment of a sum, the performance of some act, etc. As currently used, the term usually refers to a payment or performance under an order or judgment of a court. Also, the amount paid, or act performed, itself.

satisfaction piece. In law, a formal written declaration given by a creditor to a debtor stating that an indebtedness, mortgage, or legal judgment has been paid or satisfied.

saturate. Literally, to soak or charge to the point where no more can be absorbed. Hence, to *saturate* a market with advertising is to advertise in such volume that additional exposures would have no additional effect, and to *saturate* a market with goods is to make them available in such quantities that all conceivable demand will be satisfied. Similarly, *saturation* selling involves making a product available in every outlet in a area, and using every possible means of sales promotion. Such techniques may be used, for example, in an effort to obtain quick acceptance for a new product, or to fight off competition.

save. 1. In law, to reserve or hold aside; to except or exempt from otherwise expected consequences. For example, a *saving* clause in statute may exempt certain rights or acts from its provisions, and a clause in a contract may *save* one party from the consequence of his acts, or from liability for specific events.

2. In general, to preserve, or safeguard; set aside, or reserve. Hence, to *save* materials in production means to use them in such way that less is consumed, and more is preserved or reserved for future use, and *save* money is to put it aside, or to avoid using or spending it.

save-harmless. See HOLD-HARMLESS.

savings. In general, sums of money put aside, whether for future use, as a security against possible financial difficulty, or specifically to earn income. In the broadest sense, the term includes sums which are HOARDED, or simply secreted away, but statistics usually include only those funds which are invested or deposited in some recognized manner.

　　business ∼. As used in statistics on business income, that portion of income which is not distributed to suppliers, employees, creditors, stockholders, etc., but is transferred to capital or SURPLUS. See also PROFIT, UNDISTRIBUTED.

　　personal ∼. In statistics on consumer income and spending, the excess of personal income over personal consumption expenditures and taxes. It may consist of deposits in banks or savings associations, security purchases, the accumulation of life insurance reserve values, the reduction of outstanding debts, etc.

savings account. See under ACCOUNT (3).

savings and loan association. One of a number of types of mutually-owned, cooperative, savings associations, originally established for the primary purpose of making loans to members and others, usually for the purchase of real estate or homes. It may be chartered by the state, or by the federal government, in which case it is known as a *federal savings and loan association*. The deposits in such federally chartered associations are insured for up to $10,000 each by the Federal Savings and Loan Insurance Corporation. Typically, accounts in such institutions are of three types: regular savings accounts, on which interest is paid; planned accounts, in which a fixed sum is deposited at regular intervals, and on which extra interest is paid; and shares in the association, which are sold in large amounts, and on which dividends are paid. They are also known as BUILDING AND LOAN ASSOCIATIONS, home loan associations, etc.

savings bank. See under BANK.

savings bank security. See under SECURITY (1).

saving the statute. In law, an expression used to refer to the action of a creditor or other person with a claim who begins a legal action just before the expiration of the period of time set by the STATUTE OF LIMITATIONS, in order to protect his rights to press his claim in the future. For example, a creditor may have refrained from taking formal action against a customer for an unpaid account for business reasons, but may go through the steps of beginning a suit for recovery before the period for filing such a suit expires, merely to protect his position.

sc. See SCILICET.

scab. In labor slang, a worker who works under non-union conditions, or for lower than union wages. Also, one who continues working during a strike. However, a *scab* is distinguished from a FINK, who is a worker especially brought in or employed to take the place of a striking worker.

scale. 1. A balance, or weighing device. Hence, when a shipment is said to *scale* 500 pounds, it has been weighed and found to have this weight.

　　2. Any graduated measure or rule; a series or schedule of values which increases or decreases by regular amounts. For example, a *scale* of wages is a schedule of the wages to be paid for various classifications of work or degrees of skill, and to buy or sell securities ON A SCALE is to buy or sell prescribed amounts at evenly spaced price intervals as prices rise or fall.

　　3. To grade or measure according to a schedule; to increase or decrease a basic amount proportionately or according to a graduated schedule. For example, to *scale* down (or up) wages, interest, prices, etc., is to reduce or increase each level by a proportionate amount.

scalper. In general, a speculator who buys or sells to take small, quick profits; one who takes his profits off the top, as it were. In the securities and commodities markets, the *scalper* usually operates on a small scale for his own account, and is able to take a profit on smaller price movements because he pays no commissions. Also, one who makes a profit by buying up theater, sporting event, or other tickets, and reselling them at higher prices.

scalping. The practice of selling for very small profits, by reducing margins or commissions to a minimum level, in order to make larger total profits on the expected increase in volume; price-cutting.

scare buying. The heavy, unreasonable buying up of commodities which are in short supply, or are expected to be in short supply; buying to hoard. For example, when World War II began, there was an immediate outbreak of *scare buying* of such commodities as sugar, which are imported, and which the public remembered had been in short supply during World War I.

scatter diagram. In statistics, a diagram in which each item in a group, distribution, or array is portrayed as a separate point, located according to the particular values of the two variables being studied which are associated with the individual item. For example, in a *scatter diagram* of common stocks, distributed according to their market price and dividend payment, each stock would be located in the diagram according to its price, measured along one direction, and its dividend, measured in the perpendicular direction. Such a *scatter diagram* is constructed to test or demonstrate the relationship between the two variables being plotted. In this illustration, for example, it would be expected that stocks with low prices would tend to pay lower dividends, and those with higher prices pay higher dividends, so that the scatter of points representing individual stocks would tend to fall along a diagonal. See also CORRELATION.

schedule. 1. In general, a list, or table; especially one attached to or accompanying another document. Examples include the *schedule* of assets that may accompany a report on a bankruptcy, the *schedule* of prices that is included in a sales catalog, etc.

2. A detailed listing of regular or recurring events, giving the planned or expected time of occurence. Examples include a *schedule* of train or bus trips, a *schedule* of sporting events, radio programs, etc.

3. A list of planned operations, procedures, or material usages, usually including the expected or hoped for time of accomplishment of each step. For example, a machine *schedule* may list the various operations or jobs to be performed on a particular machine throughout a work period, and a shop *schedule* may list the work to be done in a plant or shop, with the timing and sequence of each phase indicated.

scheduled airline. See under AIRLINE.

scilicet. A Latin term, meaning, to wit, or that is to say, and used with this meaning in captions to clauses in some legal documents. It may be used in abbreviation, as *ss*, or *sc*.

scoop. 1. In business slang, a large profit resulting from a transaction, usually a speculative one, and usually involving advance notice over, or exclusion of competitors.

2. To beat out a rival to an advantageous position, such as being the first to obtain a news story, or the first to introduce a new product feature, or to be the successful bidder on a desirable contract.

scrap. 1. Property or equipment which no longer has any value except that of the recoverable materials contained in it. For example a machine or vehicle which is beyond repair, and which has no parts or sub-assemblies which can be SALVAGED, may be sold

for *scrap,* that is, for the value of the metal or other material it contains. See also VALUE (2), SCRAP.

2. Discarded materials; waste or trimmings. For example, in a metal stamping operation, the bits which are punched out or trimmed away from the sheet metal being worked on are *scrap,* and the bits of cloth cut away from apparel patterns are similarly *scrap.* In this sense, *scrap* is distinguished from REJECTS, which are spoiled or poor quality materials or products, not fit to be reworked, and therefore discarded. *Scrap* is intentional; rejects are not.

scrip. 1. Originally, from the Latin, any written instrument, but in current usage a certificate indicating that the bearer is entitled to some right or privilege which he has not actually received, but for which the *scrip* may be exchanged under stated conditions. For example, a city or town that is unable to meet its payroll may issue *scrip* certificates to employees, entitling them to receive the money due them at some future date. Under different conditions, shareholders in a new venture may be issued *scrip* until the actual stock certificates are ready.

2. Certificates issued in place of fractional shares of stock, when a stock dividend has been issued. Usually, such *scrip* may be bought and sold, and exchanged for actual shares when sufficient amounts are accumulated to total to one or more full shares. See also DIVIDEND, STOCK.

3. The name given to the fractional paper currency issued by the United States government during the period of the Civil War. These certificates were also known, less formally, as SHINPLASTERS due to their unwieldy size.

scrip dividend. See under DIVIDEND.

scruple. In APOTHECARIES' WEIGHT, a unit equal to 20 grains, 1/3 of a dram or 1/24 of an ounce. It is the equivalent, in the METRIC SYSTEM of 1.2976 grams.

sea. In general, the open ocean. In maritime insurance and law, it includes, as well, any bays or inlets opening into the open ocean, and the portions of rivers which are tidal. It is a broader term than HIGH SEAS, which is restricted to the *sea* beyond the low-water line, and, in international law, to the *sea* more than three miles beyond the coastline.

sea damage. In marine insurance, injury or loss to goods in ocean transit that is directly attributable to the action of the sea, as distinguished from loss that may be due to other causes, such as overheating, infestation, handling, etc.

seal. 1. Originally, from the Latin, a small image or sign. Hence, any sign or mark which is made or impressed on a document or instrument to attest to its formal execution, or to authenticate its origin. For example, a corporate *seal* is a mark or design used by a business corporation to authenticate its stocks, bonds, and other official documents.

2. To fasten or close with a *seal* or the wax impression of a *seal*. Many documents, such as wills, deeds, mortgages, etc., may be *sealed* by placing a drop of wax across two or more sheets, or across a binding ribbon or tape, and marking the wax with an embossed *seal*.

sealed and delivered. In law, a phrase used on various instruments, and usually followed by the signature of attending witnesses, attesting to the valid execution of the instrument.

sealed bid. See under BID (2).

sea mile. See MILE, NAUTICAL.

search. A step taken when title to property is to be transferred, involving the examination of available records for evidence of any ENCUMBRANCE against the property to be transferred, such as unpaid taxes, liens, judgments, etc., and for any previous deeds, mortgages, leases, and so forth. In normal procedure, such *search* is undertaken by a TITLE GUARANTY COMPANY, for a fee.

search warrant. See under WARRANT (1).

seasonal adjustment. In the treatment of statistical data, any allowance or change made in a series of weekly, monthly, quarterly, or other figures covering periods of less than one year, to compensate for changes due to seasonal factors. See also SEASONAL VARIATION; SEASONAL INDEX.

seasonal index. In statistics, a measure of the average pattern of the SEASONAL VARIATION in any activity or set of figures. There are many methods used for computing such indexes, but typically they involve determining the average level of the data during a given month over the entire period covered, and relating this average to the annual average level of the series. The index for each month or other period is usually expressed as a ratio to the average level for all months, with the average level set at 100. *Seasonal indexes* are used both to portray the seasonal pattern in a field, and as the basis of the SEASONAL ADJUSTMENT of a series of figures.

seasonal industry. In general, any field of manufacturing, processing, or similar activity in which the level of operations rises and falls periodically due to factors connected with the change of seasons. Obvious examples include the fuel industry, ice cream manufacturing, toys, food processing, etc.

seasonal tolerance. A waiving of overtime wage rates, or of limitations on hours of work, during periods of peak seasonal activity in lines of work which are seriously affected by SEASONAL VARIATIONS. Such tolerances are provided for in the federal Fair Labor Standards Act, as well as in some state labor laws and various union contracts.

seasonal variation. In economic statistics, the periodic pattern of rise and fall in any economic series which tends to repeat itself in an annual cycle. Such *seasonal variation* may be due directly to climatic factors, or it may be due to economic or social customs which are related to the calendar, but only indirectly, if at all, to the climate itself. For example, the variation in tax collections, which is a result of legislation, is as much a *seasonal variation* as the variation in soft drink consumption, which is closely related to climatic conditions.

seasoned security. See under SECURITY (1).

seat. In the securities and commodities trade, the term for a membership in a security or commodity exchange. Possession of a *seat* on an exchange entitles a member to trade directly on the exchange, or to employ someone to trade for him, and to conduct trading activities for persons who are his customers as a broker or dealer. Since the number of *seats* are limited by regulation, and a considerable income in trading commissions goes with *seat* ownership, the price of a *seat* on one of the larger security or commodity exchanges may be very high. The term derives from the fact that members of the New York Stock Exchange originally were assigned specific *seats* in the trading room.

seaworthy. In maritime usage, a term indicating that a vessel is in good repair, is properly fitted and rigged, has a capable master and crew, and is in every way ready for a voyage on the open sea. Thus, a vessel may have a sound hull and still not be *seaworthy* in the full sense of the term.

second. 1. A product or material which is of a grade or quality below the standard for a particular industry, or for its maker. In some fields, *second* is synonymous with IRREGULAR, and implies the presence of minor defects or imperfections. In other fields, however, it means simply of lower quality than the regular grade, so that one manufacturer's *second* may be of better quality than another manufacturer's FIRST, or regular product.

2. Following, later, or subordinate; junior or inferior in time or in priority. See, for example, MORTGAGE, SECOND.

3. In time measure, one 60th of a minute, or one 3600th of one hour. In circular measure, it is one 60th of a minute, or one 3600th of a degree.

secondary. Indirect, not directly connected; of less than primary importance or value. See each of the following under the principal listing: ∼ BOYCOTT; ∼ CREDITOR; ∼ STRIKE.

secondary offering. In the securities trade, a term for a sale or offering of a large block of stock, usually through an investment banker or underwriter, which stock is not a new issue but has previously been held by a large stockholder, or perhaps by the corporation itself.

second-class mail. See under POSTAL SERVICE.

second-class paper. See under COMMERCIAL PAPER.

secondhand. Not new, having previously been used; not from the original source, being offered for sale by an owner who first purchased the item in the same form in which it is being resold. Ordinarily, a sale of *secondhand* garments, equipment, or other items involves used or worn goods. In some fields, however, an item which has never been used, but has been kept in its original carton or packaging, is still *secondhand* if it is offered for sale by one who did not originally buy it specifically for resale. State laws, as well as trade regulations and customs, differ on the exact definition in particular cases.

second lien. See LIEN, JUNIOR.

second mortgage bond. See BOND (1); SECOND MORTGAGE.

second of exchange. See FIRST OF EXCHANGE.

secret. Not open, concealed; not made publicly available; kept from the knowledge of those persons likely to be affected. See each of the following under the principal listing: ∼ PARTNER; ∼ PARTNERSHIP; ∼ TRUST (1).

secretary. The officer of a corporation or other organization whose duties and responsibilities generally include the recording of all proceedings and transactions at meetings of the directors, officers, or shareholders, the issuance of all official notices or instruments by the corporation or organization, the preservation of the corporate or organizational records, and so forth. The exact duties of the *secretary* are usually set forth in the articles of incorporation, charter, or by-laws of the organization, and may be specified or limited by statute. In smaller corporations, the position of secretary is frequently combined with that of TREASURER, as *secretary-treasurer.*

secret process. In patent law, an industrial process or method which is deliberately not patented, because the owner wishes to avoid disclosing it to his competitors, who might then be able to develop a different but equally effective process. Usually, a complete description of the *secret process* is written down, dated, and witnessed, and kept in a secure place. Then, if another should independently discover the process, he could not be prevented from using it, but could be prevented from obtaining a patent by the demonstrable ANTICIPATION of the original discoverer. See also PATENT.

section. Under United States land laws, a division of land containing one square mile, or 640 acres. When the original territories were surveyed for settlement, each TOWNSHIP consisted of a square area 6 miles on each side, containing 36 sections. These were further divided into half-sections of 320 acres, and quarter-sections of 160 acres.

secular trend. In economic statistics, the long-term growth or decline of an economic series, extending over a number of BUSINESS CYCLES. The term is derived from the limited meaning of *secular,* referring to that which endures for generations, or for an age, rather than to that which is non-religious.

secured. Made safe, or backed, by a pledge or deposit of COLLATERAL, or by a LIEN; protected by a SECURITY of one sort or another. See each of the following under the principal listing: ∼ BOND (1); ∼ CREDIT (3); ∼ CREDITOR; ∼ DEBT; ∼ LIABILITY (3); ∼ LOAN; ∼ NOTE (1).

Securities and Exchange Commission. The commission created under the Securities Exchange Act of 1934, to supervise and administer the registered national SECURITIES EXCHANGES, regulate the activities of securities brokers and dealers, regulate the issuance of securities, etc. Its general objective is to protect the investing public against malpractices in the securities and financial markets. It also has special duties under the Public Utility Holding Company Act and the National Bankruptcy Act. It consists of five members, appointed by the President with the advice and consent of the Senate.

securities company. A company which depends for its income on the securities of other corporations, which it holds for investment. It may issue stocks and bonds of its own, and pay dividends and interest out of the income

319

it receives. An INVESTMENT COMPANY. See also COMPANY, HOLDING.

securities exchange. An exchange or market in which bonds and stocks are bought and sold. The actual trading is usually done by members of the exchange, who are said to have SEATS, for the accounts of customers who are members of the investing public. Under the Securities Act of 1934, national *securities exchanges,* or those which do business for customers living in more than one state, or trade in securities of corporations located in more than one state, are required to register with the SECURITIES AND EXCHANGE COMMISSION, and to comply with its regulations. See also EXCHANGE (2).

security. 1. In general, any documentary evidence of the debt or equity ownership of a corporation or other business or financial organization. As defined by the Uniform Commercial Code, it is an instrument, whether payable to bearer or registered in an owner's name, of a type commonly dealt in on securities exchanges or markets, or commonly recognized as a medium of investment. The Securities Act of 1934, as amended, lists the following as *securities:* NOTES, STOCK, BONDS, DEBENTURES, and TRUST CERTIFICATES; also, any evidence of indebtedness, certificate of beneficial interest in a profit-sharing agreement, subscription share, investment contract, fractional interest in oil, gas, or other mineral rights, etc. The principal forms and types of *securities* are listed and defined below:

assessable ∼. One which is liable to be assessed, or charged, for the obligations of the issuing corporation. Bank stocks, some insurance stocks, and any corporate stock which is not full-paid are in this class. See also STOCK, ASSESSABLE.

exempted ∼. One which is exempted, or excused, from the registration provisions and other regulations of the Securities Exchange Act. The securities of companies which restrict ownership to citizens of a single state, for example, are in this class.

gilt-edge ∼. In general, those of the highest reputation and investment quality; those which are certain to meet their dividend and interest payments, and to be redeemed in full at maturity.

inactive ∼. Any stock, bond or other traded security which is infrequently dealt in on the securities exchanges, and for which prices are reported only weekly or less often in the newspapers.

listed ∼. One which is listed for trading on a regular securities exchange. Most of the exchanges have set requirements covering the number of shares of stock or bond certificates issued, the number of holders, the total capitalization of the company, etc., which qualify a *security* for listing. Also a *security* which has been listed with the Securities and Exchange Commission for sale to the public. See also UNLISTED SECURITY, below.

marketable ∼. The term for any *security* which may readily or legally be sold. Also, one which is recognized by investors as being of reasonable investment quality. See also NON-MARKETABLE SECURITY, below.

non-marketable ∼. A *security,* such as one of various sorts of United States Treasury bonds, which is not transferrable or negotiable, but is redeemable only by the issuer. Also, one which is of such low investment quality that it cannot be readily sold to investors. See also MARKETABLE SECURITY, above.

outside ∼. One which is not traded on any of the regular exchanges, and thus an UNLISTED SECURITY, which see below. See also OVER THE COUNTER.

outstanding ∼. One which is in the hands of individual investors or holders. A share of stock which has been issued and is still individually owned, or a bond which has been placed or sold, and not yet redeemed or matured.

savings bank ∼. A term for those high-grade bonds, preferred stocks, and other *securities* which are considered sound enough for purchase by savings banks. One which the state banking laws make a legal investment for savings banks.

seasoned ∼. One which has been traded long enough, and has established a dividend payment record which is stable enough, to indicate to investors the quality or value it should have in trading.

short term ∼. One, such as a bond or note, which is due and payable in a few years or months. Such *securities* seldom fluctuate in value, and are therefore frequently purchased by trust companies and other investors whose prime aim is an assured income with little risk of capital loss.

unlisted ∼. One which is not listed for trading on any of the major securities exchanges, and which is therefore dealt in on the OVER THE COUNTER market. See also LISTED SECURITY, above.

2. Something which is given by a debtor to a creditor to assure the payment of a debt; something given to assure the performance of an obligation, or to serve as indemnification in the event of failure to perform. *Security* is a broader term than

COLLATERAL, which is a *security* with monetary value, while a *security* in general may include a pledge of personal honor or some other intangible thing. See also BOND (2).

collateral ~. Any tangible *security* which is given in addition to the personal obligation or pledge of the debtor. It may consist of money, securities, or other readily convertible things of value, or it may consist of a contract to turn over specified real or personal property in the event of default.

personal ~. A bond, pledge, or other personal obligation to repay a debt, as distinguished from a COLLATERAL SECURITY, which see above. Usually, both forms of *security* are given.

security bond. See BOND (2), SURETY.

security dividend. See DIVIDEND, PROPERTY.

security for costs. In law, the term for the security which a plaintiff in some legal actions may be required to deposit, against any award of court costs that may be made against him. Generally, this is in the form of a BOND (2), specifically prepared to cover the payment of any costs so awarded to the defendant in the event that the plaintiff's complaint is thrown out.

seignorage. Originally, a tax or charge on the coining of money, levied to pay the costs of coining, and as a source of revenue. In current usage, the profit taken by a government in issuing coins at a higher face value than the intrinsic value of the contained metal; the difference between the price paid for bullion and the face value of the coins made from it. It is sometimes called mintage. See also FREE COINAGE, which refers, however, to the amount of coinage, not to the charge or lack of charge.

seizure. The act of taking possession of property, such as for failure to pay a debt or judgment. It is usually carried out by a sheriff or other duly authorized officer. Depending on the statutes of the particular state, the seized property may be immediately sold to satisfy the debt or judgment, or further action may be required to authorize such sale. See also CONDEMNATION; CONFISCATION.

selective selling. In marketing, the policy of selling a product or service only through dealers or distributors who meet the seller's standards, with respect to size, location, character, etc., or only to a restricted number of dealers, under a FRANCHISE arrangement, rather than to all dealers and distributors willing to handle the product. In another sense, the practice of concentrating sales effort on those products in a complete line of products which produce the highest rate of profit, or the greatest amount of gross profit.

self-insurance. In insurance, the practice of creating a fund to meet possible losses directly, rather than through the use of an insurance company. Strictly speaking, *self-insurance* involves the regular setting aside of money to build a reserve fund, rather than the absorption of losses as current expenses, which is really non-insurance. *Self-insurance* is considered practical for even smaller companies for such things as glass breakage, auto collision damage, etc. Larger companies may *self-insure* WORKMEN'S COMPENSATION, small public liability claims, etc. Sometimes, a particular hazard may be *self-insured* up to a given amount, with EXCESS INSURANCE to cover losses above that amount.

self-liquidating. Capable of being converted into cash over a period of time, or through the normal course of business. Subject to the full recovery of the money invested, over a period of time. A *self-liquidating* investment, for example, is one in which the full original cost may be recovered through higher-than-average earnings over a period.

self-liquidating premium. See under PREMIUM (1).

self-reducing clause. A clause included in life insurance policies covering the value of a mortgage or other reducing debt, under which the amount of insurance automatically decreases during the term of the policy, to match the decreasing amount of the obligation covered. See also INSURANCE, LIFE, ACCIDENT, AND HEALTH.

self-service. A method of retail marketing in which customers wait on themselves, selecting the desired merchandise from shelf, counter, or rack displays. Usually, the customer takes the purchased items to a central cashier or check-out counter, where the purchase is paid for and packaged. This method is now widely used in grocery SUPERMARKETS and is being used increasingly in the retailing of apparel, housewares, and other consumer products.

sell. To dispose of by SALE; to give up title to property, or to transfer goods, or to perform services, in exchange for a monetary consideration. See also BUY.

sellers' market. A descriptive term for the situation in which demand is greater than supply so that the sellers in the market tend to set the prices and terms of sale. Hence, a market characterized by rising or high prices. It is the opposite of a BUYERS' MARKET.

seller's option. See OPTION (1, 2).

selling. The process of disposing of, or transferring, by SALE. More particularly, the active assistance or persuasion of prospective buyers to actually complete a purchase of a commodity or service. *Selling* may be direct or open, or it may be indirect, through the use of advertising, sales promotion activities, and other impersonal means.

selling agent. See AGENT, SALES.

selling expense. See under EXPENSE (2).

sell on a scale. See ON A SCALE.

sell out. 1. In the securities trade, to close out the account of a customer by selling the securities or commodities held. This may be done by a dealer or broker, for example, because of the customer's failure to provide sufficient MARGIN to cover his purchases against declining prices, because of a failure on the customer's part to complete the necessary formalities of purchase, or for some other reason.

2. To dispose of by SALE. More particularly, to liquidate an entire stock of goods, or class of products, by sale at reduced prices. See also CLOSE OUT (1).

sellout. 1. In business slang, a complete sale of all of the goods or services offered. The purchase, by the public, of all of the available supply of something offered for sale. A new issue of securities, for example, is said to be a *sellout* if the total issue is SUBSCRIBED on the initial offering. Similarly, a play or other entertainment is a *sellout* if all of available tickets are sold for a long period of time in the future.

2. In slang, a betrayal, especially one motivated by gain. One who accepts money or other material gain to desert or betray another is said to take part in a *sellout*.

sell short. See SHORT (3).

semi-durable goods. See under GOODS (3).

semi-skilled labor. Labor which is essentially skilled, but to a more limited extent. See LABOR, SKILLED.

semi-trailer. See TRAILER.

senior. Older; prior to others in rank or claim; superior to others which are JUNIOR in order of time or importance. See each of the following under the principal listing: ~ MORTGAGE; ~ PARTNER.

seniority. In general, a ranking by age, or by length of service or use. In employment practices, *seniority* based on length of service is often one of the major bases for promotion, along with performance. Similarly, when it becomes necessary to reduce a work force, union agreements frequently require that those employees with the least *seniority* be the first to be laid off. Under some agreements, a worker with high *seniority* whose position has been eliminated may claim the job of another worker in an equal or lower ranking job with lower *seniority*. See also BUMPING.

senior lien. See LIEN, PRIOR.

sentence. In law, the judgment of the court in a criminal case. The *sentence* specifies the punishment or penalty to be exacted, following a verdict of guilt by the judge or by a jury. It is not in itself an evaluation of guilt or innocence.

separability clause. A clause frequently included in various contracts, specifying that the validity of the remainder of the contract will not be affected in the event that any particular provision or requirement be declared illegal or void for any reason. Such a clause is common, for example, in union contracts.

separate. In law, the opposite of JOINT. The more common term is SEVERAL.

separate return. See under RETURN (3).

separation. In personnel management, the termination of employment. It may be voluntary, as in the case of a QUIT, or involuntary, as in the case of a DISCHARGE, or LAYOFF.

sequester. Literally, to set aside or apart. In law, to place property which is in dispute into the hands of a third person, or trustee, pending the settlement of the dispute. Also, to place property in the hands of a special officer of the court, preparatory to distributing or disposing of it. For example, the property of a bankrupt may be *sequestered* for distribution to creditors, or the property of a person or corporation may be *sequestered* to satisfy a judgment.

sequestration. The act or process of sequestering the property or funds of a person or company. *Sequestration* differs only technically from ATTACHMENT, and the situations in which each procedure is applicable differ from state to state.

sequestrator. The officer of a court or similar person who is authorized to take possession of property under an order of SEQUESTRATION. His duties and responsibilities are similar to those of a RECEIVER, in that he must report to the court on his administration or distribution of the property he takes into possession.

serial bond. See under BOND (1).

serial note. See NOTE (1), INSTALLMENT.

serial right. In publishing, the right to publish a literary product in installments in a periodical or similar publication, either before or after its appearance as a single book. This right, and the compensation connected with it, should always be specifically disposed of in any contract between an author and publisher. See also BOOK RIGHT.

servant. In common usage, a household employee, or domestic worker. In law, any person who is in the employ of another, under conditions such that the latter has full and continuous control over the former's actions, and over the particular means of accomplishing the work to be done. Thus, a *servant* or EMPLOYEE is distinguished from an INDEPENDENT CONTRACTOR, who uses his own methods to accomplish the desired work, and from an AGENT, whose employer does not have full control over his actions. See also MASTER AND SERVANT RELATIONSHIP.

service. 1. In general, any work or effort expended or performed to meet the needs of others, or to fill an existing demand; especially such work which is not connected with the manufacture or processing of a product or commodity, or the retail or wholesale distribution of goods. Examples of *services* include the public utilities, such as telephone, transportation, etc., as well as such trades as laundry, dry cleaning, maintenance and repair work, etc. Such businesses as printing are *services* to the extent that they do work for customers, but include manufacturing, retailing, etc., to the extent that they make books, sell the paper on which contract printing is done, and so forth.

2. In law, the exhibition or delivery of a writ, injunction, order, etc., to a person, who is thereby officially notified of some action or proceeding with which he is concerned, and is warned or notified of the steps which he should take or avoid taking to protect his interests. The laws of the various states differ as to what constitutes valid *service,* with regard to written and oral notification, *service* in person, on holidays, to agents or employees, etc.

service charge. In general, an extra fee added to a price for the provision of some service in connection with a sale. Examples include the charge made by a bank for handling a checking account, the charge made by a finance company for processing a loan, etc.

service cooperative. See under COOPERATIVE.

service credit. See under CREDIT (3).

service department. A department or division of a company which is not directly concerned with production, or with distribution in the case of a wholesale or retail establishment, but with the provision of supporting services for the company's primary operations. Examples include the accounting, maintenance, timekeeping, storage, wrapping, and similar operations. Also, in some companies, the department providing service to customers in connection with the products the company makes or sells.

service life. In connection with DEPRECIATION calculations, the time a piece of equipment or other capital asset is in service. The period of time from the initial installation of the equipment, whether it is new or used at the time, until it is retired from use, whether or not it has any useful life left in it at that time. Thus, the *service life* of a machine for a particular company or user may be shorter than the total useful life of the machine.

service mark. See under TRADEMARK.

Servicemen's Readjustment Act. The federal law, passed after World War II and since amended, which provided for special benefits for discharged members of the armed forces. These benefits included access to mortgage loans at low rates of interest, and insured by the Veteran's Administration, commonly known as "G. I. loans," special loans to finance new business ventures, free educational or retraining programs, etc. Many of the benefits for veterans of World War II have since expired, but some have been extended to cover veterans of the Korean conflict and other former servicemen.

service trade. As defined by the Bureau of the Census, any of those RETAIL TRADES in which the thing dispensed is a service, such as laundry, shoe repair, dry cleaning, etc., rather than a product, such as food, clothing, gasoline, or other consumer goods.

set of exchange. See FIRST OF EXCHANGE.

set-off. In legal terminology, a cross-claim filed by a defendant in a legal action, against the plaintiff. Its purpose is to reduce or completely eliminate the possible award to the plaintiff. Such a claim is filed by a defendant who seeks to reduce the claim of the plaintiff, but who does not have sufficient basis to bring an independent opposing action. See also COUNTERCLAIM.

settle. 1. In general, to adjust or liquidate an obligation. It may mean to pay off a debt or debts in full, or to pay a negotiated agreed amount, which is accepted by creditors as a discharge of the obligation. The creditors of a debtor who is facing insolvency, for example, may agree to *settle* their claim against him for an amount equivalent to 50 cents for each dollar actually owed.

2. To provide for the future enjoyment by another person of real or personal property, such as by means of a will, a marriage contract, or other form of agreement.

3. To determine and balance off amounts due and owing between parties engaging in business with each other. In the securities trade, for example, brokers who do business with each other may periodically *settle* their accounts and pay any remaining balances.

settlement. Any agreement for the adjustment, liquidation, or disposal of obligations or of property, either in the present or in the future. A debtor, for example, may reach a *settlement* with his creditors, providing for the payment of all or part of his debt. A husband may make a *settlement* on his wife at the time of marriage, providing for the present or future transfer to her of certain property.

settling price. See under PRICE.

settlor. In law, the designation for one who settles a benefit on another; the title for the person who creates a TRUST. He may also be called the grantor or donor.

severable. Capable of being divided into several independent and distinct parts, each of which is not affected by changes in the status of the other. A *severable* contract, for example, is one consisting of several distinct and independent obligations or agreements, with a separate consideration, remuneration, or payment attached to each. Under such a contract, the failure or invalidation of one part does not invalidate the other parts.

several. In law, separate, distinct, or SEVERABLE. It is the opposite of JOINT. A *several* action, for example, is one taken against a number of persons as separate individuals, rather than as joint defendants. See also TENANCY, SEVERAL.

several contract. See CONTRACT (1), JOINT AND SEVERAL.

severance pay. Any payment, over and above wages or salary due, which a company may give to an employee whose employment is terminated. Such pay is usually based on length of service, such as a given number of days' pay for each year of employment by the company. In most cases, it is given to employees who are dismissed through no fault of their own, not to those DISCHARGED. Under some union contracts, the provisions for *severance pay,* or dismissal pay, frequently do not distinguish between a temporary FURLOUGH, an indefinite LAYOFF and an actual termination of employment.

severance tax. See under TAX (2).

shade. In business slang, to reduce slightly; to make lower than the regular or established price. The term is especially used in connection with a reduction which is forced on a seller by competition, or by the pressure of a prospective buyer.

shake-out. In general, any movement or trend in an industry or trade which forces marginal or weak members of the field out of business. Also, any movement in securities prices which forces speculators to sell out their holdings in the market.

shanghai. To induce or force a person to join a ship's crew, usually under the influence of alcohol or drugs, or by threat or use of force. More broadly, to obtain any desired result by force, deceit, or unfair means. The term is believed to have begun in the China trade, through practices resorted to to make up crews for ships bound for Shanghai and other Chinese ports.

shape-up. A practice in the shipping trade, under which longshoremen and other workers assemble or line up at the beginning of the work day, so that representatives of the employers may choose work crews from among the men available. The practice has been eliminated in some ports by the formation of permanent work crews, for whom work is always available. A similar practice is sometimes followed in agricultural areas in the selection of field crews, from among itinerant workers, to harvest crops. See also DECASUALIZATION.

share. In general, a portion or proportion of something, such as a proportionate interest in a business undertaking. More particularly, a certificate representing a partial ownership of a corporation or joint stock company, and a proportionate interest in the profits and assets of the enterprise. See also STOCK (1); STOCK CERTIFICATE.

share and share alike. A phrase used in the designation of beneficiaries in wills, insurance policies, etc., meaning that the named beneficiaries are to have equal proportions or shares of the estate or proceeds. This expression is used, instead of specifying a particular percentage for each beneficiary, so that the death of one or more of the beneficiaries will not affect the terms of the designation.

shareholder. See STOCKHOLDER.

shave. 1. To make a charge, or take a discount, for the handling of a note or other instrument, especially in excess of the legal rate. Hence, to *shave* a note is to DISCOUNT it at a rate higher than the regular market rate, when the note is of low grade, or when the seller is willing to take a smaller amount for any other reason.

2. In the securities trade, a term for the premium or extra charge paid for the privilege of extending the time to deliver a security or pay a note, or for the right to alter or vary the terms of a securities contract in any particular.

sheltering trust. See TRUST (1), SPENDTHRIFT.

sheriff. Originally, in England, a shire reeve, or magistrate of a shire or district. Now, in the United States, the chief administrative officer of a county. His duties include serving various court orders, forming juries, holding sales ordered to satisfy judgments, etc. Technically, he is also the chief peace officer of the county, but today the state and municipal forces have largely taken over this function.

Sherman Act. 1. The federal law, passed in 1890, repealing the silver purchase provisions of the Bland-Allison Act, and providing for the gradual cessation of the coinage of silver dollars by the Treasury.

2. The federal law, passed in 1890, and widely known as the ANTI-TRUST LAW. It provided for the outlawing of TRUSTS (2) as such, and made illegal a variety of practices leading to the monopolization of any line of business by one or a group of companies. It provided for prison and fines for violators, and authorized persons injured by the monopolistic practices of others to sue for triple damages.

shift. In employment, a standard work period; a work day. Also, the employees or work crews making up the work force during such a standard work period. Thus, the day *shift* in a factory is the work period during normal daylight hours, but also the employees who make up the factory force during this work period. See also GRAVEYARD SHIFT; SPLIT SHIFT; SWING SHIFT.

shift differential. In wage practice, a special rate of pay given for work done on any shift or turn of work other than the regular and normal day schedule. A *shift differential* is not a form of OVERTIME pay, however, since it is paid to workers who perform their normal hours of work on the shift for which the differential is paid.

shinplaster. In slang, a derisive term applied to the fractional paper currency issued by the United States during the suspension of specie payment at the time of the Civil War. The same term has been applied to other depreciated paper currency since that time.

ship. 1. Originally, to put goods on board a vessel for transport. More broadly, to transport goods from one place to another by any form of carrier. As interpreted by the courts in various cases, to turn goods over to a carrier for transport and delivery.

2. In general, any large vessel used for navigation. In some usages, a *ship* is distinguished from a BOAT in that it is mechanically propelled, and in some usages it is distinguished by the fact that it is suitable for deep-sea navigation, but often the two terms are used interchangeably.

ship broker. See under BROKER (1).

shipment. 1. The delivery of goods to a carrier for transport, and the transport of the goods by the carrier. As held in various rulings, to make *shipment* of goods is to turn them over to a carrier, obtain a receipt, and pass control of the goods over to the carrier.

2. Any load or parcel being transported together, or as a unit. A consignment of goods prepared for transportation by carrier.

shipper. In general, the person who makes SHIPMENT of goods. More specifically, the person who has control over the goods being transported. Thus, the CONSIGNEE may be the *shipper* of the goods, if he arranges for their transport, and the documents covering the shipment show him as the one in control.

shipper's order. A term sometimes used in a BILL OF LADING covering a shipment, meaning that title to the goods remains with the shipper, and that the goods are to be held after landing, pending the *shipper's order* for delivery to a specific consignee.

shipping. In general, the transportation of passengers and goods, whether by water, land, or air. Also, collectively, the ships used for the commercial transportation of passengers and goods.

shipping document. Any one of the several commercial documents which accompany or cover a shipment in inland or foreign trade, including the INVOICE, BILL OF LADING, CERTIFICATE OF INSURANCE, BILL OF EXCHANGE, LETTER OF CREDIT, DRAFT, etc. See also COMMERCIAL SET.

shipping order. The name for one of the copies of a BILL OF LADING, specifically the copy which carries the shipper's instructions to the carrier concerning the forwarding and disposition of the goods.

shipping point. See GOLD POINT.

shipping ton. A long TON.

ship's articles. The written agreement between a ship owner or master and the members of the ship's crew, containing the terms and conditions under which the seamen agree to serve, and specifying the wages rating, period of service, etc., of each man. Usually, the *ship's articles* consist of a single document, with spaces for all of the crew to sign their names. Thus, a seaman who agrees to make a voyage is said to sign on, meaning that he has signed the *ship's articles*.

ship's manifest. See MANIFEST.

ship's option. See TON, MEASUREMENT; TONNAGE, CARGO.

shipwreck. In maritime law and insurance, any serious damage or loss to a ship or its cargo by storm, collision, foundering on rocks, etc., but not necessarily resulting in the complete or total loss of the ship.

shop. 1. Originally, a place in which goods or products were prepared for sale. Hence, a place in which goods are sold, especially at retail; a RETAIL STORE. In a more limited sense, a retail establishment in which goods or products are worked on, as well as sold, or in which a service is performed. Examples include a shoe repair *shop*, barber *shop*, tailor *shop*, etc.

2. A place, establishment, or department in which mechanical work is done. A business in which metal is worked on by machine tools, for example, is known as a machine *shop*, and the maintenance and repair department of a company is typically known as the *shop*.

3. Loosely, any place in which work is done, or in which people work. The term is especially used in labor terminology. See, for example, CLOSED SHOP; OPEN SHOP; UNION SHOP.

shop chairman. In union-management relations, a term for the senior SHOP STEWARD, who is chosen by the other department stewards, and who acts as chairman in dealing with the company management on union matters. The chief union representative in a plant, who deals with management in the adjustment of disputes that cannot be settled satisfactorily by the shop stewards and foremen.

shopper. See COMPARISON SHOPPER.

shopping center. The term now used for a collection of retail stores in a more or less cohesive grouping in one place. A *shopping center* is usually created by a single developer, who then leases the individual stores to others. Frequently, the lease arrangements provide that there will be only one store of each type in the center, that the several stores will contribute toward joint advertising and promotion, etc.

shopping goods. See under GOODS (3).

shop steward. In union-management relations, a representative chosen or elected by his fellow employees in a department to represent them in disputes arising under their union contract. The *shop steward* handles matters at the department level, and deals with the foreman or manager, while the chief steward, or SHOP CHAIRMAN, deals with management on disputes that cannot be settled at this level.

short. 1. In general, the condition of having less of something than is needed; the condition of being deficient in some quantity or quality. For example, *short* weight is less than the required or marked weight, and a *short* account is one in which the actual amount of funds is less than that stated in the records.

2. Pertaining to a relatively *short* period of time. A *short* BILL OF EXCHANGE, for example, is one with a maturity period of less than 60 days, and usually of 30 days.

3. In the securities trade, a term used to define the condition of a trader who has sold a security he does not own, with the intention of buying the security later at a lower price to cover the sale. Until the purchase to close the transaction has been made, the trader is said to be *short* on the particular stock or other security. Typically, traders who take advantage of falling prices in a market to sell *short*, or go *short*, are known as BEARS.

shortage. In business usage, a deficiency in the quantity, weight, or other measurement of a shipment or lot of merchandise. Also, an allowance made in billing for such shipments for the *shortage* discovered. In accounting, it is a deficiency in funds in an account, or in a reserve fund. See also OVERAGE.

short bill. See under BILL OF EXCHANGE.

short bit. A term sometimes used in the regional slang of the Southern and Western states, meaning a dime, or 10 cents. It derives from the BIT, which was the common name for the Mexican *real*, a small coin worth about 12½ cents.

short exchange. See BILL OF EXCHANGE, SHORT.

short haul. In railroading, the transport of freight over a relatively short distance, as distinguished from LONG HAUL transport. The distinction between the two terms is relative, rather than exact, however. In passenger transport, the term sometimes refers to travel between a major terminal and a way station, rather than direct travel between two major terminal cities.

short hundredweight. See HUNDREDWEIGHT.

short interest. See under INTEREST (3).

short-line railroad. In railroad usage, a railroad other than a Class I railroad, such as, for example, a switching or terminal railroad, or one serving as a SPUR LINE to a TRUNK LINE railroad. See also CLASSIFICATION OF RAILROADS.

short of exchange. In the financial trade, a phrase used to describe the situation in which a dealer or trader in foreign EXCHANGE has sold more foreign bills than the amount of such bills or similar instruments he has on hand to cover his sales. Until this inbalance is rectified, the dealer is said to be *short of exchange.*

short position. In securities trade usage, the aggregate of all of the amounts which have been sold SHORT in each particular stock. All short sales must be reported to the Securities and Exchange Commission, which prepares and publishes reports of the *short position* in each stock periodically. See also INTEREST (3), SHORT.

short purchase. In the securities trade, the term sometimes used for the purchase of a stock made to cover a previous SHORT sale of the same stock.

short rate. In insurance, the full PREMIUM rate charged for a policy which is for only one year, as distinguished from the LONG RATE, which is usually a reduced rate charged for policies running two or three years. Also, in some cases, the rate charged for a policy of less than one year's duration, such as, for example, the adjusted rate resulting when a policy is cancelled after a number of months, and the premium returned is less than the unearned premium. See also LONG RATE.

short sale. See SHORT (3).

short-term capital gain. See CAPITAL GAIN.

short-term loan. See under LOAN.

short-term security. See under SECURITY (1).

short ton. See TON.

show cause order. The term for an order issued by a court, directed to a person against whom an INJUNCTION or similar restraint has been asked, calling on him to appear with any statements, reasons, evidence, etc., as to why the requested injunction or other order should not be granted and be put into effect.

shrinkage. In general, any reduction in weight or amount. In one sense, it is the physical *shrinkage* or DEPLETION of an asset in use. In another sense, it is the reduction in amount of goods on hand or in inventory, due to such things as pilfering, loss and damage to goods, errors in inventory count, etc.

shut down. The closing down of a shop, plant, factory, or other place of work. Any prolonged interruption of work, or cessation of regular activities. It has been held that a plant is *shut down* although such work as maintenance, machinery repair, stock sorting, etc., is carried on.

shyster. In slang, an unscrupulous, tricky, dishonest, unethical, or sharp lawyer; a PETTIFOGGER. More broadly, any person who carries on a disreputable or dishonest business. The term is believed to have derived from an attorney named Scheuster, who practiced in New York before the Civil War, and who was frequently reprimanded by the courts for pettifoggery.

sic. A Latin word, meaning, literally, thus. With reference to a quotation from another appearing in a present work, it means that the words quoted appeared in exactly this manner in the original. The term is used especially when the quotation as it stands might be questioned, or contains an obvious error.

sick leave. In personnel practice, time off from work allowed as a result of illness or accident. It may be with or without pay, or at a reduced rate of pay, or the absence may be compensated for by disability insurance. In any event, there is ordinarily no loss of seniority or of re-employment rights when an employee is absent on authorized *sick leave.*

sickness insurance. See INSURANCE, LIFE, ACCIDENT, AND HEALTH.

side line. In general, any secondary line of business engaged in, or any secondary line of goods or merchandise taken on by a merchant, in addition to the principal one. For example, an attorney may sell real estate or insurance as a *side line,* or a bakery shop may sell dairy products as a *side line.*

sideways movement. A term used to describe the movement of business in general, or of the securities markets, when there are some industries or securities rising and others falling, with no appreciable net change in the average level. The term implies a horizontal trend over time in the aggregate or average figures, resulting from indecisive rising and falling trends in various components.

sight. As used in a bill, draft, or other negotiable instrument, a term meaning presentation, either for payment or ACCEPTANCE (3). An instrument may be made payable at *sight,* or immediately on presentation, or AFTER SIGHT, in which case a specified number of days are allowed for payment after presentation. See each of the following under the principal listing: ~ BILL OF EXCHANGE; ~ DRAFT (2); ~ LOAN.

sight note. See NOTE (1), DEMAND.

sign. 1. A mark or symbol used to express a term, idea, quantity, etc. Examples in business include the dollar *sign* ($), percent *sign* (%), etc.

2. A placard, poster, or other notice publicly displayed, carrying some message of public interest or importance. In business, for example, it might be a board carrying the name of a business, a placard warning of a dangerous area, or an advertising poster.

3. To fix one's name or mark to a document, or to any written statement or instrument. See also SIGNATURE.

signature. In general, a name written on a document or instrument by the person whose name it is. An impression made by a stamp or seal is recognized as a *signature,* and even a typewritten *signature* will be recognized in some cases. A person who is unable to write may make a MARK instead of a *signature,* which will also be recognized when properly made.

silent partner. See under PARTNER.

silver. A whitish metallic element, used primarily for coinage, jewelry, and as an electrical conductor. It is also used in special solders and for other special industrial uses. The word is also used loosely for *silver* money, and hence for any fractional coinage.

silver certificate. See CERTIFICATE (2).

silver dollar. See DOLLAR.

silver standard. A standard or basis for a monetary system in which silver is recognized as the basic medium of exchange and as the measure of value. In practice, a currency based on a *silver standard* is one whose basic monetary unit has a legally fixed value in silver of a specified fineness and weight. Typically, under a true *silver standard,* there is free and unlimited coinage of silver, and the acceptance of silver as full legal tender.

simple arbitration. See ARBITRATION OF EXCHANGE.

simple average. See under AVERAGE (1).

simple contract. See CONTRACT (1), INFORMAL.

simple correlation. See under CORRELATION.

simple interest. See under INTEREST (2).

simple trust. See TRUST (1), DRY.

sine. In Latin, without. A term appearing in several expressions used in business, always meaning without. *Sine die,* for example, means without a date, or without a definite time set for resuming. When a legislative body adjourns *sine die,* it sets no definite date for re-assembling, indicating that it has finished its work for the current session, but may be called into session again if necessary.

sinecure. Literally, without care. A position or office which has no regular duties attached to it, though it usually carries a regular compensation. Such a position, for example, might be found for a partially disabled employee who is nearing the retirement age, or for a part owner of a business whose name it is desired to show on the regular payroll, though he takes no actual part in the conduct of the business.

single bill. See SOLA.

single-entry. The name for the system of BOOKKEEPING or ACCOUNTING in which each transaction is entered only once on the account books of the company. The system is used only by small businesses, such as retail stores or professional services. The only two books involved are the JOURNAL, which is the BOOK OF ORIGINAL ENTRY, and one or more LEDGERS for making the final entries. The ledger is usually set up with multiple columns, for distributing the various income and expenditure items to the proper accounts.

single-name paper. See under COMMERCIAL PAPER.

single payment annuity. See under ANNUITY.

single premium. See under PREMIUM (2).

single standard. A MONETARY STANDARD based on the value of only one metal, usually either gold or silver, as distinguished from a BIMETALLIC STANDARD, in which both metals form the basis of the system, with a fixed ratio in value between the two.

single tax. See under TAX (2).

sinking fund. A fund of money set aside, usually out of current earnings, for some particular purpose. The usual purpose for a *sinking fund* is the extinguishment or retirement of a long term debt or obligation. The money periodically set aside is frequently invested conservatively, such as in government bonds, and the income from the investment added to the fund. In many cases, the long term debt issue itself specifies that a *sinking fund* is to be established to assure payment at maturity. A *sinking fund* for the retirement of a real estate mortgage is sometimes known as an amortization fund, and one for the repayment of a bond issue is often known as a redemption fund. See each of the following under the principal listing: ~ BOND (1); ~ DEPRECIATION; ~ RESERVE.

sit-down strike. See under STRIKE.

sixteenmo. See under BOOK SIZES.

skilled labor. See under LABOR (1).

skip. In business slang, a person who leaves town without notice, especially to avoid paying his debts. Hence, in a broader sense, any defaulting debtor, especially one who takes steps to avoid being pressed for payment, whether or not this includes actually leaving town.

skip-tracer. A person or organization engaged in the business of locating defaulted debtors, especially those who have deliberately left town to avoid payment. Such organizations are frequently employed by department stores, sales finance companies and others, to locate private persons who have defaulted on installment sale payments. Sometimes, the same organization may be employed by a corporation, bank, or transfer agent, to locate missing stockholders to whom interest, dividends, or stock redemption payments are due.

slack. In general, dull, easy, or inactive. Business is said to be *slack,* for example, when there are less than the usual number of inquiries and sales, and securities trading is said to be *slack* when the number of transactions is below the average amount.

slander. In law, the defamation of a person's character or reputation through oral utterances, as distinguished from LIBEL, which is defamation by written or printed word. In general, the same legal principles apply to slander as to libel, and it is common for a person to bring suit on both charges at the same time.

slate. A list of candidates for position, such as for political office, or for the board of directors of a corporation. The term is derived from the practice, in former times, of writing the names of the candidates on a *slate,* or board, and tallying the vote next to each candidate's name. Usually, each party in an election proposes its own *slate* of candidates, and the management of a corporation usually submits a *slate* of proposed directors for the approval of the stockholders. It is also known as a ticket.

sleeper. In business slang, any item which has an unexpectedly heavy sale, or which has a greater than expected value. A stock may be known as a *sleeper,* for example, if its worth and earning potential are not generally recognized by the investing public. A particular style or model of a product is a *sleeper* if it unexpectedly catches the public fancy and sells in large quantities.

sleeping partner. See PARTNER, SILENT.

sliding scale. In general, any scale or basis for charges or payment which progressively increases or decreases with the volume of activity, or over time. A public utility, for example, may charge for electricity on a *sliding scale,* with progressively lower rates for greater usage. Tax rates, on the other hand, may be based on a progressively increasing *sliding scale,* so that the tax on higher incomes is proportionately greater than that on lower incomes. See also STRAIGHT-LINE RATE.

slight negligence. See under NEGLIGENCE.

slow asset. See ASSET (2), FIXED.

slowdown. In labor relations, an organized action on the part of employees in a plant or other place to bring pressure on the employer, without actually going on STRIKE, by *slowing down* on the volume of production. In some cases this may be done by simply working at a slower rate, but in other cases the effect is accomplished by a strict and literal observance of all of the rules, regulations, and procedures connected with the work, such as the periodic inspection of equipment, the use of larger crews to do the work, etc.

slump. A term describing the situation in which prices fall rapidly and suddenly, or in which business activity decreases. As usually used, a slump is a dip in activity or price levels of relatively short duration, as distinguished from a RECESSION, which is of more substantial proportions. A *slump* may occur in business or prices in general, or in one particular industry or line of trade.

slush fund. A sum set aside, often by joint contributions from several persons, for purposes of bribery, purchasing special privileges, or other corrupt practices. It is said to be so called after the funds raised for pleasure and luxuries in port by the crews of sailing ships, by selling the *slush* or waste pork fat accumulated during a voyage.

small business. A term of widely differing definition, as used in various fields. In one sense, it is any business organization managed or operated by a relatively few persons, or requiring only moderate amounts of invested capital. The Small Business Administration has established a series of definitions of *small business,* for use in manufacturing, wholesaling, and retailing, depending on the number of employees, the annual net sales volume, or the annual net income. These definitions have been revised from time to time, and may be applied differently with respect to priority in obtaining government contracts, eligibility for special loans, etc.

Small Business Administration. The independent federal agency, formally established in 1953. Its primary purposes are to make loans to small businesses for plant and equipment, for working capital, or for help in recovering from a disaster such as a flood; to assist small businesses to obtain government contracts; and to provide technical, management, and financial advice and assistance to small businesses. The definition of a small business varies from field to field, and may be different for purposes of obtaining a loan or for obtaining a government contract.

small loan company. See PERSONAL FINANCE COMPANY.

smart money. 1. In business slang, a term for the investments made by clever, experienced, or well-informed investors. It may be said, for example, that the *smart money* is withdrawing from the stock market at a certain point, indicating that the well-informed groups expect a downturn in stock prices.

2. In law, a term used for those punitive DAMAGES which are awarded as a punishment for gross mismanagement or misconduct in handling an enterprise or funds. In another sense, it is an excessive amount of money paid by one who wishes to be released from an agreement or commitment.

smuggling. The act of importing goods into a country secretly or illegally, either to avoid paying the import tariff on the goods, or because they may not legally be imported. Jewelry, for example, is frequently *smuggled* to avoid payment of the tariff, while narcotics are an example of an item imported illegally by *smuggling*.

social insurance. Broadly, any of the various types of insurance or similar plans, sponsored by government, and intended to protect large groups of the general public against the uncertainties and hazards of life. Examples in general use in the United States include WORKMEN'S COMPENSATION INSURANCE, UNEMPLOYMENT INSURANCE, and OLD AGE AND SURVIVORS' INSURANCE. See also SOCIAL SECURITY.

social security. The popular name for the combination of SOCIAL INSURANCE plans sponsored by the federal government, and including OLD AGE AND SURVIVORS' INSURANCE and UNEMPLOYMENT INSURANCE. The term is especially used with reference to the wage and payroll deductions which are made to finance these insurance plans, both forms of deduction being known popularly as *social security* taxes.

social security tax. See under TAX (2).

society. In business, any association of persons brought together through common interests. A *society* may or may not be incorporated, depending on its purposes and on the laws of the state in which it is formed. Examples include a FRATERNAL SOCIETY, a SAVINGS AND LOAN ASSOCIATION, etc.

soft. A term describing the condition of a market in which the supply of goods is not supported by an equivalent and balancing demand. Hence, a market condition in which prices tend to decline. It is distinguished from a FIRM (2) market, in which supply is offset by sufficient demand to keep prices stable.

soft goods. See under GOODS (3).

sola. A term used in reference to a BILL OF EXCHANGE or other COMMERCIAL PAPER, indicating that the particular copy is the only one in existence. Such an instrument is also referred to as a sole bill, single bill, sole of exchange, etc.

solar. Literally, according to the sun. Also, according to the calendar. A *solar* DAY, for example, is usually understood to be the hours from sunrise to sunset, and a *solar* MONTH is a calendar month.

sold bill. See under BILL OF EXCHANGE.

sold note. See under NOTE (2).

sold up. A term used to describe the situation in which all of the scheduled production for a period of time has been sold in advance. In the textile industry, steel industry, and in other fields, for example, it is usual for companies to accept orders for delivery during advance periods out of the production of the period. When the total production scheduled for the period has been covered by such accepted orders, the period, such as a month or calendar quarter, is said to be *sold up*.

sole bill. See SOLA.

sole of exchange. See SOLA.

sole tenant. See under TENANT.

solicitor. 1. An agent, especially one who seeks business, subscriptions, contributions, etc. In some lines of trade, salesmen are regularly known as *solicitors* for the companies they represent.

2. In English law practice, a lawyer who practices in the courts of EQUITY, or chancery.

solvency. The ability to meet all of one's debts and obligations. In business, it is the potential ability to meet all of the just claims against a business, and hence, the state of having more ASSETS, especially liquid assets, than LIABILITIES. A business enterprise is said to be *solvent* when it is able to meet its obligations without liquidating the fixed assets of the business. See also INSOLVENCY.

S.O.P. See STANDARD OPERATING PROCEDURE.

sound. In general, in good condition, free from defects or flaws, and usable for the intended purpose. With reference to a business, the term implies that the business is in a state of SOLVENCY, is operating profitably, and can be expected to meet its obligations.

sound value. See VALUE (2), ACTUAL CASH.

space. In advertising, the place in a periodical, newspaper, or similar advertising medium which is devoted to an advertisement. Advertising *space* is usually measured in COLUMN INCHES, AGATE LINES, etc.

span. A measure of extension, now fixed at nine inches. Originally, it was the distance from the tip of the thumb to the tip of the little finger, with the fingers extended as far as possible.

span of control. In management, a term for the maximum number of subordinates, or the maximum number of functions, for which an executive or supervisor can effectively be responsible. Measurement and analysis of the *span of control* is important in determining the proper organization of a business management.

special. In various contexts, particular, limited, specific, not ordinary, restricted, etc. See each of the following under the principal listing: ∼ AGENT; ∼ BENEFIT; ∼ DEPOSIT; ∼ DEPOSITORY; ∼ ENDORSEMENT; ∼ LETTER OF ATTORNEY; ∼ LIEN; ∼ PARTNER; ∼ PARTNERSHIP; ∼ TRUST (1).

special acceptance. See ACCEPTANCE (3), QUALIFIED.

special checking account. See under ACCOUNT (3).

special contract. See CONTRACT (1), FORMAL.

special delivery. See under POSTAL SERVICE.

special dividend. See DIVIDEND, EXTRA.

special injunction. See INJUNCTION, TEMPORARY.

specialist. One who is specially trained in a particular field, or who devotes his activities to a particular field of activity. In the securities trade, for example, a *specialist* is a BROKER (2) who confines his operations to a few particular stocks, executing orders in these stocks for other brokers. The *specialist* is said to make the market for the stocks he covers; that is, he brings together buyers and sellers at a price agreeable to both.

specialization. In business, the restriction or narrowing of activity to a particular field. Particularly, the concentration of production or sales effort on a limited number of products, or on a limited and special market. It is the opposite of DIVERSIFICATION.

special legacy. See LEGACY, SPECIFIC.

special offering. In the securities trade, the sale, at a specified price, of a large block of a particular security, according to a plan which has been submitted to and approved by the Securities and Exchange Commission, under which the price, the commission offered, etc., are established. The term refers to an offering of already issued securities, not to the selling of a new issue.

specialty. 1. In law, the statutory term for any document that is delivered under seal according to the legal requirements. Examples include bonds, deeds, and in some states, judgments.

2. In commerce, any article of special or peculiar quality or character. Merchandise which is sold only by particular types of stores, or used only in particular trades. Examples include the various types of fasteners used in particular industries, a special food prepared by only one restaurant, etc.

specialty goods. See GOODS (3), SHOPPING.

specialty store. See under RETAIL STORE.

specie. Any metallic currency. Coins of precious metal, of the required weight and fineness, as distinguished from paper currency or coins of base metal. At one time, it was common for contracts, bonds, etc., to specify payment in *specie*, but today payment in any legal tender is almost universal.

specific. Pertaining to a specified or named thing; precise, or particular. See each of the following under the principal listing: ∼ LEGACY; ∼ TARIFF (2); ∼ TAX (2).

specifications. In general, a detailed statement of all of the elements involved in any matter. In patent law, it is the part of the patent application containing an exact and detailed DISCLOSURE and description of the invention, and of the methods of making, operating, and using it. In engineering and industry, it is a written statement, accompanied by drawings if necessary, of the work to be done, materials to be used, etc.

specific performance. In law, a requirement for the PERFORMANCE of an agreement or obligation in the exact and precise manner called for, as distinguished from SUBSTANTIAL PERFORMANCE, which is defined in various ways under state law. Statutes differ as to when *specific performance* is required.

spectacular. In advertising, a term for a very large outdoor sign, usually with lights and moving parts, intended to attract special attention. More broadly, any extravagant advertising operation, such as a radio or television program of unusual length, designed to attract wide attention.

speculation. In general, the act of buying, or of laying out money, with the hope of reaping a quick profit, rather than of making an INVESTMENT, or making a normal profit or reselling. It is buying in the hope or expectation of a quick rise in prices, so that there is always a risk of disappointment and loss involved. Usually, the risk in *speculation* is proportionate to the possible profits available.

speculator. One who engages in SPECULATION. One who makes a general practice of buying, especially in the fields of securities and commodities, in the hope of making a quick profit on risky ventures, rather than for long term investment. In the real estate field, a *speculator* is one who buys land or buildings with the intention of reselling, rather than with the intention of holding them for development or management.

speed-up. In labor usage, a term that describes any method of wage payment or other device, intended to force employees to increase production unreasonably. It is used especially to describe any such scheme which requires increased production merely to maintain the former level of earnings. Thus, an INCENTIVE SYSTEM that provides for legitimate increases in compensation for reasonable increases in production would not be considered a *speed-up* system. See also STRETCH-OUT.

spendthrift trust. See under TRUST (1).

spin-off. In financial and tax terminology, a distribution of stock in a newly-created corporation to the present stockholders of a parent corporation. For example, a division of the company, or a previously absorbed subsidiary, may be constituted as a separate corporation, and *spun-off* to the stockholders. This may be done as a maneuver to increase the stockholders' equity without incurring a tax liability, as a result of a court order after an anti-trust suit, or for some other reason. See also SPLIT-OFF; SPLIT UP.

split-dollar insurance. A term for a special form of life insurance purchase plan used in business, under which a company is able to buy a life insurance policy for an employee at little or no cost to the employee, and no long-term cost to the company. Briefly, the company is made the beneficiary of the policy up to its cash reserve value, and pays part of the premium, in proportion to its interest in the policy. Ordinarily, after the first few years, the employee's share of the premium is covered by the policy dividend, so that the insurance is at no cost to him. In effect, the company is making a long-term loan to the employee, which will be repaid out of the proceeds of the policy at the time of his death.

split-off. In financial and tax terminology, a distribution to stockholders, made by a parent company, of the stock of a newly created subsidiary, in exchange for a partial surrender of the stock of the parent company. Thus, it is distinguished from a SPIN-OFF, in which no stock is surrendered in exchange for that distributed. See also SPLIT UP.

split order. See under ORDER (4).

split shift. A term for a regular daily work period which is divided into two or more parts, rather than being continuous. In some types of manufacturing operations, for example, it may be necessary for some employees to make up their full 40 hours of weekly work by working part of the regular day shift one day a week, and part of one day on another shift.

split up. In financial and tax terminology, a transfer of all of the assets of a corporation to two or more newly created corporations, accompanied by a distribution to stockholders of stock in the new corporations in exchange for the surrender of the stock of the old. It is distinguished from a SPIN-OFF or SPLIT OFF in that all of the stock of the old corporation is exchanged for that of the newly created corporations, and the old corporation ceases to exist. In another sense, a STOCK SPLIT.

sponsor. In general, one who agrees to answer for, or stand behind, another. Hence, a SURETY, or one who puts up security for another's debts or actions. In advertising, a person or company undertaking to pay the costs of a radio or television broadcast, in return for which a part of the time of the broadcast is given over to advertising the *sponsor's* products or services.

spot. As used in business, a term always meaning immediate cash payment and immediate delivery. Hence, when a *spot* PRICE is quoted for a commodity, it is the price at which a sale will be made for cash, with the commodity to be delivered immediately, as distinguished from a FUTURES price, which is the price for delivery some time in the future. The term is also used to designate orders, quotations, sales, contracts, etc., which call for cash payment and immediate delivery.

spot price. See under PRICE.

spread. 1. In the securities and commodities markets, the difference between the offered and asked prices of a security or commodity at any moment. Also, in OVER THE COUNTER transactions, and in the buying and selling of currencies, the difference between the broker's buying and selling prices, which is his profit.

2. In the securities trade, the name for a form of STRADDLE, in which two prices are named instead of one. For example, if a stock is selling at 100, a speculator may buy a *spread* option for $5 per share, with a *spread* in the buying and selling prices of 5 points up or down. Thus, if the stock later goes below 90 (including the 5 point *spread* and the 5 point cost of the option), it can be sold at a profit, and similarly, if it goes above 110, it can be bought by the holder of the option at a profit.

3. In ABRITRAGE operations, a term for the situation in which the difference between two markets in the price of a currency or security is greater than usual, and hence offers momentary opportunity for profitable arbitrage, as distinguished from a BACK SPREAD situation, in which the price difference is smaller than normal.

spurious. In general, false or not genuine. As used in business and legal terminology, a synonym for COUNTERFEIT.

spur line. In railroading, the name for a relatively short line of track, running from a TRUNK LINE or BRANCH LINE at one end to a small station or an industrial plant at the other. A *spur line* is usually built and owned by the railroad, but constructed for the convenience and use of one or a few rail shippers.

squatters' rights. See POSSESSION, ADVERSE.

ss. See SCILICET.

stabilization. Any process or course of action whereby prices, such as security or commodity prices, or the value of a currency, are kept artificially steady. This may be done by buying up or selling off supplies of the security, commodity, or currency to equalize the buying and selling pressures in the market, or it may be done by regulation, establishing a fixed or pegged price for the currency in question.

staff. As used in business organization, a term describing those functions which are primarily advisory, supplementary, or consulting, or which provide facilities or services. *Staff* functions are distinguished from LINE (5) functions in that they involve no direct supervisory responsibilities, and are not directly connected with production. Examples of *staff* activities in a typical company include accounting, personnel, maintenance, research, etc. See also LINE ORGANIZATION.

stake. Originally, the amount of a bet, or an amount of money risked in any venture. More particularly, an amount of money provided to the operator of a speculative enterprise, such as an inventor, prospector, etc., on the understanding that the person who provides the *stake* is to share, equally or otherwise, in any eventual profits from the enterprise. A GRUB STAKE, for example, is that given to a mining prospector.

stale. Literally, no longer fresh. In business, out of date, or outstanding for a long time. A claim which has been outstanding and not pressed for a long period of time may be subject to LACHES, and hence unenforceable. A check which has been outstanding for a long period of time, whatever the cause, is known as a *stale* CHECK (1). See also STATUTE OF LIMITATIONS.

stamp tax. See under TAX (2).

standard. Any established measure or basis of comparison or value, by which other things are measured. In business, *standards* may be expressed in terms of weight, size, content, performance, value, etc. See also MONETARY STANDARD.

  commercial ~. One established as the basis of price and contract quotations for regular commerce and trade. *Commercial standards* have been established, for example, for many chemicals, commodities, metals, etc.

  descriptive ~. One which is stated in terms of the physical description of a commodity or product, including color, size, shape, weight, etc., rather than in terms of its performance characteristics, as in a PERFORMANCE STANDARD, which see below.

  performance ~. One which is based on the operating or performance characteristics of a commodity or product, including its durability, elasticity, hardness, output rate, speed, etc., as distinguished from a DESCRIPTIVE STANDARD, which see above.

standard average clause. See COINSURANCE CLAUSE.

standard cost. In COST ACCOUNTING, a predetermined estimated cost of production for a product or service, based on the expected costs of materials, labor, etc., and on the amounts of materials and labor included in the product. Such *standard costs* are used for comparison with actual cost performance, and as a means of compiling interim or temporary accounting reports before the detailed cost figures are available. See also UNIT COST.

standard deviation. See DEVIATION (3).

standard error of estimate. In statistics, a measure of the DEVIATION of the items in a distribution, measured from a line of relationship, such as a regression line, rather than from the arithmetic mean of the distribution. It defines the range of error to be expected in estimates of one variable in the distribution based on given values of the other variable and on the relationship between the two.

standard gauge. See GAUGE (1).

standardization. In general, any setting of basic and rational limits to which the specifications of various products must conform. In industry, for example, *standardization* has been widely accepted for such things as the alloy content of stainless steels, the pitch of threads on screws and bolts, the thickness of lumber, etc. In agriculture, *standardization has* been extended to the grading of eggs, the butterfat content of dairy products, the grading of meats, etc.

standard metropolitan area. As defined by the Bureau of the Census, a major urban center, together with the adjoining territory which is linked to it. As used in the various Censuses conducted by the Bureau, each *standard metropolitan area* contains at least one major central city with a population of 50,000 or more, and the county in which it is contained. Additional complete counties which are contiguous to the central one may also be included if they are deemed to be closely integrated economically with the central county and its central city. Since each *standard metropolitan area* is made up of complete counties, it may include some territory which is actually rural in nature, and may exclude small parts of adjoining counties which are actually urban in nature.

standard money. See MONETARY STANDARD.

standard of living. In economics, a concept consisting of the aggregate of the amounts and qualities of the goods and services which any large social group considers essential to maintaining a reasonable scale or plane of living. Strictly speaking, the abstract *standard of living* of a group differs from its actual plane or scale of living at a particular moment in time, though the term is frequently used loosely in this sense. A COST OF LIVING index, for example, measures the cost of maintaining a particular *standard of living,* not the cost of the things that people actually buy in the proportions indicated by their current scale of living.

standard operating procedure (S.O.P.). Any method of operating or of conduct which has been reduced to a set of rules and regulations which can be followed. In business, for example, most companies have established *standard operating procedures* for such widely diverse activities as obtaining supplies, handling customer complaints, processing new employees, etc.

standard time. The time for any given place or zone as established by the Standard Time Act of 1918. The Act provides for five time zones, Eastern, Central, Mountain, Pacific, and Alaska, in each of which the standard time is one hour earlier as the zones progress from east to west. Each zone is roughly 15 degrees of longitude wide, and the zones are centered on the 75th, 90th, 105th, 120th, and 150th degrees of longitude west of Greenwich, respectively. The actual boundaries of the zones, however, as set by the Interstate Commerce Commission, are designed to avoid centers of population, and vary considerably from the longitudinal lines. In eastern Canada, a sixth standard time zone, the Atlantic zone, is used. See also DAYLIGHT SAVING TIME.

staple. 1. Originally, in Medieval Europe, a market place or town designated as a central market for the trade in the principal commodities of a region or area. Hence, in current usage, any of the principal or basic commodities of an area. More broadly, any basic commodities in general, such as grain, cotton, etc.

2. In a completely different sense, from a different derivation, a *staple* is a support, or a holding device of any sort. In mining and construction, it is a U-shaped bar or rod which is driven into a wall or rock and to which a cable is attached. In business, it is a small U-shaped wire fastener used for attaching papers, and usually dispensed from a stapling machine. In some cases, usages (1) and (2) have grown to be confused, so that a *staple* diet, for example, is sometimes one that will support life, and sometimes one including the principal food commodities.

starboard. Originally, the steering side, or the side of a ship on which the rudder was hung in early times. Hence, it is the right-hand side of a ship, as distinguished from the PORT, or left-hand side, facing forward.

state. In the United States, one of the 48 basic political subdivisions of the country, or anything pertaining to one of these basic subdivisions. More generally, any sovereign political area, or the government of such a sovereign area. The *state* is sometimes distinguished from the nation, which is the people themselves, and from the country, which is the geographic area, while the *state* is the political entity. In various federal laws, such as the Bankruptcy Act, the District of Columbia and the territories of Alaska and Puerto Rico are considered as *states.*

state auditor. See AUDITOR.

state bank. See under BANK.

state bond. See BOND (1), MUNICIPAL.

stated account. See ACCOUNT (1) STATED.

statement. 1. In accounting, any of various periodic formal reports of the condition or status of a business operation, such as an INCOME STATEMENT, FINANCIAL STATEMENT, etc. In general, a statement is a declaration of the accounting facts as they exist at some particular point in time, or at the end of a defined period of time.

  2. In particular, an account summarizing the transactions between a creditor and debtor, supplier and customer, etc., over a period of time. See, for example, BANK STATEMENT; STATEMENT OF ACCOUNT.

statement of account. A statement submitted by a supplier to a customer periodically, usually monthly, listing the amounts billed or invoiced during the period, the payments received, and the amounts still outstanding. A *statement of account* is distinguished from an INVOICE in that it is not a formal request for payment. Sometimes, however, a specific request for payment of the balance may be added to a *statement of account*.

station. Originally, a standing place, or position, and hence, a status, level, or rank. In railroading, a place at which trains regularly stop, and at which passengers and freight are regularly picked up or discharged. It may be a TERMINAL, or main *station* at the end of a route, or a WAY STATION, a *station* along the way or route.

statistical quality control. The control of the quality of manufactured or purchased goods or materials, within desirable limits, by the application of statistical techniques and principles. The primary technique is the selection and testing of small SAMPLES of the product being inspected, on the basis of which conclusions are drawn concerning the lot from which the samples are drawn. Typically, control limits are set, within which the particular characteristic may vary without the sample, and thus the entire lot, being rejected for non-conformance with the desired quality level. When applied to production processes, the careful examination of the results for successive samples makes it possible to make the necessary adjustments in the process before the deviations from desired quality become so serious as to require the rejection of the product.

statistics. The science of collecting, classifying, analyzing, and interpreting mass data which can be expressed in numerical or quantitative terms. Also, any such numerical or quantitative facts, collected and arrayed in rational order. Finally, any of the various measures used in statistical analysis, such as AVERAGES (1), DEVIATIONS (3), etc.

status quo. Literally, in Latin, the situation as it is; the existing state of affairs. It may be the situation as it exists at present, or at some specified time in the past, or as it existed before the occurrence of some specified event.

statute. Broadly, a decree or enactment; a law or item of legislation. Particularly, in current American usage, a law or decree of one of the 48 states, as distinguished both from the federal laws and from municipal or other local ordinances and rules.

statute mile. See MILE.

statute of distribution. The law, enacted separately in each state and differing somewhat from state to state, providing for the manner of distribution of the ESTATE (2) of a person who dies without leaving a valid will, or without specifically disposing of all of his property. Typically, it prescribes the DISTRIBUTIVE SHARE of each class of heir, such as the widow, child, and other relatives of the deceased person.

statute of frauds. The law in each state enacted to protect persons entering into agreements and contracts from the loss of their rights or property through fraud, deceit, perjury, etc. The statute differs in each state, but generally provides for written agreements of transfer, and for the proper signature and dating of such agreements. The particular statute of the appropriate state should be consulted in any case.

statute of limitations. The law in each state which prescribes the definite time limit to the period within which a suit for redress may be brought under law or equity, to the period required for the acquisition of title to property by adverse possession, to the period within which the state must begin prosecution for certain crimes, etc. The terms in the statutes of the different states vary, but the time required for title by adverse possession is generally 20 years, and the time within which an action must be brought in commercial cases is frequently 6 years. See also POSSESSION, ADVERSE; SAVING THE STATUTE.

statutory. Provided by law; required or prescribed by law. As generally used, the term refers to any laws, regulations, ordinances, etc., not strictly to the STATUTES of a state government.

statutory reserve. See RESERVE (1), LEGAL.

stay-in strikes. See STRIKE, SIT-DOWN.

steal. In law, to commit THEFT, especially by stealth, or secretly. In common usage, the term includes both the commission of BUR-

GLARY, which is theft by stealth, and ROB-
BERY, which is theft from the person. In
business slang, anything obtained for less
than its regular price, or at an exceptional
bargain, may be called a *steal*.

step-rate premium. See PREMIUM (2), NATURAL.

sterling. 1. The basis of the currency of Great
Britain, especially the POUND (2) *sterling*.
Originally, the term is derived from a small
coin, marked with a star, so that one pound
sterling was literally the value of a pound
of these coins. It now refers to the value of
the British currency in general, at whatever
level it is established by law. See also BILL
OF EXCHANGE, STERLING; BOND (1), STERLING.
2. A standard for silver of an established
degree of FINENESS. As set by the British government, *sterling* silver is silver which is at
least 222 parts out of 240 of pure silver, and
18 parts or less of alloy metal.

steward. See SHOP STEWARD.

stet. In Latin, let it stand. A term used in
editing copy for a printer, or in annotating
any document, meaning that the original
writing is to stand, and that an intended
correction or revision is not to be made.

stipend. A regular, periodic payment for services, especially that paid to a clergyman,
teacher, public official or similar public servant; a SALARY.

stipulation. In law, any matter in agreement
between the parties to a contract, or agreed
to in advance between the parties to a dispute in court. In admiralty law, in particular, it is an agreement in the form of a
SURETY, by which the owner of a ship agrees
to indemnify another person, and to place
his ship and cargo as surety.

stirpes. See PER STIRPES.

stock. 1. A share in the ownership or equity
of a corporation; the capital invested in a
corporation, as represented by shares of this
capital held by individual persons in the
form of stock certificates. A corporation may
issue several different classifications of *stock*,
with different privileges, rights, and responsibilities. The principal classes of *stock*, and
the various types of *stock* which have developed, are listed and defined below:
A, B, etc. ∼. *Stock* of a particular series
or issue, identified by a letter to distinguish
it from other *stock* of the same class issued
by the corporation but carrying different
provisions. A and B PREFERRED STOCK, which
see below, may carry different dividend
rates, or A and B COMMON STOCK, which also
see below, may come in order of precedence
for dividend payments, etc.

accumulative ∼. See CUMULATIVE STOCK,
below.

active ∼. One in which there are frequent
trading transactions on the STOCK EXCHANGE.
Also, one for which the current market
price is reported daily in the newspapers.
See also INACTIVE STOCK, below.

assented ∼. Shares of *stock* deposited by
their owners under a REORGANIZATION agreement, when a corporation is being reformed
after becoming insolvent. See also NON-
ASSENTED STOCK, below.

assessable ∼. One which may be assessed
or charged to help meet the liabilities of
the corporation in the event of bankruptcy.
Most bank *stocks* were formerly assessable,
and insurance company *stocks* sometimes are.
Also, any *stock* which is not fully paid up
is assessable up to its par value in the event
of bankruptcy. See also NON-ASSESSABLE STOCK;
PAID-UP STOCK; PAR VALUE STOCK, below.

assigned ∼. One which has been properly
signed on the reverse by the holder for
transfer to a new owner. *Stock* may be
assigned in blank when it is deposited with
a broker for sale, or it may be *assigned* to a
particular individual when it is sold.

authorized ∼. The total number of shares
of *stock* which a corporation may issue, as
stated in its original certificate of incorporation, or as later provided by the stockholders. It is not necessary for the corporation to issue all of the *authorized stock*.

blue-chip ∼. Originally, any high quality
stock selling for $100 or more per share. As
currently used, any well-known, high-grade
stock, with a good record of earnings,
dividend payments, and price stability.

bonus ∼. The term used to describe those
shares of *stock* which may be given to an
underwriter or promoter as compensation
for his efforts in moving the *stock*. *Bonus
stock* may also be given to purchasers of the
corporation's PREFERRED STOCK, which see below, or its bonds, as an inducement to
purchase.

callable ∼. See REDEEMABLE STOCK, below.

capital ∼. The total amount of *stock*
which a corporation is authorized to issue.
It may be divided into a number of shares
of stated value, or each share may carry no
stated value. In either event, the amount
paid in by the original corporators may have
little relation to the stated value of each
share or of the total amount. When the
amount paid in exceeds the stated value of
the *capital stock*, the excess is carried as
paid-in SURPLUS on the corporate balance
sheet.

classified ∼. One which is issued in more
than one class, such as COMMON STOCK and

PREFERRED STOCK, which see below, or when the preferred *stock* is divided into classes, such as first preferred, second preferred, etc.

clearing-house ∼. The term for those *stocks* which are paid for and delivered through the STOCK CLEARING CORPORATION; thus, those which are listed on the stock exchange.

common ∼. Corporate *stock* which is not preferred over any other with regard to dividend payments, but which is usually the only class of *stock* with voting rights in the management of the corporation. Dividends on the *common stock* are declared and paid only when there is sufficient profit remaining after all other forms of securities, such as bonds, have been satisfied, and after the PREFERRED STOCK, which see below, has received its dividend. On the other hand, there is no limit to the amount of dividend that may be declared on the *common stock,* as there usually is on preferred stock.

convertible ∼. In general, any class of *stock* which may be converted into another class of *stock* in the corporation at the option of the holder. More particularly, PREFERRED STOCK, which see below, which may be converted into COMMON STOCK, which see above.

cumulative ∼. A form of PREFERRED STOCK, which see below, on which unpaid dividends accumulate until they can be paid. When profits are not great enough to meet the full dividend on such *stock,* any unpaid dividend accumulates until enough profit to cover it is earned, and meanwhile no dividends may be paid on other *stock.* When the arrears on the *cumulative stock* have been made up, dividends may again be paid on the other *stock.*

curb ∼. One traded on the CURB EXCHANGE; that is, one not listed on the New York Stock Exchange.

debenture ∼. An infrequently used term for PREFERRED STOCK, which see below. In England, it is the name of a form of mortgage bond.

deferred ∼. A class of *stock* on which dividends are not paid until some condition is met, or until some future time. BONUS STOCK, which is given to the organizers or promoters of a venture, may be deferred for a period of time.

donated ∼. A term for *stock* which may be returned, or *donated,* to the corporation by the original stockholders, so that the corporation may sell the *stock* to obtain additional funds. This may be done, for example, when it is desired to broaden the ownership of the company and obtain outside capital, but not to issue additional shares of *stock.*

double liability ∼. *Stock* which is fully

paid but assessable up to an amount equal to its par value to meet obligations of the corporation. Most bank stock was formerly of this form. See also ASSESSABLE STOCK, above.

floating ∼. In different contexts, it may be newly issued *stock* which has not yet been permanently bought by public holders, *stock* bought for speculation and held in the name of a broker since it is soon to be sold again, or that portion of a corporation's *stock* which is available on the open market for speculation.

founders' ∼. See BONUS STOCK, above.

full-paid ∼. *Stock* for which the original subscribers have paid in at least the full amount of the stated par value. Such *stock* is then NON-ASSESSABLE STOCK, which see below.

full- ∼. A term sometimes used for *stock* with a face or par value of $100. Hence, *stock* with $50 par value is known as *half-stock,* $25 par *stock* is *quarter-stock,* etc.

growth ∼. One which is expected to increase in value, in the long run, at a greater rate than the average *stock.* This growth is usually due to a combination of the increasing volume of business of the company and a policy of retaining a large share of profits to promote growth.

guaranteed ∼. One on which the payment of dividends is guaranteed by a company other than the one which originally issued it. For example, a railroad which leases the property of another may guarantee the dividends on the *stock* of the leased road.

inactive ∼. One which is infrequently traded, and thus one on which prices are reported only weekly or less often in financial reporting. See also ACTIVE STOCK, above.

industrial ∼. In securities trade usage, the *stock* of any manufacturing or trading company, as distinguished from that of a railroad or public utility.

international ∼. A term for a *stock* of a corporation in one country which is traded on the exchanges of other countries. See also DEPOSITARY RECEIPT.

issued ∼. Those shares of corporate *stock* which have been authorized and actually sold or distributed to stockholders. The term includes both OUTSTANDING STOCK, and TREASURY STOCK, which see below. See also UNISSUED STOCK, below.

listed ∼. One which has been admitted for trading on a regular stock exchange such as the New York Stock Exchange, American Stock Exchange, etc.

management ∼. *Stock* which is given special voting privileges, to assure control of a corporation's board of directors by the holders of the *management stock*. Such *stock* may be issued, for example, when a corporation is formed for a special purpose, to assure that the purpose will be carried out. Also, loosely, the *stock* held by the management group of a corporation.

non-assented ~. Shares which the holders have refused to deposit for exchange for new securities when a corporation is going through a REORGANIZATION. See also ASSENTED STOCK, above.

non-assessable ~. *Stock* which is fully paid, and which therefore may not be assessed to meet the obligations of the corporation in the event of insolvency. The words "full paid and non-assessable" are usually printed on the face of the certificate for such *stock* to identify it. See also ASSESSABLE STOCK; FULL-PAID STOCK, above.

non-cumulative ~. *Stock* on which unpaid dividends do not accumulate for future payment. When profits are not large enough to pay the full dividend on *non-cumulative* PREFERRED STOCK, which see below, the dividend due in the following year is only the regular dividend amount, and any income over this may be used immediately to pay dividends on other *stock*.

no par value ~. Capital *stock* of a corporation, each share of which bears no stated face or par value. The actual value of the *stock* may be determined by dividing the total net assets of the corporation by the number of shares outstanding at any time. Some corporations issue *no par value stock* because they are incorporated in states which place a tax on the par value of issued *stock*. It is sometimes known as unvalued, or without par value *stock*. See also PAR VALUE STOCK, below.

ordinary ~. A term for COMMON STOCK, which see above.

outstanding ~. *Stock* which has been issued and is in the hands of individual stockholders. It differs from ISSUED STOCK, which see above, in that it does not include TREASURY STOCK, which was once issued, but has been bought back by the company and is no longer *outstanding*.

over the counter ~. See UNLISTED STOCK, below.

paid-up ~. See FULL-PAID STOCK, above.

participating ~. A form of PREFERRED STOCK, which see below, which, when corporate profits are above a certain amount, is entitled to share with the COMMON STOCK, which see above, in additional dividends. Typically, the *participating stock* receives dividends at a fixed rate, after which the common *stock* receives the excess up to a given amount, beyond which both classes of *stock* share in any further dividends.

part-paid ~. Any *stock* on which the holders have paid less than the full par value, as distinguished from FULL-PAID STOCK, which see above.

par value ~. Any *stock* for which a fixed value has been set originally for each share, by dividing the total *capital stock* value by the number of shares to be issued. The *par value* of the *stock* has no necessary relation to the actual value, since the *capital stock* may be only a small part of the total net worth of the corporation, the major part being included in SURPLUS. Usually *par value common stock* has a low or nominal par value, while *par value preferred stock* usually has a value of $100, $50, or a similar amount per share. See also NO PAR VALUE STOCK, above.

penny ~. A term for a *stock* which is issued at a price of only a few cents a share, usually for the purpose of attracting buyers who feel that they are getting a bargain when they can buy many shares for less money. Such *stocks* are often highly speculative, and may be of questionable value.

potential ~. See UNISSUED STOCK below.

preferred ~. One that is preferred over other *stocks* of the same company with regard to dividend payments and any distribution of assets on liquidation. *Preferred stock* must receive its full dividend before any dividend can be paid on other *stock*. It may be CUMULATIVE or NON-CUMULATIVE STOCK, and may be PARTICIPATING STOCK, which see above, but ordinarily would not be both cumulative and participating. It is usually issued as PAR VALUE STOCK, which also see above. In many corporations, the *preferred stock* carries no privilege of voting in the management of the company.

prior preference ~. An issue of *stock*, usually of PREFERRED STOCK, which see above, which must receive its dividends before other issues, including other preferred issues.

reacquired ~. See TREASURY STOCK, below.

redeemable ~. One, usually a PREFERRED STOCK, which see above, which may be redeemed, or called in and retired, at the option of the company, after some set date and on certain conditions. Such *stock* is usually redeemed at its par value. Many companies issue preferred *stock* originally as a means of attracting capital, then redeem it as soon as funds are available to improve the dividend position of the common stock.

treasury ~. Shares which have been once issued but which have since been repurchased by the corporation and held by it.

Treasury stock receives no dividends, which is one reason why the corporation may acquire such *stock*. It is also available for distribution as bonuses to employees and others, or for sale on the market if the price should be advantageous. *Stock* which has been authorized but never issued is not *treasury stock*, but UNISSUED STOCK, which see below, though it is sometimes loosely known as *treasury stock*.

unissued ∼. *Stock* which has been authorized for issue but not yet issued to actual owners. It is not included in the capital stock of the corporation and receives no dividends. See also ISSUED STOCK, above.

unlisted ∼. One which is not listed for trading on one of the regular stock exchanges, and is therefore traded in direct negotiations, or OVER THE COUNTER. See also LISTED STOCK, above.

unvalued ∼. See NO PAR VALUE STOCK, above.

voting ∼. That which carries the right to vote in the management of the company. Ordinarily, only the COMMON STOCK, which see above, is the *voting stock* of a corporation.

watered ∼. *Stock* issued as FULL-PAID, PAR VALUE STOCK, which see above, when the total par value of the issue is actually greater than the total amount of paid in capital, so that the face value of each share represents at least partly fictitious value. The term derives from the practice of "watering" cattle, or forcing them to drink excessive amounts of water before sale, to create fictitious weight and thus obtain a fraudulently high price. Besides issuing shares for more than their true value, *watered stock* may be created by giving par value *stock* to promoters as BONUS STOCK, which see above, by accepting overvalued assets in payment for *stock*, by declaring *stock* dividends in par value *stock* when no additional value has been added to net assets, etc.

without par value ∼. See NO PAR VALUE STOCK, above.

2. Originally, the goods which were the basis of a business, the capital of a retail business. Hence, the aggregate of the goods on hand and unsold in any business; the INVENTORY. As currently used, the *stock* of a business may consist of materials for processing, or work in process, or finished *stock* held for sale. Originally, however, the term referred particularly to goods held for sale.

stock broker. See BROKER (2).

stock certificate. The written evidence of ownership of one or more shares of the stock of a corporation. Each certificate is issued in the name of one of the contributors to the capital of the corporation, and registered in that name on the TRANSFER BOOK of the corporation. As the shares of stock are bought and sold on the market, the original certificates may be retired and new ones issued to the new owners, rather than being actually transfered.

Stock Clearing Corporation. The CLEARING HOUSE operated by the New York Stock Exchange for its members. The activities of the corporation include the clearing and settling of cash balances between member traders, the checking and clearing of purchase and sale transactions, and the handling of stock transfer operations for members. The corporation issues receipts for securities in its hands during transfer, which receipts are accepted by banks as collateral on loans to members.

stock company. See under COMPANY.

stock company insurance. See under INSURANCE.

stock corporation. See under CORPORATION.

stock dividend. See under DIVIDEND.

stock exchange. See EXCHANGE (2), SECURITIES.

stock exchange seat. See SEAT.

stockholder. The name for a person who owns and holds one or more shares of the STOCK (1) of a corporation, stock company, or other stock association. Particularly, one who has contributed money, property, or something else of value to the capital stock of a corporation, or who has bought one or more shares of corporate stock, or otherwise legally obtained such stock.

stock insurance company. See under INSURANCE COMPANY.

stock in trade. In general, the things used or needed to carry on a business activity. Thus, a plumber's *stock in trade* includes not only the plumbing materials and products he uses and sells, but his tools, equipment, and other things needed to carry on his trade. In a more limited sense, the STOCK (2), carried for sale by a retail or wholesale business.

stock-jobbing. In the securities trade, a slang term used for the manipulation of stock prices by dishonest or irregular activities. More broadly, any irregular trading in securities, such as that carried on by a BUCKET SHOP or other unlicensed securities trader.

stock ledger. See under LEDGER.

stock market. Strictly, an EXCHANGE (2) on which stocks are bought and sold. More broadly, the entire business of buying and selling corporate securities, including stocks, bonds, investment company shares, etc. As frequently used, the term refers specifically to the New York Stock Exchange, which is the principal market for corporate securities in the United States.

stock note. See under NOTE (1).

stock-out. See OUT OF STOCK.

stockowner. See STOCKHOLDER.

stockpiling. The accumulation of a long-term reserve supply of critical materials which are likely to be in short supply, especially during a wartime emergency. The federal government has conducted such *stockpiling* activities since World War II, and maintains strategic *stockpiles* of such critical materials as aluminum, rubber, copper, chromium, tungsten, and other industrial materials. *Stockpiling* may also refer to the accumulation of supplies of finished goods, such as ammunition, certain machine tools, spare parts, etc.

stock power. A POWER OF ATTORNEY to transfer ownership of stock. See also ASSIGNMENT IN BLANK.

stock purchase plan. Any of various plans established by corporations to permit their employees, or selected groups of employees, to purchase stock in the corporation. In some plans, the employees are permitted to buy a limited amount of stock at less than the current market value, while in other plans the contribution of the corporation consists only of a payroll deduction for the regular purchase of stock shares. The general purpose of all such plans is to give the employees a stake in the success of the corporation, and an opportunity to share in the profits and responsibilities of the company.

stock purchase warrant. See WARRANT (4).

stock record card. A device regularly used in inventory control, on which are recorded the amount in inventory at a given date, each addition to and withdrawal from inventory, and the balance on hand at any time. Ordinarily, a separate *stock record card* is kept for each item on which separate inventory records are desired. The device itself may not literally be a card, but may be a form of any sort. At the time of each physical inventory, the actual amount on hand is compared with the running balance shown on the *stock record card,* and the card is adjusted, if necessary, to show the new balance. See also INVENTORY.

stock record date. The date established by a corporation as the date to be used in determining ownership of stock for dividend purposes. The owner of the stock on the *stock record date* receives the dividend declared payable to owners of record on that date, though the dividend may actually be paid at a later date. If a stock has been sold just before the *stock record date,* and the transfer of ownership has not yet been recorded by the corporation, the old owner who receives the dividend is required to turn it over to the new owner. See also EX-DIVIDEND.

stock register. The name for the record of stock ownership and transfers kept by the REGISTRAR of a corporation. This record is kept in addition to any kept by the transfer agent, or by the corporation itself. See also AGENT, TRANSFER.

stock registrar. See REGISTRAR.

stock right. See RIGHT (1).

stock savings bank. See under BANK.

stock split. A term for the increase in the number of issued shares of stock of a given class by a corporation, by the mechanism of substituting for the original shares a greater number of shares with the same total aggregate value, but a proportionately lower value per share. If the stock is par value stock, the total par value remains the same, and the par value of each share is reduced. It is most common for the new stock to be issued in some even multiple of the old, so that a *stock split* is commonly referred to as a two-for-one split, a three-for-one split, etc. One of the chief purposes for carrying out a *stock split* is the desire to lower the per share market price of the stock, making it more flexible in trading, and perhaps encouraging wider ownership.

stock split-down. A term for the reverse of a normal STOCK SPLIT, in which the total number of issued shares of a stock is reduced, without reducing the total value of the issue, by issuing one new share of stock in exchange for each two or more shares previously issued. The most frequent reason for such a step is the desire to raise the market price of the stock, if it had previously been selling at an extremely low price which made it appear unattractive and speculative to investors.

stock-taking. See INVENTORY.

stock ticker. See TICKER.

stock transfer. The act or process of transferring the record of ownership of shares of stock in a corporation. The actual transfer takes place at the time the stock is bought and sold, but the record of this transfer is made on the TRANSFER BOOK of the corporation by the transfer agent, and this is the official record for purposes of paying dividends, mailing meeting notices to stockholders, etc. See also AGENT, TRANSFER.

stock warrant. See WARRANT (4).

stone. A unit of weight, now used almost exclusively in Great Britain, where it is legally established as the equivalent of 14 pounds avoirdupois. It is used primarily for expressing the weight of persons, or of animals.

stop. As usually used in business, to issue an order to halt or *stop* a transaction already initiated, or to bring a transaction to completion at a specified point. See, for example, ORDER (4), STOP; STOP PAYMENT.

stop-loss order. See ORDER (4), STOP.

stop-off charge. In railroading, a charge made by a railroad to a shipper for the privilege of stopping a freight car at a point between the shipping point and the marked destination of the shipment. Such a charge might be made, for example, if the shipment is halted en route to permit the repackaging or further processing of the contents. Though a charge may be made for the handling of the freight car, the freight rate itself is usually the through rate from shipping point to destination. See also TRANSIT PRIVILEGE.

stop order. See under ORDER (4).

stoppage in transit. The legal right which a seller has to stop in passage or transit, and to repossess, any goods which have been sold but not yet delivered and paid for. This right may be exercised especially if the buyer is placed in bankruptcy before the goods are delivered. Though technically title to the goods may already have passed, the right of *stoppage in transit* enables the seller to recover them, and thus avoid having them declared part of the bankrupt estate, to be divided among all the creditors.

stop payment. An order from a depositor to a bank, requesting the bank to refuse to accept for payment a particular check which has been issued by the depositor. Such an order might be given, for example, if a check has been lost in the mail, to prevent a finder from cashing it, or if a transaction for which the check was payment has been cancelled but the check not returned. It is illegal in many states, however, to attempt to break an otherwise valid contract or agreement by placing a *stop payment* order on a check.

storage. In general, the holding of goods or materials for future use, sale, or delivery. Within a company, it is the function of holding either raw materials or finished goods, preparatory to their use in operations or their shipment to customers. As a service, it is the holding of goods, such as furniture, household effects, motor vehicles, or commercial products, in a WAREHOUSE, for which the owner of the goods pays a fee usually based on the amount of space required, the value of the goods stored, or both.

   dead ~. The *storage* of property, especially personal property such as furniture, motor vehicles, etc., for an uninterrupted long period of time, without easy access to the stored property. The charge for such *dead storage* is ordinarily considerably less than the charge for LIVE STORAGE, which see below.

   live ~. The *storage* of property in such a fashion that the owner has easy access to the stored goods. This access may be used for adding to or removing part of the goods, for referring to stored records, or for other purposes. The charge for such *live storage* is necessarily higher than the charge for DEAD STORAGE, which see above.

store. 1. To accumulate or hold goods in STORAGE; to collect and deposit goods in a WAREHOUSE or other place for storage. Also, in the plural, the goods or supplies so stored. In some cases, the term *stores* is restricted to those goods or supplies which are to be consumed or used within the company, rather than those which are to be sold, which are known as STOCK (2).
   2. A retail STORE.

store audit. See AUDIT (2).

store credit. See CREDIT (3), BOOK.

store-door delivery. In rail and truck shipping, a term for the delivery of goods direct to the receiver's place of business. This may actually be a retail store, but the same term is used for delivery to a warehouse, plant, or office. There may or may not be an extra charge for such delivery, depending on the particular class of freight shipment involved and the general practice of the particular carrier.

store order act. The name for a type of statute passed by some states, forbidding the payment of wages in any but monetary form, and specifically forbidding payment in the form of an order for merchandise or a *store order*.

stowage. The act or process of placing cargo in proper order in the hold of a ship, or sometimes in a freight car or truck. Also, the charge made for placing cargo in the hold of a ship, or the extra charge made for placing specialized cargo.

straddle. In the securities trade, a form of option which is, in effect, a combination of a PUT and a CALL (1). The buyer of a *straddle* option agrees to purchase or sell the stock at the current market price, and to complete the transaction by selling at a higher price or buying to cover at a lower price at a later time, but before a specified date. If the option is not taken up, the price paid for the privilege is forfeit. For example, if a stock is selling at 100, a person may buy a *straddle* on the stock at this price for $5 per share. Then, if the stock rises to over 105, he may take up his option to buy, and resell the stock at a profit, even including the charge for the option. On the other hand, if the stock falls to below 95, he may exercise his option to sell, buying on the market at the lower price to cover the sale at a profit. However, if the stock stays within a narrow price range during the period of the option, it will usually be dropped. See also SPREAD (2).

straight. A term sometimes meaning IRREVOCABLE. Thus, *straight* CREDIT (3) is irrevocable credit, a *straight* LETTER OF CREDIT is an irrevocable letter of credit, etc.

straight bill of lading. See under BILL OF LADING.

straight life insurance. See ORDINARY LIFE INSURANCE, under INSURANCE, LIFE, ACCIDENT, AND HEALTH.

straight line depreciation. See under DEPRECIATION.

straight-line rate. A term for any rate or basis for charges or payment which is directly proportional to the quantity, and does not increase or decrease as volume changes. A PIECE WORK wage system, for example, is a *straight-line* system if the same rate is paid for each unit of production, instead of a higher rate being paid for production over a certain amount. Similarly, a utility may charge a *straight-line rate* for some classes of service, meaning that the charge per unit of electricity or gas consumed is the same regardless of volume. See also SLIDING SCALE.

straight shipment. A term for a shipment of goods consigned to the name of a particular person or company, and not merely to the order of a person or company. See also BILL OF LADING, STRAIGHT.

straight time. The term for TIME WORK paid for at regular wage rates, as distinguished from time paid for at OVERTIME or PREMIUM (1) rates.

stratified sample. See under SAMPLE (3).

straw. As used in various business terms, not financially responsible, or generally false and worthless. *Straw* BAIL, for example, is bail put up by a financially irresponsible person, and therefore worthless. A *straw* BID is a bid submitted by one who is unable to fulfill its terms. A *straw* name added to a list of EN-DORSERS to a note, to meet the legal requirements as to the number of endorsers, is usually the name of a clerical employee or similar person who does not actually meet the requirements of financial integrity for an endorser. See also DUMMY.

straw boss. In business slang, a term for a FOREMAN, especially one who supervises a factory or contruction work crew.

street. 1. A contraction of Wall Street, and hence, the financial district, or more particularly, the securities and financial trade, or the money market in general. It is common for newspapers to quote the opinion of the *street,* meaning the financial trade, or for a person to say that he is employed in the *street,* meaning in a company connected with securities or financial operations.

2. In the securities trade, a term meaning not on the regular market, or not through the regular securities exchange channels. See, for example, PRICE, STREET. See also BROKER (2), OUTSIDE.

street name. In the securities trade, a term for the recording of the ownership of stock in the name of a brokerage house, rather than in the name of the individual purchaser. The purchaser is the legal owner of the stock, but the broker is listed on the TRANSFER BOOK as the owner, and receives the dividends, which he transfers to the owner. Purchasers frequently buy stocks in a *street name* as a matter of convenience, since the broker keeps the certificate in safe keeping, and to avoid the need of executing an ASSIGNMENT when the stock is later sold.

street paper. See under COMMERCIAL PAPER.

stretch-out. In labor usage, any system or plan under which an employee's responsibilities or duties are increased without an accompanying increase in wages. For example, an operator may be required to attend an additional machine, or an assembly line worker may be required to perform additional operations. In effect, it is the same as a SPEED-UP, applied to situations in which piece work wages are not paid.

strict construction. Any interpretation of a law, contract, regulation, etc., under which the strict letter of the document is followed as closely as possible, and any possible alternative meanings are narrowly or conservatively construed. It is the opposite of a LIBERAL CONSTRUCTION, under which the wording of the document is enlarged or stretched to have a broader or looser meaning.

strike. In labor usage, the act by a body of

workers of leaving their work at a pre-arranged time, or failing to appear for work when scheduled, in an effort to force an employer to accept their demands with regard to wages or working conditions, or perhaps to call public attention to some condition, or to voice a protest against some political or economic situation. The various kinds and classifications of *strikes* are listed and defined below.

economic ~. One which is called by workers strictly for the purpose of enforcing their economic demands on their employer. Under various laws, the right to call such a *strike* cannot be abridged by injunction or otherwise.

general ~. One which is called and effective throughout an entire community, or throughout an entire industry, or even throughout an entire country. Such *strikes* are frequently POLITICAL STRIKES, which see below.

illegal ~. One which is called in violation of the terms of a union contract providing that there shall be no *strikes* during the life of the contract. Also, one which is called without the proper authorization or prior vote of the union members. See also OUTLAW STRIKE, and WILDCAT STRIKE, below.

jurisdictional ~. One which is called as the result of a JURISDICTIONAL DISPUTE. For example, members of one trade or craft union on a project may *strike* over the assignment of certain work to members of another union.

outlaw ~. One called by a local union without the consent or against the orders of the national union organization, when such consent is required by the union by-laws or by a union contract. In common usage, it differs from a WILDCAT STRIKE, which see below, which is called against the wishes of the local union officials.

quickie ~. A term for one called suddenly, without prior notice. When the law or a contract requires advance notice of intention to *strike,* such a *strike* is illegal.

political ~. One called to enforce the political demands of workers, or to protest against some action by the government. Such *strikes* are usually GENERAL STRIKES, which see above, rather than being directed against a particular employer.

secondary ~. One called against an employer who uses materials produced in a plant which is itself on *strike,* or who has other business dealings with a company on *strike,* and not because of any direct grievances against the employer. See also SYMPATHETIC STRIKE, below.

sit-down ~. One in which the employees, instead of leaving their place of work, re-main at their places but refuse to work. Such *strikes,* in which the strikers remain on the employers' property, are also variously known as *sit-in strikes, stay-in strikes,* etc.

sympathetic ~. One called by a union in sympathy with another union, or to help another union enforce its demands. For example, members of one union in a company may *strike* in sympathy with the members of another union who are striking against the company. Also, workers in a company supplying a struck plant may *strike* in sympathy with the employees of the customer company. There is frequently an overlap between the definition of a SECONDARY STRIKE, which see above, and a *sympathetic strike.*

wildcat ~. One called by a group of employees in a company without the authorization of the local union officials, and without a vote of the union membership. For example, employees in one department, who have a particular grievance against the employer, may call such a *wildcat strike* without taking their grievance to the union membership.

strikebreaker. An employee specifically hired to take the place of an employee who has gone on strike. In another sense, a person employed to use force and violence, if necessary, to break up a strike. Also, sometimes, an employee who refuses to join a strike, and continues at his work. See also FINK; SCAB.

strong market. In securities trade usage, a market situation in which there is more buying pressure than selling pressure. Thus, a market in which prices tend to remain level, or rise, as distinguished from a WEAK MARKET in which prices tend to decline.

structure. As used in law, contracts, and business statistics, anything that is built or constructed by man, and permanently attached to land. Thus it is a much broader term than BUILDING, which is restricted to *structures* intended to be occupied by man. *Structures* include not only buildings of all kinds, but also bridges, dams, oil wells, etc. The term excludes such things as ships, however, which are not permanently attached to land.

stuffer. In advertising, an expression for any piece of advertising literature designed to be inserted in an envelope already containing other material to be mailed. A department store, for example, may include *stuffers* with its monthly mailings of invoices to charge account customers.

stumpage. A fee paid to the owner of land by a person who obtains the right to remove and utilize the stumps remaining on the land after it has been cut over for lumber

The fee paid, and the permission given, may also cover the right to remove whatever standing timber, such as scrub, still remains on the land. Also, as sometimes used, the estimated value of the remaining timber and the stumps on the land.

style. In business, a TRADE NAME, or designation under which an organization does business. The term is especially used for a name or designation which is not registered as a TRADEMARK, and is not part of a corporate name. A partnership, for example, may adopt a particular name or phrase as the STYLE under which it conducts business.

sub-contract. See under CONTRACT (1).

subject to sale. A qualifying term used in an offer to sell property, when the property has previously been offered or advertised for sale to others. It means that the offer will be automatically withdrawn if the property should be sold to another before the offer is accepted. The term *subject to prior sale* is sometimes used.

sub-lease. See under LEASE.

subornation of perjury. In law, the crime of procuring or encouraging another person to commit PERJURY, especially with regard to a matter affecting the person who does the encouraging.

subpoena. In law, a process or writ requiring a person to appear in court on a day assigned, or suffer a penalty. It is used primarily to compel witnesses to appear in investigations, grand jury proceedings, etc., as well as in actual trials. A *subpoena duces tecum* is one requiring a witness to bring with him his records, accounts, or other pertinent information.

subrogation. In law and insurance, the substitution of one person for another, especially with respect to claims, obligations, etc. For example, a person who owes a debt to a second person, who in turn owes a similar debt to a third person, may pay the debt directly to the third person, thus satisfying both debts at once. By so doing, however, he automatically places himself in *subrogation,* or in the place of the second debtor, as far as any claims of the third person are concerned. An insurance company that pays a claim to a policy holder obtains the right of *subrogation,* or the right to sue in the place of the policy holder, to attempt to recover from the party that caused the loss or damage.

subscribe. Literally, to write under, and hence, to endorse, or to agree. As used in connection with the establishment of a business, to agree or guarantee to provide a stated amount of capital for the new corporation,

in return for a number of shares of the corporation stock. More generally, to agree to receive and pay for something, such as a periodical, a series of tickets for entertainment, etc.

subscribed capital. See under CAPITAL.

subscription. Literally, a signature at the bottom of a document, contract, or application. As used in business, an agreement to provide capital for a corporation in return for stock, or an agreement to receive a periodical for a period of time.

subscription right. See RIGHT (1).

subsidiary. In general, something which is supplementary or auxiliary; subordinate or secondary. As used in business, when not otherwise specified, a company which is wholly or partially owned and controlled by another company, usually through ownership of all or a majority of the outstanding stock of the subject company. See also each of the following under the principal listing:
~ COIN; ~ COMPANY; ~ LEDGER.

subsidy. Any direct financial aid, or grant of monetary assistance, such as that by a government to farmers, which is considered to be in the public interest. Other examples of *subsidies* include those paid to steamship lines to aid in the construction of merchant ships, and those paid to railroads and airlines in the form of payments for carrying mail.

substantial damages. See under DAMAGES.

substantial performance. As used in business, the carrying out of a contract or agreement with no willful departure from its terms, and with no serious deviations. PERFORMANCE as specified, with variations only in technical and unimportant aspects of the undertaking, so that the basic purpose is adequately served. Under various statutes, *substantial performance* is an acceptable defense against a suit for breach of contract or of warranty.

substitute. In law, a person who is not named in a will as an HEIR, but to whom an inheritance will be passed along from a named heir, known as the INSTITUTE.

sub-tenant. A person who rents the use of land or housing from a person who is himself a TENANT. Usually, the *sub-tenant* is given the use or occupancy of part of the premises, or the use of the total for a period of time less than that for which the original tenant has possession. A transfer of the total property to a *sub-tenant* for the entire term of a lease is actually an ASSIGNMENT. See also SUB-LEASE, under LEASE.

subvention. A monetary grant of aid from a government or public body, such as a charitable or educational foundation, for some purpose of public benefit; a SUBSIDY.

succession. In law, the right by which an heir, especially the heir of a person who has died without leaving a will, takes possession of his inherited estate. Also, the order and process by which the heirs to such an estate are designated, as specified under the STATUTES OF DISTRIBUTION of the various states.

successor. In general, one who succeeds, or follows, another. As used in business, one who has assumed all of the rights and obligations of another, such as in the taking over of an unincorporated business from a former owner. One who replaces another as an officer, director, trustee, etc., is his *successor,* and assumes all of the rights and obligations of the one he replaces which follow from his office or title.

sue. To prosecute at law; to begin legal proceedings against another for the redress of a grievance, such as for the payment of a debt, or for the satisfaction of a claim. To institute any legal proceedings in a civil court.

sufferance. In law, permission, or the lack of opposition or objection. See, for example, TENANCY AT SUFFERANCE; TENANT AT SUFFERANCE.

sufficient consideration. See under CONSIDERATION.

suggested price. See under PRICE.

suggestion system. Any of various methods or plans under which employees are rewarded for suggestions which they submit to the management of a company. Under most plans, suggestions are reviewed by a committee, and awards are made in proportion to the actual or potential savings which adoption of the suggestion will bring to the company. The suggestions submitted may cover methods of operation, materials, sales promotion ideas, new products, working conditions, etc.

sui juris. Literally, in Latin, of his own right. A phrase used in legal terminology to describe a person who is entitled to act for himself, being of full age and mentally competent, and otherwise legally capable of taking action.

suit. In law, any legal proceeding brought in court by one person against another, for redress of a wrong suffered or injury received, or for enforcement of a right. A *suit* is sometimes distinguished from an ACTION (1), in that a *suit* is brought under EQUITY, while an action concerns matters of law. This distinction is frequently not recognized in statutes and usage, however, and in some cases the phrase *suit or action* is used to cover all possibilities.

summary. In general, any abstract, or any brief, abridged account, report, or statement. See, for example, ACCOUNT (2), SUMMARY.

summons. An order or writ by a court, used to notify the defendant that an action or suit has been begun against him, and calling on him to appear in court. Since it is used in civil cases, a *summons* does not strictly compel the defendant to appear, but it puts him on notice that if he fails to appear the action will be decided against him for non-defense.

sum-of-digits depreciation. See under DEPRECIATION.

supercargo. On board ship, an agent of the shipper or charterer, who has supervision over the cargo itself. He travels with the ship, and has authority to dispose of the cargo on reaching port, and usually the authority to obtain other cargo for the return voyage. He has no authority over the conduct of the ship, however, and may not interfere with its management.

superior. In general, higher, with more power or authority; dominant, as distinguished from INFERIOR; such as, for example, a *superior* court or a *superior* claim.

superior court. See under COURT.

supermarket. The name for a form of large RETAIL STORE selling a wide variety of consumer products, but basically food and small housewares. It is characterized by the large volume of sales, the open display of goods and self-selection by the customers, and generally by the absence of such services as credit, delivery, etc. Many, but not all *supermarkets* are operated as parts of retail chains.

supervisor. In general, one who supervises, or oversees, the work of others. As defined by the National Labor Relations Act, a *supervisor* is any individual who, in the interest of the employer, has the authority to hire, discharge, promote, assign, reward, or discipline other employees, or to direct them or to adjust their grievances, or to recommend such action, provided the exercise of such authority requires the use of independent judgment.

supplier. In general, a company which regularly supplies another with goods, materials, or services. In some fields, a *supplier* is known as a RESOURCE.

supply. 1. In general, the total available amount of any salable commodity. More specifically, the total amount of a commodity which will become available on the market at a given price, and at any given time. See also VISIBLE SUPPLY; INVISIBLE SUPPLY.

2. In the plural, those industrial or commercial goods which do not become a p

of the finished product, and which are continually consumed in the operation of a business enterprise. Examples include cleaning materials, stationery, small hand tools, etc.

upport price. See under PRICE.

upra. In Latin, above. Over, superior to, and sometimes outside of. It is the opposite of INFRA, or below.

upra protest. Literally, above or after PROTEST. After a bill or acceptance has been DISHONORED and has gone to protest, a person other than the original drawer may take up the note and accept or pay it to protect the credit of the drawer. The drawer is then obligated to reimburse the person who has accepted or paid.

upreme Court. See FEDERAL COURT SYSTEM.

urety. Any person who has bound himself, or made himself liable, for the payment of money or the performance of some act by another. He usually does this by posting a surety bond to guarantee that the payment or performance will be completed. See also BOND (2), SURETY; INSURANCE, SURETY AND FIDELITY.

rety and fidelity insurance. See under INSURANCE.

rety bond. See under BOND (2).

rety company. A corporation formed for the purpose of acting as SURETY, or providing surety bonds, for a fee, for persons occupying positions or offices of private or public trust.

plus. In general, that which is left over, or the excess. In accounting, the term may have several meanings, depending on the context. Most commonly, it is the excess of assets over the total of liabilities and capital, as shown on a BALANCE SHEET or FINANCIAL STATEMENT. In certain usages, however, it may also be the excess of income over expenses, or of receipts over expenditures. The principal forms of *surplus* are listed and defined below.

    accumulated ~. That which arises out of accumulated profits; the EARNED SURPLUS, which see below.

    appraisal ~. One arising out of a revaluation of corporate property, or out of an appreciation in the value of corporate assets. It is sometimes known as an *appreciation surplus.*

    appropriated ~. A term for a portion of the corporate *surplus* which is specifically set aside for some particular purpose, such as for the establishment of a reserve fund. It is sometimes known as a *reserved surplus.*

    capital ~. One which arises from any source other than from accumulated or re-

tained profits; all surplus except the EARNED SURPLUS, which see below. Typically, it may arise out of sales of company stock, gifts to the corporation, various conversions of securities, etc. It includes the PAID IN SURPLUS, which see below.

    contributed ~. See PAID IN SURPLUS, below.

    earned ~. One which is accumulated through the retention of profits. It is the total amount which has been accumulated over the life of the corporation out of that portion of net profits after taxes which has not been distributed to stockholders in the form of dividends, or used to increase the capital stock of the corporation. It is frequently called retained earnings, or retained income.

    initial ~. A term appearing in financial statements, meaning the *surplus* at the beginning of the period covered by the statement, before any additions to *surplus* resulting from the operations of the corporation during the period. Thus, it is the TOTAL SURPLUS, which see below, of the previous period.

    operating ~. The amount remaining at the end of an accounting or fiscal period, after the deduction of all expenses, provision for taxes, and distribution of dividends to stockholders. Thus, it is the amount transferred to EARNED SURPLUS, which see above, at the end of the period.

    paid in ~. A *surplus* arising from the original sale of the capital stock of the corporation at above the par value, so that the total subscribed, or paid in, by the stockholders is greater than the capital of the corporation, creating an immediate *surplus.* It may be added to by further sales of stock, such as sales of treasury stock at above par, or by other capital operations. It is usually the major component of CAPITAL SURPLUS, which see above.

    reserved ~. See APPROPRIATED SURPLUS, above.

    total ~. A term appearing in financial statements, meaning the total of the EARNED and CAPITAL SURPLUS, which see above, at the beginning of the period covered, plus any additions to *surplus* made during the period. The *total surplus* of one accounting or fiscal period is the INITIAL SURPLUS, which see above, of the next period.

surplus line. In insurance, a term used among insurance companies, meaning that portion of the insurance on a particular property, or on a particular class of property, which an insurance company has accepted but does not wish to retain. It is the amount of insurance assumed by an insurance company which it reinsures with other companies. See also LINE (3); REINSURANCE.

surplus profit. See under PROFIT.

surplus reserve. See RESERVE (2), EXCESS; SURPLUS, APPROPRIATED.

surrender. In law, the voluntary or involuntary relinquishment or giving up of property, rights, or interest, to another. It may be permanent, or it may be temporary, such as under a BAILMENT proceeding. Strictly, a *surrender* which is involuntary, or against the wishes of the person giving up, is a FORFEIT. Surrender differs from ABANDONMENT in that it always involves a second party, and is not necessarily permanent.

surrender charge. In life insurance practice, a term for that portion of the RESERVE VALUE of a policy which a policyholder may forfeit to the company if he surrenders his policy. Thus, it is the difference between the reserve value and the CASH SURRENDER VALUE of the policy.

surrender value. See CASH SURRENDER VALUE.

surrogate. In some states, the title of a judicial officer who administers matters relating to the PROBATE of wills, the issuance of LETTERS OF ADMINISTRATION, problems of guardianship, etc. In some states, his title may be probate judge, register, etc. Usually, the jurisdiction of a *surrogate* extends over one county, but in less populated areas one may administer affairs in several counties.

surtax. See under TAX (2).

survey. In general, a thorough examination, or inspection. Thus, a *survey* of land is an inspection by means of which the boundaries and characteristics of a particular parcel of land are determined and recorded. In insurance, it is a printed form, containing questions to be answered by the insured, on the basis of which the insurer prepares the policy. More generally, it is any inspection made by an authorized person or group, such as one made to determine the extent of loss or damage, for insurance purposes.

survivor. One who outlives another, or who outlives all others of the same class. In various forms of joint or common relationships, the *survivor* is the one on whom the rights or responsibilities of the relationship fall, after the death of the other parties.

survivorship account. See under ACCOUNT (3).

survivorship annuity. See under ANNUITY.

suspected bill. See BILL OF HEALTH.

sweatshop. A term for a factory in which employees are paid on a PIECE WORK basis, at very low rates. In the typical *sweatshop* which existed before the passage of various corrective labor laws, the rates paid were so low that the employees took work home, sometimes putting their whole family to work at it in order to earn a subsistence wage. *Sweatshops* existed primarily in the garment industries, in which work could be conveniently given out to employees to take home.

swindle. In law, to cheat or defraud. To obtain money or property from a person under false or deceitful pretenses, or by fraudulen misrepresentation. It is a form of LARCENY but is not THEFT, since the victim is induced to give up his property willingly.

swing shift. In employment practice, a wor SHIFT or period which extends beyond th usual two or three shift operations of plant on continuous operation. Thus, it ma be a week-end shift, or a third or four shift between the last shift of one day an the first shift of the next.

sympathetic strike. See under STRIKE.

syndicalism. A revolutionary political doctri based on the use of direct action by labc such as a general strike, to obtain politic and economic power. It envisioned the co trol and operation by labor of all factorie plants, etc. In modern usage, any use of t strike weapon for political purposes, rath than as a means of improving workir conditions, is frequently referred to syndicalism. In various statutes, crimir *syndicalism* is defined as the use of sabota force, or terror, rather than peaceful a orderly striking and picketing, as a weap in labor disputes.

syndicate. 1. In general, a temporary assoc tion of two or more persons formed to ca out some business venture. Usually, the me bers of a *syndicate* share in any profits losses in proportion to their individual c tributions to the *syndicate's* resources. amples include the *syndicate* of investm bankers formed to UNDERWRITE (2) a curities issue, or one formed to undert; a large real estate deal. In some cases CARTEL or TRUST (3) is called a *syndicate*.

2. An organization formed for the p pose of distributing the work of writ artists, cartoonists, etc., to newspapers periodicals. In its usual method of operati the *syndicate* buys the productions or feati from their creators, and sells or leases th to the various publications. The creator receive a flat fee, or a royalty based on number of newspapers in which his w appears, or sometimes on their total circ tion.

systematic sample. See under SAMPLE (3).

T

tab. In colloquial usage, a bill of account, or a check; a reckoning of amounts due. For example, to pick up a *tab* is to pay a bill or check, and to keep a *tab* on something or someone is to maintain a running account or record.

table. A condensed statement of facts; any collection or arrangement of facts or figures for ready reference. For example, a *table* of weights and measures, or of interest, currency exchange rates, statistical data, etc.

tabulating machine. A business machine, activated by punched cards, punched tape, or magnetic tape, which sorts, totals, computes, and otherwise manipulates the data recorded on the cards or tape. A punch-card machine. See also BUSINESS MACHINE.

tacit. Not expressed; implied or inferred. Inferred from the situation or circumstances, or from actions or lack of actions. For example, *tacit* consent is implied from failure to object when the opportunity is offered.

tacking. In law, the process or act of annexing a junior claim to a senior one, for the purpose of gaining whatever benefits may arise from doing so. For example, to attach a recent claim against a bankrupt to an earlier claim, to obtain priority treatment; to attach an older criminal complaint to a newer one, to avoid the STATUTE OF LIMITATIONS; or to attach a claim to land to an earlier claim, to permit the taking over by right of adverse possession. This procedure is possible under some circumstances, but is prohibited by many statutes. See also POSSESSION, ADVERSE.

taffeta. A fine, plain woven fabric, usually of silk or rayon, smooth on both faces, and with a surface sheen.

Taft-Hartley Act. The federal law, amending the WAGNER ACT, passed in 1947 and known officially as the Labor-Management Relations Act. It is the basic law governing all relations between employers and their organized employees. Its major revisions of the Wagner Act include specification of the rights of employers, to balance the rights of employees listed in the earlier act, and restrictions on some forms of union activity.

tag. A label or ticket; especially a price ticket. Hence, to *tag* a product at a given amount, is to place that price on it.

tail. A limitation, abridgement, or reduction, especially a legal limitation. For example, an ESTATE IN TAIL is one which passes to the lawful issue in each generation only, rather than to the heirs in general.

take. 1. Legally, to lay hold, seize, or receive into possession. In statutes which define and limit the government's right to *take* property for public use, *take* generally includes the destruction or rendering valueless of the property, or of the owner's property rights.

    2. In slang, the income, proceeds, or profit from a venture or operation, especially one of a questionable or illegal nature.

take a flier. To engage in a risky venture, or one with a possibility of high profit but also of great loss; such as the purchase of a highly speculative security. See also FLIER (1).

take-home pay. The actual wages or salary paid in cash, after deductions for withholding taxes, social security, welfare benefits, union dues, etc. In some cases, *take-home pay* may be as much as one-third less than the wages or salary paid.

take over. To assume control or management, as of a business operation, but not necessarily including the taking of ownership or title.

take stock. To take a physical INVENTORY.

take up. To pay or discharge an obligation, such as a note or bill. To retire, as a security or long-term indebtedness.

tale quale. A Latin expression, used in contracts for commodities, meaning roughly, AS IS. The term signifies that the buyer accepts the goods as they are, or as indicated by a sample submitted, and assumes any risk of damage they may later suffer, such as during transit after acceptance.

talesman. In general usage, a juror. More correctly, a person chosen for a jury from among the bystanders in a court, such as might be done when the panel of prospective jurors has been exhausted. The word derives from the Latin *tales,* meaning such persons. This is the opening word of the traditional writ ordering the sheriff or other court officer to collect such of the bystanders as may be needed for the jury. See also VENIRE-MAN.

tally. Originally, from the Latin, *talea,* a stick. In medieval times, it was the practice to mark the amount of a loan by making notches on a stick or rod. The stick was then split lengthwise, so that each party to the loan had a record of the amount. Hence, in modern usage, a *tally* is any count or record of amounts or numbers. Also, to *tally* is to count or record by making marks, called *tally* marks, or *tallies.*

tangible. Literally, touchable. That which has physical form and qualities, and can be weighed, measured, counted, etc. It is the opposite of *intangible,* or incorporeal. See each of the following under the principal heading: ~ ASSET (2); ~ NET WORTH; ~ PROPERTY.

tape. In securities trade usage, the paper ribbon on which the TICKER prints the price quotations for stocks, commodities, etc. When it is said that the *tape* is slow, or that the *tape* is behind, this means that the volume of trading activity is so heavy that the *tape* printing mechanism can not keep up with it.

tare. The difference between the gross weight of a shipment and the net weight of the goods contained, due to the weight of the packaging, container, etc. Hence, an allowance for the weight of packaging, calculated so that net weight plus *tare* weight equals gross weight.

    actual ~. *Tare* computed by actually weighing the container or packaging materials before packaging; also called the clear *tare.*

    average ~. A *tare* allowance arrived at by weighing a few containers representative of a large number of similar ones.

    clear ~. See ACTUAL TARE, above.

    customary ~. A *tare* based on a standard or established container weight for the type of goods.

    customs ~. A *tare* allowance fixed arbitrarily by customs laws and regulations.

    estimated ~. A *tare* allowance based on an estimate of the container weight, arrived at by comparison with containers of known weight.

tare weight. The total weight of the package, container, or packaging materials, which, together with the net weight of the contents,

makes up the gross weight of a package or shipment.

tariff. 1. Originally, from the Arabic, an explanation or notification. Hence, any listing or schedule, such as one of rates, charges, sizes, etc. In transportation, for example, it is a schedule of freight charges or rates, showing the costs for shipping different classes of goods between named cities or over particular routes. In the clothing industry, a *tariff* is a schedule of the sizes and size combinations, such as sleeve length and collar size, in which particular garments are normally manufactured or stocked.

    joint ~. A schedule of rates issued jointly by two or more carriers, such as two railroads, or a railroad and motor freight line, for shipments between points requiring the use of the facilities of two or more carriers.

    2. Specifically, in foreign trade, a listing or schedule of the articles and commodities on which import duties are collected, and the rate or amount to be collected on each item or class of items. Strictly, the amount collected is the DUTY, and the basis on which it is collected is the *tariff.* The various types and classifications of *tariffs* are listed and defined below.

    ad valorem ~. One which is levied as a percentage of the value of the item imported, rather than as a specific amount per unit of the item, as in a SPECIFIC TARIFF, which see below.

    anti-dumping ~. One authorized by law to discourage the DUMPING of imported goods at less than their true value. It is set at the calculated difference between the price at which the item normally sells in its country of origin and the price at which it is to be sold in the importing country. Thus, it eliminates any potential gain from selling below the true cost of the item.

    compensatory ~. A term for one which is applied to a manufactured article at the rate which would have been charged on the raw materials contained.

    compound ~. One which is based partly on value, and partly on the number of units of the item, and is thus a combination of an AD VALOREM TARIFF, which see above, and a SPECIFIC TARIFF, which see below.

    countervailing ~. A term for one which is specifically applied to a product to offset some export subsidy, bounty, or other advantage conferred on the item by the government of the exporting country, by a CARTEL etc.

    differential ~. One which differentiates between the products of different countries, setting higher rates for some than for others. Such a *tariff,* for example, would provide special rates for countries with which there are TRADE AGREEMENTS in force.

flexible ~. One providing for increases or decreases in the rates charged, such as, for example, to offset changes in the rate of exchange, or changes in domestic costs of manufacture, etc.

preferential ~. One established with special rates favoring the products of certain named countries or groups of countries; a DIFFERENTIAL TARIFF, which see above.

protective ~. One designed specifically to protect or encourage a domestic industry, by setting a high rate on the imported goods with which it competes, as distinguished from a REVENUE TARIFF, which see below. See also PROTECTION.

revenue ~. One designed primarily to raise revenues, or to defray the costs of operating the customs system, rather than to protect domestic industries or discriminate against those of foreign countries, as distinguished from a PROTECTIVE TARIFF, which see above.

specific ~. One which is levied as a specific charge per unit of quantity or weight, such as per item or per pound, rather than as a proportion of the value of the imported item, as in an AD VALORUM TARIFF, which see above.

Tariff Commission. The independent federal agency, originally created in 1916 and now operating under the various Tariff Acts as amended, which reviews and supervises the operation of the tariff laws. It checks for DUMPING activities, reviews tariff concessions under the various RECIPROCAL TRADE AGREEMENTS, and warns the President when it finds that a PERIL POINT has been reached.

tax. 1. Originally, to charge, or to blame. In modern usage, to assess, or to impose a charge. To state that an amount or contribution is payable and due, and to collect such amounts.

2. Any enforced contribution exacted from persons or property by the authority of a government, usually for the primary purpose of meeting the costs of government. Strictly, a *tax* differs from a FEE, which is usually charged for permission to perform some act; from an ASSESSMENT, which is levied directly against those who will benefit from some improvement; and from a TOLL, which is a charge for the use of some service or facility. There are a great many kinds and classes of *taxes,* the principal ones of which are listed and defined below.

ad valorem ~. One calculated as a proportion or percentage of the value of the income, wealth, goods, or property being

taxed, as distinguished from a SPECIFIC TAX, which see below.

capitation ~. Literally, a head *tax.* One levied against each individual person, or against each person in some group or classification, such as those of a certain age or sex. When connected with the voting privilege, it is usually known as a POLL TAX, which see below.

consumption ~. One which is levied on the consumption or use of named materials or products, rather than on their production or manufacture, as is the case with an EXCISE TAX, which see below.

corporate income ~. One levied on the net profits of incorporated businesses, figured before the distribution of dividends to stockholders or the transfer of any income to surplus or capital. Both the federal government and some states levy such *taxes.*

death ~. See ESTATE TAX and INHERITANCE TAX, below.

direct ~. One levied directly against the person who will ultimately bear its cost, such as an INCOME or SALES TAX, which see below, as distinguished from an INDIRECT TAX, which see below.

estate ~. One levied against the wealth left by a deceased person. Strictly, it is levied against the ESTATE itself, as distinguished from an INHERITANCE TAX, which see below, which is levied against the person who inherits from an estate.

excess profits ~. A *tax* on the profits of incorporated businesses which exceed a certain level, or which exceed those earned in previous years. Such a *tax* is usually set at a very high rate, so as to recover all or most of the excess profits for the government. Such a *tax* may be levied during wartime, for example, to recover profits due to wartime shortages, profiteering, etc.

excise ~. Strictly, one levied against the performance of some act, such as the manufacture of a product or the use of a service. As used, the term includes *taxes* on attendance at places of amusement or entertainment, on the recording of documents, etc. The federal *taxes* on various products, calculated as a percentage of their retail price, collected at the time of sale, and paid directly by the purchaser, are called *excise taxes* but are actually SALES TAXES, which see below.

franchise ~. One levied on the privilege of conducting a business. Many states collect such *taxes* on all incorporated businesses which operate within the state. Localities and states frequently collect special *franchise taxes* from bus lines, public utilities, etc.

general property ~. One levied against the value of all property owned, as distinguished from a PERSONAL PROPERTY TAX or REAL ESTATE TAX, which see below.

gift ∿. One levied as a percentage of the value of a gift made by a living person. As with an ESTATE TAX, which see above, the *tax* is levied against the giver, or against the gift itself, rather than against the recipient.

graded ∿. The name for a system of *taxes* and ASSESSMENTS, under which the specific assessments on improvements are progressively reduced and the general REAL ESTATE TAX, which see below, increased to make up the loss. The purpose is to encourage building and improvement in areas in which new assessable improvements are being made.

graduated ∿. One under which the rate per unit increases as the number of units taxed increases. Several states, for example, have taxes on chain stores under which the *tax* per store is higher the greater the number of stores in the chain. It is a form of PROGRESSIVE TAX, which see below.

hidden ∿. One which is levied in such a way that it is not apparent or identifiable to the person who ultimately pays it; an INDIRECT TAX, which see below.

income ∿. One imposed as a percentage of personal or business income from specified sources, usually after allowances for certain exemptions, deductions, expenses, etc.

indirect ∿. One which is included in the price or cost of the item or service taxed, and passed along, rather than levied separately and directly against the ultimate consumer, as is the case with a DIRECT TAX, which see above. Examples include EXCISE TAXES, which see above, and TARIFFS.

inheritance ∿. One levied on the receiver of an INHERITANCE, in proportion to the value of the property inherited. In fact, many *taxes* commonly called *inheritance taxes* are actually ESTATE TAXES, which see above, levied against the estate itself, rather than against the receiver.

internal revenue ∿. In the United States, any of the various federal *taxes,* including those on income, production, sales, etc., but excluding TARIFFS.

land ∿. A term for a property *tax* levied on the value of land only, rather than on the buildings or other improvements on it.

license ∿. One levied against some privilege or permission, such as the permission to engage in some business, or to own some type of property, or to sell some product, such as alcoholic beverages. A FRANCHISE TAX, which see above.

luxury ∿. One imposed on the manufacture, sale, purchase or use of goods or services which are classed as luxuries, rather than as necessities. The purpose of such a *tax* may be to reduce the consumption of such goods, such as in wartime, or to redistribute wealth.

occupation ∿. See FRANCHISE TAX, above.

payroll ∿. Any of various *taxes* which are collected as a proportion of business payroll values, or as a specified amount per employee on the payroll. The *tax* may be borne by the employer, or deducted from the amount paid the employee.

personal property ∿. One levied against the value of personal property owned, such as furniture, automobiles, etc. Such *taxes* are frequently levied by cities or states. *Taxes* on business inventories, machinery, and equipment are also *personal property taxes* in the strict sense.

poll ∿. A form of CAPITATION TAX, which see above, levied for the privilege of taking part in an election, or POLL. Practically all such *taxes* in the United States have now been abolished.

progressive ∿. One with proportionate rates that increase as the value of the thing taxed increases. Personal income *taxes* are the most common example of *progressive taxes.* See also REGRESSIVE TAX, below.

property ∿. Any of various forms of *taxes* levied in proportion to the value of property owned, including PERSONAL PROPERTY TAXES, which see above, and REAL ESTATE TAXES, which see below.

proportional ∿. One levied in direct proportion to the value of the thing taxed, and which is neither a PROGRESSIVE TAX, which see above, nor a REGRESSIVE TAX, which see below.

real estate ∿. A form of *property tax* levied against the value of real estate, including both the land and the improvements on it. Such *taxes* are the principal source of revenue of most localities.

regressive ∿. One which absorbs a relatively smaller proportion of the value of the thing taxed, as the value increases. Any SPECIFIC TAX, which see below, is automatically a *regressive tax.*

sales ∿. One levied as a proportion of the sales value of goods, at the time of sale. It may be a direct retail *sales tax,* paid by the purchaser of specific goods, or in the form of a gross sales or turnover *tax,* paid by the wholesale or retail merchant on the basis of his total sales.

severance ∿. One levied on the extraction of some natural resource, such as coal, petroleum, mineral ores, etc. It may be based on volume, such as tonnage or gallons, or it may be based on the value of the product extracted.

single ∿. The name for one proposed by

the economist Henry George. Under his proposal, all existing *taxes* were to be replaced by a *single tax* on the value of land.

social security ∼. Any one of the various *taxes* or contributions collected under the federal SOCIAL SECURITY program, including the old age retirement tax, unemployment insurance *tax,* etc.

specific ∼. One, such as an import TARIFF, which is levied as a specific amount per unit of weight or quantity, rather than in proportion to the value of the thing taxed. See also AD VALOREM TAX, above.

stamp ∼. Any one of the various *taxes* collected through the sale of stamps, which must be attached to certain products or documents, such as tobacco, stock certificates, title deeds, etc.

surtax. One levied on top of, or in addition to, a *tax* already being collected. Under an INCOME TAX, which see above, for example, a basic *tax* rate may be set for all incomes, with a *surtax* rate set for income above a certain amount.

tonnage ∼. See SEVERANCE TAX, above.

transfer ∼. One imposed on the transfer of documents, or of securities. It is usually collected as a STAMP TAX, which see above.

undistributed profits ∼. One imposed on those corporate profits, above a certain amount, which are not distributed as dividends to stockholders. Its purpose is to prevent the unreasonable accumulation of surpluses by corporations.

withholding ∼. One, such as an INCOME TAX, which see above, which is collected at the source by withholding the amount of the *tax* from payments due the taxpayer. The present federal income *tax,* for example, is collected largely on a withholding basis.

taxable value. The actual or theoretical value assigned to property, goods, or income, on the basis of which a tax or import tariff is collected. The *taxable value* need have no direct relation to the market or sale value of the goods, but may be based on some standard or formula, or may be the market value less certain allowed deductions and exemptions.

tax accounting. That branch of ACCOUNTING which is concerned with the establishment of systems for the keeping of tax records, the setting up of accounts to provide for the payment of taxes, the preparation and review of federal, state, and local tax reports for businesses, and the preparation of individual tax returns. The professional tax accountant is frequently called on, as well, to interpret the tax regulations in terms of accounting procedures, and to defend particular accounting procedures before the various tax authorities and the tax courts.

tax anticipation note. A term for any of a variety of short-term, interest-bearing, obligations which are specifically designed to be purchased by businesses with funds accumulated as a reserve to pay taxes. The notes are sold by the federal, state, or local governments, and serve the purpose of providing a more level inflow of revenue. The government receives its actual tax revenue over a period of time, and the tax-paying businesses simply present the notes as payment when the tax is due. See also RESERVE, TAX.

taxation. In general, the acts and practices of imposing and collecting TAXES. The processes by which taxes are imposed on individuals, companies, and property for the support of governmental units.

tax base. In TAX usage, the objective basis on which a tax is imposed or levied. For example, the *base* of a capitation tax is the individual, that of an income tax is the amount of income earned, that of an excise tax on cigarettes the number of cigarettes, etc.

tax bond. See under BOND (1).

Tax Court. The independent federal court, originally established as the Board of Tax Appeals, which hears and settles disputes between taxpayers and the Internal Revenue Service. Its decisions may be appealed to the appropriate Circuit Court of Appeals, and ultimately to the Supreme Court.

tax-exempt. Released or exempted from the necessity of paying a tax; not subject to inclusion in totals of income or value for tax purposes. For example, the income from certain municipal and other bonds is *tax-exempt;* the person receiving the income need not include it in the income he reports for income tax purposes. Such bonds are frequently known simply as *tax-exempts.*

tax lien. See under LIEN.

taxpayer. In general, any person who pays taxes, especially, as used, anyone who pays income taxes. In real estate usage, a building intended primarily to produce enough income to pay the real property taxes on the land on which it is built and on the improvement itself. Such buildings are usually one or two-story structures, designed for commercial occupancy, including stores, offices, recreation places, etc. Thus, any building of this type is frequently called a *taxpayer,* regardless of whether it was actually built for this purpose. –

tax rate. In general, the proportion of the TAX BASE which must be paid in taxes. With regard to real property taxes, it is usually quoted in terms of the number of dollars in taxes for each $100 of ASSESSED VALUATION of the property. Thus, if the *tax rate* in a community is $3.00, the tax on a $10,000 home will be $300, or 100 times the $3.00 rate. In most communities, the *tax rate* is arrived at by dividing the total necessary tax income by the total assessed valuation of the taxable property in the community.

tax reserve. See under RESERVE (1).

tax return. See RETURN (3).

tax sale. See under SALE (1).

tear. See WEAR AND TEAR.

tear sheet. A page torn from a newspaper, magazine, or other publication. It is usual practice for a publication to send *tear sheets* to advertisers or advertising agencies as proof that the advertisement was run, and for advertising agencies to submit such *tear sheets* to their clients as proof of insertion. Retail dealers who receive advertising allowances are also frequently required to submit *tear sheets* to obtain payment from the manufacturer.

technical. As used in business, formal, rather than substantial. A *technical* change in a tax law, for example, is one which changes the details or form of the statute, without changing its basic aim or content. Similarly, *technical* changes in prices on the stock exchange are those which do not affect the basic trend of prices.

technological change. The process of change in methods of production, brought about by the introduction of new and improved methods, the application of mechanical principles to replace manual labor, the development of new materials and products, etc. This process of change is the chief characteristic of the so-called industrial revolution.

technological unemployment. See UNEMPLOYMENT.

telegraphic money order. See under MONEY ORDER.

telegraphic transfer (T.T.). A term used in business communications, or in orders, referring to the transfer or forwarding of funds by telegraph. See also MONEY ORDER, TELEGRAPHIC.

teller. Literally, one who counts or reckons. In a bank, the officer or employee who is responsible for the actual handling of money, receiving deposits and paying out withdrawals, checks, etc. In larger banks, there may be a separate paying *teller,* receiving *teller,* and note *teller.* The last of these is responsible for handling the collection of notes

and drafts. In a legislature, the *teller* is the person who counts the votes when legislation is acted on.

tel quel. The French variation of TALE QUALE.

temporary. Of relatively short duration; designed or intended to last or be used for a relatively short period of time. The term is used to distinguish such things or events from those which are permanent or indefinite. See, for example, ANNUITY, TEMPORARY; INJUNCTION, TEMPORARY.

temporary bond. See BOND (1), INTERIM.

temporary receipt. A receipt given pending the performance of some duty or obligation, or the issuance of a permanent document, and intended to be redeemed or taken up on completion of the duty or obligation. Such a receipt, for example, may be given to the purchasers of stock or bonds pending the issuance and delivery of the permanent stocks and bonds themselves.

tenancy. In general, the state of being a TENANT; the occupancy of property, usually, but not necessarily, under an agreement calling for rent and a time of termination; the estate in property which one holds as a tenant. Also, the period of time during which one possesses property as a tenant.

  entire ∼. See TENANCY BY THE ENTIRETY below.

  general ∼. One which has no fixed termination date or period of duration; one which is not made definite by an agreement between the parties involved.

  joint ∼. One rising out of a grant or transfer of property to two or more parties who then jointly hold an undivided interest in the property. The interest of all of the *joint tenants* is equal but not separable. If any should become deceased, the property is then jointly held by the remaining tenants. See also TENANT, JOINT.

  several ∼. One in which a separate, identifiable, partial interest is held by each tenant. Each occupant's portion belongs to him separately, and is part of his estate. A number of persons may be given a *several tenancy* in a bond, for example, with the value held by each one separately stated, though each may not be able to realize the value of his *tenancy* unless the entire bond is sold and the proceeds distributed. It is the opposite of a JOINT TENANCY, which see above.

  ∼ at sufferance. The possession of property by a lawful tenant after the termination of his original *tenancy,* by the actual or constructive *sufferance* or permission of the landlord. Generally, if the landlord has notified the tenant that the lease will not be renewed, the holdover tenant becomes a tre passer and may be evicted. In some states, if the landlord does not act, the tenant automatically is recognized as having a TENANCY FROM YEAR TO YEAR, which see below.

~ **at will.** Generally, one that may be terminated at the will of either party. For example, a TENANCY AT SUFFERANCE, which see above, is a *tenancy at will* until the landlord takes action.

~ **by the entirety.** One created by a conveyance of property to two or more persons jointly; a JOINT TENANCY, which see above. More specifically, a *tenancy* held jointly by a husband and wife.

~ **from year to year.** One held under a general lease in which no termination is specified, but under which an annual rent is accepted, giving the tenant the right of occupancy for another year. The annual rent may actually be paid in periodic installments. If a landlord accepts a rent payment from a tenant whose lease has expired, he grants a *tenancy from year to year* by so doing. If the original lease was for a period of less than one year, the extended lease will be from quarter to quarter, month to month, etc.

tenant. In general usage, one who holds or has the use of real property which belongs to another, for a period of time and under other terms which are fixed by an agreement, or lease. In the legal sense, any person who holds, occupies, or uses property is a *tenant*, whether the property is his own or someone else's.

joint ~. One who holds property together with one or more others, under a single instrument of TENANCY, with an undivided right and interest in the entire property, rather than a separate right to a particular part of the property.

sole ~. One who holds property in his own name only, not together with others. However, a *sole tenant* may hold part of a property, of which other parts are held by others, as a TENANT IN SEVERALTY, which see below.

~ **at sufferance.** One who continues to hold property after the termination of his lease, with the sufferance, or permission of the landlord, or at least without his objection.

~ **at will.** One who holds property with no definite right, but who may be put out at any time by the landlord. A TENANT AT SUFFERANCE, which see above, is a *tenant at will* until the landlord acts.

~ **for life.** One who holds, or has an interest in, property for the duration of his life, or for the life of some named other per-

son. A widow, for example, may be made a *tenant for life* in property by the terms of a will, after which it passes to others.

~ **for years.** One who holds property under a lease with a fixed period of duration of one year or more.

~ **in common.** One who holds property together with others, but with a separate title, and perhaps in a share or proportion which is different from the others, but without having separate title to a distinct part of the property. See also JOINT TENANT, above, and TENANT IN SEVERALTY, below.

~ **in severalty.** One who holds a part of a property, of which others hold other parts, but who holds his part by a separate and distinct title. He is, in effect, a SOLE TENANT, which see above, of his part of the property.

tender. An offer, especially an offer of money in settlement of a claim or obligation. In the law of contracts, a *tender* must be an unconditional offer, and it must be of the exact amount and in the exact form called for by the contract. If a *tender,* or offer to pay, is declined, and is held open for the period of time required, the one offering it may not later be required to pay damages or interest charges. The term also refers to that which is offered, so that LEGAL TENDER, for example, is money which the law requires a creditor to accept when offered in payment.

tenement. Literally, and originally, something which is held. Hence, in law, any property which is held by one person under some form of TENURE from another, or which is held by a TENANT. In popular usage, a dwelling place held as a tenant, such as an apartment or flat. A *tenement* building was originally any building containing apartments or dwelling units leased to tenants, but has come to mean particularly such a building of the poorer type, or in a bad state of repair.

ten-forty. In the securities trade, a term for a form of United States government bond, so called because it is redeemable after ten years, and due and payable after forty years. Other similar forms of bond are known as FIVE-TWENTIES, etc. See also BOND (1), OPTIONAL.

tenor. In financial circles, a term for the period of time between the beginning of an obligation and the maturity date. For example, the period of time between the date of issue of a note and the maturity date is known as its *tenor.* Similarly, the period of time between the date of acceptance of a bill of exchange and the date of payment, as illustrated in the typical phrase, ninety days AFTER SIGHT, is the *tenor* of the acceptance.

tenure. 1. In law, the method or form by which

property is held; such as by LEASEHOLD, by FEE, by TITLE, etc.

2. The term during which an office or position is held, or the condition under which it is held. The holder of a title, for example, may have *tenure* during good behavior, the director of a corporation may have *tenure* in office for a period of one year, or a teacher may receive permanent *tenure* in his position after three years of satisfactory service, after which he may not be dismissed except on the presentation of charges against him.

term. 1. A period or space of time; the duration of an elected or appointive office, or of a court session. The time between a specified beginning and terminating date, such as the *term* of a promissory note.

2. A condition or specification; a limitation. The *terms* of a contract, for example, are the promises or agreements proposed by each side, which, when accepted, constitute the contract itself. See also TERMS OF SALE.

terminal. A boundary, or ending. In railroading, or in transportation in general, a station facility at the end of a line, or at the end of a principal route. In personnel administration, similarly, a *terminal* position is one from which no further advancement or promotion is possible.

term insurance. See under INSURANCE, LIFE, ACCIDENT, AND HEALTH.

term policy. See under POLICY (2).

term rate. See LONG RATE.

terms of sale. In general, the terms or conditions under which a sale is made, or will be made, including the period allowed for payment, insurance and transportation provisions and charges, date of shipment or delivery, stipulations as to quality, discounts allowed for prompt payment, volume orders, trade qualifications, etc. As used, however, it refers specifically to the period allowed for payment, and to any discount allowed for prompt or earlier payment. The principal *terms of sale* used in commerce are either CASH, or NET. Sales made on cash terms call for payment before delivery, or on delivery, or with the order, depending on the particular terms. Net terms call for payment of the full amount by the end of a particular period of time, usually with a discount allowed for payment within a specified number of days. For example, terms specified as "2% 10 days, net 30 days" mean that a discount of 2 percent is allowed for payment made within 10 days, and that full payment is required by the end of 30 days after submission of the invoice. Similarly, terms specified as "2%

10/EOM" mean specifically that a discount of 2 percent is allowed for payment made within 10 days after the end of the month in which the invoice is dated, and payment in full is required by the end of the month following the month in which the invoice is dated.

territorial. In general, pertaining to a particular country or state, or the area over which it has sovereignty. The *territorial* waters of a country, for example, are those adjoining or surrounding it, and over which it has sovereignty and jurisdiction.

testament. Strictly speaking, the document by which a person arranges for the disposition of his personal property after his death. Thus, it is technically distinguished from a WILL, which disposes of both real and personal property. In current usage, however, the term has disappeared, except in such phrases as, last will and *testament*.

testate. In legal terminology, having died leaving a valid will, as distinguished from INTESTATE.

testamentary. Pertaining to a WILL or TESTAMENT, or to its terms. See, for example TRUST (1), TESTAMENTARY; LETTERS TESTAMENTARY.

testator, or **testatrix.** In law, a person, male or female, who has died leaving a will. The author of a will.

testimonial. Strictly speaking, pertaining to TESTIMONY, or to evidence. *Testimonial* proof for example, is proof offered by the testimony or evidence of witnesses, rather than by document. As commonly used, a statement attesting to the quality or character of a person or product; a statement included in an advertisement, personally recommending a product or service.

testimony. In law, EVIDENCE in spoken form given by a witness under oath. Thus, it is distinguished from documents or other exhibits offered in evidence. Strictly speaking any statement under oath is *testimony*, even though it contains no evidence, in the sense of proof.

T.F. See TILL-FORBID.

theft. In law, the act of taking another's personal property feloniously or fraudulently without the consent of the owner. Thus, includes both ROBBERY, which is *theft* from one's person, and BURGLARY, which is *theft* by breaking and entering. See also LARCENY

theft insurance. See under INSURANCE, CASUALTY AND LIABILITY.

thin market. In the securities trade, a term for a market characterized by little trading a tivity, but by wide variations in prices; a market situation in which there is little support for the existing price levels. See also NARROW MARKET.

third. In commerce, merchandise or goods of very inferior quality or grade. See also SECOND (1).

third-class mail. See under POSTAL SERVICE.

third-class paper. See under COMMERCIAL PAPER.

third mortgage. One that is inferior to two other mortgages on the same property. See MORTGAGE, FIRST; MORTGAGE, SECOND.

third of exchange. See FIRST OF EXCHANGE.

third party. In law, a term applied to a person who is not a PARTY to a contract or agreement, but whose interests are affected by it. A person who becomes involved in an action or occurrence without intention, either on his part or on the part of the principal parties to the action. For example, a customer of a store, who is injured in an accident that results from the instructions given by the store owner to an employee, may bring suit, as a *third party,* against either or both the employer and employee. See also INSURANCE, CASUALTY AND LIABILITY.

thirty. In financial circles, a term sometimes used for a BILL OF EXCHANGE or other instrument payable in *thirty* days.

thirty-twomo. See under BOOK SIZES.

three-D policy. See INSURANCE, SURETY AND FIDELITY.

three-name paper. See COMMERCIAL PAPER, TWO-NAME.

thrift account. See under ACCOUNT (3).

through bill of lading. See under BILL OF LADING.

through freight. In rail transportation, the term for shipments made from one TERMINAL or originating station of a freight train or route to another terminal or the final destination. It is distinguished from LOCAL FREIGHT, which includes shipments made from an originating station to a way station, or from a way station to another or to a terminal.

through rate. See FREIGHT RATE, JOINT.

throw-away. See DODGER.

ticker. In the securities trade, the popular name for the device used to print the price quotations for stocks, bonds, and commodities. It is a form of typewriter which prints the code letters for the various securities, together with the prices at which they have been traded, on a continuous paper tape. This tape may be read directly, or may be projected on an enlarged screen in a broker's office or at the exchange itself. Similar machines are used to report news events.

ticket. 1. A brief certificate, usually printed on paper or cardboard, and stating that the bearer is entitled to some service or privilege, such as passage on a train, admission to a theater, etc. It may be either transferable or non-transferable, depending on the terms under which it is issued or sold.

2. A label or tag, attached to goods or merchandise for purposes of identification or description. For example, a price *ticket* may be attached to merchandise sold at retail, to notify prospective customers of its cost, or a *ticket* may be attached to apparel brought to a shop for cleaning or storage, so that it may be identified when called for.

3. In politics, the list of candidates of one party in an election; a SLATE.

tickler file. The name for any of several devices used to provide a set of daily reminders of actions to be taken or matters to be attended to. In its simplest form, a number of file folders, each bearing a date, in which items or reminders are stored, to be taken out and acted on at the appropriate date. More elaborate devices and appliances for use in file cabinets or on desk tops are available.

tidal. Pertaining to that part of a river or inlet in which a tide flows. *Tidal* waters are those waters of a stream, river, or inlet, as far up as where the direction of flow changes with the tides. This is usually farther upstream than the point at which the water ceases to be salty.

tidewater. Strictly, any body of water that flows with the tides. More broadly, the low coastal land areas as far inland as the point at which the tidal flow of water ceases; coastlands in general, as distinguished from the higher country or that farther inland.

tie-in sale. A term for a sale in which the buyer is required to accept one or more additional items to obtain the one he wants to purchase. A seller of industrial or commercial equipment, for example, may require buyers of the equipment to agree to buy supplies or materials to use with the equipment. Similarly, a manufacturer or wholesaler may require retail dealers to accept a certain number of less popular models of his products in order to obtain supplies of the models which are in more demand. Sales of both these types are prohibited under the Clayton Anti-trust Act. See also CONTRACT (1), REQUIREMENT.

tierce. In liquid measure, particularly in wine measure, a unit formerly used containing 42

GALLONS, or one-third of a PIPE. Also, a cask containing this quantity of wine or other liquid. In dry measure, it is a container sometimes used for meat products such as lard, with a capacity of 300 to 375 POUNDS.

tight. Strictly regulated, not readily available, difficult to come by. See, for example, MONEY, TIGHT.

till-forbid. In advertising, a term used for an order to a publisher by an advertiser or an advertising agency, instructing him to place a given advertisement in each issue of the publication until instructed to do otherwise, rather than to place it in a particular number of issues. It is frequently used as an abbreviation, *T.F.*

time. As used in business terms, a qualification usually referring to a specified period of *time,* or to a delay until some specified date. See each of the following under the principal listing: ∼ ACCOUNT (3); ∼ BILL OF EXCHANGE; ∼ CHARTER; ∼ COMMERCIAL PAPER; ∼ DEPOSIT; ∼ DISCOUNT; ∼ DRAFT (2); ∼ LOAN; ∼ NOTE (1); ∼ POLICY (2).

time and motion study. In industrial engineering, a detailed scientific analysis of the time taken by an employee to perform each segment of a particular task, and the hand and body movements made in performing it. Such a study may be made for the purpose of determining the most efficient methods for doing the task, or to evaluate the task in establishing work standards, or setting wages. The equipment used in making the study may include special stop-watch devices, photographic equipment, and so forth. The results of the study may be compared with the results of similar studies, or with predetermined time standards established on the basis of a great number of similar analyses. See also MOTION STUDY.

time bargain. In the securities trade, a term for a form of agreement under which a seller and buyer agree to exchange a particular security at a specified price at some specified future time. This form of agreement or contract is the equivalent of a FUTURES contract in commodities trading, and is a form of HEDGE against price changes. It differs from a PUT, CALL, or STRADDLE in that it is a firm agreement to buy and sell, not an option.

time measure. The universally used system for measuring elapsed time, in which 60 SECONDS equal one MINUTE, 60 minutes equal one HOUR, 24 hours equal one DAY, 365 days equal one YEAR.

time money. A term for borrowed money which is to be returned at the end of a specified period of time, or on a specified date, rather than on the demand of the lender. See also CALL MONEY; LOAN, TIME.

time paid for but not worked. An expression used in computation of wages, hourly rates of pay, and in payroll work. It consists of time such as holidays, approved leave, vacation, sick leave, etc. It also includes time allowances, such as the time paid for to complete a full day of work when less than a day is worked. See, for example, CALL-IN PAY.

time selling. See INSTALLMENT PLAN; CONSUMER CREDIT.

time study. See TIME AND MOTION STUDY.

time work. A system of wage payments based on the amount of time worked, rather than on the number of units or pieces produced. In an industry in which wages are ordinarily based on production, for example, new workers, or workers on new processes, who do not produce at a high enough rate to earn a reasonable wage on PIECE WORK rates, may be paid on the basis of time worked instead.

time zone. See STANDARD TIME.

tip. 1. An item of advice or advance information given, especially one which, if acted upon, will supposedly produce a profit. As defined under the Securities Exchange Act, for example, a *tip* is advance information, particularly information to the effect that the price of a security will, or is likely to, rise or fall.

2. A payment or GRATUITY offered for some personal service rendered. According to one account, the term derives from the initials T.I.P.S., for "to insure prompt service," which were placed on a small container or basket by the employees of taverns, inns, etc. Other authorities, however, believe that the word is of old English origin.

tithe. Literally, the tenth part of anything. Originally, a form of tax consisting of one-tenth of the produce or profit from land, such as one-tenth of the crop harvested, one-tenth of the increase in herds, etc. At one time, it was a tax levied in England for the support of the church. Today, a similar levy on a voluntary basis is still paid by some local church congregations for the support of their local church. More broadly, any tax collected IN KIND is sometimes known as a *tithe.*

title. 1. Originally, from the Latin, a descriptive writing put over, or at the head of something; a designation or appellation. Hence, an appellation of honor, or of authority. Also, a heading or description of a piece of legislation, or of a section of a legislative act.

2. In law, the means by which the ownership of land or other property is established, and by which the owner has his right to lawful possession. Also, the document which contains the evidence of the owner's right to possession.

absolute ∼. One which is exclusive to the one holding it, barring any interest of others in the property covered.

adverse ∼. See TITLE BY ADVERSE POSSESSION, below.

clear ∼. One which has no ENCUMBRANCE, or claim against it, to lessen its value. It is usual, in real estate transactions, for the seller to WARRANT that his title to the property is *clear,* and free of encumbrances.

colorable ∼. A claim to the ownership of property which has some of the conditions necessary to support ownership, but is not legally and technically sufficient to support *title.* In another sense, a *title* which exists in appearance only, but is not valid. The exact meaning depends on the context in which the term is used.

defective ∼. One which contains some defect, or is involved in litigation, or in some other manner is not in such condition that its holder is free to convey the property to another. See also GOOD TITLE, below.

doubtful ∼. One which is neither a GOOD TITLE, which see below, nor necessarily a DEFECTIVE TITLE, which see above, but one concerning which there is some doubt, sufficient so that a court will not enforce it. See also MARKETABLE TITLE, below.

good ∼. One which is free of defects, litigation, or any other conditions which would prevent its holder from conveying the property to another.

legal ∼. One which meets all of the requirements of local statutes, which differ from state to state.

marketable ∼. One which is free from plausible or reasonable obstacles to the conveyance of the property to another. One which a court will enforce in case of doubt.

∼ by abandonment. One acquired by the possession and use of property which has been abandoned by another. Local statutes differ as to the property which can be so acquired, the term of years of use required, etc. See also ABANDONMENT (1).

∼ by accession. One acquired by an innocent addition to one's property, which may occur in several ways. It may be the result, for example, of a natural occurrence such as a flood, or of an intermingling of the property of one person with that of another, etc.

∼ by accretion. One acquired in additions to property resulting from the deposit of soil by a stream, the falling of the water level, etc. See also ACCRETION.

∼ by adverse possession. One which is acquired by the exclusive, actual, and continuous possession of property, especially in the face of opposition, for the period of time required by local statutes, usually twenty years.

∼ by descent. In general, one acquired by inheritance. More specifically, one acquired by a relative under the terms of the local inheritance laws, in the absence of a will.

∼ by devise. One acquired under the terms of a will, especially the will of a person other than an ancestor of the recipient.

∼ by discovery. One acquired by the discovery or finding of concealed or abandoned property, when it is impossible to ascertain the former owner.

∼ by gift. One acquired by a person who receives a gift of real or personal property, without any valuable consideration or return.

∼ by inheritance. See TITLE BY DESCENT, above.

∼ by occupancy. The *title* acquired by one who enters, occupies, and improves unoccupied land, such as under the federal land laws. See also OCCUPANCY.

∼ by purchase. Strictly, that acquired by a person who buys property; that is, who pays the price or consideration demanded. More broadly, the *title* in real property acquired by any means other than by DESCENT, which see above.

title guaranty company. A financial organization which is in the business of searching the available records covering real estate, to uncover, if possible, any evidence of ENCUMBRANCES, DEFECTS, etc., in the title to particular parcels of property. Having made such a search, the company then guarantees to the purchaser of the property, for a fee, that his title is both clear and good. See also TITLE (2), CLEAR; TITLE (2), GOOD.

title insurance. See under INSURANCE, CASUALTY AND LIABILITY.

to arrive. A term used in selling and purchasing, indicating that the goods are ordered with the understanding that they will arrive, or be delivered, on or before a specified date. A purchase order, for example, may include the term *to arrive* March 1, meaning that the sale will be complete only if the goods are delivered by that date.

to arrive price. See under PRICE.

to boot. See BOOT.

to have and to hold. An expression traditionally used in a CONVEYANCE of property, indicating that the rights of both POSSESSION and

TENURE are transferred to the person receiving the property.

token. 1. Originally, a distinguishing sign or mark. Hence, anything used as a sign of an intention to do a thing, rather than the thing itself. For example, a company may place a *token* order for a small amount of goods, as an indication of good intentions and good faith to a supplier, and as an implication that a substantial order will be placed in the future.

2. Something of no intrinsic value, but which is accepted as having value because it bears a stamp or mark of authority. A transportation company, or public transportation authority, for example, may issue *tokens* for use as fares on its vehicles, when the fare is not the exact amount of one of the regular coins, such as a nickel or dime, or of a combination of these. Also, various states and cities may issue *tokens* to be used as fractional coins in the payment of local sales taxes.

token money. See under MONEY.

token payment. The payment of a small portion of a debt, or of an amount due, as a sign of the debtor's good intentions to pay the rest, and as a sign that the debt has not been repudiated. A person facing BANKRUPTCY, for example, may offer to make such *token payments* to his creditors, in an attempt to avoid bankruptcy proceedings.

tolerance. Literally, that which can be borne or endured. Hence, an amount or proportion which is allowed; an allowance. In coinage, for example, a small *tolerance* is allowed in the weight and metal content of a coin from the legal standard. Similarly, in engineering and quality control, specifications for size or weight are usually stated with a small *tolerance* above and below the desired amount, which will be allowed or accepted. The specification for the diameter of a drilled hole, for example, may be stated as 6 inches, plus or minus a *tolerance* of five hundredths of an inch.

toll. Originally, any excise, or tax on the permission to do something or produce something, and usually collected as a proportion of the thing produced, or as a proportion of the profits on the thing done. Today, specifically, a tax or charge on the permission to use some public facility, such as a highway or bridge, or long-distance telephone communications. In the telephone industry, for example, any call beyond the normal local calling area is known as a *toll* call, and the long distance telephone facilities themselves are known as *toll* lines.

ton. A unit of weight in the American and English systems of weight. The American *ton,* also known as the *net ton* or *short ton,* contains 2,000 pounds avoirdupois, and is the equivalent of 907.2 kilograms in the METRIC SYSTEM. The English *ton,* also known as the *imperial ton, gross ton, long ton,* or *shipping ton,* contains 2,240 pounds avoirdupois, and is the equivalent of 1,016 kilograms in the metric system. Several other measures, used in particular fields, are listed and defined below.

displacement ~. A unit used in measuring the displacement, or size, of a ship. It is 35 cubic feet of volume, roughly equivalent to the volume taken up by a *long ton* of average sea water. See also TONNAGE, DISPLACEMENT.

freight ~. See MEASUREMENT TON, below.

measurement ~. A unit of volume, used as an approximation of a *ton* of weight for the calculation of shipping charges on certain types of shipments, at the option of the carrier. It is 40 cubic feet of volume, which is figured to be the equivalent of one *gross ton* of average freight or cargo.

metric ~. A unit of weight equal to 1,000 kilograms, and the equivalent of 2,204.6 pounds, avoirdupois. Thus, it is roughly equal to one *long ton* in the English system, and is slightly larger than one *short ton.*

register ~. A unit used in determining the total registered TONNAGE of a ship. It is a volume of 100 cubic feet of internal space, which is considered to be roughly the equivalent volume of one gross *ton* of carrying capacity.

ton mile. In transportation statistics, a measure equal to the transportation of one ton of freight or cargo one mile. The total number of *ton miles* during a period for a specific route is the sum of all of the distances each ton of freight was carried during the period.

revenue ~. The measure equal to the transportation of one ton of revenue freight, or freight for which the carrier receives payment, for one mile.

~ cost. The measure of the average cost per mile of carrying each ton of freight. It is the total of all freight operation costs divided by the total number of *ton miles* of freight for the period.

~ revenue. The measure of the average receipts per mile for each ton of revenue freight carried. It is the total of all freight revenues received, divided by the total number of *ton miles* of freight for the period.

tonnage. 1. In general, weight measured in TONS; a total number of tons. Also, a charge based on the number of tons carried or processed.

2. In maritime usage, a measure of the size, or carrying capacity of a ship. Theoretically, it is the weight, in gross tons, of the maximum cargo a ship can carry, but the various measurements used have specific and arbitrary meanings, which are listed and defined below. See also TON.

cargo ∼. The measure of ship's cargo used as a basis for transportation and insurance charges. It is computed in terms of actual weight, in gross tons, or in measurement tons of 40 cubic feet, at the option of the shipowner.

dead weight ∼. The measure of the number of tons of cargo, supplies, and fuel a ship can carry. It is the difference between the number of tons of water the ship displaces when empty, and the tons of water it displaces when loaded to its load line, or PLIMSOLL LINE. See also DISPLACEMENT TONNAGE, below.

displacement ∼. Strictly, the number of tons of water displaced by the hull of a ship when afloat. Actually, it is usually measured in terms of the volume of that part of the hull that is submerged, at 35 cubic feet per ton, which is considered to be roughly the volume of one gross ton of sea water. A ship's *displacement tonnage* may be measured empty or loaded to the Plimsoll line.

gross ∼. A measure of the interior capacity of a ship, both above and below decks, in register tons of 100 cubic feet each. It is the volume of all enclosed space on the ship, whether actually available for use or not.

net ∼. A measure of that part of the interior capacity of a ship that is available for use. It is the GROSS TONNAGE, which see above, less the volume of the space taken up by the power plant, fuel storage, supplies, crew quarters, etc. Thus, it is the volume of the enclosed space available for passengers and cargo, measured in register tons of 100 cubic feet each.

registered ∼. The *tonnage* of a ship as listed on its ship's papers, and on the REGISTER (3) maintained by the port from which it sails, or that maintained by the marine insurance companies. Usually, the DEADWEIGHT, DISPLACEMENT, GROSS, and NET TONNAGE, which see above, are all listed.

tonnage tax. See TAX (2), TONNAGE.

tontine. In general, any of a variety of financial schemes in which contributions are made by a large number of persons, and the benefits eventually accrue to those who survive after a period of time. The name is based on a scheme devised by Lorenzo Tonti, a seventeenth century Italian. A typical *tontine* plan involves the payment into a fund by a number of persons of regular amounts over a period of years, with the survivors collecting an annuity from the fund at the end of a specified period. At one time, some insurance policies had a *tontine* feature, under which the dividends and other gains on a whole class of policies were deferred until a stated time, then divided among the policy holders in the class still surviving. Such policies are now generally illegal in the United States. Many company profit sharing and pension funds still have similar features, however, in that the contributions of those who leave the employ of the company accrue to those who remain.

tontine policy. See under POLICY (2).

tool. In general, any mechanical device for shaping, changing, or cutting material, especially one to be used manually. In current usage, the term includes attachments and fittings for machines that cut or shape material, such as drill bits, cutting heads, etc. As used in the bankruptcy laws, which exempt *tools* of the trade from seizure and sale, the term includes those hand *tools* and instruments normally used in the particular trade, but excludes machinery and equipment as such. See also MACHINE TOOL.

to order. A term used in negotiable instruments and endorsements, indicating that the payment is to be made to the person named, or *to his order,* so that he may endorse the instrument to another. An instrument made out *to order* is thus distinguished from one made out to BEARER, which is not restricted in payment to a specifically named person.

Torrens system. A system of land TITLE registration in use in some states, under which each owner of land is required to register his title with the office created for the purpose. He receives in turn a certificate of title, which he may then assign to another to transfer his title to the land. The system is named after its Australian originator.

tort. In law, a private injury or wrong; a wrongful act by one person against another or against the rights of another, which is grounds for a legal action, especially an action in EQUITY. Examples of *torts* include libel, slander, malicious mischief, etc. A *tort* is distinguished from a CRIME, which is a wrong against the state, or against the public in general.

total. In general, full, complete, or maximum; the opposite of PARTIAL. The exact or technical meaning of the term may depend on arbitrary definitions, as, for example, the definition of *total* deafness in state workmens' compensation laws. See also DISABILITY, TOTAL; LOSS, TOTAL.

total surplus. See under SURPLUS.

towage. The act of towing a ship; the charge made for such towing by a tug or other vessel.

town. In general, any inhabited place larger than a village, and having an independent government and administration. More particularly, in the United States, a basic political and civil subdivision of a county. The exact usage and practice differs from state to state, however. See also TOWNSHIP.

township. In United States land law, an area or division of land six miles square, and containing 36 SECTIONS of one square mile each. In some states, each county is divided into *townships* for administrative and taxing purposes, regardless of the actual location of villages, towns, and cities.

trackage. The right given to one railroad to operate its cars over the tracks of another. Also, the charge made by one railroad for granting the right of *trackage* to another, when the tracks are actually used.

trade. 1. Originally, a path, and hence, a following, or line of work. A means of earning a living; a calling, or vocation; a field of business. In one sense, the term means a calling requiring manual or mechanical skill or training, rather than professional training. In another sense, it means a line or field of business in general, such as the grocery *trade*, the commodities *trade*, etc.
2. From the same derivation, passage or travel, especially for the purpose of exchanging goods or carrying on business. Also, the exchange itself, so that the exchange of one type of goods for another is known as a *trade*. More broadly, any COMMERCE, barter, or exchange, of goods, merchandise, money, or other valuables. See each of the following under the principal listing: ~ ADVERTISING; ~ ACCEPTANCE (3); ~ BILL OF EXCHANGE; ~ CREDIT (3); ~ DISCOUNT (1); ~ PRICE.

trade agreement. An agreement or treaty between two nations, or among a group of nations, under which each agrees to grant various privileges to the others, to buy the products of the others, or to sell its own products to the others at a favorable price. Also, a customs or TARIFF agreement, under which the countries agree to give each other's goods favorable tariff treatment.
    reciprocal ~. One under which two countries agree on a mutual exchange of trade privileges or advantages. One in which a country desiring particular trade benefits agrees to give equivalent benefits in exchange. Specifically, any of the commercial treaties entered into by the United States under the Trade Agreement Act of 1934.

trade association. An association of business organizations in a common field, or in allied fields, formed for the purpose of promoting their mutual interests, collecting industry statistics, maintaining and establishing industry standards, or for similar purposes. Also, in some cases, an organization of individual business proprietors or executives, formed for the purpose of promoting their interests as executives, as well as the interests of their common line of business.

trade balance. See BALANCE OF TRADE.

trade in. To turn in one product or item of merchandise as partial payment in the purchase of a new item. For example, the purchaser of a new automobile will frequently turn in, or *trade in* his present automobile as part payment on the new one. Also, the item or product itself which is turned in. Used products in many fields are identified as *trade-ins* when resold to the public. A *trade-in* allowance, or *trade-in* price, is the value set on an item turned in as payment for a new one.

trade journal. See TRADE PUBLICATION.

trade magazine. See TRADE PUBLICATION.

trademark. Any particular device, symbol, mark, name, design, etc., which is used for the purpose of indicating the source, ownership, quality, or kind of a product or service, as a guide and protection to the buying public. It is intended and recognized as a means of protection against fraud, misrepresentation and deception, as well as a means of identifying and distinguishing the products and services of one source from those of all others. Under the present *trademark* laws, a *trademark*, once properly registered and maintained, is the permanent and exclusive property of the one registering it. Aside from the basic *trademark*, the present law recognizes several classifications of marks which may be registered with the Patent Office for protection. The principal classifications of these subsidiary marks are defined below.
    certification ~. A mark used to indicate or certify the origin, quality, method of manufacture, or other characteristic of particular goods or services. It differs from a collective mark, which see below, in that it represents a standard of quality, not merely membership in an organization. An example

is the certification mark of the Underwriters' Laboratories.

collective ~. A mark owned by an association, such as a trade union or producers' cooperative, and used by members of the association and others who are authorized to use the mark, to identify and distinguish their goods and services. Examples include the marks used by the members of various trade associations, unions, etc.

service ~. A mark used in the sale or advertising of a particular service, to identify and distinguish the service of one source from that provided by others. It includes any names, symbols, slogans, phrases, cartoon characters, etc., which may be used in any form of advertising or sales promotion for the service. An example would be the advertising slogan used by a finance company to identify the particular form of credit arrangement offered by the company. Others might offer the same arrangements, but could not identify them by the same registered *service mark*.

trade name. A name used by a business organization to identify its activities, products, or services, but which is not part of the registered or incorporated business name. In credit reference books and other business listings, for example, the corporate name or the name of an unincorporated proprietor may appear, followed by the statement, trading as, or, DOING BUSINESS AS, followed in turn by a *trade name* which is used by the business. Such a *trade name* may be registered as a TRADEMARK if it meets the requirements of the laws, but many *trade names* are not registered as trademarks.

trade paper. See TRADE PUBLICATION.

trade publication. Any regular publication which is devoted primarily to the interests of one or more particular trades, businesses, industries, or professions. It may be a newspaper, magazine, or professional journal. Such publications are known variously as trade magazines, trade journals, or trade papers. They are distinguished from BUSINESS PUBLICATIONS, which are devoted to news and material of interest in business in general, rather than to a particular trade, and which are circulated widely, rather than primarily among the members of the particular trade.

trader. In general, one who buys and sells merchandise or commodities; a person engaged in trading or dealing in a particular class of goods. Strictly speaking, a *trader* is distinguished from a BROKER (2), in that he buys and sells in his own name, and takes title to the goods he deals in, while a broker acts for others. In the securities

trade, for example, a *trader* is a member of a securities exchange who buys and sells for his own account, rather than for the accounts of customers. In many fields, however, the distinction has become blurred in current usage.

floor ~. In the securities trade, an exchange member who conducts trading operations on the TRADING FLOOR of the exchange, as a representative of brokers who take orders from investors and transmit them to the *floor trader*. Also, one who buys and sells for his own account on the floor of the exchange. He is sometimes known as a brokers' broker.

pit ~. In the commodities trade, especially the grain trade, a *trader* or broker who buys and sells speculatively for his own account on the floor or PIT of the exchange. A *trader* who buys and sells commodities, and commodities FUTURES, in the expectation of a speculative profit, rather than in the course of regular business dealings.

trade rights. A term used for those proprietary rights which belong exclusively to a person or company, as a result of having established and built up a business operation, other than regularly registered trademarks or brand names. Such rights include TRADE NAMES, established business locations, reputations among customers, etc.

trade secret. In general, any secret plan, process, or method, such as one used in the manufacture of a secret formula, which is known only to the inventor and the user. Under the patent laws, another term for a SECRET PROCESS.

trade union. See UNION.

trading area. In marketing, the area within which a manufacturer or distributor can reasonably expect to sell or distribute his products economically and profitably. The size of a *trading area* may be limited by shipping costs, by the perishable nature of the product, by voluntary restriction, or perhaps by the terms of a franchise or other agreement. Also, sometimes, the area around a city or metropolitan area in which local residents are likely to trade, and in which local advertisers can expect to obtain customers. Thus, a local newspaper may say that it is read throughout its city's *trading area,* as well as in the city itself.

trading as. See DOING BUSINESS AS.

trading difference. In the securities trade, the term for the difference of a fraction of a point in price which is charged for shares bought or sold in an ODD LOT transaction, over and above the price at which the stock is traded in regular ROUND LOT trading. On the New York Stock Exchange, for example, this difference is ⅛ of a point, or 12½ cents per share, for stocks selling at less than $40 per share, and ¼ of a point, or 25 cents per share, for stocks selling at $40 or higher. In odd lot sales, the *trading difference* is subtracted from the amount received by the seller, and in purchases it is added to the price paid. See also BROKER (2), ODDLOT.

trading floor. In the securities and commodities trades, the place in a securities or commodities exchange in which the actual trade between members of the exchange takes place. The securities broker who acts on the *trading floor* for his customers and for other brokers is known as a floor TRADER. In the commodities trade, the *trading floor* is known as the PIT, and a member of the exchange who operates on the floor is called a pit TRADER.

trading stamp. A device used by retail dealers to increase the volume of sales. Typically, it consists of a plan under which shoppers are given stamps representing a fractional part of the value of their purchases, usually about 2 or 3 percent, which are later exchangeable for merchandise premiums when a large number of stamps have been accumulated. Some *trading stamp* companies are nationwide, so that customers may accumulate stamps from a large number of stores toward their premiums.

trading unit. In the securities trade, the unit of trading for a stock on an exchange, usually 100 shares; a ROUND LOT.

traffic. 1. In one sense, the transportation of merchandise or passengers. Hence, more broadly, commerce or trade in merchandise or services. In modern usage, the term has come to have an unfavorable connotation, as, for example, in terms such as drug *traffic,* slave *traffic,* etc.

2. In business operations, the handling and transportation of materials or products, both within a company and in shipments to and from the company. In many companies, the *traffic* manager or *traffic* department is responsible for the receiving, storage, movement, and shipping of all goods. See also TRAFFIC MANAGEMENT.

3. The goods, passengers, or other things moved, or the vehicles in which they move. In this sense, *traffic* may be in either tangible or intangible form. A telephone or telegraph company, for example, has a *traffic* load in messages.

traffic density. A measure of the relative volume of passenger or freight volume handled by a carrier, or of the number of vehicles using a given highway, bridge, or other facility. It may be measured, for example, in terms of TON MILES of freight carried per mile of route operated, or in terms of vehicles per hour, or per mile of highway. See also FREIGHT DENSITY; PASSENGER DENSITY.

traffic management. That function of business management dealing with the handling and movement of materials and finished products, both within the company and in shipments to and from the company. The field includes the planning of movements, selection of carriers and routes, direction of handling and transport of goods within the company, etc., and in some cases, supervision of storage, packing, and materials handling in general.

traffic return. The term for a periodic report or statement issued by a railroad or other carrier, showing the income received from goods and passengers carried during a period. Such reports or returns are comparable to the interim financial reports issued by manufacturing or commercial companies, and serve as a guide to investors and others interested in the performance of the particular carrier.

trailer. In highway motor vehicle usage, a separate vehicle which does not have its own motive power, but must be pulled by another, called a tractor. A full *trailer* has at least four wheels, and is able to roll and stand by itself, without being attached to another vehicle, while a *semi-trailer* usually has only a full rear axle and wheels, and must be attached to the tractor vehicle, rather than merely pulled.

train mile. In railroading, a measure equivalent to the movement of one train of cars for one mile. The total number of *train miles* for a period is the sum of the miles travelled by all of the trains moving over the particular route. See also CAR MILE.

tramp steamer. A ship which does not operate on a regular schedule or route, but which picks up cargo for any port within its range, and follows each trip by one to the next port for which a cargo is available. The designation derives from the common name for a vagrant, or one who wanders from place to place on foot.

transact. To carry on, or to conduct; as, for example, a business, or negotiations for a sale or purchase.

transaction. Any agreement between two or more parties, creating or affecting a legal right or obligation. More particularly, an agreement involving the sale, purchase, lease, borrowing, lending, or other form of transfer of something of value in exchange for money or other thing of value. Thus, any contract or agreement for sale, lease, etc., may be said to be a *transaction,* but *transactions* are not necessarily in the form of contracts.

transcript. Literally, a writing over of an original. As generally used, a record in writing of any proceedings, such as a meeting, trial, speech, etc., which is a full and faithful record of the original proceedings. Also, in law, a copy of a legal record or document, such as a birth certificate, marriage record, etc., officially prepared and authenticated.

transfer. 1. In law, the passing over, or conveying of something from one person to another. A seller of property, for example, *transfers* title to the property to the new owner. In the securities trade, the *transfer* of a security is the act of placing the certificate in the name of the new owner. See also ASSIGNMENT.

2. The shifting or movement of an employee from one position to another, or from one plant to another, without any accompanying increase in responsibilities, duties, or compensation. Thus, a *transfer* is different from a PROMOTION, which involves an increase in both responsibilities and compensation. In labor agreements, the difference is frequently important, and may call for different actions under the agreement.

transferable. Assignable, or NEGOTIABLE. For example, the right granted by a ticket for admission or transportation may be *transferable* or *non-transferable.* In the latter case, it will not be honored when presented by any person other than the original purchaser, even though it may have been purchased in a completely regular and legal manner.

transfer agent. See under AGENT.

transfer book. A book or register in which are kept the names of all of the registered owners of the stock of a corporation, together with the record of the number of shares owned by each. This book or register is the basis on which dividend payments are made, and on which notices of stockholders meetings are mailed. Frequently, the *transfer book* is closed for a number of days before dividend checks and meeting notices are mailed, to give the corporation time to prepare the mailing. Notice of the closing of the *transfer book* must be included in the announcement of the dividend, if the book is closed.

transfer company. A company formed for the purpose of moving baggage to and from, or between, railroad terminals in a city. Also, a company formed to move the freight cars of one railroad to and from the terminal of another, or to and from the sidings of local shippers. Both types of company are considered to be common carriers, and are governed by any regulations or laws affecting common carriers.

transfer in blank. See ASSIGNMENT IN BLANK.

transfer payments. In national income statistics, those monetary receipts by individuals and others from government and business for which no services are rendered, including pensions, awards, etc., and payments by government and business in the form of gifts to non-profit institutions, etc. In other words, those monetary transactions which do not represent additions to the national product.

transfer tax. See under TAX (2).

transit. In general, a passage, or transportation across; a moving from one place to another. In banking, a term sometimes used for a check which is sent out by mail or otherwise for collection, while it is still in the mails and uncollected. See also IN TRANSIT; STOPPAGE IN TRANSIT.

transit advertising. See under ADVERTISING.

transit operations. In banking, the name for the nationwide operation of the exchange of checks and other instruments among local CLEARING HOUSES, as distinguished from the process of CLEARING (1) among member banks of the local clearing house itself.

transit privilege. The right granted to a shipper by a railroad, giving permission to process goods in transit without paying more than the regular through rate for the shipment. Goods shipped from New York to Chicago, for example, may be stopped at an intermediate city for manufacture, packaging, or other processing, under a single New York to Chicago freight rate, rather than under one rate from New York to the intermediate city and another rate from there to Chicago, which might come to a higher total.

transportation. In general, the carrying of goods or persons from place to place; the physical means provided for such carrying, including cars, vehicles, etc. Specifically, as defined under the Interstate Commerce Act, all the services rendered by a carrier, including the receipt, handling, delivery, and caring for goods shipped, as well as the actual carrying of them from place to place.

transportation advertising. See ADVERTISING, TRANSIT.

transshipping. 1. In transportation, the removal of goods from one vessel to another, or from the cars or vehicles of one carrier to those of another. It may be direct, or it may include storage on a wharf or in a warehouse of one of the carriers.

2. In distribution, a term for the practice of one distributor or dealer shipping goods to another dealer or distributor outside of his own regular selling territory. In some fields, for example, distributors may receive more favorable purchasing terms for larger volume. To achieve this volume, a distributor may accept delivery of more goods than he can normally sell, and then sell the excess at reduced prices to retail dealers in a territory other than his own. Similarly, a retail dealer with excessive inventory may *transship* the excess to another dealer at a reduced price to liquidate his investment.

traveler. See COMMERCIAL TRAVELER; TRAVELING SALESMAN.

travelers' check. See under CHECK.

traveler's letter of credit. See under LETTER OF CREDIT.

traveling benefit. A form of unemployment benefit, paid as a grant or loan to unemployed members by some unions, to enable them to travel to another place to seek work. Such benefits are usually granted by local unions in the skilled crafts, such as printing, plumbing, etc., to enable their members to find work.

traveling salesman. A sales representative who travels from place to place, soliciting orders for the company he represents. Usually, the term is limited to a representative who travels from town to town, rather than one who goes from store to store or house to house in the same town; a COMMERCIAL TRAVELER.

treasurer. The officer of a corporation, or of any other organization, who is charged with the responsibility for the receipt, custody, and disbursement of the corporate or organizational funds. In many corporations, he is also the SECRETARY.

Treasurer of the United States. The official in the U.S. TREASURY DEPARTMENT who is responsible for the receipt, custody, and disbursement of all of the money of the United States government, both in the Treasury and in various depositories and accounts, according to the specifications and instructions of the Secretary of the Treasury and the CONTROLLER OF THE CURRENCY. He is appointed by the President with the consent of the Senate.

treasury bill. A short-term, non-interest-bearing obligation of the U.S. Treasury, which is sold on the open market on a DISCOUNT basis. *Treasury bills* are issued and sold

periodically as the need for cash arises. They are usually 91 day negotiable instruments, issued on a BEARER basis, and sold primarily to banks in denominations of $5,000 to $1,000,000. The tax anticipation federal notes issued in recent years, with 144 day maturities, are also technically known as *treasury bills,* though not commonly known as such.

treasury bond. See under BOND (1).

treasury certificate. An intermediate term, interest-bearing obligation of the United States Treasury. They usually have a one year maturity, and pay interest on a coupon basis. *Treasury certificates* may be purchased for the purpose of establishing a reserve for the payment of taxes. See also CERTIFICATE OF INDEBTEDNESS.

Treasury Department. The federal department originally established in 1789 to manage the national finances. It is responsible for the issuance of all currency, the collection of taxes and tariffs, the Coast Guard service, etc. It administers the National Bank Act, and together with the Federal Reserve System supervises the banking system of the country. The department is headed by the Secretary of the Treasury, who is a member of the presidential cabinet.

treasury note. A long term, interest-bearing obligation of the United States Treasury, on which interest is paid by coupon. The term to maturity of *treasury notes* may be from one to five years, so that the *treasury note* falls between the TREASURY CERTIFICATE and regular government bonds in terms of maturity.

treasury stock. See under STOCK (1).

trespass. In law, any unlawful or unauthorized entry on the property of another; any forcible or violent wrong done to the property, rights or person of another. More broadly, any transgression against law, or against the rights of another person.

tret. In shipping, an allowance in the weigh of some commodities for dust, waste, etc When *tret* is allowed, the GROSS WEIGHT c the package equals NET WEIGHT plus TAR and *tret.*

trial balance. In accounting, a totalling of th debit and credit balances in all of the ledge accounts of a company, usually taken at th end of an accounting period. The purpos is to test or check whether all entries hav been made in both debit and credit account preparatory to the preparation of a FINANCIA STATEMENT. The *trial balance* does not te the absolute accuracy of the accounts, sinc an entry may easily be made incorrectly in both a credit and debit account.

triangular exchange. A form of ARBITRATION OF EXCHANGE, involving three different places.

trick. In the slang of some trades, a work period, or SHIFT.

trip charter. See under CHARTER.

trough. In economics, and specifically in the business cycle, the lowest point reached during a particular cycle. It is the low point of the DEPRESSION phase of the cycle, and the point at which the CONTRACTION phase ends and the EXPANSION begins. More generally, it is any low point in activity, such as the *trough* in sales activity after the principal selling season is over.

trover. In law, the technical name for the right to recover damages which belongs to a person whose property has been taken by CONVERSION.

troy weight. A system of measurement of weight, which is now used primarily for weighing metals and precious stones. The system is based on a POUND of 5,760 grains, or 12 OUNCES of 480 grains each. The ounce is further divided into 20 PENNYWEIGHTS of 24 grains each. See also AVOIRDUPOIS; APOTHECARIES' WEIGHT.

truckload. In motor freight usage, the amount of a commodity that will fill a truck, or the amount that is sufficient to be treated as if it filled a truck. If the capacity of a truck is 12,000 pounds, for example, 8,000 pounds of some commodities might be considered a *truckload*. In interstate commerce, motor freight carriers are required to charge lower rates per pound for *truckload* shipments than for LESS-THAN-TRUCKLOAD shipments of the same commodity.

true bill. In law, the name for the report in which a grand jury finds that the charges listed in a BILL OF INDICTMENT are sufficiently sustained by the available evidence to warrant a trial. See also BILL (2).

true discount. See DISCOUNT (2).

true value. See VALUE (2), INTRINSIC.

trunk line. In railroading, one of the principal railroads of the country, so called because these routes provide the MAIN LINES from which others branch out. Similarly, in telephone operations, a main telephone line connecting the central lines to a company telephone switchboard, from which the internal telephone connections branch off.

trust. 1. In law, the FIDUCIARY relationship existing between persons according to which one person, the TRUSTEE, holds property for the use or benefit of another, the BENEFICIARY.

The person who creates the *trust* is known as the SETTLOR, grantor, donor, or trustor. Under such an arrangement, legal title to the property involved is conveyed to the trustee, with the obligation to administer it according to the terms of the *trust* and for the period for which it is established. The various forms of *trust,* and the various methods of operation, are listed and defined below:

accumulation ∼. One created for the specific purpose of holding an estate intact, and accumulating and reinvesting any income, profits, or gains, so that upon the termination of the *trust* the larger total can be turned over according to its terms to the person specified. Such a *trust* might be established under a will for the benefit of a minor, for example. The laws of the various states may set certain maximum time limits on the life of such a *trust*.

active ∼. See SPECIAL TRUST, below.

beneficial ∼. One under which the trustee, as well as the beneficiary, will derive some benefit or advantage, such as an income. See also NAKED TRUST, below.

charitable ∼. One created for the specified purpose of providing some charitable, educational, or non-profit institution with a source of funds. Such *trusts* usually receive special treatment under the tax and other laws.

constructive ∼. One which is declared by a court to exist, though no special act to create a *trust* has occurred. See also IMPLIED TRUST, below.

direct ∼. See EXPRESS TRUST, below.

discretionary ∼. One in which the choice of the manner in which the funds involved are to be invested is left to the broad choice or discretion of the trustee, as distinguished from a NON-DISCRETIONARY TRUST, which see below.

dry ∼. One in which the trustee has no responsibilities or discretionary powers whatever, but is required merely to hold the property and turn it over at the termination of the trust. It is sometimes known as a *passive trust*. See also SPECIAL TRUST, below.

executed ∼. One that meets all of the legal requirements; one that is complete and is ready to be administered, as distinguished from an EXECUTORY TRUST, which see below.

executory ∼. One with respect to which something remains to be done or specified, to enable its intent to be carried out. Such a *trust* may result, for example, from the use of loose or ambiguous language in the creating instrument.

express ∼. One in which the purpose, persons concerned, property involved, and its distribution are all set forth clearly and unmistakably, leaving nothing to be construed or implied. Sometimes known as a *direct trust*. See also IMPLIED TRUST, below.

fixed ∼. See NON-DISCRETIONARY TRUST, below.

implied ∼. One which is not specifically declared to exist, but which arises out of the operation of the law, or is established by a court to protect the rights or satisfy the demands of a party involved. See also CONSTRUCTIVE TRUST, above; PRECATORY TRUST, below.

inter vivos ∼. See LIVING TRUST, below.

involuntary ∼. In some states a name for an IMPLIED TRUST, which see above.

irrevocable ∼. One which cannot be changed or cancelled by the settlor, once it is declared and in operation. Under the federal tax laws, such a *trust* is eligible for more favorable treatment than one which may be revoked at the will of the settlor.

limited ∼. One which is specified to continue in force for a limited and fixed period of time. See also PERPETUAL TRUST, below.

living ∼. The term for a *trust* which is made voluntarily by a settlor, usually for the support of another person, without any valuable consideration to the settlor. It may be an IRREVOCABLE, LIMITED, or other form of *trust*. It is sometimes called a *voluntary* or *inter vivos trust*.

naked ∼. One from which the trustee receives no benefit whatsoever through his administrations. See also BENEFICIAL TRUST, above.

non-discretionary ∼. One in which the trustee is strictly limited as to the type of investment that may be made, as distinguished from a DISCRETIONARY TRUST on the one hand, and a DRY TRUST, both of which see above, on the other. It is sometimes known as a *fixed trust*.

passive ∼. See DRY TRUST, above.

perpetual ∼. One which is specified to continue as long as the need for which it was established continues to exist. Thus it is seldom actually *perpetual,* but may be for the life of a beneficiary, or for as long as the class of persons it is intended to aid exists. CHARITABLE TRUSTS, which see above, are usually *perpetual trusts.*

precatory ∼. A form of IMPLIED or CONSTRUCTIVE TRUST, which see above, created by a court when the intent to set up a *trust* is clear in a will but the mechanics have not been carried through.

private ∼. One established for the benefit of one or a few private individuals, as distinguished from a CHARITABLE TRUST, which see above.

public ∼. A CHARITABLE TRUST, which see above.

resulting ∼. An IMPLIED TRUST, which see above, resulting from the actions or failure to take action of the parties concerned.

revocable ∼. One which contains a provision reserving to the settlor the right to change or revoke it. See also IRREVOCABLE TRUST, above.

secret ∼. One created in secret between the settlor and trustee, usually in verbal form only, providing that property turned over to the secret trustee will actually be held for the benefit of another person and eventually turned over to him. For example, a bankrupt may create a *secret trust* with himself as beneficiary in an attempt to keep property out of the hands of his creditors, or a person may create a *secret trust* for the benefit of a relative in an attempt to evade estate taxes.

sheltering ∼. See SPENDTHRIFT TRUST, below.

simple ∼. See DRY TRUST, above.

special ∼. One in which the trustee has some prescribed duties to perform, as distinguished from a simple or DRY TRUST, which see above. It is sometimes called an *active trust.*

spendthrift ∼. One established for the benefit of a person, such as a minor or one who might not be expected to exercise good judgment, usually providing that neither the principal nor the income of the *trust* can be attached by creditors for the debts of the beneficiary. Such restricted *trusts* may not be legal in some states.

testamentary ∼. One established under the terms of a will, to come into operation upon probate of the will.

voluntary ∼. See LIVING TRUST, above.

2. A form of business organization, now illegal, created by the transfer of all or a substantial portion of the voting stock of a number of corporations to a board of trustees, who constitute a *voting trust,* to vote the stock of the respective corporation in the interests of the entire group. Such organizations or combinations were declared illegal under the anti-trust laws. More broadly, any combination of competing companies, for the purpose of controlling market, is known as a *trust,* whether actually organized in the form of a *trust* or not.

3. A form of business organization based on the *trust* concept, under which the persons who contribute the capital of the business form a voluntary organization, rather than a corporation, company, or partnership. The title to the property and asse

of the business are transferred to a group of trustees, elected to serve for the duration of the *trust* agreement, who manage the affairs of the business for the benefit of the original owners of the assets. The owners receive CERTIFICATES OF BENEFICIAL INTEREST, representing their interest in the business, and receive payments out of the profits of the business. This form of organization is variously known as a *Massachusetts trust* (because it was most effectively developed under the laws of that state), *business trust, common-law trust,* etc.

trust certificate. A form of obligation, similar in effect to a mortgage bond, and used primarily to finance the purchase of railroad equipment. In operation, the equipment, such as locomotives, freight cars, etc., is purchased by a trustee, such as a TRUST COMPANY, and either leased to the railroad or sold to it on a conditional sales contract. Title to the equipment in either case is held by the trustee until the equipment is paid for, and *equipment trust certificates* are issued against the title to individual investors, who receive interest on their investments, and who legally own a small share of the equipment until it is paid for. The plan under which the equipment is leased to the railroad is known as the *Philadelphia plan,* and that under which it is sold under a conditional sale contract is known as the *New York plan,* but the effect of both is the same, since title to the equipment does not pass until it is paid for in either case. See also BOND (1).

trust company. A financial institution organized specifically to serve as TRUSTEE or FIDUCIARY for individuals and businesses. The trust company may be named as the executor of a will, or as the trustee of a trust fund established by any means. It will also serve as trustee under a mortgage, as a depository in ESCROW, as transfer agent or registrar for securities, etc. The laws of the various states differ as to the exact services which the company may perform, and as to its responsibilities.

trust deed. See under DEED.

trustee. In law, a person who has been named to manage and execute a TRUST. Depending on the nature of the trust, his powers and duties may range from those of a mere custodian to those of a manager of a going business enterprise. A *trustee* may be a private individual, or one of a number of such individuals, or a TRUST COMPANY. In general, a member of the governing body of any organization which is governed by a board

of *trustees,* rather than by a board of directors. See also FIDUCIARY.

trustee in bankruptcy. The name of the person assigned by the court or by the creditors to discharge the functions of trust in connection with a BANKRUPTCY. His duties include assembling the assets of the bankrupt, preparing an inventory and valuation of these, conducting the business if it is in operation, and paying off the claims of the various creditors. See also ASSIGNMENT FOR BENEFIT OF CREDITORS.

trust fund. In general, any fund of money or property established for the benefit of one or more persons, and held by a TRUSTEE. Such a fund may be set up under any of the various forms of TRUSTS (1), and may be deposited with a TRUST COMPANY or privately administered.

  common ~. One established by a TRUST COMPANY, or the trust department of a bank, or sometimes by a state agency, to provide for the common investment, administration, and safekeeping of the funds in a number of small *trust funds.* Such a fund, for example, may be used to invest the funds of a number of small pension funds or other trusts. It is sometimes known as a *commingled trust fund.*

trust officer. The title of the officer or executive in a TRUST COMPANY or other institution who has direct and immediate charge of the matters and funds in which the institution acts as trustee.

trust receipt. In banking and foreign trade, an instrument by means of which an importer is able to obtain possession of the shipping documents covering a shipment, and dispose of the shipment, before paying the bank on the BILL OF EXCHANGE covering the shipment. Under the terms of the receipt, the importer agrees to deposit the proceeds of the sale, whether the goods are sold as a lot or in parcels, immediately with the bank, until the goods are paid for. Thus, in effect, the importer gives the bank a chattel mortgage on the goods, but one which permits him to dispose of them.

trust share. See CERTIFICATE OF BENEFICIAL INTEREST.

T.T. See TELEGRAPHIC TRANSFER.

tub. A measure of capacity, used commercially for such products as butter, lard, fish, etc. In various uses, it may contain from 56 to 86 pounds, but usually contains about 60 pounds.

tun. A measure of liquid capacity, used now almost exclusively in the wine trade. In the United States, it is the equivalent of 2

PIPES or BUTTS, 4 HOGSHEADS, 8 BARRELS, or 252 GALLONS.

turn. In retail merchandising, a TURNOVER of inventory. A merchant, for example, may speak of obtaining five stock *turns* per year, meaning that his total sales to average inventory ratio is five to one. Also, in the securities trade, a transaction, especially a complete one involving both a purchase and sale of the same security; a ROUND TRANSACTION.

turnover. 1. In general, the relative activity of any stock of capital, or inventory of goods, in relation to the volume of business. The number of times a stock of capital or of goods is used in a given period of time. For example, the annual *turnover* of an inventory of retail merchandise is measured as the total annual sales volume divided by the average inventory on hand. The *turnover* of the capital invested in a business is the volume of business transacted in a period of time, divided by the average capital invested during the period.

2. In personnel management, the number of employees hired or terminated by a company in relation to the total employment during the period measured. The accepted measurement is taken as the total number of employees who are hired to replace those terminated, as a proportion of the average total employment during the period.

turnover ratio. Any of the several ratios used as a measure of the activity of capital, inventory, or other factor in a business. It may be, for example, the ratio of total sales to average inventory, of total revenue to average capital investment, of net sales to working capital, etc. See also OPERATING RATIO.

turnpike. Originally, a tollgate, or one that was turned aside only after payment of a TOLL. Now, a toll road, especially one operated by a state or public authority. More broadly, any major highway, whether operated as a toll road or not.

twelvemo. See BOOK SIZES, DUODECIMO.

twenty-fourmo. See under BOOK SIZES.

twisting. In insurance, a term for the practice of persuading a policy holder to drop one policy and replace it with another, usually with a different insurance company. Typically, the insurance salesman who resorts to *twisting* may persuade the holder of an ordinary insurance policy to turn it in for the cash value, and take out a term insurance policy at a lower premium rate. To the extent that the policy owner is not aware of the full implications of what he has done, the practice is considered highly unethical,

and is discouraged by the major insurance companies. See also INSURANCE, LIFE, ACCIDENT, AND HEALTH.

two bits. In slang, twenty-five cents. See also BIT.

two-dollar broker. In the securities trade, a popular term for a member of a stock exchange who engages only in executing orders for other brokers. The name derives from the fact that the commission for executing such orders was formerly two dollars per hundred shares bought or sold. See also BROKER (2).

two-name account. See ACCOUNT (3), JOINT.

two-name paper. See under COMMERCIAL PAPER.

two thousand hour clause. The popular name for a clause in the federal Fair Labor Standards Act, under which working schedules may be established without regard to the basic 8 hour day and 40 hour week, up to a limit of 12 hours daily and 56 hours weekly. Such longer weekly and daily schedules may be established in certain cases, provided that the employer and the union have agreed that no employee will work more than a total of 2,000 hours in any consecutive 5 weeks. Under an agreement of this sort, overtime wages need not be paid until the employee exceeds 2,000 hours of work during the year. See also BELO PLAN; OVERTIME.

tycoon. Originally, a Japanese title for a prince or high priest. Today, in business slang, an important business personage, or MAGNATE. A person who exercises a strong influence or degree of control over an area of business activity.

tying contract. See CONTRACT, REQUIREMENT TIE-IN SALE.

type size. The system for the measurement of the height of lines of type in printed material, and the size of the individual character of type. The system is based on the POINT (2), which is approximately 1/72 of one inch. The actual measurement in points, however includes a minimum allowance of space between lines, so that when type is said to be 12-point, for example, each letter is actually a little less than one sixth of an inch high. Among the basic type sizes are AGATE which is 5-point type and prints 14 lines to the inch, and PICA, which is 12-point type and print 6 lines to the inch. The pica is also the standard measure of horizontal type length, so that a 24-pica column width is 4 inches, regardless of the size of type. The measure of the relative width of a letter is the *em*, which is a width equal to the height of the line, so that an em of 12-point type is 12 points, or 1/6th of an inch wide

U

ullage. 1. In commercial usage, the difference between the full capacity of a cask and its actual contents. Hence, the term *in ullage,* with reference to wine or liquor, means kept or left in a partly filled cask or bottle, which is believed to be undesirable.

2. Sometimes, as in British customs terminology, the actual amount in a partly filled cask. In this usage, the true *ullage* is termed the VACUITY.

ultimate consumer. See CONSUMER.

ultimo. In business usage, the previous month; that is, the month before the current one. See also PROXIMO, the next month.

ultra vires. Literally, in Latin, beyond the power. In law, an *ultra vires* act is one which is beyond the lawful authority or power of a corporation, as stated in its charter. Courts have disagreed concerning the validity of *ultra vires* contracts entered into by corporate officers, and as to whether the corporation is liable for the performance of such a contract.

umpire. In disputes, such as labor disputes, an impartial party employed by both sides to decide on the correct interpretation or application of the terms of an agreement or settlement. An *umpire* may be selected, for example, when a committee of REFEREES or ARBITRATORS is unable to reach a conclusion, and the *umpire's* decision is accepted as final.

unaccrued. Not yet become due, whether received or not. A rent payment received in advance, for example, is *unaccrued* income. See also ACCRUED.

unavoidable. In law and insurance, that which could not have been prevented by reasonable and prudent care and foresight. Hence, an *unavoidable* accident is one which occurs despite reasonable precautions, and which cannot be foreseen by ordinary intelligence. An *unavoidable* event differs from an ACT OF GOD in that the former may be caused by a human agency, though beyond control or anticipation, while the latter is an event due to natural causes.

unconditional. Not limited, confined, or affected by any conditions or restrictions. See also ABSOLUTE.

unconfirmed credit. See CREDIT (3), REVOCABLE.

unconfirmed letter of credit. See under LETTER OF CREDIT.

under bond. Stored in a government warehouse, or in one licensed by the government, pending the payment of an import TARIFF or excise TAX. Imported goods may be stored *under bond* until they are either re-exported or released upon the payment of duty, and alcoholic beverages may be stored *under bond* after manufacture, until they are released for sale on payment of the excise tax. See also IN BOND.

underinsurance. Insurance in an amount less than the value of the property insured, or the amount of the risk insured against. It may be the result of a deliberate decision on the part of the insured to carry some of the risk himself, or it may be due to negligence or to ignorance of the true amount of the risk. See also INSURANCE; COINSURANCE; SELF-INSURANCE.

underlying. Prior or senior to another obligation, in order of claim though not necessarily in order of time. See, for example, BOND (1), UNDERLYING; MORTGAGE, UNDERLYING.

under protest. A term indicating that a payment is made under some compulsion, and with reservations. When a payment is made *under protest,* the payer reserves the right to open the transaction at a later time, and to take legal action, if necessary, to recover the payment.

undersell. To sell at a price lower than that of a competitor, or of the trade in general, or of the regular market value.

understanding. In law, any informal AGREEMENT, such as one implied from the express terms of another. A meeting of minds, which constitutes a valid agreement, enforceable in a court.

undertake. To agree or attempt to perform some act or service. Thus, a seller who *undertakes* to deliver a stated quantity of goods at some specified time is not absolutely bound to do so, as long as he makes a reasonable attempt to do so. Similarly, an agent who *undertakes* to find a customer for a product is bound only to use his best efforts to do so.

undertaking. 1. An engagement or promise made by one party to an agreement or contract to the other party. It is usually a stipulation or assurance by one party alone, rather than a mutual promise.

2. In legal proceedings, a promise or bond by a person appealing from a decision of a court, to the effect that he will prosecute his appeal, pay costs, and satisfy whatever judgment may be rendered against him.

3. In general, any enterprise or venture, especially a business enterprise in which one engages.

under the counter. In a furtive or surreptitious manner, or outside of normal and ethical methods of dealing. For example, an additional payment made surreptitiously to obtain better service or extra favor, is said to be made *under the counter*. Similarly, illegally obtained goods may be disposed of by a sale *under the counter*.

under the hammer. A term meaning sold at AUCTION; sold to the highest bidder.

under the rule. In the securities trade, the term used to describe a sale or purchase of securities made by the officers of a stock exchange, for the purpose of completing a transaction entered into by a delinquent member. The member who has failed to deliver or accept the securities involved is charged with any difference in price that may have developed. Similar sales or purchases *under the rule* may be made by the exchange officers to settle disputes, or otherwise to close out open matters.

underwrite. 1. In insurance, to insure another. Literally to agree to assume a risk in exchange for a premium paid, by writing one's name under an insurance contract. See also INSURANCE.

2. In the securities trade, to agree to market an issue of securities to the public, with the commitment to buy any of the issue not bought by the public. Thus, an agreement to *underwrite* a stock issue is essentially a purchase and resale agreement, though the underwriter, strictly, takes title only to those shares he cannot resell.

underwriter. 1. In insurance, a person or company agreeing to assume all or a share of a risk being insured; an INSURANCE COMPANY.

2. An officer or employee of an insurance company who passes on the desirability of risks offered to the company, and who determines whether the risk will be insured and the premium rate to be charged, if this is variable.

3. In the securities trade, a person or group who agree to UNDERWRITE an issue of securities. See also SYNDICATE.

undistributed profit. See under PROFIT.

undistributed profits tax. See under TAX (2).

undivided right. A RIGHT or title to property or an estate, held by one of two or more joint tenants or TENANTS IN COMMON. Each tenant is said to have an *undivided right* to a share of all of the property, rather than an exclusive right to any particular part, regardless of the equality or inequality of the shares of ownership.

undue influence. In law, any actions taking an unfair advantage of another person's weakness of mind, ignorance, or circumstances such as by the use of misrepresentations and exaggerations, to gain an advantage. The use of pressure, short of threats and intimidation. When exerted in connection with the making of a will or in similar situation it is considered a species of FRAUD.

unearned. Received without the performance of any work or service, or for work or service not yet performed, but due to be performed in the future. See each of the following under the principal listing: ~ DIVIDEND; ~ INCOME; ~ INCREMENT; ~ PREMIUM (2

unemployment. The condition or state of not being employed. As used in federal statistics it is the condition of not actually working and of not having a position to return to the end of a vacation, leave, or furlough, but still being a member of the LABOR FORCE in the sense that work is sought. Also, the total number of persons who are not employed. *Unemployment* may result from a decrease in business activity, known as *economic unemployment,* or it may result from the gradual displacement of employees by automatic equipment or more efficient means of production, known as *technological unemployment.* The temporary *unemployment* of workers due to changing jobs, or to seasonal shifts from industry to industry is known as *frictional unemployment.*

unemployment insurance. Insurance against unemployment from causes beyond the control of the worker. Under the Federal Social Security Act, the federal government operates with the several states in providing systems of *unemployment insurance* workers covered by the law. See also SOCIAL SECURITY.

unfair competition. Any dishonest or unlawful act by a competitor, for the purpose of gaining an unfair advantage. Particularly, as used in the federal anti-trust laws, any acts, including imitation, falsification, or deception, designed to mislead and confuse the public, and to permit the substitution of one product for another. The passing off, or the attempt to pass off, on the public the goods of one source as those of another. See also COMPETITION.

unfair labor practice. As defined by the National Labor Relations Act, any interference with, or restraint of employees in the exercise of their rights to organize and bargain collectively. Any attempt to dominate or interfere with the formation or activity of any labor organization; any discrimination in the hiring, employment, promotion, discharge, etc., of workers because of their labor organization activities; or a refusal to bargain collectively with employees or their representatives.

unfair to union labor. A term used by labor unions to refer to an employer who refuses to hire union workers, or who refuses to recognize and bargain with the union.

unfair trade practice. Any business or marketing practice considered illegal or unethical. Specifically, any practice declared illegal by the federal Robinson-Patman Act or any of the several state FAIR TRADE LAWS, such as selling a product below cost for the purpose of injuring a competitor, or granting an unfair price advantage to certain customers.

unfunded debt. See DEBT, FLOATING.

unified bond. See BOND (1), CONSOLIDATED.

uniform. As used in business, conforming to a standard, or to regulations. Not differing materially from item to item, place to place or time to time.

uniform bill of lading act. The uniform law, also included in the UNIFORM COMMERCIAL CODE, covering the BILLS OF LADING issued by common carriers. The act specifies the form, terms, and conditions of such bills, and provides for the responsibilities of the shipper and the carrier. The act has been enacted by most states.

uniform commercial code. A codification and combination of the uniform laws affecting business activities, prepared by the Commissioners on Uniform Laws. It includes such uniform laws as the UNIFORM BILL OF LADING ACT, UNIFORM NEGOTIABLE INSTRUMENT ACT, UNIFORM SALES ACT, UNIFORM STOCK TRANSFER ACT, UNIFORM TRUST RECEIPTS ACT, and UNIFORM WAREHOUSE RECEIPTS ACT. Most states have adopted only selected parts of the code thus far.

uniform conditional sales act. The uniform law, adopted by several of the states, providing for uniform terms in CONDITIONAL SALES CONTRACTS, and establishing the rights of buyers and sellers under such contracts. It also provides for a uniform procedure of repossession in the event of default in payments.

uniform delivered price. A method of pricing, under which an article sells at the same delivered price throughout the area in which it is sold, regardless of differences in delivery or freight costs. When such *uniform delivered prices* are set by a number of manufacturers jointly, this has been declared to be a violation of the anti-trust laws, but an individual manufacturer may set such prices independently. See also ZONE PRICING.

uniform law. One of a series of laws adopted by the several states in various fields of business, commerce and law, to eliminate confusion, conflicts and disputes. Most of these laws have been drawn up by the United States Commissioners on Uniform Laws, but some have been proposed by trade and professional associations and other groups. Some of the more important of these laws include the UNIFORM BILL OF LADING ACT, the UNIFORM NEGOTIABLE INSTRUMENTS LAW, the UNIFORM SALES ACT, the UNIFORM STOCK TRANSFER ACT, and the UNIFORM COMMERCIAL CODE.

uniform negotiable instruments act. The uniform law, also included in the UNIFORM COMMERCIAL CODE, which has now been adopted by all of the states. It includes a uniform definition of a NEGOTIABLE INSTRUMENT, and specifies the conditions and terms under which one may be issued, the method of endorsement and negotiation, and the rights and liabilities of the parties to the instrument.

uniform partnership act. The uniform law, defining the various forms of PARTNERSHIP, which has now been adopted by a majority of the states. The law establishes the rights and responsibilities of the various classes of PARTNERS, and the liabilities of the partnership itself.

uniform sales act. The uniform law, covering contracts of SALE, which is also included in the UNIFORM COMMERCIAL CODE, and which has been adopted by most states. It specifies the effects of the conditions and warranties of sale, and provides for the transfer of title and performance of the sale agreement.

uniform stock transfer act. The uniform law, also included in the UNIFORM COMMERCIAL

CODE, which covers the transfer of certificates of stock, and which has now been adopted by the major states. It provides for the assignment of the certificate, the disposition of lost and stolen certificates, etc.

uniform trust receipts act. The uniform law, also included in the UNIFORM COMMERCIAL CODE, which covers the issuance and use of TRUST RECEIPTS. It covers the form of the receipt, establishes the rights and liabilities of the trustee and the importer, etc.

uniform warehouse receipts act. The uniform law, also included in the UNIFORM COMMERCIAL CODE, covering the form and use of WAREHOUSE RECEIPTS. The act defines the form and terms of the receipt, establishes the obligations and rights of the warehouseman, and those of the depositors and other persons in relation to the property deposited or stored. It has now been adopted by most states.

unilateral. One-sided; applying to only one of two or more persons or things. A *unilateral* contract or agreement, for example, is one which binds or applies to only one of the parties involved. See also BILATERAL.

unimproved. With respect to property, land which is in a state of nature, whether it has never been improved, or has once been improved but has now reverted to its natural state. See also IMPROVED.

union. An organization of employees, formed for the purpose of dealing collectively with employers on matters concerned with their employment, including wages, hours, conditions of work, seniority, welfare benefits and so forth. It is also known as a *labor union,* or *trade union.* Among the many types of such *unions* are the following:

amalgamated ~. A *union* formed by the combination of two or more local or national *unions,* usually in related crafts or industries, such as the Amalgamated Clothing Workers Union.

closed ~. One which does not freely admit new members. This may be accomplished by the setting of long apprenticeship requirements, high initiation fees, or other restrictions.

company ~. One formed or sponsored by an employer for his own employees. Employers are prohibited from interfering in union organization by the National Labor Relations Act, so that true *company unions* are now outlawed.

craft ~. A *union* including workers who are all engaged in the same specialized craft, such as carpentry, electrical work, metal work, etc., regardless of the industry in which they are employed. A HORIZONTAL UNION, which see below.

dual ~. A *union* set up in a company, craft or industry in which there is already an established *union.* In the past, such *dual unions* were established by the rival A.F.L and C.I.O., by left- or right-wing groups politically opposed to the existing *union* or by independent groups dissatisfied with the established *union.*

federal labor ~. In the American Federation of Labor, a local *union* set up in a field in which there is no established organization and affiliated directly to the national Federation. The *federal labor union* may become the nucleus for a new national or international *union.*

horizontal ~. A CRAFT UNION, which see above, so called because its jurisdiction cuts across industry lines.

independent ~. One formed by the employees in a particular plant, company, craft or industry, without affiliating with an INTERNATIONAL UNION, which see below, or with a federation of *unions.*

industrial ~. A *union* including workers in a single industry, regardless of their craft or degree of skill, such as the steel, automobile, chemical, and other industries. A VERTICAL UNION, which see below.

international ~. In the American labor movement, a parent *union* with locals in Canada, and sometimes Mexico, as well as in the United States.

local ~. A *union* of workers in one company, plant, city or area, affiliated to a larger craft or industrial *union.* The *local* is the basic membership and collective bargaining unit of the *union* system.

national ~. A parent *union* which has locals throughout the country. It is distinguished from an INTERNATIONAL UNION which see above, since it does not have locals in either Canada or Mexico.

open ~. A *union* in which new members can gain relatively free admission. Such *unions* have low initiation fees, and usually require only that the new member be employed or trained in the field covered.

vertical ~. An INDUSTRIAL UNION, which see above, so called because it is organized down through an industry, regardless of craft or skill.

union contract. A written agreement or contract between an employer or group of employers and the UNION representing the employees, covering the wages, hours, working conditions and other aspects of employment policy and practice.

union jurisdiction. The craft, skill, industry

region which a union claims as the area in which it seeks members and bargains with employers, or which its parent organization has assigned to it as the basis for its membership.

union label. See under LABEL.

union rate. The standard or minimum hourly wage or piece work rate set by a union as the rate for a particular type of work, to be used as the basis for bargaining in wage negotiations. In many fields, the average rate of pay is actually considerably above the minimum floor set by the *union rate,* or union scale, as it is also known.

union scale. See UNION RATE.

union security. A principal or policy incorporated in some union-management contracts, providing that during the length of the contract all employees, or at least those who are union members at the start of the period, will continue to be dues-paying members of the union. Such a clause in a contract may be effected by having the company deduct union dues from the employees' pay and turn it over to the union, a practice known as the CHECK-OFF of dues.

union shop. A company, plant, shop or other bargaining unit in which it is agreed by the management that all new employees will join the recognized union within a stated period of time after their employment. It differs from a CLOSED SHOP, in which only union members may be employed, and from a PREFERENTIAL SHOP, in which preference must be given to union members in hiring, if available. On the other hand, an OPEN SHOP is one in which no regard is paid to union membership in hiring practices or in continued employment.

unissued stock. See under STOCK (1).

unit banking. See under BANKING.

unit control. A method of inventory or stock control in which control is maintained in terms of individual units or amounts, rather than in dollars. This method of control is widely used by department stores and other retail stores. The typical *unit control* plan involves the taking of periodic physical inventories, with current control maintained by the use of sales check information, or by the collection and tabulation of detachable tags which are removed from the merchandise as sold.

unit cost. In cost accounting, the cost of manufacturing, storing or distributing a single unit of production.

    average ∼. The *unit cost* determined by dividing the total actual cost by the total number of units to which it is applied.

    standard ∼. A computed *unit cost* determined by summing up the normal or STANDARD COSTS of the materials, labor and other cost factors involved in each unit of production.

United States depository. See DEPOSITORY, GOVERNMENT.

United States rule. A procedure for the partial settlement of debts, first established under a ruling of the Supreme Court, and since adopted as law by the majority of states for all debts of more than one year maturity. Under this rule, each partial payment is first applied to interest accrued to date, and any excess over interest is used to reduce the principal. If previous payments have not covered interest, any subsequent payments must first eliminate the arrears before there can be any reduction of the principal. See also MERCHANTS' RULE.

United States value. As defined by the Tariff Act of 1930 as amended, the price at which an imported item is being offered for sale in the United States at the time it is originally exported from the country of origin, less allowances for transportation, duties, insurance, etc. This is one of the two values used in computing import TARIFFS, the other being the FOREIGN VALUE, which is essentially the price at which the item is selling in the country of origin, plus the costs of preparing it for export.

unit load. See PALLET LOAD.

unit-of-production method. See DEPRECIATION.

unit of value. The basic MONETARY UNIT of a system of currency. In the United States, for example, the *unit of value* is the gold DOLLAR, in Great Britain, the POUND sterling, etc.

unit replacement. A method or system of maintenance of industrial equipment, under which complete units or assemblies needing repair or maintenance are withdrawn and replaced by units in perfect condition. The withdrawn units are then repaired or maintained separately and put into reserve stock until needed for similar *unit replacement.* This method is especially applicable to the maintenance of electric motors and similar self-contained units.

universal. Relating to the whole, or pertaining to all without exception. It is a broader term than GENERAL, which is usually understood to permit of exceptions.

universal agent. See under AGENT.

universal partnership. See under PARTNERSHIP.

unlisted security. See under SECURITY (1).

unlisted stock. See under STOCK (1).

unloading. In the securities trade, an extensive

selling of a stock by one or a small group of owners. In general, throwing a commodity or security on the market regardless of price.

unoccupied. Not inhabited. In fire and other insurance, it means not used as a dwelling by human beings, or not used for its normal intended purposes, in the case of a business structure. It differs from VACANT, which means empty of furnishings and equipment. See also OCCUPIED.

unsecured. In general, not backed or secured by any COLLATERAL, or other valuable obligation. See each of the following under the principal listing: ∼ CREDIT (3); ∼ CREDITOR; ∼ DEBT; ∼ LOAN; ∼ NOTE (1).

unsecured bond. See BOND (1), DEBENTURE.

unskilled labor. See LABOR, COMMON.

unvalued policy. See under POLICY (2).

unvalued stock. See STOCK (1), NO PAR VALUE.

upgrading. In general, a raising of quality or of skill. Particularly, in personnel work, an organized policy of selecting, developing, and training employees to do more skilled and more advanced work, and promoting them to better positions.

upkeep. In general, the costs of maintaining property or equipment in good condition and repair.

upset price. See under PRICE.

upstream. In business usage, further back in the process of production or distribution. For example, an *upstream* loan is one made by a subsidiary company to a parent company. See also DOWNSTREAM.

urban. Pertaining to or characteristic of the city. Within the city limits, or within the populated area surrounding the city itself.

usage. A customary or established manner or practice; the course of action usually followed in a particular country, or by those engaged in a particular trade or line of business. In the absence of specific rules, regulations or contract terms, *usage* may be recognized as binding.

usance. A period of time, which varies from country to country, allowed for the payment of foreign bills of exchange, above and beyond the formal DAYS OF GRACE. The length of the period allowed between any two countries is based on local commercial custom.

use and occupancy insurance. See BUSINESS INTERRUPTION INSURANCE, under INSURANCE, PROPERTY.

usual tare. See TARE, CUSTOMARY.

usufruct. In law, the right to use and obtain the benefits from property belonging to another, without obtaining any of the rights of ownership.

usury. Originally, any charge made for the use of money. In present-day usage, an interest rate or charge over and above that provided for by law; an illegal profit obtained from the lending of money. See also INTEREST.

utility. See PUBLIC UTILITY.

utter. In business usage, to put into circulation, to issue or publish. As usually used, to circulate or offer a forged or counterfeit note or other negotiable instrument.

V

vacancy. 1. The condition of being unoccupied or empty. Hence, in real estate usage, a house, office or apartment which is empty and available for occupancy.

2. With respect to a corporate or political office or position, one which is not occupied by a person with the legal right to hold it and exercise its rights and duties. The courts have consistently held that an office is technically vacant on the expiration of a term, though the incumbent may continue to perform the duties of the office.

vacancy ratio. In housing statistics, the percentage of available dwelling units that are vacant and fit for occupancy. It varies from zero to 100, but is usually less than 10. The vacancy ratio is also 100 minus the OCCUPANCY RATIO.

vacant. Of a corporate or political office or position, not occupied by a legally qualified incumbent. In fire and other insurance, it means completely empty of all furnishings and equipment. It differs from UNOCCUPIED, which means not being used as a dwelling or for other intended purpose.

vacate. In law, to set aside, cancel, or annul an award, order, or other proceeding; to void. In real estate usage, to move out; to make the premises empty, or VACANT.

vacation. In general, a period of time granted an employee, usually annually, for rest and relaxation, to refresh him for the coming year's work. In current usage, a *vacation* is such a time period with pay, or with partial pay, as distinguished from a FURLOUGH.

vacation pay. Regular payments made to an employee for time spent on VACATION. Also, in some industries, extra payments accepted by employees in place of taking regular vacation time off.

vacuity. In British and some other countries' customs usage, the empty space in a cask or barrel. The difference between the marked capacity and the actual contents. In American commercial usage this is known as the ULLAGE.

valid. Sound, well-grounded, sensible, proper and defensible; legally sufficient. Examples include a *valid* argument, a *valid* contract, a *valid* claim, a *valid* test, etc.

validate. To make or declare VALID; to confirm or give legal force to a claim or contract. To test or prove the validity of something; to confirm by experiment or examination.

valid consideration. See CONSIDERATION, GOOD.

valorization. Price maintenance or the fixing of prices, usually by governmental action or by a CARTEL. For example, the *valorization* of coffee in Brazil involved the purchase of coffee by the government at a fixed price, which then held the coffee off the market until the market price had recovered.

valuable consideration. See under CONSIDERATION.

valuation. The assignment or fixing of the value of something. This may be accomplished by agreement between the parties involved; by an appraisal or an arbitration decision; or by determination by an assessor, as in the case of a *valuation* for tax purposes.

valuation, inventory. See INVENTORY VALUATION.

valuation reserve. See under RESERVE.

value. 1. In economics in general, the power of a commodity, goods, or service to command other goods or services in exchange; or this power expressed in terms of money.

2. In accounting and finance, the worth of something, as stated in accordance with any of a number of rules or concepts. In most states, it has been held that the term *value*, not qualified in any way, means the price a thing will bring in a fair and open market sale, or its MARKET VALUE, which see below. This and the other classes of *values* are listed and defined below.

   actual cash ~. In insurance, a term now usually interpreted to mean "replacement cost new, less normal depreciation." However, in special cases, the *actual cash value* of insured property may be determined by an appraisal, by the current market *value*

375

of similar property, by the cost to repair or replace the loss, or by negotiation between the insurer and insured. It is sometimes called the *sound value,* or *material value.*

asset ∼. See NET ASSET VALUE, directly.

book ∼. In one sense, the *value* at which assets are carried on the books of account of a corporation. Generally, fixed assets are carried at cost less normal depreciation, while inventories may be carried at COST OR MARKET, WHICHEVER IS LOWER. In another sense, it is the total NET WORTH of a business, as shown by the excess of assets over liabilities. Thus, the *book value* of a share of corporate stock is the net worth divided by the number of shares outstanding. The *book value* may be a poor reflection of the market *value* of the stock, which is determined more by company earnings and dividend payments.

cash ∼. See MARKET VALUE, below.

cash surrender ∼. See directly.

face ∼. With reference to an instrument of indebtedness, the PRINCIPAL SUM, on which the rate of interest or discount is based. The *value* written on the face of the instrument.

fair ∼. One determined for purposes of sale or tax valuation, which may be based on a combination of, or compromise between, book *value,* earning power, good will, business prospects, and the *value* of such intangible assets as trademarks, franchises, etc.

fair market ∼. See MARKET VALUE, below.

foreign ∼. See directly.

intrinsic ∼. The *value* which a thing possesses in and of itself, rather than a *value* placed or forced on it by outside circumstances. The *intrinsic value* of a stock, for example, is its basic *value* as an investment, rather than its current price, which may be distorted by market conditions.

invoice ∼. The *value* or price of a product as it is stated on the seller's invoice. The cost of the product to the buyer, however, is its *invoice value* plus inbound freight charges, if any.

liquidation ∼. The amount that could be realized upon the liquidation or breaking up of a business, as distinguished from its *value* as a going concern.

market ∼. The amount that can be obtained for goods or services in a free and open market sale. It is sometimes called the *cash value* or *fair market value.*

material ∼. See ACTUAL CASH VALUE, above.

net asset ∼. See directly.

par ∼. The nominal *value* of a share of corporate stock, determined by dividing the total stated capital stock by the number of shares authorized. Thus, a corporation may

set its capital at $1,000,000, and issue 10,0 shares of $100 *par value* stock. In all sta except Nebraska, and except the District Columbia, it is now permissible to issue sto without a stated *par value.* See also P. STOCK.

present ∼. With respect to an annu: or an amount invested at compound inter the amount which must be invested present to produce a required number of nual payments of a given amount, or a quired future total investment, includi retained interest, at a stated rate of inter over a specified number of years.

purchase ∼. The *value* which a prud purchaser or prospective purchaser would willing to pay for a going business, the F. VALUE, which see above.

reserve ∼. See directly.

scrap ∼. The worth of a thing for scr that is, considering only the *value* of contained materials and components, not *value* for the purpose for which it is us

sound ∼. See ACTUAL CASH VALUE, abo

United States ∼. See directly.

value added by manufacture. A term used government statistics and in the measu ment of productivity, specifying that part the value of produced goods which is actua created within a given company or indust It is calculated by subtracting from sa value the costs of materials, supplies, pov and fuel, contract work, etc. Thus, it g erally includes labor costs, sales and admir tration costs, and operating profits. In sta tics, the purpose of using *value added* a: measure of production is to eliminate dupli tion at succeeding stages of extracti processing and manufacture from statistics gross product. In productivity measureme *value added* per man-hour of labor or simi unit is a commonly used standard.

value bill of exchange. See under BILL OF CHANGE.

value date. In banking, the date as of wh a deposit in an account is effective, depe ing on the time needed for the collection payment on the deposited item from bank or other place on which it is draw

valued policy. See under POLICY (2).

value of product. A term used in statistics a in financial statements, specifying the va of all goods produced during a peri whether sold or transferred to inventory, sales prices, or at the prices at which goods are turned over to a sales subsidiar

value received. A phrase used in contra implying a consideration. It is taken as me ing a valuable consideration, but not nec sarily a money consideration. See also CON-SIDERATION.

vandalism and malicious mischief insurance.
See INSURANCE, PROPERTY.

vara. A Spanish and Portuguese measure of
length, used locally in Texas, New Mexico,
and Arizona as a land measure. A *vara* is
equal to about 33 inches, or 2.75 feet.

variable annuity. See under ANNUITY.

variable budget. See under BUDGET.

variable cost. See under COST.

variance. 1. In general, a disagreement between
two sets of figures or two arguments, or
between figures and the known or assumed
facts. In accounting, it is the difference
between standard or expected costs and actual
costs of production. See also COST.
2. In statistics, a measure of the dispersion
in a distribution of observations or occurrences. It is computed by squaring the difference between each item value and the
arithmetic mean of the distribution, sum-
ming these differences, and dividing by the
number of items. The standard DEVIATION
of a distribution is the square root of the
variance.
3. In real estate practice, a permission to
vary from the zoning regulations, building
code, etc.

variety store. See under RETAIL STORE.

velocity of circulation. The rate of turnover of
money. It is the average number of times
a given monetary unit is spent during a given
time period. Thus, it may be calculated by
dividing the total amount of spending activity by the amount of CURRENCY IN CIR-
CULATION.

velvet. In business slang, any profit or income
which is unearned, unexpected or easily acquired; an extra profit.

venal. That which is offered for sale, or can be
bought. The term is usually used in a derogatory sense, implying that the thing for sale
should not morally be so; mercenary.

vend. To sell, or to offer for sale.

vendee. One to whom anything is sold; a buyer.
Also, specifically, one who receives, without
endorsement, a bill or note payable to bearer.

vending machine. A coin-operated machine for
selling merchandise on a self-service basis.

vendor. One who sells or offers for sale; a
seller. In common usage, *vendor* is often
used synonymously with source of supply. A
purchasing agent, for example, may speak
of his company's *vendors* for a given material or supply. Also, specifically, the one
who delivers, without endorsement, a bill
or note payable to bearer.

vendor's lien. See under LIEN.

vendue. From the French, *vendu,* meaning
sold; a public sale at auction.

venireman. From the Latin, to come; a member of a jury panel. A juror specifically sum-
moned to appear by a writ of *venire*. Strictly,
a *venireman* differs from a TALESMAN, a
juror selected from among the bystanders in
court.

venture. In general, a business undertaking,
especially one in which there is a considerable degree of hazard or uncertainty. See also
ADVENTURE; CAPITAL (2), VENTURE.

venue. From the Latin, *venir,* to come. In law,
the place from which the action in a legal
proceeding arises, and the place in which
the trial is to take place. Under state laws,
the county within which an action must be
brought, or a trial held.
   change of ∼. The removal of a trial of
an action from the county in which it was
originally brought to another. The impossi-
bility of obtaining a fair trial, such as might
be due to the bias of a judge, or the preju-
dices of the prospective jurors, may be the
grounds for such a change.

verbal. Strictly speaking, expressed in words.
As commonly used, however, it means expressed in spoken words; ORAL, by word of
mouth. Also, when used to refer to a written
instrument, such as a memorandum, it means
not signed or executed in a formal manner.

verbatim. Literally, in Latin, word for word;
in the same words. Thus a *verbatim* transcript of a proceeding is a word for word
reproduction of what was said, and a *verbatim* copy of a document is a word for word
copy, including the original punctuation.

verdict. From the Latin, the true words. The
decision or finding of a trial jury, as announced to the court. Strictly, the finding of
the court in a non-jury case is a DECISION.

verification. The process of declaring or in-
vestigating the truth of a statement. Thus,
in law, it is the properly subscribed and
executed written oath of a party regarding
the truth of his statements in a matter. In
accounting, it is the substantiating of entries
and values in the books of account.

vertical. In business usage, consisting of two
or more units which operate at different
levels of production or distribution in the
same field. Operating from elementary to
final stages in a field, rather than across
several fields. See also HORIZONTAL. See each
of the following under the principal listing: ∼ AGREEMENT IN RESTRAINT OF TRADE;
∼ INTEGRATION; ∼ UNION.

vertical filing. A method of filing in which the file folders are stored on edge, with the tab edge forward, instead of upright. Since *vertical filing* is usually done on open shelves, there is the possibility of conserving considerable amounts of space, if the material to be filed is of the sort that will store satisfactorily in this manner.

vest. In law, to give immediate right of either present or future possession of property; to transfer ownership.

vested estate. See ESTATE (1) IN POSSESSION.

vested interest. In law, a claim or interest which has become fixed as a right to present or future enjoyment. An interest which has become clothed with complete and legal rights.

vested pension plan. See PENSION PLAN.

vested right. A right which can't be interfered with, defeated, or canceled on ordinary grounds, and which will be protected by the law if challenged. Usually, it is a present right to the enjoyment of some future benefit. For example, an employee may receive a *vested right* in his share of a pension fund after a period of time, meaning that the funds are indisputably his, though he may not have access to them until retirement. See also VESTING.

vestibule training. Training for unskilled or semi-skilled workers, carried on away from the actual job, but in surroundings which are usually a miniature or approximation of the actual conditions. It is so called, apparently, because it was originally carried on in the vestibules near the working floor.

vesting. The acquisition by an employee of a right or interest in the contributions made by an employer to a pension fund, profit-sharing plan, or other employee benefit fund. The employee's VESTED INTEREST in a share of the fund may be limited or qualified as to amount, period of employment required, etc. Under the federal Internal Revenue Code, pension funds which do not have a *vesting* feature may not qualify for deduction as a business expense under certain circumstances. For this reason, many company pension fund plans are vested plans today. See also PENSION PLAN.

via. Originally, in Latin, by way of. A term used in routing instructions. For example, a shipment may be marked for export *via* New York, meaning it is to be shipped out of the port of New York; or a rail shipment may be marked *via* N.Y. Central, meaning it is to be routed over the New York Central railroad.

vice. 1. In law, a defect or imperfection which is serious enough to annul a sale or contract. It may be an imperfection in the goods themselves, or in the terms of the contract. Illegality, for example, is a *vice* which gives a purchaser the right to demand a refund upon the return of the goods purchased. Such a defect is known as an *inherent vice* when it is in the goods or agreement originally, and not added or imputed to it.

2. From the Latin, instead of; in place of. It is used in this sense in such terms as *vice*-president, *vice*-chairman, etc. In current usage, the term has taken on the added meaning of assistant.

vice-president. One of the principal officers of a business corporation, next in order of importance to the PRESIDENT. Some corporations may have more than one *vice-president*, in charge of various aspects of the company's operations, such as a *vice-president* for sales, one for manufacturing, etc. There may also be an executive *vice-president*, who is the senior executive officer under the president.

violating law clause. A clause found in life and accident insurance policies, under which the insurer seeks to be relieved of liability in the event that the insured meets death or an accident while violating the law. See also INSURANCE.

virgin wool. See under WOOL.

visa. From the Latin, meaning seen. An official endorsement on a PASSPORT by a consul or other representative of a country, indicating that the passport has been inspected, is in good order, and that the owner has permission to enter the country, or to continue on his journey. The French form *vise* is also widely used abroad, but the U.S. State Department prefers *visa*.

visible supply. In the commodities trade, the ascertained amount of a commodity, such as coal, ore, grain, meat, etc., which is in storage, in transit, or otherwise available to the market. It does not include potential supplies still in the ground, or growing, which are known as the INVISIBLE SUPPLY.

visible trade. That part of the trade between nations which is represented by the import and export of tangible goods, such as those on which a customs valuation may be placed, as distinguished from INVISIBLE TRADE, which includes services, tourist travel, remittances, etc.

vital statistics. Literally, the statistics of life. Thus, collected data on births, marriages, deaths, etc.

vitreous. Literally, like glass. The term is used in connection with various products made of ceramic materials, such as *vitreous* china, *vitreous* enamel, etc., which have a glass-like hardness and luster, though not actually composed of glass or glass minerals.

vocational training. Education or training for a business or trade; as distinguished from general education, or professional education.

void. That which is invalid, not binding, unenforceable at law. Contracts may be *void* for a number of reasons, including the absence of a consideration, an agreement to do that which is forbidden by law, or the use of undue influence. See also CONTRACT (1), VOID.

voidable contract. See under CONTRACT (1).

volt. The standard unit of ELECTROMOTIVE FORCE, or electric pressure. It is the force which, when steadily applied to a conductor having a resistance of one OHM will produce a current of one AMPERE. The voltage of each cell of an automobile storage battery is rated at 2 *volts,* while household circuits usually operate at 110 to 115 *volts,* or 220 to 230 *volts* in some places. In the basic relationship between *volts,* WATTS and amperes, *volts* equal watts divided by amperes. In other words, in a circuit operating at 110 volts, a 500 watt electric appliance will result in a flow of current at a rate of about 5 amperes.

voluntary. That which is done freely, at one's own initiative, without coercion. The laws of the various states differ as to what is legally a *voluntary* act. See each of the following under the principal listing: ∼ ASSIGNMENT; ∼ BANKRUPTCY; ∼ DISSOLUTION; ∼ SALE (1); ∼ TRUST (1).

voluntary chain. A group of affiliated but independent retailers who operate under the name of a single sponsoring agency, usually a wholesaler or wholesale organization. The independently owned member stores of a *voluntary chain* cooperate in various aspects of their operations, such as joint buying, cooperative advertising, promotion of joint brand names, and sometimes group control and supervision of store operation.

voluntary trust. See TRUST (1), LIVING.

voting stock. See under STOCK (1).

voting trust. See TRUST (2).

voucher. Any written instrument in proof of the payment or receipt of money, or of other monetary transactions; a receipt. As used in an accounting system based on *vouchers,* the *voucher* typically provides space for noting the date, *voucher* number, description of items covered, price, discount, net amount, approval, etc. *Vouchers* used for special purposes may carry special names. A cash *voucher,* for example, is used to record cash disbursements, a purchase or sales *voucher* for the appropriate transaction, and a journal *voucher* when vouchers are required for all journal entries.

voucher check. See under CHECK (1).

voucher register. A book of original entry, kept in connection with a VOUCHER SYSTEM of accounting. Essentially it is a combination purchase journal and accounts payable register. Each purchase or other cash disbursement is first made up in voucher form, then entered in the register. The register is divided into numerous columns providing for the date, voucher number, payee or creditor, check number, and the account to be charged with the expense. At the end of the month or other period, the various account columns are totalled, and the summary amounts entered in the proper accounts.

voucher system. A system of accounting in which all transactions are first set up in voucher form, then entered in a register. Often, only the accounts payable are kept under a *voucher system,* using a VOUCHER REGISTER, or carbon copies of the voucher sections of voucher CHECKS as the book of record.

voyage policy. See under POLICY (2).

W

wage and salary administration. The branch of personnel management dealing with the development of programs of compensation for employees, based on skills, seniority, job study, merit rating, the going rates in the community and industry and similar factors.

wage and salary receipts (or payments). A term used in the national income statistics prepared by the Department of Commerce. In these figures, *wage and salary receipts* include all wages and salaries of employees, less contributions for social insurance. Wages and salaries are counted at the time paid, rather than as earned.

wage bracket. A term used to describe the range of wage payments for a given occupation or skill. The term is often used in negotiating for wage changes.

wage differential. An established difference in the regular wages paid for the same work in different plants or areas, due to differences in working conditions or for other reasons.

wage earner. 1. In general, an employee whose compensation is based on an hourly or piecework rate; one who is paid WAGES.

2. Formerly, in federal government statistics on employment and earnings, a term used to define any employee in industry and commerce other than supervisory and administrative personnel. This has been replaced, since 1945, by the more exactly defined term PRODUCTION AND RELATED WORKERS.

wage-hour law. 1. In general, legislation by a state or by the federal government regulating minimum wage rates, maximum hours of labor and similar conditions.

2. Specifically, the federal wage-hour law, technically known as the Fair Labor Standards Act of 1938, which established minimum wages, overtime pay for hours beyond the maximum set by the law, and other rights and conditions for workers in interstate commerce. The act also prohibits the use of child labor in general.

wage rate. The amount of compensation, or WAGES, for a specified unit of work.

wager policy. See under POLICY (2).

wages. 1. In general, the income which a man receives in exchange for his labor. In current usage, *wages* refer to payments based on hourly earning rates, or on rates per unit of production, as distinguished from SALARY, COMMISSION, or FEE payments.

2. Under many state labor laws, *wages* are defined as regular earnings, exclusive of overtime pay, premium pay, holiday pay, etc., as distinguished from EARNINGS, which includes the total received.

wage stabilization. A program, government sponsored or otherwise, for keeping wages in an area or in an industry from rising above established levels.

Wagner Act. The basic federal law governing the collective bargaining between employers and unions. It defined UNFAIR LABOR PRACTICES by both employers and unions, which were either prohibited or restricted by the act. The *Wagner Act* has been substantially amended and revised by the terms of the TAFT-HARTLEY ACT.

wagon jobber. See under JOBBER.

waiting period. 1. In insurance, in policies or regulations calling for the payment of a periodic indemnity, such as accident and health insurance, workmen's compensation and so forth, the period between the occurrence or the onset of a disability and the date at which the indemnity will be paid. Under unemployment insurance regulations, it is the period between the beginning of unemployment and the start of weekly payments.

2. In the securities trade, the period usually twenty days, which must elapse between the filing of a registration for new securities with the Securities and Exchange Commission and the date on which the security may be released for public sale. This is the so-called COOLING OFF PERIOD.

3. In labor practices, the period prescribed by a union contract or by legislation which must elapse between the filing of a notice of intention to strike and the actual calling of the strike.

waiver. Any intentional renunciation of a claim, interest, privilege, or right. A *waiver* may be oral or written, express or implied.

waiver clause. In insurance, a clause in property damage, marine or inland marine insurance policies, providing that in the event of an insured accident, either the insured or the insurer may do whatever he thinks necessary to minimize the loss, without prejudicing his rights under the policy.

waiver-of-premium clause. See DISABILITY CLAUSE.

waiver of protest. A written statement which is signed by the endorser of a note or other negotiable instrument, indicating that the endorser will remain liable without having been specifically notified, in the event the note is not paid when due. See also PROTEST.

walkout. See a STRIKE.

Wall Street. 1. Literally, a street in lower Manhattan, New York City, on which or near which are located many of the important financial institutions of the country. Thus, the financial district itself, including the New York Stock Exchange, the American Stock Exchange, the several commodities and produce exchanges, the New York Clearing House, and many investment, brokerage, banking and other companies.

2. As a collective term, American financial interests and the influence they exert in world affairs; usually used in a critical sense.

3. Sometimes, the securities market in general; familiarly referred to as "the street."

Walsh-Healy Act. The federal regulation, the full title of which is the Walsh-Healy Public Contracts Act, which authorizes the Secretary of Labor to regulate the hours, wages and working conditions of employees working on government contracts involving more than $10,000. The act also prohibits the use of child labor, or convict labor, or the maintenance of dangerous or hazardous working conditions on such government contracts.

wanton negligence. See under NEGLIGENCE.

want-slip. A form or memorandum used by retail salespeople to note that a customer has requested an item, style, size or color which is not in stock. The accumulated *want-slips* are used by the BUYER as a guide in re-ordering or in selecting new items to be carried.

war baby. An industry or corporation whose prospects and securities values are enhanced by war or by defense activities. Typically these include the fields of aviation, munitions, chemicals, shipbuilding, and heavy industry in general.

war clause. A clause in an insurance policy or other contract relieving the company of liability, or reducing its liability, in the event of death, injury or other loss caused by war or wartime activities.

ward. 1. Any person who, because of his youth or because of mental or physical infirmity, has a guardian appointed to manage and protect his interests. See also GUARDIAN.

2. A territorial or political subdivision of a city or town.

warehouse. Any building or structure used for the receiving, storing, and caring for of property, merchandise, commodities, household goods, etc., for either short or long periods of time.

   bonded ∼. A warehouse, under government supervision, in which goods may be stored without the payment of duties or taxes until they are withdrawn. For example, imported goods may be stored in a *bonded warehouse* without the payment of import duties, and may then be re-exported duty-free or sold domestically after the payment of the duty. Similarly, alcoholic beverages may be stored in a *bonded warehouse* after manufacture, with the taxes not paid until they are withdrawn for sale. In many cases, various degrees of manufacture and processing may be carried on while the goods are in the *bonded warehouse*.

   field ∼. See directly.

   public ∼. A warehouse, either privately or publicly owned, in which storage space is made available to users on a rental basis. The warehouse operators usually provide or make available certain services, such as handling, packaging, crating, etc., which are either included in the rental or charged for separately.

warehouse bond. See under BOND (2).

warehouseman. A person or company operating a warehouse or providing warehouse services for others, for profit. A public warehouse company.

warehouseman's lien. See under LIEN.

warehouse receipt. A receipt given by a warehouseman for goods placed in his warehouse for storage. Such a receipt may be either negotiable or non-negotiable, and, when negotiable, is often used as collateral for a loan. Under law, a *warehouse receipt* is assignable, and the transfer of it by assignment is the transfer of the title to the goods it represents. Thus, if a loan secured by a *warehouse receipt* is not paid, the lender may sell the goods and use the proceeds to satisfy the loan.

Businesses that accumulate large inventories of raw materials seasonally, such as paper mills, or that accumulate large inventories of finished products, such as distillers, regularly use *warehouse receipts* as a means of raising working capital. To eliminate the necessity of actually placing the goods in a public warehouse, it may be arranged with a licensed warehouseman to convert part of the business' own storage space to a FIELD WAREHOUSE, and to obtain a receipt for goods stored therein. See also FIELD WAREHOUSING.

wares. Any articles, merchandise, goods or commodities offered for sale.

warrant. 1. In law, a court order, writ, or precept authorizing a public official or other person to perform some special act, to arrest, seize, search, etc.

bench ∼. A *warrant* issued by a court, or a judge "on the bench," calling for the arrest of a person in contempt, or who has disobeyed a court order, or who has been indicted. A *bench warrant* is so called to distinguish it from one issued by an inferior official.

search ∼. A *warrant* issued by a court, under a state search and seizure law, directing the proper authority to search a named premises for articles alleged to be concealed there in violation of some law. The laws of the various states differ, but the articles for which search is most usually authorized are stolen property, counterfeit money, gambling paraphernalia, etc. Such a *warrant* is made necessary by Article I of the Constitution, which forbids unreasonable search and seizure.

2. In business, a written authorization from a competent source to a proper individual to receive money or its equivalent, or to pay money to one who is entitled to receive it.

dividend ∼. An order by a dividend-paying corporation upon its treasurer to give his check to a shareholder to whom a dividend is due.

interest ∼. A term used for the order or check drawn by a corporation on its bank, directing the bank to pay a stated sum to a named person, usually a bondholder entitled to interest.

∼ of attorney. A *warrant* issued by a debtor to his attorney directing him to appear in court and to confess judgment against him in favor of a creditor named in the *warrant*. A *warrant of attorney* may also be used to enable any judgment to be confessed without the necessity of an action. Regula-

tions governing the use of such *warrants* differ from state to state. See also NOTE, JUDGMENT.

3. In government financing, a short-term obligation issued by a municipality or other governmental agency, usually in anticipation of tax revenues. May be negotiable or not depending on the issuing authority.

4. In the securities trade, a certificate evidencing the right or privilege of buying capital stock, under certain conditions. *Warrants* are often issued in connection with preferred stock or bonds, giving the purchaser the right to purchase a stated additional number of shares of stock at a stated price. A *warrant* is said to be *detachable* when it can be sold separately from the securities with which it was issued, and *non-detachable* when it cannot be sold separately. Stock *warrants* usually have an expiration date, before which they must be exercised or lose their value.

warranty. 1. In a sales contract or transaction a statement, declaration or stipulation by the vendor to the effect that the quality, character, or title to the goods sold are as he represents them. A *warranty* is enforceable under law, and any false statement included gives the buyer cause for legal action. In common usage, the terms *"warranty"* and "guaranty are often used interchangeably, though strictly speaking a GUARANTY is an entirely different matter.

express ∼. A *warranty* made in a direct statement by the seller, written or oral.

implied ∼. A *warranty* indicated by the nature of the sales contract, or by the description of the goods or their stated purpose or application. It has been held, however that general extravagant claims made in advertisements, such as "world's best," are no *warranties,* but are permissible "puffing" by the seller.

2. In insurance, a statement made or subscribed to by the insured regarding the nature of the risk. A *warranty* is regarded as voluntary undertaking by the insured, and if found false or violated to any material exten may void the insurance. In fire insurance, for example, typical *warranties* may state that the property is guarded by a watchman, that sprinklers are installed, etc.

warranty deed. See under DEED.

war risk insurance. Insurance against the hazards of war, such as those affecting merchant vessels, exposed property, or persons in military service. See also INSURANCE.

wash sale. In securities trade usage, a fictitious stock transaction in which the same stock is both sold and bought by the same person perhaps operating through an agent on one side of the transaction, for the purpose of establishing a market price, or to create the appearance of activity in the stock. Such sales are prohibited both by law and by Stock Exchange rules. When a *wash sale* involves two parties, but with no change in beneficial ownership of the stock, it is sometimes known as a MATCHED ORDER.

wastage. The loss due to use, decay, deterioration, leakage, or wear of property or equipment.

waste. 1. The normal and generally unpreventable loss of material during processing or manufacture. Also, the product or by-product of such normal loss.

2. Rags and other scrap materials used for cleaning equipment, absorbing oil or grease, and other industrial purposes. Originally, so named because the waste-ends of yarn and cloth created in textile manufacture were used for this purpose.

3. In law, any permanent or lasting injury done to an ESTATE or inheritance, such as by a life tenant in the estate. According to the laws of some states, anything done which diminishes the value of an estate.

wasting asset. See under ASSET.

watch and warning service. A service offered by a credit bureau or credit checking agency, under which members or subscribers to the service exchange derogatory information on credit customers.

watered asset. See under ASSET (2).

watered stock. See under STOCK (1).

watermark. The transparent letters, design or other symbol seen when paper is held up to the light. *Watermarks* are used to identify the maker of the paper, or to identify as genuine checks, currency, stamps or other valuable papers.

watt. The standard unit for measuring the rate at which electrical energy is used or produced. One *watt* is equal to one JOULE of energy per second. In the basic relationship of *watts* to AMPERES and VOLTS, *watts* = amperes × volts. In other words, a 500 watt appliance operating in a 110 volt circuit will cause current to flow at a rate of about 5 amperes. A KILOWATT-HOUR is the amount of energy consumed in one hour by a device using 1,000 *watts*, or one kilowatt. It is the standard measure of electrical energy consumption.

waybill. A written listing and description of goods included in a shipment by rail or motor freight. It is the authorized document which the common carrier accepts under the regulations of the Interstate Commerce Commission, and is the official description of the shipment in the event of any claim or insurance proceedings. In maritime trade, the BILL OF LADING is the equivalent document, though a *waybill* and bill of lading are not identical, since the former does not constitute a contract between the shipper and carrier.

way station. In railroad transportation, a station or stop which is along a route, rather than being a TERMINAL at one end. As used, the term excludes those principal stations which are along a route but which are considered terminals, due to their importance.

weak market. In securities trade usage, a market in which there is more selling pressure than buying pressure. Thus, a market in which prices are declining, as opposed to a STRONG MARKET, in which prices tend to rise.

wear and tear. The normal decay, deterioration and depreciation in property or equipment that is the result of its ordinary and reasonably careful usage, or the passage of time.

Webb-Pomerene Association. See EXPORT ASSOCIATION.

weighted average. See under AVERAGE (1).

welfare management. The aspect of PERSONNEL MANAGEMENT dealing with the steps taken by an employer to increase the comfort, security, and general well-being of his employees.

wharfage. The fee charged for the use of a wharf or of dock facilities for receiving, storing and removing goods which are either being shipped or landed. It may be paid by either the shipper or receiver of the goods, depending on the terms of their contract.

Wheeler-Lea Act. A federal law passed in 1938, amending the Federal Trade Commission Act, giving the Commission the power to act against "unfair or deceptive practices" in advertising, especially of food, drugs, cosmetics, etc. Under the act, the Commission may take action in the public interest, without waiting for a complaint from a competitor or customer.

when issued. A basis of pricing securities, used before the securities themselves have actually been issued and traded. When a corporation decides to split its stock shares, for example, trading in the new shares will begin after they are authorized but not yet issued, on a *when issued* basis. If the number of shares is to be doubled, the *when issued* price of the new securities will be approximately half the price of the old securities which are about to be converted. Under the Securities Act of 1933, *when issued* trading is restricted to such authorized issues as in the above example.

whipsawed. In the securities trade, to have suffered a loss at both ends of a transaction. For example, one may have bought a stock at a high price just before a decline, then sold it at a low price just before a rise; or one may have sold a stock short just before a rise, then bought to cover the sale just before a decline. See also SHORT.

white brass. An alloy of copper and zinc, with a lower than usual proportion of copper, which causes the whitish cast.

white-collar worker. Traditionally, a salaried employee, such as an office or clerical worker, or a technical or professional worker, as distinguished from a *blue-collar* worker, or one who is engaged in factory production or maintenance work. With the increasing mechanization of industry, the differentiation between *white-collar* and *blue-collar* work has been gradually disappearing.

white space. In advertising and publishing, that part of an advertisement or printed page on which no printing or art work appears.

whole life insurance. See ORDINARY LIFE INSURANCE, under INSURANCE, LIFE, ACCIDENT, AND HEALTH.

wholesale. The method of selling goods or merchandise in bulk, or in large lots; also, the method of selling for further resale, as distinguished from RETAIL, which is the method of selling in small lots, or for consumption.

wholesaler. As defined by the Bureau of the Census, any business or establishment engaged primarily in selling merchandise directly to RETAILERS; to industrial, commercial, institutional, or professional users; to other *wholesalers;* or acting as agents in buying merchandise from or selling merchandise to, such persons or companies.

　merchant ∼. A *wholesaler,* DISTRIBUTOR, or JOBBER who takes title to the goods he distributes. He may be a full-service *wholesaler,* storing goods, delivering them, making collections, etc., or he may be a DROP SHIPPER, WAGON JOBBER, or other form of limited-service *wholesaler.*

wholesale price. See under PRICE.

wholly-owned subsidiary. See SUBSIDIARY.

wide opening. In securities trade usage, a term describing a situation in which the bid and asked prices at the daily opening of the stock or commodities market are wide apart.

widow. In printing, a single word or short line at the end of a paragraph. Sometimes, more specifically, such a single word or short line carried over to the next column or page.

wildcat. 1. In the petroleum producing industry, a term for a well which is driven in land not previously proved to be oil or gas bearing. A person who prospects for oil on such lands, and who drills experimental wells in areas not known or expected to be productive is known as a *wildcatter.*

　2. In railroading, a term for a locomotive and tender operating without cars. For example, a locomotive and tender being transferred to another section, or on the way to assist another train, is known as a *wildcat* train.

　3. In general, pertaining to any enterprise, undertaking, or scheme which is unsound or risky, which is unauthorized, or which is outside of the normal standards of practice. See each of the following under the principal listing: ∼ BANK; ∼ BRAND; ∼ MONEY; ∼ STRIKE.

will. The document by which a person wills or bequeaths his property, at his death, to others. When made by a person of legal age and sound mind, in the proper form, a *will* is recognized as a legal document. The laws of the several states differ as to the proper requirements, but in most states a *will* is valid if it is in writing, signed by the maker or testator, or at his direction, and attested by witnesses.

　alternative ∼. One of two *wills,* one drawn after the other and not containing a revocation clause, but instead containing a declaration that in the event of some named contingency the first *will* shall become operative as if it were the last *will.*

　concurrent, or partial ∼. One of several *wills* drawn simultaneously by a person owning property in several states, and relating to the property in one state.

　holographic ∼. A *will* in which every word is in the handwriting of the maker or testator. Such a *will* need not be attested by witnesses to be valid.

　joint ∼. A *will* made jointly by two or more persons. It operates to pass the property of one, on his death, to the others as a group and so on to the last survivor. See also TONTINE.

　mutual ∼. A *will* in which each of two persons bequeaths his property to the other. It may be a single document, or the same intent may be accomplished by separate documents.

　nuncupative ∼. An oral *will,* made before witnesses, which is later reduced to writing. Under statutory law, it is confined to sailors at sea, and those in military service. State laws differ considerably as to details.

　partial ∼. See CONCURRENT WILL, above.

　reciprocal ∼. One of two or more *wills* prepared by two or more persons at the same time, but as separate documents, each nam ing the other as heir, and each naming the same contingent heirs. Such a *will* might be prepared, for example, when a husband and wife own much of their property jointly.

will-call. In retailing, a sale in which the buyer leaves a deposit or partial payment for the merchandise, which is put aside for him with the understanding that he will call for it at a future time with the remainder of the payment. Also, sometimes, the put-aside merchandise itself. See also LAYAWAY PLAN.

willful negligence. See under NEGLIGENCE.

windfall. An unexpected gain, or a sudden and unearned income. The term derives from the tradition that fruit blown from the tree by the wind is the property of the finder.

winding up. The closing up of all business and financial activities of a business, either voluntarily or by order of a court. During the time that the business' affairs are being wound up, it is said to be in liquidation.

window dressing. 1. The attractive and pleasing arrangement of a display in a shop-window; hence any display aimed to please, to create a false impression or to deceive.
2. An arrangement of balance-sheet items or of a financial statement to give an impression that a company is in better financial condition than is actually the case. For example, the term was formerly applied to the practice among some banks of calling in loans to make their cash balances appear larger in their periodic statements.

with all faults. In real estate and other contracts, a term meaning without a guarantee of absence of imperfections; as is. See also SALE (1) WITH ALL FAULTS.

with average. See under AVERAGE (3).

withdrawal. The removal of funds or other things of value from a bank or other place in which they have been deposited. It is the opposite of a DEPOSIT. Also, the removal of goods from a bonded warehouse, for purposes of sale or re-export.

with exchange. As applied to a DRAFT, the term meaning that the charge for the collection of the draft is to be collected from the payer, or the one who is to pay, along with the amount of the draft itself.

withholding. In taxation practice, a method of collecting taxes, such as income taxes, at the source; that is, from the person who pays the wages or salary, rather than from the person who receives the payments. The collection of income taxes by *withholding* is popularly known as PAY-AS-YOU-GO taxation.

withholding tax. See under TAX (2).

with interest. A term used in promissory notes, indicating that the note is to be repaid *with interest* added. When the term is used alone, without a specified rate of interest, it is understood that the legal or customary rate is to be paid.

without dividend. See EX-DIVIDEND.

without interest. See EX-INTEREST.

without par value stock. See STOCK (1), NO PAR VALUE.

without prejudice. A term used in an offer to settle a matter of litigation, or in a settlement itself, indicating that the party making the offer does not admit any responsibility whatever, and that all rights are not to be affected by the offer but are to stand as before.

without recourse. 1. A term used in endorsing a negotiable instrument, indicating that the endorser is no longer responsible in case the obligation is not paid. When a retailer endorses his customer's promissory note to a bank or finance company, for example, he may do so *without recourse,* so that he is no longer a party to the transaction, and it is the bank's responsibility to collect the note. The endorser remains responsible, of course, to the extent that his endorsement affirms that the note represents a valid obligation. See also ENDORSEMENT (2), QUALIFIED.
2. As a term in a sales contract, an agreement that the buyer accepts all the risks that attend the transaction, and relinquishes any rights of RECOURSE.

without reserve. A term in auction selling, meaning that the vendor or owner of the goods auctioned does not reserve the right to bid for the goods he is offering, nor to put a RESERVE PRICE, or UPSET PRICE, on the goods; but that they will be sold *without reserve* to the highest bidder.

with particular average. See under AVERAGE (3).

with recourse. 1. A term used in endorsing a negotiable instrument, indicating that the endorser remains responsible for the payment of the obligation. Thus, if the original maker of the note defaults, the endorser may be called upon to make good the note. See also ENDORSEMENT.
2. A term in a sales contract indicating that in the event of the failure of the seller to maintain his promises and warranties, the buyer has the right to endorse a claim against the seller for any damages he may have sustained.

W.O.C. See DOLLAR-A-YEAR MAN.

wolf. In the securities trade, an experienced and crafty trader; one who speculates cleverly, as distinguished from a LAMB, who is an amateur at stock speculation.

wool. The hair or fleece of sheep or lambs, or of certain goats, such as the Angora or Cashmere. Also, yarn spun from such fleece, or cloth woven of the yarn.

    reprocessed ∼. Wool which has been previously woven into cloth, or made into felt, then reprocessed and reused, usually in a mixture with new or virgin wool.

    virgin ∼. New wool; wool which has never been used to make knit, woven, or felted cloth.

woolens. Any of several types of cloth woven completely or substantially of wool.

wool tops. The long, choice wool fibers which are selected to be spun into WORSTED yarn. It is usually handled in the form of a loose, continuous rope or sliver.

work. 1. Strictly, in physics, the overcoming of a resistance by a force, resulting in motion. For example, lifting a weight against gravity, starting a wheel against inertia, or sliding a body against friction. It is measured in terms of the force applied and the distance moved; e.g. in foot-pounds.

    2. Generally, the application of physical or mental effort to do or make something. To *work*, in this sense, is to exert oneself for a purpose; hence any occupation engaged in which calls for the purposeful exertion of effort is *work*.

    3. To operate, or to cause to operate, a machine or device. For example, to *work* a lathe, or to *work* a projector.

    4. To form or shape metal or other material by hammering, rolling or other pressure. Thus, WROUGHT IRON is iron which has been hammered, or worked, to shape.

worker. See EMPLOYEE.

working capital. See under CAPITAL (3).

working capital ratio. See OPERATING RATIO.

working papers. 1. In accounting, the preliminary notes, memoranda, schedules, etc., prepared and used by an accountant or auditor as he makes his examination of the books of record of a business, and upon which he bases his final reports and statements.

    2. In some states, the official document signifying that a minor has obtained the necessary permission of his parents, school authorities, etc., and may be employed under certain conditions.

working partner. See under PARTNER.

work in process. In inventory calculations, those products and materials on which some work or processing has been done, but which are not yet completely manufactured or processed. Thus, *work in process* is distinguished from RAW MATERIALS (2), which have not yet been put into production, and from

FINISHED GOODS, which are manufactured and ready for sale.

workload. The amount of work which an individual, department or organization performs or is scheduled to perform, usually expressed in terms of standard work units.

work measurement. Any of a number of methods or systems of measuring the amount of work actually performed in relation to the man-hours expended. The purpose of *work measurement* may be to establish standards of efficiency, to set up incentive compensation plans, or to obtain cost information for accounting, pricing and budgeting purposes.

workmen's compensation insurance. Insurance purchased by an employer to cover his obligations under a workmen's compensation law. It provides for indemnities to be paid to employees who are injured or killed in the course of their employment.

workmen's compensation law. A state law, now in effect in 47 states and the District of Columbia, providing that employees are entitled to recover damages against their employers for injuries received in the course of employment. The particular amounts which may be collected, and the conditions under which the employer is liable vary from state to state. Most laws provide that the employer must take steps to assure that he will be able to meet any liabilities under the law. In some states, for example, it is compulsory for the employer to buy insurance through the state compensation fund, while in other states he has the option of insuring privately or of self-insuring. See also INSURANCE, CASUALTY AND LIABILITY.

works. A factory or manufacturing plant; a in the phrase, a steel *works*.

work sharing. The practice among workers in a plant of spreading out or sharing a limited amount of work. The workers may agree for example, to work short hours or a short week, to avoid the necessity of some of th workers being laid off.

work stoppage. See STRIKE.

worsted. Yarn spun from long-stapled, even combed, fine wool. Also, cloth woven of this fine-grade woolen yarn.

worth. 1. The value of a thing, particularly i value in exchange, as expressed in mone the market value or exchange value.

    2. The total value of the investment in going business. See also NET WORTH.

wreck. Popularly, the remains or ruins of ship which has foundered or run agroun Strictly speaking, in maritime parlance, ship that has been cast upon the shore by th sea, or goods that have been similarly cast on land. Thus, to speak of a "floating wreck" is a contradiction in terms. See also DERELICT; FLOTSAM.

writ. A mandatory order issued in the name of the state by a court, in the form of a letter, directing the person named therein to appear in court, or to perform some specified act at some specified time or suffer a penalty.

write down. To reduce the recorded value in an account, or the stated value of an asset. A value may be *written down* on the basis of judgment, as well as on the basis of some scheduled reduction such as a DEPRECIATION plan.

write off. To remove from the accounts an uncollectible debt or a worthless asset, by reducing its value to zero and making a balancing loss entry in an account such as bad-debt losses. Sometimes, the uncollectible debt itself; a bad debt.

write up. 1. To increase the stated value of an asset, or the total of an asset account. Usually, assets are *written up* for the purpose of making a financial statement appear more favorable than is the actual case.

2. To record the information in connection with a sale; thus, to make the sale itself. A salesman may speak of *writing up* $300,000 worth of sales volume.

written contract. See under CONTRACT (1).

wrought iron. A form of low-carbon malleable iron which is, typically, heated and hammered or worked into the desired shape. *Wrought* is, in fact, an otherwise obsolete form of the word *worked*.

X Y Z

yard. A standard unit of linear measurement, equal to 3 feet or 36 inches. The standard *yard* is equal to 0.9144 METERS in the metric system.

yard goods. In the textile trades, those cloths which are sold by the running yard. Also, material not yet cut to length or pattern. See also PIECE GOODS.

year. A period of 365 days (366 in leap year); twelve calendar months. See also CALENDAR YEAR, FISCAL YEAR, NATURAL BUSINESS YEAR.

year-end dividend. See under DIVIDEND.

yellow brass. Any of a class of copper alloys, containing at least 17% zinc, less than 6% tin, and traces of aluminum, manganese, nickel, iron or lead.

yellow-dog contract. The name for a formal or informal contract under which an employee, as a condition of employment, agrees not to become a member of any trade union. Less frequently, one under which the employee agrees to join a particular union or company union. Such conditions of employment have been illegal since the passage of the Norris-LaGuardia Act.

yield. 1. The percentage of return on an investment; the RATE OF INTEREST or dividend.

~ **to maturity.** A measure of the yield of a bond over its entire life, or over its remaining life. The *yield to maturity* is based on a complicated formula, depending on the price paid, the price at maturity, the term or number of years to maturity, and the annual rate of interest. Tables of *yield to maturity* for various terms, rates and prices are available. Assuming that the redemption price at maturity will be 100, a practical approximation formula for the *yield to maturity* of a bond is the following:

Yield = [(100 − P)/T + I]/P,

where P = the price paid or current price,
   T = the term or number of years to maturity,
and I = the annual dollar rate of interest on the bond.

Thus, if a 3% ten-year bond is actually

bought at issue at a price of 90, the *yield to maturity* will be approximately 4.44%, since the yield based on the price difference is $10, or $1 per year, and the yield based on the interest rate is $3 per year, for a total of $4 or 4.44% of the price of $90.

current ~. The present return on a bond or other investment. It is calculated simply by dividing the rate of interest or dividend by the price paid, or the current price. For example, a stock selling at $20 per share and paying an annual dividend of $1 per share has a *current yield* of 5%.

2. In industry, the amount recovered from refining or processing, usually expressed in relation to the amount of raw material put into production.

York-Antwerp rules. In maritime trade and marine insurance, a set of regulations covering the terms of uniform BILLS OF LADING, designed to eliminate or settle disputes in connection with losses. The rules have no statutory force, but are binding as part of standard marine contracts.

zirconium. A metallic element, used in industry in pigments, in flash photography, and lately as a structural material in atomic reactors, where its special properties relative to the non-absorption of nuclear radiation make it especially satisfactory.

zone freight rate. See under FREIGHT RATE.

zone, parcel post. One of the eight areas into which the United States is divided for purposes of setting parcel post charges. The charge per ounce from any point in any one *zone* to any point in another specified *zone* is the same, regardless of actual distance. See also POSTAL SERVICE, PARCEL POST.

zone price. See under PRICE.

zone pricing. A method of pricing delivered goods under which the same price is charged throughout a geographic area or zone, despite differences in delivery costs. The price is normally based on factory price plus an average freight charge for the zone. It is sometimes known as *zone-delivered pricing*. See also BASING POINT PRICING.

APPENDIX A

A Table of Equivalents Including Measures of Area (or Surface) Capacity, Length, Volume, and Weight

The order of information in each entry is: the *Unit* of measure, its *Abbreviation**, the *Kind* of measure, and the *Equivalents*.

acre. **; area; 10 square surveyor's chains, 160 square rods, 4,840 square yards, 43,560 square feet, 0.40469 hectare, 40.4687 ares, 4,046.8726 square meters

angstrom. A; length; 0.0000001 millimeter (10^{-10} meter), 0.0001 micron, 0.1 millimicron, 0.000000004 inch

are. a.; area; 119.5989 square yards, 1076.387 square feet, 0.02471 acre, 1 square decameter, 100 square meters

barleycorn. --; length; 0.33 inch, 8.5 millimeter

barrel, dry, for most fruits, vegetables, and other dry commodities, except cranberries. dry bbl.; capacity; 7056 cubic inches, 105 dry quarts, 3.281 bushels, 115.62 liters

barrel, dry, for cranberries. dry bbl.; capacity; 5826 cubic inches, $86\,{}^{45}\!/_{64}$ dry quarts, 2.709 bushels, 95.47 liters

barrel, liquid. lq. bbl.; capacity; 31.5 gallons, 119.237 liters

barrel, petroleum. bbl.; capacity; 42 gallons (U.S.), 34.97 gallons (imperial), 158.9 liters, 0.15899 cubic meters

barrel, U.S., beef, pork, fish. bbl.; weight; 200 pounds, 90.72 kilograms

barrel, U.S., flour. bbl.; weight; 196 pounds 88.90 kilograms

barrel, U.S., cement. bbl.; weight; 376 pounds, 170.55 kilograms

barrel, U.S. lime, small. bbl.; weight; 180 pounds, 81.65 kilograms

barrel, U.S., lime, large. bbl.; weight; 280 pounds, 127.01 kilograms

board foot. bd. ft.; volume; 144 cubic inches (12 in. × 12 in. × 1 in.)

bolt (cloth). --; length; 40 yards

bolt (wallpaper). --; length; 16 yards

bushel, British, struck measure. bu.; capacity; 1.0320 U.S. bushels, struck measure, 33.026 U.S. dry quarts, 2,219.36 cubic inches

bushel, U.S. struck measure. bu.; capacity; 32 dry quarts, 4 pecks, 2,150.42 cubic inches, 35.2383 liters

bushel, U.S. heaped. bu.; capacity; 1.278 U.S. bushels, struck measure (also commonly regarded as 1 1/4 bushels, struck measure), 2,747.715 cubic inches

bushel. bu.; weight; a wide variety of legal weights for different commodities in different states.

butt. --; capacity; 2 hogsheads, 126 U.S. gallons

cable's length, U.S. Navy. --; nautical; 120 fathoms, 720 feet, 219.456 meters

cable's length, marine measure. --; nautical; 100-120 fathoms, 600-720 feet, 182.88-219.456 meters

carat. c.; precious stones; 3.0865 grains troy, 200 milligrams

cental. --; weight; 100 pounds, 45.36 kilograms

centare, or centiare. ca.; area; 1.196 square yards, 10.764 square feet, 1 square meter, 0.01 are

centigram. cg.; weight; 0.15432 grain, 0.01 gram

centiliter. cl.; capacity; 0.3381 fluid ounce, 0.01 liter; volume, 0.6102 cubic inch

centimeter. cm.; length; 0.39370 inch, 0.01 meter, 10 millimeters

centistere. --; volume; 0.353 cubic foot, 0.01 cubic meter

chain, engineer's. ch.; length; 100 feet, 30.48 meters

chain, Gunter's or surveyor's. ch.; length; 100 surveyor's links, 4 rods, 22 yards, 66 feet, 20.117 meters

cord. cd.; volume; 128 cubic feet (usually arranged 8 feet long, 4 feet high, 4 feet wide), 8 cord feet, 3.625 cubic meters

cord foot. cd. ft.; volume; 1/8 cord, 16 cubic feet

cubic centimeter. cm^3; capacity; 0.0610 cubic inch, 0.000001 cubic meter, 0.001 cubic decimeter, 1 millimeter (precisely, 1 millimeter = 1.000027 cubic centimeters)

cubic decameter. dkm^3; volume; 1,307.942 cubic yards, 1,000 cubic meters

cubic decimeter. dm^3; volume; 61.023 cubic inches, 0.001 cubic meter, 1 liter (precisely, 1 liter = 1.000027 cubic decimeters)

cubic foot. cu. ft.; volume; 1,728 cubic inches, 0.037 cubic yards, 28.317 cubic decimeters, 0.0283 cubic meters; capacity; 7.481 gallons, 60 liquid pints, 28.316 liters

cubic hectometer. hm^3; volume; 1,000,000 cubic meters

cubic inch. cu. in.; volume; 0.000579 cubic foot, or $\frac{1}{1728}$ cubic foot, 16.387 cubic centimeters.
capacity; 0.0173 liquid quart, 0.554 fluid ounce, 4.433 fluid drams, 0.0164 liter

cubic kilometer. km³; volume; 1,000,000,000 cubic meters

cubic meter. m³; volume; 1.3079 cubic yards, 35.31445 cubic feet, 61,023.38 cubic inches, 1,000 cubic decimeters.
capacity; 264.1776 gallons, 1,000 liters

cubic millimeter. mm³; volume; 0.00006 cubic inch, 0.001 cubic centimeter

cubic yard. cu. yd.; volume; 27 cubic feet, 46,656 cubic inches, 0.76456 cubic meter

cubit. --; length; 18 inches

decagram. dkg.; weight; 0.35274 ounce, avoirdupois, 0.32151 ounce, apothecaries or troy, 10 grams

decaliter. dkl.; capacity; 2.6418 gallons, 10.5671 liquid quarts, 10 liters.
volume; 0.284 bushel, 1.1351 pecks, 9.081 dry quarts, 610.25 cubic inches

decameter. dkm.; length; 10.9361 yards, 32.8083 feet, 393.7 inches, 10 meters

decare. --; area; 0.2471 acre, 10 ares

decastere. dks.; volume; 13.08 cubic yards, 353.15 cubic feet, 10 cubic meters, 10 steres

deciare. --; area; 11.96 square yards, 0.1 are, 10 square meters

decigram. dg.; weight; 0.003527, 1.5432 grains, 0.1 gram

deciliter. dl.; capacity; 0.1816 dry pint, 0.211 liquid pint, 0.8454 gill, 3.38147 fluid ounces, 0.1 liter;
volume; 6.1025 cubic inches

decimeter. dm.; length; 0.328 foot, 3.937 inches, 0.1 meter, 10 centimeter

decistere. ds.; volume; 3.5315 cubic feet, 0.1 cubic meter, 0.1 stere

digit. --; length, 0.75 inch

dozen. doz.; count; 12 items

dram, apothecaries'. dr. ap.; weight; 2.1943 dram, avoirdupois, 0.125 apothecaries' ounce, 2.5 pennyweights, 3 scruples, 60 grains, 3.888 grams

dram, avoirdupois. dr. avdp.; weight; 0.4558 dram, apothecaries', 0.0625 avoirdupois ounce, 1.1393 pennyweights, 1.3672 scruples, 27.344 grains, 1.7718 grams

dram, fluid or liquid, British. fl. dr.; capacity; 0.9607 fluid dram, U.S., 0.125 fluid ounce, British, 60 minims, British, 0.2167 cubic inches, 3.5514 milliliters

dram, fluid or liquid, U.S. fl. dr.; capacity; 0.03125 gill, 0.125 fluid ounce,

U.S., 60 minims, U.S., 0.2256 cubic inch, 3.6966 milliliters

ell, English. --; cloth, length; $\frac{1}{32}$ bolt, 45 inches

em, pica. --; printing; $\frac{1}{6}$ in. by $\frac{1}{6}$ in.

fathom. fath.; depth; 6 feet, 8 spans, 1.829 meters

finger. --; length; 0.125 yard, 4.5 inches.
width; 0.25 hand, 0.75 to 1 inch

foot. ft.; length; 0.333 yard, 1.515 links 12 inches, 0.3048006 meter

furlong. fur.; length; 0.125 statute mile, 10 chains, 40 rods, 220 yards, 660 feet, 201.168 meters

gallon, British or imperial. gal.; capacity; 1.20094 U.S. gallons, 4 British quarts, 8 British pints, 160 British fluid ounces, 277.42 cubic inches, 4.5460 liters

gallon, U.S. gal.; capacity; 0.83268 British gallons, 4 quarts, 8 pints, 32 gills, 128 fluid ounces, 231 cubic inches, 3.7853 liters

gill, British. gi.; capacity; 1.20094 U.S. gills, $\frac{1}{8}$ British quart, $\frac{1}{4}$ British pint, 8.6694 cubic inches, 0.1421 liter

gill, U.S. gi.; capacity; 0.83268 British gill, $\frac{1}{8}$ liquid quart, $\frac{1}{4}$ liquid pint, 4 fluid ounces, 32 fluid drams, 7.2188 cubic inches, 0.1183 liter

grain. --; weight; $\frac{1}{5760}$ troy pound, $\frac{1}{7000}$ avoirdupois pound, 0.01666 apothecaries dram, 0.03657 avoirdupois dram, 0.05 scruple, 0.0648 grams, 64.799 milligrams

gram. g.; weight; 0.03215 apothecaries' ounce, 0.03527 avoirdupois ounce, 0.257 apothecaries' dram, 0.5644 avoirdupois dram, 15.432 grains

great gross. g. gr.; count; 12 gross

gross. gr.; count; 12 dozen items

hairsbreadth. --; width; $\frac{1}{4}$ line, $\frac{1}{48}$ inch

hand. --; length or height; 4 inches, 10.16 centimeters

hectare. ha.; area; 2.471 acres, 395.367 square rods, 1 square hectometer, 100 ares, 10,000 square meters

hectogram. hg.; weight; 3.5274 ounces, 0.1 kilogram, 100 grams

hectoliter. hl.; capacity; 2 bushels and 3.35 pecks, or 2.838 bushels, 26.418 gallons, 100 liters.
volume; 6102.5 cubic inches, 0.1 cubic meter

hectometer. hm.; length; 109.361 yards, 328 feet and 1 inch, or 328.083 feet, 10 decameters, 100 meters

hectostere. --; volume; 130.794 cubic yards, 3531.445 cubic feet, 100 cubic meters, 100 steres

hogshead, British. hhd.; capacity; 52.4 British or imperial gallons, 238.476 liters

hogshead, U.S. hhd.; capacity; ½ butt, 63 U.S. gallons, 2 liquid barrels, 238.476 liters

hundredweight, gross or long. gross cwt. or l. cwt.; weight; 112 pounds, 50.802 kilograms

hundredweight, net or short. cwt., or sh. cwt.; weight; 100 pounds, 45.359 kilograms

inch. in.; length; 1/12 foot, 1,000 mils, 2.540 centimeters, 25.40 millimeters

iron. --; shoe leather; 1/48 inch

keg, nail. --; weight; 100 pounds, 45.359 kilograms

kilogram. kg.; weight; 2.2046 avoirdupois pounds, 2.6792 apothecaries' pounds, 1,000 grams

kiloliter. kl.; capacity; 28.378 bushels, 264.18 gallons, 1,000 liters
volume; 1.308 cubic yards, 35.315 cubic feet

kilometer. km.; length; 0.621370 mile, 1093.611 yards, 3280 feet and 10 inches, or 3280.83 feet, 1,000 meters

kilostere. --; volume; 1,308 cubic yards, 1,000 cubic meters, 1,000 steres

knot. k.; speed; one nautical mile per hour (see mile, nautical)

league. l.; length; 3 statute miles, 4.82805 kilometers

league, marine. l.; length; 3 nautical miles, 3.45 statute miles, 5.56 kilometers

line. l.; printing; 1/12 inch (0.0833), 2.12 millimeters
button; 1/40 inch

link, engineer's. li.; length; 1/100 chain, 12 inches, 0.3048 meter

link, Gunter's or surveyor's. li.; length; 1/100 chain, 0.66 feet, 7.92 inches, 0.2012 meter

liter. l.; capacity; 1.0567 liquid quarts, 0.9081 dry quarts, 61.0250 cubic inches, 1 cubic decimeter (precisely, 1.000027 cubic decimeters)

meter. m.; length; 1.093611 yards, 3.280833 feet, 39.37 inches, 10 decimeters, 100 centimeters

metric ton. see millier

micron. μ ; length; 0.00003937 inch, 0.03937 mil, 0.001 millimeter

mil. --; wire, length; 0.001 inch, 0.0254 millimeter

mile, nautical or admiralty, British. --; length; 6,080 feet, 1.8532 kilometers

mile, nautical, geographical or sea, U.S. --; length; 1.0007 nautical miles, international, 1.1515 statute miles, 6,080.20 feet, 1.853248 kilometers

mile, nautical, International Hydrographic Bureau. --; length; 0.999 U. S.

nautical miles, 1.151 statute miles, 6,076.10 feet, 1.852 kilometers

mile, statute or land. --; length; 0.868 U.S. nautical miles, 8 furlongs, 80 chains, 320 rods or poles, 1,760 yards, 5,280 feet, 1.6093 kilometers, 1,609.3472 meters

millier. t.; weight; 0.98421 long ton, 1.1023 short ton, 2,204.622 pounds avoirdupois, 2,679.23 pounds troy, 1,000 kilograms, 1 metric ton

milligram. mg.; weight; 0.01543 grains, 0.001 gram

milliliter. ml.; capacity; 0.27052 fluid dram, 16.231 minims, 0.001 liter.
volume; 0.06102 cubic inch, 1 cubic centimeter (precisely 1.000,027 cubic centimeters)

millimeter. mm.; length; 0.03937 inch, 0.001 meter

millimicron. m ; length; 0.001 micron, 0.00003937 mil, 0.00000003937 inch

minim, British. min.; capacity; 0.96073 U.S. minim, 0.05919 milliliter

minim, U.S. min.; capacity; 1/60 fluid dram, 0.00376 cubic inch, 0.06161 milliliter

myriagram. --; weight; 22.046 pounds, 10 kilograms, 10,000 grams

myriameter. --; length; 6.2137 miles, 10 kilometers

nail. --; cloth, length; 1/16 yard, 1/4 span, 2.25 inches, 5.715 centimeters

ounce, avoirdupois. oz. advp.; weight; 0.911 troy or apothecaries' ounce, 1/16 avoirdupois pound, 16 avoirdupois drams, 437.5 grains, 28.3495 grams

ounce, fluid, British. fl. oz.; capacity; 0.96073 U.S. fluid ounce, 1.734 cubic inches, 28.4130 cubic centimeters, 28.4122 milliliters

ounce, fluid, U.S. fl. oz.; capacity; 1.041 British fluid ounces, 1/32 liquid quart, 1/16 liquid pint, 1/4 gill, 8 fluid drams, 480 minims, 29.5737 cubic centimeters, 29.5729 milliliters

ounce, troy or apothecaries'. oz. t., or oz. ap.; weight; 1.0971 avoirdupois ounces, 0.0833 troy or apothecaries' pound, 8 apothecaries' drams, 20 pennyweights, 24 scruples, 480 grains, 31.1035 grams

pace, common. --; length; 2.5, 3, or 3.3 feet

pace, military, double time. --; length; 36 inches

pace, military, quick time. --; length; 30 inches

palm. --; length; 7-9 inches.
width; 3 inches

peck, British. pk.; capacity; 1.0320 U.S. peck, 554.84 cubic inches, 9.0919 liters

peck, U.S. pk.; capacity; 1/4 bushel, 8 dry

quarts, 16 dry pints, 537.605 cubic inches, 8.8096 liters

pennyweight. dwt.; weight; 0.05 troy or or apothecaries' ounce, 0.4 apothecaries' dram, 1.2 scruple, 24 grains, 1.5552 grams

perch. see rod

pint, dry, U.S. dry pt.; capacity; $\frac{1}{16}$ peck, $\frac{1}{2}$ dry quart, 33.60 cubic inches, 0.5506 liter

pint, liquid, British. liq.pt.; capacity; 1.0320 U.S. dry pints, 1.2009 U.S. liquid pints, 20 fluid ounces, 34.6775 cubic inches, 0.5682 liters

pint, liquid, U.S. liq.pt.; capacity; 0.5 liquid quart, 4 gills, 16 fluid ounces, 128 fluid drams, 28.875 cubic inches, 0.47317 liters

pipe. --; capacity; $\frac{1}{2}$ tun, 2 hogsheads, 126 gallons, 476.952 liters

point. pt.; printing; $\frac{1}{6}$ line, 0.013837 inch (nearly $\frac{1}{72}$ inch), 0.351 millimeter

pole. p.; see rod

pound, avoirdupois. lb. advp.; weight; 1.215 troy or apothecaries' pound, 16 avoirdupois ounces, 256 avoirdupois drams, 350 scruples, 7,000 grains, 543.592 grams

pound, troy or apothecaries'. lb.t., or lb.ap.; weight; 0.82286 avoirdupois pound, 12 apothecaries' or troy ounces, 96 apothecaries' or troy drams, 240 pennyweights, 288 scruples, 5,760 grains, 373.242 grams

quart, British or imperial. qt. or imp.qt.; capacity; 1.0320 U.S. dry quarts, 1.2009 U.S. liquid quarts, 2 British or imperial pints, 69.35 cubic inches, 1.1365 liters

quart, dry, U.S. dry qt.; capacity; 0.969 British or imperial quart, $\frac{1}{8}$ peck, $\frac{1}{32}$ bushel, 2 U.S. dry pints, 67.201 cubic inches, 1.1012 liters

quart, liquid, U.S. liq.qt.; capacity; 0.833 British quart, $\frac{1}{4}$ gallon, 2 liquid pints, 8 gills, 57.75 cubic inches, 0.9463 liters

quarter. qtr.; length; $\frac{1}{4}$ mile, 440 yards, 402.34 meters

quarter. qtr.; cloth, length; $\frac{1}{4}$ yard, 1 span, 9 inches

quarter, dry, U.S. --; capacity; 8 bushels, 32 pecks

quarter, long ($\frac{1}{4}$ ton). --; weight; 560 pounds, 254.0 kilograms

quarter, long ($\frac{1}{2}$ hundredweight). --; weight; 28 pounds, 12.701 kilograms

quarter, short ($\frac{1}{4}$ ton). --; weight; 500 pounds, 226.8 kilograms

quarter, short ($\frac{1}{4}$ hundredweight). --; weight; 25 pounds, 11.34 kilograms

quartern. --; volume; $\frac{1}{4}$ pint, 1 gill weight; $\frac{1}{4}$ stone, 3$\frac{1}{2}$ pounds

quintal. q.; weight; 1 hundredweight weight, metric; 220.46 pounds, 100 kilograms

rod. --; length; $\frac{1}{320}$ mile, $\frac{1}{40}$ chain, 5.5 yards, 16.5 feet, 25 links, 5.0292 meters

roll. --; wallpaper, length; 1 bolt (wallpaper), 16 yards

score. --; count; 20 items

scruple, apothecaries'. s.ap.; weight; 0.04166 apothecaries' ounce, 0.3333 apothecaries' dram, 20 grains, 1.2959 grams

section. --; area; $\frac{1}{36}$ township, 1 square mile, 640 acres, 2.59 square kilometers

span. --; length; $\frac{1}{8}$ fathom, 9 inches, 22.86 centimeters

square. --; building; 100 square feet, 9.29 square meters

square centimeter. cm^2; area; 0.155 square inch, 0.0001 square meter, 100 square millimeters

square chain (surveyor's). sq.ch.; area; 16 square rods, 484 square yards, 4,356 square feet, 10,000 square links, 404.687 square meters

square decameter. dkm^2; area; 1 are, 155,000 square inches, 100 square meters, 1,000,000 square centimeters

square foot. sq.ft.; area; $\frac{1}{9}$ square yard (0.1111 sq. yd.), 144 square inches, 0.09290 square meter, 929.034 square centimeters

square furlong. sq.fur.; area; 10 acres, 404.7 ares

square hectometer. hm^2; area; 1 hectare

square inch. sq.in.; area; $\frac{1}{1296}$ square yard, $\frac{1}{144}$ square foot, 6.4516 square centimeters

square kilometer. km^2; area; 0.3861 square miles, 247.104 acres, 100 square hectometers, 10,000 ares, 1,000,000 square meters

square link. sq.li.; area; 0.0001 square chain, 0.0484 square yard, 0.4356 square foot, 62.7264 square inches, 0.04047 square meter

square meter. m^2; area; 1.1960 square yards, 10.764 square feet, 0.01 are, 100 square decimeters

square mil. sq.mil.; area; 0.000001 square inch, 0.000645 square millimeter

square mile. sq.mi.; area; 640 acres, 6400 square chains, 102,400 square rods, 3,097,600 square yards, 27,878,400 square feet, 2.5899 square kilometers, 258.999 hectares

square millimeter. mm^2; area; 0.00155 square inch, 0.01 square centimeter square myriameter. myr.^{2}; area; 38.610 square miles, 100 square kilometers

square perch. --; area; see square rod

square pole. sq.p.; area; see square rod

square rod, pole, or perch. sq.rd.; area; $1/160$ acre, 30.25 square yards, 272.25 square feet, 625 square links, 25,293 square meters

square yard. sq.yd.; area; 9 square feet, 1,296 square inches, 0.83613 square meter

stere. s.; volume; 1.308 cubic yards, 35.314 cubic feet, 1 cubic meter

stone. --; weight; 14 pounds, 6.35 kilograms

tierce, liquid, U.S. --; capacity; $1/3$ pipe, 42 gallons, 159 liters

ton, gross or long. gross tn., l. tn.; weight; 1.016 metric tons or milliers, 1.12 short tons, 2,240 pounds, 1.016.05 kilograms

ton, metric. --; weight; 1 millier

ton, net or short. net tn., sh.tn.; weight; 0.89286 long ton, 0.90718 metric ton or millier, 2,000 pounds, 907.18 kilograms

tonneau. --; weight; 1 millier

township. twp.; area; 36 square miles, 36 sections, 9324.0 ares

tun. --; capacity; 2 pipes, 4 hogsheads, 252 gallons, 953.9 liters

yard. yd.; length; 3 feet, 36 inches, 0.9144 meter

* Only the most common or preferred abbreviation is listed.

The National Bureau of Standards recommends that:

1. periods be omitted after all abbreviations of units except where the abbreviation forms a word.

2. exponents "2" and "3" be used to signify "square" and "cubic" respectively, in the case of the metric units, instead of the abbreviations "sq" or "cu".

3. the use of the same abbreviation for both singular and plural. This practice is already established in expressing metric units and is in accordance with the spirit and chief purpose of abbreviations.

4. unless all the text is printed in capital letters, only small letters be used for abbreviations, except in such case as A for angstrom, etc., where the use of capital letters is general.

** A. is probably the most frequently used abbreviation; however, the National Bureau of Standards and other authorities recommend that the word should be spelled out and no abbreviation used.

APPENDIX B

Centigrade and Fahrenheit Equivalents

Cent.	Fahr.	Cent.	Fahr.	Cent.	Fahr.	Cent.	Fahr.
0	32.0	25	77.0	50	122.0	75	167.0
1	33.8	26	78.8	51	123.8	76	168.8
2	35.6	27	80.6	52	125.6	77	170.6
3	37.4	28	82.4	53	127.4	78	172.4
4	39.2	29	84.2	54	129.2	79	174.2
5	41.0	30	86.0	55	131.0	80	176.0
6	42.8	31	87.8	56	132.8	81	177.8
7	44.6	32	89.6	57	134.6	82	179.6
8	46.4	33	91.4	58	136.4	83	181.4
9	48.2	34	93.2	59	138.2	84	183.2
10	50.0	35	95.0	60	140.0	85	185.0
11	51.8	36	96.8	61	141.8	86	186.8
12	53.6	37	98.6	62	143.6	87	188.6
13	55.4	38	100.4	63	145.4	88	190.4
14	57.2	39	102.2	64	147.2	89	192.2
15	59.0	40	104.0	65	149.0	90	194.0
16	60.8	41	105.8	66	150.8	91	195.8
17	62.6	42	107.6	67	152.6	92	197.6
18	64.4	43	109.4	68	154.4	93	199.4
19	66.2	44	111.2	69	156.2	94	201.2
20	68.0	45	113.0	70	158.0	95	203.0
21	69.8	46	114.8	71	159.8	96	204.8
22	71.6	47	116.6	72	161.6	97	206.6
23	73.4	48	118.4	73	163.4	98	208.4
24	75.2	49	120.2	74	165.2	99	210.2
						100	212.0

To convert Fahrenheit to Centigrade, subtract 32, multiply by 5 and divide by 9.
To convert Centigrade to Fahrenheit, multiply by 9, divide by 5, and add 32.

APPENDIX C

Roman Numerals

I = 1	X = 10	C = 100	M = 1000
II = 2	XX = 20	CC = 200	MD = 1500
III = 3	XXX = 30	CCC = 300	MM = 2000
IV = 4	XL = 40	CD = 400	MMM = 3000
V = 5	L = 50	D = 500	MMMM = 4000 or $\overline{\text{MV}}$
VI = 6	LX = 60	DC = 600	
VII = 7	LXX = 70	DCC = 700	$\overline{\text{V}}$ = 5000
VIII = 8	LXXX = 80	DCCC = 800	$\overline{\text{M}}$ = 1,000,000
IX = 9	XC = 90	CM = 900	

When a letter is repeated the value is repeated, thus XX = 20, III = 3, CCC = 300.

When a letter is followed by the same letter or a letter of less value, the value of the two letters are added; thus XI = 10 + 1 = 11.

When a letter is followed by a letter of greater value, the value of the lesser is subtracted from that of the greater; thus IX = 10 − 1 = 9.

A dash over a letter multiplies the value by 1,000; thus $\overline{\text{X}}$ = 10,000; $\overline{\text{L}}$ = 50,000; $\overline{\text{C}}$ = 100,000; $\overline{\text{D}}$ = 500,000; $\overline{\text{M}}$ = 1,000,000; $\overline{\text{DCXIV}}$ = 614,000.

APPENDIX D

Simple Interest Table

Showing at different rates the interest on $1 from 1 month to 1 year, and on $100 from 1 day to 1 year.

		3%	4%	5%	6%	7%	8%
$1.00	1 month	$.002	$.003	$.004	$.005	$.005	$.006
"	2 "	.005	.007	.008	.010	.011	.013
"	3 "	.008	.011	.013	.015	.017	.020
"	6 "	.015	.020	.025	.030	.035	.040
"	12 "	.030	.040	.050	.060	.070	.080
$100.00	1 day	.008	.011	.013	.016	.019	.022
"	2 "	.016	.022	.027	.032	.038	.044
"	3 "	.025	.034	.041	.050	.058	.067
"	4 "	.033	.045	.053	.066	.077	.089
"	5 "	.041	.056	.069	.082	.097	.111
"	6 "	.049	.067	.083	.110	.116	.133
"	1 month	.250	.334	.416	.500	.583	.667
"	2 "	.500	.667	.832	1.000	1.166	1.333
"	3 "	.750	1.000	1.250	1.500	1.750	2.000
"	6 "	1.500	2.000	2.500	3.000	3.500	4.000
"	12 "	3.000	4.000	5.000	6.000	7.000	8.000

APPENDIX E

Years in Which a Given Amount Will Double at Several Rates of Interest

Rate	At Simple Interest	At Compound Interest		
		Compounded Yearly	Compounded Semi-Annually	Compounded Quarterly
1	100 years	69.660	69.487	69.237
1½	66.66	46.556	46.382	46.297
2	50.00	35.003	34.830	34.743
2½	40.00	28.071	27.899	27.748
3	33.33	23.450	23.278	23.191
3½	28.57	20.149	19.977	19.890
4	25.00	17.673	17.501	17.415
4½	22.22	15.747	15.576	15.490
5	20.00	14.207	14.035	13.949
5½	18.18	12.942	12.775	12.689
6	16.67	11.896	11.725	11.639
6½	15.38	11.007	10.836	10.750
7	14.29	10.245	10.074	9.966
7½	13.38	9.584	9.414	9.328
8	12.50	9.006	8.837	8.751
8½	11.76	8.497	8.327	8.241
9	11.11	8.043	7.874	7.788
9½	10.52	7.638	7.468	7.383
10	10.00	7.273	7.103	7.018
12	8.34	6.116	5.948	5.862

APPENDIX F

COMPOUND INTEREST TABLE

Interest compounded semi-annually

Yrs.	1%	2%	3%	4%	4½%	5%	6%	7%	8%	10%
1	$1.0100	$1.0201	$1.0302	$1.0404	$1.0455	$1.0506	$1.0609	$1.0712	$1.0816	$ 1.1025
2	1.0201	1.0406	1.0613	1.0824	1.0930	1.1028	1.1255	1.1475	1.1692	1.2155
3	1.0303	1.0615	1.0934	1.1261	1.1438	1.1596	1.1940	1.2292	1.2646	1.3400
4	1.0407	1.0828	1.1264	1.1715	1.1948	1.2184	1.2667	1.3168	1.3678	1.4773
5	1.0511	1.1045	1.1605	1.2188	1.2481	1.2800	1.3439	1.4105	1.4794	1.6287
6	1.0616	1.1267	1.1956	1.2681	1.3004	1.3448	1.4257	1.5110	1.6002	1.7957
7	1.0723	1.1494	1.2317	1.3193	1.3643	1.4129	1.5125	1.6186	1.7307	1.9747
8	1.0830	1.1725	1.2689	1.3726	1.4264	1.4845	1.6047	1.7339	1.8720	2.1827
9	1.0949	1.1961	1.3073	1.4281	1.4913	1.5596	1.7024	1.8574	2.0247	2.4064
10	1.1059	1.2201	1.3463	1.4858	1.5592	1.6385	1.8061	1.9897	2.1899	2.6530
11	1.1170	1.2446	1.3875	1.5458	1.6301	1.7234	1.9161	2.1315	2.3687	2.9250
12	1.1281	1.2696	1.4295	1.6082	1.7044	1.8086	2.0326	2.2833	2.5619	3.2248
13	1.1394	1.2952	1.4727	1.6732	1.7820	1.9001	2.1564	2.4459	2.7710	3.5553
14	1.1508	1.3212	1.5172	1.7408	1.8631	1.9963	2.2878	2.6201	2.9971	3.9198
15	1.1623	1.3478	1.5630	1.8111	1.9479	2.0933	2.4271	2.8068	3.2417	4.3216
16	1.1740	1.3748	1.6103	1.8843	2.0365	2.2027	2.5749	3.0067	3.5062	4.7645
17	1.1857	1.4025	1.6589	1.9604	2.1272	2.3142	2.7317	3.2208	3.7923	5.2529
18	1.1976	1.4307	1.7091	2.0396	2.2240	2.4313	2.8981	3.4502	4.1018	5.7883
19	1.2096	1.4594	1.7607	2.1220	2.3252	2.5544	3.0746	3.6960	4.4365	6.3816
20	1.2218	1.4888	1.8140	2.2078	2.4310	2.6837	3.2618	3.9592	4.7985	7.0362
21	1.2341	1.5187	1.8686	2.2970	2.5415	2.8196	3.4605	4.2412	5.1900	7.7574
22	1.2465	1.5492	1.9253	2.3898	2.6572	2.9624	3.6712	4.5433	5.6136	8.5525
23	1.2590	1.5804	1.9835	2.4863	2.7781	3.1123	3.8948	4.8669	6.0716	9.4292
24	1.2716	1.6121	2.0434	2.5868	2.9045	3.2699	4.1320	5.2136	6.5670	10.3957
25	1.2843	1.6445	2.1052	2.6913	3.0367	3.4354	4.3836	5.5849	7.1030	11.4612
26	1.2973	1.6776	2.1688	2.8006	3.1749	3.6094	4.6506	5.9827	7.6826	12.6359
27	1.3103	1.7113	2.2344	2.9131	3.3193	3.7921	4.9338	6.4088	8.3094	13.9311
28	1.3235	1.7457	2.3019	3.0318	3.4703	3.9841	5.2343	6.8653	8.9875	15.3591
29	1.3367	1.7808	2.3715	3.1543	3.6282	4.1858	5.5531	7.3543	9.7208	16.9334
30	1.3501	1.8166	2.4432	3.2818	3.7933	4.3977	5.8913	7.8781	10.5143	18.6691
31	1.3637	1.8430	2.5170	3.4144	3.9660	4.6203	6.2500	8.4391	11.3742	20.5827
32	1.3773	1.8800	2.5931	3.5523	4.1465	4.8542	6.6307	9.0402	12.3024	22.6924
33	1.3911	1.9176	2.6715	3.6958	4.3351	5.0990	7.0345	9.6841	13.3062	25.0184
34	1.4051	1.9562	2.7522	3.8451	4.5324	5.3581	7.4629	10.3738	14.3920	27.5828
35	1.4192	1.9955	2.8354	4.0005	4.7387	5.6294	7.9174	11.1126	15.5664	30.4081
36	1.4334	2.0356	2.9211	4.1621	4.9543	5.9144	8.3996	11.9041	16.8367	33.5249
37	1.4478	2.0765	3.0094	4.3302	5.1798	6.2138	8.9111	12.7620	18.2105	36.9612
38	1.4623	2.1183	3.1004	4.5052	5.4146	6.5284	9.4538	13.6709	19.6965	40.7497
39	1.4770	2.1608	3.1941	4.6872	5.6610	6.8589	10.0295	14.6446	21.3038	44.9266
40	1.4918	2.2043	3.2907	4.8766	5.9288	7.2061	10.6403	15.6877	23.0422	49.5316
41	1.5067	2.2486	3.3901	5.0736	6.1986	7.5709	11.2883	16.8050	24.9224	54.6086
42	1.5218	2.2938	3.4926	5.2785	6.4807	7.9542	11.9758	18.0020	26.9561	60.2059
43	1.5371	2.3399	3.5982	5.4928	6.7756	8.3569	12.7051	19.2842	29.1857	66.3771
44	1.5545	2.3869	3.7070	5.7147	7.0840	8.7800	13.8832	20.6577	31.5348	73.1807
45	1.5701	2.4349	3.8191	5.9456	7.4062	9.2245	14.7287	22.1290	34.1080	80.6817
46	1.5858	2.4838	3.9345	6.1858	7.7430	9.6915	15.6257	23.7052	36.8813	88.9516
47	1.6017	2.5338	4.0432	6.4357	8.0954	10.1822	16.5773	25.3936	39.8908	98.0692
48	1.6178	2.5847	4.1655	6.6957	8.4638	10.6967	17.5868	27.2022	43.1459	107.1213
49	1.6330	2.6367	4.2914	6.9662	8.8490	11.2383	18.6597	29.1397	46.6666	118.1012
50	1.6494	2.6897	4.4211	7.2477	9.2516	11.8072	19.7941	31.2141	50.4746	130.2066

APPENDIX G

BOND INTEREST TABLE

Interest on $1000 from 1 Day to 6 Months

Exclude day of delivery and to the interest for the full month or months add the interest for the remaining days. Calculate 30 days to the month and 360 days to the year

Days	3½%	3¾%	4%	4¼%	4½%	4¾%	5%	6%	7%
1	$ 0.0972	$ 0.1041	$ 0.1111	$ 0.1180	$ 0.125	$ 0.1319	$ 0.1389	$ 0.1667	$ 0.1944
2	0.1944	0.2083	0.2222	0.2361	0.250	0.2638	0.2778	0.3333	0.3889
3	0.2916	0.3125	0.3333	0.3541	0.375	0.3958	0.4167	0.5000	0.5833
4	0.3889	0.4166	0.4444	0.4722	0.500	0.5277	0.5556	0.6667	0.7778
5	0.4861	0.5208	0.5555	0.5903	0.625	0.6597	0.6944	0.8333	0.9722
6	0.5833	0.6250	0.6667	0.7083	0.750	0.7916	0.8333	1.0000	1.1667
7	0.6805	0.7291	0.7778	0.8264	0.875	0.9236	0.9722	1.1667	1.3611
8	0.7778	0.8333	0.8889	0.9444	1.000	1.0555	1.1111	1.3333	1.5556
9	0.8750	0.9375	1.0000	1.0625	1.125	1.1875	1.2500	1.5000	1.7500
10	0.9722	1.0416	1.1111	1.1805	1.250	1.3194	1.3889	1.6667	1.9444
11	1.0694	1.1458	1.2222	1.2986	1.375	1.4513	1.5278	1.8333	2.1389
12	1.1667	1.2500	1.3333	1.4166	1.500	1.5833	1.6667	2.0000	2.3333
13	1.2639	1.3541	1.4444	1.5347	1.625	1.7152	1.8055	2.1667	2.5278
14	1.3611	1.4583	1.5555	1.6527	1.750	1.8472	1.9444	2.3333	2.7222
15	1.4583	1.5625	1.6667	1.7708	1.875	1.9791	2.0833	2.5000	2.9167
16	1.5555	1.6666	1.7778	1.8888	2.000	2.1111	2.2222	2.6667	3.1111
17	1.6528	1.7708	1.8889	2.0069	2.125	2.2430	2.3611	2.8333	3.3056
18	1.7500	1.8750	2.0000	2.1250	2.250	2.3750	2.5000	3.0000	3.5000
19	1.8472	1.9791	2.1111	2.2430	2.375	2.5069	2.6389	3.1667	3.6944
20	1.9444	2.0833	2.2222	2.3610	2.500	2.6388	2.7778	3.3333	3.8889
21	2.0417	2.1875	2.3333	2.4791	2.625	2.7708	2.9167	3.5000	4.0833
22	2.1389	2.2916	2.4444	2.5972	2.750	2.9027	3.0555	3.6667	4.2778
23	2.2361	2.3958	2.5555	2.7153	2.875	3.0347	3.1944	3.8333	4.4722
24	2.3333	2.5000	2.6667	2.8333	3.000	3.1666	3.3333	4.0000	4.6667
25	2.4305	2.6041	2.7778	2.9514	3.125	3.2986	3.4722	4.1667	4.8611
26	2.5278	2.7083	2.8889	3.0694	3.250	3.4305	3.6111	4.3333	5.0556
27	2.6250	2.8125	3.0000	3.1875	3.375	3.5625	3.7500	4.5000	5.2500
28	2.7222	2.9166	3.1111	3.3055	3.500	3.6944	3.8889	4.6667	5.4444
29	2.8194	3.0208	3.2222	3.4236	3.625	3.8263	4.0278	4.8333	5.6389
30	2.9167	3.1250	3.3333	3.5416	3.750	3.9583	4.1667	5.0000	5.8333
1 Mo.	2.9167	3.1250	3.3333	3.5416	3.750	3.9583	4.1667	5.0000	5.8333
2 Mos.	5.8333	6.2500	6.6667	7.0833	7.500	7.9166	8.3333	10.0000	11.6667
3 Mos.	8.7500	9.3750	10.0000	10.6250	11.250	11.8749	12.5000	15.0000	17.5000
4 Mos.	11.6667	12.5000	13.3333	14.1666	15.000	15.8332	16.6667	20.0000	23.3333
5 Mos.	14.5833	15.6250	16.6667	17.7083	18.750	19.7915	20.8333	25.0000	29.1667

APPENDIX H—INCOME TABLE

Purchase Price	1%	1½%	2%	2½%	3%	3½%	4%	4½%
10	10	15	20	25	30	35	40	45
15	6.66	10	13.33	16.66	20	23.33	26.66	30
20	5	7.50	10	12.50	15	17.50	20	22.50
22	4.54	6.81	9.09	11.36	13.63	15.90	18.18	20.45
24	4.16	6.25	8.33	10.41	12.50	14.58	16.66	18.75
26	3.84	5.76	7.69	9.61	11.53	13.46	15.38	17.30
28	3.57	5.35	7.14	8.92	10.71	12.50	14.28	16.07
30	3.33	5	6.66	8.33	10	11.66	13.33	15
32	3.12	4.68	6.25	7.81	9.37	10.93	12.50	14.06
34	2.94	4.41	5.88	7.35	8.82	10.29	11.76	13.23
36	2.77	4.16	5.55	6.94	8.33	9.72	11.11	12.50
38	2.63	3.94	5.26	6.57	7.89	9.21	10.52	11.84
40	2.50	3.75	5	6.25	7.50	8.75	10	11.25
42	2.38	3.57	4.76	5.95	7.14	8.33	9.52	10.71
44	2.27	3.40	4.54	5.68	6.81	7.95	9.09	10.22
46	2.17	3.26	4.34	5.43	6.52	7.60	8.69	9.78
48	2.08	3.12	4.16	5.20	6.25	7.29	8.33	9.37
50	2	3	4	5	6	7	8	9
51	1.96	2.94	3.92	4.90	5.88	6.86	7.84	8.82
52	1.92	2.88	3.84	4.80	5.76	6.73	7.60	8.65
53	1.88	2.83	3.77	4.71	5.66	6.60	7.54	8.49
54	1.85	2.77	3.70	4.62	5.55	6.48	7.40	8.33
55	1.81	2.72	3.63	4.54	5.45	6.36	7.27	8.18
56	1.78	2.67	3.57	4.46	5.35	6.23	7.14	8.03
57	1.75	2.63	3.50	4.38	5.26	6.14	7.01	7.89
58	1.72	2.58	3.44	4.31	5.17	6.03	6.89	7.75
59	1.69	2.54	3.38	4.23	5.08	5.93	6.77	7.62
60	1.66	2.50	3.33	4.16	5	5.83	6.66	7.50
61	1.63	2.45	3.27	4.09	4.91	5.73	6.55	7.37
62	1.61	2.41	3.22	4.03	4.83	5.64	6.45	7.25
63	1.58	2.38	3.17	3.96	4.76	5.55	6.34	7.14
64	1.56	2.34	3.12	3.90	4.68	5.46	6.25	7.03
65	1.53	2.30	3.07	3.84	4.61	5.38	6.15	6.92
66	1.51	2.27	3.03	3.78	4.54	5.30	6.06	6.81
67	1.49	2.23	2.98	3.73	4.47	5.22	5.97	6.71
68	1.47	2.20	2.94	3.67	4.41	5.14	5.88	6.61
69	1.44	2.17	2.89	3.62	4.34	5.07	5.79	6.52
70	1.42	2.14	2.85	3.57	4.28	5	5.71	6.42
71	1.40	2.11	2.81	3.52	4.22	4.92	5.63	6.33
72	1.38	2.08	2.77	3.47	4.16	4.86	5.55	6.25
73	1.36	2.05	2.73	3.42	4.10	4.79	5.47	6.16
74	1.35	2.02	2.70	3.37	4.05	4.72	5.40	6.08
75	1.33	2	2.66	3.33	4	4.66	5.33	6
76	1.31	1.97	2.63	3.28	3.94	4.60	5.26	5.92
77	1.29	1.94	2.59	3.24	3.89	4.54	5.19	5.84
78	1.28	1.92	2.56	3.20	3.84	4.48	5.12	5.76
79	1.26	1.89	2.53	3.16	3.79	4.43	5.06	5.69
80	1.25	1.87	2.50	3.12	3.75	4.37	5	5.62
81	1.23	1.85	2.46	3.08	3.70	4.32	4.93	5.55
82	1.21	1.82	2.43	3.04	3.65	4.26	4.87	5.48
83	1.20	1.80	2.40	3.01	3.61	4.21	4.81	5.42
84	1.19	1.78	2.38	2.97	3.57	4.16	4.76	5.35
85	1.17	1.76	2.35	2.94	3.52	4.11	4.70	5.29
86	1.16	1.74	2.32	2.90	3.48	4.06	4.65	5.23
87	1.14	1.72	2.29	2.87	3.44	4.02	4.59	5.17
88	1.13	1.70	2.27	2.84	3.40	3.97	4.54	5.11
89	1.12	1.68	2.24	2.80	3.37	3.93	4.49	5 05
90	1.11	1.66	2.22	2.77	3.33	3.88	4.44	5

Purchase Price	1%	1½%	2%	2½%	3%	3½%	4%	4½%
91	1.09	1.64	2.19	2.74	3.29	3.84	4.39	4.94
92	1.08	1.63	2.17	2.71	3.26	3.80	4.34	4.89
93	1.07	1.61	2.15	2.68	3.22	3.76	4.30	4.83
94	1.06	1.59	2.12	2.65	3.19	3.72	4.25	4.78
95	1.05	1.57	2.10	2.63	3.15	3.68	4.21	4.73
96	1.04	1.56	2.08	2.60	3.10	3.64	4.16	4.68
97	1.03	1.54	2.06	2.57	3.09	3.60	4.12	4.63
98	1.02	1.53	2.04	2.55	3.06	3.57	4.08	4.59
99	1.01	1.51	2.02	2.52	3.03	3.53	4.04	4.54
100	1	1.50	2	2.50	3	3.50	4	4.50
101	.99	1.48	1.98	2.47	2.97	3.46	3.96	4.45
102	.98	1.47	1.96	2.45	2.94	3.43	3.92	4.41
103	.97	1.45	1.94	2.42	2.91	3.39	3.88	4.36
104	.96	1.44	1.92	2.40	2.88	3.36	3.84	4.32
105	.95	1.42	1.90	2.38	2.85	3.33	3.80	4.28
106	.94	1.41	1.88	2.35	2.83	3.30	3.77	4.24
107	.93	1.40	1.86	2.33	2.80	3.27	3.73	4.20
108	.92	1.38	1.845	2.31	2.77	3.24	3.70	4.16
109	.91	1.37	1.83	2.29	2.75	3.21	3.66	4.12
110	.90	1.36	1.81	2.27	2.72	3.18	3.63	4.09
111	.90	1.35	1.80	2.25	2.70	3.15	3.60	4.05
112	.89	1.33	1.78	2.23	2.67	3.12	3.57	4.01
113	.88	1.32	1.77	2.21	2.65	3.09	3.54	3.98
114	.87	1.31	1.75	2.19	2.63	3.07	3.50	3.94
115	.86	1.30	1.73	2.17	2.60	3.04	3.47	3.91
116	.86	1.29	1.72	2.15	2.58	3.01	3.44	3.87
117	.85	1.28	1.70	2.13	2.56	2.99	3.41	3.84
118	.84	1.27	1.69	2.11	2.54	2.96	3.38	3.81
119	.84	1.26	1.68	2.10	2.52	2.94	3.36	3.78
120	.83	1.25	1.66	2.08	2.50	2.91	3.33	3.75
121	.82	1.23	1.65	2.06	2.47	2.89	3.30	3.71
122	.81	1.22	1.63	2.04	2.45	2.86	3.27	3.68
123	.81	1.21	1.62	2.03	2.43	2.84	3.25	3.65
124	.80	1.20	1.60	2.01	2.41	2.82	3.22	3.62
125	.80	1.20	1.60	2	2.40	2.80	3.20	3.60
130	.76	1.15	1.53	1.92	2.30	2.69	3.08	3.46
135	.74	1.11	1.48	1.85	2.22	2.59	2.96	3.33
140	.71	1.07	1.42	1.78	2.14	2.50	2.85	3.21
145	.68	1.03	1.37	1.72	2.06	2.41	2.75	3.10
150	.66	1	1.33	1.66	2	2.33	2.66	3
155	.64	.96	1.29	1.61	1.93	2.25	2.58	2.90
160	.62	.93	1.25	1.56	1.87	2.18	2.50	2.81
165	.60	.90	1.21	1.51	1.81	2.12	2.42	2.72
170	.58	.88	1.17	1.47	1.76	2.05	2.35	2.64
175	.57	.85	1.14	1.42	1.71	2	2.28	2.57
180	.55	.83	1.11	1.38	1.66	1.94	2.22	2.50
185	.54	.81	1.08	1.35	1.62	1.89	2.16	2.43
190	.52	.78	1.05	1.31	1.57	1.84	2.10	2.36
195	.51	.76	1.02	1.28	1.53	1.79	2.05	2.30
200	.50	.75	1	1.25	1.50	1.75	2	2.25
210	.47	.71	.95	1.19	1.42	1.66	1.90	2.14
220	.45	.68	.90	1.13	1.36	1.59	1.81	2.04
225	.44	.66	.88	1.11	1.33	1.55	1.77	2
230	.43	.65	.86	1.08	1.30	1.52	1.73	1.97
240	.41	.62	.83	1.04	1.25	1.45	1.66	1.87
250	.40	.60	.80	1	1.20	1.40	1.60	1.80
275	.36	54	.72	.90	1.09	1.27	1.45	1.63
300	.33	.50	.66	.83	1	1.16	1.33	1.50

Purchase Price	5%	5½%	6%	6½%	7%	7³/₁₀%	7½%	8%
10	50	55	60	65	70	73	75	80
15	33.33.	36.66	40	43.33	46.66	48.66	50	53.33
20	25	27.50	30	32.50	35	36.50	37.50	40
22	22.72	25	27.27	29.54	31.81	33.18	34.09	36.36
24	20.83	22.91	25	27.08	29.16	30.41	31.25	33.33
26	19.23	21.15	23.07	25	26.92	28.07	28.84	30.76
28	17.85	19.64	21.42	23.21	25	26.07	26.78	28.57
30	16.66	18.33	20	21.66	23.33	24.33	25	26.66
32	15.62	17.18	18.75	20.31	21.87	22.81	23.43	25
34	14.70	16.17	17.64	19.11	20.58	21.47	22.05	23.52
36	13.88	15.27	16.66	18.05	19.44	20.27	20.83	22.22
38	13.15	14.47	15.78	17.10	18.42	19.21	19.73	21.05
40	12.50	13.75	15	16.25	17.50	18.25	18.75	20
42	11.90	13.09	14.28	15.47	16.66	17.38	17.85	19.04
44	11.36	12.50	13.63	14.77	15.90	16.59	17.04	18.18
46	10.86	11.95	13.04	14.13	15.21	15.86	16.30	17.39
48	10.41	11.45	12.50	13.54	14.58	15.20	15.62	16.66
50	10	11	12	13	14	14.60	15	16
51	9.80	10.78	11.76	12.74	13.72	14.31	14.70	15.68
52	9.61	10.57	11.53	12.50	13.46	14.03	14.42	15.38
53	9.43	10.37	11.32	12.26	13.20	13.77	14.15	15.09
54	9.25	10.18	11.11	12.03	12.96	13.51	13.88	14.81
55	9.09	10	10.90	11.81	12.72	13.27	13.63	14.54
56	8.92	9.82	10.70	11.60	12.50	13.03	13.39	14.28
57	8.77	9.64	10.52	11.40	12.27	12.80	13.15	14.03
58	8.62	9.48	10.34	11.20	12.06	12.58	12.93	13.79
59	8.47	9.32	10.16	11.01	11.86	12.37	12.71	13.55
60	8.33	9.16	10	10.83	11.66	12.16	12.50	13.33
61	8.19	9.01	9.83	10.65	11.47	11.95	12.39	13.11
62	8.06	8.87	9.67	10.48	11.29	11.77	12.09	12.90
63	7.93	8.73	9.52	10.31	11.11	11.58	11.90	12.69
64	7.81	8.59	9.37	10.15	10.93	11.40	11.68	12.50
65	7.69	8.46	9.23	10	10.76	11.23	11.53	12.30
66	7.57	8.33	9.09	9.84	10.60	11.06	11.36	12.12
67	7.46	8.20	8.95	9.70	10.44	10.89	11.19	11.94
68	7.35	8.08	8.82	9.55	10.29	10.73	11.02	11.76
69	7.24	7.97	8.69	9.42	10.14	10.57	10.86	11.59
70	7.14	7.85	8.57	9.28	10	10.42	10.71	11.43
71	7.04	7.74	8.45	9.15	9.85	10.28	10.56	11.26
72	6.94	7.63	8.33	9.02	9.72	10.13	10.41	11.11
73	6.84	7.53	8.21	8.90	9.58	10	10.27	10.95
74	6.75	7.43	8.10	8.78	9.45	9.86	10.13	10.80
75	6.66	7.33	8	8.66	9.33	9.73	10	10.66
76	6.57	7.23	7.89	8.55	9.21	9.60	9.86	10.52
77	6.49	7.14	7.79	8.44	9.09	9.48	9.74	10.38
78	6.41	7.05	7.69	8.33	8.97	9.35	9.61	10.25
79	6.32	6.96	7.59	8.22	8.86	9.24	9.49	10.12
80	6.25	6.87	7.50	8.12	8.75	9.12	9.37	10
81	6.17	6.79	7.40	8.02	8.64	9.01	9.25	9.87
82	6.09	6.70	7.31	7.92	8.53	8.90	9.14	9.75
83	6.02	6.62	7.22	7.83	8.43	8.79	9.03	9.63
84	5.95	6.54	7.14	7.73	8.33	8.69	8.92	9.52
85	5.88	6.47	7.05	7.64	8.23	8.58	8.82	9.41
86	5.81	6.39	6.97	7.55	8.13	8.48	8.72	9.30
87	5.74	6.32	6.89	7.47	8.04	8.39	8.62	9.19
88	5.68	6.25	6.81	7.38	7.94	8.29	8.52	9.09
89	5.61	6.17	6.74	7.30	7.86	8.20	8.42	8.98
90	5.55	6.11	6.66	7.22	7.77	8.11	8.33	8.88

Purchase Price	8½%	9%	9½%	10%	11%	12%	15%	20%
10	85	90	95	100	110	120	150	200
15	56.66	60	63.33	66.66	73.13	80	100	133.33
20	42.50	45	47.50	50	55	60	75	100
22	38.63	40.90	43.18	45.45	50	54.54	68.18	90.90
24	35.41	37.50	39.58	41.66	45.83	50	62.50	83.33
26	32.69	34.61	36.53	38.46	42.30	46.15	57.69	.76.92
28	30.35	32.14	33.92	35.71	39.28	42.85	53.57	71.42
30	28.33	30	31.66	33.33	36.66	40	50	66.66
32	26.56	28.12	29.68	31.25	34.37	37.50	46.87	62.50
34	25	26.47	27.94	29.41	32.35	35.29	44.11	58.82
36	23.61	25	26.38	27.77	30.55	33.33	41.66	55.55
38	22.36	23.68	25	26.31	28.94	31.57	39.47	52.63
40	21.25	22.50	23.75	25	27.50	30	37.50	50
42	20.23	21.42	22.61	23.80	26.19	28.57	35.71	47.61
44	19.31	20.45	21.59	22.72	25	27.27	34.09	45.45
46	18.47	19.56	20.65	21.73	23.91	26.08	32.60	43.47
48	17.70	18.75	19.79	20.83	22.91	25	31.25	41.66
50	17	18	19	20	22	24	30	40
51	16.66	17.64	18.62	19.60	21.56	23.52	29.41	39.21
52	16.34	17.30	18.26	19.23	21.15	23.07	28.84	38.46
53	16.03	16.98	17.92	18.86	20.75	22.64	28.30	37.73
54	15.74	16.66	17.59	18.51	20.37	22.22	27.77	37.03
55	15.45	16.36	17.27	18.18	20	21.81	27.27	36.36
56	15.17	16.07	16.96	17.85	19.64	21.42	26.78	35.71
57	14.91	15.78	16.66	17.54	19.29	21.05	26.31	35.08
58	14.65	15.51	16.37	17.24	18.96	20.68	25.86	34.48
59	14.40	15.25	16.10	16.94	18.64	20.33	25.42	33.80
60	14.16	15	15.83	16.66	18.33	20	25	33.33
61	13.93	14.75	15.57	16.39	18.03	19.67	24.59	32.78
62	13.70	14.51	15.32	16.12	17.73	19.35	24.19	32.25
63	13.49	14.28	15.07	15.87	17.46	19.04	23.80	31.74
64	13.28	14.06	14.84	15.62	17.18	18.75	23.43	31.28
65	13.07	13.84	14.61	15.38	16.92	18.46	23.07	30.76
66	12.87	13.63	14.39	15.15	16.66	18.18	22.72	30.30
67	12.68	13.43	14.17	14.92	16.41	17.91	22.38	29.85
68	12.50	13.23	13.97	14.70	16.17	17.64	22.05	29.41
69	12.31	13.04	13.76	14.49	15.94	17.39	21.73	28.98
70	12.14	12.85	13.57	14.28	15.71	17.14	21.42	28.57
71	11.97	12.67	13.38	14.08	15.49	16.90	21.12	28.16
72	11.80	12.50	13.19	13.89	15.28	16.66	20.83	27.77
73	11.63	12.32	13.01	13.69	15.06	16.43	20.54	27.39
74	11.49	12.16	12.83	13.51	14.86	16.21	20.27	27.02
75	11.33	12	12.66	13.33	14.66	16	20	26.66
76	11.18	11.84	12.50	13.15	14.47	15.78	19.73	26.31
77	11.03	11.68	12.33	12.98	14.27	15.58	19.48	25.97
78	10.89	11.53	12.17	12.82	14.10	15.38	19.23	25.64
79	10.75	11.39	12.02	12.65	13.92	15.18	18.98	25.31
80	10.62	11.25	11.87	12.50	13.75	15	18.75	25
81	10.49	11.11	11.72	12.34	13.58	14.81	18.51	24.69
82	10.36	10.97	11.58	12.19	13.41	14.63	18.29	24.39
83	10.24	10.84	11.45	12.04	13.25	14.45	18.04	24.09
84	10.11	10.71	11.30	11.90	13.09	14.28	17.85	23.80
85	10	10.58	11.17	11.76	12.94	14.11	17.64	23.52
86	9.88	10.46	11.04	11.62	12.79	13.95	17.44	23.25
87	9.77	10.34	10.91	11.49	12.64	13.79	17.24	22.98
88	9.65	10.22	10.79	11.36	12.50	13.63	17.04	22.72
89	9.55	10.11	10.67	11.23	12.35	13.48	16.85	22.47
90	9.44	10	10.55	11.11	12.22	13.33	16.66	22.22

Purchase Price	5%	5½%	6%	6½%	7%	7³/₁₀%	7½%	8%
91	5.49	6.04	6.59	7.14	7.69	8.02	8.24	8.79
92	5.43	5.97	6.52	7.06	7.60	7.93	8.15	8.69
93	5.37	5.91	6.45	6.98	7.52	7.84	8.06	8.60
94	5.31	5.85	6.38	6.91	7.44	7.76	7.97	8.51
95	5.26	5.78	6.31	6.84	7.36	7.68	7.89	8.42
96	5.20	5.72	6.25	6.77	7.29	7.60	7.81	8.33
97	5.15	5.67	6.18	6.69	7.21	7.52	7.73	8.24
98	5.10	5.61	6.12	6.63	7.14	7.45	7.65	8.16
99	5.05	5.55	6.06	6.56	7.07	7.37	7.57	8.08
100	5	5.50	6	6.50	7	7.30	7.50	8
101	4.95	5.44	5.94	6.43	6.93	7.22	7.42	7.92
102	4.90	5.39	5.88	6.37	6.86	7.15	7.35	7.84
103	4.85	5.33	5.82	6.31	6.79	7.08	7.28	7.76
104	4.80	5.28	5.76	6.25	6.72	7.01	7.21	7.69
105	4.76	5.23	5.71	6.19	6.66	6.95	7.14	7.61
106	4.71	5.18	5.66	6.13	6.60	6 88	7.07	7.54
107	4.67	5.14	5.60	6.07	6.54	6.82	7	7.47
108	4.62	5.09	5.55	6.01	6.48	6.75	6.94	7.40
109	4.58	5.04	5.50	5.96	6.42	6.69	6.88	7.33
110	4.54	5	5.45	5.90	6.36	6.63	6.81	7.27
111	4.50	4.95	5.40	5.85	6.30	6.57	6.75	7.20
112	4.46	4.90	5.35	5.80	6.25	6.51	6.69	7.14
113	4.42	4.86	5.30	5.75	6.19	6.46	6.63	7.07
114	4.38	4.82	5.26	5.70	6.14	6.40	6.57	7.01
115	4.35	4.78	5.21	5.65	6.08	6.34	6.52	6.95
116	4.31	4.74	5.17	5.60	6.03	6.29	6.46	6.89
117	4.27	4.70	5.12	5.55	5.98	6.23	6.41	6.83
118	4.23	4.66	5.08	5.50	5.93	6.18	6.35	6.77
119	4.20	4.62	5.04	5.46	5.88	6.13	6.30	6.72
120	4.16	4.58	5	5.41	5.83	6.08	6.25	6.66
121	4.13	4.54	4.95	5.37	5.78	6.03	6.19	6.61
122	4.09	4.50	4.91	5.32	5.73	5.98	6.14	6.55
123	4.06	4.47	4.87	5.28	5.69	5.93	6.09	6.50
124	4.03	4.43	4.83	5.24	5.65	5.88	6.04	6.45
125	4	4.40	4.80	5.20	5.60	5.80	6	6.40
130	3.84	4.23	4.61	5	5.38	5.61	5.76	6.15
135	3.70	4.07	4.44	4.81	5.18	5.33	5.55	5.92
140	3.57	3.92	4.28	4.64	5	5.21	5.35	5.71
145	3.44	3.79	4.13	4.48	4.82	5.03	5.17	5.51
150	3.33	3.66	4	4.33	4.66	4.86	5	5.33
155	3.22	3.54	3.87	4.19	4.51	4.70	4.83	5.16
160	3.12	3.43	3.75	4.06	4.37	4.56	4.68	5
165	3.03	3.33	3.63	3.93	4.24	4.42	4.54	4.84
170	2.94	3.23	3.52	3.82	4.11	4.29	4.41	4.70
175	2.85	3.14	3.42	3.71	4	4.17	4.23	4.57
180	2.77	3.05	3.33	3.61	3.88	4.05	4.16	4.44
185	2.70	2.97	3.24	3.51	3.78	3.94	4.05	4.32
190	2.63	2.89	3.15	3.42	3.68	3.84	3.94	4.21
195	2.56	2.82	3.07	3.33	3.58	3.79	3.84	4.10
200	2.50	2.75	3	3.25	3.50	3.65	3.75	4
210	2.38	2.61	2.85	3.09	3.33	3.47	3.57	3.80
220	2.27	2.50	2.72	2.95	3.18	3.31	3.40	3.63
225	2.22	2.44	2.66	2.88	3.11	3.24	3.33	3.55
230	2.17	2.39	2.60	2.82	3.04	3.17	3.26	3.47
240	2.08	2.29	2.50	2.70	2.91	3.04	3.12	3.33
250	2	2.20	2.40	2.60	2.80	2.92	3	3.20
275	1.81	2	2.18	2.36	2.54	2.65	2.72	2.90
300	1.66	1.83	2	2.16	2.33	2.40	2.50	2.66

Purchase Price	8½%	9%	9½%	10%	11%	12%	15%	20%
91	9.34	9.89	10.44	10.98	12.08	13.18	16.48	21.97
92	9.23	9.78	10.32	10.86	11.95	13.04	16.30	21.73
93	9.13	9.67	10.21	10.75	11.82	12.90	16.12	21.50
94	9.04	9.57	10.10	10.63	11.70	12.76	15.95	21.27
95	8.94	9.47	10	10.52	11.57	12.63	15.78	21.05
96	8.85	9.37	9.89	10.41	11.46	12.50	15.72	20.83
97	8.76	9.27	9.79	10.30	11.34	12.37	15.46	20.61
98	8.67	9.18	9.69	10.20	11.22	12.24	15.30	20.40
99	8.58	9.09	9.59	10.10	11.11	12.12	15.15	20.20
100	8.50	9	9.50	10	11	12	15	20
101	8.41	8.91	9.40	9.90	10.89	11.88	14.85	19.80
102	8.33	8.82	9.31	9.80	10.78	11.76	14.70?	19.60
103	8.25	8.73	9.22	9.70	10.67	11.65	14.56	19.41
104	8.17	8.65	9.13	9.61	10.57	11.53	14.42	19.23
105	8.09	8.57	9.04	9.52	10.47	11.42	14.28	19.04
106	8.01	8.49	8.96	9.43	10.37	11.32	14.15	18.86
107	7.94	8.41	8.87	9.34	10.28	11.21	14.01	18.69
108	7.87	8.33	8.79	9.25	10.18	11.11	13.88	18.51
109	7.79	8.25	8.71	9.17	10.09	11	13.76	18.34
110	7.72	8.18	8.63	9.09	10	10.90	13.63	18.18
111	7.65	8.10	8.55	9	9.90	10.81	13.51	18.01
112	7.58	8.03	8.48	8.92	9.81	10.71	13.39	17.85
113	7.52	7.96	8.40	8.84	9.73	10.61	13.27	17.69
114	7.45	7.89	8.33	8.77	9.64	10.52	13.15	17.54
115	7.39	7.82	8.26	8.69	9.56	10.43	13.04	17.39
116	7.32	7.75	8.18	8.61	9.48	10.34	12.93	17.24
117	7.26	7.69	8.11	8.54	9.40	10.25	12.83	17.09
118	7.20	7.62	8.05	8.47	9.32	10.16	12.71	16.94
119	7.14	7.56	7.98	8.40	9.24	10.08	12.60	16.80
120	7.08	7.50	7.91	8.33	9.16	10	12.50	16.66
121	7.02	7.43	7.85	8.26	9.09	9.91	12.39	16.52
122	6.96	7.37	7.78	8.19	9.01	9.83	12.29	16.39
123	6.91	7.31	7.72	8.13	8.94	9.76	12.19	16.26
124	6.85	7.85	7.66	8.06	8.87	9.67	12.09	16.12
125	6.80	7.20	7.60	8	8.80	9.60	12	16
130	6.53	6.92	7.30	7.69	8.46	9.23	11.53	15.38
135	6.29	6.66	7.03	7.40	8.14	8.88	11.11	14.81
140	6.07	6.42	6.78	7.14	7.85	8.57	10.71	14.28
145	5.86	6.20	6.55	6.89	7.58	8.27	10.34	13.79
150	5.66	6	6.33	6.66	7.33	8	10	13.33
155	5.48	5.80	6.12	6.45	7.09	7.74	9.67	12.90
160	5.31	5.62	5.93	6.25	6.87	7.50	9.37	12.50
165	5.15	5.45	5.75	6.06	6.66	7.27	9.09	12.12
170	5	5.29	5.58	5.88	6.47	7.05	8.82	11.76
175	4.85	5.14	5.42	5.71	6.28	6.85	8.57	11.42
180	4.72	5	5.27	5.55	6.11	6.66	8.33	11.11
185	4.59	4.86	5.13	5.40	5.94	6.48	8.10	10.81
190	4.47	4.73	5	5.26	5.78	6.31	7.89	10.52
195	4.35	4.61	4.87	5.13	5.64	6.15	7.69	10.25
200	4.25	4.50	4.75	5	5.50	6	7.50	10
210	4.04	4.28	4.52	4.76	5.23	5.71	7.14	9.52
220	3.86	4.09	4.31	4.54	5	5.45	6.81	9.09
225	3.77	4	4.22	4.44	4.88	5.33	6.66	8.88
230	3.69	3.91	3.90	4.34	4.78	5.21	6.52	8.69
240	3.54	3.75	3.90	4.16	4.58	5	6.25	8.33
250	3.40	3.60	3.80	4	4.40	4.80	6	8
275	3.09	3.27	3.45	3.63	4	4.36	5.45	7.27
300	2.83	3	3.16	3.33	3.66	4	5	6.66

APPENDIX I

FOREIGN EXCHANGE

Country	Currency	Consisting of	Country	Currency	Consisting of
Aden	Shilling	100 Cents	Guadeloupe	Franc	100 Centimes
Afghanistan	Afghani	100 Puls	Guatemala	Quetzal	100 Centavos
Alaska	U.S. Dollar	100 Cents	Guiana, British	Dollar	100 Cents
Albania	Lek	100 Qintar	Guiana, French	Franc	100 Centimes
Algeria	Franc	100 Centimes	Haiti	Gourde	100 Centimes
Angola	Escudo	100 Centavos	Hawaii	U.S. Dollar	100 Cents
Argentina	Peso	100 Centavos	Honduras	Lempira	100 Centavos
Australia	Pound	20 Shillings = 240 Pence	(Republic)		
			Hong Kong	Dollar	100 Cents
Austria	Schilling	100 Groschen	Hungary	Forint	100 Fillers
Bahama Is.	Pound	20 Shillings = 240 Pence	Iceland	Krona	100 Aurar
			India	Rupee	100 Naye Pais
Bahrain Is.	Indian Rupee	100 Naye Paise	Indonesia	Rupiah	100 Sen
			Iran	Rial	100 Dinars
Barbados	Dollar	100 Cents	Iraq	Dinar	1000 Fils
Belgian Congo	Franc	100 Centimes	Ireland	Pound	20 Shillings = 240 Pence
Belgium	Franc	100 Centimes	(Republic)		
Bermuda	Pound	20 Shillings = 240 Pence	Israel	Pound	1000 Prutot
			Italy	Lira	100 Centesimi
Bolivia	Boliviano	100 Centavos	Jamaica	Pound	20 Shillings = 240 Pence
Brazil	Cruzeiro	100 Centavos			
British Honduras	Dollar	100 Cents	Japan	Yen	100 Sen
			Jordan	Dinar	1000 Fils
British North Borneo	Dollar	100 Cents	Kenya	Shilling	100 Cents
			Korea (South)	Hwan	100 Chon
British Somaliland	Shilling	100 Cents	Laos	Kip	100 At
			Lebanon	Pound	100 Piasters
Bulgaria	Lev	100 Stotinki	Liberia	U.S. Dollar	100 Cents
Burma	Kyat	100 Pyas	Libya	Pound	100 Piasters = 1000 Mill.
Cambodia	Riel	100 Sen			
Canada	Dollar	100 Cents	Liechtenstein	Franc	100 Centimes
Cape Verde Is.	Escudo	100 Centavos	Luxembourg	Franc	100 Centimes
Cayman Is.	Pound	20 Shillings = 240 Pence	Macao	Pataca	100 Avos
			Madagascar	Franc	100 Centimes
Ceylon	Rupee	100 Cents	Malaya	Dollar	100 Cents
Chile	Peso	100 Centavos	Malta	Pound	20 Shillings = 240 Pence
China	NT Dollar	100 Cents			
Colombia	Peso	100 Centavos	Martinique	Franc	100 Centimes
Costa Rica	Colon	100 Centimos	Mauritius	Rupee	100 Cents
Cuba	Peso	100 Centavos	Mexico	Peso	100 Centavos
Cyprus	Pound	1000 Mils	Monaco	Franc	100 Centimes
Czechoslovakia	Crown	100 Hellers	Morocco	Franc	100 Centimes
Denmark	Krone	100 Ore	Mozambique	Escudo	100 Centavos
Dominican Republic	Peso	100 Centavos	Netherlands	Guilder	100 Cents
			Netherlands Antilles	Guilder	100 Cents
Ecuador	Sucre	100 Centavos			
Egypt	Pound	100 Piasters = 1000 Mil	New Caledonia	Franc	100 Centimes
			New Guinea (Mandate)	Pound	20 Shillings = 240 Pence
Ethiopia	Dollar	100 Cents			
Fiji Is.	Pound	20 Shillings = 240 Pence	New Zealand	Pound	20 Shillings = 240 Pence
Finland	Markka	100 Pennis	Nicaragua	Cordoba	100 Centavos
France	Franc	100 Centimes	Nigeria	Pound	20 Shillings = 240 Pence
French Equatorial Africa	Franc	100 Centimes			
			Norway	Krone	100 Ore
French West Africa	Franc	100 Centimes	Oceania (French)	Franc	100 Centime
Germany (West)	Deutsche Mark	100 Pfennig	Pakistan	Rupee	16 Annas = 192 Pies
Ghana	Pound	20 Shillings = 240 Pence			
			Panama	Balboa	100 Centesir
Gibraltar	Pound	20 Shillings = 240 Pence	Paraguay	Guarani	100 Centimo
			Peru	Sol	100 Centavo
Greece	Drachma	100 Lepta	Philippines	Peso	100 Centavo

Country	Currency	Consisting of	Country	Currency	Consisting of
Poland	Zloty	100 Grosze	Surinam	Guilder	100 Cents
Portugal	Escudo	100 Centavos	Sweden	Krona	100 Ore
Portuguese	Escudo	100 Centavos	Switzerland	Franc	100 Centimes
Guinea			Syria	Pound	100 Piasters
Portuguese	Rupia	16 Tangas =	Tanganyika	Shilling	100 Cents
India		192 Reis	Thailand	Baht	100 Satang
Puerto Rico	U.S. Dollar	100 Cents	Timor	Pataca	100 Avos
Reunion Is.	Franc	100 Centimes	Tonga Is.	Pound	20 Shillings =
Rhodesia-	Pound	20 Shillings =			240 Pence
Nyasaland		240 Pence	Trinidad	Dollar	100 Cents
Romania	Leu	100 Bani	Tunisia	Franc	100 Centimes
Salvador	Colon	100 Centavos	Turkey	Pound	100 Piasters
Samoa	New Zea.	20 Shillings =	Uganda	Shilling	100 Cents
(British)	Pound	240 Pence	Union of	Pound	20 Shillings =
Sarawak	Dollar	100 Cents	South Africa		240 Pence
Saudi Arabia	Riyal	22 Gurshes	U.S.S.R.	Ruble	100 Kopecks
Seychelles	Rupee	100 Cents	United Kingdom	Pound	20 Shillings =
Singapore	Dollar	100 Cents			240 Pence
Solomon Is.	Austral.	20 Shillings =	Uruguay	Peso	100 Centesimos
	Pound	240 Pence	Viet-Nam	Piaster	100 Cents
South West	Pound	20 Shillings =	(South)		
Africa		240 Pence	Venezuela	Bolivar	100 Centimos
Spain	Peseta	100 Centimos	Virgin Is.	U.S. Dollar	100 Cents
St. Thomas &	Escudo	100 Centavos	Yugoslavia	Dinar	100 Paras
Principe			Zanzibar	Shilling	100 Cents
Sudan	Pound	100 Piasters= 1000 Mill.			

From the Manufacturers Trust Company

APPENDIX J

TAX-FREE VS. TAXABLE BONDS

Interest from State and municipal bonds is exempt from Federal income taxes. Taxable income is currently subject to tax rates ranging from 20% to 91%, as specified in the Internal Revenue Code of 1954. This table gives the approximate yields which taxable bonds must earn in various income brackets to produce, after tax, yields equal to those on tax free bonds yielding .75% to 5.00%.

This table is computed on the theory that the taxpayer's highest bracket tax rate is applicable to the entire amount of any increase or decrease in his taxable income resulting from a switching from taxable to tax-free bonds, or vice versa.

Figures at top of columns are the taxable income brackets and the tax rates applying to such brackets.

The rates shown are applicable to taxpayers filing single returns. To find the taxable equivalent yield for taxpayers filing joint returns, divide the entire taxable income by two, and use the income bracket column applicable to the amount thus obtained.

Tax Exempt Bonds vs. Taxable Dividends: To make approximate comparison of tax-free yields with dividend income, an individual entitled to the 4% dividends received credit should use the bracket rate column which is 4 percentage points (or the one

Individual Income Brackets—Thousands of Dollars

Tax Exempt Yields	Not Over $2 20%	$2 to $4 22%	$4 to $6 26%	$6 to $8 30%	$8 to $10 34%	$10 to $12 38%	$12 to $14 43%	$14 to $16 47%	$16 to $18 50%	$18 to $20 53%	$20 to $22 56%	$22 to $26 59%	$26 to $32 62%
.75	.94	.96	1.01	1.07	1.14	1.21	1.32	1.41	1.50	1.60	1.70	1.83	1.9
1.00	1.25	1.28	1.35	1.43	1.52	1.61	1.75	1.89	2.00	2.13	2.27	2.44	2.6
1.10	1.37	1.41	1.49	1.57	1.67	1.77	1.93	2.08	2.20	2.34	2.50	2.68	2.8
1.25	1.56	1.60	1.69	1.79	1.89	2.02	2.19	2.36	2.50	2.66	2.84	3.05	3.2
1.40	1.75	1.79	1.89	2.00	2.12	2.26	2.46	2.64	2.80	2.98	3.18	3.41	3.6
1.50	1.87	1.92	2.03	2.14	2.27	2.42	2.63	2.83	3.00	3.19	3.41	3.66	3.9
1.60	2.00	2.05	2.16	2.29	2.42	2.58	2.81	3.02	3.20	3.40	3.64	3.90	4.
1.75	2.19	2.24	2.36	2.50	2.65	2.82	3.07	3.30	3.50	3.72	3.98	4.27	4.
1.80	2.25	2.31	2.43	2.57	2.73	2.90	3.16	3.40	3.60	3.83	4.09	4.39	4.
1.90	2.38	2.44	2.57	2.71	2.88	3.06	3.33	3.58	3.80	4.04	4.32	4.63	5.
2.00	2.50	2.56	2.70	2.86	3.03	3.23	3.51	3.77	4.00	4.26	4.55	4.88	5.
2.10	2.62	2.69	2.84	3.00	3.18	3.39	3.68	3.96	4.20	4.47	4.77	5.12	5.
2.25	2.81	2.88	3.04	3.21	3.41	3.63	3.95	4.25	4.50	4.79	5.11	5.49	5.
2.40	3.00	3.08	3.24	3.43	3.64	3.87	4.21	4.53	4.80	5.11	5.45	5.85	6.
2.50	3.12	3.21	3.38	3.57	3.79	4.03	4.39	4.72	5.00	5.32	5.68	6.10	6.
2.60	3.25	3.33	3.51	3.71	3.94	4.19	4.56	4.91	5.20	5.53	5.91	6.34	6.
2.75	3.44	3.53	3.72	3.93	4.17	4.44	4.82	5.19	5.50	5.85	6.25	6.71	7.
2.80	3.50	3.59	3.78	4.00	4.24	4.52	4.91	5.28	5.60	5.96	6.36	6.83	7.
2.90	3.62	3.72	3.92	4.14	4.39	4.68	5.09	5.47	5.80	6.17	6.59	7.07	7.
3.00	3.75	3.85	4.05	4.29	4.55	4.84	5.26	5.66	6.00	6.38	6.82	7.32	7.
3.10	3.87	3.97	4.19	4.43	4.70	5.00	5.44	5.85	6.20	6.60	7.05	7.56	8.
3.25	4.06	4.17	4.39	4.64	4.92	5.24	5.70	6.13	6.50	6.91	7.39	7.93	8
3.50	4.37	4.49	4.73	5.00	5.30	5 65	6.14	6.60	7.00	7.45	7.95	8.54	9
3.75	4.69	4.81	5.07	5.36	5.68	6.05	6.58	7.08	7.50	7.98	8.52	9.15	9
4.00	5.00	5.13	5.41	5.71	6.06	6.45	7.02	7.55	8.00	8.51	9.09	9.76	10
4.25	5.31	5.45	5.74	6.07	6.44	6.85	7.46	8.02	8.50	9.04	9.66	10.37	11
4.50	5.62	5.77	6.08	6.43	6.82	7.26	7.89	8.49	9.00	9.57	10.23	10.98	11
4.75	5.94	6.09	6.42	6.79	7.20	7.66	8.33	8.96	9.50	10.11	10.80	11.59	12
5.00	6.25	6.41	6.76	7.14	7.58	8.06	8.77	9.43	10.00	10.64	11.36	12.20	13

Rev.—4-1-57

closest thereto) below his top bracket. On joint returns follow the instructions in the paragraph above and then reduce by 4 percentage points to find the appropriate column.

Maximum Tax: For taxable years beginning after December 31, 1953, the total tax cannot exceed 87% of the net income for the taxable year. For persons using the alternative capital gains tax, the tax ceiling is 87% of their ordinary taxable income plus 25% of their net long-term gain.

Bond Yield Equivalent to Banks and Other Corporations: The income tax on banks and other corporations having taxable income in excess of $25,000 is 52%, of which 30% is the normal tax and 22% the surtax. Figures in Column A are taxable equivalent yields to corporations subject to the 52%

rate. Corporations having taxable income of $25,000 or less are subject to a normal tax of 30%. For taxpayers in this position, approximate taxable bond equivalent yield comparisons may be made by using the column shown for the $6,000 to $8,000 income bracket and the Tax-Exempt Bond Yield column.

Partially Tax-Exempt Governments vs. Fully Tax-Exempt Bonds: When held by banks and other corporations having income in excess of $25,000, partially tax-exempt U.S. Government bonds are exempt from the normal tax (30%), but are subject to the surtax of 22%. Column B shows the yields of partially tax-exempt Governments which are equivalent after such 22% tax to yields of fully tax-exempt bonds.

Individual Income Brackets—Thousands of Dollars

$32 to 38 5%	$38 to $44 69%	$44 to $50 72%	$50 to $60 75%	$60 to $70 78%	$70 to $80 81%	$80 to $90 84%	$90 to $100 87%	$100 to $150 89%	$150 to $200 90%	Over $200 91%	Corporate Tax Equivalent Yields A	B	Tax Exempt Yields
.14	2.42	2.68	3.00	3.41	3.95	4.69	5.77	6.82	7.50	8.33	1.56	.96	.75
.86	3.23	3.57	4.00	4.55	5.26	6.25	7.69	9.09	10.00	11.11	2.08	1.28	1.00
.14	3.55	3.93	4.40	5.00	5.79	6.87	8.46	10.00	11.00	12.22	2.29	1.41	1.10
.57	4.03	4.46	5.00	5.68	6.58	7.81	9.62	11.36	12.50	13.89	2.60	1.60	1.25
.00	4.52	5.00	5.60	6.36	7.37	8.75	10.77	12.73	14.00	15.56	2.92	1.79	1.40
.29	4.84	5.36	6.00	6.82	7.89	9.37	11.54	13.64	15.00	16.67	3.12	1.92	1.50
.57	5.16	5.71	6.40	7.27	8.42	10.00	12.31	14.55	16.00	17.78	3.33	2.05	1.60
.00	5.65	6.25	7.00	7.95	9.21	10.94	13.46	15.91	17.50	19.44	3.65	2.24	1.75
.14	5.81	6.43	7.20	8.18	9.47	11.25	13.85	16.36	18.00	20.00	3.75	2.31	1.80
.43	6.13	6.79	7.60	8.64	10.00	11.87	14.62	17.27	19.00	21.11	3.96	2.44	1.90
.71	6.45	7.14	8.00	9.09	10.53	12.50	15.38	18.18	20.00	22.22	4.17	2.56	2.00
.00	6.77	7.50	8.40	9.55	11.05	13.12	16.15	19.09	21.00	23.33	4.37	2.69	2.10
.43	7.26	8.04	9.00	10.23	11.84	14.06	17.31	20.45	22.50	25.00	4.69	2.88	2.25
.86	7.74	8.57	9.60	10.91	12.63	15.00	18.46	21.82	24.00	26.67	5.00	3.08	2.40
.14	8.06	8.93	10.00	11.36	13.16	15.62	19.23	22.73	25.00	27.78	5.21	3.21	2.50
.43	8.39	9.29	10.40	11.82	13.68	16.25	20.00	23.64	26.00	28.89	5.42	3.33	2.60
.86	8.87	9.82	11.00	12.50	14.47	17.19	21.15	25.00	27.50	30.56	5.73	3.53	2.75
00	9.03	10.00	11.20	12.73	14.74	17.50	21.54	25.45	28.00	31.11	5.83	3.59	2.80
29	9.35	10.36	11.60	13.18	15.26	18.12	22.31	26.36	29.00	32.22	6.04	3.72	2.90
57	9.68	10.71	12.00	13.64	15.79	18.75	23.08	27.27	30.00	33.33	6.25	3.85	3.00
86	10.00	11.07	12.40	14.09	16.32	19.37	23.85	28.18	31.00	34.44	6.46	3.97	3.10
29	10.48	11.61	13.00	14.77	17.11	20.31	25.00	29.55	32.50	36.11	6.77	4.17	3.25
00	11.29	12.50	14.00	15.91	18.42	21.87	26.92	31.82	35.00	38.89	7.29	4.49	3.50
71	12.10	13.39	15.00	17.05	19.74	23.44	28.85	34.09	37.50	41.67	7.81	4.81	3.75
43	12.90	14.29	16.00	18.18	21.05	25.00	30.77	36.36	40.00	44.44	8.33	5.13	4.00
14	13.71	15.18	17.00	19.32	22.37	26.56	32.69	38.64	42.50	47.22	8.85	5.45	4.25
86	14.52	16.07	18.00	20.45	23.68	28.12	34.62	40.91	45.00	50.00	9.37	5.77	4.50
57	15.32	16.96	19.00	21.59	25.00	29.69	36.54	43.18	47.50	52.78	9.90	6.09	4.75
29	16.13	17.86	20.00	22.73	26.32	31.25	38.46	45.45	50.00	55.56	10.42	6.41	5.00